About the Authors

DAVID SADKER

Source: David Sadker

Dr. Sadker has taught at the junior and senior high school levels, as well as at universities in Wisconsin, Virginia, Arizona, the District of Columbia, and Thailand. He is professor emeritus at American University (Washington, DC), and now teaches and writes in Tucson, Arizona. Along with his late wife Myra Sadker, he gained a national reputation for work in confronting gender bias and sexual harassment. The Sadkers' book, *Failing at Fairness: How Our Schools Cheat Girls,* was published by Charles Scribner and, with Karen Zittleman, updated and retitled *Still Failing at Fairness: How Gender Bias Cheats Girls and Boys and What We Can Do About It*. David Sadker co-edited *Gender in the Classroom: Foundations, Skills, Methods and Strategies Across the Curriculum* and was on the editorial board of *The Encyclopedia of Diversity in Education.*

David Sadker is a Courage & Renewal facilitator who works with educators, physicians, patients, social workers, lawyers, political and business leaders, as well as spiritual communities. David employs poetry, storytelling, music, art, reflection, and mindfulness to create a circle of trust, a place where individuals can explore their inner landscape. (Visit www.couageaz.com)

He has directed more than a dozen federal education grants and has written seven books and more than seventy-five chapters and articles in journals including the *Harvard Educational Review* and *Psychology Today*. The Sadkers' work has been reported in hundreds of newspapers and magazines, from *The London Times* to *The New York Times*. The Sadkers appeared on radio and television, including *The Today Show, The Oprah Winfrey Show, Dateline: NBC* with Jane Pauley and *All Things Considered.* The American Educational Research Association (AERA) recognized the Sadkers' work with several national awards, including the best review of research published in the United States, their service to the profession, and for "scholarship, activism, and community building on behalf of women and education." The American Association of University Women awarded the Sadkers their Eleanor Roosevelt Award, and the American Association of Colleges of Teacher Education recognized their work with the Gender Architect Award. In 2012, David was selected as one of "Nine Most Influential Actors in Title IX History" by The American Civil Liberties Union. David Sadker was selected as a Torchbearer by the U.S. Olympic Committee and has been awarded two honorary doctorates.

KAREN R. ZITTLEMAN

Source: Karen Zittleman

Dr. Karen Zittleman attended the University of Wisconsin for her bachelor's degree and American University for her master's degree and doctorate. Karen loves teaching and has taught in elementary and middle schools. She was also a Ropes course instructor, focusing on self-empowerment, team building, and communication skills. At the collegiate level, she has taught both introductory and methodology courses, as well as online teacher professional development courses. Her articles about educational equity and teacher education appear in the *Journal of Teacher Education, Educational Leadership, Phi Delta Kappan, Principal,* and other professional journals. Dr. Zittleman is the co-author of *Still Failing at Fairness,* which documents gender bias against girls and boys in school. She also wrote *Making Public Schools Great for Every Girl and Boy,* a guide for promoting equity in math and science instruction for the National Educational Association and educational film guides for *A Hero for Daisy* and *Apple Pie: Raising Champions*. Her academic interests focus on educational equity, effective teaching, and contemplative practices in education. She also facilitates workshops on entrepreneurism, conscious aging, and purposeful living. Dr. Zittleman teaches and writes in Tucson, Arizona. You are invited to visit her Web site at www.sadker.org/zittleman.html.

Brief Table of Contents

Table of Contents

PART 3
SCHOOLS AND CLASSROOMS

Preface

If you think that *Teachers, Schools, and Society: A Brief Introduction to Education* was written to introduce you to the world of teaching, you are only half right. This book also reflects our excitement about a life in the classroom and is intended to spark your own fascination about working with children. We wrote this book to share with you the joys and the challenges we feel about teaching, as well as the importance of fairness and justice in school and society. With this fifth edition, our goals are unchanged. We work hard to provide you with information that is both current and concise, and we work even harder to create an engaging book—one that will give you a sense of the wonderful possibilities found in a career in the classroom.

The primary intent of *Teachers, Schools, and Society* is to provide a broad yet precise exposure to the realities of teaching and the role of education in our society. The text will help you answer important questions such as: Do I want to become a teacher? How do I become the best teacher possible? What should a professional in the field of education know? How are schools and teaching changing? To help you answer those questions, we offer a panoramic, diverse, and (we hope) stimulating view of education.

The text views education from several vantage points. In Part I, "Teachers and Students," we present the world of schools, teachers, and students from the teacher's side of the desk. Part II, "Foundations," examines the broad forces—historical, philosophical, financial, and legal—that shape the underpinning of our educational system. In Part III, "Schools and Classrooms," we explore the purposes of schools, daily life in and beyond school, and the obvious (and not so obvious) curriculum taught in school. In this last section, we also provide an overview and analysis of the reform movement and the many curricular changes that are now so much a part of America's schools. We conclude the text with a variety of effective teaching strategies and practical suggestions to make your first year in the classroom a success.

The fifth edition of Sadker/Zittleman's brief *Teachers, Schools, and Society* retains and builds upon the hallmark characteristics that made the fourth edition a best seller.

- **Brevity of a Streamlined Introduction to Education.** The eleven essential chapters are organized for balanced coverage of foundational, curricular, and professional topics; the brief edition provides maximum teaching flexibility while assuring coverage of crucial content areas.
- **Contemporary Focus.** Current issues and topics are presented in a balanced and exciting reading style. A few of the contemporary topics in this edition include greater attention to global and international education; a Connect site with video links to TED talks, relevant YouTube, and other video segments related to concepts in the text (see page 13–15 for more information about Connect); and a greatly expanded section on the Common Core and the arguments surrounding it. The text explores the Every Student Succeeds Act (ESSA), the federal policy that replaces No Child Left Behind—including discussion of how states may respond to changing responsibilities. The text updates topics from the role of business in educational reform to the myths surrounding our public schools. "Contemporary Issues" provides a

CONTEMPORARY ISSUES

A View from the Field: Greening Schools

Sidwell Friends Middle School in Washington, D.C., is one of a growing number of green schools. Guided by its Quaker values, Sidwell Friends is committed to practicing responsible environmental stewardship. The building itself has achieved a LEED Platinum green certification, the highest level awarded.

Every aspect of the building has been constructed or remodeled with an eye toward conservation and sustainability. Photovoltaic panels on the roof provide 5 percent of the school's energy, which helps power the computer lab. On the rooftop garden, students grow herbs and vegetables for their school lunches. A constructed wetland in front of the school looks like an attractive, sloping landscape with a variety of plants, but it is much more. The school's wastewater flows below, filtered and cleaned by the plants and microorganisms, and then is recycled and used in the school's toilets. Skylights and reflective panels maximize the natural light in classrooms, a renovation that has been shown to improve academic performance. The windows, with their light-filtering shades, are the single most energy-efficient step employed in the building: Sidwell uses 10 to 15 percent of the energy of a comparable building to light the school. Even the siding on the building is green; the wood cladding is made from reclaimed cedar wine casks. Sidwell Friends represents an amazing institutional commitment to environmental sustainability. Educators use these building innovations as teaching tools, to help students understand the importance of protecting our planet. More and more, teachers across the nation are also promoting green living. Take, for example, Andy Stephens.

Andy Stephens is a science teacher at CALS Early College High School in Los Angeles. Andy's school is not a certified green school but he incorporates environmental education into his curriculum.

> We focus on the impacts we have at our school in terms of energy usage, transportation, waste, recycling, and indoor air quality. In a culminating project, I work with a team of teachers to create an interdisciplinary (math, science, history, English) action project that includes a research paper, civic action, presentation, and reflection. Students look at the science behind an issue, mathematically analyze data, write about the history of the issue, and take action.

Andy also leads the school's environmental club, the Mean Green Team. The club's many activities include beach cleanups and peer education.

Andy was actively interested in the environment before becoming a teacher. He was an avid hiker, hunter, and fisherman growing up in Washington. "I was galvanized towards action at a young age thanks to many outdoor experiences and my connection to the land."

Courtesy of Andy Stephens.

More information about Sidwell Friends School and its green building can be found at www.sidwell.edu.

Andy Stephens has a BA in economics from Occidental College and completed his master's in science education at California State University, Northridge in 2008.

TEACHING TIP

First, You Get Their Attention

I entered teaching through the back door and did not have the advantage of an effective classroom management mentor. What I would have loved in retrospect was to have someone say to me: One of the first things you need to establish is a simple and effective method of getting your students' attention. For example, in working with elementary-age children, I experimented with holding up an object. "Hey, look at this magic marker," I would say. All eyes would automatically look up because I had given them a task to perform. And with a note of wonder in my voice perhaps there was a good reason to look up. "Hey, look at this remarkable paper clip I just found and look what I can do with it."

This method was less effective as I started to work with middle schoolers. Some colleagues used the counting down method with this age group. "By the time I get to one, starting from five everyone should be quiet." It didn't work as well for me. Then I was attending an adult workshop one weekend and the facilitator said right at the start, "When you hear me say 'Focus up!' please repeat it and stop what you are doing." Well, it worked for a roomful of two hundred adults and it worked wonders with middle schoolers as well. To repeat the words required that they interrupt what they were doing, whether it was deep engagement with their work or more likely chatting with a neighbor. Sometimes I would have to repeat it again, but rarely did it take three times to quiet them down.

Most recently, I learned from a colleague who teaches kindergarten that a few simple rhythmic claps that in turn needed to be repeated by the class would achieve the same effect—simpler and easier on the voice, and a little less militaristic than the abrupt "focus up."

It is the nature of children's minds to wander, and it is the task of the teacher to gather and hold their attention when necessary instructions or other words are being spoken. What I gleaned from these experiments over the years was that the response that I needed from them was best achieved by having them perform a simple concrete action.

Courtesy of Eric Baylin.

ERIC Baylin, an art teacher for more than 40 years, currently teaches high school art at Packer Collegiate Institute in Brooklyn, NY.

REFLECTION: Do any of Eric Baylin's techniques appeal to you? Are there other techniques that you are considering to encourage your students to focus and stay on task?

chapter focus on a specific issue in today's schools, including but not limited to the notion of gender identity challenges in the classroom, unconscious bias, merit pay, and the reintroduction of single-sex public schools. Students are also given practical, current instructional strategies in the "Teaching Tips" feature. We view this text as a living and changing narrative of today's educational issues.

- **Social Justice and Equity.** The text stresses the importance of fairness and justice in school and society, focuses on the most crucial topic areas, and integrates the most current issues in education.
- **Focus on Fairness:** Issues of social justice and equity are at the core of this text. These pages examine the racial, economic, social, and gender issues that too often erect barriers to equal opportunity.
- **Diverse Voices and Experiences:** Issues of multicultural education and diversity in learning are treated as fundamental and are infused from the very first chapter ("The Teaching Profession and You") to the very last one ("Becoming an Effective Teacher"). The authors argue that only through recognizing and appreciating diversity can teaching be both effective and joyful.
- **Standards and Testing.** Important legislation and policies are thoroughly addressed, including the arrival of national standards, the proponents and critics of the testing culture, and new federal programs. There is also a section analyzing the problems of high-stakes testing and discussing some of the alternatives to high-stakes testing.
- **Connections to INTASC Principles.** Online INTASC Reflective Activities and Your Portfolio (RAPs) activities offer readers ways to apply text content and develop portfolio artifacts that demonstrate their understanding of INTASC principles. McGraw-Hill also offers a LearnSmart Praxis Study Tool, using adaptive technology to help with Praxis exam preparation.
- **Research Updated and Expanded to Reflect Education in America Today.** As with previous editions, the goal of the fifth edition is to expose you to the issues facing education today; to ensure its currency, many new references have been added. This new edition also provides updated discussions of school reform, including vouchers and charter schools, the Every Student Succeeds Act (ESSA), Common Core and national standards, the success of educational reform in Finland, and new discussions such as the unconscious bias we all carry – not a point of shame but a marker for moving forward. Readers will also note the revised discussions of Carol Dweck's work on fixed and growth mindset theories, the impact of male and female brains on learning. There is an important explanation of wealth and the business community on school reform—what Diane Ravitch refers to as "the corporate reform movement."

New in the Fifth Edition

In addition to the updated statistics, charts, and graphs that you would expect in a new edition, we have made some other interesting changes. We want this text to be the most exciting, interesting, and useful textbook you have ever read, and to mirror the enthusiasm that we feel about education. Along those lines, we have a little bonus for you in each chapter, a little extra material which you may find helpful but will not be tested on. (Isn't that cool?) This edition includes two new features: "Digging Deeper" and "News Flash." These activities are called out in the text, but are found online, and pretty much do as you might expect: allow the reader to dig deeper into an issue or to follow an issue that appears in the news. "Digging Deeper" consists of an additional page or two and is found on the textbook's Online Learning Center. You may want to read this additional information, do the exercises, and take some additional notes. Or, if your instructor allows, you can choose to ignore it entirely (when's the last time an author gave you that option?). It's your choice—and there will be no hard feelings on our part.

The "News Flash" feature sends you to a news story about the topic you are reading in that chapter. Some questions are offered for you to consider, some additional insights are given, and you get to experience the event the way the pubic does. We think it breathes more life into the topic, and we hope you agree with us.

What's more, this edition includes many of the features you enjoyed in the fourth edition: greater attention to global and international education by way of marginal notes that highlight facts and insights about education around the world. There are videos and other relevant resources, and a wealth of practical strategies from teachers. Each chapter begins with an opening quote, which sets the tone for that chapter. Connect now has video links to TED talks, relevant YouTube, and other video segments related to concepts in the text. Connect also has an expanded collection of portfolio and contemplative activities reflecting the revised INTASC: Core Teaching Standards. These activities can add depth to your learning. Here is a brief, chapter-by-chapter description of what's new and updated in the fifth edition:

Chapter 1: The Teaching Profession and You

In this chapter, we present some often-heard comments about teaching, both pros and cons, from teachers themselves.

Practical advice and insights about life in the classroom as today's teachers experience them are also included. Different approaches to teacher preparation are analyzed and updated (TFA, teaching residences, online teacher preparation), along with the strengths and weaknesses of each. A section titled "You Are Not Alone" is added to offer new teachers the resources—human and otherwise—available to help transition into a teaching career. The section "Your First Year and Beyond" has been moved from Chapter 11 to this first chapter. This section has been edited to offer a peek into the teaching years ahead, and it also includes a graphic depicting the stages of teacher development.

Chapter 2: Different Ways of Learning

Updates to this chapter explore the growing scientific field of how we learn. Carol Dweck's research on fixed and growth mindsets is expanded, along with specific instructional strategies to help teachers develop successful mindsets in their students. New research on brain development and neuroplasticity is also included, highlighting the important connections between biology and environment to learning. The discussion on special needs students—those in gifted and special education programs—is expanded to include practical strategies to help teachers identify and meet unique educational challenges these students often encounter.

Chapter 3: Teaching Your Diverse Students

A new section titled "Unconscious Bias: When Believing is Seeing" discusses the unconscious biases we carry with us, and offers examples that the reader can relate to. Another expanded section, "Gender: From Binary to Spectrum (LGBTQA)," explores the growing litigation and challenges around gender identity. New descriptions, examples, and relevant research are provided for English acquisition programs and dual language programs. The chapter has been shortened by moving most of the exercises in distinguishing between generalizations and stereotypes to the Digging Deeper Activity online.

Chapter 4: Student Life in School and at Home

In recognition of how peer pressure, bullying, and relational aggression are significant aspects of life in school, research and discussion on how these issues contribute to students' academic and emotional well-being have been expanded. Research on how poverty and homelessness intersect with students' school experiences is updated, along with ways teachers can best support the academic and emotional needs of these underprivileged youths and their families. The section on sex education is also updated to include descriptions of both sexual risk avoidance and comprehensive sex education curricula. The growing epidemic of drug addiction in youth is also addressed.

Chapter 5: The Multicultural History of American Education

This chapter now includes a new "Closer Look" feature on Rosenwald Schools and the role of Julius Rosenwald and Booker T. Washington in creating community schools to improve the education of black children living in the Jim Crow South.

Chapter 6: Philosophy of Education

Instructors and students alike give this chapter strong reviews for effectively connecting sometimes challenging concepts. As a result, we decided to pretty much leave well enough alone (not always easy for authors!).

Chapter 7: Financing and Governing America's Schools

New cases of financial inequity in education are continuously emerging, and recently even relatively wealthy Connecticut has been in the news. The courts have ruled that the inequities in this state are striking, and so major changes have been called for. Additional evidence is provided regarding the connection with funding to educational outcomes, as well as strategies to produce positive learning results even in underfunded schools. Finally, Finland's educational successes are revisited and brought up to date.

CHAPTER 8: School Law and Ethics

Rapidly developing legal and ethical issues related to technology inside and outside the classroom—especially social networks and other cyber-communication—are explored, with practical teacher strategies suggested. New case studies discuss teacher and school responses to undocumented immigrant students and their families, as well as legal issues related to how communities, school districts, and administrators respond to a teacher's sexuality. Updated resources are provided for teachers to deal with plagiarism and cheating in the Internet age. In addition, the concept of moral voices is explained.

CHAPTER 9: Purposes of America's Schools and the Current Reform Movement

New research on charter schools is explored, including ongoing issues with outcomes, oversight, and equity. The chapter has expanded discussion of open enrollment, homeschooling, and school vouchers and their implications. It also examines today's schools' role in economic mobility,

English proficiency, and public attitudes toward U.S. education. There is new data on virtual schools indicating serious problems in following through on that promising model.

CHAPTER 10: Curriculum, Standards, and Testing

The chapter explores the Every Student Succeeds Act (ESSA), the federal policy that replaces No Child Left Behind–including discussion of how states may respond to changing responsibilities. More in-depth discussion is given to the ongoing tension among the often-competing goals and values of conveying our cultural heritage, preparing children for an unknown future, and keeping curricula from obsolescence. The growing controversy over, and resistance to, Common Core standards is also explored. The standardized testing section includes expanded discussion of cheating at school-district and state-wide levels. There is updated data on U.S. student performance in international testing, and its implications for the classroom. The "Tension Points" section includes new data on teaching climate change and helps teachers develop practical strategies for handling censorship pressures. The "Technology" section adds discussion on dealing with student use of smartphones and other personal technology in the classroom. New Online Learning activities include "The Case for High School Activities," "The Power of Textbooks," and "Teaching Controversial Topics in the Age of Micro-Aggressions, Trigger Warnings and Tweeting."

Chapter 11: Becoming an Effective Teacher

Additional insights on effective classroom management and flipped instruction are included in chapter updates. The section "Stages of Teacher Development" was moved to Chapter 1 in an effort to provide more streamlined strategies and discussion of preparing for one's first year of teaching.

connect® The fifth edition of *Teachers, Schools, and Society: A Brief Introduction to Education* is now available online with Connect, McGraw-Hill Education's integrated assignment and assessment platform. Connect also offers SmartBook for the new edition, which is the first adaptive reading experience proven to improve grades and help students study more effectively. All of the title's Web site and ancillary content is also available through Connect, including:

- A full Test Bank of multiple choice questions that test students on central concepts and ideas in each chapter.
- An Instructor's Manual for each chapter with full chapter outlines, sample test questions, and discussion topics.
- PowerPoints for instructor use in class and downloadable RAP forms.

McGraw-Hill Connect® is a highly reliable, easy-to-use homework and learning management solution that utilizes learning science and award-winning adaptive tools to improve student results.

Homework and Adaptive Learning

- Connect's assignments help students contextualize what they've learned through application, so they can better understand the material and think critically.
- Connect will create a personalized study path customized to individual student needs through SmartBook®.
- SmartBook helps students study more efficiently by delivering an interactive reading experience through adaptive highlighting and review.

Over **7 billion questions** have been answered, making McGraw-Hill Education products more intelligent, reliable, and precise.

Connect's Impact on Retention Rates, Pass Rates, and Average Exam Scores

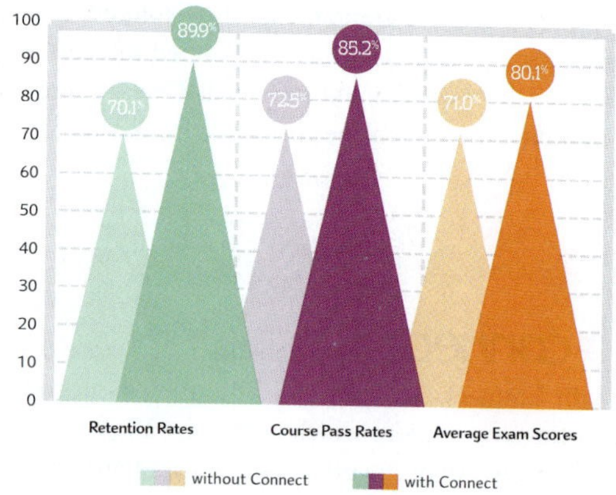

Using **Connect** improves retention rates by **19.8%,** passing rates by **12.7%, and** exam scores by **9.1%.**

73% of instructors who use **Connect** require it; instructor satisfaction **increases** by 28% when **Connect** is required.

Quality Content and Learning Resources

- Connect content is authored by the world's best subject matter experts, and is available to your class through a simple and intuitive interface.
- The Connect eBook makes it easy for students to access their reading material on smartphones and tablets. They can study on the go and don't need internet access to use the eBook as a reference, with full functionality.
- Multimedia content such as videos, simulations, and games drive student engagement and critical thinking skills.

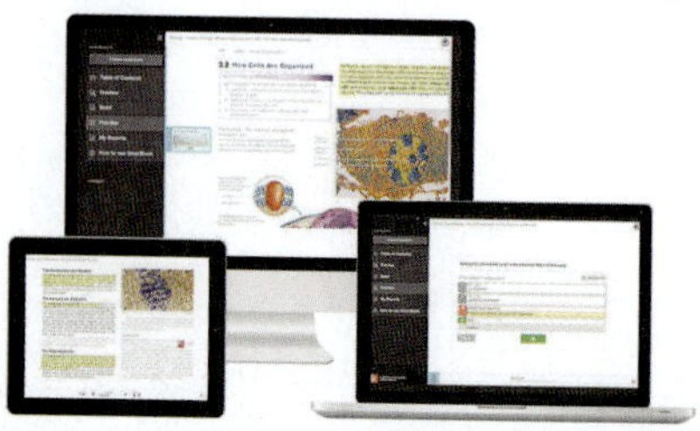

Robust Analytics and Reporting

- Connect Insight® generates easy-to-read reports on individual students, the class as a whole, and on specific assignments.
- The Connect Insight dashboard delivers data on performance, study behavior, and effort. Instructors can quickly identify students who struggle and focus on material that the class has yet to master.
- Connect automatically grades assignments and quizzes, providing easy-to-read reports on individual and class performance.

©Hero Images/Getty Images

Impact on Final Course Grade Distribution

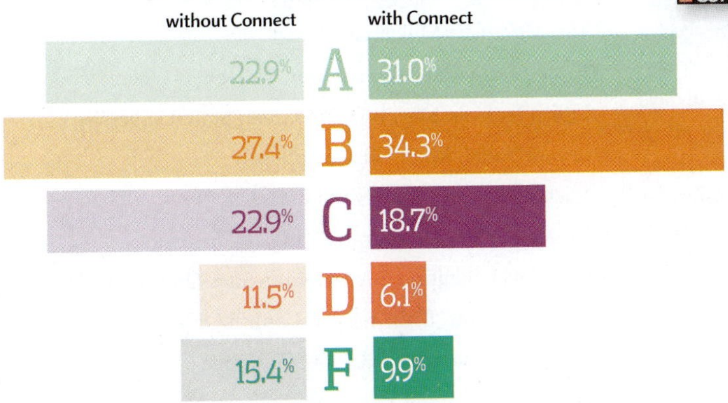

More students earn **As** and **Bs** when they use **Connect**.

Trusted Service and Support

- Connect integrates with your LMS to provide single sign-on and automatic syncing of grades. Integration with Blackboard®, D2L®, and Canvas also provides automatic syncing of the course calendar and assignment-level linking.
- Connect offers comprehensive service, support, and training throughout every phase of your implementation.
- If you're looking for some guidance on how to use Connect, or want to learn tips and tricks from super users, you can find tutorials as you work. Our Digital Faculty Consultants and Student Ambassadors offer insight into how to achieve the results you want with Connect.

www.mheducation.com/connect

Acknowledgments

Joe Kelly has become a valued partner in preparing this fifth edition. For past editions, Joe has done a great job summarizing the many new readings as well as creating new questions. But for this edition, he took on more responsibility in drafting the revision for chapters 8, 9, and 10. He has an engaging writing style that fits in well with ours, and he has the ability to learn quickly—which we hope one day to learn master! We are thankful for his contribution.

We are grateful for the contributions and insights of our colleagues. Professors John White of the University of North Florida, Ian Macgillivray of James Madison University, Scott Grubbs from Valdosta State College, and Carl Grant of the University of Wisconsin. We appreciate the contributions of the classroom teachers who provided practical insights to our "Teaching Tips." Of course, last and far from least is a force of nature, S. J. Miller, who added depth, clarity, and the spark of life to our writing.

Teachers, Schools, and Society was originally inspired by a wonderful woman and bright academic star—Myra Pollack Sadker. David's late wife co-wrote the text through several editions over a fifteen-year period. She was always the major force behind providing a student-friendly introduction to teaching. In March 1995, Myra died undergoing treatment for breast cancer. Yet her insights and passion for teaching still guide our efforts. Even when her name is no longer on the cover, her heart and mind shine through the book. We know that she will always be the primary author of this book. To learn more about Myra and her work, visit the Myra Sadker Foundation at www.sadker.org.

Managing Editor Jamie Laferrera has been the editorial godmother of this text, and we appreciate her efforts. We also owe a debt of thanks to Francesca King for her help in moving this project forward to a successful conclusion. We appreciate the effort of Ryan Warczynski, Content Production Manager, in moving this publication process forward in a smooth and efficient manner. Our development team, **ansr**source, led by editors Erin Guendelsberger, Anne Sheroff, and Reshmi Rajeesh have done an amazing job of taking on this challenging assignment and keeping the pages, footnotes, and authors all on track. We are lucky to have their services. **ansr**source was responsible for assembling the many supplements that accompany the book, including the online video album, and we appreciate their efforts in both assembling and directing development. Jasmine Stanton was the Brand Coordinator on this project and worked on coordinating manuscript and information as it passes from one set of hands to another.

We also thank the following reviewers of *Teachers, Schools, and Society: A Brief Introduction to Education* for generously sharing with us their experiences in teaching the book:

Paula Ahles, Illinois Central College

Susan Brandt, Volunteer State Community College

Theresa Capra, Mercer County Community College

Pamela Chibucos, Owens Community College

Cindi Davis, Harrisburg Area Community College

Gail Ditchman, Moraine Valley Community College

Dr. Colleen Fawcett, Palm Beach State College

Laurie Gach, Miami Dade College

Theodore Gilkey, Salisbury University

Janice Grskovic, Indiana University Northwest

Jeanine Huss, Western Kentucky University

Jody Lawrence, University of Northern Colorado

Alfred Longo, Ocean County College

Tim Mahoney, Millersville University

Anne Marie Marshall, Lehman College

Judith Jackson May, Bowling Green State University

Lesley Nadal, Miami Dade College

Michelle Proctor, College of Lake County

Kristina Rouech, Central Michigan University

Carmen H. Sanjurjo, Metropolitan State University of Denver

Susan C. Scott, University of Central Oklahoma

Dr. Constance Shepard, USC Columbia

Robert Shkorupa, College of Southern Nevada

Ron Siers, Jr., Salisbury University

Darrell Sorrells, Georgia Highlands College

Jane Spruill, Pensacola State College

Janet Stramel, Fort Hays State University

Laura Wendling, California State University San Marcos

Elizabeth Werre, Pensacola State College

Finally, we thank our students for keeping us honest, on track, and motivated. They are our inspiration.

David M. Sadker
Karen R. Zittleman
Tucson, Arizona

©Big Cheese Photo LLC/Alamy RF

> *Do not ask yourself what the world needs. Ask yourself what makes you come alive, and then go do that. Because what the world needs is people who have come alive.*
>
> **HOWARD THURMAN**

chapter 1

The Teaching Profession and You

Focus Questions

1. Is teaching a "good fit" for you?
2. What are the joys and disappointments of being a teacher?
3. Can we consider teaching to be a profession?
4. How has teacher preparation changed over the years?
5. What resources are available to help you succeed as a teacher?
6. What are the stages of teacher development?
7. Are America's schools a secret success story?

Chapter Preview

This chapter looks at classroom life through the teacher's eyes. You may be thinking: I have spent years in a classroom, watching teachers and what they do. If there is one thing I know, it is teachers and teaching! But during your years in the classroom, you have looked at teaching through "student-colored glasses," a unique but somewhat distorted view, like looking through a telescope from the lens that makes everything tiny instead of large. In this chapter, we will view the classroom from the teacher's side of the desk, a very different way of looking at school.

Some of you are taking this course because you want to learn more about schools and teaching. This text will answer many of your questions and offer useful information. We know that many of you taking this course are considering a major decision: Do I want to be a teacher? This first chapter is especially designed to help you answer that question.

The chapter is also about "us." Yes, us. We are now a team, this textbook, the authors, and you. When your authors were students, we did not much like our textbooks. They were far from exciting to read. By extension, we feared that we might not like teaching. In the end, we loved teaching—but still hated our textbooks. We want this textbook to be different—to be not only informative but also enjoyable. This first chapter offers us the opportunity to introduce the textbook and, in a sense, to introduce ourselves.

Welcome to our classroom.

A Teaching Career—Is It Right for You?

FOCUS QUESTION 1

Is teaching a "good fit" for you?

In this text, we will try mightily to include relevant information, witty insights, useful studies, and engaging chapters about teaching, school law, student diversity, and educational history—all kinds of topics that offer you a balanced view of teaching. We want you to understand the fundamentals of teaching and schooling in the United States, and we will present the information in as exciting a way as we can. To do this, we have created several features that encourage you to reflect and focus on key points. You will learn about both the positive and the negative aspects of many educational issues as you consider a possible career in teaching.

At some point, you will need to figure out if teaching is right for you. (And here's the hard part: Only you can do that.) Consider your friends' and relatives' advice, but realize that in the final analysis, it is your life, not theirs. You undoubtedly have met people who are doing work they love, and they are joyful and fulfilled. You have also met people who have made an unhappy choice, perhaps followed someone's advice that sounded good at the time—but wasn't. For them, every day is "a grind." Your goal is to find the career that puts you in that first group, a career that brings you joy and meaning. Where do you find such a vocation?

People think "vocation" is all about choosing and preparing for a career: learn about different careers, consider the external rewards and downsides of each career, weigh the pros and cons, and finally choose the one that makes the most sense. But if you haven't discovered this yet, life often defies such logic and planning. The clue about choosing the right vocation is hidden in plain sight, in the word itself. *Vocation* comes from the Latin root for *voice*; your voice. What career is your inner voice telling you to pursue? What, you don't hear an inner voice? Not surprising. In our society, schools teach us early on to be quiet and listen to others, to take notes on what others say, to study hard, and to do well on the test. But finding the vocation that is right for you is not about knowing what others believe; it is about learning about yourself. Theologian and Pulitzer Prize winner

Frederick Buechner put it nicely when he said that finding your vocation in life is discovering the place ". . . where your deep gladness and the world's deep hunger meet."[1] We hope you find reflective, quiet times in this course so you can listen to your heart and discover where your deep gladness leads you.

Like this perspective? In this chapter, you will look at classrooms from the teacher's side of the desk.

©Christopher Futcher/Getty Images RF

RAP 1.3

Why Teach?

As you read through this text, stop every now and then and ask yourself: "Does this speak to my heart? Am I enjoying what I am reading? Does teaching feel right for me?" We know, this heart talk is not what you typically read about in textbooks, but this is not a typical textbook.

In a *Peanuts* cartoon, Linus comments that "no problem is so big or complicated that it can't be run away from." Charles Schulz succinctly highlighted a human frailty shared by most of us—the tendency to put aside our problems or critical questions in favor of day-to-day routine. In fact, it is amazing how little care and consideration many of us give to choosing a career. It is always easier to catch a movie, surf the net, or even study for the next exam than it is to reflect on and plan for the future. That may be one reason why questions such as "What are you going to be when you grow up?" and "What's your next career move?" make so many of us uneasy. The big question facing many of you is: Is teaching right for me? Some of you are in college or university programs and will be teaching in the next few years. Others of you may already be in a classroom, teaching as you work toward your license in one of several alternative teacher certification programs. For some of you, teaching may become a decades-long career filled with joy and satisfaction. For others, teaching may be limited to only a few years spent in the classroom, one of several careers you explore during your working years. And still others may reach an equally useful and important realization: Teaching is not the ideal match for your interests or skills. We'd like to help you decide whether you and teaching are a good fit.

Over the years, we have heard many students ask a question that sounds something like this:

> I'm going into teaching, but almost everyone says don't do it. I've heard lots of reasons like the paperwork, the administration, money, and the current culture of education. But I am still confused. Why would you recommend that I not go into teaching, or why do you think I should ignore those warnings and go for it anyway?

This is how teachers and former teachers responded. Do any of these responses resonate with you?

FOCUS QUESTION 2

What are the joys and disappointments of being a teacher?

***Teacher A*:** It's tough. It's really hard when you start. Your principal will want to help, but half the time, won't know how. You'll never be able to provide anything nice for your family beyond the basics. It's a heck of a life. But given the choice, I'd choose it again.

***Teacher B*:** I needed to buy supplies for my students, and even food for some who are hungry. I don't make enough money for my own family. I left teaching. I earn more in retail.

***Teacher C*:** Teaching is definitely not for everyone, mostly because of classroom management. I want to teach, not police.

***Teacher D*:** A construction worker can look at their work at the end of the day and say "Man, that's a good-looking house!" Teachers don't get that kind of instant gratification.

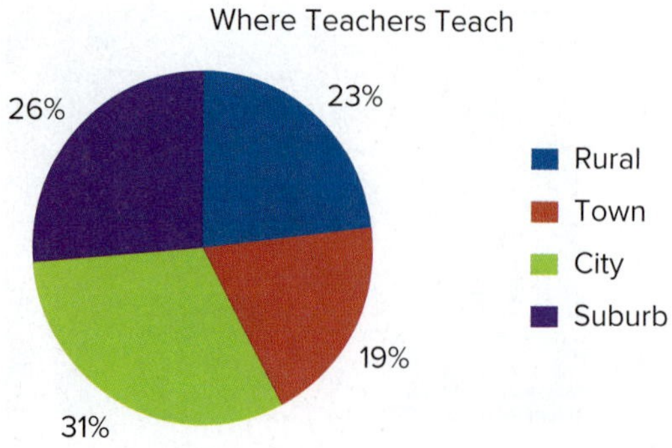

FIGURE 1.1

Where teachers teach.

SOURCE: Feistritzer, C. Emily, *Profile of Teachers in the U.S., National Center for Education Information*, Washington, DC: National Center for Education Information, 2011, p. 16. Copyright ©2011 by National Center for Education Information. All rights reserved. Used with permission.

REFLECTION: Which of these geographic regions speak to you? Why?

Teacher E: Every teaching job is different. My wife hated teaching in one community, but loved working in a small, rural school community. (See Figure 1.1.)

Teacher F: I think teaching is one of those fields that you just can't really "get" until you're inside. My advice: Email teachers and ask them out for coffee so you can pick their brains. Find out the good, the bad, and the ugly as much as you can.

Teacher G: It is an internal struggle mostly. The stresses and pressures of being a teacher versus the joy I get being with the kids. In general, it is a challenge that warms my heart.

As the comments of teachers reveal, one of the persistent challenges facing educators is inadequate pay. To be sure, there are teachers in some states and communities who are paid fairly well, but most teachers are woefully underpaid. While raising teachers' salaries across the board might well be warranted, the plans that have emerged tend to select and reward some teachers and not others. Based on classroom observations or student test scores or some criteria developed by a school board, the "better" teachers get substantial raises, and the others do not. But not everyone agrees exactly who those wonderful teachers are, or even if such a teacher versus teacher competition is a healthy idea. Here is an example of how these plans might work. How would you feel about working in a school with a pay-for-performance reward system?

Pay-for-performance, often called **merit pay,** attempts to reward the best teachers. Although many of us feel we know a good teacher when we see one, being objective can be difficult. For example, many teacher merit pay programs use student test scores to identify the most effective teachers. The idea is to link strong student test scores and teacher salaries. As test scores go up, so would the teacher's salary. The logic is that better teaching leads to better test scores. But it is not that simple. Does a high test score measure effective teaching, or student attendance, or the wealth and stability of the student's family, or just that the student had a good test day? Can you attribute rising or falling student test scores solely to teacher performance? Many teachers feel this is an example of bad policy from those who do not work in a classroom.

Here's another merit approach some advocate: Pay teachers who teach challenging subjects like physics or math more money than other teachers. Perhaps teachers who work at under-resourced schools in high-poverty areas should be paid more. (Does that mean we pay less to those who teach the gifted or work in wealthy communities?) Another problem: school politics and personality issues can influence judgment about who is a terrific teacher. It is no surprise when the principal's favorite teacher ends up getting the biggest raise. Sometimes a plan that sounds fairly easy, like paying the best teachers more money, is actually pretty difficult. Pay-for-performance has its challenges, but it is popular among many people, and it is part of the current reform movement that we will talk more about later.[2]

In addition to identifying and rewarding superior teachers, recent reform efforts have focused on identifying and removing weak teachers, even those with tenure. What is tenure? After teaching satisfactorily during a probationary period

GLOBAL VIEW

If there are international students in your class (or students who have been schooled abroad), perhaps they will be willing to discuss their experiences with teacher satisfaction in other cultures. Visit the Institute for International Education (www.iie.org) for information on teacher experiences in different countries. The site also describes opportunities to teach abroad, including the Fulbright scholarship program.

A Teaching Career

THE GOOD NEWS...

YOU ARE NOT WORKING ALONE, STARING AT A COMPUTER SCREEN OR SHUFFLING PAPERS

If you enjoy being in contact with others, particularly young people, teaching could be the right job for you. Young people are so often funny, fresh, and spontaneous. As America's students become increasingly diverse, you will find yourself learning about different cultures and different life experiences. The children will make you laugh and make you cry. "I still can't get used to how much my heart soars with every student's success, and how a piece of my heart is plucked away when any student slips away."[1]

THE SMELL OF THE CHALKBOARD, THE ROAR OF THE CROWD

You carefully plan your social protest lesson. You bring your favorite CDs and DVDs of social protest songs, and prepare an excellent PowerPoint presentation to highlight key historical figures and issues. Thoughtful discussion follows, and students are spellbound. Wow, what a lesson!

When you have taught well, your students will let you know it. On special occasions, they will come up to you after class or at the end of the year to tell you "This class is awesome." At younger grade levels, they may write you notes (often anonymous), thanking you for a good class or a good year.

I'M PROUD TO BE A TEACHER

When you become a teacher, many people will accord you respect, because they admire teachers. You will be someone whose specialized training and skills are used to benefit others. Mark Twain once wrote, "To be good is noble, but to teach others how to be good is nobler." Which would have summed up this point perfectly, except, being Mark Twain, he added: "—and less trouble."

AS A TEACHER, YOU ARE CONSTANTLY INVOLVED IN INTELLECTUAL MATTERS

You may have become very interested in a particular subject. Perhaps you love a foreign language or mathematics, or maybe you are intrigued by contemporary social issues. If you decide you want to share that excitement and stimulation with others, teaching offers a natural channel for doing so. As one teacher put it: "I want them to be exposed to what I love and what I teach. I want them to know somebody, even if they think I'm crazy, who's genuinely excited about history."[4]

PORTRAIT OF THE TEACHER AS AN ARTIST

Some people draw clear parallels between teachers and artists and highlight the creativity that is essential to both:

...THE BAD NEWS

STOP THE CROWD—I WANT TO GET AWAY

Right in the middle of a language arts lesson, when fifteen kids have their hands in the air, you may feel like saying, "Stop, everybody. I feel like being alone for the next fifteen minutes. I'm going to Starbucks." For the major part of each day, your job demands that you be involved with children in a fast-paced and intense way, which could affect behavior beyond school. One kindergarten teacher warned her 40-year-old brother "to be sure and put on his galoshes. Wow! Did he give me a strange look."[2]

IS ANYBODY THERE?

After teaching your fantastic lesson on social protest literature, you want to share your elation with your colleagues, but it is hard to capture the magic of what went on in the classroom. It is rare to have another adult spend even ten minutes observing you at work in your classroom. Once you have obtained tenure, classroom observation becomes incredibly infrequent. The word may leak out—through students, parents, or even the custodian—if you are doing a really fine job; however, on the whole, when you call out, "Hello, I'm here, I'm a teacher. How am I doing?" there will be little cheering from anyone outside your classroom.

I DON'T GET NO RESPECT

Many are quick to blame teachers, and only teachers, for all the academic problems students encounter. When students test poorly, teachers, not poverty, parents, or students are blamed. Sexist attitudes compound the problem, as majority female occupations, like teaching, are held in lower esteem. And for those who see the world through a money lens, teaching does not stack up well.[3]

THE SAME MATTERS YEAR AFTER YEAR AFTER YEAR

Teaching, like most other jobs, entails a lot of repetition. You may tire of teaching the same subject matter to a new crop of students every September. If this happens, boredom and a feeling that you are getting intellectually stale may replace excitement. Because you are just embarking on your teaching career, you may find it difficult to imagine yourself becoming bored with the world of education. However, as you teach class after class on the same subject, interest can wane.

THE BOG OF MINDLESS ROUTINE

Although there is opportunity for ingenuity and inventiveness, most of the day is spent in the three Rs of ritual, repetition, and routine. As one disgruntled sixth-grade teacher in Los Angeles said,

The Good News...

> I love to teach as a painter loves to paint, as a musician loves to play, as a singer loves to sing, as a strong man rejoices to run a race. Teaching is an art—an art so great and so difficult to master that a man [or woman] can spend a long life at it without realizing much more than his [or her] limitations and mistakes, and his [or her] distance from the ideal. But the main aim of my happy days has been to become a good teacher. Just as every architect wishes to be a good architect and every professional poet strives toward perfection.[5]

TO TOUCH A LIFE, TO MAKE A DIFFERENCE

Teaching is more than helping a child master a subject; each classroom is a composite of the anguish and the joy of all its students. You can feel the pain of the child in the fourth seat who is too shy to speak or the student who struggles to focus on any one task or project. You can be the one who makes a difference in their lives:

> I am happy that I found a profession that combines my belief in social justice with my zeal for intellectual excellence. My career choice has meant much anxiety, anger, and disappointment. But it has also produced profound joy. I have spent my work life committed to a just cause: the education of Boston high school students. Welcome to our noble teaching profession and our enduring cause.[7]

BETTER SALARIES, LONGER VACATIONS

Salaries vary enormously from one community to another. Additional salary can be earned by working in the summer or accepting extra faculty responsibilities. Occupational benefits, such as health and retirement, are generally excellent, and you will enjoy long vacations. All these considerations make for a more relaxed and varied lifestyle, one that gives you time for yourself as well as your family. Whether you use your "free time" to be with your family, to travel, or to make extra money, time flexibility is a definite plus.[8]

...The Bad News

> "Paper work, paper work. The nurse wants the health cards, so you have to stop and get them. Another teacher wants one of your report cards. The principal wants to know how many social science books you have. Somebody else wants to know if you can come to a meeting on such and such a day. Forms to fill out, those crazy forms: Would you please give a breakdown of boys and girls in the class; would you please say how many children you have in reading grade such and such. Forms, messengers—all day long."[6]

THE TARNISHED IDEALIST

We all hope to be that special teacher, the one students remember and talk about long after they graduate. But too often, idealistic goals give way to survival—simply making it through from one day to the next. New teachers find themselves judged on their ability to maintain a quiet, orderly room. Idealistic young teachers find the worship of control incompatible with their humanistic goals. Likewise, they feel betrayed if a student naively mistakes their offer of friendship as a sign of weakness or vulnerability. As a result, many learn the trade secret—"don't smile until Christmas" (or Chanukah, Kwanzaa, or Ramadan, depending on your community)—and adopt it quickly. Even veteran teachers often throw up their hands in despair. Trying to make a difference may result in more frustration than satisfaction.

BUT SALARIES STILL HAVE A LONG WAY TO GO

Although teachers' salaries have improved, they still lag behind what most people would call a good income. Teachers would need a 30 percent pay increase to become competitive with other college-educated careers. Compared with teachers in other countries, U.S. teachers work longer hours for less pay. A history teacher says, "It's really difficult to maintain a family . . . I'm not sure I could have done it then except for a wife who's not demanding or pushy. She's completely comfortable with the things we have, and we don't have a great deal."[9]

connect YOU DECIDE...

Which of these arguments and issues are most influential in determining if teaching is a good fit for you? Is there a particular point that is most persuasive, pro or con? What does that tell you about yourself? On a scale from 1 to 10, where 10 is "really committed" to teaching, and 1 is "I want no part of that job," what number are you? Remember that number as you read the text and go through this course—and see if you change that rating in the pages and weeks ahead.

(usually two to four years), teachers typically receive **tenure,** an expectancy of continued employment. Tenure is not an iron-clad guarantee of job security. It does not protect teachers who break the law, are debilitated by alcoholism, or theoretically have become terrible teachers. Tenure is intended to protect teachers from arbitrary and unfair dismissal, like an administrator who disapproves of a teacher's politics. Unfortunately, in too many school districts, it has had the unintended effect of insulating some weak teachers from dismissal. (Did you ever have an awful teacher protected by tenure? Not much fun.) But many teachers worry that without tenure, it may not be just the weak teachers who are removed. Teachers may be fired because of personality conflicts, disputes with administrators, or other reasons unrelated to teaching skills. So although tenure protections are still in place in most school districts, much consideration is being given to the best ways to identify and remove incompetent teachers—and to possibly eliminating tenure entirely.[3]

How do you feel about these possible tenure changes and the introduction of pay-for-performance? Throughout this text, we pose a variety of questions like these for you to consider, for many of them will become authentic issues you will face when you begin your career in the classroom. Much of this information is new to you and to present both sides of an issue, we have devised a feature called *You Be the Judge.* We will ask you to be the judge and consider differing opinions on an educational issue, and consider where you stand. We also want you to know that when we, your authors, have a strong opinion about these or any of the issues in the text, we will tell you up front. We are real flesh and blood people; we don't pretend to be neutral (we are not). That's being phony. When we feel strongly about an issue, like the importance of equal educational rights for all, we will tell you. We will not hide our beliefs, but we will label them as our beliefs and not put them on you. After all, our opinion is just our opinion, and in this course it is important for you to form your own ideas based on evidence. To that end, we will work hard to be fair, to present more than one side of controversial issues, and trust that you will form your own point of view. *You Be the Judge* is one way that we hope to spark your interest and thinking on critical issues.

In the first *You Be the Judge,* we highlight the joys and the concerns of a career in the classroom (see pp. 5 and 6). We include comments by teachers themselves that reflect their perceptions and feelings about their work. You will read about the assets and liabilities of a teaching career, and determine which issues speak to your heart, to help you think about the real benefits and disadvantages of a teaching career.

GLOBAL VIEW

Research teacher wages internationally. How might salary affect status and lifestyle issues abroad?

Before we move on, here is a word from your authors (remember, we said we would do that every now and then, and this is one of those times). We have seen significant changes in teaching over the past few decades, and much of that change has not been for the better. Sad but true, and we strive to give you a balanced view and let you decide. The economic situation for teachers is depressing. But looking beyond the dollars world, the psychic rewards in teaching can be extraordinary. Teaching a lesson that soars creates extraordinary energy, in you and your students. Having students leave your classroom excitedly talking about the lesson has a value beyond merit pay and tenure, a value our culture does not always recognize. And while intangible, it may be the most real thing going on in your classroom. So perhaps a key question that you should ask yourself is, can I excite, motivate, and inspire my students.

In a poll of almost a quarter of a million high school students, half said that they did not have a single teacher who inspired them.[4] (At the college level it was more dismal, with a third admitting to having no professors who excited them about learning.) The high school students who said they had at least one teacher who made them feel excited about the future were more than four times more likely to be involved in and enthusiastic about school than those who did not. So there is so much more than a teacher shortage; there is an inspiring teacher shortage. Can you respond to that need?

Here is a second question for you to consider: Are you a contrarian? Let's use economics as an example. A contrarian investor buys and sells stock in opposition to what most investors are doing. If the price of stocks is going down, the contrarian buys them anyway, enjoying a lower purchase price and betting that they will increase in the future. A contrarian bets against popular sentiment. This may be the era of contrarians in education, new teachers who understand that the value of public education is currently depressed, but believe it will gain value in the future, and want to enter teaching with an eye to the future. So if you are an educational contrarian, with a belief in the intrinsic value of education, perhaps this is a good time for you to enter the field.

RAP 1.5

Creating a Career Information Document

Professionalism at the Crossroads

> What noble employment is more valuable to the state than that of the man who instructs the rising generation?
>
> **(Cicero)**

> Education makes a people easy to lead, but difficult to drive; easy to govern but impossible to enslave.
>
> **(Lord Brougham)**

FOCUS QUESTION 3

Can we consider teaching to be a profession?

> I shou'd think it as glorius [sic] employment to instruct poor children as to teach the children of the greatest monarch.
>
> **(Elizabeth Elstob)**

> We must view young people not as empty bottles to be filled, but as candles to be lit.
>
> **(Robert Schaffer)**

> I touch the future; I teach.
>
> **(Christa McAuliffe)**

Literature, philosophy, and history are replete with such flowery tributes to teaching. In many minds, in some of our greatest minds, teaching is considered the noblest of professions. But the realities of the job do not always mesh with such admirable appraisals, resulting in a painful clash between noble ideals and practical realities.

Many teachers feel that the satisfaction they realize inside the classroom is too often jeopardized by forces beyond the classroom: politicians mandating numerous standardized tests, demanding parents offering little support, and textbook publishers or state officials deciding what should be taught and what topics are off-limits to teachers. Teachers desire more autonomy and control over their careers and, like all of us, want to be treated with more respect. Teachers increasingly see themselves as reflective decision makers, selecting objectives and teaching procedures to meet the needs of different learners.[5] They must know their subject matter, learning theory, research on various teaching methodologies, and techniques for curriculum development.[6] Some believe that the problems confronting teachers stem from the more pervasive issue of professional status and competence. Are teachers professionals? Are they treated like professionals? What does it take to be a professional, anyway? *Educating a Profession,* a publication of the American Association of Colleges for Teacher Education (AACTE), lists twelve criteria for a *profession.*

We have shortened these criteria here, and ask you to consider each one and decide if you believe that teaching meets these criteria. Take a moment and go to page 10. write down your responses to "Criteria for a Profession." After marking your reactions in the appropriate column, compare your reactions with those of your classmates.

Do not be surprised if you find some criteria that do not apply to teaching. In fact, even the occupations that spring to mind when you hear the word *professional*—doctor, lawyer, clergy, college professor—do not completely measure up to all these criteria.

Where do you place teaching? If you had a tough time deciding, you are not alone. Many people feel that teaching falls somewhere between professional and semiprofessional in status. Perhaps we should think of it as an "emerging" profession. Or perhaps teaching is, and will remain, a "submerged" profession. Either way, teachers find themselves in a career with both potential and frustration.

Why does all this "profession talk" matter? You may be more concerned with *real* questions: Will I be good at teaching? Do I want to work with children? What age level is best for me? Will the salary be enough to give me the quality of life that I want for myself and my family? You may be thinking: Why should I split hairs over whether I belong to a profession? Who cares? The issue of professionalism may not matter to you now or even during your first year or two of teaching, when classroom survival has top priority. But if you stay in teaching, this idea of professionalism will grow in significance, perhaps becoming one of the most important issues you face. Even now, as a student, you can become more reflective in your views of teaching and learning; you can begin to refine your own professional behaviors and outlooks.

But let's keep all this in some perspective. Americans like to call themselves "professionals" because the term brings some status. But there are issues far more important than status. For example, no one would argue that a lawyer is a professional, but whereas some lawyers work to ensure that the environment is protected, others work to overturn environmental laws. Some lawyers work to protect the rights of the disenfranchised, while others serve the interests of the powerful. All these lawyers are professionals, but some of them make us proud, while the work of others saddens us. There is no reservation about the value of teachers' work. Teachers move the world forward—a meaningful way to spend one's life and more relevant than the word *professional,* and perhaps even more relevant than salary.

Collectively, teachers struggle to empower their profession; individually, they struggle to empower their students.
©John Lund/Marc Romanelli/Blend Images/Getty Images RF

Criteria for a Profession	True for Teaching	Not True for Teaching	Don't Know
1. Professions provide essential services to the individual and society.	______	______	______
2. Each profession is concerned with an identified area of need or function (e.g., maintenance of physical and emotional health).	______	______	______
3. The profession possesses a unique body of knowledge and skills (professional culture).	______	______	______
4. Professional decisions are made in accordance with valid knowledge, principles, and theories.	______	______	______
5. The profession is based on undergirding disciplines from which it builds its own applied knowledge and skills.	______	______	______
6. Professional associations control the actual work and conditions of the profession (e.g., admissions, standards, licensing).	______	______	______
7. There are performance standards for admission to and continuance in the profession.	______	______	______
8. Preparation for and induction into the profession require a protracted preparation program, usually in a college or university professional school.	______	______	______
9. There is a high level of public trust and confidence in the profession and in the skills and competence of its members.	______	______	______
10. Individual practitioners are characterized by a strong service motivation and lifetime commitment to competence.	______	______	______
11. The profession itself determines individual competence.	______	______	______
12. There is relative freedom from direct or public job supervision of the individual practitioner. The professional accepts this responsibility and is accountable through his or her profession to the society.[7]	______	______	______

The unspoken dimension of this professional talk is salary. While doctors and lawyers might also fall short of professional status, many of them earn significantly higher salaries than teachers, so that must make their lives if not easier, than at least happier. Not necessarily. Psychologists and economists have found that after an economic threshold is met, the correlation between income and happiness is weak. At the University of Rochester, for example, researchers compared students who expressed extrinsic *profit* goals (wanting wealth and fame) with students who held intrinsic *purpose* goals (wanting to help others, improve their lives, grow and learn). A year or two later, the students with purpose goals in college reported being happier and more satisfied than they were in college. They had very low levels of anxiety or depression because they were finding fulfillment. But this was not the case for the graduates who had profit goals. Even though they were successfully accumulating money and status, they reported they were no happier than they were in college. Moreover, they were experiencing increased depression, anxiety, and other negative indicators. Attaining profit goals actually led to negative consequences. "People who have very high extrinsic goals for wealth are more likely to attain wealth, but they are still unhappy."[8] While all workers deserve to have an adequate salary, earning a large income is no guarantee of happiness. Living a purposeful life may well offer a happier future.

From Normal Schools to Board-Certified Teachers

FOCUS QUESTION 4

How has teacher preparation changed over the years?

As you read this brief history of teacher preparation, think about whether teachers are prepared in a way commensurate with belonging to a profession.

From colonial America into the twentieth century, teacher education scarcely existed. More often than not, teachers in colonial America received no formal preparation at all. Most elementary teachers never even attended a secondary school. Some learned their craft by serving as apprentices to master teachers, a continuation of the medieval guild system. Others were indentured servants paying for their passage to America by teaching for a fixed number of years. Many belonged to the "sink-or-swim" school of teaching, and the education of an untold number of students undoubtedly sank with them.

The smaller number of teachers working at the secondary level—in academies or Latin grammar schools and as private tutors—had usually received some college education, more often in Europe than in America. Some knowledge of the subject matter was considered desirable, but no particular aptitude for teaching or knowledge of teaching skills was considered necessary. Teaching was viewed not as a career but as temporary employment. Many of those who entered teaching, especially at the elementary level, were teenagers who taught for only a year or two. Others were of dubious character, and early records reveal a number of teachers fired for drinking or stealing.

From this humble beginning there slowly emerged a more professional program for teacher education. In 1823, the **Reverend Samuel Hall** established a **normal school** (derived from the French *école normale,* a school that establishes model standards) in Concord, Vermont. This private school provided elementary school graduates with formal training in teaching skills. Reverend Hall's modest normal school marked the beginning of teacher education in America. Sixteen years later, in 1839, **Horace Mann** was instrumental in establishing the first state-supported normal school in Lexington, Massachusetts. Normal schools typically provided a 2-year teacher training program, consisting of academic subjects as well as teaching methodology. Some students came directly from elementary school; others had completed a secondary education. Into the 1900s, the normal school was the backbone of teacher education. The lack of rigorous professional training contributed to the less-than-professional treatment afforded teachers. The following is a teacher contract from the 1920s, a contract that offers a poignant insight into how teachers were seen . . . and treated.

Many of today's noted universities began as normal schools a century ago and were established to prepare teachers.

Source: Library of Congress, Prints and Photographs Division [LC-USZ62-49011]

As the contract indicates, by the 1900s, teaching was becoming a female occupation. Both female workers and teaching being held in low regard, the reward for the austere dedication detailed in this contract was an unimpressive $75 a month. But as the twentieth century progressed, professional teacher training gained wider

Teaching Contract

Miss _______ agrees:

1. Not to get married. This contract becomes null and void immediately if the teacher marries.
2. Not to keep company with men.
3. To be home between the hours of 8 P.M. and 6 A.M. unless in attendance at a school function.
4. Not to loiter downtown in ice-cream parlors.
5. Not to smoke cigarettes. This contract becomes null and void immediately if the teacher is found smoking.
6. Not to drink beer, wine, or whiskey. This contract becomes null and void immediately if the teacher is found drinking beer, wine, or whiskey.
7. To keep the schoolroom clean:
   a. To sweep the classroom floor at least once daily.
   b. To scrub the classroom floor at least once weekly with soap and hot water.
   c. To clean the blackboard at least once daily.
   d. To start the fire at 7 A.M. so that the room will be warm by 8 A.M. when the children arrive.
8. Not to wear face powder, mascara, or to paint the lips.

Source: *Chicago Tribune*, September 28, 1975, Section 1.

acceptance. Enrollments in elementary schools climbed and secondary education gained in popularity, and so did the demand for more and better-trained teachers. Many private colleges and universities initiated teacher education programs, and normal schools expanded to 3- and 4-year programs, gradually evolving into state teachers' colleges. Interestingly, as attendance grew, these teachers' colleges expanded their programs and began offering courses and career preparation in fields other than teaching. By the 1950s, many of the state teachers' colleges had evolved into state colleges. In fact, some of today's leading universities were originally chartered as normal schools.[9]

Today, there is interest not only in how teachers are prepared, but also which teachers are the most effective. In the 1990s, the **National Board for Professional Teaching Standards (NBPTS)** was created to recognize superior teacher performance, and to name those teachers as "board certified." Now what does that mean? How do you become board certified?

Imagine that you have taught for a number of years, and decide to apply for this recognition. You would take written tests, your lesson plans examined, and your teaching observed. If you pass, you would be anointed with the title "board certified." About 3 percent of teachers are board certified, so you would be part of a select group.[10] As a board certified teacher, you might be given additional pay, more responsibility for schoolwide instruction, or perhaps given released time to work with new teachers. That may be in your future. As you enter the teaching profession, you will want to stay abreast of the activities concerning the national board and determine if you want to work toward board certification.[11] (What skills are needed for such superior teachers? See A Closer Look: About the National Board for Professional Teaching Standards. For a current update of NBPTS activities, visit www.nbpts.org.)

A CLOSER LOOK

About the National Board for Professional Teaching Standards

The National Board for Professional Teaching Standards (National Board) is a not-for-profit professional organization, created and governed by practicing teachers and their advocates. The founding mission of the National Board is to advance the quality of teaching and learning by maintaining high and rigorous standards for what accomplished teachers should know and be able to do; providing a national voluntary system certifying teachers who meet these standards; and advocating related education reforms to integrate National Board Certification into American education and capitalize on the expertise of National Board Certified Teachers.

Today, there are 25 certificate areas that span 16 content areas and four student developmental levels. The essence of the National Board's vision of accomplished teaching is captured in the enduring document: "What Teachers Should Know and Be Able to Do." The Five Core Propositions:

1. Teachers are committed to students and their learning.
2. Teachers know the subjects they teach and how to teach those subjects to students.
3. Teachers are responsible for managing and monitoring student learning.
4. Teachers think systematically about their practice and learn from experience.
5. Teachers are members of learning communities.

Source: National Board for Professional Teaching Standards, "Five Core Propositions," 2009, http://www.nbpts.org/five-core-propositions.

REFLECTION: Can you demonstrate your understanding of each proposition with a classroom example from your past? If your schooling offers little to brag about (or your memories are faded), let your imagination give credence to the task. Envision an example from the five areas to confirm you comprehend each concept.

How Teachers Are Prepared Today

Even as educators strive toward professional status, there is no consensus and much controversy on how best to prepare teachers, and today we have many different paths to becoming a teacher. These different approaches have been categorized as traditional (undergraduate preparation at a college) or alternative (post-graduate preparation at a college or school district). The traditional teacher education path is found in hundreds of colleges where undergraduates study education and subject matter, then do student teaching en route to becoming a teacher. Alternative teacher preparation typically focuses on a structured apprenticeship, a sort of on-the-job training.

There are also more controversial alternative programs, like those offered primarily online. At the end of a year, or perhaps two years, the individual is licensed to teach. As you might imagine, the quality of alternative programs (and to be fair, traditional ones as well) varies greatly.

The positive side of alternative programs is that it has opened the teaching door to a more mature and diverse teaching force. Alternative teacher education programs are more likely to graduate new teachers who are over 30, and many over 40 years of age, and about a third are male or nonwhites, quite a difference from traditional undergraduate teacher education populations. Alternative teacher preparation may also graduate teachers better able to relate to today's more diverse students—little wonder

PROFILE IN EDUCATION

Rafe Esquith

Rafe Esquith teaches Shakespeare to his fifth-grade students from Central Los Angeles, most of whom do not speak English as a first language. His students arrive early and leave late in order to work through a rigorous core curriculum, take part in a real-world environment, and, by the end of the year, perform Shakespeare.

Read a full profile of Rafe Esquith on Connect.

©Heather Harris

connect

that almost every state offers some form of alternative teacher training, and that approximately one in four new teachers have gone through an alternative teacher education program.[12]

Perhaps the best known of these alternative programs is Teach for America (TFA). Its founder, Wendy Kopp, conceptualized this program back in 1990 in her undergraduate thesis at Princeton. (That could be a motivator for you to view your class paper less as a task and more as an opportunity!) TFA recruits, called corps members, agree to teach for at least two years in under-resourced urban and rural schools. By being very selective, rejecting 9 out of 10 applicants, and drawing strong candidates to teaching, TFA has captured the imagination of many. But critics point out that its teacher preparation is too brief to be effective, usually a month or so, and many corps members leave as soon as their two-year commitment ends, adding to the already high turnover rate in these struggling schools. Moreover, even though TFA has been around for decades, its 4,000 to 6,000 yearly recruits are only a tiny fraction of the nation's 3.5 million teachers.[13] What TFA has shown America is that teaching can and should attract the very best college graduates. And that's what the public wants as well. (See Figure 1.2.)

Let's mention another teacher preparation program that forges a dramatically different path than TFA. *Teaching residencies* have been expanding in recent years, and in some critical ways, resemble medical residences. In a typical residency program, for example, talented teacher candidates commit to teaching for three years beyond their residency year. The first year of residency is mostly observing and taking graduate-level coursework, and candidates are paid for that year. They have the time to discuss educational theory and practice, and work alongside an experienced and effective mentor teacher learning how to implement these skills in a classroom. When they begin their teaching careers the second year, they feel well prepared and experienced. To the outside world, these "new" teachers look experienced. Now doesn't that sound like a thoughtful approach! Unlike TFA, it is not unusual for 70 percent or more of teachers prepared in a residency program to remain in teaching for five years or longer. Effective preparation makes a difference.[14] (To find out more, visit the National Center for Teacher Residencies at nctresidencies.org.)

So you may be asking: Which is the better path to teacher education, traditional or alternative? Trick question–strong and weak programs exist in both approaches.[15] Perhaps the better questions to ask of any teacher education program: Do the candidates have a strong background in their subject matter? Have they received effective

FIGURE 1.2

The public's view on who should become a teacher.

SOURCE: *Phi Delta Kappan*/Gallup poll in *Phi Delta Kappan*, September 2011.

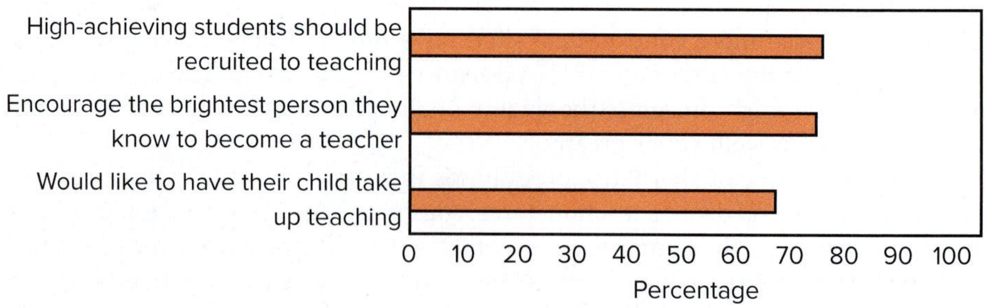

REFLECTION: Why is there such a large gap between what the public wants, and the difficulty of recruiting top students to teaching?

TEACHING TIP

First, You Get Their Attention

I entered teaching through the back door and did not have the advantage of an effective classroom management mentor. What I would have loved in retrospect was to have someone say to me: One of the first things you need to establish is a simple and effective method of getting your students' attention. For example, in working with elementary-age children, I experimented with holding up an object. "Hey, look at this magic marker," I would say. All eyes would automatically look up because I had given them a task to perform. And with a note of wonder in my voice perhaps there was a good reason to look up. "Hey, look at this remarkable paper clip I just found and look what I can do with it."

This method was less effective as I started to work with middle schoolers. Some colleagues used the counting down method with this age group. "By the time I get to one, starting from five everyone should be quiet." It didn't work as well for me. Then I was attending an adult workshop one weekend and the facilitator said right at the start, "When you hear me say 'Focus up!' please repeat it and stop what you are doing." Well, it worked for a roomful of two hundred adults and it worked wonders with middle schoolers as well. To repeat the words required that they interrupt what they were doing, whether it was deep engagement with their work or more likely chatting with a neighbor. Sometimes I would have to repeat it again, but rarely did it take three times to quiet them down.

Most recently, I learned from a colleague who teaches kindergarten that a few simple rhythmic claps that in turn needed to be repeated by the class would achieve the same effect—simpler and easier on the voice, and a little less militaristic than the abrupt "focus up."

It is the nature of children's minds to wander, and it is the task of the teacher to gather and hold their attention when necessary instructions or other words are being spoken. What I gleaned from these experiments over the years was that the response that I needed from them was best achieved by having them perform a simple concrete action.

Courtesy of Eric Baylin.

ERIC Baylin, an art teacher for more than 40 years, currently teaches high school art at Packer Collegiate Institute in Brooklyn, NY.

REFLECTION: Do any of Eric Baylin's techniques appeal to you? Are there other techniques that you are considering to encourage your students to focus and stay on task?

pedagogical training? Has there been a carefully planned and implemented clinical experience?[16] It's not too surprising to learn that teachers who feel well prepared are far more likely to stay in teaching.

Considering the strengths and weaknesses of individual teacher education programs is particularly challenging in our world, so flooded as it is with myths about teaching. So let's take a moment to debunk these myths—some of these "urban legends" which may be lurking in your own mind.

Alternative teacher education programs attract more males and minorities into teaching than traditional programs.

©Ingram Publishing RF

Urban Legends about Teacher Education

You may have heard that "Teachers are born, not made," or "To be a good teacher, all you really need to know is the subject you are teaching." Like the urban legend of alligators cavorting in the New York

City sewer system, these teaching myths have taken on a life of their own. Let's take a moment and clear the air about a few of these.

Teachers are born, not made: It is certainly true that some students enter a teacher education program with impressive instructional skills, yet training and practice is what is needed to transform a strong teacher into a gifted one. Teaching is far from unique in this. When a group of Olympians and their coaches were asked what it takes to become a champion, none of the answers suggested that they were "born" champions. On the contrary, the athletes credited well-designed practices and good coaching. Accomplished musicians attribute their performance to hours of focused practice, as do master chess players. So too, superior teachers are not born; they work at it.

All you really need to know is the subject you are teaching: Though it is true that subject mastery is critical in effective teaching, research reveals that teachers skilled in **pedagogy,** the art and science of teaching, especially teaching methods and strategies, outperform teachers with superior subject area knowledge. Clearly, the most successful teachers do not view this as an either/or proposition. Effective teaching requires both knowledge of the subject and instructional skills.

For example, one researcher observed a group of medical doctors in training, brilliant students with over the top test scores, but they were struggling nevertheless. Socially inept, awkward, and unable to communicate effectively, some of these super-strong students were weak physicians. Strong academic credentials were not enough. Today, medical schools are responding to this problem with new courses in communication skills, as well as recruiting students who may not be the top academically, but who have other, more relevant interpersonal skills. Effective teaching also requires effective communication—both knowledge of the subject and the talent to teach it.[17]

Teacher education students are less talented than other college majors: (We never liked this one, either!) It is true that education majors are less likely to score in the top 25 percent on the SATs and too many who go into teaching are not strong academically. That is disappointing but true. On the other hand, adult literacy surveys show that teachers attain scores similar to those of physicians, writers, engineers, and social workers, which is much more encouraging.[18] It saddens us that no one seems to compare those becoming teachers with others in areas such as creativity, social consciousness, diversity of workforce, and honesty, for example. Why are such important factors overlooked?

Teaching is an easy college major: Teaching is unlike most college majors, but far from easy. Unlike many college programs, teacher candidates need focused and thoughtful time not only in their college studies (like reading this fine textbook), but also in the skills necessary for success in the real world of preK–12 classrooms. Planning lessons, incorporating new technology, supervising students, interacting with parents, and in fact, just managing time, are additional competencies that education students need to learn. Effective teacher preparation programs require close partnerships with local schools, partnerships that brand teacher education as unique (but far from easy).[19]

Once you actually begin teaching in your own classroom, you continue to grow and refine your teaching skills. Like many professional programs, from medicine to engineering, those early years on the job can be years of tremendous professional growth, if you use them wisely. And here's the good news: there are wonderful on-the-job resources to help you refine and improve your teaching skills. What resources? Glad you asked.

You Are Not Alone

FOCUS QUESTION 5

What resources are available to help you succeed as a teacher?

As you enter your first classroom as a new teacher, all those empty chairs staring at you can be intimidating. Even more so when they are occupied by animated youngsters. You may feel as though you are alone. But you are not alone. First-year teachers report that they gain a great deal from discussions with fellow teachers, actual teaching experiences, and the help of mentors in the classroom.[20] You have colleagues who can offer you advice and insights and are more often than not happy to help.

Mentors and Induction

Beyond this informal network of colleagues, some schools offer a more formal introduction to teaching, often called induction. **Induction programs** "provide some systematic and sustained assistance to beginning teachers for at least one school year," in the hope that such support will create the first of many magical years.[21] While some teachers are "naturals," gifted classroom instructors from the first day they step foot in a classroom, most of us benefit from a support system that helps us refine our teaching skills. Induction programs typically match new teachers with an experienced instructor, usually called a mentor.

Mentors are experienced teachers selected to guide new teachers through the school culture and norms, shedding light on the *official* and the *hidden* school cultures (e.g., which memos need a quick response and which do not; who keeps the key to the supply room; where the best DVD players are hidden) and offering a shoulder to lean on during those difficult days. Mentors offer insights on how best to use curricular materials, hints on teaching strategies, advice on scheduling problems, and suggestions on smoothing out stressful communication with a student, a parent, an administrator, or a colleague. They can observe a class to analyze how you might improve your teaching or actually teach a class to model a skill for you to use.[22] Effective mentors offer a bridge for new teachers to become skilled professionals.

Professional Associations and Resources

Today, teaching is one of the most organized occupations in the nation, and teachers typically belong to one of two major teacher organizations, the **National Education Association (NEA),** or the **American Federation of Teachers (AFT).** Both organizations offer conferences, workshops, and publications focused on honoring and improving the lives of teachers. Teachers, as well as teacher education students like yourself, can get digital access to the publications produced by these two organizations. *NEA Today* features the latest in K-12 education trends, opinions, and news; and *Thought & Action* explores higher education issues. The AFT offers publications that address classroom resources, early childhood, and special needs students, to name but a few. To learn more, visit www.nea.org and www.aft.org. Beyond these well-known associations, there are many other professional organizations that

GLOBAL VIEW

Nearly every week, the powerful teachers union and the government officials in Finland meet to discuss education. Why are unions seen as constructive partners in Finland, but so controversial in the United States?

offer a rich array of resources. One of our favorite publications is *Rethinking Schools* (www.rethinkingschools.org). You will find articles of interest to you regardless of the subject or grade you teach, often with a social justice dimension. Publications such as *Education Week* keep teachers abreast of educational developments. (The online version is available at www.edweek.org.) Here is a short list of other professional organizations, but Google away and you will uncover more. Each underscores that you are not alone:

National Council for Teachers of English (www.ncte.org)

National Council for the Social Studies (www.ncss.org)

National Science Teachers Association (www.nsta.org)

Teachers of Speakers of Other Languages (www.tesol.org)

National Council for the Teachers of Mathematics (www.nctm.org)

The Association for Supervision and Curriculum Development (www.ascd.org)

Association for Middle Level Education (http://www.amle.org/) National Association for the Education of Young People (www.naeyc.org)

National Association for Gifted Children (www.nagc.org)

The Council for Exceptional Children (www.cec.sped.org)

Your First Year and Beyond

FOCUS QUESTION 6

What are the stages of teacher development?

When you begin teaching, you will benefit from mentors, colleagues, and your professional associations. But questions will persist. Teaching is a complex work that cannot be fully mastered in the short period of teacher education. Like doctors, lawyers, engineers, and architects, you will continue to learn on the job. You will have concerns about whether you are good enough or will you be able to manage students. And in that first year, you will likely freak out a bit when you are notified that your supervisor would like to observe your teaching. Like most beginning teachers, you will likely survive both the challenges and fears of that first year.

The two largest teacher organizations are the National Education Association (NEA) and the American Federation of Teachers (AFT)

nea NATIONAL EDUCATION ASSOCIATION nea.org

Great Public Schools for Every Child

Source: National Education Association, www.nea.org

aft

A Union of Professionals

Source: American Federation of Teachers, www.aft.org

In your second year, you will be more experienced (and more confident), and move beyond those first-year survival questions. Now you will be more familiar with the curriculum, school norms, and life as a teacher, and shift your focus to refining your teaching skills. You might be asking yourself: What worked that first year? What bombed and needs to be rethought? What can I do to improve student performance? You may find yourself spending more time analyzing the needs of individual students, exploring new approaches, and asking such questions as: How can I help this shy child? What is this student's learning problem? If you hear about a colleague achieving success using a new teaching strategy, you might ask to visit that classroom and perhaps adapt or adopt that new strategy.

Then after a few years, your interests and vision may well grow beyond your classroom. You may begin considering ways that you can influence education on a larger scale. These stages of teacher development are illustrated in Figure 1.3.[23] And keep this in mind: Although efforts to improve schools may consider many factors,

GLOBAL VIEW

If you are interested in teaching overseas, there are both private and government opportunities. Here's a start: www. educatorsoverseas .com, www.state.gov/, and www. dodea.edu/.

FIGURE 1.3

Stages of teacher development.

SOURCE: Based on the work of Lillian Katz.

Stage 1: Survival

Teachers move from day to day, trying to get through the week and wondering if teaching is the right job for them. Concerns about classroom management, visits by supervisors, professional competence, and acceptance by colleagues dominate their thoughts. Support and professional development at this stage are particularly critical.

Stage 2: Consolidation

At stage 2, the focus moves from the teacher's survival to the children's learning. The skills acquired during the first stage are consolidated, and synthesized into strategies to be thoughtfully applied in the class. Teachers also synthesize their knowledge of students and are able to analyze learning, social, or classroom management problems in the light of individual student differences and needs.

Stage 3: Renewal

Once teaching skills and an understanding of student development have been mastered, and several years of teaching experience have been completed, predictable classroom routines can become comforting, or boring. Teachers at stage 2 face a decision: stay at stage 2, comfortable in the classroom but exploring little else, or move toward stage 3, renewal. In stage 3, new approaches are sought as teachers participate in regional or national professional development programs and visit successful colleagues to seek new ideas for teaching and learning.

©Mark Edward Atkinson/ Blend Images/Corbis RF

Stage 4: Maturity

Teachers move beyond classroom concerns and seek greater professional perspective. At this stage, the teacher considers deeper and more abstract questions about broad educational issues: educational philosophy, ways to strengthen the teaching profession, and educational ideas that can enhance education throughout the school, region, or nation. Regrettably, many teachers never reach stage 4.

REFLECTION: Have you been taught by teachers representing each of these four developmental stages? Describe behaviors at each of the four levels. If you were to build in strategies to take you from stage 1 to stage 4, what might they be?

research reveals that teacher competence, your teaching skill, *is the most important factor* in improving student achievement.[24]

As you consider your own career development, you might also want to take a look at the bigger picture—how schools themselves are doing. It is discouraging for teachers-to-be to invest their talent and energy only to be told by politicians, journalists, and even the general public that our schools are doing poorly. We would like to offer another side of the story, presenting a perspective and evidence we rarely hear.

American Schools: Better Than We Think?

FOCUS QUESTION 7

Are America's schools a secret success story?

GLOBAL VIEW

Juku schools have been called cram schools. Do you see Juku-type schools taking root in the United States?

Critics decry the low performance by U.S. students on international tests, but such criticisms may be way off the mark. In fact, today's schools may be doing as well as they ever have—perhaps even better than they ever have. Low test scores sometimes reflect timing differences. Consider that Japanese middle school students score significantly higher than U.S. students on algebra tests, but most Japanese students take algebra a year or two earlier than U.S. students do. Moreover, most Japanese children attend private academies, called *Juku* schools, after school and on weekends. By 16 years of age, the typical Japanese student has attended at least two more years of classes than has a U.S. student. Yet, because of the greater comparative effectiveness of U.S. colleges in relation to Japanese colleges, many of these differences evaporate on later tests. [Perhaps there are two lessons here: (1) U.S. students should spend more time in school, and (2) the Japanese need to improve the quality of their colleges.]

Cultural differences in selecting which students take these exams also affect test scores. In some countries, students who do not speak the dominant language are routinely excluded from international exams. In some nations, only a small percentage of the most talented students are selected or encouraged to continue their education and go on to high school. As one might imagine, a highly selective population does quite well on international tests. In the United States, the full range of students is tested: strong and weak, English-speaking, and non-English-speaking students. A larger number of American test takers are likely to be poor. Comparing all of America's students with another nation's best is unfair.

Americans value a comprehensive education, one in which students are involved in a wide array of activities, from theater to sports to community service. The U.S. public typically values spontaneity, social responsibility, and independence in their children, values that are not assessed in international tests. Consider the way a South Korean teacher identifies the students selected for the International Assessment of Education Progress (IAEP):

> The math teacher . . . calls the names of the 13-year-olds in the room who have been selected as part of the IAEP sample. As each name is called, the student stands at attention at his or her desk until the list is complete. Then, to the supportive and encouraging applause of their colleagues, the chosen ones leave to [take the assessment test].[25]

U.S. students taking international exams do not engender cheers from their classmates and do not view such tests as a matter of national honor, as do the South Korean students. Too often, our culture belittles intellectuals and mocks gifted students.

Despite these obstacles, on several key tests our nation's students are doing quite well. In recent years, the proportion of students scoring above 500 on the SAT reading and mathematics tests had reached an all-time high. The number of students taking Advanced Placement (AP) tests soared, a sign that far more students are in the race for advanced college standing. Improvements have been documented on the California Achievement Test, the Iowa Test of Basic Skills, and the Metropolitan Achievement Test–tests used across the nation to measure student learning. One of the most encouraging signs has been the performance of students of color, whose scores have risen dramatically. Among African American students, average reading scores on the NAEP tests rose dramatically.[26] Decades ago, many of these students probably would not have even been in school, much less taking tests. U.S. schools are teaching more students, students are staying in school longer, and children are studying more challenging courses than ever before. According to the 2006 Lemelson-MIT Invention Index, teenagers reported that they are pleased with the problem-solving and leadership skills, teamwork, and creativity they learned in school, areas few news reports discuss. (See Figure 1.4.) Still another survey revealed that a strong majority of parents (71 percent) give an A or B to the school they know best, the one attended by their oldest child. (Interesting to note that only 53 percent of parents give a similar grade to their community's other schools, and only 18 percent give an A or B to the nation's schools.)[27]

Then why is there a national upheaval about education–why all the furor about our failing schools and why the demands for radical school reform? Educators like Diane Ravitch, David Berliner, Bruce Biddle, and others have advanced a number of possible explanations[28]:

- The current testing culture has caused great damage to, and misperceptions about, public schools. By measuring school effectiveness with yearly reading and mathematics exams, we have created perverse incentives to "teach to the test." Education is reduced to a single test score, and that score can stigmatize schools, teachers, and students. Some point out that we would learn the same information with zip codes instead of test scores: the poorest communities virtually always receive the lowest test score. This emphasis on reading and math test scores also means we devote less school time to subjects that are not tested like science, social studies, history, geography, foreign languages, art, and music.
- Public education is being attacked on ideological grounds by those who argue that the private sector is superior to the public sector. Anti–public school forces, often with big advertising budgets, demand that taxpayer money be used to support private, religious, charter, and for-profit schools. As a result, public schools have seen their budgets decrease. Students are now attending private and religious schools paid by taxpayer dollars. Yet despite all the clamor, few realize that test performance of these students at these private schools is no better, and often worse, than the local public schools.

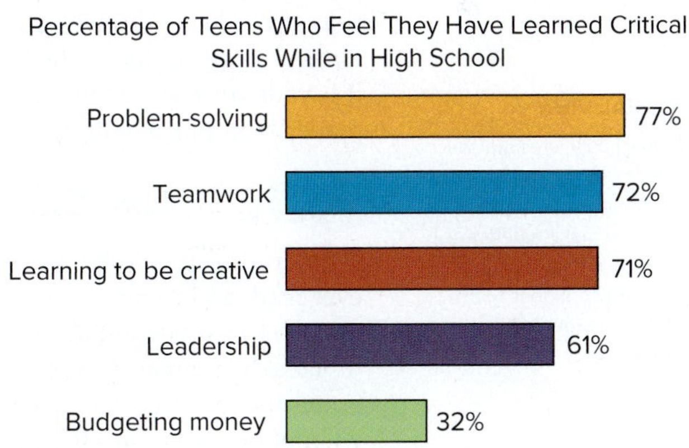

FIGURE 1.4

Critical skills.

SOURCE: The Lemelson-MIT Invention Index 2006, http://web.mit.edu/newsoffice/2006/lemelson-teens.html.

REFLECTION: Why do so few reports about U.S. schooling examine topics like these?

- Teachers' associations and tenure have been criticized for protecting incompetent teachers at the expense of student performance. This argument is weakened when we see that countries with far stronger teacher unions, like Finland, have student test scores that are at or near the top of all countries tested.
- Adults tend to romanticize what schools were like when they attended as children, for they always studied harder and learned more than their children do. (And when they went to school, they had to walk through four feet of snow, uphill, in both directions!)
- Americans hold unrealistic expectations. They want schools to conquer all sorts of social and academic ills, from illiteracy to teenage pregnancy, and to accomplish everything from teaching advanced math to preventing AIDS.
- Schools today work with tremendous numbers of poor students, non-English-speaking children, and special education students who just a few years ago would not have been attending school as long or, in some cases, would not have been attending school at all.
- The press has been all too willing to publish negative stories about schools—stories based on questionable sources. Sloppy, biased reporting has damaged the public's perception of schools.

It is helpful to remember two points. First, criticism can be fruitful. If additional attention and even criticism help shape stronger schools, then the current furor will have at least some positive impact. However, if the effect of this criticism is to drain public schools of their financial resources, more damage than good will be the result. Second, it is important to remember that there are countless students in all parts of the country who work diligently every day and perform with excellence. The United States continues to produce leaders in fields as diverse as medicine and sports, business and entertainment. To a great extent, these success stories are also the stories of talented and dedicated teachers. Although their quiet daily contributions rarely reach the headlines, teachers do make a difference. You represent the next generation of teachers who will, no doubt, weather difficult times and sometimes adverse circumstances to touch the lives of students and to shape a better America. Perhaps it is your voice and your commitment that will help bring an end to false comments made about public education.

GLOBAL VIEW

The UN estimates that we need millions more teachers worldwide. If you have a desire to make a difference and live in another culture, teaching continues to be a critical career in many countries.

Digging Deeper Online

We want this text to be the most exciting, interesting, and useful textbook you have ever read, and to mirror the enthusiasm that we feel about education. (Okay, so it's not an electrifying and frightening Stephen King novel like *Carrie,* but we work hard to make it stimulating and useful—and not scary). Along those lines, we have a little bonus for you in each chapter—a little extra material which you may find helpful, but will not be tested on. (Isn't that cool?) *Digging Deeper* consists of an additional page or two and is found on the textbook's Connect. You may want to read this additional information and take notes, or choose to ignore it entirely (when's the last time an author gave you that option?). Your choice—and no hard feelings on our part. For this chapter, the *Digging Deeper* section online offers some very practical advice for you: **What steps can I take between now and graduation to make myself an attractive teaching candidate?**

CONNECT FOR *TEACHERS, SCHOOLS, AND SOCIETY*

Check out Connect, McGraw-Hill Education's interactive learning environment, to:

Read Current and Historical Articles

Notes from an Accidental Teacher, by Carol Ann Tomlinson, *Best of Educational Leadership,* 2010–2011.

Raising Teacher Quality Around the World, by Vivien Stewart, *Educational Leadership,* December 2010/January 2011.

Against the Current, by Lisa Ann Williamson, *Teaching Tolerance,* Fall 2011.

Metaphors of Hope, Mimi Brodsky Chenfield, *Phi Delta Kappan,* December 2004.

A New Professional: The Aims of Education Revisited, by Parker J. Palmer, *Change* magazine, November/December 2007.

Analyze Case Studies

Megan Brownlee: A parent visits her children's favorite elementary school teacher and is surprised to discover that the teacher does not encourage her to enter the teaching profession.

Jennifer Gordon: A mature woman beginning a second career as an elementary school teacher struggles during her student teaching experience with how to deal with her cooperating teacher, who treats her very badly and corrects her in front of the class.

Watch Teachers, Students, and Classrooms in Action

Classroom Observation: **Teachers Discuss the Pros and Cons of Teaching.**
Our **Online Video Album** for contemporary videos related to this chapter.

KEY TERMS AND PEOPLE

American Federation of Teachers (AFT), 17
Hall, Reverend Samuel, 11
induction program, 17
Mann, Horace, 12
mentor, 17
merit pay, 4
National Board for Professional Teaching Standards (NBPTS), 12
National Education Association (NEA), 17
normal school, 11
pay-for-performance, 4
pedagogy, 16
tenure, 5

DISCUSSION QUESTIONS AND ACTIVITIES

1. This chapter introduces you to the importance of well-thought-out career decision making. You can read further on this decision-making process in one of the many career books now available. For example, Richard N. Bolles's *What Color Is Your Parachute?* contains many exercises that should help you clarify your commitment to teaching. Or you may want to visit Bolles's Web site at www.jobhuntersbible.com/. These resources, or a visit to your career center, can help you determine the best option for you.
2. Interview teachers and students at different grade levels to determine what they think are the positive and negative aspects of teaching. Share those interview responses with your classmates.
3. Suppose you could write an open letter to students, telling them about yourself and why you want to teach. What would you want them to know? When you attempt to explain yourself to others, you often gain greater self-knowledge. You might want to share your letter with classmates and to hear what they have to say in their letters. Perhaps your instructor could also try this exercise and share his or her open letter with you.
4. Check out teacher-related Web sites on the Internet. Schools and school districts, professional teacher organizations, and all sorts of interest groups sponsor not only Web sites but also listservs, chat groups, and other Internet activities. Seek out opportunities to interview practicing classroom teachers about their own classroom experiences.
5. Imagine that you are taking part in a career fair. Someone asks why you are exploring teaching. Briefly frame your answer.

Design Elements: Blue pencil: ©C.O.T/a.collectionRF/Getty Images RF; Pencils: ©Darren Greenwood/Design Pics RF; Gavel: ©Siede Preis/Getty Images RF; Students Huddled Together: ©Digital Vision/Getty Images RF; Pens with blue background: ©chiarito/Getty Images RF

©Purestock/Getty Images RF

It's not that I'm so smart, it's just that I stay with problems longer.

ALBERT EINSTEIN

chapter 2

Different Ways of Learning

Focus Questions

1. How do mindsets and multiple intelligences influence teaching and learning?
2. How does emotional intelligence influence teaching and learning?
3. How can teachers respond to students' different learning styles?
4. Is gender a learning style?
5. How are the needs of learners with exceptionalities met in today's classrooms?

Chapter Preview

At the dawn of the twenty-first century, basic educational concepts are being redefined, re-examined, and expanded. What does "intelligence" really mean? How many kinds of intelligences are there? What is EQ (emotional intelligence quotient), and is it a better predictor of success than IQ (intelligence quotient)? What are learning styles and how should instruction respond to different learning styles?

Gender issues are a hot topic in schools as some argue that girls' and boys' learning differences create the need for separate schools. Are single-sex learning environments a good idea? Do girls and boys learn differently? We want you to begin thinking about how teachers can recognize differences in learning while avoiding the dangers of stereotypic thinking, and the current gender debate is a good place to begin.

Another educational transformation is the increasing numbers of schoolchildren now identified as learners with exceptionalities—students with learning, physical, developmental, and emotional/behavioral disabilities—all of whom deserve appropriate educational strategies and materials. Students with gifts and talents represent another population with special needs too often lost in the current educational system.

This chapter will broaden your ideas of how students learn, and how teachers can teach to the many different ways of knowing.

Mindsets and Multiple Intelligences

Have you ever wondered what it really means to be a "genius"? How would you describe a genius? Have you ever met one? How would you rate your own intelligence? Above average? Average? Below average? Who decides, and what exactly is intelligence?

FOCUS QUESTION 1

How do mindsets and multiple intelligences influence teaching and learning?

Traditional definitions of *intelligence* usually include mental capabilities, such as reasoning, problem solving, and abstract thinking. The Intelligence Quotient, called IQ, was developed early in the twentieth century to measure a person's innate intelligence, with a score of 100 defined as normal, or average. The higher the score, the brighter the person. Some of us grew up in communities where IQ was barely mentioned. In many cases, that lack of communication might have been a blessing. Others of us grew up with "IQ envy," in communities where IQ scores were a big part of the culture. Because the IQ was considered a fixed, permanent measure of intellect, like a person's physical height, the scores engendered strong feelings. Today, we know that one's environment and well-being can greatly affect intellectual development.

Mindsets

A growing number of researchers now view intelligence not as a fixed, predetermined entity, but as malleable, something we can control, at least in part. Stanford professor **Carol Dweck** describes it this way: A **fixed mindset** views intelligence as ability-focused, finite, and determined at birth. An individual's IQ measures intelligence, and it does not change. **Growth mindset**, on the other hand, suggests that rather than being fixed at birth, intelligence can be developed through life, if we exert effort. But here's the key: which view you hold about intelligence affects how you go about learning. On difficult tasks, students who believe intelligence is fixed give up more quickly, blaming their intelligence (or lack of) for their failure. But on those same difficult tasks, students who embrace an incremental view of intelligence are more likely to persevere and explore more inventive strategies to solve a problem. To this group, setbacks are not considered a permanent reflection of intelligence, rather opportunities to learn and grow.[1]

Furthermore, Dweck believes that we all have elements of both fixed and growth mindsets. For example, if we want to move ourselves and students closer to a growth mindset in thought and practice, we need to stay in touch with our fixed mindsets. How? Awareness of fixed-mindset triggers is actually a first step to creating successful mindset learning strategies. Dweck recommends watching for fixed-mindset reactions when faced with challenges.[2] Do you feel overly anxious or avoid a situation? Do you feel incompetent or defeated? Do you look for an excuse? Does criticism evoke habits of a fixed mindset? Do you become defensive, angry, or crushed instead of interested in learning from the feedback? Do you feel envious and threatened, or do you feel eager to learn?

Specific instructional strategies can also assist students (and teachers) in developing growth mindsets. For example, teachers can

- Provide meaningful student feedback
- Ask open-ended questions
- Use more formative testing
- Create flexible ability groupings

(In Chapter 11, "Becoming an Effective Teacher," we explore these suggestions in-depth.)

Multiple Intelligences

Traditional assessments of intelligence emphasize language and logical-mathematical abilities, another narrow view of intelligence. Harvard psychologist **Howard Gardner** has worked to broaden this concept of intelligence, defining intelligence as "the capacity to solve problems or to fashion products that are valued in one or more cultural settings."[3]

Gardner identified eight kinds of intelligence, not all of which are commonly recognized in school settings. Gardner believes that his theory of **multiple intelligences** more accurately captures the diverse nature of human capability. Consider Gardner's eight intelligences[4]:

1. *Logical-mathematical.* Skills related to mathematical manipulations and discerning and solving logical problems ("number/reasoning smart").
2. *Linguistic.* Sensitivity to the meanings, sounds, and rhythms of words, as well as to the function of language as a whole ("word smart").
3. *Bodily-kinesthetic.* Ability to excel physically and to handle objects skillfully ("body smart").
4. *Musical.* Ability to produce pitch and rhythm, as well as to appreciate various forms of musical expression ("music smart").

Physical ability and body awareness are forms of kinesthetic intelligence.

5. *Spatial.* Ability to form a mental model of the spatial world and to maneuver and operate using that model ("picture smart").
6. *Interpersonal.* Ability to analyze and respond to the motivations, moods, and desires of other people ("people smart").
7. *Intrapersonal.* Knowledge of one's feelings, needs, strengths, and weaknesses; ability to use this knowledge to guide behavior ("self smart").
8. *Naturalist.* (Gardner's most recently defined intelligence) Ability to discriminate among living things, to classify plants, animals, and minerals; ability to nurture animals and grow plants; a sensitivity to the natural world ("environment smart").

In regard to the last intelligence, youth who engage in more outdoor activity report better health and social well-being than their peers who spend hours in front of television and computer screens. Yet, young people spend 50 percent less time playing outside than they did a decade ago. Teachers and parents increasingly worry that today's children are at risk of developing "nature deficit disorder" and that the naturalist intelligence is being lost to social media, academic pressures, and busy schedules.[5]

RAP 1.2

Multiple Intelligences Bingo

The theory of multiple intelligences goes a long way in explaining why the quality of an individual's performance may vary greatly in different activities, rather than reflect a single standard of performance as indicated by an IQ score. Gardner also points out that what is considered *intelligence* may differ, depending on cultural values. Thus, in the Pacific Islands, intelligence is the ability to navigate among the islands. For many Muslims, the ability to memorize the Quran is a mark of intelligence. Intelligence in Balinese social life is demonstrated by physical grace.

Gardner's theory has sparked the imaginations of many educators, some of whom are redesigning their curricula to respond to differing student intelligences. Teachers are refining their approaches in response to such questions as[6]

GLOBAL VIEW

Describe the varied cultural, religious, or ethnic intelligences of your classmates.

- How can I use music to emphasize key points?
- How can I promote hand and bodily movements and experiences to enhance learning?
- How can I incorporate sharing and interpersonal interactions into my lessons?
- How can I encourage students to think more deeply about their feelings and memories?
- How can I use visual organizers and visual aids to promote understanding?
- How can I encourage students to classify and appreciate the world around them?

Assessment

As instruction undergoes reexamination, so does evaluation. The old pencil-and-paper tests used to assess linguistic, math, and logical intelligences seem much less appropriate for measuring these new areas identified by Dweck, Gardner, and others. The **portfolio** approach is an example of a more comprehensive assessment, which includes student artifacts (papers, projects, multi-media productions, exhibits) that offer tangible examples of student learning. In other cases, rather than A's and B's or 80s and 90s, schools are using descriptions to report student competence. In music, for example, such descriptions might include "She plays the piano with technical competence," "His Haiku poetry reflects visual imagination," and so on. Whether the school is exploring portfolios, descriptive assessment, or another evaluation method, Gardner's multiple intelligences theory and Dweck's mindsets approach are reshaping many current assessment practices.[7]

The Five Minds

Gardner's work on multiple intelligences has greatly influenced how educators view teaching and learning. Now Gardner is at it again. In his book *Five Minds for the Future,* Gardner suggests new directions for schools. He points out that memorizing facts and cramming for standardized tests is not very useful in the twenty-first century. With huge amounts of information at our fingertips, with instant global communications, and with the growing intersections of cultures and countries, we have new lessons to learn. For schools to ignore these changes is self-defeating. So Gardner offers "five minds," really five ways of knowing, that he believes we need to develop and thrive in the twenty-first century. So, let go of the familiar, and let your imagination consider Gardner's "five minds."[8]

The Ethical Mind Did you ever notice how often we turn away from hard truths, as though ignoring them will make them disappear? We have become inured to dishonest behavior. For example, the majority of our students cheat on exams, copy homework from others, or plagiarize term papers. Depressing as that is, we still ignore it. In adult life, these unethical behaviors lead to grievous consequences on Wall Street, in corporations, in politics, and in our personal lives. Gardner believes that we must tackle this deceit head on and teach children to think reflectively about their behavior. He would like to see more young adults choose careers that advance society, rather than focus on accruing personal wealth at the cost of leading an ethical life.

The Respectful Mind How often do you listen to misogynist rap lyrics, combative talk radio, rude television commentators; laugh (even uncomfortably) at a racist joke; or witness road rage unfold before your eyes? Disrespectful behavior in our society has become commonplace, and Gardner believes we should teach children to develop respectful minds. This means honoring people with different ideas, different cultures, and different belief systems. In fact, we have much to learn from those who have experienced different lives. In an ever-shrinking world, the lack of respectful minds can have dire consequences.

The Disciplined Mind This mind may be the most familiar to you because it is part of today's school curriculum. The disciplined mind masters a field of study, such as literature, history, art, science, math, or even a craft. With a disciplined mind, one becomes a master of an area of work or a profession; without this mastery, one is destined to spend life simply following someone else's directions.

The Synthesizing Mind Today, we are inundated with information. Tomorrow, we will be inundated with even more information. We need to develop the ability to sort through this information, to figure out what is important and what is not so important, to see meaningful connections, and then to interpret how best we can use the data. In this information age, being able to eliminate the trivial while connecting the useful is key.

The Creating Mind Being creative is a timeless skill. A creative mind discovers new ways of looking at the world, and offers new insights and a fresh way of thinking. Some believe that creativity may be America's greatest (and most underdeveloped) natural resource.

How do these five minds sound to you? Perhaps you have yet another mind that you think should be part of school life. We encourage you to continually consider new ways of looking at teaching and learning.

Emotional Intelligence

FOCUS QUESTION 2

How does emotional intelligence influence teaching and learning?

While ideas of mindsets, multiple intelligences, and the five minds raise fundamental questions about different ways students learn and use information, **EQ**, or the **emotional intelligence quotient**, offers another perspective on learning. EQ "is a type of social intelligence that involves the ability to monitor one's own and others' emotions, to discriminate among them, and to use the information to guide one's thinking actions."[9] In his book *Emotional Intelligence,* psychologist Daniel Goleman suggests that EQ taps into the heart, as well as the head, and may be a better predictor of success in life than IQ. How does EQ work? The "marshmallow story" offers some useful insights[10]:

> A researcher explains to a 4-year-old that he/she needs to run off to do an errand, but there is a marshmallow for the youngster to enjoy. The youngster can choose to eat the marshmallow immediately. But, if the 4-year-old can wait and *not* eat the marshmallow right away, then an extra marshmallow will be given when the researcher returns. Eat one now, or hold off and get twice the reward.

What do you think you would have done as a 4-year-old? According to the social scientists who conducted the marshmallow experiment, decisions even at this age foreshadow an emotional disposition characteristic of a successful (or less successful) adult. By the time the children in the study reached high school, the now 14-year-olds were described by teachers and parents in a way that suggested their marshmallow behaviors predicted some significant differences. Students who 10 years earlier were able to delay their gratification, to wait a while and garner a second marshmallow, were reported to be better adjusted, more popular, more adventurous, and more confident in adolescence than the group who 10 years earlier had gobbled down their marshmallows.

The children who gave in to temptation, ate the marshmallow, and abandoned their chances for a second one were more likely to be described as stubborn, easily frustrated, and lonely teenagers. In addition to the differences between the gobblers and the waiters as described by parents and teachers, there was also a significant SAT scoring gap. The students who, 10 years earlier, could wait for the second marshmallow scored 210 points higher than did the gobblers. Reasoning and control, "the regulation of emotion in a way that enhances living," might be new, and perhaps better, measures of what we call smart, or intelligent.

Research at Pennsylvania State University also supports the importance of EQ to students' academic and social well-being. Researchers followed nearly 800 students for two decades, finding that children who share and show compassion are more

So What's Your EQ?

Like Daniel Goleman, Yale psychologist Peter Salovey works with emotional intelligence issues, and he identifies five elements of emotional intelligence. How would you rate yourself on each of these dimensions?

KNOWING EMOTIONS

The foundation of one's emotional intelligence is self-awareness. A person's ability to recognize a feeling as it happens is the essential first step in understanding the place and power of emotions. People who do not know when they are angry, jealous, or in love are at the mercy of their emotions.

Self-Rating on Knowing My Emotions *Always aware of my emotions__Usually aware__Sometimes aware__Out of touch, clueless.__*

MANAGING EMOTIONS

A person who can control and manage emotions can handle bad times as well as the good, shake off depression, bounce back from life's setbacks, and avoid irritability. In one study, up to half of the youngsters who at age 6 were disruptive and unable to get along with others were classified as delinquents by the time they were teenagers.

Self-Rating on Managing My Emotions *Always manage my emotions__Usually manage__Sometimes manage__ My emotions manage me.__*

MOTIVATING ONESELF

Productive individuals are able to focus energy, confidence, and concentration on achieving a goal and avoid anxiety, anger, and depression. One study of 36,000 people found that "worriers" have poorer academic performance than nonworriers. (A load off your mind, no doubt!)

Self-Rating on Motivation and Focus *Always self-motivated/focused__Usually self-motivated/focused__Sometimes self-motivated/focused__I can't focus on when I was last focused (and I don't care).__*

RECOGNIZING EMOTIONS IN OTHERS

This skill is the core of empathy, the ability to pick up subtle signs of what other people need or want. Such a person always seems to "get it," even before the words are spoken.

Self-Rating on Empathy *Always empathetic__Usually empathetic__Sometimes empathetic__I rarely "get it."__*

HANDLING RELATIONSHIPS

People whose EQ is high are the kind of people you want to be around. They are popular, are good leaders, and make you feel comfortable and connected. Children who lack social skills are often distracted from learning, and the dropout rate for children who are rejected by their peers can be two to eight times higher than for children who have friends.

Self-Rating on Relationships *I am rich in friendship and am often asked to lead activities and events.__I have many friends.__I have a few friends.__Actually, I'm pretty desperate for friends.__*

RATINGS

Give 4 points for each time you selected the first choice, 3 points for the "usual" or "many" second option, 2 points for the "sometimes" selection, and 1 point for the last choice.

18–20 points:	A grade—WOW! Impressive!
14–17 points:	B grade—You have considerable skills and talents.
10–13 points:	C grade—Feel free to read further on this topic.
5–9 points:	D grade—This may be a perfect subject to investigate in greater detail. Do you have a topic for your term project yet?

Source: Salovey, Peter, and Mayer, John D. *Emotional Intelligence*, Baywood Publishing, 1990.

REFLECTION: Are you satisfied with your rating? If you earned a high rating, to what do you attribute your high EQ? If your rating was lower than you liked, how can you work on increasing your EQ? How will you develop the EQ of your students?

likely to have a college degree and a job 20 years later than children who lack those social skills. Kids who interact well with others also are less likely to have substance-abuse problems and run-ins with the law. Importantly, these measures of EQ were constant across socioeconomic, racial, and gender status.[11] By the way, how would you rate your EQ? (See A Closer Look on p. 31.)

Shifting ideas of intelligence are toppling educational traditions, stretching our understanding of what schools are about. In a sense, they are increasing the range and diversity of educational ideas. The students you will teach will learn in diverse ways, and a single IQ or even EQ score is unlikely to capture the range of their abilities and skills. Your students will also bring to the classroom multiple learning styles that will further expand our grasp of how people learn.

Learning Styles

FOCUS QUESTION 3

How can teachers respond to students' different learning styles?

Many educators believe that students have different **learning styles**—diverse ways of learning, comprehending, and using information. Intriguing research suggests that learning styles may be as unique as handwriting. Some students do their best work late at night, but others set an early alarm because they are most alert in the morning. Many students seek a quiet place in the library to prepare for finals; others learn best in a noisy environment or with a crowd of people; still others study most effectively in a state of perpetual motion, constantly walking in circles to help their concentration.[12]

At least three types of factors contribute to a student's individual learning style[13]:

1. *Physiology.* Clearly, a student who is hungry and tired will not learn as effectively as a well-nourished and rested child. Other physiological factors are less obvious. Different body rhythms cause some students to learn better in the morning, whereas others excel in the afternoon. Some students can sit still for long periods of time; others need to get up and move around. Some students prefer to interact with material through touch; others like to take copious notes or doodle. Light, sound, and temperature are yet other factors to which students respond differently. How would you describe your physiological style?
2. *Affective (attitudes).* Individuals bring different levels of motivation to learning, and the intensity level of this motivation is a critical determinant of learning style. A popular descriptor of motivation is *grit,* one's passion and persistence to attain success. An individual with grit approaches achievement as a marathon, believing that his or her advantage is stamina. While disappointment or boredom signals to others that it is time give up, the gritty individual embraces "stick-to-it-iveness" and stays the course.[14] (Grit. The very word can stir up memories of perseverance. Recall a time, in or out of school, when you demonstrated grit.)

   Other aspects of the affective domain include attitudes, values, and emotions—factors that influence curiosity, the ability to tolerate and overcome frustration, a preference to learn in groups or individually, and the willingness to take risks. A fascinating aspect of the affective domain is a concept termed **locus of control.** Some learners attribute success or failure to external factors ("Those problems were confusing," "The teacher didn't review the material well," or "My score was high because I made some lucky guesses"). These learners have an external locus of control and do not take responsibility for

TEACHING TIP

Including Different Learning Styles

While not all educators agree that learning styles are important, many teachers are real advocates. Integrating different learning styles into instruction gives students a variety of learning experiences, builds new neural pathways, and has the added bonus of keeping instruction lively. Here are a few teaching tips you may want to consider:

VISUAL LEARNING: SEE IT

Learning with our eyes is common. Teachers can:

- Use textbooks, charts, course outlines, flash cards, videos, maps, and computer simulations as instructional aids.
- Ask students to highlight or color-code key lesson points.
- Note subheadings and illustrations before students read a chapter.
- Use overheads, PowerPoints, flip charts, and whiteboards to list key points of the lesson.
- Use guided imagery and illustrations.

KINESTHETIC/TACTILE LEARNING: DO IT

Often the least acknowledged learning style, kinesthetic/tactile learning is also called *haptic* (Greek for "moving and doing") or *hands-on.* Teachers can:

- Give students who need it the ability to stand or pace quietly in the back of the room during instruction to help with processing and retention.
- Use a bean bag or soft ball when calling on students or to organize discussions.
- Ask students to take notes and underline key points.
- Use skits and role-plays.
- Integrate hands-on lessons, observations, and field explorations.
- Create index or flash cards for students to manipulate.

AUDITORY LEARNERS: HEAR IT

Auditory learning focuses on conversations and lecture; students often develop strong language skills. Teachers can:

- Encourage students to recite the main points of a book or lecture.
- Include group work into class activities so students can verbally share ideas.
- Audio-tape classroom activities or record key lesson ideas.
- Suggest that students read the text or any new vocabulary words out loud.
- Listen to background music when studying.

REFLECTION: Choose a subject or topic that you want to teach. Describe how you would integrate three learning activities in your lesson that incorporate three learning styles (visual, kinesthetic/tactile, auditory). Which of these learning styles appeals to you? Why? Which one takes you most out of your comfort zone?

their behavior. Others attribute performance to internal factors ("I didn't study enough" or "I didn't read the directions carefully"). These students have an internal locus of control because they have the sense that they control their fate, that they can improve their performance. How would you describe your affective style?

Interestingly, the root of intrinsic is the Latin *intrinsecus,* a combination of two words meaning *within* and *alongside.* It's likely that most students *are* intrinsically motivated—just motivated to follow their own interests, not necessarily to passionately engage in what teachers and schools want them to do. A teacher's challenge is to know their students' interests and goals, and to develop trusting relationships that spark motivation from within.[15]

3. *Cognitive (information processing).* Individuals have different ways of perceiving, organizing, retaining, and using information, all components of the cognitive domain. Some students prefer to learn by reading and looking at material *(visual learners).* Others need to listen and hear information spoken aloud *(auditory learners).* Still others learn best using body movement, touch, and hands-on participation *(kinesthetic/tactile learners).* Some students are quick to respond; others are slower,

preferring to observe and reflect. Some learners focus attention narrowly and with great intensity; others pay attention to many things at once. Some learners can master many concrete ideas; others excel at abstract thinking. How would you describe your cognitive style? (See Teaching Tip: Including Different Learning Styles p. 33.)

Educators frequently try to shape their instruction to match a student's learning style. So if a student learns best visually, a teacher might focus instruction on photographs, videos, and drawings—but is this the best approach? Neuroscientists suggest that teachers should do more. They believe that learners benefit when teachers not only respond to a student's preferred learning style, but also integrate it with other learning styles. Teaching to a single learning style may be comfortable for the student, but it does not enhance brain development as much as involving other ways of learning does. Why? When the brain is challenged, it can grow by developing new neural pathways. This process is called **neuroplasticity.**[16] As teachers integrate different learning styles into the classroom and push students out of their comfort zone, the brain grows new neural pathways, and students retain more deeply and can apply information more creatively.[17] Teachers are wise to explore a variety of learning styles in the classroom. Flexibility and variety are the keys: Don't assume that all students learn the way you do, and take care not to undervalue students just because their learning styles differ from yours.

FOCUS QUESTION 4

Is gender a learning style?

Do Boys and Girls Learn Differently?

If your flying saucer arrived on Earth from another world and landed in a schoolyard, and you peeked through the schoolhouse windows, you might observe the following:

- In a kindergarten class, the teacher decides to put a girl between two boys in order to "calm them down."
- Throughout the school, you sense excitement as students talk about the championship spelling bee, the one that will decide if the girls or the boys are the better spellers.
- Outside, the boys have three basketball games in progress while the girls are off to the side jumping rope.
- Over the public address system, the principal announces: "Good morning, boys and girls."

It is all so obvious. You radio back to your home base: "Planet Earth dominated by two tribes: boys and girls. Will investigate further."

What are the assumptions inherent in boy-versus-girl competitions? Why are gender competitions still used, while school competitions based on race, religion, or ethnicity are seen as destructive?

©Blend Images/Alamy RF

Brain Differences

Teachers' comments and behaviors often blindly reinforce a gender divide, yet if applied to race, religion, or ethnicity, teachers would quickly regain their vision. You will search long and hard to find a teacher who announces: "We will have a spelling bee today to see who will be the champion spellers, Jews or Christians!" Or imagine, "Good morning, blacks and whites." How about, "You two Hispanics are causing too much disruption, so I am placing a Native American between you!" Although sensitive to religious, ethnic, or racial affronts, we seem rather oblivious to gender comments. This is a situation with serious consequences.

CONTEMPORARY ISSUES

A View from the Field: Single-Sex Education

In classrooms across the country, educators are experimenting with single-sex education. Some schools do it to raise test scores because they believe that boys and girls learn differently. Others argue that dividing students removes sexual distractions and is a good behavior management strategy. Such notions fit easily into traditional belief systems, but are not supported by rigorous research.[a]

A Washington, DC, middle school teacher shares his first-hand experience with single-sex education:

> At first, I felt there were some real advantages to separating the girls and boys. There was certainly less teasing, which had gotten out of hand the year before. So I saw the separation as having marginal advantages. But over time, each gender developed other discipline issues. Cliques of girls began teasing each other. They replaced the boys as the discipline problem. Boys really began acting out. They actually got goofier. Then there was a second problem: boys struggling with their sexual identity really lost out. Some of these boys had girls as their best friends, and when the separate classes began, they literally lost their best friends. They were now isolated in an alpha male environment. They were treated harshly and ridiculed. The third problem was sheer numbers: there were more girls in these classes than boys. The girls' classes got much bigger. The girls got less individualized attention. So what I thought at first would be a help for girls really failed them. It was not a good idea.
>
> I pride myself in not being an ideologue. I do not like it when people get stuck in one camp or the other. Show me something that works, and I want to find out why and how we can use it. But this did not work.[b]

[a]Melinda Anderson, "The Resurgence of Single Sex Education," *The Atlantic*, December 22, 2015, http://www.theatlantic.com/education.
[b]David and Myra Sadker, and Karen Zittleman, *Still Failing at Fairness* (New York: Scribners, 2009), pp. 253–288.

REFLECTION: Support your views about single-sex schooling.

Constant references to gender lead children to believe that teachers are intentionally signaling important differences between boys and girls. But are these differences significant, or are they stereotypes?

That's what Janet Hyde at the University of Wisconsin-Madison wanted to find out. Like most of us, she had heard that boys are more aggressive; better in math, science, and technology; and prefer an active and competitive male learning style. Girls, on the other hand, are seen as more nurturing and intuitive, preferring to personalize knowledge; they are more successful in the arts and languages, and more compliant than boys. This cooperative and personal approach to learning has been termed a female learning style. Hyde wanted to determine if these common gender assumptions were true.

Hyde used a sophisticated meta-analytic statistical procedure to review many studies on gender differences and similarities. The big surprise: there are precious few educationally relevant gender differences. She called her findings the *gender similarities hypothesis:* greater educational differences exist *within* the genders than *between* the genders. According to Hyde's work, there are no important intellectual or psychological differences between females and males that require unique teaching approaches.[18] Other studies confirm Hyde's findings and show that the greatest challenges in educational achievement have less to do with gender and more to do with race, ethnicity, and economic status.[19] (However, some disagree and believe that boys and girls should be taught in separate schools. See Contemporary Issues: A View from the Field: Single-Sex Education.)

Hyde's work did reveal a few exceptions to the gender similarities hypothesis. In some cases, her findings were counterintuitive: males overall exhibited slightly more helping behaviors than females, while self-esteem levels for adult men and women were quite similar. Hyde also found a couple of educationally relevant differences: boys

GLOBAL VIEW

In a comparison of 46 nations, females scored higher on international print-based reading tests than males. Interestingly, the gender gap diminished when digital texts were used. Boys did better with computer-based reading than print-based reading, while the opposite held true for girls. (Programme for International Student Assessment, 2015).

are generally more aggressive and have better ability to rotate objects mentally.[20] But the reason for these few differences is not clear. Are they due to nature or nurture, or a combination of the two? After all, socialization plays a big role in our culture.

For example, researchers at the University of Michigan followed more than eight hundred children and their parents for 13 years and found that traditional gender stereotypes greatly influence parental attitudes and behaviors related to children's interest in math. Parents provided more math-supportive environments for their sons than for their daughters, including buying more math and science toys. Parents, and dads especially, held more positive perceptions of their son's math abilities than of their daughters'.[21] Moreover, lack of expectations for technology prowess particularly impacts girls: Parents are three times more likely to give a smartphone or video game device to a son rather than a daughter.[22]

Lise Eliot, a neuroscientist at the Chicago Medical School, believes that such early socialization contributes to gender differences in learning. She describes how the many hours boys clock with Legos, baseball, and video games help develop spatial skills, like targeting and mental rotation, skills not taught in school. Such spatial skills figure prominently in subjects like physics, trigonometry, calculus, and engineering, subjects in which many boys excel. Girls, by contrast, are encouraged more than boys to read for pleasure outside school. Eliot and others contend that it is this practice, rather than any genetic or hormonal difference, that best predicts gender differences in reading achievement.[23] This socialization may also explain why boys tend to struggle in subjects like English, literature, and writing. Boys' underachievement may be driven by stereoptyes: what boys think it means to be a man is often at odds with succeeding in school. Clearly, socialization can be a powerful influence on academic success.

GLOBAL VIEW

High female performance on international math tests correlates with high levels of gender equity in their home countries. Females in Iceland, Norway, and Sweden score highest on such measures, while women in the United States rank twenty-third out of sixty-nine nations. (Programme for International Student Assessment, 2015)

Importantly, our understanding of how nature and nurture influences gender roles is changing. We are reminded of this whenever we see quiet boys who love reading or music or girls who soar in math or on the athletic field. We typically view genetics and learning styles as pretty much fixed from birth, but research shows that it is more complicated than that.[24] The brain, for example, rather than being fixed, is like a muscle that can be shaped and changed by our experiences. As we previously discussed, the ability of our brain to change itself and create new neural pathways is called *neuroplasticity*. You may have heard the catchy phrase, "Neurons that fire together wire together." This does describe how we learn: by physically creating neural pathways that connect some of the billions of neurons throughout the brain and the body. Linking neurons is how we acquire information, skills, attitudes, habits, emotions, and values. The more we practice something, the more we strengthen that pathway. The pathway might be learning how to conjugate a French verb, code a computer, repair plumbing, or ice skate. We indeed are very often the architects of our brains.

For teachers, this is exciting news. It means that if we offer a variety of challenging and involving activities in our classes, we not only maintain student interest, but also we can help students grow and cultivate their brains. On the other hand, if we teach to a single learning style or use stereotypes in our teaching, we limit the brain's possibilities. So teachers are wise to encourage all their students, girls and boys, to develop their brains by exploring different learning styles, incorporating both competitive and cooperative activities, integrating both personal connections and active learning, and focusing on the arts as well as traditional subjects.

Generalizing a pedagogy based on a student's gender will surely miss many students who do not fit neatly into a fixed gender mold. The same thing can be said of students with exceptional needs. We will end this chapter with a close look at teaching exceptional learners, from students with disabilities to gifted learners. Inclusion of these students may further broaden different learning styles and the range of teaching skills you will need.

Exceptional Learners

FOCUS QUESTION 5

How are the needs of learners with exceptionalities met in today's classroom?

In a typical classroom, a teacher meets students with a great range of abilities, from students reading years behind grade level to students reading years ahead. Both these groups of students are described by the same broad term: **exceptional learners.** Integrating exceptional learners into the regular classroom is yet another aspect of teaching students with different learning styles.

Typically, learners with exceptionalities are categorized as students with

- Learning disabilities
- Developmental disabilities/intellectual disabilities
- Emotional disturbances or behavior disorders
- Hearing impairments
- Visual impairments
- Speech and communication disorders
- Attention deficit hyperactivity disorder
- Autism spectrum disorder
- Traumatic brain injury
- Orthopedic impairments
- Other health impairments
- Severe and multiple disabilities

And although it seems a very different kind of category, gifted and talented students are also considered exceptional learners.[25]

Teaching exceptional learners, from students with disabilities to gifted and talented learners, offers teachers the opportunity to stretch their imagination and creativity. Let's begin with a group many people believe need little, if any, special attention. How wrong they are.

The Gifted and Talented

> In Westchester County, a suburb of New York City, a 2½-year-old boy already emulates the language abilities of his parents. He speaks and reads English, French, Hebrew, Spanish, and Yiddish, and he has mastered some Danish. He is studying music theory and is conducting scientific experiments. The parents, however, are unable to find any educational facility willing and able to educate their young, gifted child. A member of their local school board told them: "It is not the responsibility or function of public schools to deal with such children." As a result, the parents considered moving to Washington state, where there was an experimental preschool program for the gifted.[26]

FIGURE 2.1

Characteristics of giftedness.

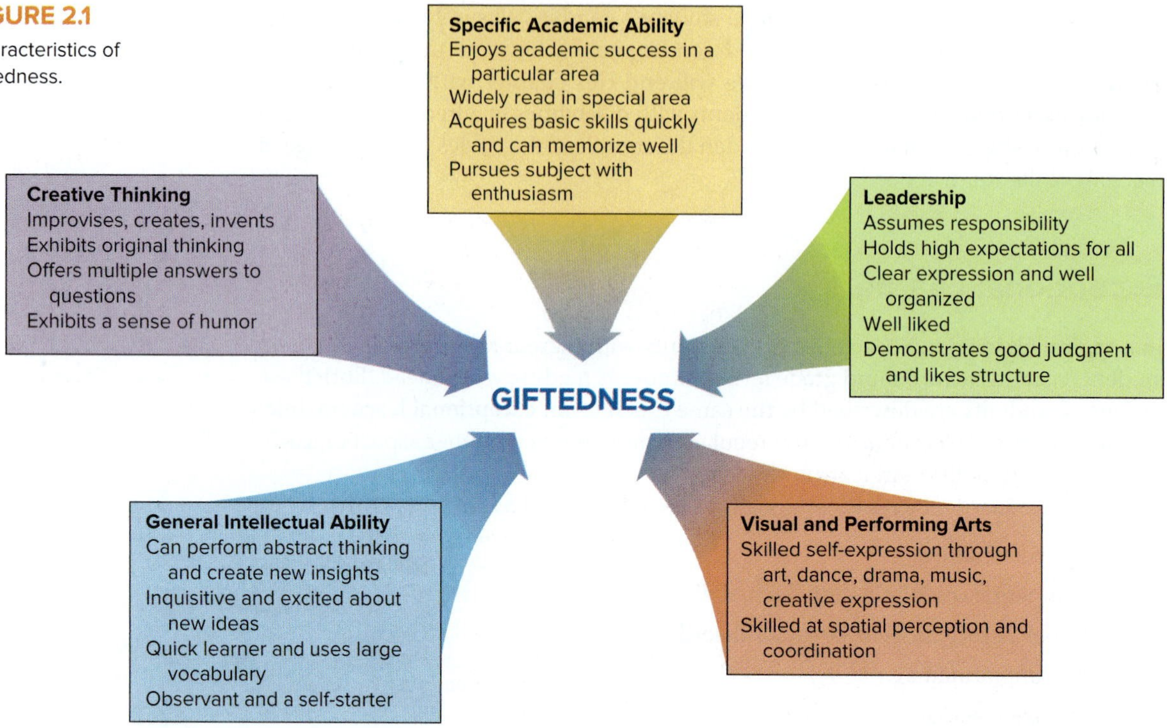

REFLECTION: Would you include Sternberg's concept of wisdom in this definition? How do these areas relate to Gardner's multiple intelligences?

If you are like most Americans, you may find it difficult to consider gifted and talented children to be in any way disadvantaged. After all, gifted learners are the lucky ones who master subject matter with ease. They are the ones who shout out the solution before most of us have a chance to write down the problem. Others may have perfect musical pitch, are athletic superstars, create scientific experiments that amaze, or demonstrate insights that inspire and inform us. Many exhibit endless curiosity, creativity, and energy.

Defining **giftedness** invites controversy.[27] To some, the traditional definition of giftedness includes those with an IQ of 130 or higher; to others, the label giftedness is reserved for those with an IQ score of 160 or higher. The National Association for Gifted Children defines five elements of giftedness: artistic and creative talents, intellectual and academic abilities, and leadership skills. (See Figure 2.1.) Noted psychologist Robert Sternberg has suggested that a new area be included: wisdom. After years of researching what it means to be gifted, Sternberg now believes that giftedness is not just about how analytical and insightful you are, but also about how you use such skills. A clever business executive who uses his or her intelligence to earn a fortune, only to leave the company and stockholders in bankruptcy, may have been quite bright, but Sternberg argues should not be considered gifted. "The world is getting too dangerous. We have to train kids not just to be smart but to be wise."[28] Sternberg looks to Gandhi, Mandela, and Martin Luther King Jr. as examples of wisdom too often ignored in current definitions.

With such varied definitions of giftedness, identifying such learners can be a challenge. Moreover, gifted students are not consistently high-achievers or well-behaved, and their giftedness can often result in apathy, lack of effort, and resentment. Only a small percentage of our population are identified with such high degrees of ability, creativity, motivation, pragmatic talent, or wisdom—making for a very exclusive club. The National Association for Gifted Children estimates that between 6 and 10 percent, or 3 to 5 million students, are identified as academically gifted. A far greater number of gifted students may remain unidentified. Intelligence testing often overlooks many students who are gifted. Students living in poverty, particularly those whose parents are uneducated or speak English as a second language, are less likely to develop the verbal skills measured by these traditional intelligence tests. Not surprisingly, students who are identified as gifted by such conventional tests are overwhelmingly White, Asian, and middle- or upper-class students. Assessments that measure spatial and mathematical intelligence as well as curiosity, artistic skills, and leadership abilities identify a more diverse crop of gifted students.[29]

For those students who are identified as gifted, school can become an unfriendly place. Gifted students may be naturally more curious and motivated to learn, but those traits often require tremendous intellectual stimulation and support. Many do not succeed on their own. Gifted students may be haunted by a sense of isolation and loneliness, pressure to achieve, fear of failure, and negative peer pressure.[30] Gifted students talk often about their feelings of isolation and feeling different, of wanting to be "normal" and "like everyone else":

> *I just want to be a regular kid and not stick out so much all the time.*
>
> *I get taken advantage of. People ask to be my partner or work with me on a paper and I am stuck doing all the work. The only thing they do is make sure their name is on my paper or project. But I'm never asked to sit with them at lunch or hang out after school.*
>
> *I get scared for the world. Being smart allows me to see the world and what trouble we're really in.*[31]

Not surprisingly then, instead of thriving in school, too many gifted students drop out. Researchers estimate that between 18 and 25 percent of gifted students drop out, and the picture is especially bleak for gifted students from lower socioeconomic backgrounds across all races.[32] The result is that many of our nation's brightest and most competent students are lost to neglect and apathy, and some of our most talented youth do not succeed at school.

Teaching gifted learners comes with its own set of challenges. To some it seems downright undemocratic to provide special services to children who already enjoy an advantage. Moreover, struggling with shrinking revenues and federal mandates that focus on improving the test scores of lower-achieving pupils, many school districts across the country are cutting programs for their most promising students. Consequently, there is often a lack of commitment to support curriculum and teachers for extremely advanced students. And while the debate over school reform focuses on efforts to help low-performing students, no federal law offers a reward for raising the scores of high achievers and punishment if their progress lags—potentially leaving gifted students behind.[33]

Despite these challenges, many educators and parents believe that we need to do a better job of "gifted inclusion" by designing regular class activities that are more responsive to the needs of the gifted. How do teachers develop an instructional plan that will be challenging, enlightening, and intriguing to students of different abilities, and still maintain a sense of community within the classroom? The regular classroom can be a major instructional resource by providing enrichment activities such as independent projects, small-group inquiry and investigations, academic competitions, and learning centers that provide in-depth and challenging content beyond regular grade-level lessons.[34] A gifted student might also spend most of the day in a regular class and be pulled out for a part of the day, perhaps an hour or so, to receive special instruction. At the secondary level, high schools have augmented their offerings with challenging courses of study, such as the **Advanced Placement (AP)** program that offers college-level courses for high-achieving high schoolers and the **International Baccalaureate (IB)** program, an internationally recognized degree program that includes rigorous science, math, and foreign language requirements along with diverse cultural studies. Special high schools, such as the Bronx High School of Science and the North Carolina School for Mathematics and Science, have long and distinguished histories of providing educational opportunities for intellectually gifted students. Other special schools have focused on programs in acting, music, and dance.

Some school districts go beyond their own resources to meet the needs of gifted students, connecting gifted high school students with the local college or community college. These students spend part of their day enrolled in college-level courses, being intellectually challenged and receiving college credit while still enrolled in high school. Still other elementary, middle, and high school gifted students receive additional support through online instruction, summer camps, or even special year-long programs that augment their regular courses. Johns Hopkins University, for example, has been sponsoring the Center for Talented Youth (CTY) in different parts of the nation for several decades. Many of these college programs are termed **accelerated programs** because they allow gifted students from all grade levels to skip grades or receive college credit early. Advanced Placement courses and exams (the APs) provide similar acceleration opportunities, permitting students to graduate before their chronological peers. Many gifted students report they feel just as comfortable, both academically and socially, with their intellectual peers as they do with their chronological peers, although cases of students who found acceleration to be a disaster are also plentiful.[35]

An important characteristic of effective gifted programs is the sense of community offered, a key step in reducing student anxiety and alienation. One student was relieved to find that "there are lots of people like me and I'm not a weirdo after all."[36] Teachers are also encouraged to help gifted students understand and manage the advantages and disadvantages that can come with their high intelligence and creativity. Moreover, when gifted students are placed in appropriate programs, they are often empowered to realize their full potential. As one 12-year-old girl said:

> I enjoy being smart because I am able to accomplish many things and I feel that being smart gives me more self-esteem. I love that I have unique interests and a place in school where I can pursue them. I enjoy challenging myself to always reach the next level.[37]

In the final analysis, it is not only the gifted who suffer from our national neglect and apathy; it is all of us. How many works of art will never be enjoyed? How many medical breakthroughs and how many inventions have been lost because of our insensitivity to the gifted?

Special Education

If a society is judged by the way it treats people who are different, our country's history of educating students with disabilities might well earn a failing grade. For many years, the legal system mirrored society's judgment that the best policy toward those with disabilities was "out of sight, out of mind." The courts typically saw education as a privilege rather than a right, and they ruled that children with disabilities should be excluded from schools. The notion was that the majority of children needed to be protected from those with disabilities: from the disruptions they might precipitate, from the excessive demands they might make, and from the discomfort their presence in classrooms might cause.

The years following World War II brought renewed hope and promise. Such pioneers as Grace Fernald, Marianne Frostig, and Heinz Werner—to name but a few—conducted research, developed programs, and gave new impetus to the field of **special education.** Their work was aided by the emergence of new disciplines, such as psychology, sociology, and social work. Parents also continued their struggle, individually and collectively, to obtain educational opportunities for children with disabilities. They took their cause to both the schools and the courts. As society's concepts of equality, freedom, and justice expanded, education's response to students with disabilities slowly changed. Educational choices have gradually shifted from patterns of exclusion and isolation to ones of integration and mainstreaming.

But change has not come easily, nor has it occurred by chance. The civil rights movements of the 1950s and 1960s began to open social, economic, and education doors once closed to those of individuals considered different—because of race, religion, culture, gender, language, or disability. The 1954 landmark case of *Brown v. Board of Education of Topeka* particularly sparked legal challenges to equal education. The case challenged the common practice of using race to segregate schools, resulting in unequal educational experiences for students of color. The U.S. Supreme Court ruled that equal education must be available to all children regardless of race and that racially separate schools are not inherently equal.[38] (See Chapter 5, "The Multicultural History of American Schools", for a more in-depth discussion of *Brown*).

Advocates for students with disabilities paid close attention to the *Brown* decision. If public schools were now required to provide Black and White children an integrated, equal education, might students with special needs also deserve similar rights? Beginning in the 1970s, a series of legal rulings and laws passed affirming that children with special needs were indeed entitled to free, equal public education. For example, in 1975 Congress passed the groundbreaking Education for all Handicapped Children Act (Public Law 94-142), establishing the right of all students with disabilities to a "free and appropriate public education." Congress has reauthorized Public Law 94-142 five times, most recently in 2004. In the 1990s, the law was renamed the **Individuals with Disabilities Education Act,** more commonly known by its acronym, IDEA.[39]

As landmark legislation, IDEA changed the face of education in the United States. IDEA requires that each child with disabilities "have access to the program best suited to the child's special needs which is as close as possible to a normal child's educational program." [40]

Six fundamental provisions are included in IDEA:

1. *Zero reject* and *A Free and Appropriate Education (FAPE).* Excluding children with disabilities from public schools violates the constitutional interpretation behind the Supreme Court's *Brown* decision, which put an end to claims of "separate but equal" schooling. The principle of zero reject asserts that *every* child with special needs must receive a free, appropriate public education. While the principle of zero reject ensures that children with disabilities will receive a free public education, it is important to recognize that this mandate goes beyond simply allowing children with disabilities to pass through the schoolhouse door. The term "**appropriate education**" means that these children have the right to an education involving the accurate diagnosis of individual needs, as well as responsive programs targeted to those needs.

PROFILE IN EDUCATION

Sally Smith

Sally Smith created a "school modeled after a party" to teach her son and others with learning disabilities. Taking an approach that encourages exploration and deep learning of academic content through arts-based instruction, over 90 percent of her school's students go on to college.

Read a full profile of Sally Smith on Connect.

Source: Courtesy of Randall Smith

connect

2. ***Parental participation.*** Through IDEA, parents or guardians are required to become full partners in all stages of decision making, including curriculum and placements. Consequently, parents or guardians of students in special education legally have a greater say in their children's education than that held by parents of any other students.
3. ***Nondiscriminatory education.*** The principle of nondiscriminatory education, based on "due process" rights of the Fifth and Fourteenth Amendments of the U.S. Constitution, mandates that children with disabilities be fairly assessed so that they can be protected from inappropriate classification and tracking. Much of the court activity in this area has centered on the disproportionate number of children of color assigned to special education classes, a situation that some claim is the result of biased testing. In one case, a court ruled that IQ tests could not be used for placing or tracking students. Other courts have forbidden the use of tests that are culturally biased, and still others have ordered that testing take place in the children's native language.
4. ***Least-restrictive environment.*** The least-restrictive environment protects children with disabilities from being inappropriately segregated. Court decisions have urged that special needs students be educated in a setting that most closely resembles a regular school environment while meeting their special needs. **Mainstreaming** has traditionally referred to placing special needs students in regular classroom settings for at least part of the day. The more recent term, **inclusion,** sometimes called *full inclusion,* reflects an even stronger commitment to educate each student in a least-restrictive environment to the maximum degree possible. Separate classes and schools are to be avoided unless a child's disabilities are such that education in a regular classroom, even with the aid of special materials and supportive services, cannot be achieved. When to include and when to separate is a source of constant debate. (See Figure 2.2.)
5. ***Procedural due process.*** As previously discussed, IDEA acknowledges that students with disabilities have important legal rights. For example, the principle of procedural due process upholds the right of students with disabilities to protest a school's decisions about their education. Due process ensures the right of children with disabilities and their parents to be notified of school actions and decisions; to challenge those decisions before an impartial tribunal, using counsel and expert witnesses; to examine the school records on which a decision is based; and to appeal whatever decision is reached.
6. ***Individualized education program (IEP).*** Because of the diversity of disabilities, IDEA requires that a "free appropriate public education" be defined on an individual basis, using a written IEP. Each IEP must be reviewed and revised annually, ensuring that the educational goals designed for a child align with his or her learning needs and that these plans are actually delivered. Teachers shoulder the responsibilities of monitoring the needs of each child with disabilities placed in their classrooms. An IEP must include the following:
   - A statement of the student's current performance, including long-term (annual) goals and short-term objectives.
   - A description of the nature and duration of the instructional services designed to meet the prescribed goals.
   - An overview of the methods of evaluation that will be used to monitor the child's progress and to determine whether the goals and objectives have been met.

School learning environments need to accommodate a wide variety of student differences.

There is no specific IEP form that must be used, as long as goals, objectives, services, and evaluation are accurately reflected. In fact, hundreds of different IEP forms are

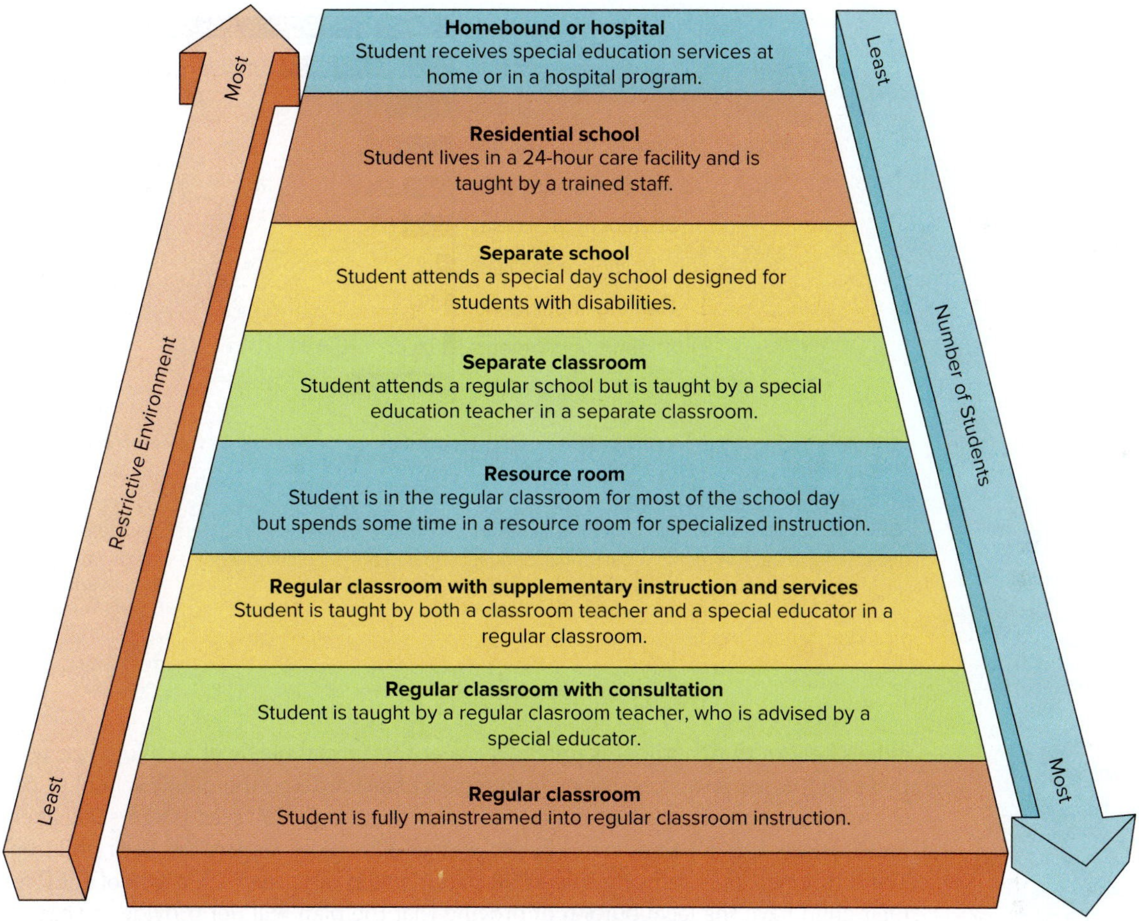

FIGURE 2.2

Appropriate education in the least restrictive environment for students with disabilities.

SOURCE: Heward, William, *Exceptional Children: An Introduction to Special Education*, 10th ed. Upper Saddle River, NJ: Macmillan/Prentice-Hall, 2013, p. 70.

REFLECTION: Why do some believe that all teachers are special education teachers?

currently in use; some run as long as twenty pages; others are only two or three pages. Remember, it is not the format that is important but, rather, whether or not the IEP accurately describes the educational needs and the related remedial plans. Even though writing these IEPs will undoubtedly consume a great deal of a teacher's time and energy, it often leads to better communication among the school staff, as well as between teachers and parents. Also, the practice of preparing IEPs will likely lead to more effective individualization of instruction for all children, not just those with disabilities.

IDEA has been one of the most thoroughly litigated federal laws in history. Parents whose children qualify for special education services can and do sue the school district if they believe their children's needs are not being met. Local courts agreeing with parents' views have ordered public schools to hire extra teachers or specialized personnel or to spend additional dollars to provide an appropriate education. When

FIGURE 2.3

Distribution of children ages 3–21 served under IDEA (rounded to nearest percent).

SOURCE: U.S. Department of Education, *Condition of Education: Children and Youth with Disabilities*, 2016.

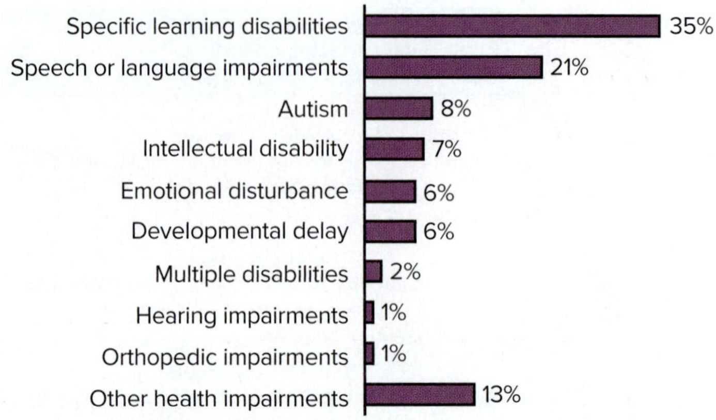

NOTE: Deaf-blindness, traumatic brain injury and visual impairments account for less than 1 percent of children served by IDEA.

REFLECTION: This distribution offers an insight into which special needs students teachers are most likely to have in regular classrooms. Suggest some of the accommodations a classroom teacher might consider for each of these special needs.

GLOBAL VIEW

More than 1 billion people worldwide live with disabilities. Mortality for children with disabilities is as high as 80 percent in many poor countries. Globally, less than 5 percent of children with disabilities have access to education.

judges believe that a school is unable to meet the special needs of a child, even with these additional resources, they can order and have ordered the public school to pay the tuition so that the student can attend a private school. However, parents will likely find it more difficult to demand better special education services for their children. The Supreme Court recently ruled that parents who disagree with a school's IEP for their child have the legal burden of proving that the plan will not provide the appropriate education. Disability advocates worry that school districts will now have little incentive to address parents' complaints or, even worse, to provide quality special education services.[41]

Today, more than 6 million students (13 percent of the total public school population) are special needs. In a few areas, such as Attention Deficit Hyperactivity Disorder (A.D.H.D.) and autism, growth has skyrocketed.[42] **Learning disabilities** constitutes the largest group of special needs students. (See Figure 2.3.) Students with learning disabilities have difficulties with listening, speaking, reading, writing, reasoning, or mathematical skills. A student with a learning disability might perform poorly in one area but extremely well in another. Uneven performance, hyperactivity, disorganization, and lack of follow-through are typical problems for these students. Educational literature reflects more than fifty terms to describe students with learning disabilities.

Meeting the growing needs of special needs students has strained education budgets nationwide. Why the upsurge? The reasons are complex–and troubling. Some believe environmental pollutants increase children's disabilities. Others argue that special needs have always been common but in past years went undiagnosed. Some wonder if today we are overdiagnosing the problem.

Consider A.D.H.D. More than one in seven American children get diagnosed with this attention problem–three times what experts have said is appropriate–meaning that millions of kids are misdiagnosed and taking medications for a neuro-behavioral

TEACHING TIP

Students with Special Needs

Effective teaching of students with special needs can be a challenging—and rewarding—experience. Here are a few practical suggestions to create an engaged *and* equitable learning environment for special needs students. In fact, these strategies are likely to improve learning for *all* students!

- **Establish and frequently review classroom rules, procedures, and academic directions.**
  Some students with special needs can become frustrated when they want to do the right thing but get confused or forget. Repeating the rules keeps them—and all students—on track.
- **Set fair, yet challenging expectations for all students, and ask higher- as well as lower-order questions.**
  Students quickly pick up when the teacher lowers expectations. For example, a teacher should not ask easy questions just to students with special needs. Asking challenging as well as simpler questions to all students is one strategy that sets a more positive tone. How challenging can the question be? With experience you will learn how to continually challenge and not frustrate learners with exceptionalities.
- **Relate new learning to previous instruction and to students' backgrounds and experiences.**
  Seeing connections is central for learners with special needs because words alone are not always adequate. Think of connections that tie class learning to students' lives and to previous work.
- **Create high student engagement by using a variety of instructional strategies, including visual and auditory methods, hands-on activities, and shorter time segments for activities.**
  The more learning channels you open, the more engaged behavior you will encourage, and the more likely that students will connect with your academic goals.
- **Model skills and strategies, and always emphasize key words.**
  Be mindful that what you say and what you do are not incidental, casual, or secondary. Be purposeful and clear because your words and behaviors teach powerful lessons.
- **Closely monitor independent work, and provide precise and immediate feedback.**
  Unlearning a behavior is more difficult than learning it correctly the first time. Monitoring and offering clear feedback can eliminate the need to unlearn and relearn.
- **Include joy and success in learning.**
  Design activities that will give students a sense of accomplishment. Provide additional time if needed to complete assignments, and don't forget to put joy and smiles in your teaching and in your students' learning.

Source: Many of these arguments are found in greater detail in Jack L. Nelson, Stuart B. Palonsky, and Kenneth Carlson, Critical Issues in Education: Dialogue and Dialectics (New York: McGraw-Hill, 2012).

REFLECTION: Describe how these strategies are likely to improve learning for non–special needs students as well.

disorder they probably do not have. The numbers rise every year. Medication often assuages the impulsiveness and inability to concentrate associated with A.D.H.D. Few dispute that attention difficulties impede success at school, work, and in one's personal life. However, educators and doctors are increasingly questioning why the A.D.H.D. label is given to so many. Is there an environmental component? Are the distractions of today's tech culture to blame? Or perhaps drug companies are marketing A.D.H.D. to increase their own profit margin? If parents and teachers emphasize patience and careful attention for students, would A.D.H.D. diagnoses decrease? Others point to affluent communities where parents hire private psychologists to ensure that their children are identified with a learning disability. Why? In wealthy communities, such labels attract additional education resources, smaller class size, and even extended test-taking time.[43]

But if special education means special privileges for the wealthy, the same diagnosis can mean fewer resources for the poor. Studies indicate that African American, Hispanic, and special education students from lower socioeconomic backgrounds are twice as likely to be educated in a more restrictive and separate setting than white and wealthier students. Poor parents struggle to make certain that the special education label is *not* attached to their children. In addition to poverty, cultural misunderstanding, low expectations, and the desire to remove "difficult" students from the classroom contribute to the high rate of African American and Hispanic students identified as having developmental disabilities or emotional disturbances. And then there is gender. Boys tend to act out their frustrations and create classroom disturbances. Because their behavior gets noticed, boys are twice as likely as girls to be (mis)labeled with a disability. Girls are quieter in class, less likely to cause discipline concerns, and more likely to turn inwardly with problems and anxieties. As a result, their special education needs often go undetected and untreated.[44] So behind the growing numbers of special education students is a disturbing imbalance of boys, and an over-identification trend of students of color.

RAP 1.10
Special Education Services

Once identified, attention focuses on how best to educate these students.[45] Students with mild disabilities typically attend regular classrooms for part of the day and leave for a period of time to receive special instruction in a resource room. These "pullout" programs have been criticized for stigmatizing students while failing to improve their academic performance. This concern has fueled the **regular education initiative,** which encourages schools to provide special services *within* the regular classroom and encourages close collaboration between classroom teachers and special educators. Today, more than half of students with disabilities are mainstreamed for 80 percent or more of the school day in a regular classroom.[46] (See You Be the Judge: Students with Special Needs on p. 45.)

Regular classroom teachers often express concerns about their ability to handle a mainstreamed classroom:

> They want us all to be super teachers, but I've got 33 kids in my class and it's really a job to take care of them without also having to deal with special needs kids too. I'm not complaining really—I wouldn't want to do anything other than what I'm doing—but it is demanding.[47]

Although classroom teachers are expected to meet many of society's obligations, including the education of special needs students, they are not always given adequate resources for the task. Frustration is often the result. To succeed, teachers need additional planning time, appropriate curricular materials, ongoing staff development programs, and sometimes, extra classroom assistance.

Despite the criticisms and problems of inclusion, one thing is certain: More students with disabilities are enjoying school life alongside their peers. Inclusion seems to thrive in schools that provide teachers with adequate planning time and resources; have open communication among teachers, administrators, and parents; promote a culture of innovation and reform; and encourage a commitment to funding the education of students with exceptional needs. (See Teaching Tip: Students with Special Needs, p. 45.)

Inclusion is at its heart a moral issue, one that raises the timeless principles of equality, justice, and the need for all of us to learn to live and grow together—not apart. This chapter is all about the rich human diversity that graces our classrooms and enables all of us—teachers and students alike—to learn from one another. We will never know how many ideas, insights, inventions, and medical breakthroughs have been lost because of our inability to honor these different ways of knowing. But we can rededicate ourselves to honoring and nurturing the unique talents of each student.

Students with Special Needs

SHOULD BE MAINSTREAMED BECAUSE . . .

WITHOUT INCLUSION, OUR DEMOCRATIC IDEAL IS HOLLOW

Segregating individuals with disabilities mirrors the historical segregation of African Americans and other groups, a segregation already rejected by the courts. Separate can never be equal, and all students quickly learn the stigma associated with those in "special" classrooms.

SOCIETY NEEDS THE TALENTS OF ALL ITS CITIZENS

Society needs the skills and economic productivity of all our citizens. Educating those with disabilities in a segregated setting decreases their opportunity for full and meaningful contributions later in life.

MAINSTREAMING IMPROVES ACADEMIC AND SOCIAL RELATIONS

Studies indicate that students with special needs perform better academically when mainstreamed in regular classes. Not surprisingly, their social adjustment is also improved.

THOSE WITHOUT DISABILITIES GAIN WHEN SPECIAL NEEDS STUDENTS ARE PRESENT

In our increasingly stratified society, students can spend years in school with peers just like themselves. Inclusion provides an opportunity for children to appreciate and work with people who do not necessarily reflect their own experiences and viewpoints.

SHOULD NOT BE MAINSTREAMED BECAUSE . . .

MERELY SITTING IN REGULAR CLASSROOMS DOES NOT GUARANTEE A FITTING EDUCATION

A rallying cry like "democracy" sounds impressive, but we need to ensure that students with special needs receive a quality education, and the best place for that is not necessarily in a regular, mainstreamed classroom.

PULLOUT PROGRAMS CAN OFFER STUDENTS WITH SPECIAL NEEDS THE RESOURCES THEY NEED TO SUCCEED

Pullout programs for children with special needs can offer an adjusted curriculum, special instructional techniques, and smaller class size. Students with special needs can soar in classrooms designed to meet their needs but flounder when they are inappropriately placed in regular classes.

GIFTED AND TALENTED STUDENTS ARE AT PARTICULAR RISK

Gifted and talented students fall within the special needs category, and for them, mainstreaming is a disaster. If the gifted are not challenged, they will be turned off from school, and the gifts of our most able students will be lost to society.

WHEN STUDENTS WITH SPECIAL NEEDS ARE MAINSTREAMED, STUDENTS WITHOUT DISABILITIES SUFFER

As teachers in regular classes adjust learning activities to accommodate the special needs students, other students lose out. The extra time, special curriculum, and attention given to students with special needs amount to time and resources taken from others in the class.

SOURCE: Many of these arguments are found in greater detail in Jack L. Nelson, Stuart B. Palonsky, and Kenneth Carlson, *Critical Issues in Education: Dialogue and Dialectics* (New York: McGraw-Hill, 2012).

connect YOU DECIDE...

What training would help you meet the special needs of students mainstreamed into your classroom? Can "separate" ever be "equal"? Whose needs are of most worth, those of students with special needs or those of "regular" students? Do their needs actually conflict? As a teacher, would you want special needs children mainstreamed or pulled out? Imagine yourself the parent of a special needs child. Would you want your child mainstreamed or pulled out?

connect CONNECT FOR *TEACHERS, SCHOOLS, AND SOCIETY*

Check out Connect, McGraw-Hill Education's interactive learning environment, to:

Read Current and Historical Articles

The Myth of Pink and Blue Brains, by Lisa Eliot, *Best of Educational Leadership,* August 2011.

Demystifying the Adolescent Brain, by Laurence Steinberg, *Education Leadership,* April 2011.

Inclusion in Two Languages: Special Education in Portugal and the United States, by Margaret Inman Linn, *Phi Delta Kappan,* May 2011.

Letters to My Younger Self, by Emilie Shafto, *Educational Leadership,* September 2011.

Analyze Case Studies

Carol Brown: A teacher, after socially integrating a diverse class, sees her efforts threatened when a child's pencil case disappears and is thought to have been stolen.

Joan Martin, Marilyn Coe, and Warren Groves: A classroom teacher, a special education teacher, and a principal hold different views about mainstreaming a boy with poor reading skills. The dilemma comes to a head over the method of grading him at the end of the marking period.

Watch Teachers, Students, and Classrooms in Action

Our **Online Video Album** for contemporary videos related to this chapter.

KEY TERMS AND PEOPLE

accelerated programs, 40
Advanced Placement (AP), 40
appropriate education, 41
Dweck, Carol, 26
emotional intelligence quotient (EQ), 30
exceptional learners, 37
fixed mindset, 26
Gardner, Howard, 27
gender similarities hypothesis, 35
giftedness, 38
Goleman, Daniel, 32
growth mindset, 26
inclusion, 42
individualized education program (IEP), 42
Individuals with Disabilities Education Act (IDEA), 41
International Baccalaureate (IB), 40
learning disabilities, 44
learning styles, 32
least-restrictive environment, 42
locus of control, 32
mainstreaming (inclusion), 42
multiple intelligences, 27
neuroplasticity, 34
nondiscriminatory education, 42
portfolio, 28
procedural due process, 42
regular education initiative, 46
special education, 41
zero reject, 41

DISCUSSION QUESTIONS AND ACTIVITIES

1. Can you develop additional intelligences beyond the ones Gardner identifies? (This is often best accomplished in groups.)
2. How would you characterize your own learning style? Interview other students in your class to determine how they characterize their learning styles. Based on these interviews, what recommendations could you offer your course instructor about using learning styles in your class?
3. Do you believe that girls and boys have different gender learning styles? Brain differences? Provide some evidence to support your position.
4. Interview people who graduated from single-sex schools and ask them about their experiences. Did they find single-sex schools to be an advantage or not? In what ways? Do males and females have different assessments? What was lost by not attending a co-ed school? What was gained?
5. Investigate a special education program in a local school. Describe its strengths. What suggestions do you have for improving it? What is your position on "full inclusion"?

©Comstock/Getty Images RF

I think we have to own the fears that we have of each other, and then, in some practical way, some daily way, figure out how to see people differently than the way we were brought up to.

ALICE WALKER

chapter 3

Teaching Your Diverse Students

Focus Questions

1. What are the challenges posed by America's increasingly diverse students?
2. How does unconscious bias influence life in the classroom?
3. How is gender fluidity influencing school life?
4. What are the instructional and political issues surrounding English Language Learners?
5. How do deficit, expectation, and cultural difference theories explain dissimilar academic performance among various racial, ethnic, and cultural groups?
6. How do phrases like "melting pot" and "cultural pluralism" both capture and mask American identity?
7. What are the purposes and approaches of multicultural education?
8. Why is culturally responsive teaching important?
9. How can teachers use culturally responsive teaching strategies?

Chapter Preview

The United States has just experienced the greatest immigration surge in its history. In the past few decades, newly minted Americans have arrived mainly from Latin America and Asia, but also from the Caribbean, the Middle East, Africa, and Eastern Europe. Today, about one in ten Americans is foreign born, and the native language of well over 30 million Americans is a language other than English. American or foreign born, about half of public school students are students of color.

But there is more to diversity than immigration.[1] Other kinds of diversity include economic, social, linguistic, sexual, and gender identity to name but a few. The growing diversity in America's schools is clearly the challenge of the twenty-first century. Disciplinary policies in schools unconsciously fall hardest on these minority and poor students. Physical and verbal abuse is too often targeted to LGBTQA students (Lesbian, gay, bisexual, transgender, queer/questioning, and Allies), students who find themselves increasingly harassed in and beyond school, and more likely to commit suicide. 2013 was a milestone year: For the first time in recent history, the majority of America's K-12 students came from low income families. More than half of the students in the United States are eligible for free or reduced-price lunch. Many teachers struggle to connect with students whose backgrounds are so different from their own. How can you as a teacher reach these students? This chapter addresses that question directly, not only with breathtaking information and some astute (we hope) insights, but with practical suggestions as well.

Student Diversity

FOCUS QUESTION 1

What are the challenges posed by America's increasingly diverse students?

Since the 1960s, more immigrants have come to this country than at the beginning of the twentieth century, a time often thought of as the great era of immigration and Americanization. Today, about one in three Americans is of color, and the majority of students in public schools are students of color. The racial composition of our nation is changing. (See Figure 3.1, The Changing U.S. Population 1965–2065.) You will teach in a nation more diverse and less Eurocentric than the one you grew up in.

So let's begin to explore our changing student population by defining some basic terms that are critical, but often used incorrectly. **Race** refers to a group of individuals sharing a common socially determined category, often related to genetic attributes, physical appearance, and ancestry. Yet, racial categories can vary by society. For example, in the United States an individual with any known African ancestry is considered black. But in Caribbean and Latin American nations, race is influenced by social class. In these countries, "money lightens": upward social mobility increases the likelihood of being classified as white. **Ethnicity** refers to shared common cultural traits such as language, religion, and dress. A sense of shared peoplehood is one of the most important characteristics of ethnicity. A Latino or Hispanic, for example, belongs to an ethnic group, but might belong to the Negro, Caucasian, or Asian race. So when a form asks an individual to indicate if he or she is white, African American, Asian, or Hispanic, the form does not capture all the information for the Hispanic, who

Being an effective teacher means being effective with culturally diverse students.

©KidStock LLC RF

FIGURE 3.1

The Changing U.S. Population 1965–2065.

SOURCE: Pew Research Center, "Modern Immigration Wave Brings 59 Million to US, Driving Population Growth and Change through 2065," 2015.

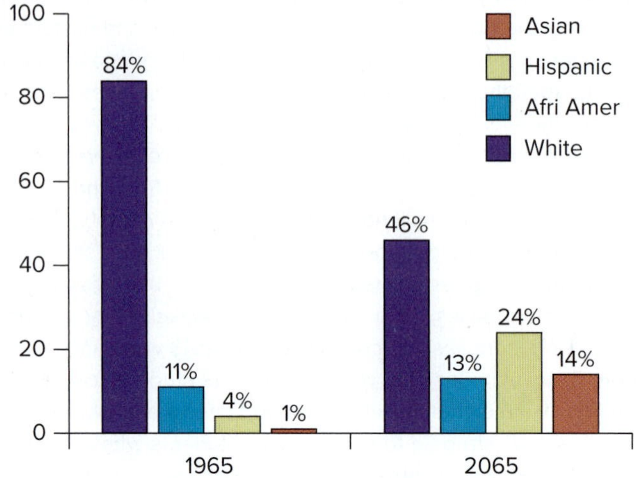

REFLECTION: Put on your prediction cap and suggest some ways—the curriculum, teaching skills, school structure, etc.—that school life might look different in 2065 than it appears today.

also belongs to one or more of those racial groups. **Culture** is a set of learned beliefs, values, symbols, and behaviors, a way of life shared by members of a society. There is not only a national culture, but also microcultures or subcultures. There are cultures related to class, religion, or sexual orientation, to offer but a few examples. These subcultures carry values and behaviors that differ from others in the same nation or the same community.[2] The willingness of people to understand and appreciate different cultures, races, and ethnicities is often at the heart of the diversity issue in the United States, while the subculture of sexual identity and orientation offers national flashpoints. The challenge for educators is to ensure that all our students achieve.

In the twenty-first century, the Census added a new demographic by asking citizens to report if they were **multiracial**—that is, claiming ancestors from two or more races. Nearly 7 million Americans responded yes, a figure that grows larger with each census (see Figure 3.2). Most of the respondents were under 18, and in at least ten states, more than a quarter of school-aged children were in the multiracial category, indicating that this group will grow in the years ahead. Few studies have investigated the specific challenges facing multiracial-multiethnic children, but we see some cultural inequities already emerging. Tiger Woods is considered by many to be our first great black golfer. Few refer to him as our first great Thai golfer. President Barack Obama is called our first black president, not our first half-white president. For them and others, any black heritage becomes shorthand for race identity. Teachers and schools have much to learn in honoring the full background of multiracial children and avoiding convenient and simplistic labels. The increased number of multiracial children can be seen against the larger picture: the population of the United States is changing, as white citizens become a smaller percentage and citizens from other racial and ethnic groups become a larger percentage (see Figures 3.1 and 3.2).

FIGURE 3.2

Multiracial children living with two parents.

SOURCE: Pew Research Fund tabulations, 1970, 1980, 1990, 2000, and 2013 American Community Surveys.

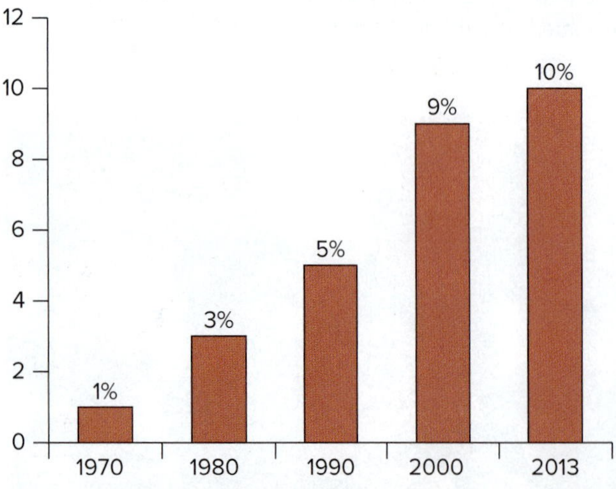

REFLECTION: What can teachers and schools do to more effectively educate multiracial children?

Unconscious Bias: When Believing Is Seeing

FOCUS QUESTION 2

How does unconscious bias influence life in the classroom?

A teacher tells the story of becoming frustrated when African American students interrupt her in class with their frequent side conversations.[3] When she told a black colleague about her frustration with this misbehavior, he had some surprising advice. Perhaps she was falling into a common pattern: noticing misbehavior among black students but "not seeing" the same misbehavior among white students. The next day she focused on white student behaviors, and she was stunned. They too were having side conversations, but they went unnoticed by her. Not unusual. Similar results emerge when gender is the factor. Teachers frequently come down hard on the boys for talking out of turn, yet when the class is videotaped, it is clear that the girls were doing the same misbehaviors, and the teacher did not notice it. There is a popular saying, "Seeing is believing." In these and other cases, it may be more accurate to say that "Believing is seeing." Teachers believe that racial minorities and boys will be the greater discipline challenge, so that's what they focus on, and that's what they see. Misbehaviors of white children and girls fly under the radar. Ask that teacher if he or she is being fair, and you will hear "yes." The teacher's intention is to be fair, but the behavior is not. Although we all like to think of ourselves as fair, our self-deception is deep. Unconscious or implicit bias permeates our culture, including our schools, and starts early (see Figure 3.3).

Let's take a look at how this is manifested. Many adults conclude that students of color are punished more in school because of their misbehaviors, but research points the finger at the unconscious bias of teachers and administrators. Here's an example: In one study teachers were given disciplinary reports of students with repeated misbehaviors. They were asked to decide what the appropriate punishment should be for each of these student infractions. But here is the heart of the study: half the student reports were randomly assigned African American sounding names (Deshawn and Darnell), and the other half were given white sounding names (Greg and Jake). Regardless of the infractions, the teachers gave more harsh punishment to the students with black sounding names.[4]

Actual school data brings this research into vivid focus. Students of color (black, American Indian, and Hispanic) are four times more likely to be given school suspensions than are white students. When black students and white students break the same rule, the black student is more likely to be sent to the office for punishment, a punishment that might lead to an in- or out-of-school suspension. Suspensions are costly. Students who are suspended or expelled are far more likely to be grade repeaters and eventually drop out of school entirely. Unconscious bias can clearly cause great damage in schools.[5]

Here's another subtle bias: Students of color are more likely to be reprimanded for subjective offenses not in the school code of conduct (insubordination, excessive noise, disrespect, and the like). These "infractions" are judgment calls by a teacher or an administrator. White students, on the other hand, are more likely to be punished for offenses written and detailed in the school code (drugs, weapons, obscene language, and the like). The results are dramatic. (See Figure 3.4.)

FIGURE 3.3

Who teachers watch.

SOURCE: Bill Hathaway, "Implicit Bias May Help Explain High Preschool Expulsion Rates for Black Children" *Yale News*. 2016.

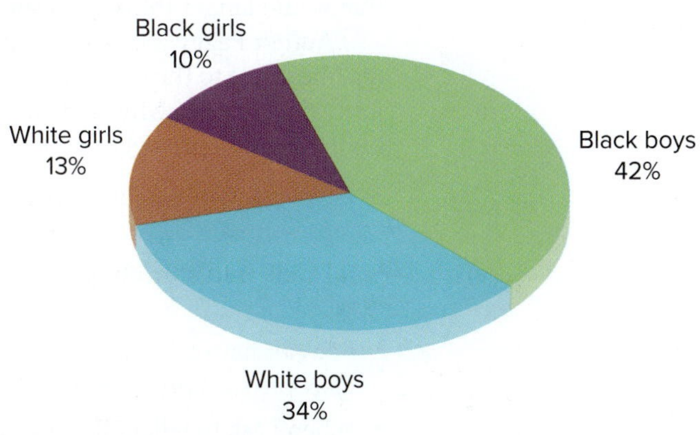

REFLECTION: Researchers used sophisticated eye-tracking technology to detect who teachers track. How can you as a teacher counteract this strong social stereotyping?

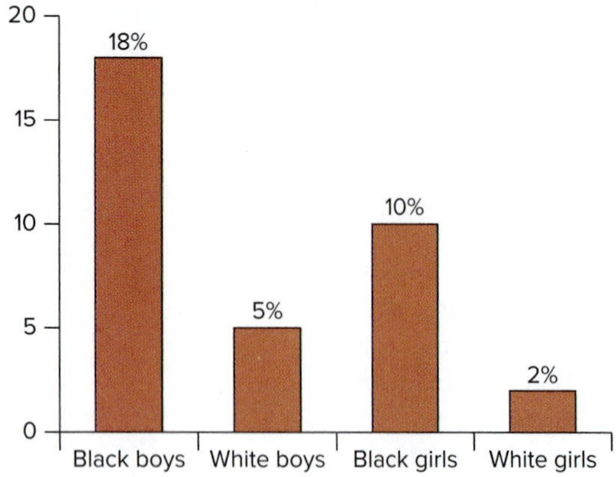

FIGURE 3.4

K–12 school suspensions.

SOURCE: U.S. Department of Education, Office for Civil Rights, "2013–2014 Civil Rights Data Collection: A First Look," 2016. Retrieved at http://www2.ed.gov/about/offices/list/ocr/docs/2013-14-first-look.pdf.

REFLECTION: These public school inequities start early. Although black students represent 19 percent of preschool students, they are almost half (47 percent) of all the preschool out-of-school suspensions. What can you do as a teacher to purge yourself of this unwanted, unconscious, implicit bias?

Such suspensions have led to a disturbing national trend: moving students out of the public school system and into the juvenile and criminal justice systems. This phenomenon has been termed the **school-to-prison pipeline.** These students, often minority children and many with histories of abuse, poverty, neglect, and learning disabilities, have their futures compromised by the unconscious bias embedded in many school disciplinary practices. Rather than receiving the educational and counseling services they need, these children are criminalized early in life and too often branded as society's exiles. The same unconscious bias is reflected in the adult world when minority defendants are more likely to be found guilty and sentenced to longer jail terms than white defendants charged with the same crime. Most people involved in these decisions—educators, judges, and lawyers—see themselves as fair, but they are not. They remain oblivious of their unconscious bias.

We can correct this. The first step is to simply acknowledge that most of us have been shaped, at least in part, by society's hidden and institutional biases. The second challenge is not to feel ashamed about it. In today's America, we are not supposed to be biased, so the images of bias emerge from the past. Although water fountains are no longer labeled for whites or "coloreds" and Jim Crow laws are now gone, bias and racism are still with us. Let's take a look at how some of these unconscious biases emerge.

When you hear the word *race*, what comes to your mind? Is it the image of a black man? Or perhaps you visualize an Asian woman? We would wager that most of you reading this text do not visualize a white person. Guess what? That's a race too! When "race" is mentioned in America, we tend to picture people of color, the ones who are not like the images that dominate newspapers, government, books, television, and much of the media. Here's another example: Have you ever listened to a news commentator point out how many African Americans are now in Congress? But when was the last time you heard a news commentator point out the number of whites in Congress? White predominance is the accepted norm, a hidden privilege that we no longer think of as special. That too is unconscious bias.

Author Peggy McIntosh helps us see the hidden privileges of being in the majority. She refers to these privileges as an "invisible knapsack," because those in the majority (in this case, whites) do not even see their advantages. Here are a few examples of the invisible privileges of being white. As a white person:

- I can watch television or read the front page of the paper and see my race widely represented.
- If I walk into a meeting late, people don't assume that my lateness reflects on my race.
- I do not have to educate my children to be aware of systemic racism for their own daily physical protection.
- When I ask to talk to the "person in charge," I can feel confident that I will be talking to a person of my own race.
- I can take a job with an affirmative action employer without having my colleagues believe that I was hired because of my race and not my qualifications.

- When I am cited for a traffic violation, I can be sure I have not been singled out because of my race.
- I can walk into a stationery store and find a card to send with pictures of my race.
- People don't ask me to explain how my race feels about a topic.

(Can you add to the list? If you'd like to see other examples, visit https://www.isr.umich.edu /home/diversity/resources/white-privilege.pdf.)

Nor is unconscious bias limited to race or ethnicity. We may hold a bias in relation to age, gender, gender identity, physical or mental abilities, religion, sexual orientation, weight . . . (and the list goes on). How do you feel about people much older than you? How do you feel about others who practice different religions? How about people who are quite heavy, or really skinny? Our brain, constantly flooded by information, needs to develop short-cuts, so we organize our world by categorizing such groups. School data illustrate that our unconscious biases are all too real (see Figure 3.5).

If you are white, or heterosexual, or Christian (and most teachers are), you have your own knapsack of hidden privileges and unconscious biases, whether you know it or not. But many students come from other backgrounds and few privileges. If teachers are to connect and communicate with the growing student diversity (and poverty!) in

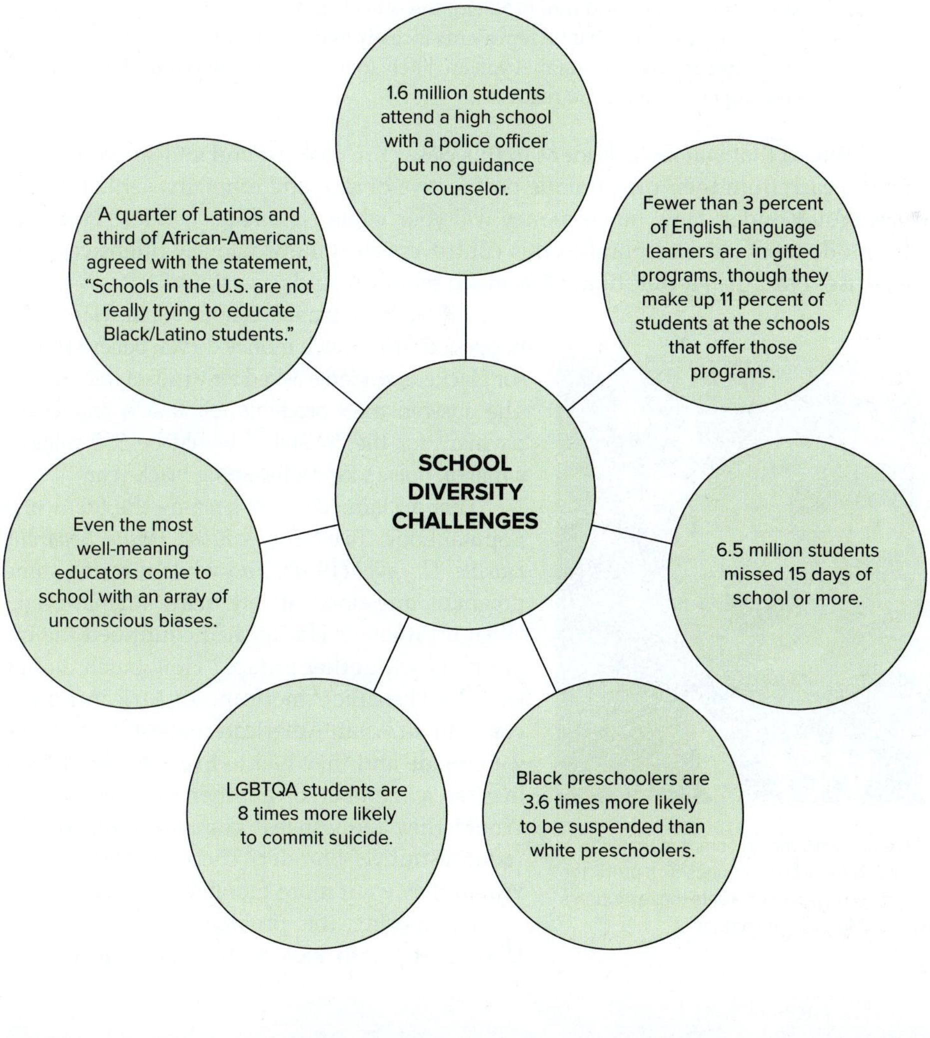

FIGURE 3.5

School diversity challenges.

SOURCE: US Dept. of Education, Civil Rights Data Collection, 2016, http://ocrdata.ed.gov/ ; Stacy Teicher Khadaroo, "Racially Diverse 'New Majority' Set to Reshape US Public Schools" *Christian Science Monitor*, April 15, 2016.

REFLECTION: Have you ever experienced one of these statistics firsthand? If so, describe your experience. If not, why do you think these stats were not part of your school life?

their classroom, they will need to learn more about students whose backgrounds are different from their own, and learn more about themselves in the process. This chapter is intended to help you do just that.

Research teaches us the many ways we accommodate our biases. For example, most people favor the group they belong to. Does this very tribal response apply to you? Research also reveals that between half and a third of the members of any stigmatized group tend to favor the "culturally valued group."[6] Does the most powerful tribe in your world receive the greatest respect? Just asking yourself these questions begins the process of bias reduction in your life, of moving beyond tribal beliefs.

If we are clever enough, we can make society's invisible biases visible. Cornell professor Andrew Hacker did just that. He began his class by greeting his students with his usual "Welcome to class!" Then he continued: "I want you to respond to the following case study. This, of course, is fictional, but suspend your disbelief, read the parable, and tell me what you think." So the students settled down and read the brief scenario:

> You are a white person and are visited by an official who explains that a mistake has been made. You were actually born to black parents who live far from where you grew up. The error has to be rectified. At midnight, you will become black, acquiring a darker skin, and body and facial features that reflect your African heritage. Your knowledge and ideas, your "inside," however, will remain the same.
>
> Now this is an unusual and rare problem, the official explains, but the error was not yours, and the organization that he represents is ready and able to offer you appropriate recompense. His records indicate that you are likely to live another 50 years. How much financial recompense would you request?[7]

Pretend that you are a student in this class. You look around and see your classmates, each from their own unique perspective of race and ethnicity, settle into the task. You wonder: How much money will your white classmates ask for? How will the students of color respond to this controversial, some would say offensive, class exercise? Now the *big* question: How much money would *you* ask for?

Although the parable is not true, the class really happened. How much money do you believe Professor Hacker's students asked for to offset the "error"? The answer: most students felt that a reasonable payment for the "mistake" would be $50 million, a million dollars for each coming black year.

That acclaimed study became the focus of a popular book, *Two Nations: Black, White, Separate, Hostile, Unequal* (1992), and while it raised some poignant questions, it left many unanswered.[7] What if Professor Hacker had continued the experiment with other groups? How much money would a Hispanic American, an African American, and an Asian American request if a mistake were made and they had to live the rest of their lives as a member of another race or culture? Would they request less compensation for the "administrative" blunder? The same $50 million? Would they want more money?

Just posing the problem underscores the U.S. tendency to look to the courts to fix any

What do you see? Hacker's anecdote unmasks the quiet racism that lurks in many adult minds as they view children's racial backgrounds as a predictor of future income and status. Could you predict what careers these students might have? How predominant was race in your prediction?

mistake, no matter how bizarre. Of course, in this story, money is the all-American panacea, a salve for any social injury. But despite these confounding issues, the parable is fascinating, and the questions it raises are intriguing.

Why did Professor Hacker construct this strange story, and how did he interpret the payment? He believed that the story unmasks America's hidden racism. Professor Hacker considers white privilege to be so commonplace that most of us are no longer able to "see" it. He uses the parable because it makes visible the hidden advantage society gives to white Americans. In Hacker's estimation, the $50 million that his students thought was "fair" compensation represents the value that white people place on the color of their own skin.

In this chapter and the next one, while we will not ask you to put a price on your bias, we will help you bring your unconscious biases to the surface, the first step in creating equitable teaching practices in your classroom. Once they become conscious, you can work to create more equitable and effective classrooms. For instance, let's look at classroom discipline. If you employ *empathetic discipline* (talking with a student who is being disruptive) rather than *punitive discipline* (threatening that same student with punishment), you are less likely to have to impose damaging suspensions. One study revealed that empathetic discipline reduced suspensions by as much as 75 percent.[8]

FOCUS QUESTION 3

How is gender fluidity influencing school life?

This chapter focuses on how issues like race, language, and sexual identity influence life in the classroom, as well as what steps you can take to be that fair and productive teacher. Chapter 4 will focus on how issues of poverty, family structure, and lifestyle impact your classroom. So let's start the process by examining one of the more contentious topics of diversity in school: gender identity and sexuality.

Gender: From Binary to Spectrum (LGBTQA)

There was a time, not that long ago, when our society had a "Pleasantville" feel to it, a time when life was viewed as simple and everyone was considered either male or female, and certainly heterosexual. Any variations were hidden from view and either disparaged or ignored. Many of today's curriculums still reflect these assumptions in subtle and not so subtle ways. Literature like *Romeo and Juliet,* math word problems like "David bought Karen one dozen roses . . . " or electing a boy and a girl homecoming king and queen are obvious examples of assumed heterosexuality for all. While intentional blindness was commonplace, we now know the world is more complex than that. It is important that today's schools recognize and respond to the needs of LGBTQA students, students already at risk in our society. **LGBTQA** is an acronym that refers to Lesbian, Gay, Bisexual, Transgender, and Queer/Questioning, with the A referring to a number of possible words, including Asexual, Allies, and/or Advocates. Being gay, lesbian, bisexual, or straight refers to a person's sexual orientation, an innate characteristic that determines who one is attracted to sexually and romantically. Being transgender refers to a person's gender identity—a person's innate sense of being male, female, or somewhere in between. Let's take a moment and learn about the LGBTQA community.

Posters like this can be found in classrooms and school offices to ensure a safe zone for LGBTQA students and others.

Source: Courtesy of Boulder County Public Health, OASOS Program

TEACHING TIP

Some Considerations for Teaching LGBTQA Students

Your visible support can help LGBTQA students achieve in school. You can do the following:

1. Post a "Safe Zone" sign in your classroom or office.
2. Don't tolerate intolerance. Immediately respond to comments like "fag" or "dyke" and explain that such bigotry is not acceptable.
3. Integrate the contributions of LGBTQA figures in science, history, athletics, the arts, and other areas of the curriculum.
4. Avoid assumptions about any particular student being gay. The range of behaviors and attitudes within each sex is enormous.
5. On the other hand, honor confidences shared with you by LGBTQA students.
6. Work to keep the school as a safe place for LGBTQA students. Think about becoming an adviser to the Gay-Straight Alliance.

SOURCE: "Ally Yourself with LGBT Students," *Teaching Tolerance*, Fall 2010, p. 35.

REFLECTION: Why is being sensitive to LGBTQA issues a good classroom strategy, even if you do not think you have any LGBTQA students in your class?

Whenever the American Dialect Society meets, one of their challenges is to name the Word of the Year. In 2015, that word was *they*, but not the plural pronoun. This *they* is a singular pronoun. It is used when an individual does not identify as male or female, or when the person's gender is unclear.[9] The term *transgender* refers to a person whose inner sense of being male, female, or something else differs from their birth sex. While research on the biology of gender is in its infancy, gender spectrum rather than the binary male or female designations might be the most useful way of understanding gender.

Integrating these fluid gender concepts at the K–12 level is not easy, and a current legal challenge concerns school bathrooms and locker assignments. Which bathroom should a transgendered student use, the one correlated with their birth sex, or the one correlated with their gender identification? As we go to press, the Supreme Court is deciding how schools should handle this question.

Schools differ in their approaches to LGBTQA students and faculty. Some schools work to be inclusive by altering traditional practices: inviting same-sex couples to the prom, providing gender-neutral or individual bathrooms and locker rooms for transgender students, and including LGBTQA people, history, and perspectives in the curriculum.[10] Other schools and communities are less accommodating, prohibiting teachers from even mentioning "transgender" or "homosexual," or requiring that such words are presented in exclusively negative terms. Such actions put LGBTQA students at risk. Violence aimed at LGBTQA students poses an ongoing danger in and beyond school. In fact, transgendered people are seven times more likely to experience physical violence even when interacting with the police.[11]

In the 1970s, feminists needed to create words like *sexism* and phrases like *sexual harassment* for a public that had no idea of what gender discrimination meant. Today, the same challenge exists in many communities grappling with the needs of LGBTQA students. On some college campuses, students introduce themselves with a name, a major, and a pronoun of choice, pronouns which reach beyond *he* and *she*. At Harvard, *E* is now a third-person pronoun to replace *he* or *she*. Facebook offers 50 different gender identities as options, including *gender fluid* for those whose gender is shifting. In the years ahead, fluid gender identities likely will touch the heart of

K–12 schools as well, influencing instruction, teacher language, curriculum, school practices, and policies, much as the concept of gender discrimination did almost half a century ago.

Depending on where you teach, you may or may not be able to include LGBTQA issues in your classroom. In California, for example, you will be required to include the contributions of gay and lesbian Americans in your teaching.[12] In other communities, you will be expected to be silent on this issue. But wherever you teach, you can ensure that democratic norms of equality are followed and that all students are respected regardless of individual differences. Students do not have to agree that "it's okay to be gay," but they should understand that "it's not okay to discriminate against those who are gay." By providing a safe place for all students, teachers can create nurturing classrooms where every child can learn and every family is welcome.

Posters like this can be placed marking bathrooms welcoming to LGBTQA.

English Language Learners (ELLs)

FOCUS QUESTION 4

What are the instructional and political issues surrounding English Language Learners?

> What is going on in America? It is amazing, and disturbing, to ride on a road and see street signs that are printed not only in English but in other languages as well. What's more, even legal documents are now being written in foreign languages. How unnerving to walk down an American street and not understand what people are talking about. Maybe this isn't America. I feel like a stranger in my own land. Why don't they learn to speak English?

Sound like a stroll through today's Miami, or San Diego, or perhaps San Antonio? Good try, but you not only have the wrong city, you are also in the wrong century. Benjamin Franklin expressed this view in the 1750s.[13] He was disgruntled that Philadelphia had printed so many things, including street signs, in another language (German, in this case). Even the Articles of Confederation were published in German as well as English, and children were taught in Dutch, Italian, and Polish.

In 1837, Pennsylvania law required that school instruction be given on an equal basis in German as well as English. In fact, that example provides us with a fairly concise definition of **bilingual education**, the use of two languages for instruction. But, almost a century later, as the United States was being pulled into World War I, foreign languages were seen as unpatriotic. Public pressure routed the German language from the curriculum, although nearly one in four high school students was studying the language at the time. Individual states went even further. Committed to a rapid assimilation of new immigrants, and suspicious of much that was foreign, these states prohibited the teaching of *any* foreign language during the first eight years of schooling. The Supreme Court found this policy not only xenophobic but unconstitutional as well, in *Meyer v. State of Nebraska*, 1923.[14]

In some bilingual education programs, English is learned as a second language while the student takes other academic work in his or her native language.

GLOBAL VIEW

Xenophobia generally means fear and hatred of strangers or foreigners. Worldwide xenophobic actions (by individuals, groups, and governments) are all too common. What contemporary or historic events can you name that demonstrate this worldwide xenophobia? How does xenophobia manifest in our nation?

Bilingual education is hardly a "new" issue, but for those who are history-challenged, it continues to provoke fierce debate. People hold strong opinions as to whether children with little fluency in English should be taught in their native language while they learn English, or immediately immersed in English. The problem: rapid English immersion has failed many students. So Congress responded with the Bilingual Education Act in 1968, providing financial incentives, what some people call "a carrot approach," to encourage schools to initiate bilingual education programs. Some schools resisted, and disillusioned parents initiated lawsuits.

During the early 1970s, disillusioned parents initiated lawsuits. In 1974, the Supreme Court heard the case of ***Lau v. Nichols.*** This class action lawsuit centered on Kinney Lau and 1,800 other Chinese students from the San Francisco area who were failing their courses because they could not understand English. The Court unanimously affirmed that federally funded schools must "rectify the language deficiency" of students. Teaching students in a language they did not understand was not an appropriate education. The Court ruled that schools must teach academics to language minority students "in their primary language until they could effectively benefit from English language instruction."[15] Under this provision, school districts must take positive steps to eliminate language barriers to learning.

Today, more than five million **English language learners (ELLs)** are enrolled in public elementary and secondary schools, nearly 10 percent of school enrollment (see Figure 3.6). Millions of students speak *hundreds* of languages and dialects, including not only Spanish but also Mandarin, French, Hmong, Urdu, Russian, Polish, Korean, Tagalog, and Swahili. Some non-English-speaking youngsters are from families that have recently come to the United States, and others were born in this country but do not speak English at home. About one in five school-age children speaks a language other than English at home, with Spanish the most common.[16] As these non-English-speaking students enter schools, most will need to make sense of a new language, a new culture, and possibly new ways of interacting with teachers and classmates.

English language learners typically work to master their new language of English as well as academic content, not an easy task. Some schools and states emphasize quick acquisition of English, while others work to maintain the first language along with mastering English.[17]

English Acquisition Programs

- The **transitional approach** uses the native language as a bridge to English language instruction. Academic subjects are first taught using the native language, but progressively students transition to English, their new language. Cultural assimilation is often stressed. The goal is to prepare for English-only classrooms, typically within 2–3 years, but that time period is not always realistic.
- In the **immersion** approach, instruction is mostly in English. **Language submersion** is an extreme example of immersion, placing students in classes where only English is spoken, a "sink or swim" approach, and not really a bilingual program.
- **English as a Second Language (ESL)** supplements immersion programs by providing special pullout classes for additional instruction in reading and writing English. The goal is to assimilate learners into the English language as quickly as possible. ESL instruction may work well for students highly motivated to be part of a mainstreamed English-only classroom.[18]

FIGURE 3.6

English language learners in public schools.

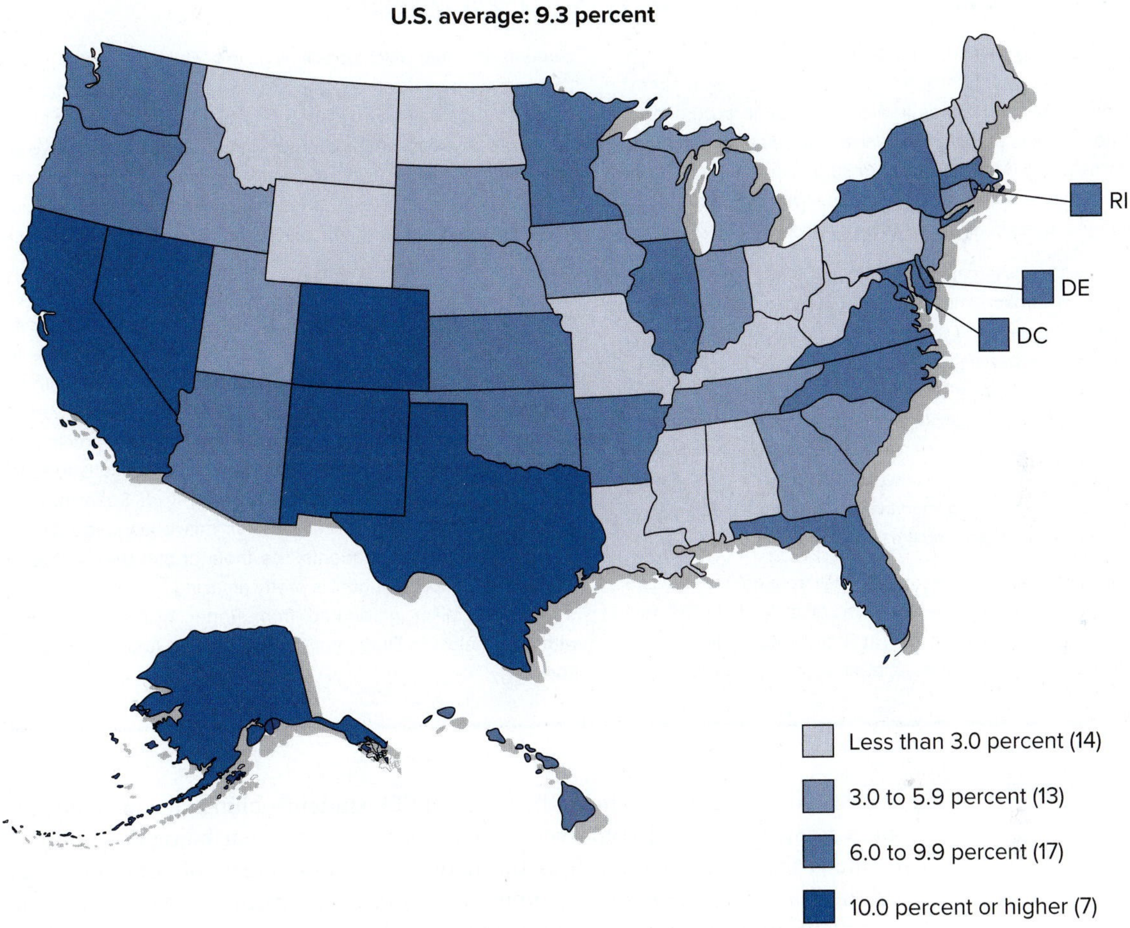

SOURCE: National Center for Education Statistics, "English Language Learners in Public Schools," May 2016.

REFLECTION: What are the implications of these demographics on your life in the classroom? How can you best prepare to teach ELL students?

Dual Language Programs

- The **maintenance** or **developmental approach** is designed to help children learn English while maintaining their native language. Instruction occurs in two languages, usually starting in kindergarten or first grade and extending for five years or longer. These programs prepare students to speak fluently in two languages (bilingual), to read and write in two languages, and to successfully complete the other academic courses.
- **Two-way immersion** programs enroll a balance of native English speakers and native speakers of the partner language. English-speaking students are enrolled to learn a second language. Classes are taught to all students in both languages.

CONTEMPORARY ISSUES

A View from the Field: Twin Classrooms

Nicole Miller, 25, is a second grade teacher at PS 108 in Brooklyn, New York, a kindergarten through fifth grade school with almost 1,000 students. Nicole teaches in a dual language program; for most of the students at PS 108, Spanish is the primary language spoken in the home. As of 2006, about 80 percent of the students were new immigrants. Although Nicole teaches in English, there are challenges to the dual language program.

> My first challenge is teaching students who are not proficient in English; my classroom is meant to be a place where only English is spoken by teachers and students. Another major challenge is the academic gap between students in my classes. For instance, I have students who only know a handful of sight words and are not able to write a complete sentence independently and I have other students who are reading books and writing five paragraph pieces. Creating lessons that don't leave anyone out is a daily challenge. It is so important to support the struggling students while still challenging the thriving students.

Picture twin classrooms across the hall from each other, one with half English-dominant students and the other half ELLs. The two teachers work together, one teaching in English—that's Nicole—and one teaching primarily in Spanish—that's Ms. Lourdes Castillo. "The students alternate which class they go to each day," explains Nicole. "We are supposed to be doing the same thing at every moment throughout the day, so we plan together. However, it is tough to find the necessary read-alouds available in both languages and we are using different texts for guided reading. Then we teach phonics; again, very different in each language. My point is that it is difficult, but my partner teacher and I collaborate. The goal is to make the daily transition as seamless as possible for our students."

Though she doesn't feel any teacher preparation program can "truly prepare you for the challenges of running a classroom," Nicole believes she was given a sound philosophical basis for her teaching career: "I was taught to be progressively minded and to be an advocate for my students." After clearing the hurdles of classroom management, Nicole is an enthusiastic participant in the dual language program. "The program's purpose is to teach all children a second language, be it English or Spanish, while still pushing them academically in their native language. That is a huge benefit to all students; the thought that they will leave elementary school bilingual is pretty amazing."

Nicole Miller graduated from Roger Williams University with dual majors in Elementary Education and Anthropology and Sociology.

As schools struggle to meet the needs of ELL students, bilingual education continues to spark political controversy. Many people worry that bilingual education threatens the status of English as the nation's primary vehicle of communication and the thing that preserves our common culture. They advocate for an English-only movement, promoting the use of one language, English, in official U.S. government operations, making English the nation's only official language. Bilingual education advocates counter this by arguing that the United States is a mosaic of diverse cultures, that diversity should be honored and nurtured, and that mastery of several languages will pay economic dividends for our country in the competitive global economy.[19] Bilingual advocates believe the English-only movement promotes intolerance, as education writer James Crawford points out, "It is certainly more respectable to discriminate by language than by race. . . . Most people are not sensitive to language discrimination in this nation, so it is easy to argue that you're doing someone a favor by making them speak English."[20]

What approach is most effective, English immersion or bilingual education? People argue over even this research. Arizona brought a case to a conservative U.S. Supreme Court (*Horne v. Flores*, 2009) and the majority of judges ruled in favor of English immersion as more effective than bilingual. This case had political overtones for sure, and the majority of educational researchers believe just the opposite, that bilingual programs are in fact more effective than English immersion. They argue that bilingual programs have a significant positive effect on student achievement in English literacy, as well as increasing student performance in other academic courses as well. There is growing evidence that bilingual education enhances brain development

TEACHING TIP

English Language Learners

Here are several strategies for teaching English language learners:

- **Get to know your students, and when possible, use their backgrounds to make connections to the material being learned.** Creating a comfortable and safe classroom climate for your students despite the language and culture differences is an important first step. By connecting to their backgrounds, you will help ELL students feel that their new classroom culture is less alien and distant.
- **Give explicit directions, emphasize key words, and offer concrete examples to enhance the understanding of ELL students.** Simple strategies such as emphasizing key words, offering examples of your main points, and using visuals such as the chalkboard, flash cards, games, graphics, and puzzles can increase the understanding of ELL students.
- **Plan for and expect the active involvement of ELL students.** It is a good idea to call on all students to keep their attention and focus. ELL students are no exception. A preferred strategy is to ask a question before calling out a specific name so that all students have time to consider their answer. Feel free to use a variety of questioning strategies, but avoid rhetorical questions, because ELL students may not understand them. Waiting a bit longer for students to respond will give ELL students more time to process the question in their new language.
- **Do not depend simply on verbal, teacher-centered learning, but incorporate a variety of instructional strategies.** Hands-on activities, cooperative learning groups, and other strategies will help ELL students develop their language skills and learn new information through avenues other than teacher talk.
- **Always provide time to check for understanding and be sure to provide precise and immediate feedback.** Unlearning the wrong word or behavior is more difficult than learning it correctly the first time. Monitoring and offering clear feedback can eliminate the need to unlearn and relearn.

REFLECTION: Although these skills are designed for ELL students, how might they enhance your teaching effectiveness for all students?

as well as social-emotional skills. School districts can still choose the English immersion approach, if they desire, and many do. It is fair to point out that careful planning and implementation is necessary for any program to succeed. Perhaps the biggest challenge, especially in bilingual programs, is recruiting teachers who themselves are fluent in two languages. And the challenge in finding those bilingual teachers is itself an argument for promoting dual language acquisition in our schools.[21]

Whether being an English language learner or not, some groups seem to struggle more in school than others. Why is that? People have advances several theories, so let's take a look at those theories and see if you connect with any of these.

Theories of Why Some Groups Succeed and Others Do Not

A number of theories have emerged to explain why some groups soar in school while others flounder. Some of the explanations are fatalistic, others are more hopeful. Here are three—deficit theory, expectation theory, and cultural difference theory. The argument for **deficit theory** is that certain students do poorly in school because they suffer some sort of deficit: cultural, social, economic, academic, linguistic, or even genetic. For instance, some studies indicate that as much as half the achievement gap can be predicted by economics. Even in wealthy suburbs, for example, black families are less wealthy than their white counterparts, and their children do less well in school. There are parenting differences as well, another line of reasoning among deficit theory advocates. Some argue that black parents are not as academically oriented in raising their children as white parents. For example, in one study, only half as many black homes as white homes owned 100 or more books, and more white parents read to their children every day. Fewer books read, fewer vocabulary

PROFILE IN EDUCATION

Carlos Ovando

Carlos Ovando immigrated to the United States with his family as a teenager. Now a professor of education, Ovando shares his first-hand experience of learning English, and how it was not until his bilingual ability was celebrated that he was able to find confidence in his academic abilities.

Read a full profile of Carlos Ovando on Connect.

©Carlos Julio Ovando

connect

FOCUS QUESTION 5

How do deficit, expectation, and cultural difference theories explain different academic performance among various racial, ethnic, and cultural groups?

words used by parents, and little understanding of the relationship between education and careers contribute to the cultural deficit. Not that this is not an easy topic to discuss. Ronald Ferguson, an African American professor who has done much of this research, is well aware that these studies anger parents. He explains, "I don't want to be another one of those people lecturing black parents. I tell them we in the black community–we–need to build stronger intellectual lives at home."[22]

It should be noted that a nefarious branch of deficit theory moves beyond these behavioral and economic issues and argues that genetic and IQ deficiencies of certain groups, especially people of color, are the root cause of academic underachievement. Most deficit theory proponents today steer clear of such genetic claims and question the research advanced to make this case.

Those who subscribe to **expectation theory** believe that some children do poorly because their teachers do not expect much of kids from certain racial and ethnic groups. As a result, they teach these students differently, and the students' academic performance suffers. This insight was first made popular by a classic study done by Rosenthal and Jacobson, which is described in greater detail later in this text. In the study, students were randomly chosen and the teachers told these students would experience an intellectual growth spurt during the year. Lo and behold, over the year, their grades improved. Teacher expectations of improved performance led to improved performance. Now imagine the opposite, teachers who expect less from certain students, and you see how harmful this "self-fulfilling prophesy" can be.

A third explanation for student achievement argues for better cross-cultural understanding. **Cultural difference theory** asserts that academic problems can be overcome if educators study and mediate the cultural gap separating school and home. Let's consider a case in point:

> Polynesian children in a Hawaiian village are performing poorly on the school reading tests. They seem unresponsive to the extra time and effort made by teachers to improve their reading performance. Why is this happening, and how can the situation be improved?

In this example, educators studied the Polynesian culture and discovered that older children, rather than adults, play a major role in educating the young. Accordingly, the school established a peer-learning center to provide the opportunity for older children to teach younger ones. By recognizing and adopting cultural traditions, the school was able to dramatically improve students' reading scores.[23]

Cultural differences are fascinating, and can be of great help to teachers who understand them, but let's not forget that successful groups and individuals also share similar traits and behaviors that lead to academic success. We talked about this a bit in the last chapter when we discussed Carol Dweck's work on growth and fixed mindset. Those with growth mindset have a more promising future than those with a fixed mindset, regardless of cultural or racial or class background. She is not alone in identifying such broad success patterns. Paul Tough, author of *How Children Succeed,* underscores the importance of perseverance, curiosity, conscientiousness, optimism, and self-control (not unrelated to a growth mindset for sure) for success in school (and in life!). Others tout resilience, the ability to overcome adversity, as a key factor for students to achieve. The authors of one popular book use the term "Triple Package" to describe the universal traits they believe are most important.[24] These authors list seemingly opposite qualities: those who succeed exhibit both a superiority and an inferiority complex. The superiority complex provides a student with a deep-seated belief in his or her innate abilities and talents. The inferiority complex sets the stage for insecurity, the feeling that even if you are bright, in some ways the cards are stacked against you, and you must work harder than others to achieve. This superior–inferior combination requires a third ingredient, impulse control, the last part of the triple package. Although you are exceptional and will be facing many obstacles, you can overcome them all with self-discipline. These authors argue that groups who have done particularly well in America (Chinese, Indians, Jews, Mormons, Nigerians, and Cuban Americans) owe their success to the triple package. But even the triple package can become problematic if taken to extreme, and can cause failure as well as success. So you see, there are no shortages of traits and qualities that people believe are central to school success. Does any of these ideas strike a chord in you?

What role do these theories play in the classroom? Deficit theory teaches us that groups bring different experiences and values to the classroom, and some of these differences do not mesh with mainstream school culture. Mainstream society terms this mismatch a deficit. The economic poverty of some groups contributes to such deficits, an issue that many believe should be addressed by the larger society. Expectation theory teaches us the power of teacher attitudes, that the attitudes you bring to the classroom influence your students, for better or worse. Cultural difference theory teaches us the rich nature of the human experience and how much we can teach each other. And despite all our group differences, there may well be qualities such as persistence, resilience, positive self-image, and mindset that apply to most if not all of us. In this chapter, we will explore our national diversity, learning what we have in common, and how our differences make us all that much richer.

From the Melting Pot to Cultural Pluralism

FOCUS QUESTION 6

How do phrases like "melting pot" and "cultural pluralism" both capture and mask American identity?

Start a discussion about cultural, racial, or ethnic differences at a social gathering—or even more challenging, in a work environment—and feel the tension grow as competing theories of group differences emerge. Introduce issues like affirmative action, immigration laws, classes being taught in Spanish or Laotian, or racial profiling, and some people become unglued. More than a few people will listen politely, carefully avoiding uttering a sound. Some might stay silent but wonder if the conversation is genuine or simply an attempt at "political correctness." Others, articulating beliefs they perceive as acceptable, may voice hopeful insights, but in their heart of hearts, they themselves do not believe them. A few may say things they will later regret, words that may spark an attack, or a charge of racism:

> "Why don't they learn to speak English? My grandparents had nothing, but they learned the language. Are people today too lazy or do they simply not care?"
>
> "I am fine with racial equality. I like it as a concept. I just wonder why all my friends are my race."
>
> "I treat all people the same, but some groups have a chip on their shoulder."

Start a discussion about cultural, racial, or ethnic differences at a social gathering, and you may wish you never did.

Many of us continue to live in silence about race and ethnicity. As a nation, we have yet to come to terms with our multicultural society. Many believe that the United States is a wondrous melting pot where the Statue of Liberty opens her arms to all the world's immigrants. This was the image painted by Israel Zangwill in a 1910 play that coined the term *melting pot.*

> America is God's Crucible, the Great Melting Pot where all races of Europe are melting and reforming . . . Germans and Frenchmen, Irishman and Englishmen, Jews and Russians—into the Crucible with you all! God is making the American . . . The real American has not yet arrived. He is only in the Crucible, I tell you—he will be the fusion of all races, the coming superman.[25]

YOU BE THE JUDGE

Separating Students By Shared Characteristics—Or Grouping All Students Together

PROVIDE GROUPS SEPARATE INSTRUCTION BY . . .

GENDER, TO FOCUS ON SPECIFIC ACADEMIC NEEDS
Same-gender classes help students focus on academics, not on each other. Girls can get extra encouragement in math and science; boys can get special assistance in reading and language arts.

COMMUNITY, TO PROMOTE RACIAL AND ETHNIC PRIDE
Let's eliminate the alienation caused by busing students out of their neighborhood. Students feel accepted and take pride in local schools, where they can study with friends and learn from a curriculum that reflects and honors their heritage.

RELIGION, TO ENCOURAGE SACRED OBSERVANCES
Secular American school norms and laws force all religious groups to make compromises. Some religious holidays are ignored, adult-led prayer in school is prohibited, school dress codes may conflict with religious requirements, and schools routinely ignore religious dietary law. By educating religious groups separately, different histories and beliefs can be honored and practiced. Students can pray as they like and pursue their religion without ridicule or taunting from peers, or interference from civil authorities.

NEED TO PROTECT LGBTQA STUDENTS
Special schools can help LGBTQA students cope with their unique personal and academic circumstances. Being with LGBTQA students protects them from comparisons and ridicule that might exist elsewhere.

TEACHING ALL CHILDREN TOGETHER PROMOTES . . .

GENDER EQUALITY
Learning and succeeding together in the classroom prepares boys and girls to live and work together as adults. Equitable instruction and curriculum will teach students how to eliminate traditional gender barriers in society.

CULTURAL AND RACIAL UNDERSTANDING
We must not allow our nation to be fractured along racial, ethnic, and class lines. Integrating children of different backgrounds mirrors our ideal of a democratic society. Cross-cultural classrooms enrich the learning experience.

RESPECT AND UNDERSTANDING OF RELIGIOUS DIFFERENCES
Religious practices are the domain of religious institutions and should not become the focal point of school life. Learning *about* different religions can help all of us to grow. Restricting each of us to one set of beliefs will eventually divide and separate Americans. By learning together, students gain valuable lessons as they prepare to live and work together as adults in a vibrant and diverse democracy. We see all too well in other countries how religion and government can create problems.

SAFETY AND HOPE FOR LGBTQA STUDENTS
Attending a regular school gives all students insight into more different lifestyles. Learning together as children can help us all live together as adults.

connect YOU DECIDE...

Do you believe equal educational opportunity is best achieved in separate or integrated classrooms? Is your position consistent or does it vary depending upon the identified group? Extend this *You Be the Judge* feature by developing the arguments for either integrating or separating two other groups discussed in this chapter (or identify new groups).

For many, "melting in" became a reality. Groups incorporated into the mainstream culture are said to have gone through **assimilation** or **enculturation.** Countless immigrants today cling to this idea of being transformed into a new citizen, a new person, an American. But the melting pot image, although enticing, describes only a part of the American reality.

Picture yourself traveling in another country and a person who has never been to America asks you to describe your country–how would you do it? Would you describe our great West, its majestic Rockies and mysterious deserts? Or perhaps you would choose South Beach in Miami, a city with a 1940s art deco feel and a beach at its doorstep. Or perhaps New York City catches your fancy, with its breathtaking skyscrapers, its world-class museums, and the wonders of Broadway theaters. Some of you might paint a picture of the magnificent Maine coast, or the rich Midwest farmlands, the pristine Alaskan wilderness, or perhaps the lush Hawaiian Islands. Okay, we will stop here because suddenly we are feeling an urge to travel. You probably already appreciate our point: A fair description of our nation would include all its diverse regions, from coast to coast.

Now, let's change the question, and imagine that you are asked not to describe America but to describe an American. How would you do it? Would you resort to the melting pot image: a white European, perhaps arriving penniless and now a rich American? Or perhaps you would take the question quite literally and describe our Native Americans, our many different Indian tribes. Or better yet, we hope that you have learned the lesson from the first question. Not only is our nation geographically diverse, our people are diverse as well. Americans live in communities called Germantown and Chinatown, maintaining traditions from their land of origin. Americans have dark skins, but they also have light skins, and every shade in between. They speak Spanish and Arabic, pray to Buddha and Christ, or perhaps look for spiritual answers in their own hearts, like the Quakers. What do we call this diversity? This is **cultural pluralism,** a recognition that some groups, voluntarily or involuntarily, have maintained their culture and their language. We now recognize that there are many kinds of Americans, and like geographic diversity, they make our nation diverse and beautiful. Different groups teach us different ways of seeing and understanding the world. As we learn to appreciate one another's experiences and viewpoints, our nation grows not only stronger but also wiser.

Schools are one of the portals where diverse Americans meet. It is a place where we can learn from one another. Teachers are the gatekeepers to that learning. If they are open to other cultures and peoples, they and their students will learn and grow.

Multicultural Education

Students in many urban and suburban schools speak scores of languages. In some urban communities, students of color comprise 70 percent to more than 90 percent of school enrollment. A successful teacher in these communities will need to bridge possible racial, cultural, and language differences. In fact, even in very stable, overwhelmingly white school districts where all students share apparently similar backgrounds and speak English, cross-cultural knowledge is important. Many of these students will

GLOBAL VIEW

With English as the most common second language in the world (and the language of international business, air travel, and technology), why do today's educators need bilingual skills?

graduate, leave these communities, and work and live in more diverse areas. The success of their transition may depend on what they learned—or did not learn—in school. Moreover, communities that appear uniform and static may have differences in religion, social class, gender, and sexuality. The controversial question facing the nation: how best to teach our multicultural students?

The Multiculturalism Debate

FOCUS QUESTION 7

What are the purposes and approaches of multicultural education?

You enter teaching in a time of harsh and divisive "culture wars," as people argue about how diversity should be recognized in schools.[26] Some worry that overemphasizing diversity may pull us apart and fear that multiculturalism will lead to a Dis-United States. Adversaries of multiculturalism point to Yugoslavia and Czechoslovakia, nations dissolved by the power of ethnic differences. They argue for a uniform national identity and urge schools to promote one set of common beliefs based on our English and European traditions. In their eyes, time spent teaching about different cultures poses a double threat: pulling apart the national fabric while taking time from important academic subjects like math and reading. They would prefer that students focus on academic achievement and adopt what they see as core values of the United States.

Others claim that multiculturalism is the nation's future. They believe that schools can no longer ignore or devalue cultural and ethnic differences, either in this country or throughout the world. National demographics are changing, and schools must recognize these changes. They argue that current practices are failing in their mission to unite and educate all our students equitably and point to statistics like these to underscore their point[27]:

- Although schools were ordered to desegregate in the 1954 *Brown* decision, since the 1980s, schools have been resegregating.
- Since the 1990s, the segregation of students of every racial group has increased.
- Nationally, Asian Americans are more likely than students of other races to attend multiracial schools.
- White students are the least likely to attend multiracial schools and are the most isolated group.
- More than three-quarters of intensely segregated schools are also high-poverty schools.
- High school graduation rates are around 70 percent, and in many communities only 50 or 60 percent of Hispanic American, African American, and Native American students are graduating from high school.

Is multicultural education part of the answer to these troubling statistics? A sacred belief of many religions is "We are one," that all humans are connected. Perhaps one path for moving ahead and avoiding yet another culture war is for us to learn balance, to honor ourselves and others, and to celebrate our group and individual differences.

Approaches to Multicultural Education

When multiculturalism began, the focus was on fighting racism. Over time, these programs expanded to confront not only racism, but also injustices based on gender, social class, disability, and sexual orientation. Today, there are many dimensions to **multicultural education,** including (1) *expanding the curriculum* to reflect America's diversity; (2) *using teaching strategies* that are responsive to different learning styles; (3) *supporting the multicultural competence of teachers* so they are comfortable and knowledgeable working with students and families of different cultures; and (4) *a commitment to social justice,* promoting efforts to work and teach toward local and global equity.

Multiculturalism has come to mean different things to different educators.[28] Some focus on *human relations,* activities that promote cultural and racial understanding among different groups. Others teach *single-group studies,* which you may know as Black Studies, Hispanic Studies, or Women's Studies programs. Some educators believe multicultural education is all about creating close links between home and school so that minority children can succeed academically, an approach termed *teaching the culturally different.* Another tack, called simply *multicultural,* promotes different perspectives based on race, class, and culture; in a sense, developing new eyes through which students learn. And finally, the *multicultural reconstructionist* approach mobilizes students to examine and work to remediate social injustices. As you can see, multicultural education can mean different things to different people.

The Curriculum

James Banks focuses specifically on developing a multicultural curriculum.[29] Banks believes that one way to achieve greater understanding and more positive attitudes toward different groups is to integrate and broaden the curriculum to make it more inclusive and action oriented. He defines four approaches to a multicultural curriculum that are related to several proposed by others.[30] (See Figure 3.7.) As you read each description, consider if any of these approaches were used in your own schooling.

1. Multicultural education often begins with the *contributions approach,* in which the study of ethnic heroes (for example, Sacagawea, Rosa Parks, or Booker T. Washington)

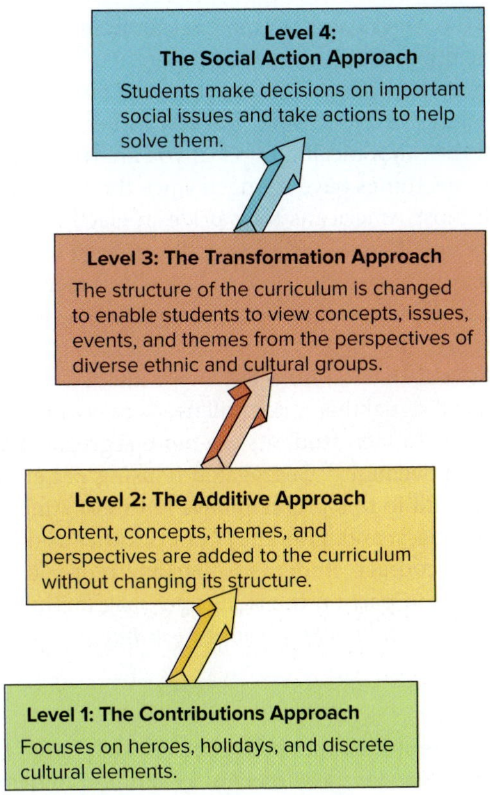

FIGURE 3.7

Banks' approach to multicultural education.

REFLECTION: Think back to your own schooling. At which of Banks's levels would you place your own multicultural education? Provide supporting evidence. As a teacher, which of these levels do you want to reach and teach? Explain.

is included in the curriculum. At this superficial contributions level, one might also find "food and festivals" being featured or holidays such as Cinco de Mayo being described or celebrated.

2. In the *additive approach,* a unit or course is incorporated, often during a "special" week or month. February has become the month to study African Americans, and March has been designated "Women's History Month." Although these dedicated weeks and months offer a respite from the typical curricular material, no substantial change is made to the curriculum as a whole.

RAP 1.8

If the Walls Could Speaks

3. In the *transformation approach,* the entire Eurocentric nature of the curriculum is changed. Students are taught to view events and issues from diverse ethnic and cultural perspectives. For instance, the westward expansion of Europeans can be seen as manifest destiny through the eyes of European descendants or as an invasion from the east through the eyes of Native Americans.
4. The fourth level, *social action,* goes beyond the transformation approach. Students not only learn to view issues from multiple perspectives, but also become directly involved in solving related problems. At this level, a school would address social and economic needs here and abroad, advocate human rights and peace, and work to ensure that the school building and activities did not harm the environment. Rather than political passivity (the typical by-product of many curricular programs) this approach promotes decision making and social action to achieve multicultural goals and a more vibrant democracy.

Multicultural education also seeks to help all students develop more positive attitudes toward different racial, ethnic, cultural, and religious groups. According to a 1990s survey of more than 1,000 young people between the ages of 15 and 24 conducted by People for the American Way, most respondents felt their attitudes toward race relations were healthier than those of their parents. Yet about half described the state of race relations in the United States as generally bad. Fifty-five percent of African Americans and whites said they were "uneasy" rather than "comfortable" in dealing with members of the other racial group.[31] If you are thinking that the 1990s were a while ago, and perhaps things have changed since then, they have not changed for the better. Although most Americans took pride in electing a multiracial president in 2008 and 2012, the media gave little in-depth coverage to race. "Black and white people have a different notion of the need to talk about race," notes *Chicago Tribune* reporter Clarence Page. Ninety-two percent of journalists reported that when it came to covering race relations, the media was not doing its job effectively.[32]

The 2016 presidential election reflected a very divided nation on issues like race and ethnicity, a powerful signal that much still needs to be done in repairing personal and group relationships. In fact, students are more segregated today than any time since the Civil Rights movement.[33] Segregated housing patterns and federal courts no longer willing to attend to this problem have left most American school children segregated by race and class, and ignorant of one another's cultures, languages, and experiences. How to encourage students to become more "comfortable" with one another depends at least in part on the skills and insights the teacher brings to the classroom, what some term *culturally responsive teaching.*

RAP 1.6

A Novel Read

Teaching

FOCUS QUESTION 8

Why is culturally responsive teaching important?

A key assumption of multicultural education is that students learn in different ways and that effective teachers recognize and respond to these differences.

Culturally responsive teaching focuses on the learning strengths of students and mediates the frequent mismatch between home and school cultures. **Gloria Ladson-Billings,** a professor at the University of Wisconsin, offers a powerful example of culturally relevant teaching. She wanted to find out what behaviors make some teachers successful with African American children, while others are not. She asked parents and principals in four schools serving primarily African American students to nominate "excellent teachers," teachers they would rate as successful. As you might expect, principals chose teachers who had low numbers of discipline referrals, high attendance rates, and high standardized test scores. Parents, on the other hand, selected teachers who were enthusiastic, respectful, and understood that students need to operate in both the white world and their local community. Nine teachers, white and black, made both lists, and eight of them agreed to participate in her study. After several years of observations and interviews, she was baffled: their personalities, teaching strategies, and styles were entirely different; there seemed to be no common patterns. She was close to throwing in the towel when she finally saw the subtle, but striking, commonalities.

First, all of these eight teachers had chosen to teach in these more challenging schools and felt responsible for the academic success of each student. Second, they were sensitive to race discrimination in society; they actively fought bias and prejudice and wanted their students to do the same. For example, some of these teachers had students rewrite out-of-date textbooks or work on projects to improve their community. And finally, the teachers viewed both the home and school as connected and seized opportunities to learn from their neighborhoods. They honored the crafts and traditions in the community, inviting parents to share traditional cooking in the school. One teacher allowed students to use "home English" in class but required that students also master Standard English. Students were expected to learn both languages well. Teachers realized that they, too, were learners and needed to be open to new information. Gloria Ladson-Billings developed three promising culturally responsive principles for teaching not only African American children, but also others[34]:

1. **Students must experience academic success, which leads to a stronger self-esteem. Esteem is built on solid academic accomplishment.** We intuitively know that students who do not feel good about themselves have a tough time in (and beyond) school. But this is not enough. For school success, students' self-esteem needs to be built on solid academic accomplishment. Teachers must create lessons that are responsive to student learning styles *and* allow student mastery of the basic knowledge and skills necessary for success in today's society. The bottom line: Students feel good about themselves when there is real academic progress.
2. **Students should develop and maintain cultural competence, and the student's home culture is an opportunity for learning.** Too many teachers have been taught only about classroom teaching skills and not about community outreach possibilities. Ladson-Billings's research teaches us that we must expand our concept of the classroom to include the community. When there is friction between school and home, academic progress suffers. Put more positively, when teachers move beyond their classroom and integrate learning with the local community, they can create a more positive, seamless, and mutually supportive academic environment. For example, a local African storyteller can visit the class and relate an African folktale. Students could use the experience as a springboard for their writing or drawing. Or a local politician could be invited to class to share his or her public service work, challenging students to develop their own vision of community service and social activism. Following the presentation, students might do just

A CLOSER LOOK

Myths about Culturally Responsive Teaching

Myth 1—Culturally responsive teaching is a new approach intended to meet the needs of poor, urban students of color. Teaching has always been culturally responsive, but primarily responsive to the values of white, Euro-American, middle-class students. That is why schools historically have emphasized individual success more than group success, strict adherence to time schedules, knowledge valued through analytical reasoning, self-sufficiency, and even dress codes. More inclusive culturally responsive teaching embraces the values and experiences of other cultures as well.

Myth 2—Only teachers of color can actually be culturally responsive to students of color. Race is not an obstacle to culturally responsive teaching; ignorance is. Through teacher training, teachers of any cultural background can gain the knowledge, skills, and attitudes needed to teach children from diverse cultures. In turn, because most teachers are white, they can share important lessons about the dominant culture.

Myth 3—Culturally responsive teaching is little more than a collection of teaching ideas and practices to motivate students of color. Culturally responsive teaching offers a new way of looking at the roles of teachers and students. Culturally relevant teachers are committed to valuing the experiences of their students and working toward a more just society, far more profound goals than simply a collection of teaching ideas.

Myth 4—Culturally relevant teachers must master all the critical details of many cultures. It is unrealistic to expect teachers to master the intricacies of many cultures. But over time, thoughtful teachers will abandon simplistic, stereotypic thinking as they gain insights into cultural differences that influence behavior and learning.

Myth 5—Culturally relevant teaching categorizes children, which feeds stereotypic thinking. Actually, culturally relevant teaching reduces stereotypic thinking by asking teachers to be reflective. They must consider student experiences and backgrounds, create teaching opportunities that respond to student learning styles, hold high expectations for all students, and help students experience academic success.

SOURCE: Jacqueline Jordan and Beverley Jeanne Armento, *Culturally Responsive Teaching* (Boston: McGraw-Hill, 2001).

REFLECTION: Why do you think these myths are so prevalent? What additional myths about culturally relevant teaching can you add? How has your understanding of culturally relevant teaching expanded by reading this chapter?

that: organize a class project to improve the quality of community life. Identifying community resources and connecting classroom activities to those resources are keystones to creating a fruitful academic climate for students.

3. **Students must develop critical consciousness and actively challenge social injustice.** A culturally relevant teacher needs to do more than connect with student needs and the local community; a culturally relevant teacher also works to improve the quality of life in the school and community. Do you remember the disconnect you may have felt among life in school, the world you read about in textbooks, and "the real world" you lived in? Schools too often live in a sanitized bubble, separate from the world's problems. Culturally relevant teachers break that bubble and, along with their students, work to improve the quality of life. For instance, if school textbooks are weak and dated, a teacher might encourage students to rewrite them. The result would be more realistic and current texts, as well as student practice in writing. Or perhaps there are serious health problems in the community. Students might volunteer to attract additional resources to the community health clinic and in the process learn how local government works. Confronting and eliminating real social problems is the third component of a culturally relevant classroom.

As you prepare to teach, it is helpful for you to consider what it means to be a culturally responsive teacher, to broaden your view of what it takes to be successful in the classroom. Let's take a moment to think about what this means for your own teacher preparation. To be competent in each of Ladson-Billings's three points, you will need to acquire certain skills, attitudes, and knowledge. What teaching *skills* will you need to be a culturally responsive teacher for all your students? You will want to diagnose different student needs and plan for different learning styles. You will want to develop critical thinking skills and include all your students in an equitable manner. You will even want to make certain that you can be silent and listen to the answers that are volunteered by all the students (a skill called "wait time"). Studies show that even teachers with the best of intentions too often fail to use these skills. (We describe equitable teaching skills later in this text in Chapter 11, "Becoming an Effective Teacher.")

What *attitudes* will you need to be a culturally responsive teacher? How do you approach teaching students whose background may be quite different from your own? Because most of us have grown up in a segregated community, there is an excellent chance that most of your friends are similar to you in race, class, and ethnicity. You probably share a common set of values and opinions, seeing the world through a lens forged in your own socialization. As you prepare to teach, you may want to make an extra effort to move out of your familiar milieu and seek different views. The more voices you hear, the more likely you will be able to appreciate different life experiences and develop attitudes that are accepting of people who at first glance may seem very different from you.

Finally, as you prepare to teach, you will want to acquire *knowledge* about different group experiences in order to be a culturally responsive teacher. You already bring to the classroom some knowledge of other groups, but this knowledge is limited, and some of it may be inaccurate. You will want to educate yourself about your future students and the educational implications of their cultural backgrounds. This chapter helps you move down that path. For example, many African American communities often emphasize aural and participatory learning over writing. If you ignore this insight and use only writing activities in class, student performance may suffer.[35] As another example, research suggests that many girls and women personalize knowledge and prefer learning through experience and first-hand observation.[36] Creating personal connections and examples may increase the success of your female students. In fact, responding to all types of student diversity is simply good teaching. A Head Start teacher in Michigan, in this case teaching poor, white, rural students, shares her view of culturally responsive teaching:

> I believe that it is my responsibility to learn as much as I can about the child's family and their culture and then implement that into my classroom, so that the child can see his/her culture is a part of our classroom and that I respect them and their family and their culture. It can be hard; I don't want to present any new stereotypes to these kids, so I ask the parents a lot of questions. Sometimes I get the answers and sometimes I don't, but at least they see I am trying.[37]

The challenge for teachers is to acquire useful and accurate cultural insights that help connect classroom and the culture, while avoiding the trap of stereotypic thinking. What's the difference between a useful cultural insight and a damaging stereotype? That critical distinction is explored in the next section.

Stereotypes

The way we use the terms stereotype and generalization can be very confusing, so let's try to be more precise. **Stereotypes** are absolute beliefs that all members of a group have a fixed set of characteristics. The word *stereotype* originated in the print shop. It is literally a type—a one-piece plate that repeats a pattern with no individuality. Today's cultural stereotypes also ignore individuality and are repeatedly applied to all members of a group. People who use stereotypes try to save time by

TEACHING TIP

What You Can Do to Learn about Your Students

1. Walk around the neighborhoods where your students live. If your students are older, they can be your guides. (They love doing this!)
2. Learn how to ask culturally acceptable questions. Your colleagues at school can be a big help here.
3. Before you start teaching, learn about the history and the cultures of the students you will serve.
4. Schedule home visits. Be open, honest, and humble, and tell families that such visits can help you be a more effective teacher.
5. Build community in your class by inviting parents to school to share their cultures.
6. In many cultures, teachers are invited to community and family events. Go! This can be an incredibly fulfilling (and delicious) part of your job!
7. If your students are immigrants, connect with community centers or refugee assistance organizations and ask questions like: "As these children's teacher, what do you think are the most important things for me to know?"
8. Get specific information about each of your students. Mexican American children born in the United States are quite different from Nicaraguan children who just arrived here. Avoid assumptions.
9. Talk to your colleagues and ask them about the mistakes they made in their own teaching—mistakes you can work to avoid.
10. In the beginning of the year, have a potluck and connect with students, families, and the community. Breaking bread together nourishes the body and the soul. How can that experience help you in your teaching?

SOURCE: E. Aguilar, "Teaching Secrets: When the Kids Don't Share Your Culture," *Teacher Magazine*, July 14, 2010.

REFLECTION: Have you ever visited or lived in another culture? How did you learn about it?

short-circuiting the thinking process, just like the original stereotype saved time in the printing process. A set of characteristics with no qualifiers are attributed to individuals based on their membership in a group. Simplistic sentences are used with words like "all Hispanics are" and are applied to every member of the group without distinction. Actually, stereotypes are examples of sloppy thinking that undermine the critical reflection that we want our students to develop. For example, a stereotype might naively proclaim that Hispanics are poor students, Asians are math geniuses, Jews are wealthy, and African Americans are great athletes. Stereotypes are impervious to contradictory information. Find a poor Jew, a Hispanic with a doctorate, an Asian dropping out of school, or an unathletic African American and each is thought to be an anomaly, the exception to the rule. The rule, the stereotype, endures. Stereotypes not only hurt people, they block learning. Stereotypic thinking obstructs a search for new information—not just "contradictory" information, but any information that might add to the complex, rich understanding of an individual or a group. Stereotypes ignore nuances, qualifiers, and subtleties that might more accurately characterize the group. This willingness to engage in complex thinking is what students need; unfortunately, stereotypes short-circuit thoughtful reflection.

Stereotype Threat

Let's look at an example of how damaging stereotypes can be. Opinion polls suggest that about half of white America endorses common stereotypes about blacks and Hispanics, such as the belief that they are not very intelligent. Such stereotypes influence expectations and behaviors not only of whites who hold them, but also of blacks and Hispanics who must live in a society marked by such beliefs. For example, an African American called on in class realizes that an incorrect answer may confirm the stereotype of inferior intelligence. For this student, speaking in class can be risky. As you might imagine, the risk intensifies on high-stakes tests. Consider the following studies: African American and white college students were asked to take a difficult standardized verbal examination. In the control group, the test was presented in a typical way, as a measure of intelligence. In the nonthreatening experimental group, the students were told that ability was not being assessed; rather, the psychology of their verbal problem-solving was being researched. The two groups were matched so that student abilities, time to take the test, and the test itself were similar. In the nonthreatening experimental groups, black test takers solved about twice as many problems as the ones in the control group where the students believed intelligence was being measured; the white students solved the same number in both groups. In a similar study, researchers found that simply asking students to record their race before taking a test had a similar devastating impact on black performance.[38]

Consider these three students. On the basis of this photo, what assumptions do you make about them? Are those assumptions based on stereotypes?

©Image Source RF

This dramatic outcome has been termed **stereotype threat,** a measure of how social context, such as self-image, trust in others, and a sense of belonging, can influence academic performance. When an individual is aware of a stereotype, he or she is more likely to behave like the stereotype than if it did not exist. Studies indicate that students who care the most about their academic performance are the most vulnerable to stereotype threat. Stereotype threat may explain in part why African Americans (and others) perform better in college than their SAT scores predict, and why standardized test scores can be so misleading. Nor are blacks alone. Latinos on English tests, females on math tests, and elderly people on short-term memory tests also fall victim to stereotype threat. In fact, even students with strong test scores can fall prey. White male engineering students with very high SAT scores were told that their performance on a test would help researchers understand the math superiority of Asians. Hearing about the comparison to strong Asian students, their scores fell. None of us is immune from stereotype threat.

Stereotypes limit students by teaching them that intellect is a fixed trait, that some groups are naturally brighter than others, and that their future was determined at birth. The belief that group differences are unchangeable is not a helpful construct for teachers. A person's intellect, like a person's brain, grows and changes. Human potential is amazing. If students see their brain and their intellect as muscles that can be taught to grow and become stronger, stereotype threat is diminished, and test scores rise.[39] Imagine the impact of stereotypes not only on intellectual performance, but also on other characteristics. Teaching also deals with ethics, values, and character of students, and damaging stereotypes can inhibit this learning as well. Fortunately, stereotype threat can be overcome with proper instruction.[40]

You can diminish stereotype threat by ensuring that your curriculum represents diversity across race, ethnicity, gender, religion, and socioeconomic class. Or perhaps you prefer to confront the problem directly: Explain stereotype threat in class and explore with your students strategies to neutralize it. The one thing you do not want to do is ignore the damage done by stereotype threat.

Generalizations

Generalizations recognize that there are trends over large numbers of people. Members of religious, racial, or ethnic groups share certain experiences and may share certain similarities. Generalizations offer insights, not hard and fast conclusions like stereotypes, and unlike a stereotype, a generalization does not assume that everyone in a group has a fixed set of characteristics. So the generalization that many Japanese value and seek higher education still holds if one encounters a Japanese dropout who dislikes school. The generalization is never intended to be applied to all; it is open to modification as new information is gathered, and there are always exceptions. Note that generalizations use words like "many," "often," or "tend to." Moreover, whereas stereotypes view people in one group or another, generalizations recognize that people belong to many groups simultaneously. Some Jews are Hispanic, some are Asian, and some are Arab, yet they are all Jews.

Generalizations offer us a hunch or clue about a group, and sometimes these clues are useful in planning for teaching. When you begin teaching you may know very little about your students, and a generalization offers a useful starting point. Think of it as an educated guess. As you learn more and more about each student, you will realize which generalizations are appropriate and which are not.

How can we use generalizations to develop culturally responsive teaching? Let's assume that a teacher has many Native American students in class; the teacher does some research and discovers that most Native American students prefer to learn in a cooperative group, valuing community and family over individual competition. Rather than teaching in the familiar teacher-centered manner, she modifies her plan and creates student groups to work on several academic topics. Using open-ended questions, she asks the groups to share their experiences, and patiently waits for each group response, realizing that Native American children may prefer to carefully consider their comments and compose their thoughts. When she can, the teacher uses natural phenomena in her explanations, because Native Americans often value both natural and supernatural forces. She may also integrate Indian words, symbols, or legends as appropriate. By building the learning on sharing rather than competition, and on valuing tribal experiences and beliefs, the teacher is increasing her chance of connecting with most of her students.[41] Because generalizations are flexible, the teacher is free to use a different approach with some or all of her students if she later discovers that they prefer a different learning style.

As you become a more experienced teacher, you will become more skilled at confronting all kinds of limiting stereotypes, developing useful teaching generalizations, and becoming a more culturally responsive teacher. In fact, let's start that process right now.

Today's Classroom

Consider yourself a teacher working with the nation's diverse students. If you are teaching in a community that reflects the nation's population, your class of 40 students might include[42]

17 white children

6 Hispanic children

6 children who do not speak English at home

5 poor children

5 African American children

1 Asian American child

The class might also include a Jewish, Native American, or Arab heritage child, not to mention multiracial or biracial students. Although we lack firm statistics concerning the number of gay, lesbian, bisexual, or transgendered children, estimates are that perhaps two or three of your students would fall into those categories. Planning for this class is quite a challenge!

The reality is that hyper-segregation of our schools makes it unlikely that you will be teaching students from all these groups in the same class at the same time. Unlikely, but not impossible. And certainly, over time, you may teach many if not all of them.

Meet Your Seventh-Grade Class

FOCUS QUESTION 9

How can teachers use culturally responsive teaching strategies?

In this section, we profile eight students: two students in the text, and six more online at the OLC feature "Digging Deeper." While you may not teach students from all of these diverse backgrounds, you will likely teach some of them. Each student is from a cultural, an ethnic, a racial, or some other group, bringing to your class a rich history and different learning preferences. It is important to keep in mind that each student is an individual and that any generalizations you make initially may change over time. But for now, let's take step one of culturally responsive teaching and learn about our students. For each student, we ask you to identify a generalization that might influence your teaching and enhance learning. As you read each student's description, you will encounter hints about potential generalizations. You may want to draw on your own knowledge as well. When you teach, you will want to learn more about your students through reading and personal interactions. But for now, let's establish your baseline, what you know about groups as you begin your teacher education program, and what you will want to learn in the future.

This exercise is not simple. You may be pushed beyond your comfort zone, and formulating generalizations will be a demanding task. If you are baffled, venture your best guess. At the end of the section, we shall provide you with sample generalizations that should help you think in new and constructive ways.

We will start you off by suggesting a few generalizations for the first student, Lindsey Maria Riley, who is Navajo. Then you are on your own. Try to identify at least one generalization for each of the other students. Later in the section, you can compare your responses with our suggestions.[43] Now, meet (and begin thinking about) your students.

Lindsey Maria Riley (Navajo)

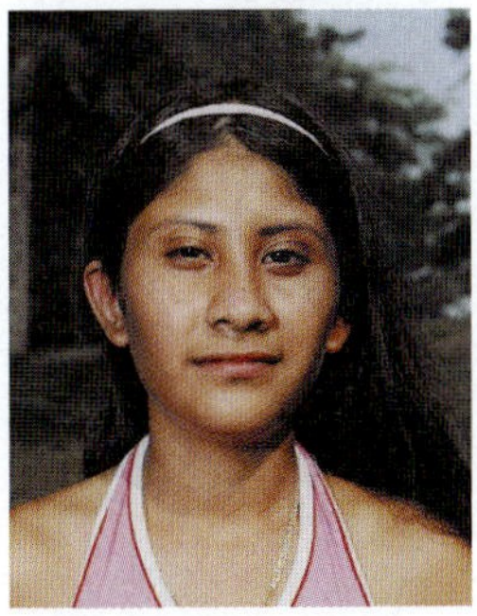

©Erin Patrice O'Brien/Taxi/Getty Images

Lindsey grew up in a small, poor town in the Southwest. Although Lindsey did not live on a reservation, her family adhered to traditional Navajo ways. Lindsey followed tradition when not at school and spent time mostly with girls and women learning to cook, make pottery, and weave at an early age. Navajo boys would hunt, make tools, and live more physical lives, quite separate from the girls. Lindsey's family did not have a lot of money and received assistance for her school supplies from Save the Children, a nonprofit organization. Lindsey enjoyed the school she attended that was run by the Bureau of Indian Affairs. But this year, her family moved to your community and she is a new student in your class.

Most of the other students in your class have seen Indians only in movies, such as *The Last of the Mohicans,* or on television. Some of Lindsey's classmates believe that Indians lived a long time ago on the frontier and are surprised to learn they still exist. Some have heard their parents say that Indians make a fortune running casinos. But neither casinos nor movies explain Lindsey. And Lindsey does not explain herself—she does not talk much. The students in your class like Lindsey, although they haven't really "figured" her out. To put it politely, Lindsey is a curiosity to them.

You recently asked the class to write a brief report on a president for Presidents' Day. Lindsey never handed in her report. When you asked her about it, she said that all the presidents had done bad things to her people and that she would rather report on a different topic. Today, she told you that the school mascot, an Indian chief, bothers her.

Potentially Useful Generalization: ____________________

____

____

Sample Response

[Note: Native Americans are not one group but hundreds of tribal nations with different languages and beliefs. Learning about tribal distinctions is a useful first step for teachers and students.] In this sample response, we will offer you a series of possible and well-accepted generalizations, but there are others as well. If we do not mention your generalization, you may want to research it to see if you are correct.

Potentially Useful Generalization: Many tribes revere modesty. Group, rather than individual, recognition is typically preferred, as is cooperation over competition and patience rather than immediate gratification (qualities too often lost in contemporary classrooms). Additionally, visual and artistic learning and "hands-on learning" are valued by many tribal cultures. Using American Indian cultural beliefs and insights during a lesson can help Native American students feel connected to the academic program. The supernatural, intuition, and spiritual beliefs are valued by many tribes and could also be incorporated in classroom instruction.

[In terms of the casino-to-riches stereotype mentioned in the profile, less than 1 percent of Indians work in casinos, and the casino profits often go to schools and community improvement projects.]

©Comstock/Getty Images RF

Marcus Griffin (African American)

Marcus is in your class because of your school district's policy to voluntarily bus African American students from across the county line, a rare event these days. He lives with his mother, who works at the post office, about ten miles from school. His elder brother never attended this school; in fact, he never graduated from high school. You hear rumors that he is in and out of trouble. Marcus has only a few friends in class, a situation made worse by the bus schedule. After his last class, he hurries to catch his bus for the long ride home. Because of this schedule, he cannot participate in after-school activities, sports, and clubs. Marcus's neighborhood friends do not really talk much about school. They do not like the fact that Marcus chooses to bus to a white community instead of hanging out with them. Marcus feels that he is growing further and further away from his roots.

Marcus loves reading and writing, but feels like an alien in his new school. Virtually everything he sees or reads in school is about the history, accomplishments, and interests of whites. Only rarely are his people discussed, and then it is not in a very positive light. Marcus finds the teachers in your school pretty serious, and he decides not to rock the boat by suggesting different ideas in class. There is only one African American teacher in your school and only a few black students. Marcus would like to go to college, but his family's finances are limited. Some of the black kids talk about going to college on an athletic scholarship, but Marcus is not very athletic. You wish that you could connect with him, but when you try, he rarely looks at you. Like several other students in your school, he sometimes interrupts in class, a habit you find annoying. You hope for the best for Marcus, but you are not optimistic.

Potentially Useful Generalization: ______________________________

____

____

Teaching Skills

Recognizing the experiences and histories of all your students is an important first step in creating a climate that honors and celebrates diversity. Your teaching behaviors should also reinforce your commitment to equity. All students benefit when they feel safe, their unique needs and interests are recognized, and they are part of classroom discourse. Teachers need to share their time and talent fairly, offering helpful feedback and encouragement to each student, and ensuring that the curriculum is meaningful. We will describe equitable teaching skills in Chapter 11, but here are some suggestions for effective and equitable teaching strategies. To help you remember them, we created the acronym *DIVERSE.*

RAP 1.1
Getting to Know Whom?

Diverse Instructional Materials: Some say that an effective curriculum is both a window and a mirror. Are all your students able to see themselves in your curricular mirror? Are all parts of the world seen through your curricular window? Are diverse thoughts, views, and people woven into the curriculum? Do class and school displays reflect all the world's cultures and peoples?

RAP 1.9
Nontraditional Hero

Inclusive: Does your teaching provide opportunities for each student, especially those very quiet students, to participate in class discussions? Sometimes careful planning, thoughtful selection of particular students to respond, and patience can encourage even shy students to participate. Every student deserves a public voice and should be heard.

Variety: Using different teaching strategies—learning styles, sensory channels, and intelligences—can do wonders to involve all. Kinesthetic and artistic activities, cooperative learning, and other approaches honor different ways of learning and allow each student to experience success.

Exploration: Teachers should encourage students to explore new cultures and beliefs, and be open themselves to new ideas. Learning how different peoples view the world can unlock student (and teacher) minds.

Reaction: Often, teacher feedback is given too quickly, with little thought, and is of little help. Each student deserves the teacher's specific, timely, honest, and precise comments. With effective feedback, patience, encouragement, and high expectation, all children can learn, and can learn well.

Safety: Without safety and security, little learning is possible. Offensive comments about religion, race, ethnicity, or sexuality and verbal or physical bullying should be quickly confronted and stopped by the teacher.

Diversity is a potential asset to every classroom.
©Stockbyte/Getty Images RF

RAP 1.7

Planning for Diversity: A Lesson Plan

Evaluation: Teachers often forget that the achievement tests, aptitude tests, and high-stakes tests are often designed for white, middle-class culture. Teachers should consider a variety of evaluation strategies to assess the unique strengths of each student. Evaluation can assist in student diagnosis and planning effective instruction. It can serve a more constructive purpose than simply ranking and rating students.

These skills should help you to reach out to all your students. While they promote equity, they also promote good teaching. How fortunate we are that equitable teaching skills are also effective teaching skills.

We Are One

In this chapter, we recognize that group differences offer a way of broadening our perspective on what it means to be truly educated. We should treat our wondrous diversity "as one of the most exciting parts of our education—an enormous opportunity to see the world in new ways and understand more about humanity. What is education about if not that?"[44]

As Hindu tradition reminds us, as we honor one another's differences, we need also to honor what we hold in common. So let's close this chapter by recognizing that we are all part of the human family. In his 1963 commencement speech at American University, John F. Kennedy said: "For in the final analysis, our most basic common link is that we all inhabit this small planet, we all breathe the same air, we all cherish our children's futures, and we are all mortal." Those words still ring true today. According to genome research, human beings are 96 percent alike, no matter where we live, no matter what experiences we have, no matter our color, our language, or our God.[45] Yes, we can do both: honor our common humanity and the richness of our differences.

An eighth-grade language arts teacher shared Langston Hughes's poem "I, Too, Sing America" with her students, and asked her students to create a similar poem based on their own experiences.[46] Her students wrote remarkable poems that underscored the continuing racism and sexism in society, as well as profound universal desires to accept and be accepted by others. We use this same activity in our teacher education classes, and each year we learn from our students. Here are two poems written by our teacher education students. We invite you to write and submit your own.

I, too, am an American
I am the trusting farm girl who grew up knowing no strangers
I ventured to the city, where they tell me I am too naïve
But I am not what my white, non-diverse, God-fearing, conservative roots suggest
I have experiences with the good and the bad this world has to offer
Yet, each day I choose to smile and look for the good
Maybe
I am the beginning of this cycle
One smile, one act of trust, one stranger turned friend at a time
I, too, am an American.

—Lacey Rosenbaum

Courtesy of Lacey Rosenbaum

I, too, am an original American.
But concealed by my blond locks

and ocean deep blue eyes,
Red Man's blood
courses through these veins.
Undetected.

The White Man joke about the gamble
they think they are safe
"I can spot an ingine a mile a way!"
They spout without a single thought.

Then I smile
and take their then trembling hand
"Rainwater, and yes, it's Cherokee"
is all I say
as I walk away.

I am an Original American.

—Mandie Rainwater

CONNECT FOR *TEACHERS, SCHOOLS, AND SOCIETY*

Check out Connect, McGraw-Hill Education's interactive learning environment, to:

Read Current and Historical Articles

Learning from Latino Families, by Susan Auerbach, *Educational Leadership,* May 2011.

Understanding Unconscious Bias and Unintentional Racism, by Jean Moule, *Phi Delta Kappan,* January 2009.

The Threat of Stereotype, by Joshua Aronson, *Educational Leadership,* November 2004.

How Good Are the Asians: Refuting Four Myths About Asian-American Academic Achievement, by Yong Zhao and Wei Qiu, *Phi Delta Kappan,* January 2009.

I, Too, Am an American: Preservice Teachers Reflect upon National Identity, by Nancy Gallavan, *Multicultural Teaching,* Spring 2002.

Analyze Case Studies

Helen Franklin: A teacher who uses parents as volunteers to help with her unique classroom organization notices that a parent volunteer who has questioned the teachers' methods will work only with white students.

Leigh Scott: A teacher gives a higher-than-earned grade to a mainstreamed student on the basis of the boy's effort and attitude and is confronted by a black student with identical test scores who received a lower grade and who accuses her of racism.

Watch Teachers, Students, and Classrooms in Action

Our **Online Video Album** for contemporary videos related to this chapter.

KEY TERMS AND PEOPLE

assimilation (enculturation), 67
Banks, James, 69
bilingual education, 59
cultural difference theory, 64
cultural pluralism, 67
culturally responsive teaching, 71
culture, 52
deficit theory, 63
English as a Second Language (ESL), 60
English language learners (ELLs), 60
ethnicity, 51
expectation theory, 64
generalizations, 76
immersion, 60
Ladson-Billings, Gloria, 71
language submersion, 60
Lau v. Nichols, 60
LGBTQA, 57
maintenance (developmental) approach, 61
multicultural education, 68
multiracial, 52
race, 51
school-to-prison pipeline, 54
stereotypes, 73
stereotype threat, 75
transitional approach, 60
two-way immersion, 61

DISCUSSION QUESTIONS AND ACTIVITIES

1. Observe a classroom, noting how many times teachers call on each student. Compare the amount of attention each student receives. Now determine group representation in the classroom. Does one group (boys or whites or native-English speakers) get more than its fair share of teacher attention?
2. How do you react to the various issues raised in this chapter? On a separate sheet of paper complete the following sentences as honestly as you can. If you wish, share your responses with your classmates.
   - To me, the phrase *invisible race privilege* means . . .
   - A great example of expectation theory is . . .
3. Given demographic trends, pick a region of the country and a particular community. Develop a scenario of a classroom in that community in the year 2030. Describe the students' characteristics and the teacher's role. Is that classroom likely to be affected by changing demographics? How are cultural learning styles manifested in the way the teacher organizes and instructs the class?
4. Choose a school curriculum and suggest how it can be changed to reflect one of the four approaches to multicultural education described by Banks. Why did you choose the approach you did?
5. Discuss the two main approaches to bilingual education in the United States: transitional and maintenance. Which do you favor, and why?

You will either step forward into growth, or you will step backward into safety.

ABRAHAM MASLOW

©Image Source/Getty Images RF

chapter 4

Student Life in School and at Home

Focus Questions

1. What rituals and routines shape classroom life?
2. How does the teacher's gatekeeping function influence classroom roles?
3. What is tracking, and what are its advantages and disadvantages?
4. How do gender and peer groups influence children in elementary and middle school?
5. In what ways does the adolescent culture shape teenage perceptions and behaviors in high school?
6. What impact do changing family patterns and economic issues have on children and schools?
7. How can educators respond to social issues that place children at risk?

Chapter Preview

School is a culture. Like most cultures, it is filled with its own unique rituals and traditions, and its own set of norms and mores. In school, even the familiar, such as time, is made new. Time is told by subjects ("Let's talk before math") or periods ("I have bank seventh period"). Students are pinched into passive roles, following schedules created by others, sitting still rather than being active, and responding to teacher questions but seldom asking any of their own. Such a system challenges and confines both teachers and students. Peer groups create friendships and popularity, a strong subculture that makes winners and losers of us all—at least for a brief time. Adults pick up where children leave off, assigning students to what amounts to an academic caste system through *de facto* tracking or ability grouping. While adults focus on academics, many adolescents and preadolescents are focused on relationships and sexuality.

Economic and social factors are also powerful forces in today's classrooms, and have reshaped the family unit. New family patterns abound, challenging the traditional view of the mother, father, and two children (did we forget the dog?) as the "typical" American family. With these changes, economic and social problems threaten our children and challenge teachers. We will describe these challenges so that educators can work to create schools that are safe havens and institutions of hope.

Rules, Rituals, and Routines

Schools create their own cultures, replete with norms, rituals, and routines. Even simple tasks, such as distributing textbooks and iPads, are clothed with cultural cues, but they are cues that differ for students and teachers.

"Poetry Lesson": A Teacher's Perspective

FOCUS QUESTION 1

What rituals and routines shape classroom life?

"Okay, class, quiet down," said Mr. Thompson. "Your iPads are now loaded with the new poetry unit. Please open the poetry folder and click on 'Stopping by Woods on a Snowy Evening,' by Robert Frost. Yes, Rosa?"

"Mine has no power!"

"Please look on Jessica's for now. Yes Ethan?"

"I can't find the folder."

"I will show you later. Jordan, could you share your screen with Ethan?

Now, as I was about to say, I'd like you to read the poem and think about the questions that I've written on the Smart Board: Why does the speaker wish to stop, and what makes him realize that he must go on? Why does he say, 'I have miles to go before I sleep'? Is he looking for a motel?"

(A few minutes pass as students read the poem. Keyboard clicks, shuffling feet, students getting up to plug in their laptops all create growing distractions in the room. Two students finish quickly and begin whispering.) "April! Maxine! This is not a time for your private chat room."

"Okay, class, I think most of you have had enough time to read the poem. Who has an answer?"

"I think he wants to stop because . . . ," but Maxine's answer was cut short by the abrasive ring of the fourth-period bell.

"For homework, I'd like everyone to answer the posted questions. Alice?"

"Do we submit our work online?"

"Yes. Any other questions? Okay, you'd better get to your next-period class."

As the last student left, Tom Thompson slumped over his desk and wearily ran his fingers through his hair. He had forgotten to give his brief explanation on the differences between prose and poetry. He had even forgotten to give his motivating speech on how interesting the new poetry unit promised to be. Well, no time for a postmortem now. Stampede-like noises outside the door meant the fourth-period class was about to arrive.

"Poetry Lesson": A Student's Perspective

From her vantage point in the fourth seat, fifth row, Maxine sat enthralled with the poem. She didn't care that it wasn't "in" to like poetry; she liked it much better than technology. She read the poem quickly and understood how Robert Frost felt, wanting to get away from life's hassles, like the noise and confusion going on in the classroom right now. As she turned around to share her observation with April Marston, Mr. Thompson's sharp reprimand interrupted her. "Private chat room!", she thought. "What's with him? Half the class is talking. I'm the only one who appreciates the poem. Oh well, I'll answer one of those questions on the Smart Board so he will see that I really am paying attention." Maxine shot her hand in the air, but her answer was interrupted in mid-sentence, this time by the fourth-period bell. "Well, next period is science. Maybe I will finish the English homework there."

Watching the Clock

You have just read two replays of a seventh-grade English lesson, one from the vantage point of the teacher, the other from the vantage point of a student. Mr. Thompson and Maxine play different roles, which cause them to have very different experiences in this class. For example, Mr. Thompson was continually leapfrogging from one minor crisis to the next while Maxine was sitting and waiting.

How does time unfold in schools? Research suggests that while teachers are typically very busy, students are often caught in patterns of delay that force them to do nothing. Are you surprised to learn that between one-quarter and one-half of time available for learning is lost to attendance problems, non-instructional activities (such as class changes and assemblies), administrative and organizational activities, and behavioral disruptions? Indeed, most teachers spend a good deal of time giving out things: paper, pencils, art materials, science equipment, books, computer tablets, exam booklets, erasers, happy faces, special privileges—the list goes on and on.[1] The classroom scene described shows Mr. Thompson greatly involved in timekeeping activities. Within the limits set by school buzzers and bells, he determines when the iPads will be distributed, when and for how long the reading activity will take place, and when the class discussion will begin.

What do students do while teachers are busy organizing, structuring, talking, questioning, handing out, collecting, timekeeping, and crisis hopping? According to multiple studies, they do little more than sit and wait.[2] They wait for the materials to be handed out, for the assignment to be given, for the questions to be asked, for the teacher to call on them, for the teacher to react to their response, and for the slower class members to catch up so that the activity can change. Furthermore, while trying to concentrate on work and to ignore social temptations, students are beset by frequent interruptions—the end-of-class bell interrupting a lively discussion, a teacher's reprimand, or a student's question derailing a train of thought.

GLOBAL VIEW

U.S. public school students typically attend school for 180 days a year, much less than the school calendars in Europe (190–210 days) and Japan (240 days).

GLOBAL VIEW

"On-time behavior" is considered one of the most powerful cultural lessons in the school's hidden curriculum. Throughout the world however, people have a varied sense of time. Arriving 10 minutes after a scheduled appointment in the states might be considered "pretty much on time." Being an hour late in some other cultures is not at all impolite, and in fact arriving punctually at the exact appointment time might be seen as quite strange. How might you as a teacher cope with the differences between school time norms and cultural time norms students bring to your classroom?

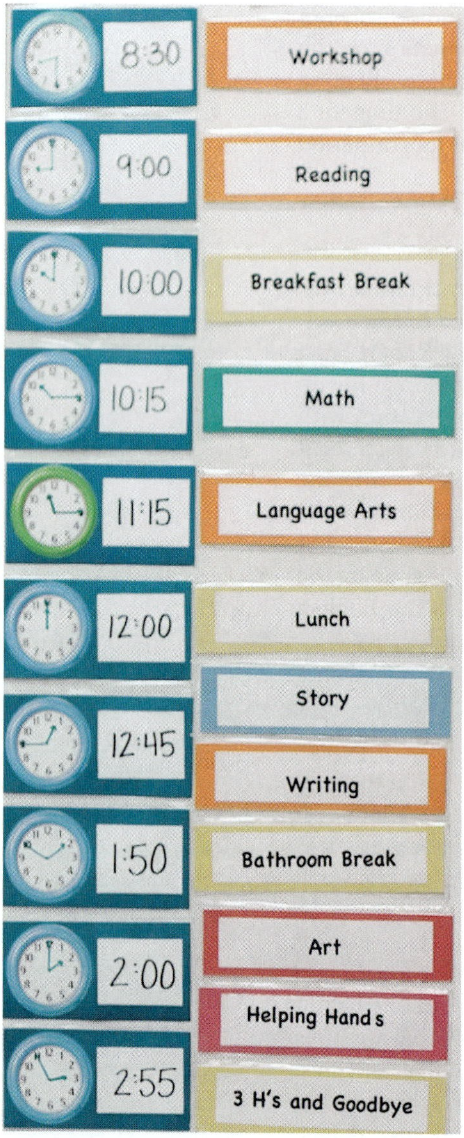

What are the pluses and pitfalls of posting a schedule like this? Do you recall your own feelings as a student about the routine and regimentation of school life?

Consider how Maxine in Mr. Thompson's English class had to cope with delay, denial of desire, social distraction, and interruptions. She waited for the delivery of her new iPad. She waited to be called on by the teacher. Her attempt to concentrate on reading the poem was disturbed by frequent interruptions. Her brief communication with a classmate was interrupted by a reprimand. Her head was filled with ideas and questions. In short, there was a lot she would like to have said, but there was almost no opportunity to say it.

If students are to succeed in school, they must be able to cope with continual delay. Many do not. Student disengagement is a very real issue, and one that widens with time: Between fifth and twelfth grades, the number of students who report feeling involved with school declines steadily each year. A majority of elementary school students—almost eight in ten—feel engaged by classroom life. By middle school that number drops to six in ten students. And when students enter high school, it plummets to four in ten. Knowing this, it becomes all the more crucial to maximize learning opportunities during the 1,260 hours or more students spend in the classroom each school year.[3]

Whereas the business world may suggest "time is money," for educators, time is learning. As one teacher points out,

> Time is the currency of teaching. We barter with time. Every day we make small concessions, small trade-offs, but, in the end, we know it's going to defeat us. After all, how many times are we actually able to cover World War I in our history courses before the year is out? We always laugh a little about that, but the truth is the sense of the clock ticking is one of the most oppressive features of teaching.[4]

Research shows that when more time is allocated to subject-matter learning, student achievement increases.[5] When this valuable resource is spent handing out supplies, reprimanding misbehavior, and test preparation, it is lost for learning. Looked at from this perspective, Mr. Thompson's class not only was frustrating but also deprived students of a precious and limited resource—the time to learn.

The Teacher as Gatekeeper

Teachers are typically involved in more than one thousand verbal exchanges with their students every day.[6] Count the number of verbal exchanges Mr. Thompson had with his students during our abbreviated classroom scene and you will get some idea of how much and how often teachers talk. One of the functions that keeps teachers busiest is what researchers term **gatekeeping.** As gatekeepers, teachers must determine who will talk, when, and for how long, as well as the basic direction of the communication.

A CLOSER LOOK

Patterns of the Classroom

After observing in more than one thousand classrooms, *John Goodlad* and his team of researchers at UCLA found that the following patterns characterize most classrooms:

- Much of what happens in class is geared toward maintaining order among twenty to thirty students restrained in a relatively small space.
- Although the classroom is a group setting, each student typically works alone.
- The teacher is the key figure in setting the tone and determining the activities.
- Most of the time, the teacher is in front of the classroom, teaching a whole group of students.
- There is little praise or corrective feedback; classes are emotionally neutral or flat places.
- Students are involved in a limited range of activities—listening to lectures, writing answers to questions, and taking exams.
- A significant number of students are confused by teacher explanations and feel that they do not get enough guidance on how to improve.

Goodlad concluded that "the emotional tone of the classroom is neither harsh and punitive nor warm and joyful; it might be described most accurately as flat."

SOURCE: John Goodlad, *A Place Called School* (New York: McGraw-Hill, 1984/2004).

REFLECTION: How many of these findings characterized your classroom life? How will you make learning more joyful and engaging?

FOCUS QUESTION 2

How does the teacher's gatekeeping function influence classroom roles?

Consider what effect patterns of classroom interaction have on both teachers and students[7]:

- Roughly two-thirds of classroom time is taken up by talk; two-thirds of that talk is by the teacher.
- While questioning signals curiosity, it is the teachers, not the learners, who do most questioning, asking as many as 348 questions a day. The typical student rarely asks an academic question.
- Most classroom questions require that students use only rote memory.
- Students are not given much time to ask, or even answer, questions. Teachers usually wait less than a second for student comments and answers.
- Teachers interact less and less with students as they go through the grades.

Ironically, although a major goal of education is to increase students' curiosity and quest for knowledge, it is teachers, not students, who most often dominate and manage classroom interaction (see A Closer Look: Patterns of the Classroom). Consequently, classroom interactions do not teach students to become active, inquiring, self-reliant learners. Students are expected to be quiet and passive, to think quickly (and perhaps superficially), to rely on memory, and to be dependent on the teacher. Not surprisingly, silent, disengaged students have less positive attitudes and lower achievement. Studies show that participating in class discussions, getting the opportunity to excel, and feeling that their schoolwork matters makes for an engaging education experience, regardless of the grade or age of students.[8] (See You Be the Judge: Homework Should Be, p. 88.) Perhaps the challenge new teachers should keep before them is finding a way to turn their gatekeeping role into a benefit for students, instead of a hindrance.

YOU BE THE JUDGE

Homework Should Be

A MAJOR PART OF A STUDENT'S LIFE BECAUSE . . .

THERE IS TOO MUCH MATERIAL TO BE MASTERED ONLY DURING SCHOOL TIME

Given demands on students to learn more and to increase their test scores, much study and learning needs to take place at home. After all, students are in school for just five hours of a twenty-four-hour day.

IT BRINGS PARENTS INTO THE LEARNING PROCESS

School cannot accomplish its goals alone. Students achieve much more when academics are reinforced at home. By providing guidance and monitoring homework, parents demonstrate their support of learning, becoming true partners with teachers. Closing the school–home gap fosters competent and attentive students.

MANY STUDENTS DO NOT USE THEIR TIME WISELY

The average student comes home from school, talks on the phone with friends, "hangs out" at the mall, watches television for hours, and then plays a computer game or two before going to bed. Homework at least gives students something meaningful to do with their time.

LIMITED AND BRIEF BECAUSE . . .

TOO MUCH STRESS IS PLACED ON STUDENTS AS IT IS

Schools have been taken over by this growing obsession with tests. The last thing we need to do is extend this angst to home life. Besides, homework is mostly busywork, unrelated to real learning.

IT FAVORS SOME STUDENTS AND PENALIZES OTHERS

Some children have highly educated parents, home computers, and the resources needed to produce quality homework. Other students have poor and uneducated parents, who may not even speak English, and who may be working two or more jobs. All too often, homework is simply a measure of family resources.

MANY STUDENTS DO NOT HAVE THE LUXURY OF EXTRA TIME

Many students go directly from school to their part-time job. Their families may need the money. Other students must care for younger siblings at home while parents are at work. Increasing homework would place an enormous burden on these families.

connect YOU DECIDE...

How much homework do you think is beneficial? Do you have a plan to handle differences in family resources? How will you help students manage the stresses of homework? Add one additional argument to each side of this debate.

The Other Side of the Tracks

FOCUS QUESTION 3

What is tracking and what are its advantages and disadvantages?

We have seen how teachers function as gatekeepers, controlling the amount and flow of student talk in the classroom. Let's step back a moment and consider an even more basic question: Which students sit in which classrooms? That very crucial decision falls on teachers, counselors, and administrators. Many believe that it is easier for students with similar skills and intellectual abilities to learn together, in same-ability, *homogeneous* classes. Educators following this belief test and sort students according to their abilities and, as a result, send them down different school paths, profoundly shaping their futures. Students of different abilities (low, middle, and high) are assigned to different *tracks* of courses and programs (vocational, general, college-bound, honors, and AP). **Tracking** is the term given to this process, and though some teachers believe that tracking makes instruction more manageable, others believe that it is a terribly flawed system. Either way, tracking is one of the oldest of school traditions.

Decades of research analyzing school as a social system reveal that the college selection process begins in elementary school and is virtually sealed by the time students finish junior high.[9] These findings have significant implications, suggesting that future roles in adult life are determined by student achievement in elementary school. The labeling system, beginning at an early age, determines who will wear a stethoscope, who will carry a laptop computer, and who will become a low-wage laborer.

Jeannie Oakes's *Keeping Track* offered a scathing indictment of racial influence on tracking. She found that race, far more than ability, determines which students are placed in which tracks: black, Hispanic, and Native American students with similar test scores as their white peers are three times more likely to be enrolled in low-track classes. Oakes also documented how these lower-tracked students have fewer learning opportunities and how teachers expect little from them. Their instruction covers less content, involves more drill and repetition, and places more emphasis on classroom management problems.[10]

Students in low-ability tracks have difficulty moving into higher tracks. Ray Rist observed a kindergarten class in an all-black urban school. By the eighth day of class, the kindergarten teacher, apparently using such criteria as physical appearance, socioeconomic status, and language usage, had separated her students into groups of "fast learners" and "slow learners." She spent more time with the "fast learners" and gave them more instruction and encouragement. The "slow learners" got more than their fair share of control and ridicule. The children soon began to mirror the teacher's behavior. As the "fast learners" belittled the "slow learners," the low-status children began to exhibit attitudes of self-degradation and hostility toward one another. This teacher's expectations, formed during eight days at the beginning of school, shaped the academic and social treatment of children in her classroom for the entire year and perhaps for years to come. Records of the grouping that had taken place during the first week in kindergarten were passed on to teachers in the upper grades, providing the basis for further differential treatment.[11]

Consider some additional disturbing facts on race, socioeconomic status, and tracking[12]:

- Teachers with the least experience and the lowest levels of qualifications are assigned to students in the lowest tracks.
- Schools with predominately poor and minority populations offer fewer advanced and more remedial courses in academic subjects.
- Asian, white, and wealthy students are more likely than black, Hispanic, and poor students to be recommended for advanced classes and gifted programs, even with equivalent test scores.
- Low-track students are seldom required to take as many math and science classes as high-track students.
- Students are more likely to choose their friends from their tracked classes in elementary through high school. These social networks can further entrench racially segregated academic tracks.
- When parents intervene, counselors place middle- and upper-socioeconomic class students with low grades and test scores into higher tracked groups.

PROFILE IN EDUCATION

Jeannie Oakes

Jeannie Oakes became a teacher for a conventional reason, but as a teacher, became an unconventional advocate for social change and equity. Oakes's first-hand experiences as a teacher and a researcher transformed her into one of the leaders in detracking. Her work focuses on not only doing away with tracking, but also increasing the quality of curriculum and instruction for all students.

Read a full profile of Jeannie Oakes on Connect.

Source: Courtesy Dr. Jeannie Oakes

connect

Low teacher expectations and unchallenging courses may encourage student passivity and boredom.

©Monkey Business Images/Shutterstock RF

Such findings add momentum to the effort to *detrack,* or eliminate tracking practices from the nation's schools. Several civil rights and educational organizations, including the National Education Association (NEA), the NAACP, and the Children's Defense Fund, support detracking initiatives. But the task is not easy. Jeannie Oakes characterizes the tracking debate as symbolic of a larger struggle over the purpose of education:

> [A] norm that bolsters and legitimizes tracking is the American emphasis on competition and individualism over cooperation and the good of the community—a norm suggesting that "good" education is a scarce commodity available only to a few winners. Although the American system of public education was designed to promote the common good and to prepare children for participation in a democratic society, more recent emphasis has been placed on what a graduate can "get out" of schooling in terms of income, power, or status.[13]

"True," tracking advocates argue, "it would appear more democratic to put everyone in the same class, but such idealism is destined to fail." They contend that it is unrealistic to think everyone can or should master the same material or learn it at the same pace. Without tracking we have *heterogeneous,* or mixed-ability, classes. Tracking advocates are quick to point out that mixed-ability classes have their own set of problems: In heterogeneous classes, bright students get bored, slower students have trouble keeping up, and we lose our most talented and our most needy students. Teachers find themselves grading the brighter students on the quality of their work, and the weaker ones on their "effort," which is a big problem (especially with parents!). Teachers get frustrated trying to meet each student's needs, and hardly ever hitting the mark. Putting everyone in the same class simply doesn't work.[14]

Detracking advocates, as you might imagine, offer a different take on the issue: "No sorting system is consistent with equality of opportunity. Worse yet, the tracking system is not based on individual ability. It is badly biased in favor of white middle-class America. We must face the reality that poor children, often children of color, come to school far from being ready to learn. And the school, whose job it is to educate all our children, does little to help. The built-in bias in instruction, counseling, curricular materials, and testing must be overcome. Students get shoveled into second-rate courses that prepare them for fourth-rate jobs. Their track becomes 'a great training robbery,' and the students who are robbed may be ones with great abilities."

Whereas the social pitfalls of tracking have been well documented, tracking's efficacy has not. More than three decades of research documents how tracking fails to foster outcomes Americans value, such as academic excellence and educational equity. Tracking is especially inconsistent with today's national goal of having all students meet high academic standards.

Yet, meeting the needs of all students is not easy. Schools that serve both poor and affluent students tend to have an enormous range in student achievement levels.

Ability grouping offers an alternative to tracking. Whereas tracking suggests permanence, ability grouping is more transitory. In elementary school, students can be grouped by achievement for part of the day (say, for reading and math), and then heterogeneously for the rest of the day (say, for social studies, science, art, music, and physical education). Reading and math instruction can be more narrowly targeted to students' current ability levels, while in their other classes, students can benefit from the social and academic advantages of diversity. In middle and high schools, a student may find herself in a high-ability math group and a low-ability English class one year. The following year, that same student might be reassigned to a new set of learning groups. Blended learning will likely offer additional solutions, as students spend part of their day learning online, with lessons customized to their achievement levels and learning styles.

Although students often arrive at school from very different backgrounds, learning from one another and together has great advantages. Detracked schools can be authentic places of learning, academically challenging to all while teaching a living lesson in democracy. What is needed is time, careful planning, and adequate training for teachers so that they can succeed and all students can learn.[15]

One of the ironies of tracking is that it simply builds on an already divided school culture. What educators do not do to divide students, students often do to themselves.

The Gendered World of Elementary and Middle Schools

FOCUS QUESTION 4

How do gender and peer groups influence children in elementary and middle school?

In the first grade, when so much about school seems gigantic and fearful, children look to adults for safety: What am I supposed to do in the classroom? Where do I get lunch? How do I find the bus to ride home from school? Children go to their first-grade teacher not only for this practical information but also for hugs, praise, and general warmth and affection. But by the second grade, a new world emerges, a world where gender shapes identities and relationships and intensifies during the school years. By the second grade, boys break away from teacher dependence and place more importance on their peer group—other boys. Boys claim their own territory on the athletic field and in the lunchroom, and sometimes even challenge the teacher. Male identity and entitlement are strengthened during elementary school years, but not for all boys, not for the boys considered sissies. Over time, many of these excluded males exhibit an increasing number of social, emotional, and academic problems.[16]

Girls spend the first few elementary school years helping the teacher, behaviors that are rewarded, in part, with good report card grades. Girls also form best-friend relationships in which pairs of girls pledge devotion to one another. By the upper elementary grades, girls begin to fantasize about the "cute" boys in their class and about what being married and having a family would be like. Being a good student and having a pleasing personality are important to girls, but by the upper elementary grades, appearance often becomes the key to social status.

Social exclusion is a painful reality for many students from elementary to high school.

©BananaStock/Getty Images RF

As popularity pressures mount, girls (and yes, some boys) use relational aggression to improve their peer status by hurting others. Sometimes referred to as emotional bullying or the "mean girl phenomenon", relational aggression often begins as early as preschool and peaks during the middle-school years. A myriad of reasons, from jealousy to attention needs to fears of competition, can spark this form of bullying.[17]

Relational aggression includes:

- Spreading rumors
- Excluding and intimidating others
- Breaking confidences or sharing secrets

FIGURE 4.1

Sociogram: A teacher's tool.

REFLECTION: Construct your own sociogram, drawing a circle for each person in your class or in a class that you are observing, or even in a lunchroom or during recess. Draw a line every time there is an interaction. Can you detect friends, cliques, and isolates? How does class seating affect relationships? What might you do as a teacher to influence these patterns?

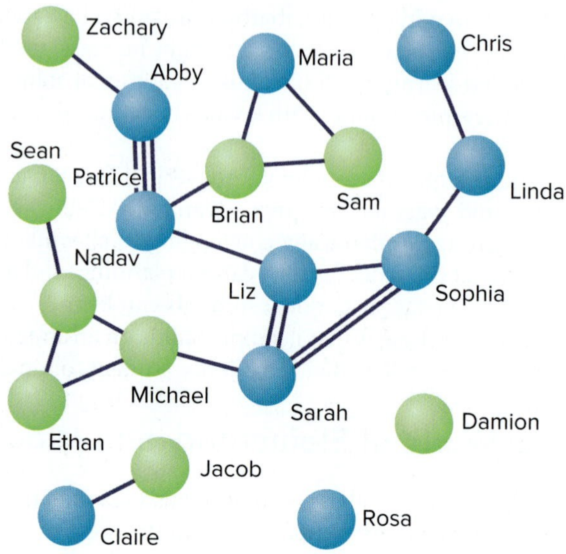

Sociograms provide insights into the social life of a class. In this sociogram, circles represent students, and colors indicate gender. Lines are drawn connecting circles when students interact with one another. Each line reflects a verbal communication: the more lines, the greater number of interactions. In this sociogram, it appears that Abby and Patrice are friends; Liz, Sarah, and Sophia may form a clique; while Damion and Rosa appear to be isolates. Charting several sociograms of these children over time would confirm or refute these initial perceptions.

- Making fun of others for who they are, the way they dress, or how they look
- Leaving hurtful or mean messages on cell phones, social media, desks, and lockers

When students respond to questions designed to measure their friendship patterns, ten percent of them emerge as not being anybody's friend (isolates). About half of these are just ignored. The other half become the victims of active peer group rejection and hostility. In fact, elementary school sociometric measures predict social adjustment better than most other personality and educational tests do.[18] These social preferences can be graphically presented in **sociograms**. (See Figure 4.1.) Most friendless children are aware of their problem and report feeling lonely and unsuccessful in relating to others. Rejection by the child's peer group is a strong indicator of future academic, emotional, or physical problems.

Teachers must work every day to create humane and caring classrooms. An insightful teacher can structure a classroom to minimize negative and hurtful interaction and maximize the positive power of peer group relations. For instance, eliminating social cliques and race- and gender-based segregation is a precursor to successful cooperative groups. An intentional teacher often assigns students to seats or to group work to counter pupil favoritism and bias. A teacher's perceptiveness and skill in influencing the social side of school can mean a world of difference in the student's environment. These social needs only grow as students transition into middle school.

Was your transition from elementary to middle school smooth, filled with the excitement of new friends and independence? Or did the move spark angst as you navigated new buildings, teachers, and friendships? The transition is important because adolescence is a time of so much change: physical, psychological, and social.

Since the 1960s, many policymakers have advocated that middle school—generally grades 6, 7, and 8—should be a time when children have a chance to adjust to puberty. Attention to the emotional and physical developmental growth of adolescents is seen as the primary purpose of middle school life. However, some critics see middle schools as having gone "soft," overemphasizing self-esteem building at the expense of academic rigor. Describing the middle school years as the "Bermuda Triangle of American education," such critics call for a return to K–8 schooling and a more discipline-focused curriculum.[19] Because some adolescents can struggle with change, they argue that K–8 schools provide stability in neighborhood, building, peers, and staff for parents and students alike. Such efforts are supported by a recent study that found students moving into middle school frequently experience a sharp drop in math and language arts achievement in the transition year that plagues them as far out as tenth grade, even risking their ability to graduate high school and go on to college.[20] Yet, advocates for middle schools argue that simply changing the grade configuration is no magic bullet. What happens in the classroom is what matters most. Noted one principal, "The challenge for us as middle-school educators in the age of high-stakes testing is to encourage teaching for understanding while addressing the myriad of social and emotional issues. Kids develop at their own rates; what's important is how you are personalizing that environment for them." What do students believe is important to support their success in middle school? Five characteristics top their list[21]:

RAP 2.1
Scoping School Culture

- Recognition for academic success
- Having the opportunity to do well
- Homework that is meaningful
- A best friend at school
- Feeling safe at school

While the future of middle schools is in doubt, one adolescent struggle remains omnipresent: the need to develop an identity, including what it means to be male or female:

> "I feel pressure from my parents and teachers to do well in school. But when I do, boys won't ask me to the school dance and even my girlfriends call me a 'nerd.' So now I talk less in class and don't study as much. The teasing hurts, so it's easier to hide being smart."

> "Boys can't take music class without being called a fag. So I hide my musical talents, like playing Mozart on the keyboard."

These are the voices of today's middle school students. Their words reveal how gender and peer relations play significant roles in their lives, expanding some options, but more often limiting academic and social development. When we asked more than four hundred middle schoolers to identify the "best and worst thing about being a boy or girl," their stories lifted the veil on the pervasive sexism in today's schools and society.[22] Students unequivocally had more positive things to say about being a boy than about being a girl. Male advantages focused on physical and athletic prowess, underscoring the central role physicality plays for boys. Students also noted that boys are listened to more, are naturally smarter,

A CLOSER LOOK

Popularity Perils

They were the *cool kids,* viewed by their middle school classmates with envy, admiration, and awe. The girls wore makeup, had boyfriends, and went to parties held by older students. The boys boasted about sneaking beers on a Saturday night and swiping condoms from the local convenience store.

Whatever happened to them? To find out, researchers at the University of Virginia followed a diverse group of 184 *cool kids* from age 13, when they were in seventh and eighth grades, to age 23.[1] "Cool kids," according to this study, were those early teens (ages 13 to 15) trying to impress their peers by acting older than their years. They had precocious romantic relationships, committed relatively minor acts of bad behavior—such as shoplifting—and surrounded themselves with good-looking friends. Their brazen behavior (what psychologists call *pseudo-mature* behavior) earned them a blaze of popularity. But such fame is fleeting and destructive. By high school, the once cool kids' popularity faded. They began struggling. By early adulthood, the once cool kids were at greater risk for alcohol and drug problems, more serious criminal behavior, and struggled with relationships.

What sent these young teenagers on a downward spiral? Researchers suggest that while these middle schoolers were chasing popularity, they were missing opportunities to develop self-identity, confidence, and mature social skills. It's also likely that as they got older, they felt a need to engage in ever-greater acts of rebellion to command respect from their peers. They were trapped in their middle-school world.

[1] J.P. Allen, M.M. Schad, B. Ouderkerk, and J. Chango, "What Ever Happened to the 'Cool' Kids? Long-Term Sequelae of Early Adolescent Pseudomature Behavior," *Child Development* 85, no. 5 (2014), pp. 1866–1880.

REFLECTION: As a teacher, what strategies might you use to help *cool kids* in your class develop healthy social and emotional behaviors?

are allowed to do more, have the dominant role in marriage, and receive greater respect. Yet middle school boys face challenges, too. When asked to describe the worst thing about being a boy, behavioral aggression and discipline topped the list, followed by poor grades and homophobia.

What are the joys for adolescent girls? Appearance was mentioned most often as the best reason for being a girl. Appearance comments included buying clothes, playing with hair styles, and taking beauty treatments, underscoring the need for females to seek approval outside themselves. One seventh-grade girl vividly captured this salience of appearance: "Clothes make it fun to be a girl. THE perfect outfit can make you feel pretty and worth something."[22] Academic advantage was another "best" reason for being a girl and included two opposing sets of comments, one that spoke to undue favoritism given girls—the "teacher's pet" idea—and the other described the extra effort given by girls and the intellectual satisfaction derived from their higher grades.

Students had little difficulty identifying negative aspects of being female. Relational aggression ranked highest with students describing a peer culture of gossip, rumors, and distrust among friends. Girls also noted their deliberate efforts to perform poorly on tests and assignments and "act dumb" to gain popularity or have a boyfriend. Girls further expressed frustration at being the "second-class gender," describing limited career options, responsibility for domestic chores, and the fear of sexual harassment/rape. At the other end of the spectrum, girls also felt they need to be "supergirls"—everything to everyone all the time. Three-quarters of the girls described feeling "a lot of pressure" to please everyone. A ninth-grader shared her frustration: "There is way too much pressure to be skinny, popular, athletic, and have a boyfriend. Girls should be respected more as people than so-and-so's girlfriend."[23]

These experiences of middle-schoolers are similar for students in urban, suburban, and rural America; in wealthy and poor communities; in schools that are diverse as well as those that are homogeneous. Such shared experiences underscore how gender stereotypes can create pressures that detract from both the academic emphasis and the social well-being of a school community.

High School: Lessons in Social Status

FOCUS QUESTION 5

In what ways does the adolescent culture shape teenage perceptions and behaviors in high school?

More than 15 million students arrive at 20,000 public high schools every day. These schools run the gamut from decaying buildings plagued by vandalism and drugs to orderly, congenial places with modern technology and attractive facilities. They vary in size from fifty to five thousand students, who spend days divided into either six or seven 50-minute periods or perhaps fewer, longer blocks of time. What happens in these schools greatly shapes the academic and social lives of millions of teenagers.

For many high school students, peer relationships are central to school life. When asked to identify the one best thing about their high school, "my friends" usually ranks at the top of the list. Sports activities rank second. "Nothing" ranks higher than "classes I'm taking" and "teachers."[24] When asked to describe her school, one high school junior said,

> The classes are okay, I guess. Most of the time I find them pretty boring, but then I suppose that's the way school classes are supposed to be. What I like most about the place is the chance to be with my friends. It's nice to be a part of a group. I don't mean one of the clubs or groups the school runs. . . . But an informal group of your own friends is great.[25]

David Owen is an author who returned to high school undercover to study peer culture. He discovered first-hand how difficult it can be to navigate adolescent society. Posing as a student who had just moved into the area, he enrolled in what he calls a typical American high school, approximately two hours outside of New York City. He was struck by the power of the peer group and how socially ill at ease most adolescents are. He likened adolescents to adults visiting a foreign country and a different culture. Experimenting with new behavior, they are terrified of being noticed doing something stupid:

> Being an adolescent is a full-time job, an all-out war against the appearance of awkwardness. No one is more attentive to nuance than a seventeen-year-old . . . When a kid in my class came to school one day in a funny-looking pair of shoes that one of his friends eventually laughed at, I could see by his face that he was thinking, "well, that does it, there goes the rest of my life."[26]

Peer groups tend to define the quality of students' school life.

©Marc Romanelli/Blend Images LLC RF

For those who remember jockeying unsuccessfully for a place within the inner circle of the high school social register, it may be comforting to learn that the tables do turn. Few studies show any correlation between high status in high school and later achievement as an adult. Those who are voted king and queen of the prom or most likely to succeed do not appear to do any better or any worse in adult life than those whose yearbook description is less illustrious. What works in that very insular adolescent environment is not necessarily what works in the

RAP 2.9

Reflections of a High School Yearbook

outside world. One researcher speculates that it is those on the "second tier," those in the group just below the top, who are most likely to succeed after high school. He says, "I think the rest of our lives are spent making up for what we did or did not do in high school."[27]

Along with navigating the social world of adolescence, the academic pressures that engulf teenagers are palpable:

> She has six exams in five days plus an analytical paper due. Her stomach hurts, she can barely eat. Some of her friends have panic attacks, while others study until 2 A.M. No, these are not law students; they are eleventh graders.

Many adolescents spend their high school years in a seemingly endless contest for the best grades, highest test scores, and the most impressive collection of resume-building accolades, all the tools they need to pry open the doors to a top college. Despite their tremendous abilities and stellar performances, many of these students succumb to the pressure. They experience a sense of purposeless, emptiness, and fear that emerge as mental health problems.[28] This stressful adolescent world is not sustainable.

With the best of intentions, adults can undermine the normal process of youthful growth and idealism, eliminating exploration, engagement, risk-taking, and the freedom to experiment. Overprotective and over-involved parents, sometimes referred to as "helicopter parents" for all their "hovering," contribute to a hyper-competitive teenage world where getting into the "right" college is not the most important thing; it's the only thing. These parents expect schools to teach-to-the-test, and even beyond school, they engage in an often costly and commercialized college admissions process. Youngsters caught in this pressure-cooker can suffer both physical and mental consequences, as their own interests and desires are submerged. Nearly 80 percent of adolescents feel they are not engaged in purposeful activities in school or other aspects of their lives.[29] While some parents recognize and rail against these unhealthy patterns, many others are swept into the prevailing cutthroat culture that craves academic status above all else. (Parental concerns often start early during elementary school years. See the Teaching Tip: How to Work with "Helicopter Parents.")

But this need not be the case, and educators can make a difference. Studies indicate that unhealthy student stress can be alleviated by personal, caring relationships at school. In fact, positive teacher–student relationships are associated with[30]:

- Increasing student understanding and meaningfulness of what is being taught
- Feeling a sense of personal empowerment
- Decreasing incidences of depression
- Improving self-confidence
- Reducing student stress
- Developing resiliency
- Improving creativity

Caring school relationships build trust and a healthier academic and social climate for adolescents. Given the growing array of social challenges you are likely to confront in your classroom, stronger student–teacher relationships have never been more needed.

TEACHING TIP

How to Work with "Helicopter Parents"

It was the day before my first year of teaching, my room was all set up, and I felt ready. But I hadn't much thought about one thing: the other adults involved with my students—their parents! I learned *very* quickly to focus on parent relationships. My first semester teaching, I learned these lessons.

BE PREPARED FOR ANYTHING

"Meet the Teacher Day" brought students with their parents, and I was taken by surprise. I had a parent yell at me for having an "inappropriate book series" in my classroom (even though this is a well-loved children's series that had been approved by our school board). I had a parent inform me that they had searched me on the Internet and knew where I'd gone to school, my past jobs, that I'd recently gotten married, my age, etc. Thankfully, there wasn't any negative information for her to find.

STAND YOUR GROUND

About two months after our first class science experiment, I had a parent e-mail me saying she was very unhappy with the grade her child received and wanted an explanation. The parent made it very apparent that she wanted me to change the grade and also threatened to pull the child from the school. This was demoralizing. However, I knew in my gut it wouldn't be fair to change the grade and it wouldn't help the student in the long run. Following an in-person meeting, the grade stayed, and so did the child. I learned that some parents just want to test their power.

COMMUNICATE REGULARLY

Each week I send home a brief newsletter with announcements, updates from the classroom, and a list of what we learned in each subject that week. Parents are e-mailed unless they request otherwise at Parent Night. It takes me about 15 minutes to put it together. Several parents have thanked me, as they didn't feel they had ever been so informed of their children's daily work. They also like feeling part of a team.

COMMUNICATE POSITIVELY

I wanted students to realize how much I value effort in class, so I came up with an "Honor Roll." All students have to do to earn a place on the Honor Roll is turn in all of their homework; they don't have to perform perfectly. When I posted my first honor roll, students were so excited and proud. What I think they valued even more was the note I sent home to their parents. I had many tell me that their son or daughter had never been recognized for any sort of effort or achievement, or that a positive note had ever been sent home.

By Amie Kemberling, a veteran educator in Tucson, Arizona

Courtesy of Amie Bergersen

REFLECTION: Which of Amie's strategies resonate with you? Did any surprise you? Do you have a strategy to add?

Social Challenges Come to School

Have you ever felt the cold slap of rejection because of your social class? Have you ever denied a family history that includes divorce or unplanned pregnancy? Has your life been touched by depression, an eating disorder, substance abuse, or bullying? Children across all racial, ethnic, and socioeconomic backgrounds may be plagued by such difficulties, affecting their academic and emotional well-being. Your students will likely carry these struggles and concerns with them as they walk through your classroom door. Although schools and teachers cannot completely solve these social issues (as much as we may try), education can bring purpose, hope, and empowerment to our most troubled youth.

FOCUS QUESTION 6

What impact do changing family patterns and economic issues have on children and schools?

Family Patterns

Today's families are becoming smaller, older, and more diverse. Families typically include two children or fewer, and these children are born increasingly to older and more educated mothers. Approximately one in five children is born to a mother at least 35 years

FIGURE 4.2

The American family: a racial/ethnic group snapshot.

SOURCE: U.S. Census Bureau, *Current Population Survey*, 2015.

REFLECTION: These graphics of children's living arrangements are only a snapshot. They don't capture the quality of family relationships. For example, are children in a loving, stable, and supportive environment? What other family patterns remain invisible when you only look at these numbers?

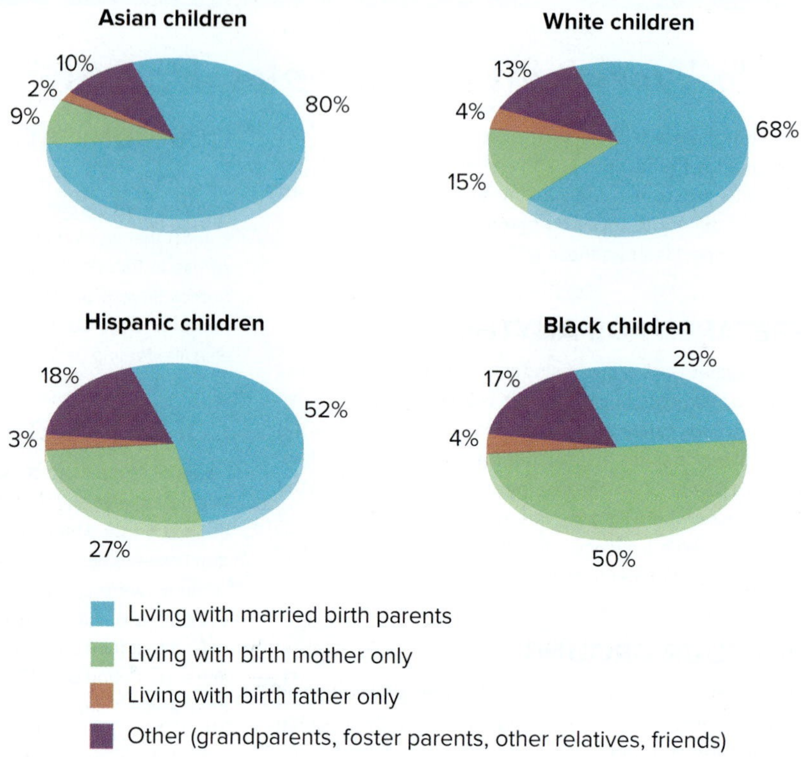

old, and more than 50 percent of new mothers have at least some college education. More than half of American families are remarried or recoupled, creating diverse stepfamily patterns: biological and legal relationships with stepparents, stepsiblings, and/or multiple sets of grandparents. Other families are created through same-sex, cross-cultural and racial unions.[31] It was only in 1967 that the Supreme Court overruled anti-miscegenation laws, which had banned interracial marriage.

Diverse patterns further emerge when we view American families by race and ethnicity. Eight in ten Asian-American kids live with married birth parents, compared with about seven in ten European-American kids, five in ten Hispanic-American kids, and only about three in ten African-American kids.[32] (See Figure 4.2.) Research shows that children from single-parent families, especially those living in poverty, often face greater academic and behavioral challenges in school.[33]

Working mothers represent yet another changing family dynamic. For generations, few women with children worked outside the home. Today, more than two-thirds of women with children participate in the salaried workforce. In fact, women with children are the primary breadwinners or co-breadwinners in more than half of American families. Although parenting and household responsibilities still fall more on women (between sixteen and twenty hours a week), more and more fathers are also assuming parenting responsibilities (about eight to ten hours a week). Not surprisingly, working fathers and mothers desire more flexible work schedules, equal pay, redesigned family and medical leave, and comprehensive child-care policies.[34]

One trend that hasn't changed is paying women less. Although equal pay has been the law since 1963, employers still find ways to pay women less, even when education, skills, and experience are the same. Women working full time in the United States typically average just 80 percent of what men earn. The pay gap grows wider for Hispanic and Latina, African American, American Indian, and Native Hawaiian and other native women. Pay inequities not only cost women, but also their children. For the first time in recent history, more than half of K–12 public school students in the United States live in low-income homes.[35] In the next section, we explore more deeply how poverty puts students at risk, and consider how, and if, schools will respond.

Students often enjoy school life better when their families are supportive.

©Buccina Studios/Getty Images RF

Poverty

Today, children are the poorest group in our society, and current programs and policies are woefully inadequate to meet their growing needs. Stanford's Michael Kirst sums it up this way:

> Johnny can't read because he needs glasses and breakfast and encouragement from his absent father. Maria doesn't pay attention in class because she doesn't understand English very well and she's worried about her father's drinking and she's tired from trying to sleep in her car. Dick is flunking because he's frequently absent. His mother doesn't get him to school because she's depressed because she lost her job. She missed too much work because she was sick and could not afford medical care.[36]

The year 2013 marked a watershed moment in our country: For the first time in more than 50 years, a majority of students attending K–12 education were from low-income homes and qualified for free or reduced-price school lunches. Sadly, the trend continues. More than one in five children (11 million) of all racial and ethnic backgrounds lives below the poverty line.[37] Many educators believe that economic inequality has emerged as a more significant risk factor than race.

GLOBAL VIEW

Our child poverty rate is substantially higher—often two to three times higher—than that of other developed nations (LIS Data Center, 2016). For example, in 2014 the child poverty rate in the United States was 22 percent; only Romania had a higher poverty rate.

Consider how the civil rights movement and school desegregation helped bring a measure of equity to student achievement. Today, despite some setbacks, racial disparities in education have narrowed significantly. The test-score deficit of black 9-, 13- and 17-year-olds in reading and math had been reduced by as much as 50 percent compared with four decades ago. Achievements like these signal hope. Racial disparities are still a stain on American society, but they are no longer the main divider. Yet, for all the progress in improving educational outcomes among African-American children, the achievement gaps between more affluent and less privileged children are wider than ever. Proficiency gaps in reading and math between the poor and the rich are nearly twice as large as that between black and white children.[38] Indeed, family socioeconomic status may be the biggest threat today to the American dream.

American parents of all socioeconomic levels want similar things for their children: for them to be healthy and happy, honest and ethical, caring and compassionate. Psychologists agree that there is no best parenting style or philosophy, and across income groups, 92 percent of parents say they are doing a good job at raising their children. Yet even before they walk through school doors, the lives of children from rich and poor families look more different than ever before. Research reveals that many middle- and higher-income parents see their children as projects in need of careful cultivation. Well-off families are ruled by calendars and organized activities, ranging from art, music, language, and sports activities. These children are also taught to question authority and how to navigate organizations, like schools. Working-class parents, meanwhile, believe their children will naturally thrive, and give them far greater independence and time for free play. They are taught to be compliant and deferential to adults. Most believe there are benefits to both approaches. Working-class children report feeling more independent, complain less and are closer with family members. Higher-income children are more likely to experience boredom and expect their parents to solve their problems.[39]

Yet, children from poverty enter school with distinct disadvantages, often coping with issues that other children (and many adults) seldom, if ever, contemplate. Though most parents of poor children work (often at multiple jobs), many don't earn enough to provide their families with basic necessities—adequate food, shelter, child care, and health care. Each of these disadvantages makes only a small contribution to the educational struggles of youth, but cumulatively they can easily overwhelm.

Poor children enter school with distinct disadvantages. They are more likely to live in single-parent families, typically receive less adult attention, have fewer books to read, and are not read to as often. Also, children from low-income homes hear only 13 million spoken words by age 4 compared to 46 million words heard by upper-income children. As a consequence, they are not exposed to complex language or large vocabularies. A child's vocabulary is part of the brain's tool kit for learning, memory, and cognition. Moreover, students living in low-income neighborhoods usually have fewer adults with professional careers who can serve as role models. In fact, simply getting out of the neighborhood to visit museums or zoos or cultural activities is difficult. Such isolation deprives these children of experiences beyond the familiar and also chips away at their self-confidence. Their neighborhood reality is often filled with crime and drugs, so safety concerns can dominate daily existence. Equally troubling, poverty can have a significant impact on the brain's development. Perhaps as toxic as drugs and alcohol to a young child's brain, the stresses and lack of resources available in poverty can limit the development of cognitive skills. Childhood poverty can also change the way the brain tissue itself matures during the critical brain developmental periods of early childhood.[40]

How can teachers understand the unique needs of children living in poverty? We can start by considering that poverty itself may be a culture. The concept of the *culture of poverty* was coined by anthropologist Oscar Lewis and describes how people in poverty often have their own behavioral norms, communication skills, and even ways of viewing the world.[41] Because schools tend to reflect middle-class values, the culture of poverty can clash with school culture. This culture clash often alienates the poor from school, and school from the poor.

One of the most common misperceptions of individuals from low socioeconomic backgrounds is that they do not value education. When poor parents do not attend a back-to-school night or miss a parent–teacher meeting, many in the middle or upper class simply assume that they are not committed to education. In reality, these absences may be due to working several jobs, struggling with unreliable transportation and child care, or difficulty with understanding or speaking English.

U.S. schools have historically been thought of as the great equalizer—the social institution best suited to ensure that all children have an equal opportunity to learn, develop, and thrive. Yet, it is unrealistic to think that school-based strategies alone will eliminate today's stark disparities in academic success. Economic policies that reduce inequality; family support policies that ensure children grow up in stable, secure homes and neighborhoods; and early-childhood education policies that promote cognitive and social development need to be part of a comprehensive strategy to close the economic achievement gap. The impact of such programs is profound: Children from low-income homes who participate in early childhood programs, such as Head Start, are four times more likely to graduate from college than their peers who do not participate.

What does poverty look like in your community?

©Jewel Samad/AFP/Getty Images

So, what is the role of schools in easing the effects of poverty and making education work for all students? The good news is that school policies and effective teaching can help these students succeed. Consider the following issues[42]:

1. *Time in School.* Growing evidence suggests that more time in school—extending the school day or year or providing after-school or summer-school programs—may help to improve academic achievement, keep kids in a safe environment, and help forge new constructive peer relationships. Extracurricular activities also expand cultural, artistic, and athletic opportunities.
2. *Vocabulary.* Teachers can help expand vocabulary across the curriculum. Words help children represent, manipulate, and reframe information. Working with poor children on expanding their vocabulary not only reduces the language deficit but also uses words to take the child beyond a local neighborhood to see a broader world perspective.
3. *Cognitive Skills.* Children from low socioeconomic backgrounds often exhibit short attention spans, high levels of distractibility, trouble monitoring the quality of their work, and difficulty generating new solutions to problems. These deficits may lead students to act out or shut down. Cognitive skills are teachable. Classroom activities can help students learn how to organize, study, take notes, prioritize, remember key ideas, problem-solve, process, and build working memory.
4. *Health and Nutrition.* Children from poor families are less likely to exercise, get proper diagnoses, receive appropriate and prompt medical attention, or be prescribed appropriate medications or interventions. Poor health affects attention, reasoning, memory, learning, and behavior. Schools can offer students breakfast, recess, and physical education, while teachers can integrate into instruction games, movement, drama, and yoga, all of which boost the level of oxygen and glucose in the brain and fuel learning.
5. *High Expectations.* Too often poor children's behavior is characterized as "lazy," when what they are really demonstrating is lost hope or depression. Avoid what has been termed "soft bias," the lowering of academic expectations for poor children. Build relationships with students; introduce novelty, excitement, and competition into learning activities; make connections between the curriculum and students' everyday lives; give more positive comments than negative; set high goals and motivate students to meet them; show them real-world success stories of adults who came from similar circumstances; and give daily feedback so students see that effort matters.

Hidden America: Homeless Families

Homelessness may conjure up images of cardboard boxes, sleeping bags, and heating grates. The realities are more complex. By federal definition, "homeless child and youth includes minors living in shelters with or without family, doubling up with friends or extended family, settling into motels, campgrounds, trailer parks, or living in vehicles." The strain on families as they face declining fortunes can be soul draining. Survival needs such as food, safety, and shelter become daily struggles.

More than 1 million public school students in the United States (one in every forty-five children) have no room to call their own, no desk to do their homework, and no bed to rest on at night. Homelessness touches children of every racial and ethnic background, as well as those in urban, suburban, and rural environments. LGBTQA students are increasingly joining the ranks of the homeless.[43] These homeless youth face significant school challenges. Although most attend school, there is constant turmoil and frequent transfers. Many arrive at school hungry, tired, distracted, and lacking even rudimentary study facilities. Add to this equation the drugs, crimes, violence, and prostitution often found in their lives, and it is clear that these children struggle against overwhelming odds. Children whose address has been in flux for more than a year are more likely than their peers to be labeled as learning disabled, to drop out of school, and to experience physical and sexual abuse.[44]

In 1987, Congress passed the **McKinney-Vento Homeless Assistance Act,** which requires homeless students to have the same access to school as everyone else. Before this law, school districts often required proof of residency, birth certificates, and immunization documents—simple tasks for most families, but challenging enough to keep many homeless children out of school. McKinney-Vento eliminated such barriers, allowing students to enroll immediately without proof of permanent address. The act also requires schools to provide the homeless with emergency food services, adult literacy programs, and access to job literacy programs. Homeless students also have the right to participate in all extracurricular activities as well as all support programs, including meal services, before- and after-school care, special education, and gifted programs. School districts must provide transportation so that highly mobile students can stay in the same school, a place of familiar faces and stability. McKinney-Vento also mandates that school districts provide a homeless liaison to connect families to appropriate social and educational services. Importantly, illegal immigrant children, who are often homeless, have the right to attend public schools.[45] Efforts such as McKinney-Vento give schools the potential to act as a stabilizing force for homeless youth and their families.

FOCUS QUESTION 7

How can educators respond to social issues that place children at risk?

Children: At Promise or At Risk?

It was not too long ago that teachers were concerned about students talking out of turn, chewing gum, making noise, running in the halls, cutting in line, and violating dress codes. More than half a century later, teachers' top student concerns reflect the devastating changes in the lives of their pupils: drug and alcohol abuse, pregnancy, suicide, bullying, low graduation rates, and weight issues.

Many teenagers smoke, do drugs (prescription and nonprescription), and engage in unprotected sex. Adolescents view this period between childhood and adulthood as a time for fun, and being adolescents, they feel protected by their own youth, by a sense of invulnerability. A second group of teenagers take similar risks for different reasons: They believe they have little to lose. Native American, Hispanic, black, and low-income teens may especially view the future with a sense of hopelessness, a fatalistic belief that risky behavior is not so risky if life offers few options, if death may come at any time.[46]

Dropping Out

Lamar was finishing junior high school with resignation and despair. He had just managed to squeak through with poor grades and no understanding of how this frustrating experience called school would help him. He wasn't good at schoolwork and felt that the classes he had to sit through were a waste of time. He wanted to end these long, boring days, get a job, and get a car. He'd had enough of school.

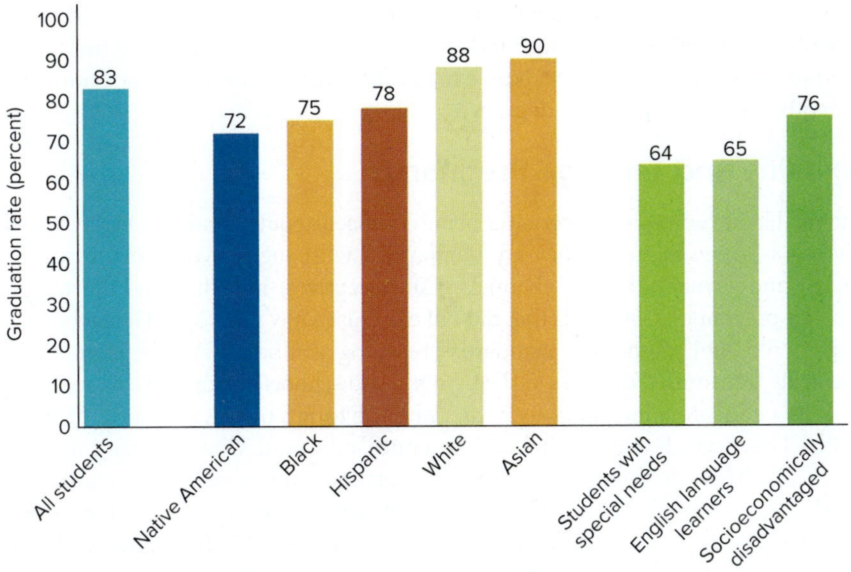

FIGURE 4.3

National high school graduation rates.

SOURCE: U.S. Department of Education, *Public High School Four-Year On-Time Graduation Rates*, 2016.

REFLECTION: What strategies would you suggest to improve graduation rates? Do these strategies vary according to the race and gender of students? Language abilities? Special needs? Socioeconomic status? Why or why not?

Lamar is a good candidate to join the nation's dropouts. Students who eventually drop out often start struggling academically in the first grade, are likely to repeat a grade at least once, frequently transfer between different elementary and middle schools, and attend poor schools.[47] One teacher described the academic slide of dropouts like this: "Kids who fail math or English in sixth grade go on to start failing *everything* in ninth grade."[48]

Are you surprised to learn that nationwide only about 80 percent of students graduate from high school? Every day 7,000 or more students give up on school, resulting in more than 1 million American high school students who drop out every year. Racial, ethnic, and gender patterns offer an even more disturbing picture of educational attainment. And not surprisingly, dropouts reflect challenges faced by other disadvantaged groups, including English language learners, students with special needs, and those from low-income backgrounds (see Figure 4.3).[49]

GLOBAL VIEW

The United States ranks 21st in the world for high school graduation rates. Portugal, Slovenia, Japan, and Finland rank highest. Why? Researchers suggest these countries place a greater emphasis on academics while U.S. schools focus more on social aspects of schooling (Organization for Economic Development, 2016).

Most students don't drop out because they can't do the work. In fact, nearly 90 percent have passing grades when they leave school. The major reasons for opting out? Classes are too boring, and students feel academically and socially disengaged. Others are more worried about pregnancy, family issues, or financial concerns. Indeed, the immediate monetary rewards of the workplace lure some students. Yet, dropouts earn on average $10,000 less a year than high school graduates and almost $40,000 less than their peers with college degrees. They are also far more likely to need government assistance or end up in jail. Many educators believe that the dropout rate can be reduced through early intervention, early literacy programs, one-on-one instruction, mentoring and tutoring, more relevant curricular materials, service learning, and family involvement. Another growing effort, especially for low-income students, is a blended high school and college program with a career-focused curriculum that allows students to earn both a high school diploma and an associate's degree or credits toward a bachelor's degree.[50]

Sexuality and Teenage Pregnancy

GLOBAL VIEW

Teen pregnancy rates remain much higher in the United States than in many other developed nations—twice as high as in New Zealand, England, and Canada. The lowest teen pregnancy rates are found in Japan, Switzerland, and Singapore (Guttmacher Institute, 2016).

Who can blame today's adolescents for being confused about sexuality? On the one hand, they see a "green light," as they are bombarded with suggestive advertising, graphic movies, and sexualized cable channels. Contraceptives, including the morning-after pill, offer pregnancy safeguards that did not exist just a few years ago. Then students see a bright "red light" of morality standards preaching abstinence and the looming threat of sexually transmitted diseases (STDs). So how do schools respond to this conflict?

Many educators feel anxious in tackling the topics of sex, sexuality, and sexual health. They may feel overwhelmed or confused about what to teach and when to teach it. (How do you feel?) Yet, the importance of sex education cannot be ignored. Nearly half of all high school students are sexually active. Though the teen birth rate has declined to its lowest level in decades, the United States still has the highest teen birth rate in the industrialized world. Roughly one in four girls will become pregnant at least once by their 20th birthday. Many teens report regretting engaging in sex: more than 70 percent of girls and more than half of boys wish they had waited.[51]

What students learn (or do not learn) in school about sex depends on the school they attend. In many districts, sex education is avoided. Where it is offered, two curricula–Sexual Risk-Avoidance (SRA) curriculum and Comprehensive Sex Education–are most common, each with a very different focus. SRA (formerly labeled abstinence-only) teaches students how to voluntarily refrain from nonmarital sexual activity. While SRA programs do include information on contraception and treating sexually transmitted infections, SRA is designed to promote abstinence from sex as the best choice for adolescent well-being. Comprehensive sex education, on the other hand, focuses on a range of issues concerning sexuality: from abstinence to body image, contraception, gender, human growth and development, human reproduction, pregnancy, relationships, sexually transmitted infections, sexual attitudes and values, sexual anatomy and physiology, sexual behavior, sexual health, sexual orientation, and sexual pleasure. (Whew! How many of these topics did you explore as a student?) Such comprehensive programs hope to provide students with developmentally appropriate knowledge and skills so that they can make healthy decisions about their sex lives now and in the future. While both SRA and comprehensive sex education can spark controversy, most middle and high schools students and their parents value the inclusion of sex education in the curriculum.[52]

GLOBAL VIEW

Cigarette smoking and alcohol use are less prevalent for U.S. tenthgraders than in almost all European nations. The lifetime use of marijuana and other illicit drugs is higher in the United States than in any European country (World Health Organization, 2016).

Substance Abuse

Emerging teenage substance abuse data may give educators and parents reason to feel hopeful. Compared to adolescents over the last two decades, today's teenagers are less likely to smoke cigarettes, try alcohol, binge drink, or experiment with illicit drugs such as LSD and cocaine.[53] But not all trends are so encouraging.

While alcohol remains the most common form of substance abuse–more than half of high schoolers report drinking–teenagers face new threats such as high rates of e-cigarette smoking, prescription drug abuse, greater marijuana smoking, and heroin addiction. Almost half of adolescents experiment with vaping–inhaling nicotine-infused water vapor from e-cigarettes, pipes, pens, hookahs, and other devices. While trying conventional cigarettes may no longer be a teen rite of passage, each day more than 2,000 youth become daily cigarette smokers. Interestingly, teens who smoke agree that cigarette smoking of any kind is bad for their health. Teens, however, hold the opposite opinions for marijuana, believing the drug is safe to smoke regularly, and its use is growing. More than one in three teens smoke weed.[54]

Although marijuana is the most popular first-time choice for teens trying drugs, prescription drugs and inhalants are a close second and third. Today's youth grow up in a world where it is routine to reach for a prescription bottle to enhance performance, to focus better in school, and to stay awake or calm down. Not surprisingly, prescription painkillers such as Vicodin and Oxycontin are abused by one in ten high schoolers. One million teens have tried an inhalant–such as glue, paint, felt-tip markers, and air fresheners–to get high. Of growing concern is teen experimentation with illicit drugs, like acid, ecstasy, methamphetamine, cocaine, and heroin, tried by more than half of all students by the time they finish high school.[55]

What leads youth to substance abuse? Some blame the mixed messages children receive. Although parents and teachers may talk about the physical, emotional, and academic dangers, the media and pop culture often glorify alcohol and other drugs as methods for coping with stress and loneliness or to improve performance. Other contributing factors include family instability and the materialistic, success-driven nature of our culture that creates tremendous pressure on youth (and adults). We know all too well that substance abuse paves a risky, downward path[56]:

- Grades go down as alcohol consumption and drug use go up.
- Substance abuse interferes with IQ and normal brain development.
- The more teenagers drink and use drugs the more likely they are to be involved in violent crime, such as murder, rape, or robbery, either as victim or as perpetrator.
- Alcohol and drug abuse is associated with more unplanned pregnancies, more sexually transmitted diseases, and more HIV infections than any other single factor.
- Approximately 50 percent of all youth deaths from drowning, fires, suicide, and homicide are alcohol-related.

Schools often adopt programs such as Drug Abuse Resistance Education (D.A.R.E.) to help youth understand the facts about drugs and cope with peer pressures. Funded and run by local police departments, D.A.R.E. costs school districts very little and is popular in schools nationwide. Yet research reveals that D.A.R.E. and its "Just Say No" message are ineffective in curtailing drug use. Similar criticism has been leveled at the U.S. Department of Education's Safe and Drug-Free Schools program. Given the poor track record of these national programs, many local schools choose to develop their own substance abuse curricula and policies, which are often designed to improve open communication between students and staff.[57]

Obesity and Eating Disorders

What does forty hours a week watching television and playing video and computer games, and playing outside for only two hours a week and eating junk food get you?

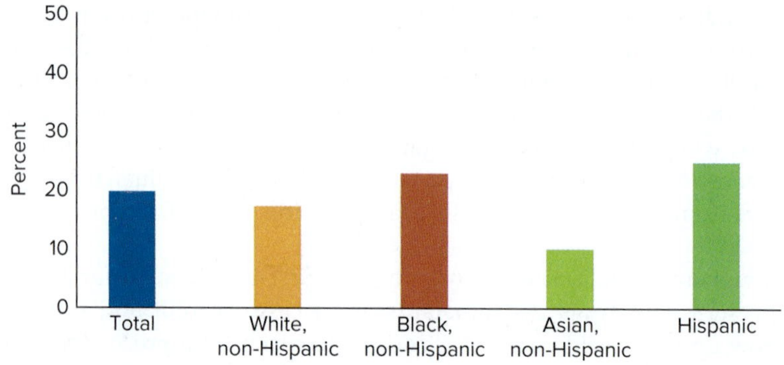

FIGURE 4.4

Obese children by race and Hispanic origin.

SOURCE: Centers for Disease Control and Prevention, *Childhood Obesity Facts*, 2016.

REFLECTION: Suggest at least three factors contributing to these obesity patterns. What role, if any, should schools have in promoting a healthy lifestyle?

Pounds, lots of extra pounds. More than 12 million American children ages 2 to 19—one in five—are overweight or obese. (See Figure 4.4.) At special risk are children from low socioeconomic backgrounds, as well as Hispanic, black, and Native American youth. The consequences of obesity are staggering. Besides potential health problems such as diabetes, arthritis, and heart disease, overweight children are more likely to have low self-esteem and be absent from school. Overweight students, particularly girls, are more likely to engage in sexual activity earlier and without protection and are less likely to attend college.[58]

School meals play a role in creating healthy (or unhealthy) students. The National School Lunch Program, signed into law by President Truman in 1946, was designed to feed hungry children who needed extra calories. Today, it serves 31 million kids, most of whom don't. Although school meals are subsidized by the government and should follow nutritional standards, that doesn't always translate into apples and cucumbers. For decades, many schools did not offer any fresh fruits or raw vegetables on a daily basis. What's more, vending machines, some stocked with cookies and soda, could be found in nearly all middle and high schools. But these nutritional failings are slowly changing. The Healthy, Hunger-free Kids Act gives the federal government power to set new nutrition standards for all food served in schools, from lunchrooms to vending machines. Schools must serve up more fruits, vegetables, whole grains, and low-fat milk and less sodium.[59] (See Table 4.1.) We encourage you to see if your local schools follow these recommendations.

The good news? Some schools are stepping up to this challenge by planting organic gardens and harvesting the food that they then use for school lunches or sell at their own farmers' markets. Some ban vending machines completely, while others are filling them with low-sugar and low-salt snacks, juices, and water. Several major school food suppliers are doubling the amount of fresh

TABLE 4.1 What's in a meal?

SOURCE: United States Department of Agriculture, Healthy, *Hunger-free Kids Act*, 2012.

A Typical School Lunch Before and After the Passage of Healthy, Hunger-Free Kids Act.

Old Menu	New Menu
Bean and cheese burrito (5.3 oz) with mozzarella cheese (1 oz)	Sub sandwich (1 oz turkey, ½ oz low-fat cheese on whole wheat roll)
Applesauce (1/4 cup)	Refried beans (1/2 cup)
Orange juice (4 oz)	Jicama (1/4 cup)
Low-fat (1%) chocolate milk (8 oz)	Green pepper strips (1/4 cup)
	Cantaloupe wedges (1/2 cup)
	Low-fat ranch dip (1 oz)
	Reduced mayonnaise (1 oz)
	Low-fat (1%) milk (8 oz)
Old Menu	**New Menu**
Cheese pizza (1 slice)	Whole-wheat cheese pizza (1 slice)
Tater tots (1/2 cup)	Baked sweet-potato fries (1/2 cup)
Ketchup (2 tablespoons)	Grape tomatoes, raw (1/4 cup)
Canned pineapple (1/2 cup)	Applesauce (1/2 cup)
Low-fat (1%) chocolate milk (8 oz)	Low-fat (1%) milk (8 oz)
	Low-fat ranch dip (1 oz)

REFLECTION: What are your impressions about the new school nutrition guidelines? Who might oppose these changes?

produce they provide. Former First Lady Michelle Obama initiated the Let's Move campaign to encourage parents, school leaders, PTAs, food manufacturers, and elected officials to make physical activity and healthy foods an integral part of school life.

But obesity is not our only weight issue. Some children are taught by our culture that you cannot be too thin, and they take drastic measures to diminish their bodies. Eating disorders among youth are prevalent, and an estimated 30 million Americans struggle with anorexia, bulimia, or binge eating, 90 percent of whom are females and 10 percent males between the ages of 12 and 20. Anorexia is the third most common chronic illness among adolescents. For most kids, eating disorders typically start when they are 11 to 13 years old, but they can begin much earlier. By age six, children, especially girls, start to express concerns about their weight and body shape. Sadly, four out of five teen girls fear being fat and consider losing weight a priority.[60] Persistent, chronic dieting puts an enormous stress on youth, one that takes a toll on physical well-being and the energy needed to learn in school.

While movies, magazines, and television tell females that being thin is the ticket to success, males receive a different message: Bulk up those muscles and flatten those abs! Boys say, "I'm getting into shape," not, "I'm fat and need to go on a diet." Yet the fitness quest can quickly turn life-threatening. Boys as young as 8 years old have been diagnosed with eating disorders, and 40 percent of all youth binge-eaters are male. The numbers may be much higher because males believe that food issues are "female issues" and are likely to deny or fail to recognize their own struggles with eating.

More than ever, American boys are trying to find perfect bodies not just by dieting or going to the gym but also from steroids. Nearly half a million boys are taking steroids, and boys as young as 10 are bulking up simply because they want to look good. Although steroids can guarantee a rack of rippling muscles, many of these substances can stifle bone growth and lead to cancer, hair loss, acne, and testosterone-driven rage.[61]

Americans of all ages have a long way to go in freeing themselves from media images of one ideal body type. Healthy bodies come in many shapes, and it is not necessary for all females to be incredibly thin or all males to look like professional athletes.

Bullying

> *Loser* and *Fag* are scribbled on binders littering a classroom. A huddle of popular girls glare at the classmate they've chosen as outsider of the week. A broad-shouldered ninth-grade boy shoves his scrawny, bespectacled friend of yesterday into the stretch of lockers.[62]

Metal detectors and extra security measures have sharply reduced school violence, but bullies still stalk. Cell phones, social networks, and online game rooms have joined playgrounds, hallways, cafeterias, and school buses as places where students interact informally with little adult supervision—prime areas for bullying. Bullies seek control over others by taking advantage of imbalances in perceived power, such as greater size, physical strength, carrying weapons, or social status. Bullies can use physical force or threats, but sticks and stones aren't the only tools. Social weapons, such as taunts and teases, name-calling, gossip-mongering, and exclusion, can cut children much deeper. One-third to a half of America's children report being bullied. In a typical classroom of twenty students, two or three come to school every day fearing being bullied, harassed, or worse. Although most youth describe bullying as harmful, a gap exists between that belief and students' behaviors. More than 40 percent of students admit to bullying a classmate at least once; more than half have witnessed bullying and not stopped or reported it.[63]

Bullies in the schoolyard now have a new place to wield their punches—cyberspace.

©Exactostock/SuperStock RF

Bullying has been an accepted school tradition for decades, if not centuries, often because so many teachers accept the myths surrounding bullying: Only a small number of children are affected, students are just "tattling, it's a natural behavior," and "boys will be boys." But those myths are dangerous. Boys *and* girls engage in bullying, though often with different behaviors. Boys are more likely to engage in physical bullying, whereas girls often revert to relational bullying, such as gossip and exclusion. Both are likely to cyber-bully. Bullying is linked to academic difficulties, withdrawal from activities, depression, suicide, and eating disorders. And children who bully are more likely to get into fights, vandalize property, and drop out of school.[64] Cyber-bullying is a relatively new phenomenon. The term didn't even exist a decade ago, but the problem is pervasive in children's lives today, with increasingly deadly consequences. Through e-mail, social media such as Instagram and Facebook, and electronic gadgets such as smartphones, cyber-bullies forward and spread hurtful images and/or messages. Bullies use this technology to harass victims at all hours, in wide circles, and at warp speed. Noted one teacher:

> You can pass around a note to classmates making fun of a peer, and it stays in the room. But when you post that same note online, thousands can see it. The whole world becomes witness and is invited to participate. Wherever kids go with their computers or phones, which is nearly everywhere, the bullies come with them.[65]

RAP 2.10
Support Staff Interview

The cost of bullying is high, and officials—from the law to schools—are finally "getting it." Courts are declaring that bullying is *not* protected by freedom of expression, and more than forty states have laws against bullying in school. Massachusetts, for example, defines bullying as both cyber-bullying and any act that creates a "hostile learning environment." In that state, even bullying occurring away from the school can be punishable if the learning environment is affected. Teachers are required to report any instance of bullying to the school principal, who must take action. Every school in the state is required to provide age-appropriate anti-bullying instruction.[66]

School leaders are also stepping up, sending the message that bullying will not be tolerated and creating a climate where students know there are adults they can trust and to whom they can safely report information. Effective anti-bullying practices ask teachers to be involved and interested in students, set firm limits on unacceptable behavior, and act as authorities and positive role models. At one Illinois school district, students can call an anonymous tip line to report instances of bullying. The school system's policy handbook makes clear that staff members must report acts of bullying and protect students who report bullying from retaliation.[67]

Creating a safe classroom climate is the first step in effective teaching. Another is teaching empathy and community-building throughout the curriculum. Schools have devised some interesting ways of doing this. In one New York school, English classes discuss whether Friar Laurence was empathetic to Romeo and Juliet. In other schools, students share snacks and board games with autistic classmates or receive recognition for sitting with a new student at lunch or helping a panicked classmate on the rock-climbing wall. To help students better relate to life with a disability, a common assignment asks students to spend a day in a wheelchair and then write a short story or poem about the experience. Meditation and yoga are increasingly offered to promote compassion and kindness. Schools are also implementing peer mediation programs to help reduce bullying and school violence. Students are trained to help classmates peacefully solve problems, becoming empowered advocates against bullying.[68]

As our awareness of bullying increases, some educators are offering new ways to address the issues. For example, Colby College Professor Lyn Mikel Brown recommends a deeper look at the factors underlying bullying. Accordingly to Brown, educators need to[69]:

- *Talk accurately about behavior.* Bullying is a broad term. If it's sexual harassment, call it sexual harassment; if it's homophobia, call it homophobia. Calling behaviors what they are encourages more complex and meaningful solutions.

CONTEMPORARY ISSUES

A View from the Field: Cyberbullying

Nadia,* 24, teaches seventh-grade reading, writing, and history in a suburb outside Chicago. Though she's been teaching for only two years, she's already witnessed several incidents of cyberbullying at her school. "It was recently brought to the attention of the teachers and staff that one student used his cell phone to record girls at our school and then placed these videos on YouTube," Nadia explains.

> I believe the title said something to the effect of "Fat Girls at Our School Just Being Fat." Just two weeks ago, three boys ganged up on another male student. Two of the boys participated in the actual assault while the third student took a video of it on his cell phone. Another student [pretended to be a teacher] and created a MySpace page for "the teacher," which painted her in an extremely unfavorable light. Another girl via Instant Messenger has repeatedly bullied one girl in my class. It seems as though these kids grow very courageous when they do not have to say things face-to-face.

Nadia's school has gone beyond simple reprimands to deal with cyberbullying.

> I definitely address all types of bullying in my class and will not stand for it. My school administrators deal with specific incidents: parents are called in, the student is required to shut down the Web site or at least get rid of all objectionable material, and a suspension is given. We have a police liaison who deals with a variety of issues at our school. Her job description now includes surfing student social media pages and checking for signs of bullying and harassment. Next year we will be introducing the Positive Behavioral and Intervention Supports system. I think my school will benefit from this as I see a definite need for it right now. Although I am very near in age to my students, with a difference of 10–11 years, I am shocked to see all that is out there! I consider myself to be pretty technologically savvy, but never would have thought to use this tool as a form of humiliation or aggression against others. I would love to learn more about what the classroom teacher can do to address and prevent these issues.

Nadia earned a B.S. in elementary education from Illinois State University. To learn more about the Positive Behavioral and Intervention Supports system, please visit www.pbis.org.

Courtesy of Nadia

*Name has been changed.

- *Move beyond the individual.* To understand why a child uses aggression toward others, it's important to understand what impact race, ethnicity, social class, gender, religion, and ability have on his or her daily experiences in school. How do these realities affect the kinds of attention and resources a child receives, where he fits in, or whether she feels marginal or privileged in school?
- *Stop labeling students.* Bully prevention programs typically put kids into three categories: bullies, victims, and bystanders. Labeling focuses on the child as the problem, downplaying the roles of parents, teachers, the school system, a powerful media culture, and societal injustices children experience every day. Labels also simplify the issue: We are all complex individuals with the capacity to do harm and to do good.
- *Accentuate the positive.* Instead of labeling kids, affirm their strengths and believe that they can do good, brave, remarkable things. The path to safer, less violent schools lies less in adults' control over children than in appreciating their need to have more control in their lives, to feel important, to be visible, to have an effect on people and situations.

We don't have to accept bullying as a part of growing up. Teaching acceptance and kindness toward others can be as much a part of schools as algebra or social studies.

CONNECT FOR *TEACHERS, SCHOOLS, AND SOCIETY*

Check out Connect, McGraw-Hill Education's interactive learning environment, to:

Read Current and Historical Articles

Bullying and the Culture of Peers, by Philip C. Rodkin, *Educational Leadership,* September 2011.

Challenging Assumptions: Helping Struggling Students Succeed, by Lois Brown Easton and Michael Soguero, *Phi Delta Kappan,* February 2011.

Keeping Youth in School: An International Perspective, by Nancy Hoffman, *Phi Delta Kappan,* February 2011.

The Engaged Classroom, by Sam M. Intrator, *Educational Leadership,* September 2004.

The Myth of the Culture of Poverty, by Paul Gorski, *Educational Leadership,* April 2008.

Analyze Case Studies

Marsha Warren: A teacher is overwhelmed by the problems created by her students, including eight children who have unique home problems and personal situations that are affecting their schooling.

Anne Holt: This case follows an experienced teacher through her morning routine with a diverse group of first-grade children. The case presents a detailed look at her organization and the climate she creates in the classroom.

Watch Teachers, Students, and Classrooms in Action

Our **Online Video Album** for contemporary videos related to this chapter.

KEY TERMS AND PEOPLE

ability grouping, 90
gatekeeping, 86
McKinney-Vento Homeless Assistance Act, 102
Oakes, Jeannie, 89
sociograms, 92
tracking, 88

DISCUSSION QUESTIONS AND ACTIVITIES

1. Observe in a local elementary school. What are the rules and regulations that students must follow? Do they seem reasonable or arbitrary? Do students seem to spend a large amount of time waiting? Observe one student over a 40-minute period and determine what portion of those 40 minutes she or he spends just waiting.
2. Do you think that tracking is a valid method for enhancing student performance? Or do you think it is a mechanism for perpetuating inequality of opportunity based on social class, race, or sex? Debate someone in your class who holds an opposing point of view.

3. We have noted the vividness with which many people recall their high school years. Try to answer the following:
   - Who was voted most likely to succeed in your high school class? (Do you know what he or she is doing today?)
   - What was your happiest moment in high school? Your worst?
   - Name five people who were part of the “in crowd” in your class. What were they like?
   - Is there any academic experience in high school that you remember vividly? If so, what was it? If not, why?
4. Research the issue of adolescent alienation. Make some recommendations on how secondary schools could get students to become more involved in academic and extracurricular activities.
5. What can schools do to address each of the following issues?
   - Poverty
   - Different family structures
   - Parental income
   - Substance abuse
   - Dropping out
   - Obesity and eating disorders
   - Bullying

Source: Library of Congress Prints and Photographs Division [LC-USZ62-42810]

> *Education then, beyond all other devices of human origin, is the great equalizer of the conditions of men, the balance-wheel of the social machinery.*
>
> **HORACE MANN**

chapter 5

The Multicultural History of American Education

Focus Questions

1. What was the nature and purpose of colonial education?
2. How did the Common School Movement promote universal education?
3. What developments mark the educational history of Native Americans?
4. How did teaching become a "gendered" career?
5. How did secondary schools evolve?
6. What were the main tenets of the Progressive Education movement?
7. What role has the federal government played in American education?
8. How did history shape the educational experiences of African Americans, Hispanics, Asian Americans/Pacific Islanders, and Arab Americans?
9. What educational barriers and breakthroughs have girls and women experienced?
10. Who are some of the influential educators who have helped fashion today's schools?

Chapter Preview

In this chapter, we will trace American education from colonial times to the present. You will discover how social class, race, ethnicity, gender, and religion influenced American education throughout history. Education during the colonial period was intended to further religious goals and was offered primarily to white males—typically, wealthy white males. Over time, educational exclusivity diminished and learning goals changed, but even today, wealth, race, and gender continue to have an impact on educational quality. In this chapter, we share the story of America's struggle to honor its commitment to equality by opening the schoolhouse door to more of our diverse citizens.

Understanding the history of America's schools offers you perspective—a sense of your place in your new profession. Your classroom is a living tribute to past achievements and sacrifices. We will begin by looking into the classroom of Christopher Lamb, a New England teacher in one of the earliest American schools, more than three centuries ago.

Christopher Lamb's Colonial Classroom

The frigid wintry wind knifed through Christopher Lamb's coat, chilling him to the bone as he walked in the predawn darkness. The single bucket of firewood that he lugged, intended to keep his seventeenth-century New England schoolroom warm all day, would clearly not do the job. Once the fire was started, Christopher focused on his other teaching tasks: carrying in a bucket of water for the class, sweeping the floor, and mending the ever so fragile pen points for the students. Margaret, who loved school, was the first student to arrive. Like most girls, she would stay in school for only a year or two to learn to read the Bible so that she could be a better wife and mother. With any luck, she might even learn to write her name before she left school. But that was really not important for girls. The other students found their way to either the boys' bench or the girls' bench, where, in turn, they read their Testament aloud.

Christopher was amazed at how poorly some students read, tripping over every other word, whereas others read quite fluently. The last student to finish, Benjamin, slowly rose from the bench, cringing. Christopher called out, "Lazy pupil," and a chorus of children's voices chimed in: "Lazy pupil. Lazy pupil. Lazy pupil." Benjamin, if not totally inured to the taunts, was no longer crushed by them, either. After the recitation and writing lessons, all the children were lined up and examined, to make certain they had washed and combed. For ten minutes, the class and the teacher knelt in prayer. Each student then recited the day's biblical lesson.

Christopher Lamb had been an apprentice teacher for five years before accepting this position. He rejected the rod approach used so frequently by his master teacher. Using the children to provide rewards and punishments was far more effective than welts and bruises, marks left by a teacher's rod. Yes, Christopher was somewhat unorthodox, perhaps even a bit revolutionary, but the challenges of contemporary seventeenth-century society demanded forward-thinking educators such as Christopher Lamb.

Colonial New England Education: God's Classrooms

FOCUS QUESTION 1

What was the nature and purpose of colonial education?

One of the striking differences between Christopher Lamb's colonial classroom and today's typical public school is the role of religion in education. The religious fervor that drove the Puritans to America also drove them to provide religious education for their young, making New England the cradle of American education. In Christopher Lamb's time, school was meant to save souls. Education provided a path to heaven, and reading, writing, and moral development all revolved around the Bible.

Early colonial education, both in New England and in other colonies, often began in the home. (Today's homeschooling movement is not a *new* approach.) The family was the major educational resource for youngsters, and the first lessons typically focused on reading. Values, manners, social graces, and even vocational skills were taught by parents and grandparents. Home instruction eventually became more specialized, and some women began to devote their time to teaching, converting their homes into schools. These "dames" taught reading, writing, and computation, and their homes became known as **dame schools.** A "dame," or well-respected woman with an interest in education, became (for a fee) the community's teacher.

This colonial recitation lesson includes a boy sitting in the corner with a dunce cap. By today's standards, "time out" back then was quite humiliating.

©North Wind Picture Archives/ Alamy

An *apprenticeship* program rounded out a child's colonial education. While boys, sometimes as young as 7 years of age, were sent to live with masters who taught them a trade, girls typically learned homemaking skills from their mothers. Apprenticeship programs for boys involved not only learning skilled crafts but also managing farms and shops. Many colonies required that masters teach reading and writing as well as vocational skills. The masters served ***in loco parentis***—that is, in place of the child's parent. The competencies of the masters guiding apprentices varied greatly, as did the talents of family members, dames, ministers, and others fulfilling the teaching role. Not surprisingly, this educational hodgepodge did not always lead to a well-educated citizenry; a more formal structure was needed.

Twenty-two years after arriving in the New World, the Puritans living in the Commonwealth of Massachusetts passed a law requiring that parents and masters of apprentices be checked periodically to ensure that children were being taught properly. Five years later, in 1647, Massachusetts took even more rigorous measures to ensure the education of its children. The Massachusetts Law of 1647, more commonly known as the **Old Deluder Satan Law**—the Puritans' attempt to thwart Satan's trickery with Scripture-reading citizens—required that

- Every town of fifty households must appoint and pay a teacher of reading and writing.
- Every town of one hundred households must provide a (Latin) grammar school to prepare youths for the university, under a penalty of £5 for failure to do so.[1]

By 1680, such laws had spread throughout most of New England. The settlement patterns of the Puritans, who lived in towns and communities rather than scattered throughout the countryside, made establishing schools relatively uncomplicated. After learning to read and write, most girls returned home to practice the art of housekeeping. Boys who could afford to pay for their education went on to a **Latin grammar school.** In 1635, only fifteen years after arriving in America's wilderness, the Puritans established their first Latin grammar school in Boston. The Boston Latin Grammar School was not unlike a "prep" school for boys and was similar to the classical schools of Europe. The Boston Latin Grammar School was a rather exclusive school for boys of wealth, charging tuition to teach boys between the ages of 7 and 14. (Within a year of the founding of the Boston Latin Grammar School, Harvard College was established specifically to prepare ministers. Founded in 1636, Harvard was the first college in America, the jewel in the Puritans' religious and educational crown.)

Many consider the Boston Latin Grammar School to be the first step on the road to creating the American high school, although the school's curriculum reflected European roots. Students were expected to read and recite (in Latin, of course) the works of Cicero, Ovid, and Erasmus. In Greek, they read the works of Socrates and Homer. (Back to basics in colonial times meant back to the glory of Rome and Greece.) By the eighteenth century, the grammar school had incorporated mathematics, science, and modern languages. Classes started at 7 a.m., recessed at 11 a.m., and picked up from 1 p.m. until 5 p.m. Graduates were expected to go on to college and become colonial leaders, especially ministers.

For attendance at exclusive schools, such as Boston Latin Grammar, or at college, wealth was critical. The least desirable educational and apprenticeship opportunities were left to the poor. Some civic-minded communities made basic education in reading and writing more available to the poor, but only to families who would publicly admit their poverty by signing a "Pauper's Oath." Broadcasting one's poverty was no less offensive in colonial times than today, and many chose to have their children remain illiterate rather than sign such a public admission. The result was that most poor children remained outside the educational system.

Blacks, in America since 1619, and Native Americans were typically denied educational opportunities. In rare cases, religious groups, such as the Quakers, created special schools for children of color.[2] But those were the exceptions. Girls did not fare much better. After they had learned the rudiments of reading and writing, girls were taught the tasks related to their future roles as mother and wife. They were taught handicrafts. Girls memorized the alphabet and then learned to stitch and display their accomplishments. They also learned to reproduce and attractively display religious sayings, on the road to becoming good Christian wives and mothers. Much as we value these beautiful samplers today, they are a sad reminder of a time when they marked the academic finish line for girls, the diploma of a second-rate education, a depressing denial of equal educational rights. Later in this chapter, we will describe in more detail the barriers separating many Americans from a quality education.

Location greatly influenced educational opportunities. The northern colonies were settled by Puritans, who lived in towns and communities relatively close to one another. Their religious fervor and proximity made the creation of community schools dedicated to teaching the Bible a predictable development.

In the middle colonies, the range of European religious and ethnic groups (Puritans, Catholics, Mennonites, the Dutch, and Swedes) created, if not a melting pot, a limited tolerance for diversity.[3] Various religious groups established schools, and apprenticeships groomed youngsters for a variety of careers, including teaching. In the middle colonies, the development of commerce and mercantile demands promoted the formation of private schools devoted to job training. By the 1700s, private teachers and night schools were functioning in Philadelphia and New York, teaching accounting, navigation, French, and Spanish.

The first city in North America was St. Augustine, Florida, where there is evidence that the Spanish settlers established schools. The southern English colonies trailed behind in education. The rural, sparsely populated southern colonies developed an educational system that was responsive to plantation society. Wealthy plantation owners took tutors into their homes to teach their children not only basic academic skills but also the social graces appropriate to their station in life. Plantation owners' children learned the proper way to entertain guests and "manage" slaves, using such texts as *The Complete Gentleman.* Wealthy young men seeking higher education were sent to Europe. Poor white children might have had rudimentary home instruction in reading, writing, and computation.

Black children made do with little if any instruction and, as time went by, encountered laws that actually prohibited their education entirely.[4]

Education has come a long way from colonial days and from Christopher Lamb's class—or has it? Consider the following:

1. The colonial experience established many of today's educational norms:
   - Local control of schools
   - Compulsory education
   - Tax-supported schools
   - State standards for teaching and schools
2. The colonial experience highlighted many of the persistent tension points challenging schools today:
   - What is the role of religion in the classroom?
   - How can we equalize the quality of education in various communities?
   - How can the barriers of racism, sexism, religious intolerance, and classism be eliminated so that all children receive equal educational opportunity?
   - How can we prepare the most competent teachers?

A New Nation Shapes Education

The ideas that led to the American Revolution revolutionized our schools. European beliefs and practices, which had pervaded America's schools, were gradually abandoned as the new national character was formed. Importantly, none of these European beliefs had been more firmly adhered to than the integration of the state and religion.

In addition to serving two terms as president of the United States, Thomas Jefferson was the colonial era's most eloquent spokesperson for education and was the founder of the University of Virginia.
©Hisham Ibrahim/Getty Images RF

In sixteenth- and seventeenth-century England, the Puritans' desire to reform the Church of England was viewed as treason. The Puritans encountered both religious and political opposition, and they looked to the New World as an escape from persecution. However, they came to America *not* to establish religious freedom, as our history books sometimes suggest, but to establish their own church as supreme, both religiously and politically. The Puritans were neither tolerant of other religions nor interested in separating religion and politics. Nonconformers, such as the Quakers, were vigorously persecuted. The purpose of the Massachusetts colony was to establish the "true" religion of the Puritans in America. Schools were simply an extension of the religious state, designed to teach the young to read and understand the Bible and to do honorable battle with Satan.

During the 1700s, American education was reconstructed to meet broader, nonsectarian goals. Such leaders as **Thomas Jefferson** wanted to go beyond educating a small elite class or providing only religious instruction. Jefferson maintained that education should be more widely available to white children from all economic and social classes. Public citizens began to question the usefulness of rudimentary skills taught in a school year of just three or four months. They questioned the value of mastering Greek and Latin classics in the Latin grammar schools, when practical skills were in short supply in the New World.

In 1749, **Benjamin Franklin** penned *Proposals Relating to the Youth of Pennsylvania,* suggesting a new kind of secondary school to replace the Latin grammar school—the

A CLOSER LOOK

Early Textbooks

As a teacher, you will come across references to some of the limited but influential curriculum materials of the past. Here is a brief profile of the best-known instructional materials from yesterday's schools.

HORNBOOK

The most common teaching device in colonial schools, the **hornbook** consisted of an alphabet sheet covered by a thin, transparent sheet made from a cow's horn. The alphabet and the horn covering were tacked to a paddle-shaped piece of wood and often hung by a leather strap around the student's neck. Originating in medieval Europe, the hornbook provided colonial children with their introduction to the alphabet and reading.

NEW ENGLAND PRIMER

The first real textbook, the ***New England Primer*** was a tiny 2½- by 4½-inch book containing 50 to 100 pages of alphabet, words, and small verses accompanied by woodcut illustrations. First published in 1690, it was virtually the only reading text used in colonial schools until about 1800. The Primer reflected the religious orientation of colonial schools. A typical verse was

> In Adam's Fall
> We sinned all.
> Thy Life to mend,
> This Book attend
> The idle fool
> Is whipt at School.

AMERICAN SPELLING BOOK

The task undertaken by Noah Webster was to define and nourish the new American culture. His ***American Spelling Book*** replaced the *New England Primer* as the most common elementary textbook. The book contained the alphabet, syllables, consonants, rules for speaking, readings, short stories, and moral advice. The bulk of the book was taken up by lists of words. Royalty income from the sale of millions of copies of this book supported Webster in his other efforts to standardize the American language, including his best-known work, which is still used today, the *American Dictionary.*

MCGUFFEY READERS

William Holmes McGuffey was a minister, professor, and college president who believed that clean living, hard work, and literacy were the virtues to instill in children. He wrote a series of readers that emphasized the work ethic, patriotism, heroism, and morality. It is estimated that more than 100 million copies of *McGuffey Readers* educated several generations of Americans between 1836 and 1920. ***McGuffey Readers*** are noteworthy because they were geared for different grade levels and paved the way for graded elementary schools.

REFLECTION: Can you detect the morals and traditional values being promoted in today's texts? Can you cite any examples?

academy. Two years later, the *Franklin Academy* was established, free of religious influence and offering a variety of practical subjects, including mathematics, astronomy, athletics, navigation, dramatics, and bookkeeping. Students were able to choose some of their courses, thus setting the precedent for elective courses and programs at the secondary level. The Franklin Academy accepted both girls and boys who could afford the tuition, and the practical curriculum became an attractive innovation. Franklin's Academy sparked the establishment of six thousand academies in the century that followed. The original Franklin Academy eventually became the University of Pennsylvania.[5]

Jefferson's commitment to educating all white Americans, rich and poor, at government expense and Franklin's commitment to a practical program of nonsectarian study offering elective courses severed American educational thought from its European roots. Many years passed before these ideas became widely established practices, but the pattern for innovation and a truly American approach to education was taking shape. (For a description of texts that shaped early American education, see A Closer Look: Early Textbooks.)

The Common School Movement

FOCUS QUESTION 2

How did the Common School Movement promote universal education?

During the early decades of the nineteenth century, the democratic ideal became popular as many "common people"—immigrants, small farmers, and urban laborers—demanded greater participation in the democracy. With the election of Andrew Jackson in 1828, the voices of many poor white people were heard, particularly their demands for educational access. Many more decades would pass before additional voices—particularly those of people of color—would also be heard.

Horace Mann became the nation's leading advocate for the establishment of a **common school** open to all. Today, we know this common school as the public **elementary school**. Historians consider Horace Mann to be the outstanding proponent of education for the common person (the Common School Movement), and he is often referred to as "the father of the public school." Mann helped create the Massachusetts State Board of Education and in 1837 became its secretary, a position similar to today's state superintendent of schools. In this role, Mann began an effort to reform education, believing that public education should serve both practical and idealistic goals. In practical terms, both business and industry would benefit from educated workers, resulting in a more productive economy. In idealistic terms, public schools should help us identify and nurture the talents in poor as well as wealthy children, and schools should ameliorate social disharmony.[6] Mann decried the rifts between rich and poor, Calvinists and religious reformers, new Irish immigrants and native workers. A common school instilling common and humane moral values could reduce such social disharmony (a popular belief today as well). Mann attempted to promote such values, but he encountered strong opposition when the values he selected revealed a distinct religious bias, one that offended Calvinists, atheists, Jews, Catholics, and others. His moral program to create a common set of beliefs had the opposite impact, igniting a dispute over the role of religion in school.

The idea of public education is so commonplace today that it seems difficult to imagine another system. But Horace Mann, along with such allies as Henry Barnard of Connecticut, fought a long and difficult battle to win the acceptance of public elementary schools. The opposition was powerful. Business interests predicted disaster if their labor pool of children were taken away. Concerned taxpayers protested the additional tax monies needed to support public education. There was also the competition. Private schools and religious groups sponsoring their own schools protested the establishment of free schools. Americans wondered what would become of a nation in which everyone received an elementary education. Would this not produce overeducated citizens, questioning authority, and promoting self-interest? The opposition to public elementary schools was often fierce, but Horace Mann and his allies prevailed.

GLOBAL VIEW

The United States has not ratified the *Convention on the Rights of the Child* (1990), which requires free compulsory primary education and equal treatment regardless of gender, race, or cultural background for children worldwide.

As he fought for public schools for all, Mann also waged a battle for high-quality schools. He continually attempted to build new and better schools, which was a problem, because so many Massachusetts schools were in deplorable condition. By publicly disseminating information about which communities had well-built or poorly built schools, he applied public pressure on districts to improve their school buildings. He worked for effective teacher training programs as well and promoted more stringent teacher licensing procedures. As a result of his efforts, several **normal schools** were founded in Massachusetts, schools devoted to preparing teachers in pedagogy, the best ways to teach children. He opposed the routine practice of corporal punishment and sought ways to positively motivate students to learn. Mann emphasized practical subjects useful to children and to adult society, rather than the mastery of Greek and Latin. Mann saw education as a great investment, for individuals and for the country, and he worked for many years to make free public education a reality. He worked for the abolition of slavery, promoted women's educational and economic rights, and even fought alongside the temperance movement to limit the negative impact of alcohol. He was not only a committed educator but a committed reformer as well.

By the time of the Civil War, this radical notion of the public elementary school had become widespread and widely accepted. Educational historian Lawrence Cremin summarized the advance of the common school movement in his book *The Transformation of the School:*

> A majority of the states had established public school systems, and a good half of the nation's children were already getting some formal education. Elementary schools were becoming widely available; in some states, like Massachusetts, New York, and Pennsylvania, the notion of free public education was slowly expanding to include secondary schools; and in a few, like Michigan and Wisconsin, the public school system was already capped by a state university. There were, of course, significant variations from state to state and from region to region. New England, long a pioneer in public education, also had an established tradition of private education, and private schools continued to flourish there. The Midwest, on the other hand, sent a far greater proportion of its school children to public institutions. The southern states, with the exception of North Carolina, tended to lag behind, and did not generally establish popular schooling until after the Civil War.[7]

Native American Tribes: The History of Miseducation

FOCUS QUESTION 3

What developments mark the educational history of Native Americans?

While the notion of universal education, especially at the elementary level, spread slowly among Americans of European ancestry, many who lived here were not European. In fact, Europeans were the late arrivals. It is estimated that 50 to 100 million Native Americans occupied both North and South America before Columbus arrived.[8] Within a relatively brief time following European arrival, more than 90 percent of them would be dead from disease, starvation, and conquest. The survivors in the United States would soon experience what many describe as an attempt to kill their culture through education. Church missionaries educated Native peoples to abandon their history and language to become "civilized Christians." Native beliefs, customs, and languages were systematically ridiculed and repressed.[9] (Do today's school mascots continue the denigration of Native culture? See You Be the Judge: School Mascots on p. 121.)

Despite adverse conditions, Native Americans achieved some extraordinary educational accomplishments. For example, when their oral traditions and beliefs were discredited, Sequoyah invented a Cherokee syllabary in 1822. This permitted the Cherokee language to be written. Books were published in Cherokee; Cherokee schools became bilingual; and the Cherokee nation wrote, edited, and published the *Cherokee Phoenix*, a bilingual weekly newspaper. However, as federal interventions became more systematic, the tribes' control over their own education diminished.

In 1824, the federal government established the Bureau of Indian Affairs (BIA) and began placing whole tribes of Native peoples on reservations. The BIA continued to use education as a tool of cultural conquest. Indian reservations saw more white superintendents, farm agents, teachers, inspectors, and missionaries. Indian boarding schools were established to assimilate young Native Americans into the dominant European American values: veneration of property, individual competition, European-style domesticity, toil, and European standards of dress. Many Native Americans refused to send their children to reservation schools. Arrest and kidnapping were common practices in forcing Native American children to attend. Rations were often withheld from parents as a means of compelling them to send their children to school.

YOU BE THE JUDGE

School Mascots

SHOULD CHANGE WITH THE TIMES BECAUSE . . .

MASCOT NAMES CAN BE HURTFUL

A pep rally featuring chanting "Indians" shaking rubber tomahawks trivializes meaningful rituals and cultural differences. Names such as the "Lady Navajos" or "Tigerettes" perpetuate an image of female inferiority and the second-class status of their sports.

MASCOT NAMES PROMOTE VIOLENCE

Stands filled with "Redskins" wielding tomahawks and chanting insults bring us all closer to potential violence and injury. Mascots should build a positive climate, not a destructive one.

WE SHOULD SET AN EXAMPLE FOR STUDENTS

We must teach by example, and changing offensive mascot names gives us that opportunity. By adopting names like "Freedom" or "Liberty," we teach our children how names can model our historical best, not our historical bigotries, and how adults can learn from past mistakes.

SHOULD NOT CHANGE OVER TIME BECAUSE . . .

IT'S JUST A NAME

There are more important issues to address than changing names of athletic teams. Exaggerated complaints about mascot names consume hours of school board meetings—and only show how political correctness is driving the times.

MASCOT NAMES BUILD SCHOOL SPIRIT

Proud mascot names like the "Warriors" highlight courage and bravery. Mascot names instill school spirit, a trait sorely needed by today's young people.

TRADITION MATTERS

Some things really do need to stay the same. Building a positive and stable school community is hard enough with people constantly moving and families splitting. School mascot names provide stability, and do not mindlessly mirror every passing fad.

connect YOU DECIDE...

You and your classmates may want to share your own experiences on this hot-button issue. Should any mascot names be changed? Which names and why (or why not)? Brainstorm positive team names and mascots. This may be more challenging than you think. To understand more about mascots and American Indians, visit www.racismagainstindians.org.

Today, more than half of the Native Americans in this country do not live on reservations. The vast majority of Native children are educated in public schools where they have lost their "critical mass," which is often associated with higher achievement. Native American students have the highest dropout rate of all students and are more likely to struggle with alcohol and drug addiction.[10]

In an effort to improve the lives of Native people, recent decades have witnessed renewed efforts by Native Americans to win control of the reservations, including the schools. Tribes feel strongly that such control will maintain cultural identity, as well as increase the academic achievement of their children.

Spinsters, Bachelors, and Gender Barriers in Teaching

Although today's perception is that teaching is predominantly a female career, in fact, men dominated teaching well into the mid-nineteenth century. Teaching was (and still is) a **gendered career,** and it was initially gendered "male." Although a few women taught at home in *dame schools,* the first women to become teachers in regular school settings, earning a public salary, were viewed as gender trespassers, "unsexed" by their ambition, and considered masculine. Concerned by this negative characterization, early feminists such as Catherine Beecher implored female teachers to accentuate their

FOCUS QUESTION 4

How did teaching become a "gendered" career?

feminine traits, highlight their domestic skills, and continue their preparation for marriage.[11] Despite the national reluctance to allow women into the workforce, and despite the perception that teachers should be male, the demand for more and inexpensive teachers created by common schools made the hiring of women teachers inevitable.

By the early part of the twentieth century, women constituted upward of 90 percent of teachers. But not all women were equally welcome. School districts preferred "spinsters," women unmarried and unlikely to marry. Such women would not suffer the dual loyalties inherent in "serving" both husband and employer. Unmarried women were hired so frequently in the late nineteenth and early twentieth century that teaching and spinsterhood became synonymous. Cartoonists, authors, and reporters made the spinster schoolteacher a cultural icon. Boarding and rooming houses, and eventually small apartments, sometimes called *teacher-ages,* were built to provide accommodations for this new class of workers. Teaching was gendered again, but now it was gendered "female."

As women came to dominate teaching, the gender tables were turned, and a new concern arose: the fear that female teachers were "feminizing" boys. There were demands to bring men back to teaching and to halt the "feminization" of young schoolboys. President Theodore Roosevelt added a touch of racism to the debate, arguing that because so many white women were choosing teaching over motherhood, they were committing "race suicide," and the continuance of the white race was in jeopardy.[12] School districts responded by actively recruiting male teachers, and male educators carved out their own niches in school systems. Administration, coaching, vocational education, and certain high school departments, specifically science and math, became male bastions.

For women, teaching meant economic and financial liberation. But not without cost. The dedicated teaching *spinsters* of the nineteenth century became the object of ridicule in the twentieth century. Women choosing teaching over motherhood were considered unnatural by a mostly male cadre of psychologists, physicians, and authors. Articles and books began to appear early in the twentieth century arguing that being unmarried caused women to be spiteful, hateful, and disgusting. The eminent psychologist G. Stanley Hall wrote an article entitled "Certain Degenerative Tendencies among Teachers," explaining why unmarried women were frustrated, bitter, and otherwise unpleasant. Stage shows and movies picked up the theme, portraying lesbian relationships in and beyond school settings. The National Education Association reacted by campaigning for school districts to drop their ban against hiring married women. But when the depression hit in the 1930s, the idea of hiring wives and creating two-income families was anathema: The scarce jobs were to be funneled to women living alone or to men, the family "breadwinners." It was not until the end of World War II that most school districts even employed married women.

Men who remained in teaching also paid a price. Conventional wisdom early in the twentieth century held that effeminate men were gay men and that gay men were naturally drawn to teaching. Worse yet, gay men were considered to be a teaching time bomb, because they would be poor role models for children. All male teachers became suspect, and few were drawn to teaching. School districts avoided hiring men who did not possess a clearly masculine demeanor. (Married men with children were preferred.) The Cold War and the accompanying McCarthy anti-Communist scare of the 1950s declared war on liberal ideas and unconventional choices: Homosexuality was seen as a threat to America. "There was a list of about twenty-one things that you could be fired for. The first was to be a card-carrying Communist, and the second was to be a homosexual."[13] Single teachers declared their "healthy" heterosexuality, and gay teachers stayed hidden. During this time, the number of married teachers doubled.

A View from the Field: Male Teachers

As an elementary school teacher, Kyle Birstler, 25, is unusual: He is one of only five male teachers at Jackson Road Elementary School in Silver Spring, Maryland. But Kyle feels that the fact that he is a male elementary teacher makes a difference to his students.

> In my first year of teaching I was given a class that I've now become quite accustomed to: a class of all or almost all boys, most of them from broken homes with absent father figures. These students can be tough, but sometimes it takes a man's approach, or just the presence, to win them over. Every year, I have had students lose their tough guy images and come talk to me about what is going on in their lives. I chose to teach in this school because it is a Title I school; I knew there were needs that I hoped to be able to meet.

Kyle was drawn to teaching at an early age by the compassion of a concerned teacher.

> I had wanted to be a paleontologist when I was growing up. I wanted to discover dinosaurs and name them after myself. On a first-grade field trip I met a real paleontologist and I told him my dream. He told me my dream was next to impossible. I cried and my first-grade teacher comforted me. Next thing you know, I wanted to teach. I have always wanted to teach younger students but during my student teaching I worked in a phenomenal fifth-grade classroom; I was hooked. I couldn't believe how independent the students could be. It was very fun and I've been teaching fifth grade since.

Though Kyle feels that the challenges he faced as a new teacher had more to do with his inexperience than his gender, he does advise new male teachers to find confidants.

> I'd advise male teachers to find mentors of their own, a professor or a male teacher in their building. They'll want a buddy to talk to and bounce ideas off of, and sometimes it's nice to get away. I know the things I learned in my first week of being in the classroom far outweighed anything I learned in the university setting. I was one of three men in my program and it (the issue of men as early childhood educators) simply didn't come up. In general, I think you cannot learn enough about classroom management and the social and emotional issues that impact your students. It's the hardest, most exciting job I can think of.

Courtesy of Kyle Birstler.

Kyle Birstler graduated from American University in Washington, D.C.

Although recent years have witnessed a loosening of gender straitjackets, sex stereotypes, myths, and bigotry against gays continue to restrict and confine both women and men. Men drawn to teaching young children and women seeking leadership roles confront both barriers and social sanctions. As long as these gender and sexual barriers persist, we are all the poorer. (See Contemporary Issues: A View from the Field.)

The Secondary School Movement

FOCUS QUESTION 5

How did secondary schools evolve?

With Horace Mann's success in promoting public elementary schools, more and more citizens were given a basic education. In 1880, almost 10 million Americans were enrolled in elementary schools, and, at the upper levels of schooling, both private and public universities were established. But the gap between the elementary schools and the universities remained wide.

Massachusetts, the site of the first tax-supported elementary schools and the first college in America (Harvard), was also the site of the first free secondary school. Established in Boston in 1821, the **English Classical School** enrolled 176 students (all boys). The notion of a public high school was slow to take root. It was not until 1852 that Boston was able to maintain a similar school for girls.

As secondary schools spread, they generally took the form of private, tuition-charging academies. Citizens did not view the secondary schools as we do today, as a free and natural extension of elementary education. A major stumbling block to

A CLOSER LOOK

The Development of American Schools

ELEMENTARY SCHOOLS

Dame Schools (1600s) These private schools taught by women in their homes offered child care for working parents willing to pay a fee. The dames who taught here received meager wages, and the quality of instruction varied greatly.

Local Schools (1600s–1800s) First started in towns and later expanded to include larger districts, these schools were open to those who could afford to pay. Found generally in New England, these schools taught basic skills and religion.

Itinerant Schools (1700s) and Tutors (1600s–1900s) Rural America could not support schools and full-time teachers. As a result, in sparsely populated New England, itinerant teachers carried schooling from village to village; they lived in people's homes and provided instruction. In the South, private tutors taught the rich. Traveling teachers and tutors, usually working for a fee and room and board, took varying levels of education to small towns and wealthy populations.

Private Schools (1700s–1800s) Private schools, often located in the middle colonies, offered a variety of special studies. These schools constituted a true free market, as parents paid for the kind of private school they desired. As you might imagine, both the curricula and the quality of these schools varied greatly.

Common (Elementary) Schools (1830–present) The common school was a radical departure from earlier ones in several ways. First, it was free. Parents did not have to pay tuition or fees. Second, it was open to all social classes. Previously, schools usually taught either middle-class or upper-class children. Horace Mann's common school was intended to bring democracy to the classroom. By the mid-nineteenth century, kindergarten was added. In the past few decades, many common schools, now called *elementary schools,* have added Head Start and other prekindergarten programs.

SECONDARY SCHOOLS

Latin Grammar Schools (1600s–1700s) These schools prepared wealthy men for college and emphasized a classical curriculum, including Latin and some Greek. From European roots, the curriculum in these schools reflected the belief that the pinnacle of civilization was reached in the Roman Empire.

English Grammar Schools (1700s) These private schools moved away from the classical Latin tradition to more practical studies. These schools were viewed not as preparation for college but as preparation for business careers and as a means of instilling social graces. Some of these schools set a precedent by admitting white girls, thus paving the way for the widespread acceptance of females in other schools.

Academies (1700s–1800s) The academies were a combination of the Latin and English grammar schools. These schools taught English, not Latin. Practical courses were taught, but history and the classics were also included. Some academies emphasized college preparation, and others prepared students to enter business and vocations.

High Schools (1800s–present) These secondary schools differed from their predecessors in that they were free; they were governed not by private boards but by the public. The high school can be viewed as an extension of the Common School Movement to the secondary level. High schools were open to all social classes and provided both precollege and career education.

Junior High Schools (1909–present) and Middle Schools (1950s–present) Junior high schools (grades 7–9) and middle schools (grades 5–8) were designed to meet the unique needs of preadolescents and to prepare them for the high school experience.

Charter Schools (1991–present) Charters are tax-supported elementary and secondary schools that are free from some of the rules and regulations that apply to other public schools. A type of choice school, charters are created with unique missions, instructional strategies, or curriculum designs.

REFLECTION: If you were responsible for creating a new school based on contemporary needs, what kind of school would you create?

GLOBAL VIEW

Choose any country in the developing world. Explore how gender, race, class, and geography affect educational opportunities.

the creation of free high schools was public resistance to paying additional school taxes. (Sound familiar?) But, in a series of court cases, especially the **Kalamazoo, Michigan, case** in 1874, the courts ruled that taxes could be used to support secondary schools. In Michigan, citizens already had access to free elementary schools and a state-supported university. The courts saw a lack of rationality in not providing a bridge between the two.[14] The idea of public high school slowly took hold.

During the last half of the nineteenth century, the nation moved from agrarian to industrial, from mostly rural to urban, and people viewed the elementary school as inadequate to meet the needs of a more sophisticated and industrialized society.

More parents viewed the high school as an important stepping stone to better jobs. With the gradual decrease in demand for teenage workers, high school attendance grew. The high school became a continuation of elementary education, a path to public higher education, and an affirmation of democracy. (See A Closer Look: The Development of American Schools on p. 124.)

Although the high school grew in popularity, it did not meet the needs of all its students. The junior high school, first established in 1909 in Columbus, Ohio, included grades 7, 8, and 9, and was designed to meet the unique needs of preadolescents. More individualized instruction, a strong emphasis on guidance and counseling, and a core curriculum were designed to respond to the academic, physiological, social, and psychological characteristics of preadolescents. The junior high school concept was further refined in the middle school, which included grades 5 through 8.

During the last decades of the twentieth and into the twenty-first centuries, the academic effectiveness of public schools was being questioned, and sparked calls for reform.

A Brief History of Educational Reform

> Our Nation is at risk. Our once unchallenged prominence in commerce, industry, science, and technological innovation is being overtaken by competitors through-out the world. . . . If an unfriendly foreign power had attempted to impose on America the mediocre educational performance that exists today, we might well have viewed it as an act of war. . . . We have, in effect, been committing an act of unthinking, unilateral educational disarmament.[15]

So began the 1983 report of the National Commission on Excellence in Education, ***A Nation at Risk: The Imperative for Educational Reform.*** The report cited declining test scores, the weak performance of U.S. students compared with students in other industrialized nations, the fear that the United States is losing ground economically to other countries, and the high number of functionally illiterate Americans. *A Nation at Risk* put school reform in the national spotlight. In response to the report, states increased the number of course requirements needed for graduation and required more testing of both students and teachers. Today, decades later, even more importance has been given to these tests. (See Chapter 9 for a detailed discussion on current reform efforts.) Although low international test scores and the global economy fuel the demand for better schools, reforming schools actually began more than 100 years ago.

By the late 1800s, the United States was undergoing profound economic and social transformations. Vast new industries and giant corporations were being formed and factory labor was being exploited; massive numbers of immigrants were arriving, the population was surging, and urban America was growing; traditional agrarian life was disappearing. How should schools respond? In 1892, the National Education Association (NEA) established the *Committee of Ten* to develop a national policy for high schools. The Committee, composed for the most part of college presidents and professors, wanted consistency and order in the high school curriculum for an easier transition into college. The committee report required that high schools teach certain required courses four or five times a week for one year and that student progress be measured by *Carnegie Units.* Now it became easier for colleges to decide which students were prepared to do college-level work.

The NEA repeated the process in 1918, but this time committee members focused not on transition to college but on preparing adults for their life roles. The truth is, very few Americans went on to college at that time; most went on to work and family. The committee wanted to know: What can high school do to improve the daily lives of citizens in an industrial democracy? This committee's report, *Cardinal Principles of*

Secondary Education, identified seven goals for high school: (1) health, (2) worthy home membership, (3) command of fundamental academic skills, (4) vocation, (5) citizenship, (6) worthy use of leisure time, and (7) ethical character. The high school was seen as a socializing agency, an opportunity to improve all aspects of a citizen's life. (More than a century later, those 1918 goals still sound balanced and useful.)

John Dewey and Progressive Education

FOCUS QUESTION 6

What were the main tenets of the Progressive Education movement?

Efforts to improve pubic high schools marked one important reform movement; the growth of progressive education signaled another. **Progressive education** includes several components. First, it broadens the school program to include health concerns, family and community life issues, and a concern for vocational education. Second, progressivism applies new research in psychology and the social sciences to classroom practices. Third, progressivism emphasizes a more democratic educational approach, accepting the interests and needs of an increasingly diverse student body.

This model of education assumes that students learn best when their learning follows their interests. Progressivists believe that knowledge is not an inert body of facts to be committed to memory; rather, it consists of experiences that should be used to help solve present problems. Passively listening to the teacher, according to the progressive movement, is not the most effective learning strategy. Students' interests should serve as a springboard to understanding and mastering contemporary issues. The role of the teacher is to identify student needs and interests and provide an educational environment that builds on them.

Progressive principles, such as student-centered, problem-based learning, began influencing education as early as 1875 when Francis Parker, superintendent of schools in Quincy, Massachusetts, introduced them to his teachers. But it took decades for progressive education to take root and challenge traditional teaching practices in other places. Not until the 1920s and 1930s did the progressive education movement spread to schools across the country, due in large part to the advocacy of **John Dewey,** considered by many to be the most influential educator of the twentieth century. (Dewey was born on the eve of the Civil War in 1859 and died during the Korean War in the early 1950s.) Many considered Dewey as a savior of schools, while others accused him of nearly destroying them.

The criticism of Dewey and progressive education came from individuals who felt that the school curriculum was not academically sound and undermined traditional American values. Hyman Rickover, a famous admiral and developer of the nuclear submarine, and Arthur Bestor, a liberal arts professor, were among the foremost critics decrying the ills of progressive education. They called for an end to "student-centered" and "life-adjustment" subjects and a return to a more rigorous study of traditional courses. While the arguments raged, the launching of *Sputnik* by the Soviet Union in 1957 put at least a temporary closure on the debate. The United States was involved in a space race with the Soviets, a race to educate scientists and engineers, a race toward the first moon landing. Those arguing for a more rigorous, science- and math-focused curriculum won the day. Although many still argued vociferously over the benefits and shortcomings of progressive education, traditionalists were setting the direction for the nation's curriculum.

Before leaving progressive education, however, it will be beneficial to examine one of the most famous studies of the progressive movement. The Progressive Education Association, formed in 1919, initiated a study during the 1930s that compared almost three thousand graduates of progressive and of traditional schools as they made their way through college. The study, called the Eight-Year Study, was intended to determine which educational approach was more effective. The results indicated that graduates of progressive schools:

1. Earned a slightly higher grade point average
2. Earned higher grades in all fields except foreign languages
3. Tended to specialize in the same fields as more traditional students
4. Received slightly more academic honors
5. Were judged to be more objective and more precise thinkers
6. Were judged to possess higher intellectual curiosity and greater drive

The Federal Government

FOCUS QUESTION 7

What role has the federal government played in American education?

As World War II drew to a close, the United States found itself the most powerful nation on earth. For the remainder of the twentieth century, the United States reconstructed a war-ravaged global economy while confronting world communism. In fact, the United States viewed education as an important tool in accomplishing those strategic goals. When the Soviets launched *Sputnik,* for example, the government enlisted the nation's schools in meeting that new challenge. Consequently, Congress passed the **National Defense Education Act (NDEA)** in 1958 to enhance "the security of the nation" and to develop "the mental resources and technical skills of its young men and women." The NDEA supported the improvement of instruction and curriculum development, funded teacher training programs, and provided loans and scholarships for college students that allowed them to major in subjects deemed important to the national defense (such as teaching). However, looking back in history, it is not at all clear how the federal government was legally able to do that. After all, the framers of the Constitution made their intentions clear: Education was to be a state responsibility, and the federal government was not to be involved. How did the NDEA and other federal acts come to pass?

Many people are unaware that the responsibility for educating Americans is not even mentioned in the Constitution. Under the **Tenth Amendment,** any area not specifically stated in the Constitution as a federal responsibility is automatically assigned to the states. Why was education a nontopic? Some historians believe that because the individual colonies had already established disparate educational systems, the framers of the Constitution did not want to create dissension by forcing the states to accept a single educational system. Other analysts believe that education was deliberately omitted from the Constitution because Americans feared control of the schools by a central government, any central government, as had been the case in Europe. They saw central control as a possible threat to their freedom. Still others suggest that the framers of the Constitution, in their haste, bartering, and bickering, simply forgot about education. (What a depressing thought!) Whatever the reason, distinct colonial practices continued as each state created its own educational structure—its own approach for preparing teachers and funding schools.

Over time, however, the federal government discovered ways to influence education. (A Closer Look: Selected Federal Legislation on p. 128 offers a snapshot of some federal education roles.) As early as the revolutionary period, the new nation passed the **Land Ordinance Act** of 1785 and the **Northwest Ordinance** of 1787. These acts required

A CLOSER LOOK

Selected Federal Legislation

The following is a partial list of legislation indicating the long history of federal involvement in education.

1. *Land Ordinance Act* and *Northwest Ordinance* (1785 and 1787). These two ordinances provided for the establishment of public education in the territory between the Appalachian Mountains and the Mississippi River. In these new territories, one square mile out of every thirty-six was reserved for support of public education, and new states formed from these territories were encouraged to establish "schools and the means for education."
2. *Morrill Land Grant College Acts* (1862 and 1890). These acts established sixty-nine institutions of higher education in the various states, some of which are among today's great state universities. These acts were also called simply the *Land-Grant College Acts,* because public land was donated to establish these colleges.
3. *Smith-Hughes Act* (1917). This act provided funds for teacher training and program development in vocational education at the high school level.
4. *Servicemen's Readjustment Act* (G.I. Bill of Rights, 1944). This act paid veterans' tuition and living expenses for a specific number of months, depending on the length of their military service.
5. *National Defense Education Act* (1958). In response to the Soviet launching of *Sputnik,* the NDEA provided substantial funds for a variety of educational activities, including student loans, the education of school counselors, and the strengthening of instructional programs in science, mathematics, and foreign languages.
6. *Elementary and Secondary Education Act* (1965). This law provided financial assistance to school districts with low-income families, to improve libraries and instructional materials, and to promote educational innovations and research. In the 1970s, this legislation was expanded to include funding for bilingual and Native American education, drug education, and school lunch and breakfast programs.
7. *Project Head Start* (1964–1965). This act provides medical, social, nutritional, and educational services for low-income children 3 to 6 years of age.
8. *Bilingual Education Act* (1968). In response to the needs of the significant number of non-English-speaking students, Congress authorized funds to provide relevant instruction to these students. The primary focus was to assist non-English speakers, particularly Spanish-speaking students, almost 70 percent of whom were failing to graduate from high school. Although many other languages besides Spanish are included in this act, a relatively limited percentage of non-English-speaking students participate in these programs because of funding shortfalls.
9. *Title IX of the Education Amendments* (1972). This regulation prohibits discrimination on the basis of sex. The regulation is comprehensive and protects the rights of both males and females from preschool through graduate school, in sports, financial aid, employment, counseling, school regulations and policies, admissions, and other areas. Title IX enforcement has been lax, and many schools violate one or more parts of the regulation.
10. *Individuals with Disabilities Education Act* (1975, 1991, 1997, 2004). This act provides financial assistance to local school districts to provide free and appropriate education for the nation's 8 million children with disabilities who are between 3 and 21 years of age.
11. *No Child Left Behind Act* (2001). This act revises the Elementary and Secondary Education Act (ESEA, 1965) and calls for standards and annual testing of math, reading, and science. Schools that test poorly face the possibility of being closed and teachers being fired. Parents are given greater freedom to select schools, with increased federal support for charter schools.
12. *Every Student Succeeds Act* (2015). This act continues the federal government's commitment to educational funding established by the Elementary and Secondary Education Act of 1965, but rolls back much of the federal role in setting education policy, from testing and curriculum to teacher and school performance standards. States are increasingly granted more freedom to set policies that hold under-performing schools and teachers accountable.

Source: Joel Spring, *American Education*, 17th ed. (New York: McGraw-Hill, 2015).

REFLECTION: Legislation often reflects the history of the time it was enacted. Identify what was happening in the country when these different educational acts were made law. What legislation do you believe will be enacted in the years ahead? Why?

townships in the newly settled territories bounded by the Ohio and Mississippi rivers and the Great Lakes to reserve a section of land for educational purposes. The ordinances contained a much-quoted sentence underscoring the new nation's faith in education: "Religion, morality, and knowledge being necessary to good government and the happiness of mankind, schools and the means of education shall forever be encouraged."

The federal government also exerted its influence through targeted funding, or categorical grants. For example, by using federal dollars for specific programs, the government was able to create new colleges and universities, as well as promote agricultural and industrial research efforts. During the Great Depression of the 1930s, the federal government became even more directly involved with education, constructing schools, providing free lunches for poor children, instituting part-time work programs for high school and college students, and offering educational programs to older Americans. With unemployment, hunger, and desperation rampant in the 1930s, states welcomed these federal efforts. More and more Americans were coming to realize that some educational challenges were beyond the resources of the states. But federal involvement in education was sometimes resisted by states and local communities. In the case of African American education, it took nearly a century for the federal government to move forcefully to end racial segregation.

Black Americans: The Struggle for a Chance to Learn

FOCUS QUESTION 8

How did history shape the educational experiences of African Americans, Hispanics, Asian Americans/Pacific Islanders, and Arab Americans?

Much of the history of African American education in the United States has been one of denial. The first law prohibiting education of slaves was passed in South Carolina in 1740. During the next hundred years, many states passed similar and even stronger compulsory-ignorance laws. For example, a 1823 Mississippi law prohibited six or more Negroes from gathering for educational purposes. In Louisiana, a 1830 law imposed a prison sentence on anyone caught teaching a slave to read or write. However, because education has always been integral to African Americans' struggle for equal opportunity, they risked the penalties of these laws and even the dangers of violence for a chance to learn. They formed clandestine schools throughout most large cities and towns of the South. One student described what it was like to attend one of those secret schools in Savannah, Georgia:

> We went every day about nine o'clock with our books wrapped in paper to prevent the police or white persons from seeing them. We went in, one at a time, through the gate, into the yard to the L Kitchen which was the schoolroom.[16]

The Civil War brought an end to official policies of compulsory ignorance. Most of the schooling of African Americans immediately following the Civil War was carried out by philanthropic societies. Many of these associations worked with the Freedmen's Bureau, a federal agency established to provide various services, including the establishment of schools. Individual social activists also made extraordinary commitments to creating schools for poor, under-served black youth. (See A Closer Look: The 5,000 Schools You Probably Never Heard of, on p. 130.) School staffs were usually a mixture of instructors from the North, blacks of Caribbean island heritage, and formerly enslaved literate blacks.

Many white Southerners responded to the education of blacks with fear and anger. Sometimes there was terrorism against black schools. State after state passed laws that explicitly provided for segregated schools. With the 1896 ***Plessy v. Ferguson*** Supreme Court decision, segregation became a legally sanctioned part of the American way of life. In this landmark case, the Court developed the doctrine of **separate**

A CLOSER LOOK

The 5,000 Schools You Probably Never Heard of

Julius Rosenwald was the genius behind the success of Sears, Roebuck and Co. The son of Jewish-German immigrants, his business innovations grew Sears from a small Chicago-based mail-order house into the largest merchandiser in the country. Sears distributed merchandise throughout the nation; it was the Amazon.com of its day. Rosenwald was a business genius, but as B.C. Forbes wrote, "The greatest thing about Julius Rosenwald is not his business but himself, not what he has but what he is."[1] Julius Rosenwald's life purpose went far beyond business: He wanted to improve the lives of all Americans.

After reading the autobiography of black educator Booker T. Washington, Rosenwald sought him out to explore strategies to improve the education of black children living in the Jim Crow South. In the early twentieth century, blacks were excluded from public libraries, playgrounds, and lacked even a segregated school building. To have a school and teachers meant that the next generation would have a chance to move beyond the often grinding poverty that permeated the South. Together, Rosenwald and Washington, who became friends, worked to create a place where poor, rural black children could receive an education—the beginning of the Rosenwald Schools.

©AP Photo/The Daily Herald, Jenny Gray

From 1915 to 1932, Rosenwald funded schools throughout the South, thousands of schools, schools that would eventually educate over one-third of all black children living in the South. Rosenwald Schools were special in many ways. Necessity made them early practitioners of "green architecture." Located in communities of extreme poverty, these schools had to function with minimal resources. Classrooms had tall ceilings and exceptionally large double-hung windows, typically arranged for maximum daylighting, needed because many of the sites lacked electricity. To tackle the heat of the South, cross-ventilation was facilitated by "breeze windows"—internal openings—and the buildings were raised off the ground on piers to facilitate cooling. But perhaps most critical: these buildings were designed for success. Classrooms were flexible, often separated by movable partitions so they could serve one large space, or smaller spaces as needed. A library, auditorium, and a room for shop and cooking classes were included, offering experiences few black students had ever imagined. Vestibules and cloakrooms completed the school layout, luxuries for these children, amenities that spoke of their worth.

In the 1954 Supreme Court case *Brown v. Board of Education of Topeka,* segregation in education was declared unconstitutional, and the 5,000 Rosenwald Schools became obsolete. Once the pride of their communities, many were abandoned or demolished. Today, preservationists work to restore at least some of these schoolhouses that improved the lives of so many.

Source: Norman Finkelstein, *Schools of Hope: How Julius Rosenwald Helped Change African American Education.* Honesdale, PA: Boyds Mills Press (2014).

[1]Quoted in P. Ascoli, *Julius Rosenwald: The Man Who Built Sears, Roebuck and Advanced the Cause of Black Education in the South.* Bloomington: Indiana University Press (2015), p. 173.

REFLECTION: What philanthropic efforts to improve education are available today? How do they compare with the Rosenwald Schools? To learn more about Julius Rosenwald's efforts to improve the lives of disadvantaged blacks, visit the Web site www.rosenwaldfilm.org, dedicated to the documentary, *Rosenwald.* (Or better yet, watch the film!)

but equal. Separate but equal initially legalized separate railway passenger cars for black and white Americans and was also used to justify a legally segregated school system, which in many states lasted for more than half a century.

"Separate but equal" was not equal. In 1907, Mississippi spent \$5.02 for the education of each white child but only \$1.10 for each black child. In 1924, the state paid more than \$1 million to transport whites long distances to schools. No money was spent for blacks, and for them a daily walk of more than twelve miles was not out of the question. Attending schools without enough books, seats, space, equipment, or facilities taught

African American children the harsh reality of "separate but unequal." In the South, a dual school system based on race was in existence. This was **de jure segregation**—that is, segregation by law or by official action.

Scenes like this one became commonplace all across America in the years following the landmark *Brown v. Board of Education of Topeka* decision in 1954 and the passage of the Civil Rights Act in 1964.

Source: Library of Congress Prints and Photographs Division [LC-DIG-ppmsca-03128]

In the North, school assignments were based on both race and residence. **De facto (unofficial) segregation** occurred as the result of segregated residential patterns, patterns that were often prompted by discriminatory real estate practices. As housing patterns changed, attendance zones were often redrawn to ensure the separation of white and black children in schools. Even in schools that were not entirely segregated, black children were routinely placed in special classes or separate academic tracks, counseled into low-status careers, and barred from extracurricular activities. Whatever the obstacle, however, African Americans continued their struggle for access to quality education. As W. E. B. DuBois noted: "Probably never in the world have so many oppressed people tried in every possible way to educate themselves."[17]

Political momentum for civil rights reform grew with the participation of African Americans in World War II and the 1954 Supreme Court decision that schools must desegregate "with all deliberate speed." In *Brown v. Board of Education of Topeka* (Kansas), the court ruled unanimously that "in the field of public education the doctrine of 'separate but equal' has no place. Separate educational facilities are inherently unequal." Yet a decade after *Brown,* almost 91 percent of all African American children in the South still attended all-black schools.

In 1964, President Lyndon B. Johnson and Congress moved boldly to eradicate racial segregation. The Civil Rights Act gave the federal government power to help local school districts desegregate (Title IV) and, when necessary, to initiate lawsuits or withhold federal school funds to force desegregation (Title VI). The Civil Rights Act produced more desegregation in the next four years than the Supreme Court's *Brown* decision had in the preceding decade. All branches of the federal government now moved in concert to desegregate the nation's schools, supporting racial quotas and busing to end segregation in both the North and the South.

Even as some schools became more racially balanced, a new barrier to equality appeared. In the same school building, black and white students found themselves separated by tracking, treated differently by teachers and administrators, and even gravitating to different areas of the school.[18] (See Chapter 4 for more on tracking.) This within-school segregation was termed **second-generation segregation.** In the 1960s, the Kerner Commission warned: "Our nation is moving toward two societies, one black, and one white—separate and unequal." The commission charged that white society must assume responsibility for the black ghetto. "White institutions created it, white institutions maintain it, and white society condones it."[19]

But the Kerner Commission's warning was not heeded. As the century drew to a close, affirmative efforts such as busing were abandoned, and in the *Hopwood* (1996) and the *University of Michigan* decisions (2003), firm racial set-asides for college and law school admissions were eliminated. In a 2007 ruling, the Supreme Court further backed away from desegregation efforts by striking down plans in Seattle and Louisville that used race to assign K–12 students to public schools.[20]

The consequences of these actions are now evident in the nation's schools, as residential patterns and the diminished legal pressures have re-segregated the nation's schools. Today's students are more segregated than they were four decades ago, with white students experiencing the most segregated educational environment.[21]

PROFILE IN EDUCATION

Marian Wright Edelman

Marian Wright Edelman is a voice for children. With views shaped by parents devoted to service and an upbringing in the segregated South, Edelman founded the Children's Defense Fund (CDF) in 1973 to ensure that every child has a Healthy Start, a Head Start, a Fair Start, a Safe Start, and a Moral Start in life.

Read a full profile of Marian Wright Edelman on Connect.

©AP Photo/Bob Burgess

connect

Should desegregation still be a goal? Has its time passed? Some believe that even the idea that African American or Latino children can learn effectively only when they sit next to a white student is demeaning. Others see segregation as a way to protect African American and Latino cultures.

Researcher Gary Orfield of the UCLA Civil Rights Project does not agree. His research suggests that students who attend integrated schools are more comfortable with peers from diverse racial, cultural, and socioeconomic backgrounds and more understanding of different points of view. As schools re-segregate, those benefits are lost. Others argue that racial isolation puts minority children in poorer schools with less experienced teachers, weaker pre-collegiate courses, and lower achievement and graduation rates.[22] As one advocate for desegregation decried, "[African Americans] who favor resegregation are doing whites the great favor of relieving both their guilty conscience and their pocketbooks."[23]

Hispanics: Growing School Impact

More than 50 million Hispanics live in the United States, most as U.S. citizens, and are the largest minority group in the nation. Only Mexico has a larger Hispanic population than the United States. Ongoing legal and illegal immigration (often to escape economic and political repression) together with high birth rates for young families in their childbearing years, have made Hispanics the youngest and fastest growing school-age population in the United States. Hispanic children are more than 25 percent of the school-aged population and often confront numerous educational barriers as they work to master English. As early as kindergarten, many Hispanic students are less able than their white peers to identify colors, recognize letters, count to fifty, or write their first name. More than half of Hispanics drop out of school.[24]

Hispanics consist of several subgroups, which share some characteristics, such as language, but differ in others, such as race, location, age, income, and educational attainment. The three largest Hispanic subgroups are Mexican Americans, Puerto Ricans, and Cuban Americans. There is also significant representation from other Latin American and Caribbean countries, such as the Dominican Republic, El Salvador, Nicaragua, and Honduras. (See Figure 5.1.) In contrast to these new immigrants, many

FIGURE 5.1

U.S. Hispanic subgroups.

SOURCE: *Hispanic Americans by the Numbers.* U.S. Census Bureau, 2016.

REFLECTION: Although many refer to Hispanics as a homogeneous community, they are not. What distinctions can you make for each of these subgroups? What similarities have you observed or studied?

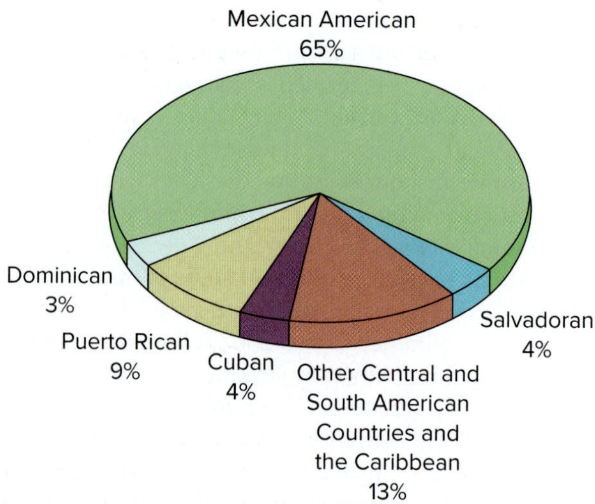

U.S. Hispanic subgroups

from war-torn or poverty-stricken countries, there is also an "old" population of Mexican and Spanish descent living in the Southwest with a longer history on this continent than those who trace their ancestors to the New England colonies. Let's briefly look at some of the groups that make up the Hispanic community.

In the late 1960s, César Chávez led the fight of migrant Mexican American laborers to organize themselves into a union and to demand a more responsive education that included culture-free IQ tests, instruction in Spanish, smaller classes, and greater cultural representation in the curriculum.

©Arthur Schatz/The LIFE Picture Collection/Getty Images

Mexican Americans

At the end of the United States' war with Mexico (1846–1848), the Mexicans who decided to stay in the new U.S. territories were guaranteed full citizenship. By 1900, approximately 200,000 Mexican Americans were living in the Southwest, having built the cities of Los Angeles, San Diego, Tucson, Albuquerque, Dallas, and San Antonio. The methods used to deny educational opportunity to Mexican Americans were similar to those imposed on African Americans. By 1920, a pattern of separate and unequal Mexican American schools had emerged throughout the Southwest.

A significant number of Mexican American families migrated once or twice a year, exploited as a source of cheap labor in rural, agricultural communities. With constant transitions, children's learning suffered. One superintendent in Texas, reflecting deeply engrained prejudice, argued that education was actually dangerous for Mexican Americans:

> Most of our Mexicans are of the lower class. They transplant onions, harvest them, etc. The less they know about everything else, the better contented they are . . . so you see it is up to the white population to keep the Mexican on his knees in an onion patch. . . . This does not mix well with education.[25]

Today, families continue to cross the border every day, hoping to improve their economic lives. More than one in three public schools enroll migrant and immigrant students, mostly Mexican Americans. The greatest numbers are in California, Illinois, Texas, Arizona, and Florida. Importantly, schools are legally required to open their doors to all students, even those living undocumented in our country.[26] Threats of deportation and divided families are mounting stresses for many students.

Puerto Ricans

During the nineteenth century, many of the Puerto Ricans in the United States were highly respected political exiles striving for the independence of their homeland. But all that changed in 1898, when Puerto Rico was acquired from Spain and became a territory of the United States. Citizenship, through the Jones Act in 1917, provided free movement between the continent and the island. Migration to the mainland peaked during the 1950s, with the majority of Puerto Ricans settling in New York City. Currently, about half the Puerto Rican population lives within the fifty states, and the other half lives in Puerto Rico.[27] The frequent passage between the island and the United States, as families search for a better economic life, makes schooling all the more difficult for Puerto Rican children.

GLOBAL VIEW

The very high 96 percent adult literacy rate in Cuba is often tied to policies of former President Fidel Castro. Go to UNICEF's Web site (www.unicef.org/statistics) to find out other international literacy rates.

Cuban Americans

Following the Castro-led revolution in the 1950s, Cuban immigration to the United States increased significantly. During the 1960s, Cubans who settled in the United States were primarily well-educated, professional, and middle- and upper-class. By 1980, 800,000 Cubans—10 percent of the population of Cuba—were living in the United States. For the most part, Cubans settled in Miami and other locations in southern Florida, but there are also sizable populations in New York, Philadelphia, Chicago, Milwaukee, and Indianapolis. Cubans, considered one of the most highly educated people in American immigration history, tend to be more prosperous and more conservative than most of the other Latino groups.[28] In the second immigration wave, during the 1980s, there were many more black and poor Cubans, who have not been accepted as readily into communities in the United States.

Asian Americans and Pacific Islanders: The Magnitude of Diversity

The term "Asian Americans and Pacific Islanders" embraces peoples from nations as diverse as India, Vietnam, China, Pakistan, Korea, Samoa, Japan, and Native Hawaii, about half the world's population. More than 18 million Americans have roots in Asia. As a group, these Americans have attained a high degree of educational and economic success. This section will describe the differing experiences of four of the largest Asian immigrant groups—Chinese, Filipinos, Asian Indians, and Japanese—as well as problems faced by refugees from Southeast Asia.[29]

Many of these cultures hold education in high esteem, and well-mannered, respectful, and studious Asian American students have earned themselves the moniker of *model minority*. In kindergarten, Asian American children consistently outscore their peers in reading and math. More than 50 percent of Asian American/Pacific Islanders students graduate from college. One year after graduation, they have a higher starting salary than any racial or ethnic group. However, diversity within the Asian community is often overlooked, and as with many stereotypes, misconceptions abound. Fewer than half of Vietnamese and Samoan Americans graduate from high school. Asian New Wavers reflect the current countercultural pattern, with baggy pants, combat boots, and dyed hair, challenging the model minority stereotype.

The United States is a nation of immigrants. Our country's motto, *E Pluribus Unum*, means "from many, one." How to educate and honor the individual while creating a unified nation is a longstanding tension for American schools.

©Image Source/Getty Images RF

Chinese Americans

When the Chinese first began immigrating to the West Coast in the 1850s, they were mostly young, unmarried men who left China, a country ravaged by famine and political turmoil, to seek their fortune in the "Golden Mountains" across the Pacific and then take their wealth back to their homeland. The California gold mines were largely depleted by the time they arrived, and the completion of the transcontinental railroad signaled a loss of jobs for Chinese laborers. Many found that the hope of taking fortunes home to their families in China was an impossible dream.

By 1880, approximately 106,000 Chinese had immigrated to the United States, fueling a vicious reaction: "The Chinese must go." With the passage of the Immigration Act of 1882, along with a series of similar bills, further Chinese immigration was blocked. The Chinese already in this country responded to increasing physical violence by moving eastward and consolidating into ghettos called Chinatowns. Inhabited largely by male immigrants, these ghettos offered a grim and sometimes violent lifestyle, one with widespread prostitution and gambling. Chinatowns, vestiges of century-old ghettos, can still be found in many of America's cities.

In 1949, the institution of a Communist government in mainland China caused Congress to reverse more than a century of immigration quotas and naturalization and antimiscegenation laws and grant refugee status to five thousand highly educated Chinese in the United States. Despite facing active prejudice and discrimination, Chinese Americans today have achieved a higher median income and educational level than that of white Americans. And the Chinese language Mandarin is the second most popular foreign language in U.S. schools, second only to Spanish. (See Newsflash on Connect: Chinese Language Immersion.)

GLOBAL VIEW

From 1910 to 1940, Chinese immigrants were detained and interrogated at Angel Island station in San Francisco Bay. For further information on U.S. immigration history, visit the Angel Island Web site at www.angelisland.org. Ellis Island was the New York gateway for European immigration from 1900 to 1920 (www.ellisisland.com). An extensive collection of primary resource photographs and immigration history for educators can be found at *Americans All* (www.americansall.com).

Filipino Americans

After the 1898 Spanish-American War, the United States acquired the Philippines. Filipinos, viewed as low-cost labor, were recruited to work in the fields of Hawaii and the U.S. mainland. Thousands left the poverty of their islands to seek economic security.

With a scarcity of women (in 1930, the male–female ratio was 143 to 1) and the mobility of their work on farms and as field hands, the Filipinos had difficulty establishing cohesive communities in the United States. Like other Asian immigrants, they came with the goal of taking their earnings back to their homeland; like other Asian immigrants, most found this an impossible dream. Finding acceptance in the United States also proved a struggle.

The Tydings-McDuffie Act of 1934 was a victory for those who wanted the Filipinos excluded from this country. Promising independence to the Philippines, this act limited immigration to the United States to fifty per year. All that changed in 1965, when a new immigration act allowed a significant increase in Filipino immigration. Between 1970 and 1980, the Filipino population in the United States more than doubled. The earlier presence of the U.S. military in Manila generated an educated elite who spoke English, studied the American school curriculum, and moved to the United States with professional skills, seeking jobs commensurate with their training. Concentrated in urban areas of the West Coast, Filipinos are the second-largest Asian American ethnic group in the United States.

Although often grouped together, Asian Americans and Pacific Islanders reflect great ethnic and cultural diversity.

©Bonnie Kamin/PhotoEdit

Asian Indian Americans

Traders from India arrived in New England in the 1880s, bartering silks and spices. Intellectuals Henry David Thoreau, Ralph Waldo Emerson, and E. M. Forster *(Passage to India)* gravitated to the culture, religion, and philosophy of the Eastern purveyors. On the West Coast, Indians from Punjab migrated to escape British exploitation, which had forced farmers to raise commercial rather than food crops. With farming conditions in California similar to those in

India, Punjabees became successful growers and landowners. They were destined to lose their lands, however, and even their leasing rights, under the California Alien Land Law, which recalled the ownership of land held by Indians and Japanese.

In addition to legal restrictions, Indian laborers were attacked by racist mobs in Bellingham, Washington, in 1907, triggering other riots and expulsions throughout the Pacific region. U.S. government support for British colonial rule in India became the rationale to further restrict Indian immigration. It was not until 1946 that a law allowing Indian naturalization and immigration was passed. During the past three decades, tens of thousands of Indians arrived in America. Most Indians are extremely well educated, and many are professionals. Their educational and income levels are the highest of any group in the United States, including other Asians.

Japanese Americans

Only when the Japanese government legalized emigration in 1886 did the Japanese come to the United States in significant numbers. For example, in 1870, records show only 50 Japanese in the United States, but by 1920, the number had increased to more than 110,000.

With immigration of the Chinese halted by various exclusion acts, Japanese immigrants filled the need for cheap labor. Like the Chinese, the early Japanese immigrants were males who hoped to return to their homeland, an unfulfilled dream. Praised for their willingness to work when they first arrived in California, the Japanese began to make other farmers nervous with their great success in agriculture and truck farming. Anti-Japanese feelings became prevalent along the West Coast. Such slogans as "Japs must go" and warnings of a new "yellow peril" were frequent. In 1924, Congress passed an immigration bill that halted Japanese immigration to the United States.

After Japan's attack on Pearl Harbor on December 7, 1941, fear and prejudice about the "threat" from Japanese Americans were rampant. On February 19, 1942, President Franklin Roosevelt issued Executive Order No. 9006, which declared the West Coast a "military area" and established federal *relocation camps.* Approximately 110,000 Japanese, more than two-thirds of whom were U.S. citizens, were removed from their homes in the "military area" and were forced into ten *internment (relocation) camps* in California, Idaho, Utah, Arizona, Wyoming, Colorado, and Arkansas. Located in geographically barren areas, guarded by soldiers and barbed wire, these internment camps made it very difficult for the Japanese people to keep their traditions and cultural heritage alive. Almost half a century later, the U.S. government officially acknowledged this wrong and offered a symbolic payment ($20,000 in reparations) to each victim.

Despite severe discrimination in the past, many of today's Japanese Americans enjoy both a high median family income and educational attainment. Their success is at least partially due to traditional values, a heritage some fear may be weakened by increasing assimilation.

Southeast Asian Americans

Before 1975, the United States saw only small numbers of immigrants from Southeast Asia, including Vietnam, Laos, and Kampuchea/Cambodia. Their arrival in greater numbers was related directly to the end of the Vietnam War and resulting communist rule. The refugees came from all strata of society. Some were wealthy; others were poverty stricken. Some were widely traveled and sophisticated; others were farmers and fishing people who had never before left their small villages. Most came as part of a family, and almost half were under age 18 at the time of their arrival. Refugee camps were established to dispense food, clothing, medical assistance, and temporary housing, as well as to provide an introduction to U.S. culture and to the English language.

By December 1975, the last refugee camp had closed and the U.S. government had resettled large numbers of Southeast Asians across the nation without too high a concentration in any one location. This dispersal was well intentioned but often left the refugees feeling lonely and isolated. In fact, many moved from original areas of settlement to cities where large numbers of Asian Americans were already located.

A second wave of Southeast Asian refugees followed in the years after 1975. Cambodians and Laotians migrated to escape poverty, starvation, and political repression in their homelands. Many tried to escape in small fishing boats not meant for travel across rough ocean seas. Called *boat people* by the media, almost half of them, according to the estimates, died before they reached the shores of the United States.

Similar to war refugees from Latin America, these children brought memories of terrible tragedy to school. For example, a teacher in San Francisco was playing hangman during a language arts lesson. As the class was laughing and shouting out letters, she was shocked to see one child, a newcomer, in tears. The girl spoke so little English she could not explain the problem. Finally, another child translated. The game had triggered a traumatic memory. In Cambodia, the girl had watched the hanging of her father.[35] Since the fall of Saigon in 1975, more than 1.4 million Southeast Asians have resettled in the United States. Their struggle to find a place in this society remains conflicted, because most Americans associate Vietnam with war.

Arab Americans: Moving beyond the Stereotype

The nearly four million Arab Americans are as diverse as their countries of origin, with unique immigration experiences that have shaped their ethnic identity in the United States. Arab Americans can trace their roots to every Arab country, from northern Africa to southwest Asia, but the majority has ancestral ties to Lebanon, Syria, Palestine, Egypt, and Iraq (see Figure 5.2). Where do they call home in the

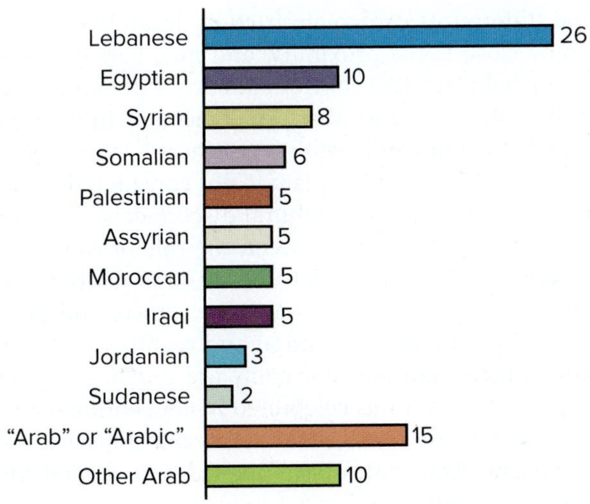

FIGURE 5.2

Arab Americans by ancestry.

Note: Other Arab (10 percent) includes Yemeni, Kurdish, Algerian, Saudi, Tunisian, Kuwaiti, Libyan, Berber, Emirati (United Arab Emirates), Omani, Bahraini, Alhuceman, Bedouin, Rio de Oro, and the general terms Middle Eastern and North African.

SOURCE: Arab American Institute, "Demographics" 2013, www.aaiusa.org.

REFLECTION: As a teacher, what steps can you take to help your students appreciate the diversity obscured by broad labels such as "Arab American"?

United States? Arab Americans live in every state, but more than two-thirds of them call just ten states home: California, Michigan, New York, Florida, Texas, New Jersey, Illinois, Ohio, Pennsylvania, and Virginia. Contrary to many cultural assumptions, most Arab Americans are native-born, and nearly 82 percent of Arabs in the United States are citizens.[30]

Misunderstanding and intolerance are all-too-common facts of life for Americans of Arab descent. Arab Americans' quality of life is often influenced by events taking place in other parts of the world. The Iraq wars, the September 11, 2001, attacks on the World Trade Center and the Pentagon, and the continuing conflict between Israelis and Palestinians create tension and anxiety for Americans of Arab descent. These news events are troubling enough, but media portrayals can exacerbate the problem. Books and movies depict a strange mélange of offensive Arab caricatures: greedy billionaires, corrupt sheiks, immoral terrorists, suave oil cartel magnates, and even romantic, if ignorant, camel-riding Bedouins. Nor are children's books immune from such characterizations. Caroline Cooney's *The Terrorist*, a popular book for children in grades 5 through 10, is the fictional tale of an American teenager who tries to find the Arab terrorist responsible for her younger brother's death. It is not surprising that polls taken as far back as the 1980s reveal that most Americans perceive Arabs as anti-American, violent, wealthy from oil, and oppressive of women. The challenge to educators could not be clearer. Students and teachers need to learn about Arab Americans, as well as the Arab world.

GLOBAL VIEW

Friendship through Education is a consortium of groups linking U.S. students and students in countries with Arab populations. www.FriendshipThroughEducation.org

Many Americans confuse Arabs and Muslims, mistaking Islam, a religion practiced by Muslims, with Arabs, a cultural group. Although Islam is the predominant religion of the Middle East, and most Arabs living there are Muslims following Islam, there are also millions of Christian Arabs (as well as those who are Jewish or Druse). In the United States, however, the vast majority of Arab Americans are Christian and the majority of America's Muslims are not Arab. (Remember: Arabs are a cultural group. Muslims are a religious group practicing the Islamic faith.) Although Arabs practice different religions, they do share the same language and culture, a culture that is at times in conflict with Western values.[31]

Such cultural differences can create friction, in and beyond school. For example, Arabs enjoy close social proximity, and members of the same sex often walk arm-in-arm or hold hands, behaviors at odds with American practice. Features of the Arabic language, including loudness and intonation, may be perceived in America as too loud and even rude. Whereas punctuality is considered a courtesy in the United States, being late is not considered a sign of disrespect in Arab culture. In addition to these cultural disconnects, more profound differences emerge, such as the disparity between the role of women in Arab society and the role of women in Western society. Many Arab nations cast women in an inferior position, denying them education, inheritance, and power. Saudi Arabia, for example, still prohibits coeducation and requires that women wear veils in public. Arranged marriages and polygamy are practiced in several Arab nations. Whereas the birth of a son is celebrated in conventional Arab families, the birth of a daughter may be met with silence. Yet, change is also sweeping part of the Arab world. Several Arab states have opened schools and the workplace to women, with dramatic results.

Today, students of Arab heritage can be found in all fifty states and, as a group, do well in American schools. The proportion of Arab Americans who attend college is higher than the national average, and Arab Americans earn postgraduate degrees at a rate nearly double the national average. Yet, they still face challenges. They learn from textbooks that have little if anything to say about their history or experiences. American teachers lack basic information about Arab culture, which may present problems. For example, a traditional Arab student may be troubled or confused in an American school where women can be both teachers and principals. In a similar way, an American teacher who criticizes an Arab student in public may have unintentionally erected a wall of hard feelings. Arabs put a lot of emphasis on personal and family honor, and public ridicule is a serious matter.

If an Arab student happens to be of Muslim faith, additional issues emerge. Muslims discover that although schools typically celebrate Christmas, they ignore Muslim holidays. For instance, during Ramadan, Muslims fast for a month during daylight hours, yet few schools recognize this observance, much less make provisions for it. In terms of dietary restrictions, school cafeterias serve, but do not always label, pork products, a food Muslims are prohibited from eating. Clearly, Arab and Muslim American students are all but invisible in the official and hidden curriculum of most American schools. Teacher training, curricular revision, and a greater understanding of these cultural and religious issues are needed if equal educational opportunities are to become a reality for these Americans.

Women and Education: A History of Sexism

The peopling of America is a story of voluntary immigration and forced migration. The story of women's struggle for educational opportunity may be just as hard to uncover but equally important to reclaim.

For almost two centuries, girls were barred from America's schools. Although a woman gave the first plot of ground for a free school in New England, female children were not allowed to attend the school. In 1687, the town council of Farmington, Connecticut, voted money for a school "where all children shall learn to read and write English." However, the council quickly qualified that statement by explaining that "all children" meant "all males." In fact, the education of America's girls was so limited that fewer than a third of the women in colonial America could even sign their names.[32] For centuries, women fought to open the schoolhouse door.

In colonial America, secondary schools, called female seminaries, appealed to families financially able to educate their daughters beyond elementary school. **Emma Hart Willard** wrote and disseminated her views on opening higher education to women and won favorable responses from Thomas Jefferson, John Adams, and James Monroe. Eventually, with local support, she opened the Troy Female Seminary, devoted to preparing professional teachers, thus providing a teacher education program years before the first normal (teacher training) school was founded. In Massachusetts, Mary Lyon created Mount Holyoke, a seminary that eventually became a noted women's college. Religious observance was an important part of seminary life in institutions such as Mount Holyoke. Self-denial and strict discipline were considered important elements of molding devout wives and Christian mothers. By the 1850s, with help from Quakers such as Harriet Beecher Stowe, Myrtilla Miner established the Miner Normal School for Colored Girls in the nation's capital, providing new educational opportunities for African American women. While these seminaries sometimes offered superior educations, they were also trapped in a paradox they could never fully resolve: They were

FOCUS QUESTION 9

What educational barriers and breakthroughs have girls and women experienced?

GLOBAL VIEW

Even in the twenty-first century, the schoolhouse door remains closed to far too many. About 100 million primary-school aged children in developing countries do not attend school. About one-fifth of the world's adult population still cannot read or write. Around the world (including the United States) students who are poor, female, or live in rural areas face an uphill battle for equal educational opportunities.

educating girls for a world not ready to accept educated women. Seminaries sometimes went to extraordinary lengths to reconcile this conflict. Emma Willard's Troy Female Seminary was devoted to "professionalizing motherhood." (And who could not support motherhood?) But, en route to reshaping motherhood, seminaries reshaped teaching.

For the teaching profession, seminaries became the source of new ideas and new recruits. Seminary leaders, such as Emma Hart Willard and Catherine Beecher, wrote textbooks on how to teach and on how to teach more humanely than was the practice at the time. They denounced corporal punishment and promoted more cooperative educational practices. Because school was seen as an extension of the home and another arena for raising children, seminary graduates were allowed to become teachers—at least, until they decided to marry. More than 80 percent of the graduates of Troy Female Seminary and Mount Holyoke became teachers. Female teachers were particularly attractive to school districts—not just because of their teaching effectiveness but also because they were typically paid one-third to one-half of the salary paid to male teachers.

By the end of the Civil War, a number of colleges and universities, especially tax-supported ones, were desperate for dollars. Institutions of higher learning experienced a serious student shortage because of Civil War casualties, and women became the source of much-needed tuition dollars.

Female funding did not buy on-campus equality. Women often faced separate courses and hostility from male students and professors. At state universities, male students would stamp their feet in protest when a woman entered a classroom.

In *Sex in Education* (1873), Dr. Edward Clarke, a member of Harvard's medical faculty, argued that women attending high school and college were at risk because the blood destined for the development and health of their ovaries would be redirected to their brains. The stress of study was no laughing matter. Too much education would leave women with "monstrous brains and puny bodies . . . flowing thought and constipated bowels." Clarke recommended that females be provided with a less demanding education, easier courses, no competition, and "rest" periods so that their reproductive organs could develop. He maintained that allowing girls to attend such places as Harvard would pose a serious health threat to the women themselves, with sterility and hysteria potential outcomes.

M. Carey Thomas, future president of Bryn Mawr and one of the first women to earn a PhD in the United States, wrote in her diary about the profound fears she experienced as she was studying: "I remember often praying about it, and begging God that if it were true that because I was a girl, I could not successfully master Greek and go to college, and understand things, to kill me for it."[33] In 1895, the faculty of the University of Virginia concluded that "women were often physically unsexed by the strains of study." Parents, fearing for the health of their daughters, often placed them in less-demanding programs reserved for females, or kept them out of advanced education entirely. Even today, the echoes of Clarke's warning resonate, as some people still see well-educated women as less attractive, view advanced education as "too stressful" for females, or believe that education is more important for males than for females.

In the twentieth century, women won greater access to educational programs at all levels, although gender-segregated programs were the rule well into the 1970s. Even when females attended the same schools as males, they often received a less valuable education. Commercial courses prepared girls to become secretaries, and vocational programs channeled them into cosmetology and other low-paying occupations. After World War II, it was not unusual for a university to require a married woman to submit a letter from her husband granting her permission to enroll in courses before she would be admitted. By the 1970s, with the passage of Title IX of the Education Amendments of 1972, females saw significant progress toward gaining access to educational programs, but not equality. The opening section of Title IX states

> No person in the United States shall, on the basis of sex, be excluded from participation in, be denied the benefits of, or be subjected to discrimination under any education program or activity receiving federal financial assistance.

Low teacher salaries can be traced back to the late nineteenth century, when communities found that they could hire capable female teachers for approximately 60 percent of what male teachers were paid.

Source: Library of Congress, Prints and Photographs Division [LC-DIG-ppmsc-04830]

The law is straightforward, but misperceptions are common. For example, many equate Title IX only with athletics; yet, the law prohibits gender discrimination in admissions, treatment of students, counseling, financial aid, employment, and health benefits, to name but a few. Nor is Title IX only about females; males are protected from gender discrimination as well. Ignorance of the law is widespread, one reason it is so rarely enforced. In fact, in almost four decades since Title IX became law, no school has ever been financially penalized by the federal government for violating Title IX.[34]

Unfortunately, sexism still thrives in today's classrooms, affecting attitudes and careers. Nursing, teaching, library science, and social work continue to be predominantly female while engineering, physics, and computer science are male domains. Even in medicine and law, where women have made progress, they find themselves channeled into the least prestigious, least profitable specialties. A "glass wall" still divides the sexes, and some call for the glass wall to become permanent, believing that males and females are so different that the nation should return to single-sex schools, an idea that was popular in colonial America, bringing us full circle in this chapter.

At the beginning of the chapter, we peeked into Christopher Lamb's colonial classroom to watch our school traditions take root. Unfortunately, one such tradition was that education was reserved for some and denied to others. We still struggle to create fair schools. In a sense, today's teachers stand on the shoulders of Christopher Lamb and other educators as each generation makes its own contribution to creating fairer, more effective schools. We have chosen to conclude this chapter with a Hall of Fame, a small tribute to those whose shoulders we stand on.

Hall of Fame: Profiles in Education

A "hall of fame" recognizes individuals for significant contributions to a field. Football, baseball, rock and roll, and country music all have halls of fame to recognize outstanding individuals. We think education is no less important and merits its own forum for recognition. In fact, Emporia State University in Kansas houses a Teachers' Hall of Fame. Following are the nominations we would offer to honor educators who we believe should be in a hall of fame.

FOCUS QUESTION 10

Who are some of the influential educators who helped fashion today's schools?

RAP 3.4
Self-Fulfilling Prophecy

Obviously, not all influential educators have been included in these brief profiles, but it is important to begin recognizing significant educational contributions. Indirectly or directly, these individuals have influenced your life as a student and will influence your career as a teacher.

©Bettmann/Getty Images

For establishing the kindergarten as an integral part of a child's education—

Friedrich Froebel (1782–1852). Froebel frequently reflected on his own childhood. Froebel's mother died when he was only 9 months old. In his recollections, he developed a deep sense of the importance of early childhood and of the critical role played by teachers of the young. Although he worked as a forester, chemist's assistant, and museum curator, he eventually found his true vocation as an educator. He attended Pestalozzi's institute and extended Pestalozzi's ideas. He saw nature as a prime source of learning and believed that schools should provide a warm and supportive environment for children.

In 1837, Froebel founded the first **kindergarten** ("child's garden") to "cultivate" the child's development and socialization. Games provided cooperative activities for socialization and physical development, and such materials as sand and clay were used to stimulate the child's imagination. Like Pestalozzi, Froebel believed in the importance of establishing an emotionally secure environment for children. Going beyond Pestalozzi, Froebel saw the teacher as a moral and cultural model for children, a model worthy of emulation. (How different from the earlier view of the teacher as disciplinarian.)

In the nineteenth century, as German immigrants came to the United States, they brought with them the idea of kindergarten education. Margaretta Schurz established a German-language kindergarten in Wisconsin in 1855. The first English-language kindergarten and training school for kindergarten teachers were begun in Boston in 1860 by Elizabeth Peabody.

©North Wind Picture Archives via AP Images

For her integrity and bravery in bringing education to African American girls—

Prudence Crandall (1803–1889). Born of Quaker parents, Prudence Crandall received her education at a school in Providence, Rhode Island, founded by an active abolitionist, Moses Brown. Her upbringing within Quaker circles, in which discussions of abolition were common, may have inspired her interest in racial equality, an interest that led her to acts of personal courage as she strove to promote education among people of all colors.

After graduating from the Brown Seminary about 1830, Crandall taught briefly in Plainfield, Connecticut, before founding her own school for girls in the neighboring town of Canterbury. However, her decision to admit a black girl, Sarah Harris, daughter of a neighboring farmer, caused outrage. Although African Americans in Connecticut were free, a large segment of the white population within Canterbury supported the efforts of the American Colonization Society to deport all freed blacks to Africa, believing them to be inherently inferior. Many were adamant that anything but the most basic education for African Americans would lead to discontent and might encourage interracial marriage. The townspeople voiced fears that Crandall's school would lead to the devaluation of local property by attracting a large number of blacks to the area. Prudence Crandall was pressured by the local population to expel Sarah Harris. However, she was determined to defy their wishes. When the wife of a prominent local clergyman suggested that if Harris remained, the school "could not be sustained," Crandall replied, "Then it might sink then, for I should not turn her out."

When other parents withdrew their children, Crandall advertised for pupils in *The Liberator,* the newspaper of abolitionist William Lloyd Garrison. A month later, the school reopened with a student body comprising fifteen black girls. However, the townspeople made life difficult for Crandall and her students. Supplies were hard to obtain, and Crandall and her pupils faced verbal harassment, as well as being pelted with chicken heads, manure, and other objects. Nonetheless, they persisted.

In 1833, only one month after Crandall had opened her doors to African American girls, the Connecticut legislature passed the notorious "Black Law." This law forbade the founding of schools for the education of African Americans from other states without the permission of local authorities. Crandall was arrested and tried. At her trial, her counsel advised the jury, "You may find that she has violated an act of the State Legislature, but if you also find her protected by higher power, it will be your duty to acquit." Her conviction was later overturned on appeal, but vandalism and arson continued. When a gang stormed the school building with clubs and iron bars, smashing windows and rendering the downstairs area uninhabitable, the school finally was forced to close.

Prudence Crandall's interest in education, racial equality, and women's rights continued throughout her life. Several of her students continued her work, including her first African American student, Sarah Harris, who taught black pupils in Louisiana for many years.

For her work in identifying the educational potential of young children and crafting an environment in which the young could learn—

Maria Montessori (1870–1952). Montessori was no follower of tradition, in her private life or in her professional activities. Shattering sex-role stereotypes, she attended a technical school and then a medical school, becoming the first female physician in Italy. Her work brought her in contact with children regarded as mentally handicapped and brain damaged, but her educational activities with these children indicated that they were far more capable than many believed. By 1908, Montessori had established a children's school called the Casa dei Bambini, designed to provide an education for disadvantaged children from the slums of Rome.

Montessori's view of children differed from the views held by her contemporaries. Her observations led her to conclude that children have an inner need to work at tasks that interest them. Given the right materials and tasks, children need not be rewarded and punished by the teacher. In fact, she believed that children prefer work to play and are capable of sustained periods of concentration. Young children need a carefully prepared environment in order to learn.

Montessori's curriculum reflected this specially prepared environment. Children learned practical skills, including setting a table, washing dishes, buttoning clothing, and displaying basic manners. They learned formal skills, such as reading, writing, and arithmetic. Special materials included movable sandpaper letters to teach the alphabet and colored rods to teach counting. The children developed motor skills as well as intellectual skills in a carefully developed sequence. Montessori worked with each student individually, rather than with the class as a whole, to accomplish these goals.

The impact of Montessori's methods continues to this day. Throughout the United States, early childhood education programs use Montessori-like materials. A number of early childhood institutions are called *Montessori schools* and adhere to the approach she developed almost a century ago. Although originally intended for disadvantaged students, Montessori's concept of carefully preparing an environment and program to teach the very young is used today with children from all social classes.

©Bettmann/Getty Images

For her contributions in moving a people from intellectual slavery to education—

Mary McLeod Bethune (1875–1955). The first child of her family not born in slavery, Bethune rose from a field hand, picking cotton, to an unofficial presidential adviser. The last of seventeen children born to South Carolina sharecroppers, she filled the breaks in her fieldwork with reading and studying. She was committed to meeting the critical need of providing education to the newly freed African Americans, and when a Colorado seamstress offered to pay the cost of educating one black girl at Scotia Seminary in Concord, New Hampshire, she was selected. Bethune's plans to become an African missionary changed as she became more deeply involved in the need to educate newly liberated American blacks.

With $1.50, five students, and a rented cottage near the Daytona Beach city dump in Florida, Bethune founded a school that eventually became Bethune-Cookman College. As a national leader, she created a number of black civic and welfare organizations, serving as a member of the Hoover Commission on Child Welfare, and acting as an adviser to President Franklin D. Roosevelt.

Mary McLeod Bethune demonstrated commitment and effort in establishing a black college against overwhelming odds and by rising from poverty to become a national voice for African Americans.

©Black Star

For her creative approaches placing children at the center of the curriculum—

Sylvia Ashton-Warner (1908–1984). Sylvia Ashton-Warner began her school career in her mother's New Zealand classroom, where rote memorization constituted the main avenue for learning. The teaching strategies that Ashton-Warner later devised, with their emphasis on child-centered learning and creativity in the classroom, stand in opposition to this early experience.

Ashton-Warner was a flamboyant and eccentric personality; throughout her life, she considered herself to be an artist rather than a teacher. She focused on painting, music, and writing. Her fascination with creativity was apparent in the remote New Zealand classrooms, where she encouraged self-expression among the native Maori children. As a teacher, she infuriated authorities with her absenteeism and unpredictability, and in official ratings she was never estimated as above average in her abilities. However, during the peak years of her teaching career, between 1950 and 1952, she developed innovative teaching techniques that influenced teachers around the world and especially in the United States.

Realizing that certain words were especially significant to individual pupils because of their life experiences, Ashton-Warner developed her "key vocabulary" system for teaching reading to young children. Words drawn from children's conversations were written on cards. Using these words, children learned to read. Ashton-Warner asserted that the key to making this approach effective lay in choosing words that had personal meaning to the individual child: "Pleasant words won't do. Respectable words won't do. They must be words organically tied up, organically born from the dynamic life itself. They must be words that are already part of the child's being."

Bringing meaning to children was at the center of Ashton-Warner's philosophy. This belief provided the foundation of several reading approaches and teaching strategies used throughout the United States. Her work brought meaning to reading for millions of children. In her best-selling book, *Teacher,* she provided many future teachers with important and useful insights. Her emphasis on key vocabulary, individualized reading, and meaningful learning is evident in classrooms today in America and abroad.

For his work in identifying the crippling effects of racism on all American children and in formulating community action to overcome the educational, psychological, and economic impacts of racism—

©William E. Sauro/ New York Times Co./Getty Images

Kenneth Clark (1914–2005). Kenneth Clark attended schools in Harlem, where he witnessed an integrated community become all black and felt the growing impact of racism. He attended Howard University, was the first African American to receive a doctorate in psychology from Columbia University, and in 1960 became the first black to be tenured at City College of New York. His concern with the educational plight of African Americans generally, and the Harlem community in particular, was always central in his professional efforts.

Beginning in the 1930s, Clark and his wife, Mamie Phipps Clark, assessed black children's self-perceptions. They bought black dolls for 50 cents each at a store in Harlem, one of the few places where black dolls could be purchased. They showed black and white children two white dolls and two black dolls, and asked the children to pick out the "nice" doll, the "pretty" doll, and the "bad" doll. Both groups tended to pick the white dolls as nice and pretty, and the black doll as bad. He repeated the study in the 1950s in South Carolina, where white students received far more funds for education than black children. The results were similar. He concluded that the lesson of black inferiority was so deep in society that even young black children understood it and believed it. As Clark noted, "A racist system inevitably destroys and damages human beings; it brutalizes and dehumanizes blacks and whites alike." In *Brown v. the Topeka Board of Education* (1954), the Supreme Court cited Clark's "doll" study in deciding that "separate was inherently unequal."

For his global effort to mobilize education in the cause of social justice—

©Jeremy E. Bigwood

Paulo Freire (1921–1997). Abandoning a career in law, Brazilian-born Freire committed himself to the education of the poor and politically oppressed. His efforts moved literacy from an educational tool to a political instrument.

Freire denounced teacher-centered classrooms. He believed that instructor domination denied the legitimacy of student experiences and treated students as secondary objects in the learning process. Freire championed a *critical pedagogy,* one that places the student at the center of the learning process. In Freire's pedagogy, student dialogues, knowledge, and skills are shared cooperatively, legitimizing their experiences. Students are taught how to generate their own questions, focus on their own social problems, and develop strategies to live more fruitful and satisfying lives. Teachers are not passive bystanders or the only source of classroom wisdom. Freire believed that teachers should

TEACHING TIP

Elusive History

Napoleon said that history is a myth that we agree to believe; Henry Ford thought history was "bunk"; Mark Twain was even more cynical, characterizing the very ink used to write history as "fluid prejudice." History always has a bias because only one side writes it, and more often than not, it is the side of power.

When you teach history, as well as some other subjects, you may want to leave your pre-learned ideas outside the classroom, and start fresh along with your students. Primary sources like original letters, correspondence, eyewitness reports, and print and media accounts will likely offer a more complete and accurate perspective than a single textbook version. (Even this one!)

Let's take the Civil War as an example. Most of us were taught that the Civil War was fought over states' rights, or slavery, or two colliding economic systems. (Which one were you taught?) But in *A People's History of the Civil War* (2005) by David Williams, we learn a very different story, a story of greed and class warfare. Poor southern farmers and northern factory workers were exploited and drafted to fight and often die in a war many opposed. Wealthy southerners and northerners were protected from the bloodshed by law, but used the war as an opportunity to grow their fortunes. Northern factory owners gladly bought southern cotton to make uniforms, because trading with the enemy to make a profit was fine for both sides. But profits did not mean quality products. In fact, the word "shoddy" comes from the Civil War. Back then, shoddy was a grade of cotton, the lowest quality cotton. When used to make uniforms, the uniforms would quickly disintegrate. It wasn't long before "shoddy" was applied to the poor quality of most things sold to the governments, north and south. This may not be the Civil War history many of us learned, but Williams provides an abundance of primary source documents to support his findings.

REFLECTION: What are the advantages of working with primary sources to help students reach their own insights? What are the downsides of this kind of learning?

facilitate and inspire, that teachers should "live part of their dreams within their educational space." Rather than unhappy witnesses to social injustice, teachers should be advocates for the poor and agents for social change. Freire's best-known work, ***Pedagogy of the Oppressed,*** illustrated how education could transform society.

Freire's approach obviously threatened the social order of many repressive governments, and he faced constant intimidation and threats. Following the military overthrow of the Brazilian government in 1964, Freire was jailed for "subversive" activities and later exiled. In the late 1960s, while studying in America, Freire witnessed racial unrest and the antiwar protests. These events convinced Freire that political oppression is present in "developed nations" as well as third world countries, that economic privilege does not guarantee political advantage, and that the pedagogy of the oppressed has worldwide significance.

We invite you to read about some additional hall of famers in the Profiles in Education section on Connect.

RAP 3.9

Publication of the Month

©De Agostino/Getty Images

Comenius (1592–1670), profiled for his pioneering work in identifying developmental stages of learning and his support of universal education.

©Georgios Kollidas/Alamy RF

Jean-Jacques Rousseau (1712–1778), profiled for his work in distinguishing schooling from education and for his concern with the stages of development.

©Hulton Archive/Getty Images

Johann Heinrich Pestalozzi (1746–1827), profiled for his recognition of the special needs of the disadvantaged and his work in curricular development.

©Hulton Archive/Getty Images

Johann Herbart (1776–1841), profiled for his contributions to moral development in education and for his creation of a structured methodology of instruction.

©Everett Collection Historical/Alamy

Emma Hart Willard (1787–1870), profiled for opening the door of higher education to women and for promoting professional teacher preparation.

©Everett Collection Historical/Alamy

Horace Mann (1796–1859), profiled for establishing free public schools and expanding the opportunities of poor as well as wealthy Americans, and for his vision of the central role of education in improving the quality of American life.

Source: Library of Congress, Prints and Photographs Division [LC-USZ62-49568]

Booker T. Washington (1856-1915), profiled for his contributions to the vocational education of black Americans and for establishing Tuskegee University.

©Historical/Corbis/Getty Images

John Dewey (1859–1952), profiled for his work in developing progressive education, for incorporating democratic practices in the educational process.

Source: Library of Congress Prints and Photographs Division [LC-USZ62-16767]

W. E. B. DuBois (1868–1963), profiled for cofounding the National Association for the Advancement of Colored People (NAACP) and for his efforts to encourage black Americans to pursue higher education.

©Bettmann/Getty Images

Jean Piaget (1896–1980), profiled for his creation of a theory of cognitive development.

©Science Source

Burrhus Frederick (B. F.) Skinner (1904–1990), profiled for his contributions in altering environments to promote learning.

CONNECT FOR *TEACHERS, SCHOOLS, AND SOCIETY*

Check out Connect, McGraw-Hill Education's interactive learning environment, to:

Read Current and Historical Articles

My Pedagogic Creed, by John Dewey, *School Journal,* January 1897.

Text excerpts from ***Narrative of the Life of Frederick Douglass: An American Slave,*** by Frederick Douglass, 1845.

Text excerpts from ***The Education of Free Men,*** by Horace Mann, 1846.

Reviving the Goal of An Integrated Society: A 21st Century Challenge, by Gary Orfield, *The Civil Rights Project,* January 14, 2009.

Analyze Case Studies

Hamilton High: From the 1950s through the 1980s, this case presents how a school has changed in reaction to societal and educational changes.

Watch Teachers, Students, And Classrooms In Action

Our **Online Video Album** for contemporary videos related to this chapter.

KEY TERMS AND PEOPLE

DISCUSSION QUESTIONS AND ACTIVITIES

1. In the colonial period, a number of factors influenced the kind of education you might receive. Describe how the following factors influenced educational opportunities:
   - Geography
   - Wealth
   - Race/ethnicity
   - Gender
2. Progressive education has sparked adamant critics and fervent supporters. Offer several arguments supporting the tenets of progressivism, as well as arguments against this movement.
3. In what ways are terms such as African Americans, Asian Americans, Hispanic Americans, or Arab Americans helpful? In what ways are these labels misleading?
4. Identify the contributions made by the following educators, whom some might consider candidates for the Hall of Fame: Septima Poinsette Clark, Madeline C. Hunter, Johnetta Cole, and Henri Mann.
5. Some teacher preparation programs do not consider or discuss the history of education, whereas other programs devote courses reviewing and analyzing educational history. Set up a debate arguing the pros and cons of the following proposition. Resolved: Teacher preparation programs should focus on current issues and not consider the history of education.

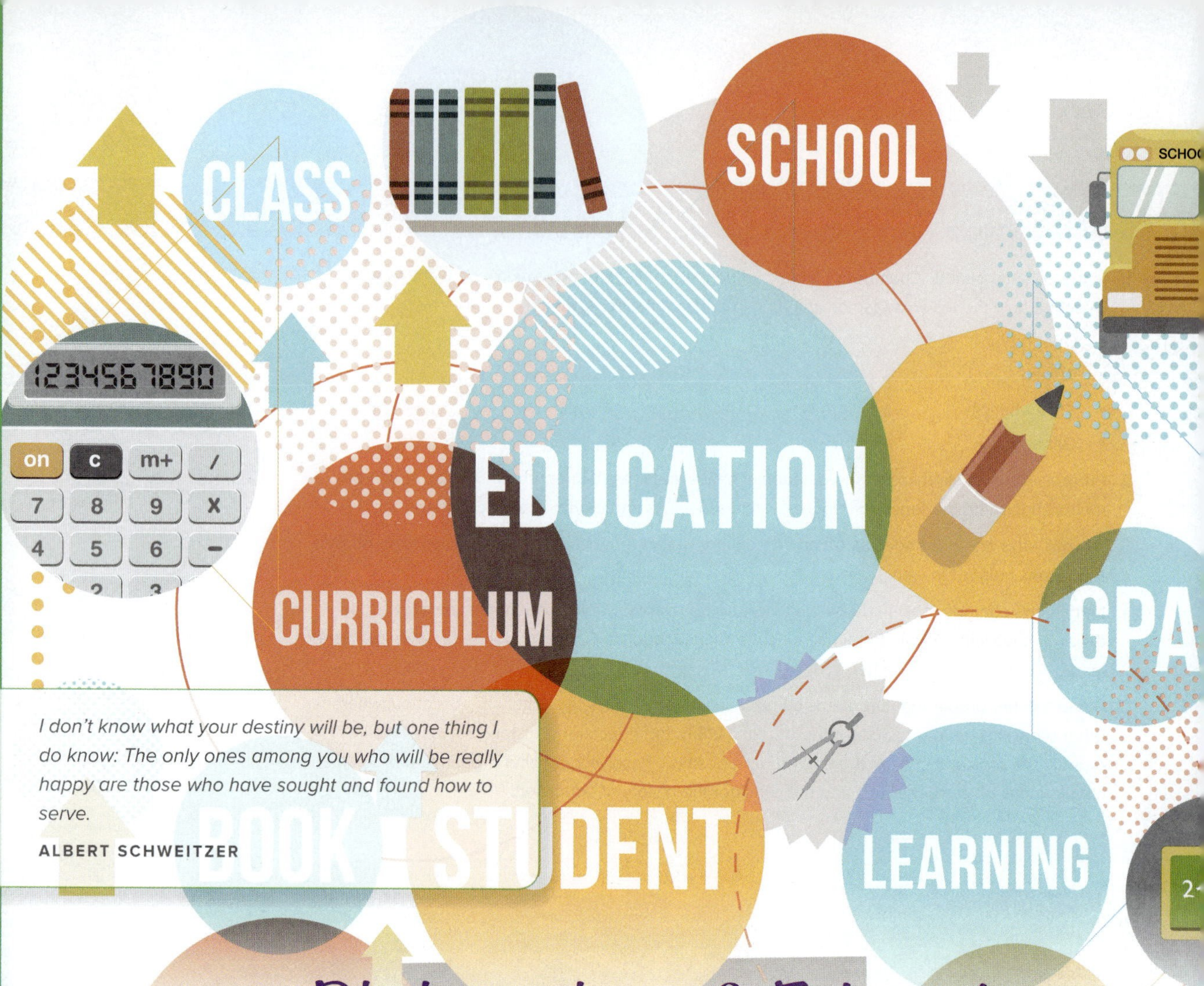

I don't know what your destiny will be, but one thing I do know: The only ones among you who will be really happy are those who have sought and found how to serve.

ALBERT SCHWEITZER

chapter 6 Philosophy of Education

Focus Questions

1. What is a philosophy of education, and why should it be important to you?
2. How do teacher-centered philosophies of education differ from student-centered philosophies of education?
3. What are some major philosophies of education in the United States today?
4. How are these philosophies reflected in school practices?
5. What are some of the psychological and cultural factors influencing education?
6. What were the contributions of Socrates, Plato, and Aristotle to Western philosophy, and how are their legacies reflected in education today?
7. How do metaphysics, epistemology, ethics, political philosophy, aesthetics, and logic factor into a philosophy of education?

Chapter Preview

The root for the word **philosophy** is made up of two Greek words: *philo,* meaning "love," and *sophos,* meaning "wisdom." For thousands of years, philosophers have been wrestling with fundamental questions: What is most real—the physical world or the realm of mind and spirit? What is the basis of human knowledge? What is the nature of the just society? Educators must take stances on such questions before they can determine what and how students should be taught.

Because educators do not always agree on the answers to these questions, different philosophies of education have emerged. Although there are some similarities, there are also profound differences in the way leading educators define the purpose of education, the role of the teacher, the nature of the curriculum and assessment, and the method of instruction.

This chapter is intended to start you on a path of thoughtfully considering your values and beliefs. Five influential philosophies will be described, and you will see how each can shape classroom life. We invite you to consider how psychological and cultural beliefs can also affect schools. We then revisit the roots of Western philosophy with three ancient Greeks as our guides: Socrates, Plato, and Aristotle. Finally, we briefly examine the building blocks of philosophy, the divisions within philosophy that focus on questions pertinent to educators: What is of worth? How do we know what we know? The ideas in this chapter will spark some very basic questions about your role in the classroom, and the school's role in society. Your answers to these questions will help you frame your philosophy of education.

Finding Your Philosophy of Education

What is a philosophy of education? Do you have one? Do you think it matters? If you are like most people, you probably have not given much thought to philosophy, in education or elsewhere. Being a practical person, you may be more concerned with other questions: Will I enjoy teaching? Will I be good at it? How will I handle discipline problems? Believe it or not, underlying the answers to those practical questions *is* your philosophy of education.

FOCUS QUESTION 1

What is a philosophy of education, and why should it be important to you?

At this point, your philosophy may still be taking shape (not a bad thing). Your beliefs may reflect an amalgam of different philosophies. Unfortunately, they may also be filled with inconsistencies. To help shape a coherent and useful educational philosophy, you must consider some basic—and very important—questions, such as:

What is the purpose of education?

What content and skills should schools teach?

How should schools teach this content?

What are the proper roles for teachers and students?

How should learning be measured?

Still not sure what a philosophy of education is all about, or how it shapes classroom and school life? Let's listen to some teachers discussing the direction a new charter school should take. You'll see that each teacher has very clear ideas about what schools are for, what students should learn, and how teachers should teach.

Hear that noise coming from the faculty room down the hall? Your potential colleagues sometimes get a bit loud as they debate the possible directions for the new charter school. As you listen in, try to sort out which of these educational directions appeals to you.

JACOB POLLACK: I am so excited! This new charter school can be just what we need, a chance to reestablish a positive reputation for the quality of public education! Let's face it, we are competing in a global economy, against nations whose students outscore ours on all the standardized tests that matter. It's embarrassing. I'd love to see a school with a strict code of conduct and core courses, like literature, history, math, and science, and no silly electives. It's all about rigorous standards.

MYRA MILLER: Jacob, you and I both would like to teach in a more rigorous school, but the truth is I'm fed up with testing. I'll tell you a secret: I don't much care whether South Korean kids or those at Country Day School score better than us on a multiple-choice test. Kids thirst for meaningful ideas. The school I envision would focus on classic works of literature and art. How about a school where we discuss Great Books like *Moby Dick, The Old Man and the Sea,* Plato's *Republic,* and Homer's *Iliad.* Maybe we can re-invent the all-but-extinct American student: One who knows not only how to read, but a student who actually *wants* to read, *enjoys* reading, and best of all, knows how to *think.*

MARCUS WASHINGTON: I agree with Myra that we need to move beyond today's tyranny of testing, but Hemingway and Homer are not the answers. Our job as teachers is to make certain that our students can do well in the real world. When I was in eighth grade, my class took a three-week trip around the Midwestern states by train. We researched and planned where to go; figured out how to read train schedules; used maps; and ended up learning math, history, geography, and writing. Talk about an integrated curriculum! We learned by doing. I want students to learn how to solve real-world problems, not just answer test questions or discuss books.

TED GOODHEART: At last, reality! But there are more pressing issues than a train trip. I want students to do more than simply fit into society; I want them to leave the world a better place than they found it. Behind our community's pretty façade are people in pain. Rather than insulate them from real-world concerns like poverty, violence, pollution, bigotry, and injustice, we should help our kids develop a social conscience and the political skills needed to improve our society. Teaching in a socially responsible charter school would be my dream.

CARA CAMUS: Everyone in this room has been trying to design a charter school backwards. Let's set aside what we as teachers want and consider a revolutionary idea: building a school based on what students want. Students must assume primary responsibility for their own learning. I would like our charter school staffed by teachers who are skilled in facilitating children to reach their personal goals. Believe it or not, I trust students, and I would give every child (even the youngest or least able) an equal voice in decision making. We have forgotten the purpose of schools: to help students find their way.

These teachers are not only discussing different approaches to a proposed charter school, but are also shedding light on five major educational philosophies. Do any of these diverse views sound attractive to you? Do any sound particularly unappealing? If so, note which of these teachers you thought reflected your own beliefs, and which were really off the mark. If you found that you had strong opinions—pro or con—about one or more of these ideas, then you are beginning to get in touch with your educational philosophy. Let's leave the faculty-room conversation and take a closer look at your own philosophical leanings. The following inventory can help you sort out tenets of your educational philosophy.

Inventory of Philosophies of Education

As you read through the following statements about schools and teaching, decide how strongly you agree or disagree. We will help you interpret your results. Write your response to the left of each statement, using the following scale:

5 Agree strongly
4 Agree
3 Neither agree nor disagree
2 Disagree
1 Disagree strongly

_____ 1. A school curriculum should include a common body of information that all students should know.

_____ 2. The school curriculum should focus on the great ideas that have survived through time.

_____ 3. The gap between the real world and schools should be bridged through field trips, internships, and adult mentors.

_____ 4. Schools should prepare students for analyzing and solving the social problems they will face beyond the classroom.

_____ 5. Each student should determine his or her individual curriculum, and teachers should guide and help them.

_____ 6. Students should not be promoted from one grade to the next until they have read and mastered certain key material.

_____ 7. Schools, above all, should develop students' abilities to think deeply, analytically, and creatively, rather than focus on transient concerns like social skills and current trends.

_____ 8. Whether inside or outside the classroom, teachers must stress the relevance of what students are learning to real and current events.

_____ 9. Education should enable students to recognize injustices in society, and schools should promote projects to redress social inequities.

_____ 10. Students who do not want to study much should not be required to do so.

_____ 11. Teachers and schools should emphasize academic rigor, discipline, hard work, and respect for authority.

_____ 12. Education is not primarily about workers and the world economic competition; learning should be appreciated for its own sake, and students should enjoy reading, learning, and discussing intriguing ideas.

_____ 13. The school curriculum should be designed by teachers to respond to the experiences and needs of the students.

_____ 14. Schools should promote positive group relationships by teaching about different ethnic and racial groups.

_____ 15. The purpose of school is to help students understand themselves, appreciate their distinctive talents and insights, and find their own unique place in the world.

_____ 16. For the United States to be competitive economically in the world marketplace, schools must bolster their academic requirements to train more competent workers.

_____ 17. Teachers ought to teach from the classics, because important insights related to many of today's challenges and concerns are found in these Great Books.

_____ 18. Students learn effectively through social interaction, so schools should plan for substantial social interaction in their curricula.

_____ 19. Students should be taught how to be politically literate, and learn how to improve the quality of life for all people.

_____ 20. The central role of the school is to provide students with options and choices. The student must decide what and how to learn.

_____ 21. Schools must provide students with a firm grasp of basic facts regarding the books, people, and events that have shaped the nation's heritage.

_____ 22. The teacher's main goal is to help students unlock the insights learned over time, so they can gain wisdom from the great thinkers of the past.

_____ 23. Students should be active participants in the learning process, involved in democratic class decision making and reflective thinking.

_____ 24. Teaching should mean more than simply transmitting the Great Books, which are replete with biases and prejudices. Rather, schools need to identify a new list of Great Books more appropriate for today's world, and prepare students to create a better society than their ancestors did.

_____ 25. Effective teachers help students to discover and develop their personal values, even when those values conflict with traditional ones.

_____ 26. Teachers should help students constantly reexamine their beliefs. In history, for example, students should learn about those who have been historically omitted: the poor, the non-European, women, and people of color.

_____ 27. Frequent objective testing is the best way to determine what students know. Rewarding students when they learn, even when they learn small things, is the key to successful teaching.

_____ 28. Education should be a responsibility of the family and the community, rather than delegated to formal and impersonal institutions, such as schools.

Interpreting Your Responses

RAP 3.5

Putting Your Philosophy into the Classroom

Write your responses to statements 1 through 25 in the columns provided on p. 155; then tally up your score in each column. (We will return to items 26 to 28 in a bit.) Each column is labeled with a philosophy and the name of the teacher who represented that view in this chapter's opening scenario (the charter school discussion). The highest possible score in any one column is 25, and the lowest possible score is 5. Scores in the 20s indicate strong agreement, and scores below 10 indicate disagreement with the tenets of a particular philosophy.

Your scores in columns A through E, respectively, represent how much you agree or disagree with the beliefs of five major educational philosophies: essentialism, perennialism, progressivism, social reconstructionism, and existentialism. Check back to see if your scores reflect your initial reactions to these teachers' points of view. For example, if you agreed with Jacob's proposal to create an "Academy," then you probably agreed with a number of the statements associated with essentialist education, and your score in this column may be fairly high.

A Essentialism (Jacob)	B Perennialism (Myra)	C Progressivism (Marcus)	D Social Reconstructionism (Ted)	E Existentialism (Cara)
1. ____	2. ____	3. ____	4. ____	5. ____
6. ____	7. ____	8. ____	9. ____	10. ____
11. ____	12. ____	13. ____	14. ____	15. ____
16. ____	17. ____	18. ____	19. ____	20. ____
21. ____	22. ____	23. ____	24. ____	25. ____
Scores ____	____	____	____	____

Compare your five scores. What is your highest? What is your lowest? Which three statements best reflect your views on education? Are they congruent and mutually supporting? As you look at the statements that you least support, what do those statements tell you about your values? You may notice that your philosophical leanings, as identified by your responses to statements in the inventory, reflect your general outlook on life. For example, your responses may indicate whether you generally trust people to do the right thing, or if you believe that individuals need supervision. How have your culture, religion, upbringing, and political beliefs shaped your responses to the items in this inventory? How have your own education and life experiences influenced your philosophical beliefs?

Now that you have begun to examine varying beliefs about education, you may even want to lay claim to a philosophical label. But what do these philosophical labels mean? In the following pages we will introduce you to all five of these educational philosophies and look at their impact in the classroom.

Five Philosophies of Education

Essentialism, perennialism, progressivism, social reconstructionism, and existentialism. Taken together, these five schools of thought do not exhaust the list of possible educational philosophies you may consider, but they present strong frameworks for you to refine your own educational philosophy. We can place these five philosophies on a continuum, from teacher-centered (some would say "authoritarian") to student-centered (some would characterize as "permissive").

Let's begin our discussion with the teacher-centered philosophies.

Teacher-Centered Philosophies

Traditionally, *teacher-centered philosophies* emphasize the importance of transferring knowledge, information, and skills from the older (presumably wiser) generation to the younger one. The teacher's role is to instill respect for authority, perseverance, duty, consideration, and practicality. When students demonstrate through tests and writings that they are competent in academic subjects and traditional skills, and through their actions that they have disciplined minds and adhere to traditional morals and behavior, then both the school and the teacher have been successful. (In Chapter 9, we will revisit these teacher-centered philosophies

FOCUS QUESTIONS 2–4

How do teacher-centered philosophies of education differ from student-centered philosophies of education?

What are some major philosophies of education in the United States today?

How are these philosophies reflected in school practices?

and explore how they view the primary purpose of schools as "passing the cultural baton.") The major teacher-centered philosophies of education are essentialism and perennialism.

Essentialism

Essentialism strives to teach students the accumulated knowledge of our civilization through core courses in the traditional academic disciplines. Essentialists aim to instill students with the "essentials" of academic knowledge, patriotism, and character development. This traditional or **back-to-basics** approach is meant to train the mind, promote reasoning, and ensure a common culture among all Americans.

American educator **William Bagley** popularized the term *essentialism* in the 1930s,[1] and essentialism has been a dominant influence in American education since World War II. Factors such as the launching of *Sputnik* in 1957, the 1983 report *A Nation at Risk,* standardized testing mandated by *No Child Left Behind,* intense global economic competition, and increased immigration into the United States have all kept essentialism at center stage. Some educators refer to the present period as neo-essentialism because of the increased core graduation requirements, stronger standards, and more testing of both students and teachers.

Not all essentialists are the same. Author Allan Bloom, *The Closing of the American Mind,* contends that immigration and multiculturalism threaten the traditional "American" identity. He advocates for a time-honored, Anglo-Saxon curriculum reflecting European traditions. On the other hand, **E. D. Hirsch Jr.** advocates for a more inclusive curriculum that offers all students a shared knowledge, a common curriculum (not unlike Horace Mann's idea of a common school). Hirsch wrote *Cultural Literacy: What Every American Needs to Know* and *The Knowledge Deficit,* and he suggests facts and ideas that might be included in his curriculum. Although people refer to his work by the popular title of his book, cultural literacy, he prefers to call it "core knowledge," a knowledge that would be shared by all Americans.[2]

Most of you reading this chapter have been educated in essentialist schools. You were probably required to take many courses in English, history, math, and science. Such a program would be typical in an essentialist school.

The current emphasis on pen-and-paper testing is an example of essentialism in action.

©Tom Grill/Corbis RF

The Essentialist Classroom Essentialists urge that traditional disciplines such as math, science, history, foreign language, and literature form the foundation of the curriculum, which is referred to as the **core curriculum.** Essentialists frown upon electives that "water-down" academic content. Elementary students receive instruction in skills such as writing, reading, measuring, and computing. Even when studying art and music, subjects most often associated with the development of creativity, students master a body of information and basic techniques, gradually moving to more complex skills and detailed knowledge. Only by mastering the required material are students promoted to the next higher level.

Essentialists maintain that classrooms should be oriented toward the teacher, who should serve as an intellectual and moral role model for the students. The teachers or administrators decide what is most important for the students to learn and place little emphasis on student interests, particularly when such interests divert time and attention from the academic curriculum. Essentialist teachers rely on achievement test scores to evaluate progress. Essentialists expect that students will leave school possessing not only basic skills and an extensive body of knowledge but also disciplined, practical minds, capable of applying schoolhouse lessons in the real world.

Essentialism in Action: Rancho Elementary School Rancho Elementary School in Marin County, California, proudly promotes its essentialist philosophy, and announces on its Web page that "students will participate in a highly enriched environment exposing them to rigorous academics, foreign language, citizenship/leadership opportunities, and grade appropriate technology." Its mission is the acquisition of basic skills through direct instruction in the core academic areas, including reading through phonics. As a testament to its success, the school boasts high test scores. Beyond academics, the school also emphasizes "firm, consistent discipline" and close parent–teacher relationships.

RAP 3.3
What You See and What You Get

If you do not live in Marin County, you may not have heard of Rancho, but you may have heard of a school belonging to The Coalition of Essential Schools, as two hundred schools nationwide are members. But don't be misled by the name. Although these schools promote intellectual rigor, test students for mastery of information, and emphasize strong thinking skills across subjects, they are not pure examples of essentialism. The schools do not share a fixed core curriculum, they emphasize the study of single topics or issues in depth, and they incorporate components of perennialism, which brings us to the other teacher-centered philosophy.

Perennialism

Perennialism is a cousin to essentialism. Both advocate teacher-centered classrooms. Both tolerate little flexibility in the curriculum. Both implement rigorous standards. Both aim to sharpen students' intellectual powers and enhance their moral qualities. So what are the differences?

Perennialists organize their schools around books, ideas, and concepts and criticize essentialists for the vast amount of factual information they require students to absorb in their push for "cultural literacy." Perennial means "everlasting"—a perennialist education focuses on enduring themes and questions that span the ages. Perennialists recommend that students learn directly from the **Great Books**—works by history's finest thinkers and writers, books as meaningful today as when they were first written.

Perennialists believe that the goal of education should be to develop rational thought and to discipline minds to think rigorously. Perennialists see education as a sorting mechanism, a way to identify and prepare the intellectually gifted for leadership, while providing vocational training for the rest of society. They lament the change in universities over the centuries, from institutions where a few gifted students (and teachers) rigorously pursued truth for its own sake, to a glorified training ground for future careers.

Those of you who received a religious education might recognize the perennialist philosophy. Many parochial schools reflect the perennialist tradition with a curriculum that focuses on analyzing great religious books (such as the *Bible*, the *Talmud*, or the *Quran*), discerning moral truths, and honoring those moral values. In the classroom description that follows, we will concentrate on secular perennialism as formulated in the twentieth-century United States by such individuals as Robert Hutchins and Mortimer Adler.

In a perennialist classroom, primary sources rather than textbooks are the center of learning.

©Brand X Pictures/Getty Images RF

The Perennialist Classroom As in an essentialist classroom, students in a perennialist classroom spend considerable time and energy mastering the three "Rs," reading, 'riting, and 'rithmetic. Greatest importance is placed on reading, the key to unlocking the enduring ideas found in the Great Books. Special attention is given to teaching values and character training, often through discussion about the underlying values and moral principles in a story. High school marks an increase in academic rigor as more challenging books are explored, including works of Darwin, Homer, and Shakespeare. Few elective choices are allowed. In an extreme example, **Mortimer Adler** proposed in his *Paideia Proposal* (1982) a single elementary and secondary curriculum for all students, with no curricular electives except in the choice of a second language.

Electives are not the only things perennialists go without. Critics chastise perennialists for the lack of women, people of color, and non-Western ideas in the Great Books they teach, but many perennialists are unmoved by such criticism. To them, "training the mind" is ageless, beyond demographic concerns and transient trends. As Mortimer Adler wrote,

> The Great Books of ancient and medieval as well as modern times are a repository of knowledge and wisdom, a tradition of culture which must initiate each generation.[3]

You also find few if any textbooks in a perennialist class. **Robert Hutchins,** who as president of the University of Chicago introduced the Great Books program, once opined that textbooks "have probably done as much to degrade the American intelligence as any single force."[4] Because perennialist teachers see themselves as discussion seminar leaders and facilitators, lectures are rare.

Perennialism in Action: St. John's College The best-known example of perennialist education today takes place at a private institution unaffiliated with any religion: St. John's College, founded in 1784 in Annapolis, Maryland (www.sjcsf.edu). St. John's College uses the Great Books as a core curriculum and assigns readings in the fields of literature, philosophy and theology, history and the social sciences, mathematics and natural science, and music. Students write extensively and attend seminars twice weekly to discuss assigned readings. They also complete a number of laboratory experiences and tutorials in language, mathematics, and music, guided by the faculty, who are called *tutors.* Seniors take oral examinations at the beginning and at the end of their senior year and write a final essay that must be approved before they are allowed to graduate.

Although grades are given to facilitate admission to graduate programs, students receive their grades only upon request and are expected to learn only for learning's sake. Because the St. John's experience thrives best in a small-group atmosphere, the college established a second campus in 1964 in Santa Fe, New Mexico, to handle additional enrollment.

A CLOSER LOOK

Essentialists and Perennialists: Different Core Curricula

Although both essentialism and perennialism promote a traditional approach to education, these teacher-centered philosophies draw their curricula from different sources. The first column includes excerpts from a typical essentialist list (we included a few of the words and phrases under the letter "c"); the second column provides selections from the perennialists' *Great Books* curriculum. Remember, these are only a few suggestions from very long lists!

THE LIST (ESSENTIALISM)

centigrade
center of gravity
cerebellum
Calvary
capital expenditure
Cèzanne
Canberra
Cain and Abel
Caesar Augustus
Candide
cast pearls before swine
Cascade Mountains
carbon dioxide
carte blanche
Caruso, Enrico
cathode ray tube

GREAT BOOKS (PERENNIALISM)

Aristotle, *Sense and Sensible*
The Bible
Geoffrey Chaucer, *Canterbury Tales*
Charles Darwin, *On the Origin of Species*
Charles Dickens, *Oliver Twist*
F. Scott Fitzgerald, *The Great Gatsby*
Homer, *The Iliad*
James Joyce, *Ulysses*
The Koran
Karl Marx, *Das Kapital*
Herman Melville, *Moby Dick*
Thomas Paine, *Common Sense*
Plato, *Charmides*
Jonathan Swift, *Gulliver's Travels*
Virginia Woolf, *Night and Day*
Leo Tolstoy, *War and Peace*

REFLECTION: Does this list make you feel culturally literate—or illiterate? Do you believe that lists like this one should be important? Why or why not?

Student-Centered Philosophies

Student-centered philosophies are less authoritarian, less concerned with the past and "training the mind," and more focused on individual needs, contemporary relevance, and preparing students for a changing future. Progressivism, social reconstructionism, and existentialism place the learner at the center of the educational process: Students and teachers work together on determining what should be learned and how best to learn it. School is not seen as an institution that controls and directs youth, or works to preserve and transmit the core culture, but as an institution that works with youth to improve society or help students realize their individuality.

Progressivism

Progressivism organizes schools around the concerns, curiosity, and real-world experiences of students. The progressive teacher facilitates learning by helping students formulate meaningful questions and devise strategies to answer those questions. Answers are not drawn from lists or even Great Books; they are discovered through real-world experience. Progressivism is the educational application of a philosophy called pragmatism. According to **pragmatism,** the way to determine if an idea has merit is simple: Test it. If the idea works in the real world, then it has merit. Both pragmatism and progressivism originated in America, the home of a very practical and pragmatic people. John Dewey refined and applied pragmatism to education, establishing what became known as progressivism.

John Dewey was a reformer with a background in philosophy and psychology who taught that people learn best through social interaction in the real world. Dewey believed that because social learning had meaning, it endured. Book learning, on the other hand, was no substitute for actually doing things. Progressivists do not believe that the mind can be disciplined through reading Great Books, rather that the mind should be trained to analyze experience thoughtfully and draw conclusions objectively.

Dewey saw education as an opportunity to learn how to apply previous experiences in new ways. Dewey believed that students, facing an ever-changing world, should master the scientific method: (1) become aware of a problem, (2) define it, (3) propose various hypotheses to solve it, (4) examine the consequences of each hypothesis in the light of previous experience, and (5) test the most likely solution. (For a biography of John Dewey, visit Connect.)

Dewey regarded democracy and freedom as far superior to the political ideas of earlier times. Dewey saw traditional, autocratic, teacher-centered schools as the antithesis of democratic ideals. He viewed progressive schools as a working model of democracy. Dewey wrote:

> To imposition from above is opposed expression and cultivation of individuality; to external discipline is opposed free activity; to learning from texts and teachers, learning through experience; to acquisition of isolated skills and techniques by drill is opposed acquisition of them as means of attaining ends which make direct vital appeal; to preparation for a more or less remote future is opposed making the most of the opportunities of present life; to statistics and materials is opposed acquaintance with a changing world.[5]

The Progressive Classroom Walk into a progressivist classroom and you will not find a teacher standing at the front of the room talking to rows of seated students. Rather, you will likely see children working in small groups, moving about and talking freely. Some children might be discussing a science experiment while another group works on a model volcano and a third prepares for a presentation. Interest centers would be located throughout the room, filled with books, materials, software, and projects designed to attract student interest on a wide array of topics. Finally you notice the teacher, walking around the room, bending over to talk with individual students and small groups, asking questions and making suggestions. You sense that the last thing on her mind is the standardized state test scheduled for next week.[6]

Progressivists build the curriculum around the experiences, interests, and abilities of students, and encourage students to work together cooperatively. Teachers feel no compulsion to focus their students' attention on one discrete discipline at a time, and students integrate several subjects in their studies. Thought-provoking activities augment reading, and a game such as Monopoly might be used to illustrate the principles of capitalism versus socialism. Computer simulations, field trips, and interactive Web sites on the Internet offer realistic learning challenges for students and build on students' multiple intelligences.

Progressivism in Action: The Laboratory School In 1896, while a professor at the University of Chicago, Dewey founded the Laboratory School as a testing ground for his educational ideas. Dewey's writings and his work with the **Laboratory**

Learning by doing is a touchstone of progressivism.

©Ariel Skelley/Blend Images LLC RF

School set the stage for the progressive education movement. Based on the view that educators, like scientists, need a place to test their ideas, Dewey's Laboratory School eventually became the most famous experimental school in the history of U.S. education, a place where thousands observed Dewey's innovations in school design, methods, and curriculum. Although the school remained under Dewey's control for only eight years and never enrolled more than 140 students (ages 3 to 13) in a single year, its influence was enormous.

Dewey designed the Lab School with only one classroom but with several facilities for experiential learning: a science laboratory, an art room, a woodworking shop, and a kitchen. Children were likely to make their own weights and measures in the laboratory, illustrate their own stories in the art room, build a boat in the shop, and learn chemistry in the kitchen. They were unlikely to learn through isolated exercises or drills, which, according to Dewey, students consider irrelevant. Because Dewey believed that students learn from social interaction, the school used many group methods such as cooperative model-making, field trips, role-playing, and dramatizations. Dewey maintained that group techniques make the students better citizens, developing, for example, their willingness to share responsibilities.

Children in the Laboratory School were not promoted from one grade to another after mastering certain material. Rather, they were grouped according to their individual interests and abilities. For all its child-centered orientation, however, the Laboratory School remained hierarchical in the sense that the students were never given a role comparable to that of the staff in determining the school's educational practices.

Social Reconstructionism

Social reconstructionism encourages schools, teachers, and students to focus their studies and energies on alleviating pervasive social inequities and, as the name implies, reconstruct society into a new and more just social order. Although social reconstructionists agree with progressivists that schools should concentrate on the needs of students, they split from progressivism in the 1920s after growing impatient with the slow pace of change in schools and in society. **George Counts**, a student of Dewey, published his classic book, *Dare the Schools Build a New Social Order?* in which he outlined a more ambitious, and clearly more radical, approach to education. Counts's book, written in 1932, was no doubt influenced by the human cost of the Great Depression. He proposed that schools focus on reforming society, an idea that caught the imagination and sparked the ideals of educators both in this country and abroad.

Social challenges and problems provide a natural (and moral) direction for curricular and instructional activities. Racism, sexism, climate change and environmental pollution, homelessness, poverty, substance abuse, homophobia, and violence are rooted in misinformation and thrive in ignorance. Therefore, social reconstructionists believe that school is the ideal place to begin ameliorating social problems. The teacher's role is to explore social problems, suggest alternative perspectives, and facilitate student analysis of these problems. Although convincing, cajoling, or moralizing about the importance of addressing human tragedy would be a natural teacher response, such adult-led decision making flies in the face of reconstructionist philosophy. A social reconstructionist teacher must model democratic principles. Students and teachers are expected to live and learn in a democratic culture; the students themselves must select educational objectives and social priorities.

The Social Reconstructionist Classroom A social reconstructionist teacher creates lessons that both intellectually inform and emotionally stir students about the inequities that surround them. A class might read a book and visit a photojournalist's exhibit portraying violent acts of racism. If the book, the exhibit, and the class discussion that follows move the students, the class might choose to pursue a long-term project to investigate the problem. One group of students might analyze news coverage of racial and ethnic groups in the community. Another student group might conduct a survey analyzing community perceptions of racial groups and race relations. Students might visit city hall and examine arrest and trial records to determine the role race plays in differential application of the law. Students might examine government records for information about housing patterns, income levels, graduation rates, and other relevant statistics. The teacher's role would be as facilitator: assisting students in focusing their questions, developing a strategy, helping to organize visits, and ensuring that the data collected and analyzed meet standards of objectivity. Throughout, the teacher would be instructing students on research techniques, statistical evaluation, writing skills, and public communications.

In a social reconstructionist class, a research project is more than an academic exercise; the class is engaged in a genuine effort to improve society. In this case, the class might arrange to meet with political leaders, encouraging them to create programs or legislation to respond to issues the students uncovered. The students might seek a *pro bono* attorney to initiate legal action to remedy a social injustice they unmasked. Or the students might take their findings directly to the media by holding a press conference. They might also create a Web page to share their findings and research methods with students in other parts of the country, or other parts of the world. How would the teacher decide if the students have met the educational goals? In this example, an objective, well-prepared report would be one criterion, and reducing or eliminating a racist community practice would be a second measure of success. (See p. 163, Contemporary Issues: A View from the Field to learn how an entire school and an individual teacher follow the social reconstructionist philosophy to improve the environment.)

Digital social activism—often coined "clicktivism"—extends the impact of social reconstructionism to a global stage. Here are a few examples[7]:

1. *The Ryan's Well Project*. In first grade, Ryan learned that many people around the world don't have access to clean water. Since then, he's raised money and awareness, helping to build more than 700 wells in poor communities. (http://www.ryanswell.ca/)
2. *25 Days to Make a Difference*. When she was in fourth grade, Laura lost her grandfather to brain cancer. To honor him, she decided to do simple things to improve the world. She blogged about her 25-day effort, and watched her plan grow into a 16-month worldwide effort. (http://twentyfivedays.wordpress.com/about/)
3. *Be Straw Free*. Nine-year-old Milo was shocked to learn that 500 million plastic straws are used every day, and they take thousands of years to break down in landfills. So Milo created a Web site that describes how people can make their communities straw-free zones. (http://ecocycle.org/bestrawfree)

PROFILE IN EDUCATION

Jane Roland Martin

Jane Roland Martin advocates the development of "schoolhomes" that support what she calls the three Cs—caring, concern, and connection. Her social reconstructionist vision focuses on fostering students' individual emotional and cognitive needs.

Read a full profile of Jane Roland Martin on Connect.

©Jane Roland Martin

connect

GLOBAL VIEW

The Council on Global Education is dedicated to the development of a new model of education for the child in the twenty-first century. Its four building blocks are universal values, global understanding, excellence in all things, and service to humanity. www.globaleducation.org

CONTEMPORARY ISSUES

A View from the Field: Greening Schools

Sidwell Friends Middle School in Washington, D.C., is one of a growing number of green schools. Guided by its Quaker values, Sidwell Friends is committed to practicing responsible environmental stewardship. The building itself has achieved a LEED Platinum green certification, the highest level awarded.

Every aspect of the building has been constructed or remodeled with an eye toward conservation and sustainability. Photovoltaic panels on the roof provide 5 percent of the school's energy, which helps power the computer lab. On the rooftop garden, students grow herbs and vegetables for their school lunches. A constructed wetland in front of the school looks like an attractive, sloping landscape with a variety of plants, but it is much more. The school's wastewater flows below, filtered and cleaned by the plants and microorganisms, and then is recycled and used in the school's toilets. Skylights and reflective panels maximize the natural light in classrooms, a renovation that has been shown to improve academic performance. The windows, with their light-filtering shades, are the single most energy-efficient step employed in the building: Sidwell uses 10 to 15 percent of the energy of a comparable building to light the school. Even the siding on the building is green; the wood cladding is made from reclaimed cedar wine casks. Sidwell Friends represents an amazing institutional commitment to environmental sustainability. Educators use these building innovations as teaching tools, to help students understand the importance of protecting our planet. More and more, teachers across the nation are also promoting green living. Take, for example, Andy Stephens.

Andy Stephens is a science teacher at CALS Early College High School in Los Angeles. Andy's school is not a certified green school but he incorporates environmental education into his curriculum.

> We focus on the impacts we have at our school in terms of energy usage, transportation, waste, recycling, and indoor air quality. In a culminating project, I work with a team of teachers to create an interdisciplinary (math, science, history, English) action project that includes a research paper, civic action, presentation, and reflection. Students look at the science behind an issue, mathematically analyze data, write about the history of the issue, and take action.

Andy also leads the school's environmental club, the Mean Green Team. The club's many activities include beach cleanups and peer education.

Andy was actively interested in the environment before becoming a teacher. He was an avid hiker, hunter, and fisherman growing up in Washington. "I was galvanized towards action at a young age thanks to many outdoor experiences and my connection to the land."

Courtesy of Andy Stephens.

More information about Sidwell Friends School and its green building can be found at www.sidwell.edu.

Andy Stephens has a BA in economics from Occidental College and completed his master's in science education at California State University, Northridge in 2008.

Social Reconstructionism in Action: Paulo Freire **Paulo Freire** believed that schools were just another institution perpetuating social inequities while serving the interests of the dominant group. Like social reconstructionism itself, Freire's beliefs grew during the Great Depression of the 1930s, when he experienced hunger and poverty firsthand. Influenced by Marxist and neo-Marxist ideas, Freire accused schools of perpetuating the status quo views of the rich and powerful "for the purpose of keeping the masses submerged and content in a culture of silence."[8] Schools were endorsing **social Darwinism,** the idea that society is an ingenious "sorting" system, one in which the more talented rise to the top, while those less deserving find themselves at the bottom of the social and economic pecking order. The conclusion: Those with money deserve it, those without money deserve their lot in life, and poverty is a normal, preordained part of reality.

In social reconstructionism, students not only learn by doing, they learn to make the world a better, more just place to live.

©JGI/Jamie Grill/Blend Images LLC RF

Freire rejected this conclusion. He did not believe that schools should be viewed as "banks," where the privileged deposit ideas such as social Darwinism to be spoon-fed into the limited minds of the dispossessed. He envisioned schools as a place where the poor can acquire the skills to regain control of their lives and influence the social and economic forces that locked them in poverty in the first place. Freire engaged the poor as equal partners in dialogues that explored their economic and social problems and possible solutions. Freire believed in **praxis,** the doctrine that when actions are based on sound theory and values, they can make a real difference in the world. (It is no accident that the term *praxis* is also the name given to the teacher competency tests required by many states.) Freire's ideas took hold not only in his native Brazil but in poor areas around the globe. As poor farmworkers became literate and aware, they organized for their self-improvement and began to work for change. It is not surprising that the autocratic leaders of his country eventually forced him into exile, for he had turned schooling into a liberating force. (For a biography of Paulo Freire, see the "Hall of Fame: Profiles in Education" in Chapter 5.)

Existentialism

Existentialism, the final student-centered philosophy we shall discuss, places the highest priority on students directing their own learning. **Existentialism** asserts that the purpose of education is to help children find the meaning and direction in their lives, and it rejects the notion that adults should or could direct meaningful learning for children. Existentialists do not believe that "truth" is objective and applicable to all. Instead, each of us must look within ourselves to discover our own truth, our own purpose in life. Teaching students what adults believe they should learn is neither efficient nor effective; in fact, most of this "learning" will be forgotten. Instead, each student should decide what he or she needs to learn, and when to learn it. As the Buddhist proverb reminds us: When the student is ready, the teacher will appear.

There is little doubt that for many readers this is the most challenging of all the philosophies, and schools built on this premise will seem the most alien. We are a culture very connected to the outside world, and far less connected to our inner voice, or as an existentialist might say, our essence. We compete with one another for material goods, and we are distracted by hundreds of cable channels, iPads, smartphones, and a constant array of external stimuli. Thinking about why we are here and finding our purpose in life is not what schools typically do, but existentialists believe it is precisely what they should do. Schools should help each of us answer the fundamental questions: Why am I here? What is my purpose?

The Existentialist Classroom Existentialism in the classroom is a powerful rejection of traditional, and particularly essentialist, thinking. In the existentialist classroom, subject matter takes second place to helping the students understand and appreciate themselves as unique individuals. The teacher's role is to help students define their own essence by exposing them to various paths they may take in life and by creating an environment in which they can freely choose their way. Existentialism, more than other educational philosophies, affords students great latitude in their choice of subject matter and activity.

The existentialist curriculum often emphasizes the humanities as a means of providing students with vicarious experiences that will help unleash their creativity and self-expression. For example, existentialists focus on the actions of historical individuals, each of whom provides a model for the students to explore. Math and the natural

Teacher- Versus Student-Centered Approaches To Education

TEACHER-CENTERED APPROACHES ARE BEST BECAUSE ...

AFTER CENTURIES OF EXPERIENCE, WE KNOW WHAT TO TEACH

From Plato to Orwell, great writers and thinkers of the past light our way into the future. We must pass our cherished cultural legacy on to the next generation.

TEACHERS MUST SELECT WHAT IS WORTH KNOWING

The knowledge explosion showers us with mountains of new, complex information on a daily basis. Selecting what students should learn is a daunting challenge. Teachers, not students, are trained and best equipped to determine what is of value. To ask students to choose what they should learn would be the height of irresponsibility.

SCHOOLS MUST BE INSULATED FROM EXTERNAL DISTRACTIONS

Students can be easily distracted by the "excitement" of contemporary events. Although academic and rigorous school-based learning may be less flashy and less appealing, in the long run, it is far more valuable. Once schoolwork has been mastered, students will be well prepared to leave the sanctuary of learning and confront the outside world.

DISCIPLINED MINDS, RESPECTFUL CITIZENS

Students who listen thoughtfully and participate respectfully in classroom discussions learn several important lessons. For one, they learn the worth and wisdom of Western culture. They also learn to appreciate and to honor those who brought them this heritage, the guardians of their freedom and culture: their teachers.

STUDENT-CENTERED APPROACHES ARE BEST BECAUSE ...

GENUINE LEARNING ORIGINATES WITH THE LEARNER

People learn best what they want to learn, what they feel they should or need to learn. Students find lessons imposed "from above" to be mostly irrelevant, and the lessons are quickly forgotten.

THEY BEST PREPARE STUDENTS FOR THE INFORMATION AGE

The knowledge explosion is actually a powerful argument for student-directed learning. Teachers can't possibly teach everything. We must equip students with research skills, then fan the flames of curiosity so they will want to learn for themselves. Then students can navigate the information age, finding and evaluating new information.

EDUCATION IS A VITAL AND ORGANIC PART OF SOCIETY

The most important lessons of life are found not on the pages of books or behind the walls of a school but in the real world. Students need to work and learn directly in the community, from cleaning up the environment to reducing violence. Social action projects and service learning can offer a beacon of hope for the community while building compassionate values within our students.

HUMAN DIGNITY IS LEARNED IN DEMOCRATIC CLASSROOMS

Democracy is learned through experience, not books. Students flourish when they are respected; they are stifled when they are told what and how to think. As students manage their own learning, they master the most important lessons any school can teach: the importance of the individual's ideas and inner motivation.

connect YOU DECIDE...

Do you find yourself influenced more by the arguments supporting teacher-centered approaches or student-centered approaches? Are there elements of each that you find appealing? How will your classroom practices reflect your philosophy?

sciences may be de-emphasized because their subject matter is less fruitful for promoting self-awareness. Career education is regarded more as a means of teaching students about their potential than of teaching a livelihood. In art, existentialism encourages individual creativity and imagination more than it does the imitation of established models.

Existentialist learning is self-paced and self-directed and includes a great deal of individual contact with the teacher. Honest interpersonal relationships are emphasized; roles and "official" status are de-emphasized. According to philosopher Maxine Greene, teachers themselves must be deeply involved in their own learning and questioning: "Only a teacher in search of his freedom can inspire a student to search for his own." Greene asserts that education should move teachers and students to "wide awakeness," the ability to discover their own truths.[9]

Although elements of existentialism occasionally appear in public schools, this philosophy has not been widely disseminated. In an age of high-stakes tests and standards, only a few schools, mostly private, implement existentialist ideas. Even Summerhill, the well-known existentialist school founded in England by A. S. Neill in 1921, struggles to persevere with its unusual educational approach.

Existentialism in Action: The Sudbury Valley School Visit Sudbury Valley School just outside Boston, Massachusetts, look around, look closely, and you still may not see the school. The large building nestled next to a fishing pond on a ten-acre campus looks more like a mansion than a school. Walk inside and you will find students and adults doing pretty much as they please. Not a "class" in sight. Some people are talking, some playing, some reading. A group is building a bookcase over there, a student is working on the computer in the corner, another is taking a nap on a chair. All ages mix freely, with no discernible grade level for any activity. In fact, it is even difficult to locate the teachers. If there is a curriculum, it is difficult to detect. Instead, the school offers a wide variety of educational options, including field trips to Boston, New York, and the nearby mountains and seacoast, and the use of facilities that include a laboratory, a woodworking shop, a computer room, a kitchen, a darkroom, an art room, and several music rooms.

Sudbury Valley provides a setting, an opportunity, but each student must decide what to do with that opportunity. Students are trusted to make their own decisions about learning. The school's purpose is to build on the students' natural curiosity, based on the belief that authentic learning takes place only when students initiate it. The school operates on the premise that all its students are creative, and each should be helped to discover and nurture his or her individual talents.

Sudbury Valley is fully accredited, and the majority of Sudbury Valley's graduates go on to college. The school accepts anyone from 4-year-olds to adults and charges low tuition, so as not to exclude anyone. Evaluations or grades are given only on request. A high school diploma is awarded to those who complete relevant requirements, which mainly focus on the ability to be a responsible member of the community at large. More than thirty schools follow the Sudbury model, including schools in the United States, Canada, Europe, Israel, and Japan.[10]

Can Teachers Blend These Five Philosophies?

Some of you might be drawn to (and let's face it, sometimes resistive to) one or more of these philosophies. A social reconstructionist idea such as students learning as they work to improve the world sounds perfect to some of us, whereas a more traditional approach focused on reading and discussing great books is a dream come true to others. For many, elements from both of these approaches are appealing. So you might be wondering if this is an either/or proposition; must we be purists and choose one philosophy, or can we mix and match, blending two or more philosophies?

A CLOSER LOOK

After 35 Years in the Classroom, Would I Do It Again?

When I began my teaching career in 1969, I left the intoxicating atmosphere of a University of California campus in the 60s for a high school English classroom in a traditional public school. I was determined to defy tradition, to infuse my teaching with educational strategies relevant to students growing up in a rapidly changing world. Fortunately for me, the school's curriculum guidelines were stowed away in an administrator's filing cabinet somewhere, and there were no standardized tests to worry about. My principal granted me a reasonable amount of latitude.

If I thought something might be valuable for my students, I tried it out. I did my best to teach them about literature and language, and they, by the looks on their faces and the quality of their work, taught me how to teach. I listened to my students, possibly more closely than they listened to me. I built on what worked and discarded what didn't.

Through all my successes and failures, I always kept one goal in mind. I tried to be myself in the classroom—or, more accurately, I tried to be the best version of myself I could bring to school every day.

Students learned in my classes, I know that. Whether they learned what is considered important by today's standards—whether they would have done well on "the test"—that's something I'll never know.

I was obsessed with teaching during those first few years. I loved it; I hated it; it drove me crazy. After four years I took time off to look for another line of work, but I didn't find one. The next year I returned to the classroom and stayed there until I retired thirty years later.

By the time high-stakes testing began in earnest, I was five years from retirement. My teaching style and strategies were still my own idiosyncratic mix, but time and experience had smoothed out the rough edges. I found that incorporating a little bit of test prep into my curriculum was enough to help my students do well on the state tests.

Would I choose to become a teacher today, faced with the constraints of common core standards and high-stakes testing? I hope so. I loved teaching. I hate to think a younger version of myself would miss out on that. If I could still find room to innovate, and to be the best version of myself I could bring to school every day, I think I could make it work.

Courtesy of David Safier

David Safier taught high school near Portland, Oregon for more than 30 years. He now lives in Tucson where he blogs about educational issues in Arizona.

REFLECTION: What philosophy or philosophies did this teacher embrace?

As you probably have guessed, people differ on the answer, which means you get to think it through and come to your own conclusion. Some schools blend philosophies. For example, the YES College Preparatory School in Houston and Wakefield High School in Maryland mix several philosophies in their programs. There is both traditional academic emphasis on content mastery, with many AP tests being offered, and a more progressive approach as students create independent senior projects. And the faculty and students seem to appreciate the blending. But others are not so sure this is a good idea.

Advocates of a purist model argue that although blending sounds like a comfortable and reasonable compromise, much is lost. For example, if we want children to be independent problem solvers, then we must promote that approach. Blending independent problem solving with a traditional philosophy of teachers telling students what they are to learn might not work. Either students are taught how to think for themselves, or they are told what to think, and compromise is not an option. More traditional teachers fear that much of progressive education, although replete with lofty goals, actually leads to little real learning. They claim that blending student-centered philosophies with a demanding traditional curriculum actually dilutes learning.[11] As you consider where you want to teach geographically, you might also want to consider where you want to teach philosophically. Are you comfortable with the school's educational philosophy? If you have some freedom in structuring your classroom, which philosophy or philosophies will you follow? Are you a purist, or will you be blending several philosophies? (See Table 6.1. on p. 168.)

RAP 3.2
Philosophy on The Big Screen

	Focus of Curriculum	Sample Classroom Activity	Role of Teacher	Goals for Students	Educational Leaders
Student-Centered Philosophies					
Progressivism	Flexible; integrated study of academic subjects around the needs and experiences of students	Learning by doing—for example, students plan a field trip to learn about history, geography, and natural science	Guide and integrate learning activities so that students can find meaning	To become intelligent problem solvers, socially aware citizens who are prepared to live comfortably in the world	John Dewey, Nel Noddings
Social Reconstructionism	Focus on social, political, and economic needs; integrated study of academic subjects around socially meaningful actions	Learning by reconstructing society—for example, students work to remove health hazards in a building housing the poor	Provide authentic learning activities that both instruct students and improve society	To become intelligent problem solvers, to enjoy learning, to live comfortably in the world while also helping reshape it	George S. Counts, Jane Roland Martin, Paulo Freire, bell hooks
Existentialism	Each student determines the pace and direction of his or her own learning	Students choose their preferred medium—such as poetry, prose, or painting—and evaluate their own performance	One who seeks to relate to each student honestly; skilled at creating a free, open, and stimulating environment	To accept personal responsibility; to understand deeply and be at peace with one's own unique individuality	A. S. Neill, Maxine Greene
Teacher-Centered Philosophies					
Essentialism	Core curriculum of traditional academic topics and traditional American virtues	Teacher focuses on "essential" information or the development of particular skills	Model of academic and moral virtue; center of classroom	To become culturally literate individuals, model citizens educated to compete in the world	William Bagley, E. D. Hirsch, Jr.
Perennialism	Core curriculum analyzing enduring ideas found in Great Books	Socratic dialogue analyzing a philosophical issue or the meaning of a great work of literature	Scholarly role model; philosophically oriented, helps students seek the truth for themselves	To increase their intellectual powers and to appreciate learning for its own sake	Robert Hutchins, Mortimer Adler

TABLE 6.1 Five philosophies of education.

REFLECTION: How many of these philosophies have you experienced in your own education? Describe the circumstances. Would you like to encounter others as a student? As a teacher? Explain.

Psychological Influences on Education

FOCUS QUESTION 5

What are some of the psychological and cultural factors influencing education?

Essentialism, perennialism, progressivism, social reconstructionism, and existentialism are influential philosophies of education, but they are far from the only forces shaping today's schools. The following descriptions offer a glimpse into some other forces guiding current school practices.

Constructivism

Constructivism, like progressivism, social reconstructionism, and existentialism, puts the learner at the center of the educational stage. **Constructivism** asserts that knowledge cannot be handed from one person to another (from a teacher to a learner) but must be *constructed* by each learner through interpreting and reinterpreting a constant flow of information. Constructivists believe that people continually try to make sense of and bring order to the world.

Built on the work of Swiss and Russian psychologists, Jean Piaget and Lev Vygotsky, constructivism reflects cognitive psychologists' view that the essence of learning is the constant effort to assimilate new information. In a constructivist classroom, the teacher builds knowledge in much the same way, gauging a student's prior knowledge and understanding, then carefully orchestrating cues, penetrating questions, and instructional activities that challenge and extend a student's insight. Teachers can use **scaffolding,** that is, questions, clues, or suggestions that help a student link prior knowledge to the new information. The educational challenges facing students in a constructivist classroom could be creating a new way to handle a math problem, letting go of an unfounded bias about an ethnic group, or connecting the role of religion in political movements. In a constructivist classroom, students and teachers constantly challenge their own assumptions. (If you check back to the philosophy inventory, see how you responded to item 26, which captured this aspect of constructivism.)

Although constructivism runs counter to the current emphasis on uniform standards and testing, it is enjoying popularity, especially among school reformers. Perhaps part of the reason for its growing acceptance is that constructivism dovetails with authentic learning, critical thinking, individualized instruction, and project-based learning, ideas popular in reform circles.

Behaviorism

In stark contrast to constructivism, **behaviorism** is derived from the belief that free will is an illusion and that human beings are shaped entirely by their environment. Alter a person's environment and you will alter his or her thoughts, feelings, and behavior. People act in response to physical stimuli. We learn, for instance, to avoid overexposure to heat through the impulses of pain our nerves send to our brain. More complex learning, such as understanding the material in this chapter, is also determined by stimuli, such as the educational support you have received from your professor or parents and the comfort of the chair in which you sit when reading this text.

Harvard professor **B. F. Skinner** became the leading advocate of behaviorism, and he did much to popularize the use of positive reinforcement to promote desired learning. (For a biography of B. F. Skinner, visit Connect.) Behaviorists urge teachers to use a system of reinforcement to encourage desired behaviors, to connect learning with pleasure and reward (a smile, special privilege, or good grades). In a program termed **behavior modification**, extrinsic rewards are gradually lessened as the student acquires and masters the targeted behavior. By association, the desired

A CLOSER LOOK

Voices of Five Philosophies

YESTERDAY'S VOICES

William Bagley (1874–1946) *Essentialism* Bagley believed that the major role of the school is to produce a literate, intelligent electorate; argued against electives while stressing thinking skills to help students apply their academic knowledge. Source: Teachers College, Columbia University

Robert M. Hutchins (1899–1979) *Perennialism* During the sixteen years he served as president of the University of Chicago, Hutchins abolished fraternities, football, and compulsory attendance, and introduced the Great Books program. ©Keystone/Getty Images

John Dewey (1859–1952) *Progressivism* A founder of progressivism, Dewey not only worked to democratize schools but also fought for women's suffrage and the right of teachers to form unions. ©Historical/Corbis/Getty Images

George S. Counts (1907–1974) *Social Reconstructionism* Counts viewed education as an important tool to counter social injustices, and, if educators questioned their own power to make critical decisions, Counts's plea was to "Just do it!" ©AP Photo

A. S. Neill (1883–1973) *Existentialism* Neill's attitude toward education stemmed from his own problems as a student, problems that fueled his creation of Summerhill, a school that encouraged youngsters to make their own decisions about what and when to learn. Source: Courtesy of A.S. Neill

TODAY'S VOICES

E. D. Hirsch Jr. (1928–) *Essentialism* He established the Core Knowledge Foundation to develop a prescribed curriculum in subject areas. Visit your local bookstore and browse through his books delineating what educated people should know. Source: The Core Knowledge Foundation

Mortimer Adler (1902–2001) *Perennialism* He renewed interest in perennialism with the publication of *The Paideia Proposal* (1982). Adler advocated that all students be educated in the classics and that education be a lifelong venture. ©Bettmann/Getty Images

Nel Noddings (1929–) *Progressivism* She believes that an ethic of care can best be cultivated when the curriculum is centered on the interests of students. Schools are challenged to nourish the physical, spiritual, occupational, and intellectual development of each child. ©Lee L. Jacks/Professor Emeritus of Education/Stanford University

bell hooks (1952–) *Social Reconstructionism* Her theory of education, *engaged pedagogy,* helps students and teachers develop a critical consciousness of race, gender, and class biases. A prolific writer, her books include *Ain't I a Woman: Black Women and Feminism* (1981) and *Teaching to Transgress: Education as the Practice of Freedom* (1994). ©Pinderhughes Photography

Maxine Greene (1917–2014) *Existentialism* She believes that it is crucial for students and teachers to create meaning in their lives. Greene sees the humanities and the arts as catalysts for moving people to critical awareness and conscious engagement with the world. Source: Teachers College, Columbia University

REFLECTION: How do historical and political events influence whose voices are heard? Whose voices are being heard in education today, and why?

behavior now produces its own reward (self-satisfaction). This process may take minutes, weeks, or years, depending on the complexity of the learning desired and on the past environment of the learner. The teacher's goal is to move the learner from extrinsic to intrinsic rewards. (If you check the inventory at the chapter's opening, behaviorism was represented by statement 27. How did you respond?)

Critics of behaviorism decry behaviorists' disbelief in the autonomy of the individual. They ask, Are people little more than selfish "reward machines"? Can clever forces manipulate populations through clever social engineering? Are educators qualified to exert such total control of students? Those who defend behaviorism point to its striking successes. Behaviorism's influence is apparent in the joy on students' faces as they receive visual and auditory rewards via their computer monitor, or in the classroom down the hall where special needs learners make significant progress in a behaviorist-designed curriculum.

Cultural Influences on Education

Most of the ideas and philosophies discussed in this chapter are drawn from Western culture. As a nation, we rarely identify or reflect on the ideas that derive from many parts of Asia, Africa, Eastern Europe, and Latin America. We are guilty of **ethnocentrism,** the tendency to view one's own culture as superior to others and (perhaps worse) to fail to consider other cultures at all. Let's broaden our view and examine education as practiced in other cultures.

In much of the West, society's needs dictate educational practices, with statewide standards, national goals, and high-stakes testing. In the rest of the world, that is to say, in most of the world, the child's education is primarily a concern of the family, not the society. A child's vocational interests, for example, might mirror the occupation of a parent or be built around the unique interest or talent of the child, rather than respond to the broader employment market or societal priorities. Family and community are foremost; the nation is a weaker influence.

GLOBAL VIEW

William. G. Sumner introduced the cultural concept of *ethnocentrism* early in the 1900s. Culture captures the concepts of national character, perception, time and space, thinking, language and nonverbal communication, values, behavior (norms, rules, manners), social groupings and relationships.

In Western society, formal schools, formal certification and degrees are valued; in other societies, more credence is placed on actual knowledge and mastery rather than educational documentation. The notion of *teachers* and *nonteachers* is foreign in many cultures, since all adults and even older children participate in educating the young. Children learn adult roles through observation, conversation, assisting, and imitating, all the while absorbing moral, intellectual, and vocational lessons. This shared educational responsibility is called **informal education.**[12] What does calling this practice "informal education" reveal about Western values and assumptions? Would someone in a culture practicing this integrated education call it "informal education"? In the process, adults also learn a great deal about the children in the community. Strong bonds are forged between the generations. (As you probably already concluded, item 28 on our opening inventory describes informal education. You might want to check your answer to that statement.)

Oral traditions enjoy particular prominence in many parts of the world, even in literate societies where reading and writing are commonplace and valued. In the **oral tradition,** spoken language becomes a primary method for instruction: Word problems teach reasoning skills; proverbs instill wisdom; and stories, anecdotes, and rhymes teach lessons about nature, history, religion, and social customs. The oral tradition refines communication and analytical skills, and reinforces human connections and moral values. Not infrequently, religious and moral lessons are passed on initially through oral communication, only later to be written.

The practices and beliefs of peoples in other parts of the world offer useful insights for enhancing–or questioning–our own educational practices, but they are

GLOBAL VIEW

The word *Qur'an* (*Koran*) is often translated as "the Recitation."

insights too rarely considered, much less implemented. Perhaps this will change in the years ahead as immigration, the global economy, and technology continue to bring all world cultures closer together. For now, however, our education philosophies are rooted in the ideas and thoughts of Western thinkers. Let's visit some of these powerful thinkers and their influential, enduring contributions.

The Three Legendary Figures of Classical Western Philosophy

FOCUS QUESTION 6

What were the contributions of Socrates, Plato, and Aristotle to Western philosophy, and how are their legacies reflected in education today?

To understand Western philosophy, we must look back to its birthplace—ancient Greece. Specifically, we must begin with a trio of philosopher-teachers: Socrates, Plato, and Aristotle. Together they laid the foundation for most of Western philosophy. It is likely that you are familiar with at least their names. Let's review their lasting contributions to the world of philosophy.

The name **Socrates** is practically synonymous with wisdom and the philosophical life. Socrates (469–399 B.C.E.) was a teacher without a school. He walked about Athens, engaging people in provocative dialogues about questions of ultimate significance. Socrates is hailed as an exemplar of human virtue whose goal was to help others find the truths that lie within their own minds. In that regard, he described himself as a "midwife." By repeatedly questioning, disproving, and testing the thoughts of his pupils on such questions as the nature of "love" or "the good," he helped his students reach deeper, clearer ideas. Today we call his approach the **Socratic method.**

RAP 3.8

The Great Lecture Theory of Learning

Socrates' method did not just promote intellectual insights in his students; it also challenged the conventional ideas and traditions of his time. Socrates offended many powerful people and was eventually charged with corrupting the youth of Athens. Even in that, Socrates provides a lesson for today's teachers: Challenges to popular convention may lead to community opposition and sanctions. (Luckily, sanctions today are less severe than those meted out to Socrates, who was condemned to death for his "impiety.")

We know about Socrates and his teachings through the writings of his disciples, one of whom was **Plato** (427–347 B.C.E.). Plato's writing is renowned for its depth, beauty, and clarity. His most famous works were dialogues, conversations between two or more people that present and critique various philosophical viewpoints. Plato's dialogues feature Socrates questioning and challenging others and presenting his own philosophy. After Socrates was put to death, Plato became disillusioned with Athenian democracy and left the city for many years. Later, he returned to Athens and founded the **Academy,** considered by some to be the world's first university.

Plato held that a realm of eternally existing "ideas" or "forms" underlies the physical world. In Plato's philosophy, the human soul has three parts: intellect, spirit, and appetite (basic animal desires). Plato believed that these faculties interact to determine human behavior. Plato urged that the intellect, the highest faculty, be trained to control the other two. In his famous "Allegory of the Cave," Plato describes his unique political philosophy where he envisions a class of philosopher kings who rule over the warriors and common people. You can explore this epic piece at http://www.historyguide.org/intellect/allegory.html.

Just as Plato studied under Socrates, **Aristotle** (384–322 B.C.E.) studied under Plato. Aristotle entered Plato's Academy at age 18 and stayed for twenty years! In 342 B.C.E., Aristotle went to northern Greece and, for several years, tutored a young boy named Alexander, later known as Alexander the Great. After educating Alexander, Aristotle returned to Athens to set up his own school, the *Lyceum,* adjacent to Plato's Academy.

A CLOSER LOOK

The Socratic Method in Action

TEACHER: Today we will try to understand what we mean by the concepts of right and wrong. What are examples of conduct you consider wrong or immoral?

STUDENT: Lying is wrong.

TEACHER: But what if you were living in Germany around 1940 and you were harboring in your house a certain Jewish man named Nathan Cohen, who was wanted by the Nazis? If asked by a Nazi if you knew the whereabouts of that Mr. Cohen, wouldn't it be acceptable, even obligatory, to lie?

STUDENT: I suppose so.

TEACHER: So could you rephrase what you meant when you said that lying is wrong or immoral?

STUDENT: I think what I meant is that it is usually wrong to lie. But it is true that there are times when lying is acceptable, because the overall effects of the lie are good. Look at how much your Mr. Cohen was helped; the lie about where he was may have saved his life.

TEACHER: So you are saying that it is okay to lie, as long as the consequences of the lie are positive. But consider this hypothetical situation: I am a business tycoon who makes millions of dollars selling diamonds to investors. I sell only to very rich people who can afford to lose the money they invest in my diamonds. I tell my customers that my diamonds are worth $10,000 each, but they really are fakes, worth only $2,000 each. Rather than keeping the profits myself, I give all the money to the poor, helping them obtain the food and shelter they need to live. If you look at the obvious consequences of my business—the rich get slightly poorer and the needy are helped out immensely—you may conclude that my business has a generally positive effect on society. And, yet, because the business is based on fraud, I find it immoral. Do you agree?

STUDENT: Yes, I find it immoral. I suppose I was wrong in saying that whenever a lie has generally good results it is morally acceptable. In your diamond example, unlike the Nazi example, the lie was directed at innocent people and the harm done to them was significant. I want to change my earlier statement that a lie is acceptable whenever it has generally good results. What I want to say now is that you should never lie to innocent people if that would cause them significant harm.

As is typical of Socrates' dialogue, this one could go on indefinitely, because there is no simple, "correct" solution to the issues being discussed—the meaning of right and wrong and, more specifically, the contours of when a lie is morally acceptable. By asking questions, the teacher is trying to get the student to clarify and rethink his or her own ideas, to come eventually to a deep and clear understanding of philosophical concepts, such as right and wrong.

REFLECTION: Have you ever experienced the Socratic Dialogue as a student? What were your reactions? Would you like to develop this teaching technique? Why or why not?

The depth and breadth of Aristotle's ideas were unsurpassed in ancient Western civilization. In addition to tackling philosophical questions, Aristotle wrote influential works on biology, physics, astronomy, mathematics, psychology, and literary criticism. Aristotle placed more importance on the physical world than did Plato. Aristotle's teachings can, in fact, be regarded as a synthesis of Plato's belief in the universal, spiritual forms, and a scientist's belief that each animal, vegetable, and mineral we observe is undeniably real.

Aristotle also won renown for his ethical and political theories. He wrote that the highest good for people is a virtuous life, fully governed by the faculty of reason, with which all other faculties are in harmony. Aristotle promoted the doctrine of the **Golden Mean,** or the notion that virtue lies in a middle ground between two extremes. Courage, for example, is bordered on the one side by cowardice and on the other side by foolhardiness.

Basic Philosophical Issues and Concepts

FOCUS QUESTION 7

How do metaphysics, epistemology, ethics, political philosophy, aesthetics, and logic factor into a philosophy of education?

Philosophy has many subdivisions that are of particular significance to educators: metaphysics, epistemology, ethics, political philosophy, aesthetics, and logic. (See Figure 6.1.) These fields are where key educational questions are raised, including: How do we know what we know? What is of value? What is education's role in society? As you

A CLOSER LOOK

Why We Remember Socrates, Plato, and Aristotle

- **Socrates.** His philosophical lifestyle; the Socratic method, in which students are provocatively questioned so that they can rethink what they believe; his noble death.
- **Plato.** Discussions of philosophy through eloquent dialogues; the theory of "forms," or "ideas," that exist in an eternal, transcendent realm.
- **Aristotle.** The breadth of his knowledge; the synthesis of Plato's belief in the eternal "forms" and a scientist's belief in the "real" world that we can see, touch, or smell; the theory of the Golden Mean (everything in moderation).

Many of the ideas first formulated by Socrates, Plato, and Aristotle have long been integrated into Western culture and education.

REFLECTION: How might your current classroom instruction change if your education professor was Dr. Socrates, Plato, or Aristotle? Detail aspects of a "typical" lesson.

FIGURE 6.1
Branches Of philosophy.

REFLECTION: This view of philosophy is like a tree. Are any of these branches new to you?

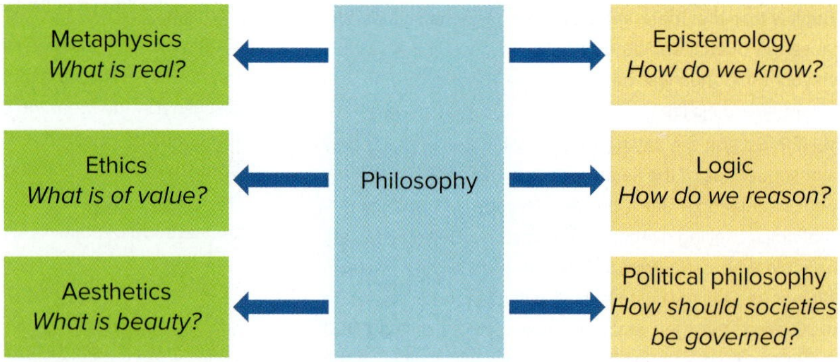

ponder these questions, you should find elements of your philosophy of education coming into sharper focus.

Metaphysics and Epistemology

Metaphysics deals with the origin and the structure of reality. Metaphysicians ask: What really is the nature of the world in which we live? **Epistemology** examines the nature and the origin of human knowledge. Epistemologists are interested in how we use our minds to distinguish valid from illusory paths to true knowledge. It may be the easiest to remember the scope of these closely related disciplines by considering that epistemology and metaphysics address *how* we know (epistemology) *what* we know (metaphysics) about reality.

Is Reality Composed Solely of Matter? One of the most basic metaphysical issues is whether anything exists other than the material realm that we experience with our senses. Many philosophers assert the existence only of the physical, affirming fundamentally the existence of matter, a philosophy called **materialism.** By emphasizing in their curriculum the study of nature through scientific observation, modern public schools clearly deem that the material world is real and important. Other philosophers contend that the physical realm is but an illusion. They point out that matter is known only through the mind. This philosophy is called spiritualism or **idealism.** The physical world exists to teach us higher principles and meaningful lessons, and life is far more than a drive to acquire physical things. Educators focused on idealism might teach students the importance of finding their place and purpose in the world, the importance of helping one another, and the need to protect the environment. A third group of philosophers asserts that reality is composed of materialism and idealism, body and mind, a belief associated with French philosopher René Descartes and called **Cartesian dualism.**

Is Reality Characterized by Change and Progress? Metaphysicians question whether nature is constantly improving through time. The belief that progress is inevitable is widely held in the United States. On the other hand, some philosophers hold that change is illusory and that a foundation of timeless, static content underlies all reality. Still others believe that change is cyclical, swinging widely from one side of center to the opposing side.

Teachers who believe in the inevitability of progress seek new approaches to teaching and new subjects to be taught, thereby "keeping up with the times." Other teachers pay little heed to current trends and technologies. They may prefer to teach everlasting, timeless truths described in the Great Books or discussed by great thinkers, such as Plato and Aristotle. Finally, some teachers suggest that, with change such a constant, it is pointless to try to keep pace. They choose to ignore these cycles and to simply select the teaching methods they find most comfortable.

What Is the Basis of Our Knowledge? Empiricism holds that sensory experience (seeing, hearing, touching, and so on) is the source of knowledge. Empiricists assert that we experience the external world by sensory perception; then, through reflection, we conceptualize ideas that help us interpret that world. For example, because we have seen the sun rise every day, we can formulate the belief that it will rise again tomorrow. The empiricist doctrine that knowledge is gained most reliably through scientific experimentation may be the most widely held belief in Western culture. People want to hear the latest research or be shown documentation that something is true. Teachers expect students to present evidence before drawing conclusions. Even children demand of one another, "Prove it."

Rationalism emphasizes the power of reason—in particular, logic—to derive true statements about the world, even when such realities are not detected by the senses. Rationalists point out that the field of mathematics has generated considerable knowledge that is not based on our senses. For example, we can reason that seven cubed equals 343 without having to count seven times seven times seven objects to verify our conclusion experientially. Whereas educational empiricists would support hands-on learning activities as the primary source for discovery and validation of information, rationalists would encourage schools to place a greater emphasis on teaching mathematics, as well as such nonempirical disciplines as philosophy and logic.

Logic

Logic is the branch of philosophy that deals with reasoning. Logic focuses on how to move from a set of assumptions to valid conclusions and examines the rules of inference that enable us to frame our propositions and arguments. Whereas epistemology defines reasoning as one way to gain knowledge, logic defines the rules of reasoning.

Schools teach children to reason both deductively and inductively. When teaching **deductive reasoning,** teachers present their students with a general rule and then help them identify particular examples and applications of the rule. Inductive reasoning works in the opposite manner. When teaching **inductive reasoning,** teachers help their students draw tentative generalizations after having observed specific instances of a phenomenon.

A teacher who explains the commutative property of addition ($a + b = b + a$) and then has the student work out specific examples of this rule (such as $3 + 2 = 2 + 3$)

TEACHING TIP

Writing Your Philosophy Statement

Writing your philosophy of teaching statement can feel like a daunting experience, but it's a lot more manageable when you do it one step at a time. Here a few ideas to help you get started.

1. Review the philosophies described in this chapter. Which one(s) most closely aligns with your beliefs about education? Why?
2. Now, ask yourself some specific questions about learning, teaching, and schools:
    - What qualities do good teachers have?
    - What is the role of a teacher?
    - What is the role of a student?
    - What adjectives describe your teaching style?
    - What is the most effective way to motivate students?
    - What should students learn in school?
    - What is the most effective way to assess student learning?
    - What is the purpose of school?

Your answers to these questions are the beginning of your philosophy statement! A philosophy of teaching statement might be just one or two typed pages, but collecting your thoughts into a single document helps you reflect on how you will apply your knowledge and insights to your actual teaching practice. Your philosophy is a work in progress. As your teaching experience grows and reflections deepen, see how much your ideas change, or stay the same.

REFLECTION: What new insights did you learn about yourself, teaching, or learning from drafting your philosophy statement?

is teaching deductive reasoning. Contrast this with a teacher who begins a lesson by stating a series of addition problems of the form $3 + 2 = 5$ and $2 + 3 = 5$, then asks, "What do you notice about these examples?" If students can draw a generalization about the commutative property of addition, they are reasoning inductively. Whereas math is a natural field to isolate examples of deductive and inductive reasoning, logic equips students to think more precisely in virtually any field.

Ethics, Political Philosophy, and Aesthetics

Whereas metaphysics focuses on what "is," ethics, political philosophy, and aesthetics are concerned with what "ought to be." In these disciplines, philosophers grapple with the issue of what we should value. As you read on, consider the place of ethics, political philosophy, and aesthetics in the classroom.

Ethics is the study of what is "good" or "bad" in human behavior, thoughts, and feelings. It asks, What is the good life? and How should we treat each other? (What should schools teach children about what is "good" and what is "bad"?)

Political philosophy analyzes how past and present societies are arranged and governed and proposes ways to create better societies in the future. (How might schools engage in an objective evaluation of current governments, including our own?)

Aesthetics probes the nature of beauty. It asks, What is beauty? Is beauty solely in the eyes of the beholder? Or are some objects, people, and works (music, art, literature) objectively more beautiful than others? (How can teachers help students understand how their personal experiences, peer group values, and cultural and ethnic history shape their standards of what is beautiful?)

Your Turn

[I]n modern times there are opposing views about the practice of education. There is no general agreement about what the young should learn either in relation to virtue or in relation to the best life; nor is it clear whether their education ought to be directed more towards the

> intellect than towards the character of the soul. . . . [A]nd it is not certain whether training should be directed at things useful in life, or at those conducive to virtue, or at nonessentials. . . . And there is no agreement as to what in fact does tend towards virtue. Men [sic] do not all prize most highly the same virtue, so naturally they differ also about the proper training for it.[13]
>
> Aristotle

More than 2,300 years later, we still find that reasonable people can come to entirely different points of view on all kinds of issues in education. (Remember the charter school discussion in the faculty room at the beginning of the chapter?) If everyone agreed on what should be taught, and how to teach it, there might be just one philosophy of education. But it is not so simple.

Re-reading the inventory statements at the beginning of this chapter can help you determine if one of the five major philosophies speaks for you. You may be more eclectic in your outlook, picking and choosing elements from different philosophies. Your responsibility as an educator is to wrestle with tough questions, to bring your values to the surface, and to forge a coherent philosophy of education.

You might say a clear philosophy of education is to a teacher what a blueprint is to a builder—a plan of action, reassurance that the parts will fit together in a constructive way. With a clear philosophy of education, you will not ricochet from one teaching method to another and will not confuse students, parents, and administrators with conflicting messages about the role of students and teacher in the classroom. If you have a well-honed philosophy of education, you will be better able to assess whether you will find a comfortable fit in a school and a community. Simply put, a philosophy brings purpose and coherence to your work in the classroom.

CONNECT FOR *TEACHERS, SCHOOLS, AND SOCIETY*

Check out Connect, McGraw-Hill Education's interactive learning environment, to:

Read Current and Historical Articles

The Humanities: Why Such a Hard Sell? by David J. Ferrero, *Educational Leadership,* March 2011.

Text excerpts from ***Experience and Education***, by John Dewey, copyright 1938, 1998 by Kappa Delta Pi.

Text excerpts from ***Escape from Childhood,*** by John Holt, 1974, New York: E.P. Dutton. The excerpt is taken from *Taking Sides* (2009).

Analyze Case Studies

Brenda Forester: A pre-service education student is concerned that one of her methods classes will not prepare her for teaching. Her philosophy of education is challenged when she observes a writing process classroom.

Michael Watson: A teacher finds that the assistant principal's evaluation of his class calls into question his teaching style as well as his philosophy of education. The evaluation suggests that his style and rapport with the students are getting in the way of his being more demanding.

Watch Teachers, Students, and Classrooms in Action

Our **Online Video Album** for contemporary videos related to this chapter.

KEY TERMS AND PEOPLE

Academy, 172
Adler, Mortimer, 158, 170
aesthetics, 176
Aristotle, 172
back-to-basics, 156
Bagley, William, 156, 170
behaviorism, 169
behavior modification, 169
Cartesian dualism, 175
constructivism, 169
core curriculum, 156
Counts, George, 161, 170
deductive reasoning, 175
Dewey, John, 160, 170
empiricism, 175
epistemology, 174
essentialism, 156
ethics, 176
ethnocentrism, 171
existentialism, 164
Freire, Paulo, 163
Golden Mean, 173
Great Books, 157
Greene, Maxine, 170
Hirsch Jr., E. D., 156, 170
hooks, bell, 170
Hutchins, Robert, 158, 170
idealism, 174
inductive reasoning, 175
informal education, 171
Laboratory School, 160
logic, 175
Martin, Jane Roland, 162
materialism, 174
metaphysics, 174
Neill, A. S., 170
Noddings, Nel, 170
oral tradition, 171
perennialism, 157
philosophy, 151
Plato, 172
political philosophy, 176
pragmatism, 160
praxis, 164
progressivism, 159
rationalism, 175
scaffolding, 169
Skinner, B. F., 169
social Darwinism, 163
social reconstructionism, 161
Socrates, 172
Socratic method, 172

DISCUSSION QUESTIONS AND ACTIVITIES

1. Suppose that you are a student who must choose one of five schools to attend. Each reflects one of the five major philosophies. Which would you choose and why? Which school would you choose to work in as a teacher? Why?
2. Interview a teacher who has been teaching for several years. Find out what that teacher's philosophy was when he or she started teaching and what it is today. Is there a difference? If so, try to find out why.
3. Re-read the five statements by the teachers in the faculty room at the beginning of the chapter. In what areas do you think these teachers agree? In what areas are their philosophies different? What do you predict will be the result of their meeting? Which of the statements by the five teachers do you agree with most?
4. How would you describe your own philosophy of education? Imagine you are a teacher. Create a three-minute talk that you would give to parents on back-to-school night that outlines your philosophy of education and identifies how it would be evident in the classroom.
5. The key terms and people in this chapter could be dramatically expanded by including Far Eastern and Middle Eastern philosophy. Consider the following additions: Buddhism, Confucianism, Hinduism, Islam, Jainism, Judaism, Mohammed, Shinto, Taoism, Zen Buddhism. Research and briefly describe each of these. What has been (or might be) the impact of these religions, principles, and individuals on our present school philosophy?

Design Elements: Blue pencil: ©C.O.T/a.collectionRF/Getty Images RF; Pencils: ©Darren Greenwood/Design Pics RF; Gavel: ©Siede Preis/Getty Images RF; Students Huddled Together: ©Digital Vision/Getty Images RF; Pens with blue background: ©chiarito/Getty Images RF

The school is that last expenditure upon which Americans should be willing to economize.

FRANKLIN D. ROOSEVELT

©Stockbyte/Getty Images RF

chapter 7

Financing and Governing America's Schools

Focus Questions

1. Why do teachers need to know about finance and governance?
2. How is the property tax connected to unequal educational funding?
3. What is the distinction between educational equity and educational adequacy?
4. What are the sources of state revenues?
5. How does the federal government influence education?
6. How does commercialization at home and in school affect children?
7. What current trends are shaping educational finance?
8. How do school boards and superintendents manage schools?
9. What is the "hidden" government of schools?
10. How does the business community influence school culture?
11. How are schools being made more responsive to teachers and the community?

Chapter Preview

Do you know who pays for U.S. schools, and how? You might be surprised. In this chapter, we introduce you to the decentralized, politically charged systems of school funding and school governance in the United States. You will become familiar with the sources of financial inequity in schooling and the attempts to keep effective education within the reach of all, not just the very wealthy. Both the formal structure of power in school governance (school boards, school superintendents, and the like) and the informal, hidden government will affect your life in the classroom. By understanding the mechanics behind school finance and governance, you will be more empowered as a classroom teacher and better able to influence decisions that shape the education of our nation's children.

Local and state governments have long grappled with the difficult proposition of raising enough public funds to adequately support education. Students in wealthy neighborhoods attend modern, well-equipped schools; poorer children make their way to decaying, ill-equipped school buildings in impoverished communities. Courts have attempted to forge solutions aimed at reducing these glaring disparities and bring a measure of fairness to education. But even in these under-resourced schools, educators and parents are finding ways to create successful learning environments.

Day-to-day classroom life is influenced not only by economic issues but also by the ways in which schools are governed. In this chapter, you will learn how schools are managed, officially and unofficially. Your knowledge of educational decision making can be a powerful ally in shaping a successful teaching career. We will also give you a quick look at what is possible, how Finland had constructed a successful educational system.

Follow the Money: Financing America's Schools

Why Should Teachers Care Where the Money Comes From?

FOCUS QUESTION 1

Why do teachers need to know about finance and governance?

Why should a teacher be concerned about school finance? (Put another way, why should I want to read this chapter?) Doesn't a teacher's responsibility pretty much start and end at the classroom door?

Sounds reasonable, but here is where the authors jump in. We believe that it is unwise, and even dangerous, for teachers to invest their time and talent in a career in which the key decisions are considered beyond their knowledge or influence. Educational finance may well determine not just the quality of life you experience as a teacher but also the very futures of the students you teach. Common sense tells us that the amount of money spent in a school is directly related to how well students learn, but not everyone agrees. What is the wisest way to invest educational dollars–and who should decide?

We believe that teachers should be major participants in financial and governance policy decisions. The recent trend toward testing teachers and rating schools is an example of what happens when teachers are left out of policy circles. The emphasis on standards and testing too often casts the teacher in the role of a technician, implementing other people's goals with the limited resources other people give them–a dysfunctional system that shortchanges teachers and students alike. We believe that teachers should be advocates for children, children who themselves are excluded from policy decisions. Teachers and students find themselves the victims of rising educational expectations but limited educational resources. All society's economic and social inequities are left for schools and teachers to remedy. If they are not successful, it is their fault. Even the bare necessities of classroom resources are often inadequate, and teachers are forced to dig into their own pockets to buy school supplies. Teachers spend about $500 a year buying classroom materials.[1] (See Contemporary Issues: A View from the Field: Schools in Need.)

CONTEMPORARY ISSUES

A View from the Field: Schools in Need

James Rosenberg, a mergers and acquisitions attorney, founded Adopt-A-Classroom after mentoring a student at a school for physically and mentally delayed children. He couldn't believe the lack of resources available to the school and how much money teachers across the country spend each year on classroom supplies. James wanted to lend a hand. With a law school friend he started Adopt-A-Classroom, partnering under-resourced classrooms with caring individuals. An interested donor can visit the Web site and find a specific classroom to assist or let the organization choose a needy classroom in the donor's community. The teacher receiving the donation can use the funds to shop online with retailers participating in the Adopt-A-Classroom program. If the teacher is unable to locate the needed resources, Adopt-A-Classroom will work with that teacher to fill the request.

Leana Borges, a teacher at P.S. 175 in New York City, has been a recipient of a classroom donation from the organization. "My class has benefited so much from the Adopt-A-Classroom program," Leana writes on the Adopt-A-Classroom Web site. "We have received plenty of products that we use on a daily basis to help in science class, such as measuring tools, safety tools (goggles), and various math manipulatives. These products have enabled my students to get a clearer understanding of the concepts I have taught." Another teacher, Kristina Kim of Sutro Elementary in San Francisco, found much more than an anonymous donor when she asked for help.

> Little did I know just how big an impact Adopt-A-Classroom would make. When Constance adopted us, she did so for the long haul. For the last two years, she has supported us with her never-ending generosity, impenetrable spirit and enormous heart. Without her, we would not have our new center table, paper cutter, crayons and markers, not to mention all of the little things that we teachers must often purchase with our own money . . . glue, construction paper, scissors. . . . Those "little things" add up. . . . Our kids benefit from her priceless friendship every year, and every year I have the joy and honor of introducing this incredible woman to a whole new class of kids.

SOURCE: Adopt-A-Classroom at www.adoptaclassroom.org. For a list of other organizations that help classrooms in need, please visit http://www.donorschoose.org/.

Teachers should have a voice, and be a voice for children as well. Consider this chapter a step in that direction, and a primer on both the economics and the governance of schools.

The Property Tax: The Road to Unequal Schools

FOCUS QUESTION 2

How is the property tax connected to unequal educational funding?

> The method of financing public schools . . . can be fairly described as chaotic and unjust.
>
> **(Supreme Court Justice Potter Stewart)**

To someone from another country, the way the United States funds its schools must seem bizarre, and certainly unfair. Unlike many other nations, which use a centralized funding system, we have a decentralized system. In fact, we have three levels of government—local, state, and federal—all raising and distributing funds. Currently, the local and state governments share the biggest burden of funding schools, with the federal government responsible for just 6 to 8 percent of the total. What a tangled web we weave when fifty states, 14,000 local governments, and one enormous federal government become involved in funding and managing 100,000 schools.

How did this financial hodgepodge begin? In colonial America, schools were the concern of local communities. Then, at the birth of our nation, the Constitution did not designate a federal role in education, effectively leaving it the responsibility of the states. "Local control" of schools became a well-established tradition, one that still holds sway today.

GLOBAL VIEW

Most poor countries spend more on servicing foreign debt than on educating their own children. See Oxfam International at www.oxfam.org.

In the agrarian society of colonial times, wealth was measured by the size of people's farms. So to raise money for schools, colonial towns and districts assessed a **property tax.** So if you had a large farm, you paid a large bill for schools; no farm, you pay nothing. Although today only 2 percent of Americans still work the land, the property tax continues to be the major source of school revenue. Today, it is less likely the value of your farm, but more likely the value of your house that determines how much of your tax money you pay toward schools. Today's property taxes are levied on real estate (homes and businesses) and sometimes personal property (cars and boats). Whether a school district will find itself rich in resources or scrambling to make ends meet depends largely on the wealth of the community being taxed. Not surprisingly, a tax on a Beverly Hills mansion raises many more thousands of dollars than a tax on a house in South Central Los Angeles. Communities blessed with valuable real estate can easily raise funds for their schools. Impoverished communities are not so fortunate. Urban areas struggle the most, suffering not only from lower property values but also from the need to use those limited resources to fund more police officers, hospitals, subways, and other services than their suburban counterparts, a phenomenon known as *municipal overburden.*[2]

Reforming Education Finance

Unequal school funding results in stark differences. In 1968, 48-year-old sheet-metal worker Demetrio Rodriguez looked with despair at his children's school in a poor Latino section of San Antonio, Texas. Not only did Edgewood Elementary School lack adequate books and air conditioning, the top two floors were condemned, and barely half the teachers were certified.[3] Ten minutes away, in affluent Alamo Heights, children were taught by certified teachers, in comfortable surroundings with ample materials. The educational cards were stacked against Rodriguez and his neighbors: even though Edgewood residents paid one of the highest tax rates on their property of any Texas community, their property was not worth much. Edgewood raised only $37 per student; Alamo Heights raised $412 per student. Rodriguez went to court, claiming that the system violated the U.S. Constitution's guarantee for equal protection under the law.

In a landmark decision, ***San Antonio v. Rodriguez*** (1973), the Supreme Court ruled against Rodriguez, deferring to the long history of local communities funding neighborhood schools. The Court declared that education was not a "fundamental right" under the U.S. Constitution and that preserving local control was a legitimate reason to use the property tax system. Although the Court recognized that educational funding through the property tax was a seriously flawed system, it was left up to the states to change it. Change has been slow. Texas is one of many states in which wealthy communities have strong schools, and poor ones have under-resourced schools.

Reformers had more courtroom success under state constitutions' equal protection clauses. The California Supreme Court, in ***Serrano v. Priest*** (1971), struck down the state's financing system as unconstitutional. The California court, faced with the glaring differences between Beverly Hills, spending $1,232 per student, and nearby Baldwin Park, spending only $577 per student, declared that education was a fundamental right under the California constitution and that the property tax system violated equal protection of that right. The court found that heavy reliance on the local property tax "makes the quality of a child's education a function of the wealth of his parents and neighbors. . . . Districts with small tax bases simply cannot levy taxes at a rate sufficient to produce the revenue that more affluent districts produce with a minimum effort." *The Serrano v. Priest* decision ushered in both a wave of litigation in other states and an increase in the state share of school funding[4] (see Figure 7.1).

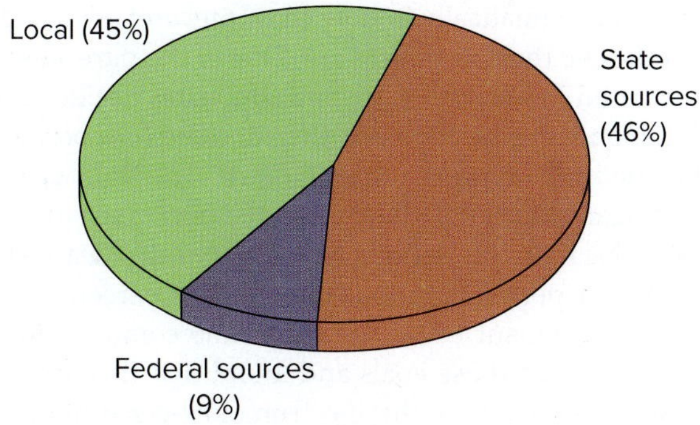

FIGURE 7.1

The public education dollar: Where the money comes from.

SOURCE: National Center for Educational Statistics, 2013; See also *Public Education Finances*, 2014 U.S. Census Bureau, Public Elementary-Secondary Education Finance Data, 2013, June 2, 2015.

NOTE: These proportions are averages, and actual percentages vary significantly from state to state.

REFLECTION: Is the proportion of revenue spent by local, state, and federal governments on education different from your initial perceptions? If you were able to suggest changes in this pie graph, what would they be? Why?

Robin Hood reformers, as they were called, won a victory as they took funds from wealthy districts and redistributed the monies to the poorer districts, much like the Robin Hood hero of Sherwood Forest fame. Robin Hood was a wonderful hero for those in need; those who were rich had a different view.

From Robin Hood to Adequacy

As the effort to equalize funding disparities grew, so did the opposition. In New Jersey, for example, the legislature was dominated by wealthy interests and middle-class communities who fought the Robin Hood idea. The state court shut down the schools to force the legislature to distribute more funds to poorer districts. In *Abbott v. Burke* (1990, 1998), the state court identified twenty-eight failing districts (known as "Abbott districts") where the rights of poor students were being denied. The court mandated that significantly greater funds be spent to transform their students into "productive members of society."[5]

The *Abbott* cases in New Jersey contributed to a new line of litigation focusing on *educational outcome* (student achievement) rather than *financial input* (per-pupil expenditures). State constitutions do not guarantee that every student is entitled to either an equal education or equal funding, but they do guarantee a basic education to all. States use different words to express this right. Some states require that every student receives an "efficient" education, others a "sound basic" education or a "thorough" education, or that all schools need to be "free and uniform."[6] Together, these constitutional clauses are referred to as **adequate education** guarantees, intended to ensure that all students have the basic skills they need to be effective citizens and compete in the labor market. Do you believe that literacy is a part of an adequate education? The state of Michigan does not. In a recent court case, poor parents sued because their children graduating from Detroit Public Schools were unable to read. They argued that the state of Michigan was not meeting its constitutional obligation for an adequate education. Michigan argued that other factors, like poverty and poor parenting, were the reasons behind the students' illiteracy. Michigan said that an adequate education was being provided even if the graduating high school students could not read. Interesting, isn't it? The case is currently going through the courts.[7]

PROFILE IN EDUCATION

Marian Wright Edelman

Edelman attended Yale University Law School and became the first black woman to pass the bar exam in Mississippi. Children "had no one to speak out on their behalf—no one to make sure that there were laws and government policies in place to protect them." During the next four decades, Marian Wright Edelman became their voice. She founded the Children's Defense Fund (CDF) in 1973, with the mission to "Leave No Child Behind." (Yes, her organization's motto was appropriated by others in later years.)

Read a full profile of Marian Wright Edelman on Connect.

©AP Photo/Bob Burgess

connect

Clearly, states differ dramatically in how they interpret adequate education, and how effective or ineffective their responses are. One of the purest examples of the adequacy approach is found in Maryland. Historically, states decided how much money they could afford to spend on education and then decided how best to distribute those funds. Maryland turned that approach upside down. The state appointed a commission that defined adequate education, then computed how much money was needed to achieve it. Adequate education was defined as a school with at least 94 percent student attendance, less than a 4 percent dropout rate, and 70 percent or more of the students passing state achievement tests. Then the state commission studied successful schools that were meeting those goals and found that they were spending about $6,000 per pupil. At the other end of the spectrum, low-performing schools had high numbers of poor children, non-English speakers, and children with special needs. Maryland determined that those schools would require an additional $4,500 per pupil to reach the goals of an adequate education: Maryland would need to add more than a billion education dollars. The state tackled the problem voluntarily, and without litigation.[8] Maryland called its program "The Bridge to Excellence" and invested about 80 percent of the additional funds for teacher salaries and hiring, particularly teachers working with poor and special education students, as well as English Language Learners. *Education Week* ranked the state's schools first in the nation.[9]

FOCUS QUESTION 3

What is the distinction between educational equity and educational adequacy?

Maryland is one of those states continuously ranked at or near the top in school funding, as are Massachusetts and New Jersey. Other states, like Louisiana, Arizona, Alabama, Kansas, and Mississippi, are typically relegated to the bottom of that list as they struggle with under-resourced schools and unfavorable tax structures. (Check https://wallethub.com/edu/states-with-the-best-schools/5335/ to see which states are rated near the top—and bottom—this year.) But before we get too comfortable with our perceptions of states that adequately fund education and those that don't, financial difficulties can be found in every state. Each state has wealthier and poorer communities, and even states with good educational reputations can come up short in funding schools in poorer communities.

A recent example is Connecticut, a wealthy state with a good educational standing. But as a judge noted, Connecticut educational performance was not equitable and serious problems were under the surface of the state's high ratings. He noted that nearly all the high school students in affluent communities like Darien and Westport scored incredibly well on state math and reading tests, but one-third of the students in nearby Bridgeport and other poor cities did not even reach the most basic level in math, and did only slightly better in reading. The judge said that the idea of local communities controlling education has given the state an excuse to avoid meaningful school improvement in poor communities. He scolded Connecticut for evaluating "virtually every teacher in the state" as proficient or exemplary, while a third of students in many of the poorest communities could not read. The judge ordered the state to revamp nearly every facet of its education policies and practices, from graduation requirements to special education. He threw out the state's school financing system, declaring it unconstitutional. His far-reaching decision rejected business as usual in Connecticut's schools.[10]

There is a growing pattern of courts finding grievous injustices in school funding, but too often, states fail to act. Courts cannot enforce their decisions, and many state politicians simply ignore them or stall. This is unfortunate from both human potential and economic perspectives. Investments in schools pay rich dividends. When one economist calculated the impact of effective schools on a community, in this case Virginia Beach, Virginia, he found that the school district produced about $1.53 of community value for every $1 spent. On a national scale, the cost of poor achievement is beyond the imagination. In 2009, the consulting firm McKinsey & Co. estimated that the under-education of poor and minority students costs the United States' between $1.3 trillion and $2.3 trillion (yes, trillion!) in gross domestic product a year.[11] When communities and nations cut back their educational spending, they lose far more than they save.

When local and state budgets get tight, school budgets become a ready target for cuts.

©Hayne Palmour IV/ZUMA Press Inc/Alamy

While adequate education has become the new rallying cry for more equitable school funding, adequate funding remains problematic. The 2008 recession caused most states to make deep cuts to school budgets, often affecting the neediest students, but when the recovery took hold and the economy improved, many states decided not to restore the money to public education.[12] The Center on Budget and Policy Priorities surveyed twenty-four states and found that twenty-one of them were spending less on education in 2012 than they did in 2011; when the rate of inflation was considered, seventeen of the twenty-four were actually spending less than they did in 2008, even though costs for education and other services had risen. Texas terminated preschool services for 100,000 (mostly at-risk) children. Why did the cuts remain after the economy improved?

Sometimes it is the economy; sometimes it is politics that take funding from public schools. When the economy recovered, politicians in some states, like California, voted to approve a higher sales tax and a higher income tax to support schools. Between 2011 and 2016, California increased its education funding by 51 percent.[13] But politicians in other states, including Wisconsin, Arizona, and Kansas, simply refused to restore much of public school funding. Nevada, Montana, and South Dakota, for example, determined that additional funds were not needed to educate English-language learners, students in poverty or special needs students. Political agendas at the state level reduced the funding for public schools, their teachers and students. (See Figure 7.2.) Will this be allowed to continue? Once again, the courts will decide, and we wll wait and see if states comply.[14]

Now let's leave the courtroom (finally!) and pose a more basic (and fascinating) question about school funding: Does money matter?

Does Money Matter?

Common sense would say yes, more money, better schools, but for many years the relationship between spending and student learning was surprisingly inconclusive. Those wishing to keep taxes low would argue that some school districts that received a significant increase in funding were doing no better academically, so "throwing money at schools" does not work. And often, they were right: more money went to schools with little apparent effect. Clearly, these funds were being used in ways that did not improve learning. Money for money's sake is not the answer. But money spent wisely in schools can make a significant difference.

A striking, recent national study looked at test scores on the National Assessment of Educational Progress (NAEP) in 49 states, comparing states that increased funding to poorer communities with states that did not. The study revealed that the test scores improved in states that invested additional money to improve classroom

FIGURE 7.2

Report card on state support of public education.

SOURCE: Valerie Strauss, "How Do States Support Their Public Schools? Badly, a New 50-State Report Card Shows," *Washington Post*, February 2, 2016.

State	GPA	Grade	State	GPA	Grade	State	GPA	Grade
Iowa	2.50	C	Rhode Island	1.83	D	Virginia	1.33	D
Nebraska	2.50	C	Wisconsin	1.83	D	Washington	1.33	D
Vermont	2.50	C	Wyoming	1.83	D	Louisiana	1.17	D
Montana	2.33	C	DC	1.80	D	Arkansas	1.00	D
West Virginia	2.33	C	Alabama	1.67	D	Colorado	1.00	D
Alaska	2.17	C	Hawaii	1.67	D	Nevada	1.00	D
Massachusetts	2.17	C	Maine	1.67	D	New Mexico	1.00	D
New Hampshire	2.17	C	Minnesota	1.67	D	Oklahoma	1.00	D
New Jersey	2.17	C	South Carolina	1.67	D	Tennessee	1.00	D
North Dakota	2.17	C	Delaware	1.50	D	Florida	0.83	F
South Dakota	2.17	C	Michigan	1.50	D	Georgia	0.83	F
Connecticut	2.00	C	Pennsylvania	1.50	D	Indiana	0.83	F
Maryland	2.00	C	Utah	1.50	D	North Carolina	0.83	F
Illinois	1.83	D	California	1.33	D	Arizona	0.67	F
Kansas	1.83	D	Missouri	1.33	D	Idaho	0.67	F
Kentucky	1.83	D	Ohio	1.33	D	Texas	0.67	F
New York	1.83	D	Oregon	1.33	D	Mississippi	0.50	F

REFLECTION: Are there any surprises on this report card? Do these grades influence where you would want to teach? Do these grades motivate you to take political action?

instruction in their lowest-income school districts. States that did not invest in improving the instruction of poorer students experienced no such test gains. Money targeted to instruction made a significant difference on NAEP test scores.[15] But test scores are not the only measure of success.

Another study looked not at test scores, but assessed student success after graduation. That study found that for poor children, a 10 percent increase in per-pupil spending each year of elementary and secondary school was associated with a 10 percent increase in wages these students earned after graduation. More money invested in educating poorer students produced adults who made a better living. As you might imagine, there was also a drop in the incidence of adult poverty. In fact, this increased aid encouraged students to stay in school longer, roughly six additional months.[16] The researchers suggested that money spent on improving instruction and reducing class size resulted in a more effective educational experience and greater income upon graduation for poorer students. So money, wisely spent, does indeed make a difference. But unfortunately, the public often does not provide these extra funds.

Why do Americans tolerate such dramatic inequities in school funding? Here are a few explanations[17]:

1. *Local control.* In colonial times, it was left to individual communities in rural America to support their local schools. The Constitution codified this practice, and even after urbanization and suburbanization, Americans continue to believe that local taxes should be used to educate neighborhood children.

"Equity" or "Adequacy"

WE SHOULD SEEK EDUCATIONAL "EQUITY" BECAUSE . . .

MONEY TALKS

The gap between wealthy and poor communities makes a mockery of democracy and fairness. Poor students attend schools with leaking roofs and uncertified teachers; wealthy students learn in schools with computers, swimming pools, and well-paid and qualified teachers. No real democracy can ignore such glaring inequities.

EQUALIZING INPUT IS CRUCIAL

Isn't it strange that those who advocate business values like choice and competition ignore the most fundamental business value of all: money. Wealth creates good schools; poverty creates weak ones. Invest money wisely over a period of time, and watch those once-poor schools thrive.

EQUITY IS POWERFUL

Democracy and equity are powerful words representing powerful ideals. Adequacy is a feeble word subject to interpretation and compromise. What's adequate? Is it the ability to read at a high school level, or at an eighth-grade level? Does an adequate education lead to a minimum wage job? Only "Equity" can serve as a rallying cry.

WE SHOULD SEEK EDUCATIONAL "ADEQUACY" BECAUSE . . .

MONEY DIVIDES

Robin Hood is dead. Wealthy communities are not going to fund poor ones, happily sending their hard-earned dollars to fund someone else's school. The cornerstone of democracy is local control, and trying to redistribute wealth is fundamentally unfair, and smacks of the approach used by communists (another failed system).

EQUALIZING INPUT IS INEFFECTIVE

We will never make schools more effective by throwing dollars at them. When California moved toward equitable input, the quality of its public schools deteriorated. Our goal is not to increase school budgets and per-pupil expenditures, but to increase student achievement.

ADEQUACY IS ATTAINABLE

Equity is a powerful dream, but adequacy is an attainable one. We are unlikely to achieve a completely equitable school system, but we can demand reasonable and reachable educational standards. Moreover, we are on firmer legal footing, because state constitutions guarantee not identical expenditures but an adequate education for all.

connect YOU DECIDE...

Do you believe that adequacy or equity provides the best foundation for reforming schools? Explain. Can these approaches be blended, or are they mutually exclusive?

2. *Horatio Alger.* The rags-to-riches story of fictional Horatio Alger symbolizes the strongly held American belief that wealth and success are the fruits of individual effort, and that an individual's circumstances are merely obstacles to be overcome. It stands to reason, therefore, that if hard work and motivation alone are responsible for success, poverty comes from a lack of effort and a lack of talent. Individualism absolves communities from any collective responsibility for the poverty of others.
3. *Genetics.* For centuries, genetic differences have been used to explain why some succeed and others fail. The notion that certain groups are genetically brighter than others is a recurring theme in America.
4. *Culture of poverty.* Some believe that poor people live in and are shaped by the problems inherent in impoverished communities, problems that cannot be remedied through additional school funding.

5. *Flawed studies.* Back in the 1960s, the classic Coleman study reported that school quality and funding had less of an effect on student achievement than family background or peer groups, that schools mattered very little. (Note: Such studies have been cited for major methodological flaws, and more recent research has shown that money can make a difference–but the mis-belief that it does not persists.)
6. *Previous funding increases have not resulted in achievement gains.* Critics point out that although education spending has increased, test scores have not. However, most new funds were not targeted at improved instruction, but spent on specific educational needs, like special education, dropout prevention, expanded school lunch programs, or regular teacher salaries. These are important areas for sure, but not necessarily directly related to test scores.
7. *Unaware of how other nations fund and manage schools.* Other countries fund and manage schools quite differently, and we can learn much from their methods. Later in this chapter, we will discuss Finland, a nation that approaches education with great freedom and flexibility, spends far less money, and often scores at the very top on international tests. In Finland, the federal government assumes about 57 percent of the costs of education, the local government the remaining 43 percent. Teachers are given great autonomy to decide the direction of education, and the key approach in schools is collaboration: successful schools, managed differently and costing far less. (See Figure 7.3.)

In the United States, unequal school spending is a painful fact of life. Wealthier schools attract better prepared teachers and create smaller classes.[18] Poorer schools cannot afford this.[19] In Illinois, for example, one wealthy district spends about $20,000 more per student (not $20,000 per student, which is amazing, but $20,000 *more* per student) than a poor district in that state.[20] All across America, schools with educational everything continue to exist alongside schools struggling to keep the

FIGURE 7.3

Comparison of per student expenditures in the United States and Finland.

SOURCE: *Annual Expenditure by Educational Institutions per Student for All Services.* CIEB: Finland.

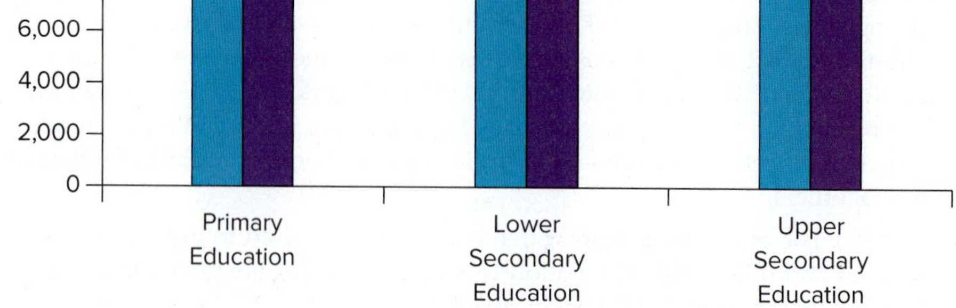

REFLECTION: How does the way schools are managed affect the impact of the effectiveness of funding? Why is collaboration working in Finland, but not being used here?

heat in and the rats out. Research suggests that well-spent funds can reduce the achievement gap, but adequate education does not even attempt to equalize spending; it simply tries to ensure a fundamental level of learning for all students.[21] Despite the Horatio Alger "rags-to-riches" myth, studies show that children born into poor families in the United States are less likely to rise out of poverty than those in other industrialized nations.[22] Schools disappoint the poor, and states need the money to reform them.

States Finding the Money

FOCUS QUESTION 4

What are the sources of state revenues?

Let's assume that you have been asked by your (choose one or more of the following) (a) education professor, (b) teacher association, (c) favorite political candidate, or (d) spouse to find out where states find the money for our schools. Here are some common sources[23]:

1. *Sales tax* (a charge added to all sales). Consumers pay a few extra pennies for small purchases or a few extra dollars for large purchases. The sales tax accounts for 30 percent of the typical state's income. More than 40 states use a 2 percent to 8 percent sales tax. Sounds easy, but there are problems: Some people avoid the tax by taking their business to a neighboring state. The tax is regressive; that is, it hurts poor families more than rich ones because the poor spend most of their income buying necessities, so most of their money is being taxed.
2. *Personal income tax* (used in more than 40 states). The personal income tax brings in more than 25 percent of state revenues. The personal income tax is collected through payroll deductions, money deducted even before you receive your paycheck. The tax is a percentage of income, and each state determines how equally, or unequally, the tax burden falls on the poor, the middle class, and the rich.
3. *Other revenue sources.* Other common state sources of funding include excise taxes (on tobacco, gasoline, and liquor, sometimes known as a *sin tax*), severance tax (based on the state's mineral wealth), motor vehicle license fees, estate or gift taxes, and state lotteries. Although state lotteries offer holders of winning tickets the chance to collect millions in prize money, a disproportionate higher percentage of the poor purchase these long-shot lottery tickets. Most states use lottery revenues to supplement, not fund, parts of an established education budget.[24]

Your brief course in "State Finance 101" is over. You can see some of the limits of state revenue sources. For extra credit, can you devise an entirely new scheme to raise state funds? As you can tell from Figure 7.4, states vary widely in how much money is invested in education.

But before we get too depressed at these heartbreaking inequities, here is some good news: Even in underfunded schools, teachers like you can make a difference. A number of low-income communities in Tucson, Arizona were experiencing high school graduation rates as high as those in higher income communities. How were they doing it? While the instructional approaches varied widely, these schools shared several commonalities, including a strong connection to their communities. As we discussed in Chapter 3 on culturally relevant teaching, the school's staff and teachers worked closely with the community and families. The schools held high expectations for staff and students alike and provided assistance to both when it was needed. Students were assessed frequently, and targeted teaching was provided when necessary. Teachers helped each other become better at their craft, and worked as teams to plan

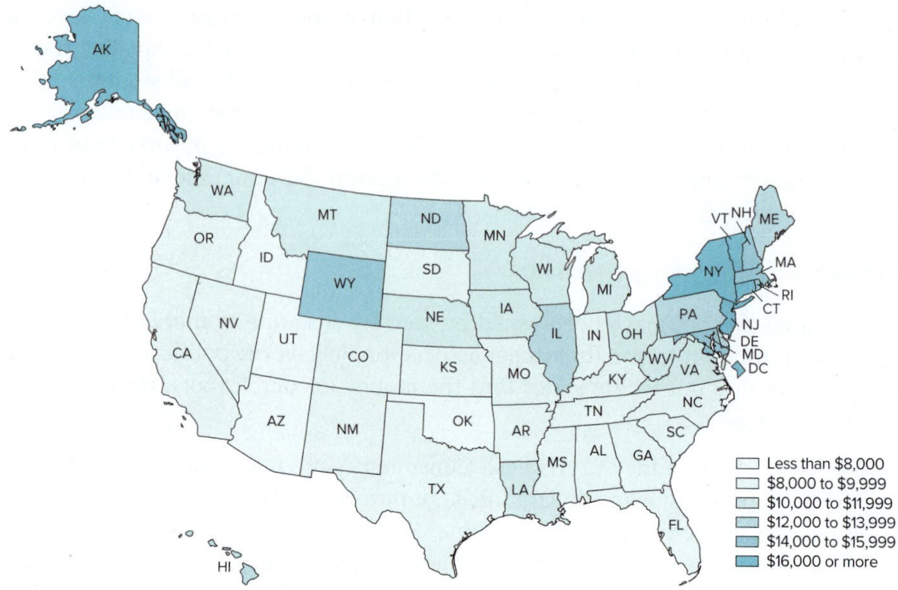

FIGURE 7.4

Public elementary and secondary school system spending per pupil.

SOURCE: US Dept. of Commerce, US Census Bureau, *Annual Survey of School System Finances,* 2014, Issued June 9, 2016.

REFLECTION: Do your teaching plans include any of the states that spend the most or least amount per-pupil? Will this spending information influence your decision on where to teach? For more information on how different states respond to the needs of children, visit www.childrendefense.org.

lessons and analyze challenges. These teachers built trusting relationships not only among the faculty, but among the students and parents as well. Building a positive school culture transformed even the poorest schools.[25]

The Federal Government's Role in Financing Education

FOCUS QUESTION 5

How does the federal government influence education?

At this point, some of you might be thinking: Even if every state provided every school district with adequate funding and a great education plan, the economic gaps among the states would still be enormous. If you thought about that, congratulations; you have put your finger on a systemic problem. For instance, students in New York or Connecticut typically receive far more education dollars than students in Mississippi or Arizona, regardless of the state's revenue plan. Because of the Constitution, this is a problem the United States seems unable to correct.

If the Constitution had assigned education as a federal responsibility, we might expect to see the federal government close the economic gap between states. U.S. schools might be centrally financed and governed; or at the very least, the Supreme Court might rule funding inequities among states unconstitutional. But this is not the case. The Supreme Court has ruled that education is not a "fundamental right" under the U.S. Constitution and has left education to the states. Accordingly, the federal government's role in the financing of education is relatively small. In fact, the federal government typically pays an average of 9 percent of the cost of public schools in the United States. How much is this of the entire federal budget? About 3 percent (and much of that is for higher education, not pre-K-12). That's 3 cents of every federal dollar going to pre-K through university education–a small role indeed.[26] (See Figure 7.5.)

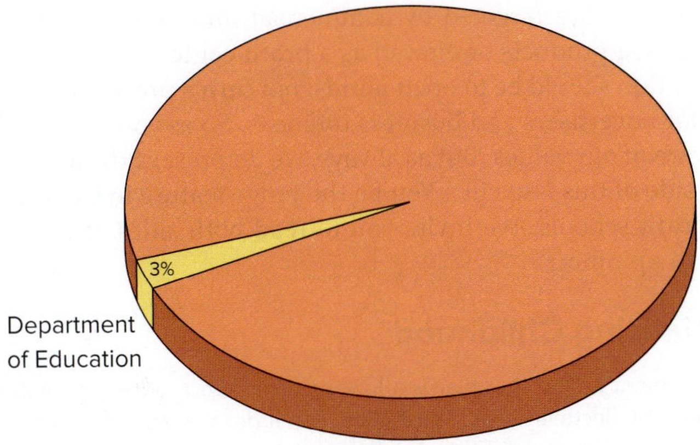

FIGURE 7.5

Federal budget and education. Within the federal budget, education expenditures remain quite small. This 3 percent includes elementary, secondary, vocational and higher education, as well as research and educational assistance.

SOURCE: Center on Budget and Policy, "Policy Basics: Where Do Our Federal Tax Dollars Go?" March 4, 2016.

REFLECTION: Can you think of any other major area of the federal budget that receives fewer dollars than education?

However, the federal government still manages to influence schools. How does it do this? One way has been through **categorical grants**–funds directed at specific categories and targeted educational needs. Categorical grants have provided funding for preschool programs for poor children, library construction, acquisition of new technology, educational opportunities for veterans, the training of teachers and administrators, educational reform, lunches for low-income youth, and loans to college students. By targeting funds, federal aid, although limited, has had a significant impact in schools.

RAP 3.1

Money Matters

The federal government also funds schools through **block grants,** large sums of money given directly to the states with few strings attached. Block grants reduce the obligations, rules, and even competition associated with seeking federal dollars. You can see that each type of grant has strengths and weaknesses. Categorical grants identify critical education areas for federal financial support. Block grants give the states the power to make their own spending decisions.

The federal government also influences education through the courts. For example, the 1954 Supreme Court's *Brown* decision desegregated the nation's schools, a monumental change that affected every state in the union. The civil rights laws that followed increased educational opportunities for students of color, limited speakers of English, students with disabilities, and females. Federal courts matter, and so do targeted federal laws such as No Child Left Behind (2001), which ushered in an era of high-stakes testing that persists today. When the 2008 recession put public school at risk, the federal government provided crucial extra funding.[27] But the bottom line is that the federal government's role is limited. The United States may well be the only nation to fund elementary and secondary education based on local wealth. If schools are to improve, it will be local communities and state governments that will make that happen.[28]

Schools, Children, and Commercialism

FOCUS QUESTION 6

How does commercialism at home and in school affect children?

This section is about the impact of businesses on children and schools, and we want to tell you up front that we are not neutral on this topic. Business dollars are shaping our children, and not in good ways. Along with other writers and educators, the authors of this text have deep reservations about what happens to children when they are targeted by commercial interests and when schools are used for marketing products or viewed as a profit center. We believe that the goal of public education should be to open minds, not turn a profit, and children should be off limits for advertisers and business interests. So as you read this section, you should be aware of our values. But as always, we do present the arguments of those on the other side of this issue in a You Be the Judge feature in Chapter 9, where we explore for-profit schools. We invite you to read both sides of the argument and form your own opinion.

Commercializing Childhood

> We have become a nation that places a lower priority on teaching its children how to thrive socially, intellectually, even spiritually, than it does on training them to consume. The long-term consequences of this development are ominous.[29]

Just a few decades ago, the children's advertising industry spent $100 million selling products to kids, mainly through television ads. More than a decade ago, food companies were already spending $1.6 billion marketing carbonated beverages, fast-food restaurants, and breakfast cereals to children.[30] Today, marketing is not just television ads. Computer games, cell phones, MP3 players, DVDs, and even school itself have become advertising hubs. Children are the target for 20 billion advertising dollars annually.

Why the surge in commercializing childhood? Politics, changing lifestyles, and electronic innovation all contribute to this problem. In the 1970s, corporate pressure moved Congress to prohibit the Federal Trade Commission (FTC) from banning television marketing to children under 8 years old. In the 1980s, children's television was deregulated even further, and television programs focused on selling products directly to children. As single-parent and two-working-parent families increased, so did the number of children watching television. Today, almost half of 3-month-old babies regularly watch television, and 10 percent of babies under 1 year of age have a television in their bedroom. The recent surge in personal electronic gadgets means that companies now target ads directly to children on iPods and other devices.[31] Advertisers influence children through product placement (in movies and computer games), brand licensing (a company's brand name placed on other products), viral marketing (advertising done on preexisting social networks), and guerrilla marketing (selling things in unconventional and unexpected places).

Are children a legitimate target for advertisers?

©David Woolley/Getty Images RF

Today's children spend a trillion consumer dollars annually. Their allowances, their paychecks, and the influence they exert on parents' spending make them prime targets for advertisers. Marketing experts film children at play, study their behaviors, and analyze their tastes. Based on that research, sophisticated and effective sales pitches are created, and children are persuaded to buy products from fast food to cosmetics.

Here is one example of how this research shapes the buying habits of children: Advertisers have learned that younger children want to be like older children, so *aspirational marketing* was born. Advertisers intentionally market older products to younger children. Young girls are targeted for sexy adolescent clothes, although they lack the maturity to understand the strong social messages wearing such clothes sends. Abercrombie and Fitch sells thong underpants to 8-year-olds with slogans such as "wink wink" and "eye candy," and girls under 5 go to "spas" such as Sak's Fifth Avenue's Club Libby Lu to get "makeovers."[32] Rather than developing their creativity and self-expression, young girls emulate the older girls they see in *High School Musical* and *Hannah Montana*. The result is that young girls become consumers of weight-reduction products, makeup, clothes, and dating.

For young boys, it is about emulating the physical strength and toughness of older boys, so rough competitions are valued. Young boys watch wrestling matches on television, play violent video games, and sometimes experiment with steroids. The Federal Trade Commission has criticized the entertainment industry for continuing to market R-rated movies, M-rated video games, and explicit-content recordings on television shows and Web sites with substantial teen audiences.[33] For both genders, sex-role stereotyping is emphasized at the expense of authentic relationships. Creative play, innocence, and connecting with nature, all healthy childhood activities, are lost to commercialism.

Other industrialized nations do not let this happen. Television marketing to children is banned in Norway and Sweden, junk-food ads for the young are banned in Britain, and Greece never allows war toys to be advertised. America's children are virtually defenseless in the face of sophisticated marketing, and they pay a price. Allen Kanner, a clinical child psychologist, finds that children now talk about making money and their friends' clothes and designer labels, but "not the person's human qualities."[34]

Commercialism promotes self-gratification: "It's about me, and I want it now." Happiness is achieved by acquiring things, and one can never have enough things. Such values have led to assaults, as students attack each other to steal designer jackets or Nike shoes. Marketing to the young teaches all kinds of lessons, few if any of them good. When the marketing occurs at school, the costs are even greater.

Brand Name Education: Should Schools Be Open for Business?

To increase attendance, some schools are offering prizes, paid for by local businesses, just for showing up. For example, in Hartford, Connecticut, a 9-year-old won a raffle for students with perfect attendance and was given the choice of a new Saturn Ion or $10,000. (His parents chose the money.) At Oldham County High School in Kentucky, a high school senior was awarded a canary yellow Ford Mustang. Krispy Kreme doughnuts awards students in Palm Beach County, Florida, a free doughnut for every report card A. Describing his quest for additional school funds, one high school principal noted, "My approach is Leave No Dollar Behind."[35]

Schools also promote specific products by entering "exclusive agreements" so that no competitive products are sold on school grounds. About 75 percent of high schools have signed exclusive soft drink contracts. Coca-Cola promised Oakland, California, half a million dollars to support a community youth program in return for a ten-year agreement banning the sale of competing soft drinks on city property. Such exclusive contracts may turn out to be a very bad business deal if schools

GLOBAL VIEW

Investigate how other countries handle marketing to children.

are sued for contributing to America's obesity epidemic,[36] while keeping vendors of healthy snacks and drinks from selling on school grounds.[37]

Branding schools does not stop with products; school districts now sell the naming rights of athletic facilities, school buildings, and offer companies the opportunity to put their corporate logos on textbooks. Sometimes the corporation pays the school for getting students and parents to buy their products. General Mills donates funds to schools according to the number of boxtops turned in or other coupons showing proof of purchase. Channel One broadcasts commercials in school and on school time. Students admit they are more likely to remember the ads than the educational programs. If children grow up with Nike and McDonald's in school, they are likely to stay with those companies as adult consumers. As one critic noted, if you teach business values early enough, children accept it as truth.[38]

Schools and teachers can be persuaded to echo the tactics of advertisers. Tom Farber, an advanced-calculus teacher in San Diego, decided that a good way to pay the cost of photocopying tests was to sell advertising space to local businesses and parents. He charges $10 for an ad on a quiz, $20 for an ad on a test, and $30 for an ad on the final exam. He raised $625 and explained, "When money is tight, you really have to be creative."[39]

These are overt examples of commercialism, but it is wise to remember that the influence of business can be far more subtle. Everyday school practices that seem so familiar also teach students corporate values such as neatness, conformity, and punctuality. As educator Linda Darling-Hammond has noted:

> The short segmented tasks stressing speed and neatness that predominate in most schools, the emphasis on rules from the important to the trivial, and the obsession with bells, schedules, and time clocks are all dug deep into the ethos of late nineteenth-century America, when students were being prepared to work in factories on predetermined tasks that would not require them to figure out what to do.[40]

Commercial interests can overwhelm schools, but we are not helpless. When in the Seminole County, Florida, school district was paid by McDonald's to put student report cards in envelopes covered by McDonald's advertising and offering free Happy Meals, almost 2,000 parents protested. The county was forced to stop the practice. *Scholastic* magazine promoted Bratz items at their book clubs and book fairs. (Bratz is the brand for provocative and sexualized dolls made under suspect labor conditions in China.) More than 5,000 e-mails persuaded *Scholastic* to stop the practice. Massachusetts and Vermont have introduced legislation to prohibit marketing in school, and citizens and organizations continue to lobby the federal government to regulate childhood commercialization in and beyond school.

Teachers can make an enormous difference as well. Teaching media literacy empowers children to understand and confront the market messages that manipulate them. Classrooms can be places where children discuss the underlying values implicit in consumerism and its impact on the planet and themselves. Rather than sitting by as young lives become focused on consuming, educators can help children connect with healthy alternatives, such as exploring nature, developing creative talents, discovering the joys of community service, and forming authentic relationships. For those who want to learn more about confronting childhood commercialism, we recommend the Campaign for a Commercial Free Childhood as a helpful resource (http://www.commercialfreechildhood.org/).

TEACHING TIP

Finance Lessons

Learning about school finance is important for educators, but learning about personal finance is useful for everyone, students and teachers alike. Remember your first paycheck? You knew how much you were earning, but when the check appeared, it was way less than you expected. Your $500 a week job was netting you just over $300 a week. Now how did that happen? Things you never heard of, like FICA, seemed to be getting some of your money. (By the way, FICA is how your social security deductions are reported.) Most students leave school woefully unprepared for the everyday world of finance.

This need not be the case. When financial literacy programs are taught, students learn the importance of savings, how compound interest works, when and how to buy items, and what tricks advertisers use to lure customers into an unwise purchase. Students understand the importance of credit scores and how to protect their credit ratings. When financial literacy is acquired, young (and older) adults can navigate the world of finance.

Although financial literacy is increasingly taught in schools, many schools are still without such a program in their curriculum. If your school is one of these, you can make an important difference by accessing relevant financial literacy lesson plans online. (But a word to the wise: Avoid Web sites that promote a particular bank or financial institution.) One program not aligned with a particular institution is FoolProof. Educators who want to teach financial literacy in their classrooms can sign up for lesson plans at www.foolproofteacher.com. (And for teachers who need to update their own financial literacy skills, there's Pollinate, at www.pollinateproject.org/.)

REFLECTION: With capitalism so highly valued in U.S. society, how do you explain why the practical world of finance is often missing from the school curriculum?

What the Future May Hold for School Finance

FOCUS QUESTION 7

What current trends are shaping educational finance?

Today, we are in a period of shifting governmental responsibility for the financing of schools. Reformers are focusing less on financial inequity and more on educational inadequacy. What are some other trends in educational finance, issues that are likely to surface in the years ahead?

Accountability

RAP 3.6

Assessing the Assessor

The public wants to see academic progress for their tax dollars—in short, **accountability.** Schools are often ranked by their students' standardized test scores, as the testing culture persists. Teachers find that student test scores can influence their pay and careers, while tenure itself has become more difficult to obtain, or retain. But there is a growing negative reaction to too many tests.

Choice Programs, Vouchers, and the Neighborhood School

The neighborhood school, long a mainstay of public education, is being challenged by school competition and the growth of charter schools. Many neighborhood schools are disappearing or being reconstituted. Vouchers move funds from public schools to private ones, leaving the public school at greater financial risk. Parents can be misled through deceptive advertising or other business techniques, posing a constant danger to effective schools as education and commercialism become intertwined. (See Chapter 9.)

Longer School Day and School Year

A number of charter schools have extended their school day and their school year as one tangible way to improve student performance. Some public schools are now following this trend, but it is difficult to determine what will happen when longer school days and years collide with shrinking educational budgets.[41]

The Economy's Impact on School Budgets

When the economy takes a downturn, state and local budgets are cut, and education suffers. This means fewer teachers, larger class sizes, and the elimination of sports, extracurricular activities, art, and music. Few state and local governments maintain the financial reserves necessary to avoid such cutbacks. This may become a steady pressure in the years ahead.[42]

The Rich–Poor School Divide Is Likely to Grow

While poor schools struggle, wealthier districts are developing creative strategies to ensure that their schools are not endangered by funding redistribution plans. Through Parent–Teacher Association donations, online fund-raisers, cooperative agreements with local business endowments, unequal local funding that gives more to schools that have more experienced teachers, and tax-sheltered private educational foundations, additional educational dollars find their way to schools in wealthier neighborhoods. Wealthy communities defend such practices as a way to prevent parents from fleeing "to private school if they don't perceive the public education to be excellent."[43]

Decaying Infrastructure

Here we are in the twenty-first century, using schools that were built in the nineteenth century. When local governments need to replace these aging buildings, they usually resort to issuing bonds. A **bond** is a certificate of debt issued by a government guaranteeing payment of the original investment plus interest by a specified future date. Bonds give the local communities the money they need to build the schools and fifteen to twenty years to pay off the debt.

But for most schools, repair, not replacement, is the remedy for antiquated buildings. Although rewiring for computer and Internet installation is needed, teachers and principals give higher priority to "adequate" heating, lighting, acoustics, ventilation, and air conditioning. The Department of Education estimates that tens of thousands of schools need major repairs, repairs that range from $279 billion to $500 billion.[44] In a nationwide survey of elementary and secondary public school

Dilapidated inner-city schools are sad examples of the decaying infrastructure.

©Janine Wiedell Photolibrary/Alamy

principals, more than 40 percent reported that poor building conditions were impairing teacher instruction and student learning.[45]

Commercializing Children and Schools

Many educators and psychologists believe that marketing to the nation's children, especially in school, has an adverse affect on their health and the quality of their lives. Sophisticated marketing techniques create a thirst for consumption and selfishness that replaces healthy, caring, and creative childhood activities. Although other nations protect their young from marketers, the United States does not.

Governing America's Schools

School Governance Quiz

The following quiz should help you focus on how schools are governed. If you are stumped by some of these questions, fear not; the remainder of the chapter is organized around a discussion of these questions and their answers.

1. Most school board members are (Choose only one.)
   a. White, male, and middle or upper class.
   b. Middle-class women, about half of whom have been or are teachers.
   c. Middle of the road politically, about evenly divided between men and women, and representing all socioeconomic classes.
   d. So diverse politically, economically, and socially that it is impossible to make generalizations.
2. State school boards and chief state school officers are
   a. Elected by the people.
   b. Elected by the people's representatives.
   c. Appointed by the governor.
   d. Appointed by officials other than the governor.
   e. All of the above.
   f. None of the above.
3. During the past two decades, the influence of local school boards has
   a. Increased.
   b. Decreased.
   c. Remained unchanged.
4. Local school district superintendents are (You may choose more than one.)
   a. Often mediating conflicts.
   b. Civil service–type administrators.
   c. Elected officials.
   d. Sometimes powerless figureheads.
5. Who might be considered part of the "hidden school government"? (You may choose more than one.)
   a. The school principal.
   b. The state school superintendent.
   c. The U.S. secretary of education.
   d. The school secretary.
   e. Parents.
   f. The Teacher Arbitration and Labor Relations Board.

6. The influence of the business community in U.S. schools can best be characterized as
   a. Virtually nonexistent.
   b. Felt only in vocational and commercial programs.
   c. Extensive and growing.
   d. Usually illegal.
7. In most schools, teachers are expected to
   a. Design the policies guiding their schools.
   b. Collaborate with principals and district officials to create policies to suit their schools.
   c. Comply with policies made by principals and by district and state officials.
   d. Comply with policies that seem appropriate and change those that do not.

School Governance Answer Key

1. a	2. e	3. b	4. a, b, d	5. d, e	6. c	7. c

0 to 1 wrong: You receive the Horace Mann Award.

2 wrong: You may want to run for school board.

3 wrong: Read the rest of the chapter carefully.

4 or more wrong: Take detailed notes on this part of the chapter; become a frequent visitor to the text Web page; find a friend to quiz you; and whatever you do, stay away from TV quiz shows.

The Legal Control of Schools

FOCUS QUESTION 8

How do school boards and superintendents manage schools?

The following sections review and discuss the quiz you have just taken, beginning with the first two questions:

1. Most school board members are . . . *white, male, and middle or upper class.*
2. School boards and chief state school officers are . . . *elected by the people, elected by the people's representatives, appointed by the governor, or appointed by officials other than the governor.*

GLOBAL VIEW

The World Data on Education (WDE) Web site provides access to information for 144 national education systems.

School boards, whether at the state or local level, determine educational policy, and their members tend to be male (more than 60 percent), white (more than 85 percent), and not young (most are 50 years of age or older). In short, many school board members look like the leaders we find in corporate America or government.[46] As for the second question, in some states, school boards and chief state school officials are elected; in others, they are appointed. Even the name for the chief state school officer differs from place to place: superintendent, commissioner, or even secretary of education. Why the differences? The **Tenth Amendment** reminds us: "The powers not delegated to the United States by the Constitution, nor prohibited by it to the States, are reserved to the states, respectively, or to the people." More than 200 years ago, the authors of the Constitution did not discuss education, so each state was free to create its own school system. While most nations have a national ministry of education to determine what and how all students will be taught, in our country, each of the fifty states, the District of Columbia, and several U.S. territories make those decisions.

The governor, legislature, state superintendent, or the state school board consider different ideas for improving education. One state might require that all schools have a certain number of computers, and another state might decide that all high school students must pass four years of science. Suppose you apply for a position in a state that passed a new requirement: all new teachers must pass a course in "Instructional

Strategies for Improving Student Test Performance." The state superintendent and the state department of education would inform all teacher candidates (including you) of the new course requirement. If you applied to teach in the state, someone in the state department of education would review your transcript to make certain that you had successfully completed the new course on improving test scores before issuing you a teacher's license. If you took that course and completed all the state's requirements, voilá, you will be issued your teacher's license. But (nothing personal) don't expect the state to hire you.

Although states issue teacher licenses, hiring and firing of teachers is done by the local school district, about 14,000 of them across the country. So you don't apply to the state for a teaching position, but to the local district. The district will check to make certain that you have your teacher's license, and then consider you for a position. Figure 7.6 describes these levels of school governance.

State Board of Education The **state board of education** is responsible for formulating educational policy. The members are usually appointed by the governor, but sometimes they are chosen in a statewide election.

Chief State School Officer Called *superintendent, commissioner, secretary of education,* or *director of instruction,* the **chief state school officer** is responsible for overseeing, regulating, and planning school activities, as well as implementing the policies of the board of education. The state superintendent is usually selected by the board of education but sometimes campaigns for the position in an election.

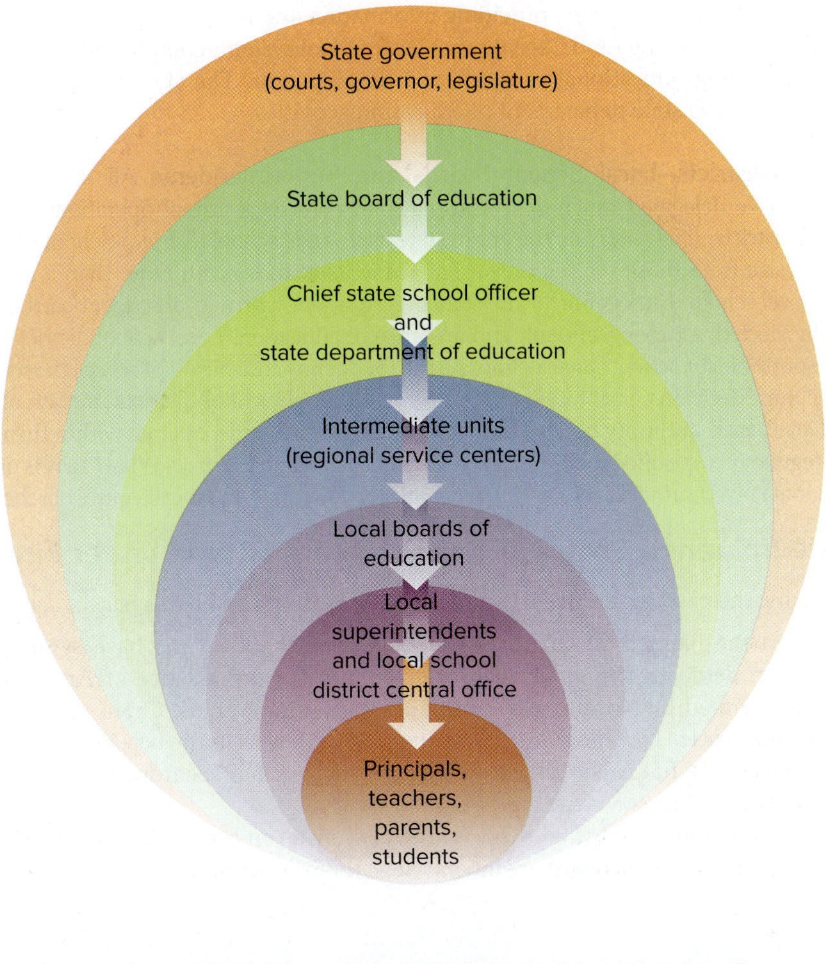

FIGURE 7.6

Structure of a typical state school system.

REFLECTION: What are some of the difficulties in these many levels of governance? Do you favor elected or appointed school boards? Why?

A CLOSER LOOK

Who Controls What? Levels of Educational Power

STATE GOVERNMENTS

- Levy taxes
- License teachers and other educators
- Set standards for school attendance, safety, etc.
- Outline minimum curricular and graduation standards (sometimes including specific textbooks to be used and competency tests for student graduation and teacher certification)
- Regulate the nature and size of local school districts

LOCAL SCHOOL DISTRICTS

- Implement state regulations and policies
- Create and implement local policies and practices for effective school administration
- Hire school personnel
- Provide needed funds and build appropriate facilities
- Fix salaries and working conditions
- Translate community needs into educational practice
- Initiate additional curriculum, licensing, or other requirements beyond state requirements
- Create current and long-range plans for the school district

REFLECTION: As a classroom teacher, offer some examples of the issues that would lead you to deal with state government. Which issues would send you down a path to the local government?

State Department of Education The **state department of education** performs the administrative tasks needed to implement state policy. This includes licensing teachers, testing student progress, providing information and training to teachers, distributing state and federal funds, seeing that local school systems comply with state laws, and conducting educational research and development. The state superintendent usually manages state department of education activities.

School Districts—Local School Boards and Superintendents All states except Hawaii have delegated much of the responsibility for local school operations to local school districts. (Hawaii treats the entire state as a single school district.) School districts vary in size from those serving only a few students to those with more than a million. Most local school districts mirror the state organization, with a local school board that is usually elected, a superintendent, and an office of education. Local school districts may be responsible for school construction, taxing, budgeting, the hiring of school personnel, curriculum decisions, and local school policy. Although school districts operate at the local level, their authority derives from the state, and they must operate within the rules and regulations specified by the state. (A Closer Look: Who Controls What? Levels of Educational Power, summarizes the relationships between state and local control of schools.)

State Influence Grows as School Boards Come under Fire

3. During the past two decades, the influence of local school boards has . . . *decreased.*

Forged in the hamlets of colonial New England, school boards have symbolized small-town democracy. School board meetings evoke the essence of Americana—the kind painted by Norman Rockwell and made into a Frank Capra movie titled *Mr. Deeds Elected to the School Board* (starring Jimmy Stewart as the beleaguered school board president). But Americana aside, many criticize school boards as unresponsive and entrenched bureaucracies.

Part of the problem is that there is little consensus on how school boards should operate.[47] Most school board members view themselves as *trustee representatives,* selected to serve because of their educational expertise and good judgment. But others, including many voters, see school board members as *delegate representatives,* responsible for implementing the will of the public (or being voted out of office if they do not). The type of elections used to select school board members can shape the kind of school board that will emerge. When school boards are selected through "at-large" elections, in which the entire school district votes for all the members of the school board, the school board is expected to represent the interests of the entire community (trustee representatives). But some school districts choose board members to represent the interests of specific neighborhoods (delegate representation).

District-wide, at-large elections typically result in more elite, politically conservative, and upper-class individuals being elected to school boards. After all, it is the well-established individual who is likely to have the financial resources and educational and business background needed to win a big, district-wide election. Poorer citizens, people of color, and women are less likely to find themselves on at-large school boards. Unfortunately, many citizens feel disenfranchised when it comes to school board elections.

RAP 3.10
Get on Board

Other criticisms include the following:

- School boards have become *immersed in administrative details,* at the expense of more important and appropriate policy issues. One study of West Virginia school boards showed that only 3 percent of all decisions made concerned policy.
- School boards are *not representing local communities,* but only special interest groups. Elections to the school board receive little public support. In a New York City school board election, for instance, only 7 percent of the voters participated.
- The *politics of local school board elections* has a negative impact on attracting and retaining superintendents and leads to conflict with state education agencies.
- The composition of the boards is *not representative,* with individuals of color, women, the poor, and the young unrepresented or underrepresented.
- School boards have been in the *backseat when it comes to educational change and reform.* As a matter of fact, many school boards do not support current educational reform proposals, and members have lagged behind public opinion on such issues as school choice and charter schools.
- The education of children goes beyond school issues to include health, social, and nutritional concerns. School boards are *too limited in scope* to respond to all the contemporary concerns of children.
- If schools continue to be *financed less from local funds and more from state funds,* local boards could become less influential.
- Many of the new reforms call for *new governance organizations,* site-based management, or choice programs that relegate the school board to a less important, perhaps even unnecessary, role.[48]

Although these criticisms suggest a dismal future for school boards, preparing their obituary may be premature. School boards have endured a long time and may be around long after many of the reform recommendations are forgotten.

The School Superintendent and Principal

4. Local school district superintendents are . . . *often mediating conflicts, civil service–type administrators, sometimes elected and sometimes powerless figureheads.*

The first superintendents were hired to relieve school boards of their growing administrative obligations. The year was 1837, and these new superintendents worked in Buffalo and Louisville. As the nineteenth century progressed, more communities followed this example. Superintendents were expected to supervise and hire teachers, examine students, and buy supplies, which had become too burdensome for the school boards themselves. Superintendents also kept school records, developed examinations, chose textbooks, and trained teachers.

By the twentieth century, the superintendent's role had changed from the board's administrative employee to its most knowledgeable educational expert–from helper to chief executive officer. Today, the superintendent is the most powerful education officer in the school district, responsible for budgets, buildings, new programs, daily operations, long-term goals, short-term results, and recruiting, hiring, demoting, and firing personnel. When things are going well, the superintendent enjoys great popularity. But when things are going poorly, or school board members are not pleased, or local community groups are angry, or teacher organizations turn militant, or . . . you get the picture. When there is a problem, it is usually the head of the system, the superintendent, who gets fired. The superintendent lives and works in a fishbowl, trying to please various groups while managing the school district. It is a very insecure existence of sidestepping controversies, pleasing school board members, responding to critics, juggling many different roles and goals, and living with conflict. In many urban school districts, superintendents serve only a few years before they are fired, resign, or retire. Many believe that this high-visibility, high-stress position is also subject to subtle forms of racism and sexism. Over 60 percent of superintendents are male, and more than 90 percent are white.[49]

One need not look hard for the reasons for this turnover. Successful superintendents must win and maintain public support and financing for their schools. This involves forming political coalitions to back their programs and to ward off attacks from those more concerned with rising taxes than with the school budget. In an era in which most citizens in many communities do not have children in schools, this becomes a real test of political acumen. Superintendents find themselves serving on a number of civic committees, speaking to community groups, and being the public relations spokesperson for the school district. Yet, despite feeling high levels of stress, nine out of ten superintendents find their work rewarding and believe they made the right career choice.[50]

School superintendents who survive and thrive are the politically savvy administrators who can "read" their school board. In *The School Managers: Power and Conflict in American Public Education,* Donald McCarty and Charles Ramsey provide a useful classification system that matches school board types with different superintendent styles.[51]

School Boards in Communities That Are . . .	*Prefer a Superintendent Style That Is . . .*
Dominated: School boards run by a few local elite who dominate community and school policies	Functionary: Follows wishes of the board
Factional: Divided community, competing factions	Political: Balances often opposing concerns, avoids appearance of favoritism
Pluralistic: Competition among interest groups	Adviser: Moves cautiously as adviser among shifting community coalitions
Inert: No visible power structure, little interest in schools	Decision maker: Board relies on superintendent for leadership and decision making

An effective superintendent must be an effective manager, and a number of new superintendents of large school districts have been selected for their management skills rather than their educational expertise. New York City, San Diego, Seattle, and Los Angeles have chosen generals, lawyers, and a former governor to lead their schools.[52] Although well-known figures may bring visibility and hope, there is no superman to "fix" the problem. An effective superintendent is a good manager who builds solid relationships and persists at the job for more than a few years.[53] And good management is essential. Superintendents have been terminated when textbooks or school buses arrive late. In fact, some school districts have adopted performance-based contracts that link superintendent compensation directly to student performance.[54]

While the superintendent is the focal point of district pressures, the principal bears the brunt of school pressure. "Stress, testing, and social problems are all in the schools now: AIDS education, security, parenting classes, language programs. There are so many things that they are responsible for that they might not have control over, and it's led to concern about principal burnout."[55] Even at the elementary level, where many consider the stress most tolerable, a typical elementary principal supervises thirty teachers, fourteen other staff members, 425 students, and works an average of nine or ten or more hours a day, sixty or even seventy hours a week.[56] When budget cuts reduce support staff, they juggle roles as teachers, community liaisons, nurses, athletic directors, crisis managers, and budget managers. Surveys have revealed that 9 in 10 principals (and 74 percent of teachers) say that a principal should be held responsible for *everything* that happens to the children in a school. Everything. That includes addressing the needs of diverse learners, engaging the community, managing school needs despite depleted budgets, and trying to stay on top of a job that is becoming more complex.[57] Principal recruiters struggle to overcome persistent racial and ethnic imbalances as well.[58] (Figure 7.7 provides insight into

GLOBAL VIEW

Twenty countries originally signed the Convention on the Organization for Economic Co-operation and Development (OECD) in 1960, and since then, fourteen additional countries have joined. Many but not all are among the world's most advanced nations. Only five of these nations have lower high school completion rates than the United States.

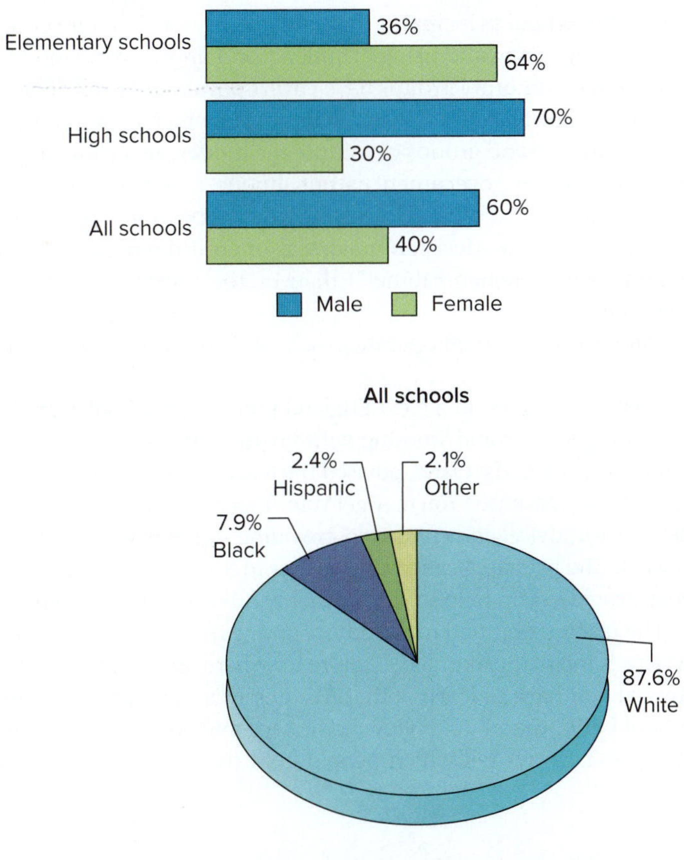

FIGURE 7.7

Elementary and high school principals.

SOURCE: Amy Bitterman, Rebecca Goldring, and Lucinda Gray, (2013). *Characteristics of Public and Private Elementary and Secondary School Principals in the United States: Results From the 2011–12 Schools and Staffing Survey,* (NCES 2013-313), U.S. Department of Education. Washington, DC: National Center for Educational Statistics, 2013. Retrieved January 24, 2017 at https://nces.ed.gov/pubsearch/.

REFLECTION: Why are more women principals at elementary rather than secondary schools? What are the potential challenges for schools with white principals and a majority of students of color?

principal demographics.) Because of the central role of the school principal, it is not a surprise to learn that their competence is second in importance only to teacher quality in improving schools.[59]

These statistics underscore the tough challenges that superintendents and principals face, and you may be wondering, "Why would anyone want these jobs?" Here's one reason: Talented educational leaders take satisfaction from making a real difference in the lives of thousands of students. If you are considering teaching, then making a positive difference in the lives of the students in your class is a motivator for you. Magnify that and you can see why some are drawn to administration. School districts committed to serious reform know that principals and superintendents can make a difference, and New York City is a case in point. The city established its own Leadership Academy to prepare a new generation of administrators. Once they graduate, these new principals manage schools that have been made smaller to increase their effectiveness. The new principals exert greater authority, control their own budget, and hire their faculty. They also shoulder a greater responsibility for the academic performance of their students and take home a larger paycheck than past administrators. Many of these new principals are only in their 30s. In fact, more than half of New York City's principals are now under 50. Why does the city seek younger (and less experienced) leaders? "I wanted to change the old system," former Schools Chancellor Joel Klein said. "New leadership is a powerful way to do that."[60]

Covert Power in Schools

FOCUS QUESTION 9

What is the "hidden" government of schools?

5. Who might be considered part of the "hidden school government". . . *the school secretary and parents.*

So you think that the school principal is the only one responsible for school personnel decisions, including hiring and firing? Think again. Parents, vocal individuals, the school secretary, and community groups have **covert power** and can bring significant pressure to bear on which teachers stay in a school, and which leave. These unofficial but highly involved people and groups constitute the **hidden government** of schools.[61]

The concept of hidden government is not unique to schools. In fact, most of our institutions, including the White House, have developed their own unique forms of hidden government. There, decision making is often influenced more by old colleagues back home (the "kitchen cabinet") than by the president's official advisers and cabinet members.

How does hidden government operate in schools? Following are some examples.

Example 1 A first-year teacher in a New England junior high school spent long hours after school preparing lessons and working with his students. Admirable as all this appeared, the school secretary, Ms. Hand, advised the teacher not to work with female students after school hours, because "You may get your fingers burned." The teacher smiled, ignored the secretary's advice, and continued providing students with after-school help.

Within a week, the principal called the teacher in for a conference and suggested that the teacher provide extra help to students only if both male and female students were present. The teacher objected to the advice and to the secretary's complaining to the principal. The principal responded, "You're new here, and I can understand your concern. But what you have to learn is that Ms. Hand is more than a secretary. She knows this school better than I do. Follow her advice and you'll do just fine."

Lesson: You can't always tell which people hold the real power by their official position.

Lesson: The school secretary is often the eyes and ears of the principal. In some cases, the secretary manages the day-to-day operations of the school.

The school secretary holds a position that can exert significant covert power in his or her pivotal role as the principal's "eyes and ears."

©Silvrshootr/Getty Images RF

Example 2 A young teacher in an elementary school in the Midwest was called into the principal's office for a conference. The principal evaluated her teaching as above average but suggested that she maintain greater discipline. Her classroom was simply too noisy, and the students' chairs were too often left in disarray. The conference was over in ten minutes.

The teacher was offended. She did not feel her classroom was too noisy, and the chairs were always arranged in a neat circle. Moreover, the principal had visited her class for only five minutes, and during that time the students had said hardly a word.

The next day, in the teacher's lounge, all became clear when she discussed the conference with another teacher. The teacher nodded, smiled, and explained:

"Mr. Richards."

"The custodian?"

"Yup. He slowly sweeps the halls and listens for noisy classrooms. Then he tells the principal. He also hates it when the chairs are in a circle, since it makes sweeping harder. Nice straight rows are much easier. Just make sure your classroom is quiet when he's in the halls and have your students put the chairs in neat, straight rows at the end of the day. That's the ticket for getting a good evaluation!"

Lesson: School custodians are often a source of information for principals and of supplies for teachers. They make very helpful allies and powerful adversaries.

Example 3 An elementary school teacher in a rural southern community was put in charge of the class play. Rehearsals were under way when the teacher received a note to stop by the principal's office at 3:00 P.M.

The principal had received a call from a parent who was quite disappointed at the small part her daughter had received in the play. The principal wanted the teacher to consider giving the child a larger part. "After all," he explained, "her mother is influential in the PTA, and her father is one of the town's most successful businessmen. It's silly for you to alienate them. Give her a bigger part. Life will be easier for both of us."

Lesson: Parents can also be influential in school decisions by applying pressure on principals, school boards, and community groups. When you decide to make a stand in the face of parental pressure, choose a significant issue and be able to substantiate your facts.

FOCUS QUESTION 10

How does the business community influence school culture?

Business and Schools

6. The influence of the business community in U.S. schools can best be characterized as . . . *extensive and growing.*

Even before there were "for-profit charter schools" directly competing with (and taking funds from) public schools, business values had long influenced schools. In fact, a century ago educators adopted a business vocabulary for school jobs and work. *Superintendent,* the title originally given to a factory supervisor, was assigned to the

Corporate influence in schools can be seen in the emphasis on competition, punctuality, and the growing trend to advertise to children.

©RJ Sangosti/The Denver Post/Getty Images

school district leader. Both a factory and a school have been called a *plant. Quality control, accountability, management design,* and *efficiency* were also expropriated. Little surprise that many superintendents come from the business sector. School values often mirror those of business: hard work, competition, dependability, punctuality, neatness, conformity, and loyalty.[62] Companies that formalize a relationship with a school, by dedicating personnel or products or signing exclusive rights contracts, are said to have formed an **educational partnership.** A number of educators express concerns about these developments, an issue we explored earlier in this chapter. But whether we are comfortable or uncomfortable with this trend, "the most far-reaching initiative in education to emerge in recent years is the growing corporate interest in public schools."[63]

Making Schools More Responsive

7. In most schools, teachers are expected to . . . *comply with policies made by principals and by district and state officials.*

While parents, community groups, and the business sector carve out their roles in schools, teachers traditionally have been omitted from meaningful involvement in school governance.

Teachers, who know more than most people in the educational chain about the needs and interests of individual students, have often been excluded from school management and policy making.

©fotoinfot/Shutterstock RF

Teachers, as a rule, do not participate in hiring new teachers, in developing criteria by which their teaching will be evaluated, in setting graduation requirements, or in scheduling classes. One reason is sheer size: Over the past centuries, schools and school districts have continued to grow. Larger districts are considered more cost-effective because they lower the per-pupil expenses, from preparing food to building maintenance, and bigger school districts are able to offer more courses, extracurricular activities, and sports programs.[64] Merging smaller schools and districts into larger ones is called **consolidation.** In 1940, more than 117,000 school districts existed in the United States. Today there are fewer than 14,000.[65] Larger schools and school districts also mean more red tape, greater student alienation, and reduced parent–teacher involvement; in other words, less responsive schools.[66] Many districts are now reversing the trend, creating smaller schools and smaller districts, a process called **decentralization,** or creating charter schools operating without central office involvement.[67]

In addition to size, top-down decision making by principals and superintendents also contributes to a sense of teacher powerlessness.[68] Efforts to empower teachers include site-based or school-based management and collaborative decision making. **Site-based or school-based management** shifts decision making from the central district office to individual schools, and **collaborative decision making** creates teacher committees to share power between the principal and the faculty.[69] If you find yourself teaching in a school using one or both of these approaches, keep in mind that the results have been mixed. Some teachers enjoy making curricular and budgetary decisions, but others feel such participation simply becomes "just another meeting you've got to go to." One of the challenges facing you as a teacher or an administrator will be to create more responsive and humane school climates, both for yourself and your students.

Schooling Beyond the United States

FOCUS QUESTION 11

How are schools being made more responsive to teachers and the community?

> Imagine you are teaching in a country created by teachers: The Wonderful Land of Learning. In our mythical country, warmth and respect for children and teachers are the norm. This reverence is demonstrated in many ways, one of which is that play and free time are school priorities. In fact, until high school, students receive a 15-minute break every hour to go outside and run around. (Great idea, right?) Teachers understand that play outside helps students focus better inside. Nutritious meals and convenient transportation support learning as well, and in our make-believe country healthy meals are free even in college. Unlike the rich–poor economic divide that characterizes U.S. schools, all schools in our Wonderful Land of Learning are equally well funded. All of them! And we do not stop at free time and free meals; all of these terrific schools are tuition-free as well, from preschool to college. (I'm liking this, aren't you?)
>
> In the Wonderful Land of Learning, teachers have the autonomy to make key educational decisions, like how best to organize classrooms and promote learning. When do they do this? During the school day, of course, with a lighter teaching load to give them adequate time to collaborate and explore each student's learning needs. Guess what? This positive learning environment is supported by the almost total absence of tests. But the absence of tests during the school years do not inhibit how well these students do on the few international tests they take at the end of high school. Graduates from Wonderful Land of Learning schools score near the top of all students in the world (significantly higher than U.S. students). No wonder that teaching here is a respected and sought-after career. In fact, 90 percent of those who apply to become teachers are rejected.
>
> Has our imagination gotten the best of us? Are we hallucinating? Is this magical thinking? No, it's Finland.[70]

In the early 1970s, Finland had much in common with today's United States: there was a popular belief that schools were not doing well. Their economy was in dire straits, dependent on a quickly disappearing natural resource, lumber. The Finns knew that to compete in the world economy, they would have to make fundamental changes to their schools and rebuild their economy. But unlike our reform efforts (discussed in Chapter 9), Finland did not focus on competition, school choice, merit pay, or standardized testing: Finland focused on teachers. First, teacher education was revamped and turned into a five-year program of study, research, and practice. Finnish teachers were prepared to work with all students with learning disabilities and given more time to study their subject fields; when they completed their preparation, they received a master's degree. Now they were ready to begin teaching. This high-quality preparation led to a highly honored career: teaching. A career in teaching is now highly selective; nine out of every ten people who apply to become teachers are rejected. People who go into teaching enjoy their careers, and few leave.

Finland has a national curriculum not unlike our current effort to create national core standards. But in Finland, the curriculum is quite general, and teachers are given great autonomy in designing and teaching their own lessons. Unlike the United States, there are no national tests, and no emphasis on test preparation.

FIGURE 7.8

Rankings on international PISA tests.

SOURCE: Programme for International Student Assessment, 2015

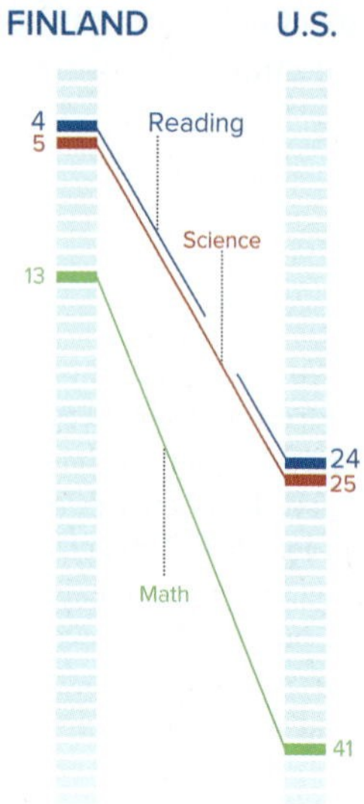

REFLECTION: What lessons do you take away from how Finland manages its schools, and how its students score on international tests?

In fact, most Finnish students take their first standardized test when they graduate high school. The few tests given before then are used for school comparisons and are not for public consumption. Finland is at or near the top on international tests, like PISA. (See Figure 7.8.)

Now you have the key clues to Finland's success (as well as Japan's and Singapore's educational success): *trusting teachers.* Parents trust teachers because they are professionals, and teachers trust one another and regularly collaborate to solve mutual problems. Trust is seen every day as teachers work in teams, continually improving their curriculum and each other's teaching. Their motto is "Trust Through Professionalism." The evidence indicates that trust is far more effective in raising test scores than test preparation.

Some might point out that Finland and the United States are too different to make useful comparisons. Certainly, there are differences, and those differences are worth pointing out. For one, Finland is less diverse than the United States, but it is far from a homogenous nation. Fifteen percent of the population speaks a second language, and 45 languages are spoken in Helsinki schools. Another difference favors the United States: we are wealthier. But our willingness to tolerate one out of five Americans living in poverty detracts from school achievement. Less wealthy Finland has a poverty rate of only 3 to 4 percent, but their poor receive more services than the poor here, and poverty is far less crushing. Finland's national policies to mitigate the impact of poverty are evident in school performance: The difference between the highest performing school and the lowest performing school in Finland is less than 4 percent. When one compares Finland to individual U.S. states, comparisons are even easier to make. Finland is the size and population of about thirty-three states, but it outperforms all of them on international tests.

U.S. schools are managed and to some degree financed with an eye to high-stakes testing, competition, and school choice. When Finnish educators view the way we run our schools, they are astonished. The idea of merit pay, teacher competition, and evaluating teachers by students' test scores make no sense to them. The very idea of promoting teacher competition rather than teacher collaboration is alien. Students feel less pressure, have frequent breaks for physical activity during their relatively short school day, and don't begin school until they are 7 years old. Finnish children typically get free school meals and tuition-free education, even at the college level. (Yes, there really is a Wonderful Land of Learning!)

By focusing on quality teaching rather than testing, Finland regularly attains the highest test scores in the Western world, and its economy is rated among the most innovative, creative, and successful. It is a nation that respects its educators and gives them the autonomy to design and measure each student's education without working under the fearful shadow of testing and competition. We have much to learn from Finland.

CONNECT FOR *TEACHERS, SCHOOLS, AND SOCIETY*

Check out Connect, McGraw-Hill Education's interactive learning environment, to:

Read Current and Historical Articles

Finding Fairness for Rural Students, by Marty Strange, *Phi Delta Kappan,* March 2011.

Respect—Where Do We Start? by Marie-Nathalie Beaudoin, *Educational Leadership,* September 2011.

School Funding's Tragic Flaw, by Kevin Carey and Marguerite Roza, *Education Sector Reports,* May 15, 2008.

Where Have All the Strong Poets Gone? by Alan C. Jones, *Phi Delta Kappan,* April 2007.

Analyze Case Studies

Kate Sullivan: A principal faces the problems endemic to the students served by her school, which is located in a very low socioeconomic area. Issues of drugs, poverty, neglect, hunger, and homelessness are compounded by the underfunding for the school.

Jane Vincent: A teacher is asked by her principal to reconsider her grading of a student whose numerical average for the marking period is just below the department's cutoff score for that grade.

Watch Teachers, Students, and Classrooms in Action

Our **Online Video Album** for contemporary videos related to this chapter.

KEY TERMS AND PEOPLE

DISCUSSION QUESTIONS AND ACTIVITIES

1. Create a plan for (a) raising funds for education and (b) distributing funds equitably to all school districts within a state.
2. What is your opinion of the "adequacy" argument? Do you have any reservations about this approach? Do you believe that educational expenditures and educational quality are directly related? Support your position.
3. Research the average costs of educating a student in a local district. Discuss with classmates as you compare district programs, tax base, facilities, and student achievement.
4. Which of the four types of school boards would you prefer to serve on, or work for? Why? Which of the four types of school superintendents would you prefer to be, or to work for? Why?
5. Have you had any personal experience in an organization that had both a formal and a "hidden" government? Explain how these governments operated.

©Win McNamee/Getty Images

Ethics is knowing the difference between what you have a right to do and what is right to do.

SUPREME COURT JUSTICE POTTER STEWART

chapter 8

School Law and Ethics

Focus Questions

1. What are your legal rights and responsibilities as a teacher?
2. What legal rights do students enjoy (and do they have legal responsibilities)?
3. What are the ethical responsibilities of teachers and students?
4. How might teachers thoughtfully and safely manage social media in and outside the classroom?
5. What classroom strategies promote moral education?

Chapter Preview

- An honors student sues the school district after being randomly strip-searched.
- A teacher is reprimanded for allowing a first-grader to read a Bible story to the class.
- A teacher is suspended for texting a student.
- A student complains that peer grading of assignments violates her privacy.
- A homosexual teacher sues a school district for discrimination.

In this chapter, you will respond to actual legal and ethical situations that confront teachers and students. A number of case studies—based on actual court rulings—will help you to determine your RQ— rights quotient. You'll also learn some pragmatic "self-defense" steps that may help you avoid potential legal problems. In addition, we will explore penetrating issues of right and wrong, including questions that go beyond the law, such as: How should teachers deal with legal, ethical, and constitutional issues that emerge in school? Should teachers take public positions on moral issues? To handle these important ethical dilemmas, we will offer some suggestions for ways teachers can organize their classroom environments and develop crucial professional skills.

Classroom Law

You have probably heard it before: The United States is a litigious society. "Take them to court," "I'll sue," and "Have your lawyer call my lawyer" are phrases that have worked their way into the American lexicon. And actions match words. People sue companies. Companies sue people. Governments sue companies. Companies and people sue governments. Today, parents sue teachers. Students sue teachers. Teachers sue schools. Lawyers and judges are increasingly a part of school life. Such a litigious world has an impact on instruction. Four out of five teachers and nearly that many principals describe "defensive teaching"–meaning that their educational decisions are motivated by a desire to avoid legal challenges. Educators believe that fewer laws would reduce their legal concerns and improve the quality of education.[1]

Despite the growing concern over legal issues, many educators are still unaware of their basic legal rights and responsibilities.[2] This can be a costly professional blind spot. What rights do you have in the classroom? Consider this exchange between a college professor and a former associate superintendent of public instruction for California[3]:

> SUPERINTENDENT: "Teaching is a privilege, not a right. If one wants this privilege, he or she has to give up some rights."
>
> PROFESSOR: "Just what constitutional rights do people have to give up in order to enter teaching?"
>
> SUPERINTENDENT: "Any right their community wants them to give up."

Arbitrary school rules, regulations, and attitudes still exist in some communities and create serious difficulties for teachers and students. Over the past few decades, state and federal court decisions have given teachers and students more freedom to fight arbitrary decisions and pursue legal action if they believe that their constitutional rights are being threatened. But these changes don't guarantee all the protections you might imagine or hope that they do. Community and political interests sometimes pressure school leaders to bypass or ignore the spirit and/or letter of the law. Students' and teachers' ability to fight for their rights can be hindered by ignorance of one's rights, fear of retribution, and/or lack of resources to launch legal action. Meanwhile, new legislation and Supreme Court rulings can change the law over time. And, in the end, legal rulings are made by judges–fallible human beings with philosophies, attitudes, and prejudices which may or may not align with the interests of individual teachers and students.

A CLOSER LOOK

School Law Basics

Federal, state, and local governments all have a voice in education, although they don't necessarily speak in unison. Here's a brief look at how the different branches and levels of government influence education law.

THE U.S. CONSTITUTION

The U.S. Constitution does not mention education, but it does guarantee people basic rights that concern schools. Three constitutional amendments are of special interest to teachers and students (for more, see constitutioncenter.org/interactive-constitution#).

- The **First Amendment** protects freedom of religion, speech, the press (or media), and peaceful assembly. The Amendment's **establishment clause** prohibits government (including schools) to promote or prohibit religion.
- The **Fourth Amendment** prohibits violation of privacy and security without a court warrant.
- The **Fourteenth Amendment** protects citizens' rights to due process and equal protection under the law, no matter where they live in the United States (rights for non-citizens are murkier).

FEDERAL LAWS

Many federal laws influence education. The Civil Rights Act of 1964 bars discrimination on the basis of race, color, or national origin. Title IX of the Education Amendments Act of 1972 prohibits discrimination on the basis of sex. The Individuals with Disabilities Education Act ensures students with a disability are provided with free public education tailored to their individual needs. By funding some programs, and withholding funds from others, the federal government exerts a significant influence on all levels of education.

STATE AND LOCAL LAWS

State and local laws (and state constitutions) also affect education, leading to significant local and regional differences throughout the nation. For example, state and local statutes often deal with school financing, collective bargaining, teacher certification, and compulsory attendance.

THE COURTS

The United States has a dual judicial system. Each state has its own local or district courts, along with one or more courts of appeal. The federal court system has district courts, 13 regional courts of appeal, and the U.S. Supreme Court. State courts initially hear most legal issues in education. Federal courts only hear cases related to the U.S. Constitution or federal laws.

SOURCE: Michael LaMorte, *School Law: Cases and Concepts*, 10th ed. (Upper Saddle, NJ: Prentice Hall 2011).

REFLECTION: What are the advantages and the disadvantages of different government jurisdictions determining school law?

As a classroom teacher, what can you legally say and do? Can you "friend" students on Facebook? What disciplinary methods are acceptable? How does your role as teacher limit your personal life? Knowing the answers to these questions *before* you step into a classroom can help you avoid costly mistakes.

While teachers would like to know definitively what is legal and what is not, courts often set forth standards with such terms as "reasonable care" or "appropriate under the circumstances." Ideally, courts try to balance legitimate concerns raised on both sides of an issue and to keep their options open. Staying legally up-to-date is an ongoing professional task.

What Is Your Rights Quotient?

The following case studies focus on court cases or federal law.[4] The vignettes are divided into two parts: teachers' rights and students' rights. In each case, an issue is identified, a situation is described, and you are asked to select an appropriate (legal) response. After your selection, the correct response and relevant court decisions or laws are described. Keep track of your rights and wrongs; a scoring system at the conclusion will help you determine your "Rights Quotient" (RQ). Good luck!

FOCUS QUESTION 1

What are your legal rights and responsibilities as a teacher?

I. Teachers' Rights and Responsibilities

Issue	*Situation 1*
Applying for a position	You did it! You finished student teaching (you were great!) and the school district you most want to teach in has called you for an interview. Mr. Thomas, from the personnel office, seems impressed with your credentials and the interview is going well. He explains that the school district is very committed to its teachers and invests a great deal of resources in training. He wants to make certain that this investment makes sense, so he asks you for your long-range plans: "Are you planning to get married or have children in the near future?"

_____ You answer the question realizing that the district is entitled to know about your long-range plans.

_____ You avoid answering the question. You think it's none of his business, but you are worried that you won't get the position.

Legal Decision Not too long ago, school districts regularly considered marital and parenthood status in employment decisions. For women these were critical factors in being offered a job, and the "right" answer was: "No, I am not going to get married or have children." For male candidates, the question was less important and rarely asked. Now a variety of federal and state laws and court decisions make such inquiries illegal. Interview questions must be related to the job requirements. Questions about race, creed, marital status, sex, religion, age, national origin, and physical or other disabilities and even a request for photographs along with an application are generally illegal. **Title IX of the Education Amendments (1972)** and **Title VII of the Civil Rights Act (1964)** are two federal laws that prohibit many of these practices. In situation 1, the questions are inappropriate and illegal, and you need not answer them. The challenge, of course, is how you could answer such questions without ruining your chances of being offered a position—that is, if you still want the job.[5]

Issue	*Situation 2*
Sexual harassment	After surviving the gender discriminatory interview, you are offered a teaching position and decide to take it. After all, you like the community and the children. You are very excited as you prepare for your first day. You enter the school, feeling hopeful and optimistic. You enjoy and respect your new colleagues, but you feel strange around Mr. Gray, the assistant principal. You spend the next year dodging his lewd comments, his unwanted touches, and his incessant propositions. You share your concerns with the other teachers, but you are alone in your experience. Finally you approach the school principal, who assures you that Mr. Gray means no harm, but promises to have a chat with him. You feel good about giving voice to the problem but soon realize the only thing that has changed is that Mr. Gray is now spreading rumors about you with other staff. The harassment continues. At the end of the year, you find yourself emotionally drained and contemplating a leave of absence. You decide that

_____ Your emotional well-being is at risk. You will resign before things get worse.

_____ Enough is enough. You sue the district for damages.

Legal Decision The assistant principal's behavior, both verbal and physical, is clearly sexual harassment. Sadly, nearly half of women are subjected to unwanted sexual contact or touching at work. The Supreme Court ruled that victims of sexual harassment are also victims of sex discrimination under Title IX, and can, in theory, recover monetary damages. (See Situation 16 on p. 231 for more.) However, in the real world, sexual harassment is both illegal and very difficult to stop. To find legal relief, nearly all of the burden falls on the victim. Family, friends, and colleagues may ask: "Are you sure? Did you lead him on? Do you want to expose yourself and your school to public embarrassment?" Too often, supervisors or human resource departments opt to protect the school—or even retaliate—rather than support the person being harassed. To successfully fight the harassment, the victim has to keep a record of the harasser's behavior and have witnesses willing to corroborate what happened—even in the face of possible retaliation toward *them*. Federal law requires charges of sexual harassment to be filed with the Equal Opportunity Employment Commission (EEOC) before going to court. The EEOC has at least 180 days to complete an investigation (and often takes much longer). In the end, the EEOC dismisses most cases. Only then can the victim sue in federal court—as long as they do it within 90 days, and can afford an attorney experienced in sexual harassment cases (bearing in mind that few such attorneys work in rural areas). Unfortunately, defendants (like a school district) choose to, in effect, put the victim on trial by dragging out elements of her personal life. Suing can lead to justice and awards for damages and distress—but it can be a rough path, despite growing awareness of sexual harassment's prevelance.[6]

Title IX also prohibits sex discrimination against female *and* male employees and students in federally funded institutions—like schools, colleges, vocational training centers, public libraries, and museums. It is designed to ensure fairness in athletics, employment, counseling, financial aid, admissions, and treatment in classrooms.

Issue	*Situation 3*
Personal lifestyle	After your first few months, your reputation is established: You are known as a creative and effective teacher and are well liked by students and colleagues. (Isn't that wonderful!) But school leadership does not appreciate your life outside the classroom. You are single and living with your "significant other." Several school officials strongly believe that this makes you a poor role model for your elementary-aged students. The school system publicly announces your suspension because your cohabitation is having a negative influence.

_____ You are the victim of an illegal action and should sue to be reinstated.

_____ The school board is within its rights in dismissing you and removing a bad role model from the classroom.

Legal Decision This case hinges on how much personal freedom an individual gives up as a teacher and role model for students. Although court decisions have varied, the following general standard should be kept in mind: Does your behavior significantly disrupt the educational process or erode your credibility with students, colleagues, or the community? If the school district can demonstrate that you have disrupted education or have lost credibility, then you may be fired.

A CLOSER LOOK

How Private Is Your Personal Life?

Courts are regularly asked to draw the line between a teacher's personal freedom and the community's right to establish teacher behavior standards. Although each case must be judged on its own merits, some trends do emerge. Courts have ruled that a teacher can be fired for:

- Incorporating sexual issues into lessons and ignoring the approved syllabus
- Inciting violent protest among students
- Engaging in sexual acts with students
- Encouraging students to attend certain religious meetings
- Allowing students to drink alcohol
- Drinking excessively
- Using profanity and abusive language toward students
- Stealing school property (even if it is returned later)
- Not living within his or her district if that is a condition of employment
- Wearing inappropriate clothing, such as short skirts or jeans

On the other hand, courts have ruled that teachers should not be fired for

- Unwed cohabitation
- Private homosexual behavior
- Obesity (unless it inhibits teaching performance)
- Adultery
- Use of vulgar language outside school
- HIV or disability

Why are teachers dismissed in some cases and not in others? Often, the standard the courts use is whether the behavior under question reduces teacher effectiveness. Public behavior, or behavior that becomes public, may compromise a teacher's effectiveness. In such cases, the courts find it reasonable and legal to terminate the teacher. If the behavior remains private, and if the teacher shows discretion, the teacher's "right to privacy" often prevails.

SOURCE: Nathan L. Essex, *School Law and the Public Schools: A Practical Guide for School Leaders*, 5th ed. (Boston: Allyn & Bacon, 2011).

REFLECTION: Courts have disagreed on whether the following three situations constitute grounds for dismissal of a teacher. If you were the judge, how would you rule on the following issues?

- Sex-change operation
- Unwed parenthood
- Conviction for shoplifting

In the case outlined here, the teacher sued the school district (*Thompson v. Southwest School District*). The court indicated that until the school district took action to suspend the teacher on grounds of immorality, the public was generally unaware of the teacher's cohabitation with her boyfriend. The court decided that it was unfair of the board of education to make the issue public to gain community support for its position. Furthermore, the court ruled that the teacher's behavior had not interfered with her effectiveness in the classroom. Unable to show a loss of credibility or a significant disruption of the educational process, the board lost its case and the teacher kept her job.

What if teachers have a same-sex partner? Do LGBTQA teachers have legal protection from dismissal and discrimination? In 1989, the Supreme Court said that sex discrimination includes sex stereotyping–and therefore it is illegal to mistreat employees when they don't comply with gender norms. In 2015, the Court ruled that the Constitution protects same-sex couples' right to marry. However, a 2016 lawsuit sought to end Houston's benefits for city employees' same-sex spouses, and North Dakota legislators refused to change the state's now-unconstitutional statute banning gay marriage. Clearly, legal precedents don't immediately change community values—or necessarily prevent discrimination against LGBTQA educators.

When holding school districts accountable for allowing harm to LGBTQA people in an educational environment, there's substantial uncertainty. Some federal courts have ruled that the Fourteenth Amendment and Title VII of the Civil Rights Act provide protection, but other federal judges have ruled that sexual orientation falls outside constitutional protections. Fortunately, major education organizations like the National Association of Secondary School Principals and the National Association of Elementary School Principals are vigorously promoting inclusion of LGBTQA educators and students.

Court decisions regarding the personal lifestyles of teachers differ from state to state. Driving while intoxicated or smoking marijuana was grounds for dismissal in one state but not in another, depending on whether the behavior resulted in "substantial disruption" of the educational process. On the other hand, an attempt to dismiss a teacher because she did not attend church was not upheld by the court.

What about your personal appearance? What can a school district legally require in regard to personal grooming and dress codes for teachers? Courts have not been consistent in their decisions, although they may uphold the legality of dress codes for teachers if the dress requirements are reasonable and related to legitimate educational concerns.[7] (See A Closer Look: How Private Is Your Personal Life?)

Do you believe that a teacher's sexuality is a legitimate consideration for employment?

©Creatas/Getty Images RF

Issue	*Situation 4*
Teachers' academic freedom	As a social studies teacher, you are committed to teaching about the futility of hate and discrimination. You assign your middle school students *The Terrorist*, a mystery novel that evokes strong feelings on ethnic and religious issues. Class discussions and activities focus on challenging stereotypes and creating peaceful responses to violence. Your students find the novel engaging, and class discussions are lively and respectful. But some parents are upset with the book's title, and the school board asks you not to teach such a controversial lesson. Committed to your beliefs, you persist. At the end of the school year, your teaching contract is not renewed.

______ Because you think your academic freedom has been violated, you decide to sue to get your job back.

______ You realize that the school board is well within its rights to determine curriculum, that you were warned, and that now you must pay the price for your indiscretion.

Legal Decision The right to **academic freedom** (that is, to teach without coercion, censorship, or other restrictive interference) is not absolute. The courts will balance your right to academic freedom with the school system's interests in students learning appropriate subject matter in an environment conducive to learning. Courts look at such factors as whether your learning activities and materials are inappropriate, irrelevant to the subjects to be covered under the syllabus, obscene, or substantially disruptive of school discipline. In this case, the lesson related to ethnic and religious differences appears to be appropriate, relevant, and neither obscene nor disruptive. If you were to sue on the grounds of academic freedom, you would probably get your job back.[8]

Academic freedom protects a teacher's right to teach about sensitive issues, such as immigration, as long as the topic is relevant to the course, is not treated in an obscene manner, and is not disruptive of school discipline.

©Jonathan Nourok/Getty Images

Issue	*Situation 5*
Legal liability (negligence)	You are assigned to cafeteria duty. Things are quiet, and you take the opportunity to make copies of an article for your next class. While you are gone from the cafeteria, a student slips on some spilled milk and breaks his arm. His parents hold you liable for their son's injury and sue you for damages.

_____ You will probably win, because you did not cause the fall and were on educational business when the accident occurred.

_____ The student's parents will win, because you left your assigned post.

_____ The student who spilled the milk is solely responsible for the accident.

_____ No one will win, because the courts long ago ruled that there is no use crying over spilled milk. (You knew that was coming, right?)

Legal Decision In recent years, litigation against teachers has increased dramatically. The public concern over the quality of education, the bureaucratic and impersonal nature of many school systems, and the generally litigious nature of our society all contribute to this rising tide of lawsuits. Negligence suits against teachers are common. In the cafeteria example, you would be in considerable jeopardy in a legal action. A teacher who is not present at his or her assigned duty might be charged with negligence unless the absence is "reasonable." The courts are very strict about what is "reasonable." (Leaving your post to put out a fire is reasonable, but going to make photocopies is unlikely to be viewed as reasonable.) It is a good practice to stay in your classroom or assigned area of responsibility unless there is an emergency.

"[O]ne of the most significant words in the field of law, **liability**, means legal responsibility for one's acts or omissions."[9] Failure of a person (like a teacher) or entity (like a school) to meet that responsibility leaves him/her/it open to being accused of negligence and sued for damages. Courts generally use two standards in determining negligence: (1) whether a reasonable person with similar training would act in the same way and (2) whether or not the teacher could have foreseen the possibility of an injury. Following are some common terms and typical situations related to teacher liability:

- **Misfeasance.** Failure to conduct in an appropriate manner an act that might otherwise have been lawfully performed; for example, unintentionally using too much force in breaking up a fight.
- **Nonfeasance.** Failure to perform an act that one has a duty to perform; for example, the cafeteria situation is nonfeasance, since the teacher did not supervise an assigned area of responsibility.
- **Malfeasance.** An act that cannot be done lawfully regardless of how it is performed; for example, starting a fistfight or bringing marijuana to school.

So what is your "take-away" from this case? Here are some reasonable precautions you can take to avoid liability:

- Establish safety rules for students.
- Try to anticipate and avoid dangerous situations.
- Warn students of any potential dangers.
- Provide proper supervision.
- If an accident does occur, document the specifics and how you helped the victim.

Many teachers believe that insurance to cover liability claims is essential. It is wise to check with your district's personnel office to determine the limits of professional liability protection. Teacher associations and organizations usually offer additional and voluntary liability policies for you. One common risk that teachers unwittingly take is to offer rides to their students for school events. Check your district's liability policy about autos before doing this. Remember, your personal insurance policy may not cover student injuries.[10]

Although liability usually involves physical injury to students because of what a teacher did or failed to do, a developing line of litigation, called **educational malpractice,** is concerned with "academic damage." Some students and parents have sued school districts for failing to provide an adequate education. Many courts have rejected these cases, pointing out that multiple factors affect learning and that failure to learn cannot be blamed solely on the school system.

Issue	*Situation 6*
Teachers' freedom of speech	As a teacher in a small school district, you are upset with the way the school board and the superintendent are spending school funds. You are particularly troubled about all the money being spent on high school athletics, because these expenditures have cut into your proposed salary raise. To protest the expenditures, you write a lengthy letter to the local newspaper criticizing the superintendent and the school board. After the letter is published, you find that the figures you cited in the letter were inaccurate. The following week, you are called into the superintendent's office and fired for breaking several school rules. You have failed to communicate your complaints to your superiors and you have caused harm to the school system by spreading false and malicious statements. In addition, the superintendent points out that your acceptance of a teaching position obligated you to refrain from publicizing critical statements about the school. The superintendent says although no one can stop you from making public statements, the school system certainly does not "have to pay you for the privilege." You decide to

_____ Go to court to win back your position.

_____ Chalk it up to experience, look for a new position, and make certain that you do not publish false statements and break school rules in the future.

Legal Decision This situation is based on a suit instigated by an Illinois teacher named Marvin Pickering. (***Pickering v. Board of Education***). After balancing the teacher's interests as a citizen in commenting on issues of public concern against the school's interests in efficiently providing public services, the Supreme Court ruled in favor of the teacher. It found that the disciplined operation of the school system was not seriously damaged by Pickering's letter and that the misstatements in the letter were not made knowingly or recklessly. Moreover, there was no special need for confidentiality on the issue of school budgets. Hence, concluded the Court, prohibiting Pickering from making his statements was an infringement of his First Amendment right to freedom of speech. You, too, would probably win in court if you were to issue public statements on matters of public concern, unless your statements were intentionally or recklessly inaccurate, disclosed confidential material, or hampered either school discipline or your performance of duties.[11]

A teacher's freedom of speech often involves gray areas and may not always come out in the teacher's favor. Consider these two cases. A federal judge ruled that a southern California public high school history teacher violated the First Amendment when he made disparaging statements during a classroom lecture about Christians and their beliefs and called creationism "religious, superstitious nonsense." The First Amendment prohibits teachers from displaying religious hostility.[12] Can a teacher wear a political button in the classroom? During the 2008 presidential campaign, many New York City public school teachers wore buttons to school in support of their candidate. Critics argued that the buttons created an environment of intimidation and hostility toward students who did not share their teacher's opinion. The teachers insisted that the students were able to distinguish between personal and institutional views. A federal judge ruled against the teachers.

Here is an example of disruptive speech not being protected. A Pennsylvania teacher created a blog for friends, where she complained about and disparaged her students. However, a student found and shared the blog on Facebook. The teacher was fired and subsequently she sued on First Amendment grounds. A federal appeals court dismissed her suit, ruling that "The speech at issue here was not protected because the disruption diminished any legitimate interest in its expression."[13]

Issue	*Situation 7*
Copying published material	You read a fascinating two-page article in *The New York Times Magazine*. Because the article concerns an issue your class is discussing, you duplicate the article and distribute it to your students. This is the only article you have distributed in class, and you do not bother to ask either the author or the magazine for permission to reprint it. You have

_____ Violated the copyright law, and you are liable to legal action.

_____ Not violated any copyright law.

Legal Decision A teacher's right to freely reproduce and distribute published works is limited by **copyright laws**. Copyright protects **intellectual property**: the printed, visual, digital, and analog work created by publications, writers, composers, lyricists, performers, artists, and so on. With so much content available on the Internet, many people presume that all of that content is free for them to use however, wherever, and whenever they want. Using a piece of intellectual property (like a magazine article) without permission and/or compensation is like taking and using your neighbor's bicycle without telling her. Taking intellectual property amounts to stealing the creator's income and erodes the incentive for professionals (like researchers, journalists, and authors) to keep producing reputable material. Another consequence is the flood of "fake news," rumors, unsubstantiated claims, and outright falsehoods inundating the Internet. Protection of intellectual property has been around for centuries; for example, Article I, Section 8 of the U.S. Constitution (1787) states that "Congress shall have the power . . . To promote the Progress of Science and useful Arts, by securing for limited Times to Authors and Inventors the exclusive Right to their respective Writings and Discoveries."[14] (The U.S. government does not copyright its publicly available content–so you are free to use it.) Teachers may use copyrighted materials in class under three conditions:

- Written permission is obtained from the creator, author, or publisher.
- Material is in the public domain (it is more than 75 years old or is published by the government).
- Reproduction of material is considered *fair use.*

Fair use is legal principle that allows the limited use of copyrighted materials without written permission or payment. Examples of fair use materials include commentary, criticism, parody, news reporting, library archiving, teaching, scholarship, or research. Teachers must observe three criteria in selecting the material: brevity, spontaneity, and cumulative effect.

1. *Brevity.* A work can be reproduced if it is not overly long. It is always wise to contact publishers directly, but typical limits might include the following criteria. Poems or excerpts from poems must be no longer than 250 words. Articles, stories, and essays of less than 2,500 words may be reproduced in complete form. Excerpts of any prose work may be reproduced only up to 1,000 words or 10 percent of the work, whichever is less. Only one illustration (photo, drawing, diagram) may be reproduced from the same book or journal. The brevity criterion limits the length of the material that a teacher can reproduce and distribute from a single work. If you were the teacher in this example and you reproduced only a two-page article, you probably would not have violated the criterion of brevity. If there is any doubt on whether the content can be used the teacher should remember the critical step of first checking with the publisher of the work.
2. *Spontaneity.* If a teacher has an inspiration to use a published work and there is simply not enough time to receive written permission, then the teacher may reproduce and distribute the work. The teacher in our vignette has met this criterion so is acting within the law. If the teacher wishes to distribute the same article during the next semester or the next year, written permission would be required because ample time exists to request such permission.
3. *Cumulative effect.* The total number of works reproduced without permission for class distribution must not exceed nine instances per class per semester. Within this limit, only one complete piece or two excerpts from the same author may be reproduced and only three pieces from the same book or magazine. Cumulative effect limits the number of articles, poems, excerpts, and so on that can be reproduced, even if the criteria of spontaneity and brevity are met. As far as we know, the teacher in our vignette has not reproduced other works and therefore has met this criterion also.

What are the three criteria for fair use of copyrighted materials in your classroom—and can you answer this without peeking at the text?

©Rainer Holz/Getty Images

Under the fair use principle, single copies of printed material may be copied for your personal use. Thus, if you want a single copy for planning a lesson, that is not a problem. Whenever multiple copies are made for classroom use, each copy must include a notice of copyright.

What about video recordings, computer software, mixed media, and the vast amount of material published online? These resources are also *intellectual property* and are copyrighted. Text, graphics, Web page code, online videos (including YouTube), multimedia materials, and even e-mail and Facebook postings are copyright protected. Therefore, teachers must follow fair use guidelines when using videos, photos, and information obtained from the Internet and gleaned from e-mail attachments. With so much information at our fingertips, both teachers and students need to assume that all work posted on the Internet is copyright protected, whether or not a specific notice is included. It is always advisable to check with your local school district officials to determine school policy and procedures.[15]

Issue

Labor rights

Situation 8

Salary negotiations have been going badly in your school district, and at a mass meeting teachers finally vote to strike. You honor the strike and stay home, refusing to teach until adequate salary and benefits are provided. During the first week of the strike, you receive a letter from the school board, stating that you will be suspended for fifteen days without pay at the end of the school year, owing to your participation in the strike. You decide

_____ To fight this illegal, unjust, and costly suspension.

_____ To accept the suspension as a legal action of the school board.

Legal Decision State courts vary in upholding teachers' right to strike. In some states, courts have determined that teachers provide a vital public service and therefore cannot strike. Although more than 30 states have laws that prohibit strikes, many communities choose not to prosecute striking teachers.[16] You need to understand your state laws and community norms to know if you are breaking the law by honoring the strike. The decision to strike is a difficult one. Under what circumstances, if any, would you choose to strike?

In a number of cases, courts have recognized the right of teachers to organize, to join professional organizations or unions such as the NEA (National Education Association) and the AFT (American Federation of Teachers), and to bargain collectively for improved working conditions. Yet, even though membership in teacher organizations and the right to collective bargaining have been upheld by the courts, some states and communities are adamantly opposed to such organizations and refuse to hire or to renew contracts of teachers who are active in them. Such bias is clearly illegal; nevertheless, it is still a factor.[17]

In summary, law and reality do not always coincide. Legally speaking, teachers may be prohibited from striking by state law but are rarely prosecuted or penalized.

In some places, active involvement in teacher organizations (albeit legal) may result in discriminatory school board actions. If you choose to join a union, strike, or participate in collective bargaining, do so with the realization that such activity may make you liable to legal sanctions or, at the very least, community hostility.[18]

II. Students' Rights and Responsibilities

FOCUS QUESTION 2

What legal rights do students enjoy (and do they have legal responsibilities)?

Issue	*Situation 9*
Student records	You are a high school teacher who has decided to stay after school and review your students' records. You believe that learning more about your students will make you a more effective teacher. As you finish reviewing some of the folders, Brenda, a 16-year-old student of yours, walks in and asks to see her folder. Because you have several sensitive comments recorded in the folder, you refuse. Within the hour, the student's parents call and ask if they can see the folder. At this point, you

_____ Explain that the information is confidential and sensitive and cannot be shared with nonprofessional personnel.

_____ Explain that the parents can see the folder and describe the procedure for doing so.

Legal Decision *The Family Educational Rights and Privacy Act,* commonly referred to as the **Buckley Amendment,** allows parents and guardians access to their children's educational records. The amendment also requires that school districts inform parents of this right and establish a procedure for providing educational records on request. Moreover, written parental permission is needed before these records can be shared with anyone other than professionals connected with the school the student attends, or another school in which the student seeks to enroll, health or safety officials, or individuals reviewing the student's financial aid applications. If the student has reached 18 years of age, he or she must be allowed to see the folder, and is responsible for granting permission for others to review the folder.

In *Owasso Independent School District v. Falvo*, the common teacher practice of asking students to exchange and grade others' papers tested the limits of the Buckley Amendment. The Supreme Court ruled that students can grade their peers' academic work (and even announce the results in class) without violating the privacy act. The Court determined that under the Buckley Amendment, grades do not become private and part of students' educational records until they are recorded in a teacher's grade book. In this situation, you should have chosen the second option, because parents do have the right to see this information.[19]

Issue	*Situation 10*
Suspension and discipline	You are teaching a difficult class, and one student is the primary source of trouble. After a string of disorderly episodes on this student's part, several iPads in the classroom mysteriously disappear. You have put up with more than enough, and you send the student to the principal's office to be suspended. The principal backs you up, and the student is told not to return to school for a week. This action is

_____ Legal and appropriate (and probably long overdue!).

_____ Illegal.

Legal Decision Although troublesome and disorderly students can be disciplined, suspension from school represents a serious penalty, one that should not be taken lightly. When considering suspension, the Supreme Court has ruled (***Goss v. Lopez***) that teachers and administrators are required to follow certain procedures to guarantee the student's **due process** rights granted by the **Fourteenth Amendment** to the Constitution. Students must be informed of the specific rule(s) they break, and see the evidence. Students are also entitled to tell their side of the story in self-defense. School officials can be held personally liable for damages if they violate a student's clearly established constitutional rights (*Wood v. Strickland*).

If you look back at this vignette, you realize that you do not know for sure which student is responsible for the missing iPads, nor does the "problem" student get the opportunity for self-defense. If you selected "illegal," you chose the correct response.

Every student has the right to learn in a school that is safe and equitable. Conflicts arise daily, and many schoools use a zero-tolerance approach to discipline. A **zero-tolerance policy** typically results in automatic detention, suspension, or expulsion for misbehavior, regardless of the circumstances or disciplinary history of the student involved. Zero-tolerance dates back to 1994, when Congress required states receiving federal education money to expel students for bringing guns onto school property. States and local governments broadened this mandate to expel children for other infractions, including possession of weapons, alcohol, drugs, and tobacco, as well as incidents of violence and stealing. Courts have generally ruled that students' constitutional right to due process is not violated by zero-tolerance policies. However, opponents point out that zero-tolerance policies are inherently unfair and can backfire. For example, one 6-year-old was expelled after his grandmother placed a "weapon" in his lunch sack—a plastic knife for spreading peanut butter.

The American Bar Association has denounced zero-tolerance policies that mandate expulsion or referral to juvenile court for minor offenses that do not compromise school safety. Studies show that suspensions and expulsions do nothing to improve the school climate, while at the same time increasing the risk that children will experience long-term social and academic problems. Children who are removed from school are at heightened risk for low achievement, being held back, dropping out, or becoming entangled in the courts, probation, and the "schools-to-prison" pipeline—a crisis for students of color because nearly 75 percent of students involved in school-related incidents involving police are Hispanic and African-American (see more in Chapter 3). Black students are three times more likely than their white peers to be suspended or expelled. In the 2011–2012 school year, 12 percent of *all* African American preK-12 girls were suspended—six times the rate for white girls and higher than rates for white, Asian, and Latino boys. Too often, students in the juvenile justice system are barred from their original school, and are permanently pushed out of school. Revealing another pattern of discrimination, gay, lesbian, and bisexual youth are more likely to be punished than their straight peers. Are minority students committing more infractions, or are they receiving tougher punishment for similar incidents?[20]

Such questions are sparking schools to re-think zero-tolerance policies. A promising alternative is *restorative-justice practices*. Restorative-justice programs aim to keep students in school and learning. They teach people how to resolve conflict and repair potential harm caused by their behavior. Restorative-justice practices include listening circles and teen courts where peers participate in conflict resolution. Schools engaging in such practices report declines in student suspensions, improved attendance, and higher test scores.[21]

While considering discipline, let us look at the legality of **corporal punishment.** In *Ingraham v. Wright* (1977), the Supreme Court said that physical punishment may be

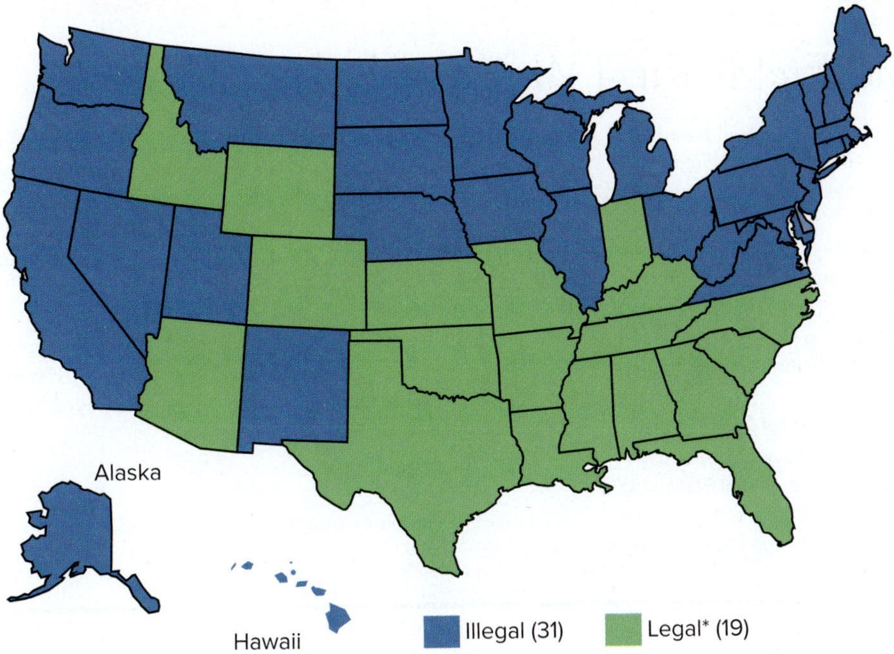

FIGURE 8.1

Corporal punishment.
*In states where corporal punishment is legal, not all school districts choose to implement the policy.

SOURCE: Gundersonhealth .org, Center for Effective Discipline, "Discipline at School," 2017.

REFLECTION: Knowing whether corporal punishment is legal in your state and in your school is only part of the issue; sorting out your philosophy on discipline is more to the point. As a teacher, would you use physical punishment against a student? Explain your reasoning.

authorized by the states. The Court ruled that corporal punishment should be "reasonable and not excessive," and such factors as the seriousness of the student offense, the age and physical condition of the student, and the force and attitude of the person administering the punishment should be considered. Although the courts allow corporal punishment, many states and school districts do not believe in it and have prohibited the physical punishment of students; other districts and states provide very specific guidelines for its practice. You should be familiar with the procedures and norms in your district before you even consider this disciplinary strategy.[22] (See Figure 8.1.)

Issue	*Situation 11*
Freedom of speech	During your homeroom period, you notice that several students are wearing "I ♥ Boobies" T-shirts. You call them to your desk and they explain that they are promoting breast cancer awareness. You tell them that you support their cause but that wearing overly sexualized T-shirts is specifically forbidden by school rules. You explain that you will let it go this time because they are not disturbing the class routine, but that if they wear them again, they will be suspended. Sure enough, the next day the same students arrive at school wearing the T-shirts, and you send them to the principal's office. The students tell the principal that although they understand the rule, they refuse to obey it. The principal suspends them. The principal's action is

_____ Legally justified, because the students were given every opportunity to understand and obey the school rule.

_____ Illegal, because the students have the right to express their opinions through dress.

CONTEMPORARY ISSUES

A View from the Field: First Amendment Rights

Max and Templeton were in real trouble. The school board had decided that they were to be expelled. But their school friends rallied behind them, evidence that Kate Lyman's lessons were taking root.

Kate Lyman is a Madison, Wisconsin, teacher and her students were second and third graders—and Max and Templeton were the pet rats kept in their classroom. The school board ruled that no animals could be kept in school, so Max and Templeton had to go. But the board had not counted on the commitment and tenacity of Kate's students.

Kate encouraged her students to speak out. She discussed persuasion and let students know they could send their objections to the school board. As Kate writes in the journal *Rethinking Schools*, "The students practiced a lot of writing skills in those few days. They edited their letters, typed them on the computer, and learned how to send them via e-mail to the school board members and superintendent." One student suggested sending the letters to a local newspaper; four were printed. Six of Kate's second- and third-grade students took their advocacy beyond letter writing and spoke at a school board meeting. "I was proud of them for speaking out in that daunting setting, in front of at least a hundred people, including school board members, the superintendent, and the school district lawyer." The school board decided to allow animals to return to the schools. Alas, it was too late for Max and Templeton. They had already been adopted by the local humane society.

To read more about Kate's work with her students, please visit http://rethinkingschools.org.

Legal Decision In December 1965, three students in Des Moines, Iowa, demonstrated their opposition to the Vietnam War by wearing black armbands to school. The principal informed them that they were breaking a school rule and asked that they remove the armbands. They refused and were suspended. The students' parents sued the school system, and the case finally reached the Supreme Court. In the landmark ***Tinker v. Des Moines Independent Community School District*** case, the Court ruled that students do not "shed their constitutional rights to freedom of speech or expression at the schoolhouse gate." Students were entitled to wear the armbands, as long as they did not substantially disrupt the operation of the school or deny other students the opportunity to learn. Because there was no disruption, the Court ruled that the school system could not prohibit students from wearing the armbands or engaging in other forms of free speech.[23]

Courts have upheld students' freedom of speech so long as the protests did not disrupt other students' right to learn and were not obscene or hateful.

©Nigel Sawtell/Alamy RF

The principal in the "I ♥ Boobies" T-shirt vignette acted illegally. Demonstrating the enduring power of *Tinker*, a Pennsylvania appeals court found that the T-shirts were neither lewd nor disruptive, but instead were starting useful conversations about breast cancer. The school could not prohibit students from wearing the controversial shirts.[24] (See Contemporary Issues: A View from the Field for another perspective on students' freedom of speech.)

Hate speech is another matter and reveals limits placed on students' freedom of speech. For example, a California high school prevented a student from wearing a T-shirt with the slogan "Homosexuals are shameful." The student argued that such a dress code policy violated his First Amendment right to free speech. But a federal court ruled that "demeaning of young gay and lesbian students in a school environment is detrimental not only to their psychological health and well-being, but also to their educational development" and that students should feel safe from attacks based on sexual orientation, race, religion, and gender while at school.[25]

Student freedom of expression does not extend to vulgar and indecent speech, according to the Supreme Court. In *Bethel School District v. Fraser,* justices evaluated the First Amendment rights of a high school senior, Matthew Fraser, who presented a speech at a school assembly that contained numerous sexual innuendos, but no explicit, profane language. Fraser was suspended for his speech and told that he could not speak at his class's graduation. His father then sued the school district. The Court upheld the suspension on the grounds that the language in the speech was indecent and offensive and that minors should not be exposed to such language.[26]

Does freedom of speech apply in cyberspace? Maybe.

Although the courts have not definitively resolved the issue, several "cyber-Tinker" decisions support First Amendment rights. A Missouri high school suspended Brandon Buessink for creating a Web site that criticized his school administration. However, the site caused no documented disturbance at the school—and Brandon built it outside school on his home computer. A federal district court reversed the suspension, ruling that the principal's simple dislike of the content was "unreasonable justification for limiting it."[27]

Yet, tech-savvy students are increasingly paying a price, including criminal arrest, for parodying their teachers on the Internet. A National School Boards Association study found that more than one in four teachers have been targeted by students via online pranks. Tired of digital ridicule, some teachers and schools are fighting back with lawsuits, long-term suspensions, and/or permanent expulsions.[28]

Issue	*Situation 12*
School prayer	A student in your class objects to the daily prayer recitation. You are sensitive to the student's feelings, and you make certain that the prayer is nondenominational. You also tell the student that he may stand or sit silently without reciting the prayer. As a teacher, you have

______ Broken the law.

______ Demonstrated sensitivity to individual needs and not violated the law.

Legal Decision You were sensitive, but you violated the law. Teachers are not allowed to lead a class in prayer. The Supreme Court has ruled that educators must be completely neutral with regard to religion. You may neither encourage nor discourage prayer (***Engel v. Vitale***). Public schools can, however, offer courses on comparative religion, and teachers may read from the *Bible,* the *Quran,* or any religious text as an example of literature, as long as no religious doctrine is promoted or defamed.

Although the First Amendment prevents educators from promoting or denigrating religious activities, it provides more freedom for students. For example, students may engage in private prayer and religious discussion during school as well as form religious clubs on school property—but only if other, *nonreligious* clubs can also use school space. School personnel may not offer "official" prayers during graduation ceremonies (despite the law, school officials often do lead prayers at graduation and other events). Meanwhile, state laws vary on whether a *student* graduation speech can include prayer. However, the Supreme Court has declared that student-led public prayers at athletic events constitute school sponsorship of religion, which violates the establishment clause of the First Amendment. School prayer is a deeply emotional, heated, and controversial issue, with critics claiming that courts have driven God out of school—damaging students and causing many of today's educational problems.

PROFILE IN EDUCATION

Morris Dees

Suing to desegregate the Montgomery, Alabama YMCA and winning multi-million dollar civil judgments against white supremacist groups, attorney Morris Dees fights inequality in court. In 1971, he cofounded the Southern Poverty Law Center (SPLC), which worked with teachers across the country to create Teaching Tolerance (Tolerance.org), which provides materials to K-12 teachers, students, and parents that promote multiculturalism, social activism, and greater interaction between social groups.

Read a full profile of Morris Dees on Connect.

©Acey Harper/The LIFE Images Collection/Getty Images

connect

GLOBAL VIEW

The nonprofit WE gives young people a powerful and legitimate voice in the creation of their own future. Children study and redesign education, family environments, business, and politics. www.we.org

A CLOSER LOOK

Religion and Public Schools

The First Amendment guarantees freedom of religion in our nation. It also requires *a separation of church and state* so that one religion is not preferred over any other in government institutions. What does this mean for public schools? The following United States Supreme Court decisions offer some guidance.

Yes . . .	Yes . . .	No . . .	No . . .
Parents can enroll their children in a private, religious school instead of a public school. *Pierce v. Society of Sisters* (1925)	Schools must provide equal access to public facilities to all groups, including religious organizations. *Board of Education v. Mergens* (1990)	Teachers cannot require students to recite prayers in class. *Engel v. Vitale* (1962)	Schools cannot require a moment of silence for silent prayer. *Wallace v. Jaffree* (1985)
Students can refuse to salute the American flag. *West Virginia State Board of Education v. Barnette* (1943)	Students may not say public prayers at school athletic events. *Santa Fe Independent School District v. Jane Doe* (2000)	Schools cannot ban religious clothing and symbols. *Tinker v. Des Moines School District* (1969)	Teachers cannot teach creation science instead of evolution. *Edwards v. Aguillard* (1987)
Students may be excused from public school to attend religious classes away from school property. *Zorach v. Clauson* (1952)	Parents can use public money (vouchers) to send their children to private religious schools. *Zelman v. Simmons-Harris* (2002)	Schools cannot post a copy of the Ten Commandments. *Stone v. Graham* (1980)	Teachers and school leaders cannot lead prayer at public school graduation ceremonies. *Lee v. Weisman* (1992)

REFLECTION: What place, if any, do you believe religion has in school?

The Pledge of Allegiance also sparks heated controversy in public schools. Many state and local school districts champion the need for patriotism, and require students to recite the pledge. However, it is illegal to compel a student to salute the flag. A 1943 Supreme Court decision, *West Virginia State Board of Education v. Barnette* (319 U.S. 624), ruled that compelling someone to say the pledge violates their First and Fourteenth Amendment rights. This was at the height of World War II, a time of enormous pressure to demonstrate patriotism. But the Court still found for Marie and Gathie Barnette, grade school students who were Jehovah's Witnesses, a religion that prohibits saluting or pledging to symbols, like flags. (In 1930s Germany, Jehovah's Witnesses who refused to salute the Nazi flag were sent to concentration camps.) State statutes and school district policies have striven to reinstate the Pledge since *Barnette*, but federal appeals courts have disagreed about their constitutionality—and the Supreme Court hasn't settled (or resettled) the dispute.

Finally, the courts say that schools can observe a moment of silence as long as its purpose is secular and does not encourage prayer over any other quiet, contemplative activity. However, students can choose to silently pray during this time.[29] (See A Closer Look: Religion and Public Schools for a detailed review of religion in schools.)

Issue	*Situation 13*
Search and seizure	The drug problem in your school is spreading, and it is clear that strong action is needed. School authorities order a search of all student lockers, which lasts for several hours. Trained police dogs are brought in, and each classroom is searched for drugs. The school principal randomly chooses several students, who are taken to the locker rooms and strip-searched.

_____ School authorities are well within their rights to conduct these searches.

_____ Searching the lockers is legal, but strip-searching is inappropriate and illegal.

_____ No searches are called for, and all these activities present illegal and unconstitutional violation of student rights.

Legal Decision Courts have ruled that school authorities have fewer restrictions than do the police in search-and-seizure activities. Moreover, the school has a parent-like responsibility (known as ***in loco parentis***) to protect children and to respond to reasonable concerns about their health and safety. Courts have indicated that schools are responsible for school property, including things like lockers and cars parked in the school lot. School officials may search a student's locker if there is *reasonable suspicion* that it contains something illegal or dangerous. At the same time, courts have determined that randomly conducting strip searches or spot-checking lockers for drugs, weapons, or other illicit materials violates students' rights under the Fourth Amendment. (The **Fourth Amendment** protects basic individual privacy and ensures due process.)

In this situation, the locker search is legal because the lockers were not randomly searched and the increased drug problem at the school gave the school principal reasonable suspicion. However, the strip search is illegal, because students were *randomly* selected with no grounds for suspicion.

The second choice is the correct response. Although school personnel have great latitude in conducting school search and seizures, educators should be familiar with proper legal procedures and think carefully about the related ethical issues.[30]

Issue	*Situation 14*
Freedom of the press	*The Argus* is the official student newspaper, written by students as part of a journalism course, but it has run afoul of school administrators. First, it ran a story critical of the school administration. In the next edition, the paper included a supplement on contraception and abortion. With their patience worn thin, school administrators closed the publication for the remainder of the school year.

_____ Closing the student newspaper is a legal action.

_____ Closing the student newspaper is an illegal action.

Legal Decision The Supreme Court ruled in ***Hazelwood School District v. Kuhlmeir*** that student newspapers written as part of a school journalism course should be viewed as part of the official school curriculum. School administrators, according to the Court, can readily censor such a paper. In situation 14, because the publication is part of a journalism course, closing the school newspaper would be legal.

On the other hand, if the newspaper is financed by the students and not associated with an official school course, the students would enjoy a greater degree of freedom. Additional grounds for censoring a school newspaper include obscenity, psychological harm, and disruption of school activities.[31]

Issue	***Situation 15***
Immigration problems	Your U.S. History classmate Julia seems distracted, and has been for the last several weeks. You ask if anything is wrong, and she says, "No, I'm fine." But during your lesson on Ellis Island and nineteenth century immigration, she starts crying, grabs her backpack, and leaves the room. You find Julia after school, and ask her again what's wrong. She finally tells you that her father returned to El Salvador for his mother's funeral last month, and now he can't get back into the United States. "I'm afraid I'll never see him again—and I'm sick of other kids calling me names," Julia says. "Plus, my mother has no papers, and neither do I; we could get deported, and no one here would ever know what happened to us!" You promise to help, and go to your principal, who:

_____ Tells Julia she must leave school for good, because her family doesn't pay taxes or belong in the country; plus, her illegal status puts the school at risk.

_____ Calls U.S. Immigration and Customs Enforcement (ICE) to report Julia and her family for breaking the law.

_____ Explains that she is developing a "sanctuary school" program to protect students like Julia from ICE and from harassment by other students.

Legal Decision In 1982, the U.S. Supreme Court ruled that, regardless of citizenship or immigration status, all children are entitled to a free public K-12 education. The ***Plyler v. Doe*** decision found that Texas violated the Fourteenth Amendment by allowing school districts to refuse enrollment or charge tuition to undocumented immigrant children. Therefore, the first choice in this situation is illegal. In fact, despite major controversies over immigration bans, as of this writing, school personnel have no legal obligation to enforce U.S. immigration laws. Schools can't require students or parents to disclose their immigration status, or ask questions that might expose it. Schools can't discriminate against undocumented students, deny them admission, or "chill" their right of access to school.

However, immigration status remains a volatile issue in schools, as it is for the rest of society—often influenced by beliefs unsupported by facts. Here are some facts: Today's immigrants are dramatically more law-abiding than native-born people, more likely to be employed, more fluent in English than past immigrants, and a smaller part of the U.S. population (13 percent) than most people think (and, of those, only 15 percent are undocumented). Unfounded beliefs have serious consequences; for instance, 2014 polling showed that more than half of Americans oppose public education for undocumented students. Shifts in public political agendas and mood can change the environment severely and suddenly; for instance, option two could become a requirement and option three could become illegal. Or vice versa. The effects of immigration policy will ripple (or flood) through your classroom in the years ahead. That means you must stay abreast of your legal obligations *and* serve the needs of students without documentation. Many are fleeing traumatic poverty and/ or violence. They may be staying with unknown relatives, separated from parents and siblings who are still "back home." Immigration courts or agents can deport them or relatives with little or no warning (children have been arrested on the way to school at bus stops, homes, and neighborhoods). Still, even if they've had little formal school before now, most of these children are eager to learn. Recognize that students' English language skills don't necessarily reflect their aptitude, knowledge, or intelligence. (It's likely that they speak more languages than you do!) Finally, remember that acculturation is a lifelong process, not a single event.[32]

Issue	***Situation 16***
Sexual harassment	Christina, an eleventh-grader, confided in her guidance counselor: "I didn't do too well on a pop quiz in Mr. Armando's algebra class. Mr. Armando suggested I repeat the quiz after school in his office. I thanked him for the second chance, especially since I want to make highest honors this year. But before I began the quiz, he touched my knee and whispered that I'd have to be nice to him if I really wanted to bring up my grade. I felt really uncomfortable." Sexual harassment?

______ This is a clear example of an unwanted sexual request, and therefore, sexual harassment.

______ While the teacher's behavior is suggestive, sexual harassment cannot be proven based on a student's uncomfortable feelings. Without witnesses or evidence, this is a classic "he said–she said" scenario.

Legal Decision Educators wrestle every day with the challenge of helping students be and feel safe in schools. Teachers also have a legal and an ethical responsibility to prevent and respond to bullying, discrimination, and harassment. So, what is **sexual harassment?** Does it happen when a male student or teacher accidentally bumps into a girl in the hallway? Does it mean teachers can't give students an encouraging hug? That students holding hands is wrong? Not at all, but these are common misconceptions. Sexual harassment is *unwelcome* behavior of a sexual nature, whether it occurs in person or virtually. (Chapter 4 discusses cyberbullying, which frequently includes sexual harassment.) It also includes *unwanted* sexual comments, sexual gestures, and physical touch. It reflects and reinforces societal attitudes about gender and sexuality that normalize sexual assault and contribute to what many call our "rape culture," where sexual assault is a pervasive and harrowing part of everyday life—even in school.[33]

Contrary to popular belief, both females and males are victims of sexual harassment and assault. The consequences are troubling, and sometime devastating. They interfere with students' and teachers' abilities to learn, study, work, achieve, or participate in school activities. Students fear attending school, withdraw from friends and activities, have trouble sleeping, develop eating disorders and other mental illnesses, are more likely to harm themselves, and more likely to attempt suicide. Nearly half of U.S. students report being harassed at school or online. Nevertheless, the problem usually remains hidden. Fewer than half of harassed students tell anyone about it. Only one in four talks with a family member, and *only 9 percent* report the harassment to an adult at school.[34]

These facts mean that teachers and administrators must challenge one another to actively create safe, inclusive, and welcome environments for work and learning. We must be respectful, humble, and open to learning new ways to understand difference, inclusion, and how they affect our work. When administrators, districts, and communities turn their backs on these recognized best practices, their shortsighted approach harms students and increases school liability. Nevertheless, some schools still ban same-sex prom dates, and/or require sex-specific clothing for yearbook photographs—actions that defy court rulings that "have consistently found these restrictions violate a student's First Amendment right to freedom of expression."[35] Meanwhile, eight states have statutes requiring teachers to portray LGBTQA people in a negative or inaccurate way. For instance, Alabama teachers must "emphasize . . . that homosexuality is not a lifestyle acceptable to the general public and that homosexual conduct is a criminal offense under the laws of the state"—even though the Supreme Court (in 2003) ruled that same-sex sexual activity is legal and protected by the Constitution.[36] For everyone's sake, we hope that legislation, court rulings, and emerging professional standards will move us closer to "normalizing" safe, fair, and inclusive education.

Title IX of federal education legislation prohibits sex discrimination in schools, and that includes sexual harassment. The courts recognize two broad categories of sexual harassment: *quid pro quo* and *hostile environment*. (These principles also apply to Situation 2 on p. 214.) *Quid pro quo*, a Latin phrase meaning "this for that," describes trading favors. It happens in sexual harassment when someone like Mr. Armando abuses his authority by trying to get a student to "trade" sexual acts in exchange for something the student wants or needs—like a higher grade, job or college recommendations, avoiding the consequences of misbehavior, and so on. *Hostile environment* describes unwelcome sexual behavior so severe and/or widespread that the entire community abuses a person and violates his or her rights. This includes hostile, harassing, abusive spoken or written comments or physical conduct.[37] Here's an example of a hostile environment:

> Albert is slender and not athletically inclined. In the locker room before gym class, his male peers tease him about his weight and clumsiness. They call him "fag," "sissy," and "girl," and snap their wet towels on his butt. Several times when Albert opened his locker, he found a bra and girls' panties with his name written on them. Albert now tries to skip gym class.

In ***Franklin v. Gwinnett County Public Schools,*** the Supreme Court extended the reach of Title IX, allowing students to sue a school district for monetary damages in cases of sexual harassment. The 1992 ruling involved a Georgia high school student who was sexually harassed and abused by a teacher. The school district was instructed to pay monetary damages to the student—establishing a precedent.[38]

RAP 3.7
Students' Bill of Rights and Responsibilities

However, more recent Court decisions make collecting personal damages from school districts more difficult, although an *individual* accused of sexual harassment can still be sued for personal damages. In *Gebser v. Lago Independent School District* (1998) and *Davis v. Monroe County Board of Education* (1999), the Supreme Court ruled that a school district must show "deliberate indifference" to complaints about teacher and peer sexual harassment before a district would be forced to pay damages. That means that complaining to a teacher or even a principal is now not enough; the complaint has to go higher.[39]

Sexual harassment complaints against teachers have been increasing. While most teachers or school staff members don't sexually harrass or abuse children, some do. The results are tragic. Teachers need to realize that sexual harassment laws prohibit not only overt actions but also offensive words and inappropriate touching. While a teacher's intention might be pure and caring, a student's perception can be quite different. Schools are places where children come to learn. They expect those places to be safe and nurturing. Sexual harassment shatters that trust.

Scoring What is your RQ (rights quotient)?

13 to 16 correct:	Legal eagle
11 or 12 correct:	Lawyer-in-training
9 or 10 correct:	Paralegal
7 or 8 correct:	Law student
6 or fewer correct:	Could benefit from an LSAT prep course

This brief review of some legal realities that surround today's classroom is not meant to be definitive. These situations are intended to highlight the rapid growth and changing nature of school law and the importance of this law to teachers. It will be your responsibility to become informed about, and stay current on, legal decisions that influence your actions inside and outside your classroom. Ignorance of the law is no defense. More positively, knowledge of fundamental legal principles allows you to develop a "proactive practice" that helps you to avoid or resolve potential legal conflicts and attend to your major responsibility: teaching.

Teaching and Ethics

FOCUS QUESTION 3

What are the ethical responsibilities of teachers and students?

How important are ethical issues in (and for) U.S. schools? Beyond simply following the law, students need to understand right from wrong. Cheating, for example, is not only against the rules, most consider it morally wrong. Social networking creates an ever-growing hyper-connective world that creates new ethical challenges for schools. Child abuse is yet another moral issue most teachers confront.

Cheating: The Dishonor Role

How do students grade themselves when it comes to ethics? An overwhelming majority say: "It's not worth it to lie or cheat, because it hurts your character." The problem is, most teens admit they cheat. (See Figure 8.2.) Why this troubling disconnect? Students blame pressure to perform, the competitive college-admissions process, and apathy toward schoolwork. Adult role models demonstrate similar hypocrisies. For instance, individual teachers and entire school districts have been caught falsifying standardized test scores (see Chapter 10). From politicians and preachers to athletes and celebrities, students can see many examples of a less-than-honest culture. People always seem to find good reasons to do not-so-good things That does not excuse cheating; it means looking within and beyond schools to remedy the problem.[40] Cheating in school has become easier; cell phones and smart watches, along with other sophisticated (and tiny) gadgets, are today's cheat sheets, and the World Wide Web is a powerful temptation at home. The Internet has made it easy for students to cut and paste their way to a term paper, downloading a few sentences or even entire essays before weaving them into their papers—without crediting the original sources. This is blatant plagiarism, grounds for suspension for many schools. Yet many students admit to completing assignments with this "cut-and-paste" method. Some do not even go to that much trouble; they purchase ready-made term papers from online sellers.[41]

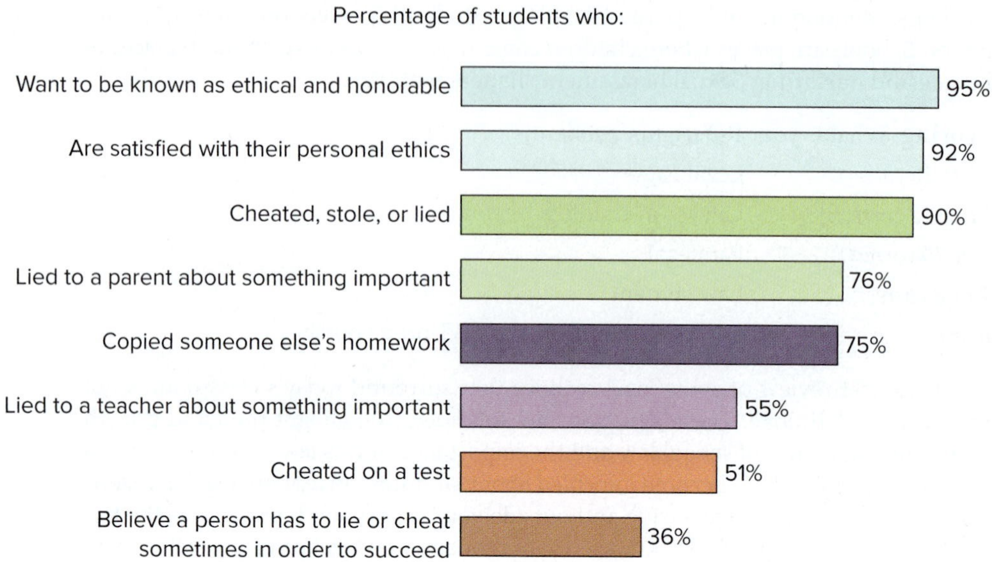

FIGURE 8.2

The dishonor role.

SOURCE: Josephson Institute for Youth Ethics: *The Ethics of American Youth* (2012).

REFLECTION: This is from a study of 20,000 public and private high school students. Has unethical behavior become an acceptable norm? Why or why not? As a teacher, how will you address ethics?

Fortunately, several online resources offer plagiarism detection. Many (like Grammerly) offer limited free service. Companies designed specifically for teachers (like Turnitin) charge fees, but also provide feedback to help students to revise papers–along with tools for teachers to check plagiarism and otherwise evaluate students' work. Some teachers simply Google a suspicious sentence to identify plagiarized material.

Perhaps most important, teachers can be proactive and work with students to promote honesty over deceit–and improve their learning skills. For instance, plagiarism may be a signal that students lack certain academic skills, such as using citations properly, synthesizing and then summarizing information, and developing their own insights. When you help students develop those skills, their learning improves now and for the future (with the side benefit of decreasing the motivation to plagiarize). Finally, when teachers and students explore values like integrity and honesty while observing a consistent no-cheating policy, students learn lifelong lessons. (See the conclusion of this chapter for more on moral education.)[42]

Social Networking Comes to School

FOCUS QUESTION 4

How might teachers thoughtfully and safely manage social media in and outside the classroom?

The digital world brings many other tricky ethical challenges. It starts with the troubling connections between children's technology use and developmental, behavioral, and health problems in and beyond the classroom. Screen time for children under age 3 is linked to delayed language acquisition.[43]

Toddler screen time is associated with problems in later childhood, including lower math and school achievement, reduced physical activity, and victimization by classmates.[44]

TEACHING TIP

Social Networking Guidelines

Teachers are held to a high standard of professional conduct. Anything you share online could be seen by your students, their parents, or school administrators. Before you post any information or images, consider whether it could cause you embarrassment or potentially damage your reputation or career. Here are some tips to consider when using social media and/or posting online.

- Do not accept students as social networking friends.
- Create *separate* professional and personal sites.
- Do not discuss students, parents, or co-workers, or publicly criticize school policies or personnel.
- Do not post images that include students without parental permission.
- Check personal sites regularly if the public has access to them. Even if you don't post inappropriate material, that doesn't mean your "friends" won't.
- If you plan to use texting, the Internet, or other technology to communicate with students and/or their parents/guardians, establish clear rules, and then follow and enforce those rules. Communicate *only* about classroom and school matters.
- If you plan to use texting, the Internet, or other technology to communicate with students, inform *all* the parents/guardians, and allow the adults to "opt-out" for themselves or their students.
- Limit personal information made available to students.

REFLECTION: Do you think these guidelines are fair? Why or why not? What additional social networking suggestions would you offer to teachers, or to anyone?

Children with two or more hours of daily screen time are more likely to have increased psychological difficulties, including hyperactivity, emotional and conduct problems, and difficulties with peers.[45] Screen time is linked to sleep disturbance in 6- to 12-year-olds.[46] Researchers also find that total media consumption predicts "ill-being" for children *and* preteens. Video gaming and electronic communication predict ill-being for preteens. For teenagers, nearly every type of technological activity predicted poor health.[47]

Nearly all U.S. teens (ages 13–17) report going online daily, and 24 percent say they are online "constantly." In addition, 71 percent say they are on two or more social network platforms. Girls dominate social media, while boys are more likely to play video games. Nearly two-thirds of "multitasking" teens say doing homework while watching TV, using social media, or texting does not affect the quality of their work. Of the 88 percent of teens with access to a cell phone, 90 percent text—receiving an average of 30 texts each day. Teens average nearly nine hours a day—outside of school—using media. Tweens (ages 8–12) average about six hours.[48]

In the face of such rocketing popularity, do students (and adults) have the skills and ethics to responsibly participate in social media? Do students understand their privacy rights and personal information they should share online? How will they decide what to share? What are the potential consequences of their social media choices? Brainstorming questions like these will help you, as a teacher, provide lessons in *digital citizenship.*

Some teachers use social media tools to improve class discussions, build rapport, answer questions about class assignments, and keep students informed about school activities. Teachers report that by connecting with students through social networking, they often discover interests or hobbies that help them engage kids in the classroom, positively affecting academic performance. Posting class schedules and assignments online can keep students and their parents up-to-date on school happenings.

Digital social networking is an integral part of students' lives. What might be the impact on learning? Brain development? Social skills?

©Frederick Bass/Getty Images RF

But potential pitfalls loom, which is why some schools prohibit any cyber-communications between teachers and students. Because most e-communication lacks essential communication clues (like body language and tone of voice), even well-intentioned interactions can be misinterpreted. Boundaries can quickly blur when teachers "friend" their students; some may find it "creepy" or want to keep a firm distinction between school and private life. Others may worry about looking like a "teacher's pet." And a small but increasing number of teacher–student cyber-interactions have led to sexual encounters and other criminal activity.[49] It's a challenge to find what role, if any, social networking, texting, and other cyber-communications play in schools and your classroom. (See the Teaching Tip: Social Networking Guidelines for specific suggestions on how to safely and ethically navigate the online world with your students.)

Protecting Your Students

Your new student, Sam, seems very awkward in school, and he is often late. Each time you ask him why he can't get to class on time, he mumbles, "I dunno." What's more, his behavior is strange. He seems to have an aversion to chairs, and, whenever possible, he stands in the back of the room alone. You have never seen Sam laugh or even smile. He wears a long-sleeve shirt every day, even when it's hot. What is that all about? Then, one day, Sam arrives in class with some bruises on his face, and you begin to suspect that there is more to his story. You ask Sam, who shrugs it off and says that he fell and bumped his face. But you are not so sure. You think: Could Sam be an abused child?

In this case, you confront a legal and ethical challenge. Most states require that teachers report suspected cases of abuse, and failure to report such cases can result in the loss of a teacher's license. Most of these laws also protect teachers from any legal liability for reporting such cases.[50] But if you're not sure, then what do you do? Should you speak to Sam's parents or press Sam for more information? Should you check with other teachers to see how they would handle the problem or go to the administration and let them handle it? Wait a second. What if you are wrong? Maybe Sam really did fall down and he's just incredibly shy. Are you responsible for Sam's family situation, which is, after all, a private concern? You should not go around accusing people without solid evidence. Maybe the prudent course of action is to monitor the situation for now and keep your suspicions to yourself. What would you do?

You can't ignore your ethical responsibility. The potential for harm to Sam is simply too great to remain silent. An ethical course to follow is to share your concerns with an appropriate person—perhaps a psychologist, counselor, or administrator at school, or Child Protective Services, which can accept a confidential report. Sharing your concern doesn't mean you're accusing anyone of child abuse. By bringing the situation to the school's attention, you start the wheels in motion to uncover facts. **Child abuse** and neglect include a range of mistreatments, including physical, emotional, and sexual harm. (See A Closer Look: Child Abuse on p. 237.) Child abuse occurs at every socioeconomic and educational level, and across religious, ethnic, and cultural lines. More than six million children are reported abused each year—but many cases remain unreported, because of shame or the threat of more abuse. Only 17 percent of child abuse reports come from educators. Nevertheless, as a teacher, you are a "mandatory reporter" and your ethical responsibility to report suspicion of child abuse is reinforced by the law.[51]

As a teacher, you will be called to follow your ethical compass to protect the physical and emotional well-being of your students and to guide students' own ethical

A CLOSER LOOK

Child Abuse

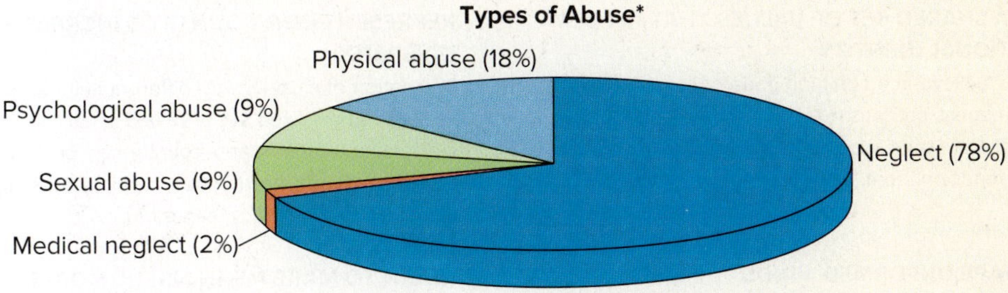

*A child may suffer multiple types of abuse, so numbers add to more than 100 percent

Children who suffer abuse and neglect may

- Exhibit signs of injury, e.g., burns, black eyes, welts, or bite marks
- Wear long sleeves even in very warm weather
- Not show emotion, e.g., joy, pain, or anger
- Be apathetic toward school and friends
- Be frequently absent or tardy
- Be unusually eager to please
- Demonstrate hostility or distress
- Be dirty or unbathed
- Show signs of alcohol and/or drug abuse
- Show symptoms of an eating disorder
- Exhibit signs of extreme hunger
- Exhibit unusually sophisticated knowledge of sexual behavior
- Create stories or drawings of an unusually sexual nature
- Have difficulty sitting or walking
- Show signs of depression
- Lack concentration
- Fear adults

SOURCE: Childhelp USA (2014), www.childhelpusa.org.

REFLECTION: If one of your students showed warning signs of abuse, whom in your school would you approach first? How would you phrase your concern?

development. Here is an idea to help you along this ethical path. Do an Internet search of "Teacher Code of Ethics." Both the National Education Association (NEA) and the American Federation of Teachers (AFT) have teacher codes of ethics. Read them to get an idea about what they believe is important. Also, it might be interesting to read the ethical codes of other careers to see how they are similar and different. Ethics are too little talked about in our culture, but also at the heart of leading an honorable personal and professional life.

FOCUS QUESTION 5

What classroom strategies promote moral education?

Moral Education: Ethics & Values in the Classroom

During the American colonial experience, schools transmitted a common set of values. Back then (and in many places today), the teacher inculcated ideas of diligence, hard work, punctuality, neatness, honesty, conformity, and respect for civil and religious authority. It was thought that instilling these values in children would produce virtuous adults. This approach continued in college: The most important course was moral philosophy, which was a requirement for all students and often taught by the college president. But not everyone agrees that preaching moral values is the only or best way to produce moral citizens. Today, schools choose from different approaches to moral education and ethics.

YOU BE THE JUDGE

Moral Values are Best Developed by

CARING AND WISE ADULTS WHO . . .

INSTILL A SHARED SET OF VALUES THAT AFFIRM OUR NATIONAL IDENTITY

Americans believe in a common code of values to teach our children: respect, patriotism, trustworthiness, and responsibility. Our national fabric is built on such values, and our nation's future depends on them.

HELP SHAPE UNFORMED MINDS

Throughout history, educators have recognized that children have "impressionable" minds. Teaching common values develops an ethical compass. Without moral direction at a young age, as Theodore Roosevelt once noted, youth can quickly become "a menace to society."

COUNTER MEDIA CORRUPTION

Ubiquitous media on hundreds of platforms bombard children with commercialism, violence, and sex. Schools must be proactive in helping families instill traditional moral values, such as hard work and citizenship, in an effort to counter the disturbing and negative influences of the media.

ENGAGED AND INDEPENDENT STUDENTS WHO . . .

REPRESENT OUR COUNTRY'S INCREASING DIVERSITY

In a nation of citizens with different cultural backgrounds, instilling a single fixed set of values is unrealistic and undemocratic. Our students and country can celebrate and benefit from values nurtured in different cultures, creating a safe, caring, and fair democracy marked by tolerance and acceptance.

LEARN TO MAKE MEANINGFUL MORAL CHOICES

Instead of telling students what values to follow, teachers must help them become reflective and critical thinkers. When students learn to develop their moral sense, they are more likely to be responsible for their values and act upon them in meaningful ways.

CHALLENGE SOCIAL INJUSTICE

Instilling traditional American values may overlook chronic problems like poverty, violence, racism, and sexism. When students investigate the world, they uncover these injustices, become active in eliminating them, and help to create a more just and vibrant democracy.

connect YOU DECIDE...

What role should moral education play in public schools? Examine textbooks and curriculum used in a local school to determine the major values being taught to students. Are students expected to accept the values or to critically examine them? Which strategy do you support?

Most states use federal grants or state statutes to provide **character education** programs, which aim to teach core attributes of a moral individual directly to children in school. Ideally, school curriculum, culture, conduct codes, and community service promote values including trustworthiness, respect, responsibility, fairness, caring, and good citizenship. For instance, a teacher may ask younger students to find examples of these qualities in literature and history, while older students use ethical reasoning exercises to consider these values. Along with developing core moral qualities, character education programs can challenge students to act on these values. For example, students may debate how best to implement a school's honor code, organize a food drive, or plan a ceremony honoring local military veterans. Some character education programs include training in conflict resolution and problem-solving skills.[52]

While supporters say this approach teaches children universal and essential ideas about how people should treat each other, not everyone is enamored with character education. Opponents say this approach is superficial, and artificially forces diverse student populations into a simplistic and narrow set of unexamined values. Furthermore, critics argue, teaching a list of values does not really alter behaviors or promote ethical thinking–instead, it rewards students for parroting adult-determined values. Who selects the values and how they are taught are at the heart of these concerns.[53]

So how can teachers help students develop and ultimately act upon their values? Perhaps we should have students explore questions such as: What qualities do you value in a friend? When is lying acceptable? How do you feel about competition? How would you include a person of a different race in your neighborhood community? Would you donate your body to science when you die? Why or why not? These sort of **values clarification** exercises challenge students to analyze and evaluate their personal values in a public light, and plan how to put them into action. In the process, students also respond to each other's beliefs, consider different points of view, and rethink their own values. Many educators (and others) believe that this approach provides the thoughtful nurturing that morality needs in order to develop fully. Of course, this approach has critics, too. They argue that treating all values equally undermines our moral responsibility to promote good, constructive values and condemn harmful, evil ones. What if students decide that bigotry or cheating is ethical? A "value neutral" stance is not designed to contradict that view, or any other.

So far, we've discussed teaching morals and ethics without asking the question: What are they, exactly? From Plato in 300 BCE to Sissela Bok in our own century, philosophers have wrestled with the answer(s) to this essential question. In the context of education, we'll focus on two psychologists. First, **Lawrence Kohlberg** (1927–1987), who developed the **moral stages of development** concept, based on the work of psychologist Jean Piaget (1896–1980), who identified stages of *intellectual* development (see "The Hall of Fame" on Connect). According to Kohlberg, the earliest stages of moral development involve children learning "right" and "wrong" by avoiding punishment and striving for rewards. Most adults function at a middle (what he calls the "conventional") stage where they obey society's laws, even ones that they believe are unjust. At the highest level, individuals act on principles (such as pacifism) which may violate conventional laws and norms. Kohlberg developed a curriculum that facilitates growth toward higher stages of morality by having students analyze moral dilemmas presented in brief scenarios. For example, a man breaks into a store and steals something. Is such stealing always wrong, or can it be justified? What if the man was a father stealing unaffordable medicine needed to save his child's life? Would that justify the theft? In theory, these intellectual explorations of moral principles help people live more ethically.

Kohlberg's model draws critics who argue that it erodes traditional values, can advocate violating the law, ignores how behavior is a better measure of one's morality than intellect, and disregards moral frameworks that diverge from Western intellectual thought. For instance, research by ethicist and psychologist **Carol Gilligan** (Kohlberg's former research assistant) found that women and men tend to react differently to moral dilemmas. Because Kohlberg studied only males in developing his framework, Gilligan says he missed experiences and perspectives that society identifies as female. In response, Gilligan developed the concept of **"moral voices."** She explains that the masculine voice is "logical and individualistic," and bases moral decisions on protecting individual rights and upholding concepts of justice. The female voice is relational, basing moral decisions on the nurturance of human bonds and caring for other individuals. She argues that people can best reach their moral potential by integrating both voices, since their combined value helps women and men become more ethical and fully human.[54]

Classroom Climates That Promote Ethical Reflection

How can teachers handle matters of ethics that appear every day? Imagine encountering these situations:

- A student complains that Christian and Western classroom activities are demeaning her Vietnamese heritage and culture.
- A student with learning disabilities is ignored by classmates at lunchtime. Rather than sitting alone in the cafeteria, he hides in the bathroom.
- A gifted student with advanced verbal skills is bullied frequently by a classmate in the locker room before gym class. Other students remain bystanders, and do not stop or report the bullying.
- You discover that the A-plus student you just recommended for a special award has stored exam answers on her cell phone.

GLOBAL VIEW

Seeds of Peace is a nonprofit, nonpolitical organization that helps teenagers from regions of conflict learn the skills to end the cycles of violence and make peace. Visit www.seedsofpeace.org

How are teachers to navigate this tricky moral minefield? Experienced educators suggest how the right classroom climate can help such exploration:

The School & Classroom Setting

Climate. Create an environment where both teachers and students respect and encourage diverse points of view—and promote sharing of diverse opinions.

School and class rules. Democratic values are trampled when teachers require students to follow rules unquestioningly. At the very least teachers must clearly explain school and class rules, and the reasons behind them. Many teachers go beyond this minimum threshold and work collaboratively with students to establish the classroom rules.

Parents and community. It is helpful when parents, citizens, and community leaders participate in developing the school's mission and its ethical codes of responsibility. One way to encourage such cooperation is to plan joint efforts that tie students' families and civic organizations into school-sponsored programs. This approach reinforces ethical lessons in the school, home, and community.

The Teacher

Modeling. Demonstrate the ethical lessons you teach in small and large ways—every day. Teacher behavior should reflect and model tolerance, compassion, forgiveness, and open-mindedness. After all, values are more often "caught" than "taught."

Interpersonal skills. A critical component of interpersonal skills is empathy—the ability to see problems from more than one point of view, including through the eyes of students. Continually develop effective communication skills to encourage students to share their concerns, thoughts, ideas, and emotions.

Commitment. Practice the personal determination and courage to confront ethical dilemmas, rather than hide within the path of indifference, inattention, or least resistance.

Reflection. To unravel moral questions, you must know how to analyze a dilemma objectively and evaluate its essential components. The more you develop effective and deliberate reasoning skills, the better suited you are for ethical challenge.

Personal opinions. There may be a tendency to create students in your own image. Avoid indoctrinating students with your personal points of view, but don't shy away from showing students that you have strong beliefs. The key is to create a classroom in which individuals can freely, responsibly, and respectfully agree or disagree.[55]

Laws tell us what is legal or illegal—but laws aren't capable of guiding us through many of the moral quandaries that we will undoubtedly encounter in (and beyond) our classrooms. It's often said that integrity is doing the right thing, even when no one is watching. That's a high standard to meet. Yet, just as they do today, moral issues will continue to have major influence in the future. How you as a teacher and a person respond will shape you, your students, and our culture. Indeed, even as our nation grows in wealth, great scientific strides, and technological breakthroughs, the final measure of our worth may ultimately be the way we treat one another. As the late U.S. Supreme Court Justice Potter Stewart says on the first page of this chapter: "Ethics is knowing the difference between what you have a right to do and what is right to do."

CONNECT FOR *TEACHERS, SCHOOLS, AND SOCIETY*

Check out Connect, McGraw-Hill Education's interactive learning environment, to:

Read Current and Historical Articles

Putting a Face to Faith, by Charles C. Haynes, *Educational Leadership,* September 2011.
Improve Relationships to Improve Student Performance, by Richard Arum, *Phi Delta Kappan,* October 2011.
Ethics: From Thought to Action, by Robert J. Sternberg, *Educational Leadership,* March 2011.
Please Help Me Learn Who I Am, by Barry Boyce, *Shambhala Sun,* January 2007.

Analyze Case Studies

Amanda Jackson: A teacher discovers that her principal has a drinking problem, which is well known but never discussed among the staff. She faces a dilemma when she realizes that the principal is planning to drive a student home during a snowstorm.
Ellen Norton: A teacher whose concern for a shy, underachieving student has led to the student becoming her "shadow" learns that another student may be the victim of child abuse at home. The teacher has to decide if she should become involved.

Watch Teachers, Students, and Classrooms in Action

Our **Online Video Album** for contemporary videos related to this chapter.

KEY TERMS AND PEOPLE

DISCUSSION QUESTIONS AND ACTIVITIES

1. If you were to suggest a law to improve education, what would that law be? Would you make it federal, state, or local? Why?
2. The role of religion and prayer in schools has always been controversial, and teachers are advised to neither *encourage* nor *discourage* religious observances. As a teacher, what religious celebrations or practices might you encounter in your class? How would you respond to these issues while maintaining your neutrality?
3. Construct an argument to support the principle that students and their property should not be searched without the students' consent.
4. Watch the short, student-created film at https://vimeo.com/98149849. In your classroom, how would you answer the questions and address the issues raised?
5. Which of the paths to moral education (values clarification, moral development, character education, or an integrated approach) appeals to you most? Why?
6. Describe some steps you might explore to promote ethical student behavior in your classroom.

It is the foremost task of education to insure the survival of these qualities: an enterprising curiosity, an undefeatable spirit, tenacity in pursuit, readiness for sensible denial, and above all, compassion.

KURT HAHN

chapter 9

Purposes of America's Schools and the Current Reform Movement

Focus Questions

1. What are the goals of America's schools?
2. What school goals are important to you?
3. Why has school reform become a national priority?
4. What new school options are replacing the traditional neighborhood public school?
5. What are the advantages and disadvantages of teaching in a virtual school?
6. What are the characteristics of effective schools?
7. What are the roles of teachers and students in reforming our schools?
8. What are the unintended consequences of school reform?

Chapter Preview

Although most of us take school for granted, its actual purpose continues to evoke heated debate. Are schools meant to prepare students for college, vocation, or high scores on standardized tests? Are schools also responsible for developing effective interpersonal relationships, patriotism, acculturation, social mobility, or active social change? And are these diverse purposes counterproductive?

In this chapter, you will examine the roles that society assigns to schools—and your own views on appropriate school goals. We'll explore the way that U.S. education is being reformed and reshaped through charter schools, green schools, virtual schools, homeschooling, and more. We will look at research into what a school must do to be effective. The purpose of today's schools is greatly influenced by the economy, political viewpoints, and cultural values. Ironically, teachers and students have much less influence on education goals and reform than you would imagine. Defining the place, purpose, and effectiveness of schools has never been more challenging. We conclude this chapter by asking if school reform is headed in the right direction.

Why Do Schools Exist?

After a bad day in class, you may have muttered (or screamed), "Why do schools exist?" However, any attempt to provide an "answer" shows that the question is deceptively complex. Of course, students go to school to learn. But what are they (we) supposed to learn? That depends on who you ask.

Imagine that you hold one of the following positions in society. Then, imagine your top priority for the nation's schools.

FOCUS QUESTION 1

What are the goals of America's schools?

Business executive, member of Congress, farmer, artist, first-year public school teacher, person of color, K-6 student, taxpayer, devout religious believer, state legislator, school bus driver, governor, physician, white person, professor of education, woman, professor of nuclear physics, armed forces member, veteran public school teacher, salesperson, man, middle-school student, parent, social worker, U.S. President, transgender, peace officer, school principal, psychologist, recent immigrant, grandparent, musician, mechanic, IT professional, government employee, middle-level manager, philosopher, historian, Secretary of Education, journalist, high school student, political consultant, software developer, entrepreneur, prison warden, athlete, member of the clergy, stockholder in a school testing company.

This list could easily be three times as long, and a moment's reflection reveals our views of what schools should do are diverse, sometimes superficial, and even contradictory.[1] Let's illustrate this reality by looking at some common **school goals** that different groups favor:

Academic Competitiveness. Our students need to rank first in the world on international tests of science, math, and technology. U.S. students currently rank lower than too many other countries, and we certainly do not want to fall behind rapidly emerging economies like China and India. Being the best country on earth means being a world leader on international tests.

Academic Curiosity. Not enough students have internal motivation to learn. We need to create self-directed students and citizens. We can't predict what tomorrow will demand, so to maintain our creativity, innovation and inventiveness, schools need emphasize curiosity over learning a fixed body of information.

Academic Basics. Too many students graduate or drop out of school without basic literacy and numeracy skills. Old-time schools succeeded by focusing on the "three Rs" (reading, 'riting, and 'rithmetic). We need to make sure every student learns to master math, and to speak, read, and write English proficiently. Let's return to tradition, rather than continue the waves of disruptive and unproven "reform."

Work Readiness. "If you want to get a good job, you better get a good education!" The nation's economic well-being depends on an educated workforce that can compete in the global economy. Tens of thousands of U.S. jobs go unfilled because people don't have the skills to perform those jobs well enough. Our nation can't survive generations of unemployed or underemployed citizens.

Civic Loyalty and Responsibility. Our students should be citizens first, with deep love of country and firm understanding of their civic obligations. We must teach them to value our country and its democracy enough to die in their defense. They must learn to engage in the larger community by volunteering, voting, participating in politics, respecting different opinions, and enduring the uncomfortable compromise inherent in a democracy.

Social Change. Our world is far from ideal, and school is a perfect tool for making the needed repairs. For example, Baltimore school students organized a photo exhibit of their decaying school buildings. While lobbying for increased construction and repair funds, they gave state legislators a guided tour via their photos, exposing broken heaters, moldy walls, library shelves without books, cockroaches, a stairwell filled with garbage, and broken windows.[2] Students must face society's critical challenges, and as adults become social change agents.[3]

GLOBAL VIEW

Japan's Hiroshima memorial explains that "the situation in Pearl Harbor hurtled Japan into the Pacific war." There is no mention of Japan's surprise attack on Pearl Harbor and no explanation of the Japanese invasion and occupation of China years earlier. Can you cite examples of how other nations (as well as our own) "whitewash" history?

Artistic Creativity. Schools should promote creativity in the arts and develop each student's skills and talents. New York City's High School of Music & Art and High School of Performing Arts have done this since 1936 and 1947, respectively.[4] Honing artistic skills, preparing for performances, and presenting work to the public all teach students real-life applications of math, literature, science, and interpersonal skills.

Social Mobility. For decades, U.S. public schools provided a ladder out of poverty and illiteracy, fulfilling the "American Dream." Now, people who are citizens of many other nations are able to advance themselves through education more successfully than Americans. One reason is that a college degree has become "the new high school diploma," necessary for good-paying jobs and economic mobility in the twenty-first century.[5] But these degrees are out of the financial reach of many Americans. We must change this, make college more accessible, and give K–12 students the vocational skills to move forward even if they don't attend college.

GLOBAL VIEW

Should the values that U.S. schools practice and promote be disseminated abroad? Is the equal treatment of women a U.S. value, or a universal value? Do we only have an economy that is global, or is promoting human rights part of our role in the world?

Passing the Cultural/Historical Baton. Schools should teach the nation's most important historic events and figures—along with our culture's most influential books, authors, artists, and inventors. Society depends on **social cohesion,** so schools must provide all students with some common, basic knowledge they share. This is the most effective way to unite our population and preserve our heritage.

Acculturation. This is a nation of immigrants, and schools still have a major obligation to integrate immigrant children into U.S. culture. Some states—Arizona and Massachusetts, for example—passed laws requiring that schools only use English when teaching non-English speaking students. **Acculturation** is essential, so schools should teach students to adopt our language and values quickly so that they can navigate successfully in our culture.[6]

A CLOSER LOOK

What's in a Name?

Ever wonder how schools get their names—and which names are the most popular? The National Education Resource Center researched the most popular proper names for U.S. high schools: Washington, Lincoln, Kennedy, Jefferson, Roosevelt (both Franklin and Teddy), and Wilson. (Presidents do well.) Lee, Edison, and Madison round out the top ten names. But proper names are not the most common high school names. Directions dominate: Northeastern, South, and Central High School are right up there. Creativity obviously is not a criterion, but politics is. Citizens fight over whether schools should be named after George Washington or Thomas Jefferson—who, after all, were slaveholders—and over why so few African Americans, Hispanics, and people of non-European ancestry are honored by having a school named after them. And, considering how many women are educators, it is amazing that so few schools are named to honor women—Eleanor Roosevelt, Amelia Earhart, Christa McAuliffe, and Jacqueline Kennedy are exceptions. Some schools have honored writers (Bret Harte, Walt Whitman, and Mark Twain) or reflect local leaders and culture. (In Las Vegas, you will find schools named Durango, Silverado, and Bonanza, which some complain sound more like casinos than western culture.)

REFLECTION: What choices do you think educators might make if they were responsible for school names? If students were in charge, would schools be named after sports figures or music and media stars? Can you name 10 influential women who aren't sports or media stars? How do our school names reflect the power and culture in a society? What's in a name?

Global Knowledge. As many other countries do, our schools advance a U.S. view of history, values, self-interests, and culture. Students learn little about the history, geography, language, and culture of other countries–or of our own cultural diversity. For students to thrive in our ever-more-connected world, today's schools must create multilingual global citizens who thrive by knowing and appreciating wider horizons of cultures, histories, and values.

Empowering the Powerless. There's a big difference between schools and education. Radical educator **Paulo Freire** argued that schools often miseducate, working to control and oppress people, while true education liberates.[7] We must help disadvantaged peoples learn to read, act collectively, and improve their living conditions, even if it means taking on current social norms. We should also educate privileged students to be allies with the dispossessed and build a better, more equitable society. (See the Education Hall of Fame in Connect for more information about Freire.)

Ethical Personal Development. Schools should focus on making students more honest, ethical, kind, and compassionate. The disturbing degree of white-collar crime, business and political corruption, and cheating in and beyond school speaks to the need of stronger ethics in our nation. This includes each of us learning to make responsible decisions in our daily lives, like avoiding products made by exploited children overseas.[8] Being an ethical person is the most important goal any school can have.

Service Learning. In 1992, Maryland began requiring students to perform community service before they could get their high school diploma.[9] All schools should use **service learning** to connect students with the larger community and develop their personal responsibility for improving society.[10] More than half of students in grades 6 through 12 already do service learning, but we must reduce gender, race, and other factors that reduce participation. [11]

Child Care. Since a large majority of U.S. parents now work for pay–most of them outside of the family home[12]–schools should be a caretaker for their children, or our

Is the purpose of schools just academic learning, or might the goals include fostering an awareness of the benefits of community service, such as volunteering to tutor others?

©Tony Freeman/PhotoEdit

RAP 2.7

A Real Inservice Program

entire society will be in jeopardy. We should simply accept that "school isn't actually about efficient teaching; it's about free all-day babysitting while parents work."[13] Schools also function to delay the day when young people enter the workforce and compete with their elders for jobs. We should embrace these societal benefits, and stop pretending that a school's top priority is academic advancement.

Some people object to most of these goals of schooling. John Taylor Gatto, who taught for 30 years in New York City public schools, agrees with Paulo Freire, arguing that compulsory, government-run schooling has more to do with control than learning. Referring to them as more prisons than learning centers, Gatto writes that schools produce "a population deliberately dumbed down and rendered childlike in order that government and economic life can be managed with a minimum of hassle."[14] He says the U.S. school system ultimately intends to generate barely literate, conformist consumers without real knowledge or much capacity to get knowledge.

GLOBAL VIEW

Should the values that U.S. schools practice and promote be disseminated abroad? Is the equal treatment of women a U.S. value, or a universal value? Do we only have an economy that is global, or is promoting human rights part of our role in the world?

What do we want from our schools? Everything. (Just maybe we are overreaching here.)

In his massive 1980s study, *A Place Called School*, **John Goodlad** confirmed these broad expectations of schools. He examined a wide range of documents defining the purposes of schooling for over 300 years of history. He and his colleague found four broad goals: 1) Academic, 2) Vocational, 3) Social and civic, and 4) Personal. (See Figure 9.1.)

Goodlad then asked parents, teachers, and students to rate the relative importance of these goals. The result: they listed all four as "very important!" (Not so helpful.) When pushed to select one top priority goal, approximately half the teachers and parents selected academics, while students spread their preferences fairly evenly among all four categories, with high school students giving a slight edge to vocational goals. It seems that no one wants to interpret the purpose of schools narrowly.[15]

RAP 2.5

A Public Service Announcement: The Purpose of School

FIGURE 9.1
Goals of schools.

REFLECTION: Under each goal, list specific efforts a school could make to reach the goal. How would you prioritize these goals? Explain.

Perhaps that's why, after conducting a major study of secondary education, another researcher, Ernest Boyer concluded:

> Since the English classical school was founded over [180] years ago, high schools have accumulated purposes like barnacles on a weathered ship. As school population expanded from a tiny urban minority to almost all youth, a coherent purpose was hard to find. The nation piled social policy upon educational policy and all of them on top of the delusion that a single institution can do it all.[16]

As early as 1953, Arthur Bestor wrote, "The idea that the school must undertake to meet every need that some other agency is failing to meet, regardless of the suitability of the schoolroom to the task, is a preposterous delusion that in the end can wreck the educational system."[17] Meanwhile, more than two-thirds of Americans believe that schools are responsible for the academic, behavioral, social, and emotional needs of all students.[18] It seems like the public (does this include you?) continues to expect and demand schools to fulfill a myriad of roles.

Where Do You Stand?

FOCUS QUESTION 2
What school goals are important to you?

It seems like everyone has one or more essential goal(s) for schools. The result? A list of goals that is unrealistic, short-sighted, self-contradictory, or brilliant (depending on your point of view).

Let's see what *you* believe schools should be doing. Different groups have advocated the following goals at different times. How do you feel about each one? Circle the number that best reflects how important you think each school goal is.

1. Very unimportant
2. Unimportant
3. Moderately important
4. Important
5. Very important

Write down your responses, and we will show you how your priorities mesh with other people's.

	Very Unimportant				Very Important
1. To transmit the nation's cultural heritage, preserving past accomplishments and insights	1	2	3	4	5
2. To encourage students to question current practices and institutions; to promote social change	1	2	3	4	5
3. To prepare competent workers to compete successfully in a technological world economy	1	2	3	4	5
4. To develop healthy citizens aware of nutrition, exercise, and good health habits	1	2	3	4	5
5. To lead the world in creating a peaceful global society, stressing an understanding of other cultures and languages	1	2	3	4	5
6. To provide a challenging education for America's brightest students	1	2	3	4	5
7. To develop strong self-concept and self-esteem in students	1	2	3	4	5
8. To nurture creative students in developing art, music, and writing	1	2	3	4	5
9. To prevent unwanted pregnancy, AIDS, drugs, addiction, alcoholism	1	2	3	4	5
10. To unite citizens from diverse backgrounds (national origin, race, ethnicity) as a single nation with a unified culture	1	2	3	4	5
11. To provide support to families through after-school child care, supplemental nutrition, medical treatment, and so on	1	2	3	4	5
12. To encourage loyal students committed to the United States; to instill patriotism	1	2	3	4	5
13. To teach students our nation's work ethic: punctuality, responsibility, cooperation, self-control, neatness, and so on	1	2	3	4	5
14. To demonstrate academic proficiency through high standardized test scores	1	2	3	4	5
15. To provide a dynamic vehicle for social and economic mobility, a way for the poor to reach their full potential	1	2	3	4	5
16. To prepare educated citizens who can undertake actions that spark change	1	2	3	4	5
17. To ensure the cultural richness and diversity of the United States	1	2	3	4	5
18. To eliminate racism, sexism, homophobia, anti-Semitism, and all forms of discrimination from society	1	2	3	4	5
19. To prepare as many students as possible for college and/or well-paid careers	1	2	3	4	5
20. To provide child care for the nation's children and to free parents to work and/or pursue their interests and activities	1	2	3	4	5

Now, like John Goodlad, we'll press you to pick the three goals for schools that you value the most. Write them here:

______________________, ______________________, ______________________

Where do your responses cast you along the continuum of people concerned about the purpose of schools? Imagine that some people are focused on transmitting the culture, and conserving what we have, while others look toward change or restructuring society. (We know, it's a bit simplistic, but bear with us.)

To help you determine where your beliefs take you, we weighted our list of purposes to help you see if you lean toward being a **cultural transmitter**, or if you are more interested in **reconstructing society**. Record your scores below, and see which way you lean:

Purpose of Schools

Transmitter		**Reconstructionist**	
Focused Item		*Focused Item*	
1	______	2	______
3	______	5	______
10	______	9	______
12	______	15	______
13	______	16	______
19	______	18	______
Total	______	*Total*	______

REFLECTION: Do your responses reflect the school experiences you had, or the ones you had hoped for? What did you learn about your *values* and your view of schools? How will being a transmitter or reconstructionist influence your work as a teacher?

The Schools We Create

FOCUS QUESTION 3

Why has school reform become a national priority?

We now have a sense of how differently people see the purpose of schools. For most of our history, school did not matter much to most Americans. In 1918, compulsory elementary school attendance finally became the law in all states, but even then only 20 percent of teens aged 14 through 17 attended some form of high school—without necessarily graduating.[19] School was someone else's problem—and usually a wealthier someone else. Today the norm is for most children to attend school for many years, a huge historical change. How are we doing? Sometimes even that is difficult to tell. Polling suggests that most Americans give their local public schools an A or B grade. Good news. But less than 20 percent rate the rest of the nation's schools that highly. Bad news. (Everybody's local school is fine and dandy, but when you add up all those fine and dandy schools, it is a big failure. You're right, doesn't make much sense.)[20] These contradictory perceptions of school performance, which began with a national report issued in the 1980s, have led to an erratic school reform movement. [21]

As we look at some major school reforms today, we invite you to ponder one of Goodlad's important findings: "[I]t doesn't matter how many bills and how many policies you lay down from on high—when it comes right down to it, the individual school has an incredible capacity for rejecting it passively or taking it on and doing something about it."[22]

How are schools responding to this challenge? You decide.

Let's look at how schools are morphing today. While we describe these different schools, consider which sounds attractive to you. Where would you like to teach? We start by giving special attention to the most influential reform product, **charter schools.**

Charter Schools

In the early 1990s, Minnesota created the first charter school, launching an idea that mushroomed into more than 5,000 charters, teaching more than six percent of all public school students, with higher rates in many urban districts.[23] The charter movement created new competition for neighborhood public schools—and all of public education today. Some states, like Arizona, California, Texas, and Florida, created many charter schools; other states have been more cautious. Most Americans support charter schools, and view them as more effective than their neighborhood school.[24] (See Figures 9.2 and 9.3.) At the same time, polling shows that most parents don't fully understand how charters work. Half thought charters were not public schools (they are) and 48 percent thought they could teach religion (they can't). A majority thought they admit students based on academic ability and charge tuition (they can't do either).[25]

The charter school concept is simple. A charter school is a tax-supported *public* school with legal permission (called a charter or a contract) to operate an "alternative" school. In effect, charter schools gain greater freedom to operate outside many normal public school regulations—but only for a fixed period. A local or state school board issues the charter (usually for five years) with the right to renew if the school is successful. Most charter schools are publicly funded and privately run, often by a for-profit corporation.

A charter school typically:

- Creates its own curriculum and structure
- Cannot use admission tests
- Builds a new school, converts an existing building, or creates a virtual school
- Hires its own (often non-unionized) staff
- Receives public funding based on the number of students enrolled
- Accepts additional private funding
- Solicits parents to enroll their children

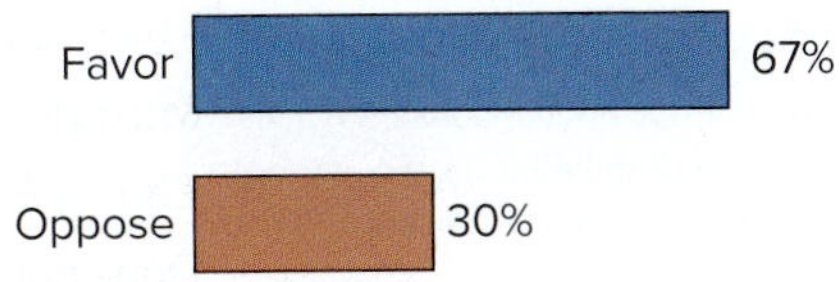

FIGURE 9.2

Do you favor or oppose charter schools?

SOURCE: Phi Delta Kappa International, "2014 PDK/Gallup Poll of the Public's Attitudes Toward the Public Schools." August, 2014, p. 10. Retrieved November 16, 2016, at http://pdkintl.org/files/2014-PDK-Gallup-Poll-Presentation.pdf.

REFLECTION: In the year 2000, less than half of the public supported charter schools. Why the big change? Do you believe support will grow or diminish in the years ahead?

Rank	School District	State	Charter Students	Non Charter Students	Total	Enrollment Share
1	Orleans Parish School District	LA	42,860	3,340	46,200	93%
2	Detroit City School District	MI	52,420	47,040	99,460	53%
3	School District of The City of Flint	MI	5,660	6,490	12,150	47%
4	District of Columbia Public Schools	DC	37,680	47,550	85,230	44%
5	Kansas City, Missouri School District	MO	9,980	14,230	24,210	41%
6	Gary Community School Corporation	IN	5,010	7,570	12,580	40%
7	The School District of Philadelphia	PA	64,090	130,660	194,750	33%
8	Hall County Schools	GA	8,200	17,080	25,280	32%
	Victor Valley Union High School District	CA	4,390	9,500	13,890	32%
9	Indianapolis Public Schools	IN	13,830	30,100	43,920	31%
	Grand Rapids Public Schools	MI	6,900	15,610	22,510	31%
10	Dayton City School District	OH	6,220	14,220	20,440	30%
	San Antonio Independent School District	TX	17,000	40,450	57,450	30%
	Cleveland Municipal School District	OH	16,220	38,730	54,950	30%

FIGURE 9.3

The highest percentage of public charter school students by school district, 2014–15.

SOURCE: National Alliance for Public Charter Schools, "A Growing Movement: America's Largest Charter School Communities, Tenth Annual Edition," November 2015. Retrieved November 15, 2016, at http://www.publiccharters.org/wp-content/uploads/2015/11/enrollmentshare_web.pdf.

REFLECTION: What commonalities can you detect in these districts where charters are numerous?

FOCUS QUESTION 4

What new school options are replacing the traditional neighborhood public school?

- Must be nonsectarian
- Must demonstrate improvement in student performance
- Can be closed if it does not meet expectations
- Does not need to conform to most state education rules and regulations
- Must follow government health, safety, and civil rights rules

Who would take on such a big task? Tom Watkins, director of the Detroit Center for Charter Schools, describes three types of charter advocates: reformers, zealots, and entrepreneurs. Reformers want to expand public school options for parents and children, and promote a specific approach, such as student-centered learning. Watkins says zealots tend to use a private school model, emphasize traditional, teacher-centered curriculum, and avoid teachers' unions. Entrepreneurs believe schools operating like efficient businesses can teach students well, reward investors, and turn education into a profit center.[26]

Some particularly brave teachers can take on this challenge as well. After three years in the classroom, six young Newark, New Jersey, teachers grew frustrated with seeing so much failure, so they designed and won a charter for their own K–8 school. They became teacher-leaders who decide what to teach and how long the school day and school year would be. In teacher-led schools from Los Angeles to New York, studies show higher teacher morale, less turnover, and greater motivation.[27]

By their nature, charter schools face some different economic and academic pressures than neighborhood public schools. Most income comes from per-pupil funding (see Chapter 7), so charters must often find additional ways to pay for unique programs and goals. And, since it's easier to close under-performing charter schools, their leaders can be under intense pressure to meet academic goals (usually measured by standardized tests). But some states that favor charter schools continue to support them even if their performance is weak.

But poor test results are one source of pressure that can lead to serious malfeasance in charter schools. Sometimes it is just bad management. For example, the Louisiana Department of Education found that ReNEW SciTech Academy in New Orleans violated state testing regulations and diverted special-education money to close a $300,000 hole in its budget. The state imposed an outside monitor and required that ReNEW hire a consultant with expertise in charter school administration. Wealthy individuals and family foundations invest in, and sometimes help to design, charter schools—not always with success. Detroit's charter school system is one example, where private financial influence led to little oversight or accountability, lower reading scores, and "what even charter advocates acknowledge is the biggest school reform disaster in the country." On the other hand, when Louisiana state government took over failing New Orleans charter schools, test scores, graduation rates, and college admissions all increased—while suspensions, expulsions, and school-switching all dropped. Sometimes, government is the answer.[28]

Charter schools are often considered the vanguard of education reform, but public discussion rarely addresses their impact on non-charter public schools. Children with severe disabilities seldom attend charters, and are far more expensive for "traditional" schools to educate effectively—forcing them to bear a disproportionate cost at the expense of their other students. Traditional schools must still pay fixed costs (maintenance, electricity, heat, bond service, administration) even as they lose funding when their students move to charter schools. In addition, lotteries for spots in charter schools skim select students away from their non-charter peers.

David Hornbeck once lobbied for new charter schools as Superintendent of Schools in Philadelphia and for the State of Maryland. He now argues against them,

CONTEMPORARY ISSUES

A View from the Field: Teaching at a Charter School

Casey Mason, 28, teaches ninth-grade social studies and is one of two certified special education teachers at Amy Biehl High School (ABHS), a charter school of 250 students in Albuquerque, New Mexico.

"I have not once planned a class in isolation. Our curriculum is planned with our colleagues; we decide what is enduring and important about New Mexico history, the quadratic equation, and biology. We have academic discussions where we explore what we will teach our students. At times, I feel as though I'm still in college. It's wonderful. I chose ABHS because I knew creative lessons that value critical thinking and differentiation would be expected here."

Casey earned a BA in women's studies and African American studies and an MA in special education from the University of New Mexico before teaching in a traditional middle school for two years. Because ABHS is so small, students are picked by lottery.

"There are no prerequisites for attending ABHS; it is a public school. I have wonderful students not because they are the highest achievers, the most talented, or the best behaved. Through the luxury of a small learning community, I can build more personal relationships with my students and really get to know their learning needs. At traditional public schools, I taught 150 students per day, with up to 35 students in each class. At ABHS, I have no more than 20 students in a class.

"At our small school, my students get to be who they are without fear of being the 'other.' The size of ABHS allows for and mandates this. You can't hide in a small school. The same goes for the teachers. The power of small personal communities makes my school magical."

Courtesy of Casey Mason.

citing the loss of services for Baltimore's remaining 70,000 students after funding shifts to the city's 13,000 charter students.

> Chartering schools is not education reform; it's merely a change in governance. ... Remaining children face the prospects of larger class sizes and cuts in core academic programming, music, art, and other inequities. ... [And,] when a local charter fails, the local system picks up the children.[29]

Civil rights advocates argue that charter schools increase racial and economic segregation in the nation's public schools.[30] The NAACP, the United States' oldest civil rights organization, called for a moratorium on privately managed charters because they lack transparency and accountability, expel too many children of color, and perpetuate de facto segregation.[31] For instance, Arizona has the highest rate of charter school attendance of any state (17 percent), but its charters have fewer minority students than neighborhood schools. Only one in six Hispanic students in Arizona attends a charter school. Among other groups, 33 percent of Asian students, 25 percent of white students, and only 10 percent of Native American students attend charter schools.[32] Nationwide, few charter schools have student transportation—a major barrier for less affluent families without the flexibility or means to get their children to schools outside the neighborhood. Language barriers, family socioeconomic status, and parental social networks also affect charter school access.[33] Research by the ACLU found that 20 percent of California charter schools have policies which violate students' rights; for example, discouraging or precluding immigrant students from attending by requiring information about the pupils' or their parents' immigration status.[34]

What are charter school classrooms like? Some charters offer teachers more freedom than the traditional neighborhood school, allowing educators to create their own standards and curriculum, establish rules for discipline, plan programs with colleagues, and even make budget decisions. (See Contemporary Issues: A View from the Field: Teaching at a Charter School.) For example, New American Academy uses large, open rooms with 60 students and four teachers. Teachers float between groups of students working in different areas and on different activities. Headmaster **Shimon Waronker** created the school to function like a trusting family, rather than an education factory. Teachers move up grade levels with the same children year after year, so relationships are long term. You might not expect Waronker to revitalize one of New York City's most violent junior high schools or create a radically different charter school. He grew up speaking Spanish in South America, became a U.S. Army intelligence officer, and is an observant Jew. Many doubted that a bearded white man in a traditional black suit and yarmulke could relate to poor minority students. But he succeeded at using globally researched practices that prepare students for today's collaborative world—replacing traditional U.S. schools, which Waronker believes are based on twentieth-century Prussian schools that strove to create docile subjects and workers.[35]

Other charters place greater demands on teachers and have more structured operations. At Edge Charter High School in Tucson, more than half of students enroll with reading and/or math skill deficiencies below the sixth-grade level and nearly all are more than a year behind in academic credits. Nearly 70 percent come from low-income families. Students attend school four hours a day, either in the morning or afternoon, and focus on three academic classes at a time. The curriculum ranges from the non-reader to the twelfth-grade level, and every student participates in DOL (Daily Oral Language) and DOM (Daily Oral Math) activities to prepare for state-mandated standardized tests. Small class sizes and a high level of individualized instruction with students at risk of school failure place intense demands on teachers. They use extensive Web-based and classroom curriculum to build basic reading, writing, and math skills to overcome deficiencies and ensure academic success.[36] Both Edge and New American Academy have had success with children who struggled in neighborhood schools.

But is such success the norm? Not according to researchers. A Stanford University study found that about one in five charter schools offered a better education than local schools, while 37 percent were "significantly worse," and the rest offered a quality of education similar to traditional schools.[37] Other studies find similar results: As a group, charter schools are no more effective than public schools. Low-income students "would on average be more likely to score better in a public school than a charter school."[38] In Wisconsin, researchers found that attendance at charter schools had *more* negative impact on public school student test scores than poverty did.

Shimon Waronker's New American Academy illustrates that people of different backgrounds can thrive in a school based on trusting relationships.

©James Estrin/The New York Times/Redux Pictures

Many charters struggle to find appropriate facilities, retain qualified teachers, and develop adequate technology or library resources.[39] After all, they also have fixed costs (maintenance, electricity, heat, rent, administration), and per-pupil funding may not cover it all. This can create a vicious circle, since neighborhood schools simultaneously lose per-pupil funding to the charter school. To make up the shortfalls, corporations and even some state governments are funneling more public and private money into charters. This raises concerns about financial oversight, influence exerted by corporate and other donors—as well as incidents where charter dollars may be spent unwisely or illegally.[40]

Advocates hoped that charter schools would enhance education and discover innovative teaching strategies that traditional schools would then adopt. But in fact, very little of what works for charter schools has found its way into regular classrooms.[41] So far, chartering is not eliminating the struggles of neighborhood public schools. Charters have exciting potential to experiment with and promote new schooling options and approaches. Yet their promise may be overblown, given the academic outcomes they produce, and the uneven application of assessment and accountability.

Can we make neighborhood schools experiment and grow more effective without having to create new semi-independent schools? Will the charter school movement eventually improve or weaken American education? Time will tell.

Vouchers

An educational **voucher** functions as an admission ticket to any school. In a voucher system, the government gives parents a certain amount of money (variable by state) which parents can use to "shop" for the best public or private school. In effect, vouchers are public taxpayer money that parents use in any school they want. The chosen school gets paid by turning in the student's voucher to a local or state government, and the government pays the money the voucher is worth. In theory, good schools will attract many students, collect their vouchers, redeem them with the local government, and receive cash. The theory goes, good schools will thrive, and perhaps even expand. Meanwhile, weak schools will have difficulty attracting "customers" and eventually go out of business. Voucher-fueled competition would leverage tried-and-true market forces to reform schools, and once again the ideas of choice and competition will make a wonderful difference.

An underlying belief of this model is that private schools are more effective than public ones—and that rewarding the former will force the latter to change their ways. Supporters of vouchers are often quite enthusiastic, but the research data on vouchers is far from persuasive. In fact, vouchers appear to have little impact on student achievement while reducing funding to public schools.[42] Nevertheless, many of the same forces promoting the charter school movement are also pushing for greater acceptance of vouchers. The Walton Family Foundation, founded and governed by the family that founded Walmart, has spent more than $1 billion to promote charter and voucher programs, and Betsy DeVos, who became Secretary of Education in 2017, actually owned for-profit schools that depended on vouchers—but those schools posted academic tests that were quite weak.[43]

A major barrier for vouchers historically was that most private schools were and (and still are) religious schools. In 1990, Wisconsin lawmakers approved the first publicly financed voucher program. Students in Milwaukee (Wisconsin's largest city) could receive about $3,000 each to attend one of Milwaukee's few nonsectarian (and expensive) private schools. Since that didn't generate much movement, legislators amended the law in 1995 so students could also attend parochial schools—which generally have lower tuition rates. In general, vouchers offer too little financial support for elite and expensive private schools but enough to cover the modest cost of many parochial schools. Unsurprisingly, religious schools are the prime beneficiaries of vouchers, receiving upward of 90 percent of voucher students.

But doesn't the First Amendment of the Constitution ensure separation of church and state—and prohibit using taxpayer money to send children for religious instruction? Wisconsin's inclusion of Milwaukee religious schools in the voucher plan, and a similar plan in Cleveland, sparked a heated controversy and rounds of lawsuits. The result is a legal picture in flux. In the pre-voucher 1970s, the U.S. Supreme Court constructed clear walls limiting the use of public funds to support religious education. In ***Lemon v. Kurtzman*** (1971) the Court established three criteria for using government funds in religious schools. The so-called Lemon test says that the funds (1) must have a secular purpose, (2) must not primarily advance *or* prohibit religion, and (3) must not result in excessive government entanglement with religion. The wall separating church and state got lower in 2002, when a more conservative court revisited the issue. In a narrow 5–4 decision, the Supreme Court ruled in ***Zelman v. Simmons-Harris*** that publicly funded vouchers could be used to send children to Cleveland's private religious schools. How could this be done? The majority argued that government-funded vouchers were not public monies going to support religious schools. Rather, the court interpreted vouchers as public funds going to parents. It is the parents who decided to spend the money at a religious school, not the government. Critics claimed that this was tortured reasoning and a flimsy attempt to paper over unconstitutional state funding of religious institutions. Writing for the majority, Chief Justice William Rehnquist disagreed—stating that vouchers permit a "genuine choice among options public and private, secular and religious." Justice John Paul Stevens dissented, writing, "Whenever we remove a brick from the wall that was designed to separate religion and government, we increase the risk of religious strife and weaken the foundation of our democracy."[44]

Despite the *Zelman* decision, some state constitutions still restrict public aid to private and religious institutions.[45] Many states and school districts forego vouchers altogether.[46] Moreover, as we noted above, evaluations of the few existing voucher programs indicate that they are not particularly effective. For example, students using Louisiana's statewide voucher program are doing dramatically worse than the students in the New Orleans charter schools run by the state (see above). Once again, an idea that sounds good in theory doesn't always work out in the real world—especially when we don't have rigorous assessment and accountability. Perhaps that's why public support for universal vouchers is falling. And in a reversal of opinion, more Democrats than Republicans now favor universal vouchers.[47] But after a pro-voucher administration took office in 2017, it is anyone's guess where the voucher debate will end.

Open Enrollment

In 1988, Minnesota eliminated the requirement that students must attend the public school closest to their home. The state moved to **open enrollment,** which allows parents to send their student to any Minnesota public school with available space. In most cases, this means switching to another school in the same school district, or one in a neighboring district. Arkansas, Iowa, Nebraska, and other states soon followed and introduced open enrollment legislation to increase school choice. In 2015, the only states without open enrollment were Maryland, North Carolina, and Indiana (outside of Indianapolis). However, several states only allow choice within the student's local school district.[48]

As with charter schools, some aspects of open enrollment look better on paper than they do in real life. Take geography, which plays a major role in a family's school choice options. For example, more than half of Minnesota's 5.5 million people live within about a 50-mile radius of Minneapolis-St. Paul. If you're a parent, your child can choose dozens of urban and suburban high schools across the metropolitan area

PROFILE IN EDUCATION

Jonathan Kozol

For almost four decades, Kozol has given voice to the poor. In his best-selling book, *Savage Inequalities* (1991), he describes life in destitute schools from East St. Louis to the Bronx.

Read a full profile of Jonathan Kozol on Connect.

©Bettmann/Getty Images

connect

(depending on your tolerance for traffic). But say you live 300 miles north in International Falls (population 6,300) on the Canadian border; your child's nearest "alternative" high schools (all rural) are 22, 69, and 101 miles away.[49] Open enrollment (and other reforms) is beyond the reach of many rural families.

When smaller school districts gain students through open enrollment, increased per-pupil funding can allow those districts to expand programs for both local and open enrollment students. Not all competition centers on academics, however. For example, some smaller districts in "first-ring" suburbs offer all-day kindergarten, free breakfast, and transportation to attract families who live in nearby, large, urban districts.[50]

How does open enrollment affect academic performance? As with charter schools, the evidence is mixed. A 10-year study of open enrollment in Mahoning County, Ohio (including the "rust belt" city of Youngstown) found that students who moved to a new district for open enrollment performed at similar levels as those remaining in the home district. However, open enrollment students performed, on average, slightly above their peers in the *new* district, even if they had lower scores when they arrived. Researchers determined that both effects were amplified for students who left Youngstown City Schools, the very lowest-performing district in the county.[51]

Magnet Schools

A **magnet school** attracts students by offering one or more special programs, such as math, music production, language immersion, science, technology, and/or other specialties. Some magnets are associated with local institutions like museums or industry. In theory, highly regarded programs draw students from near and far like a magnet.

Some magnet-like schools have been around for many decades. In 1936, New York City founded the High School of Music & Art, whose graduates include Jennifer Aniston, Ellen Barkin, Al Pacino, and Wesley Snipes. Known today as LaGuardia School of Arts, prospective students still must pass a rigorous audition to get in. As many as 20,000 students are tested each year for admission to New York's Stuyvesant High School (founded 1904), specializing in mathematics, science, and technology. Only 800 or so are accepted. Over the decades, four Stuyvesant graduates went on to become Nobel Laureates. A few other large cities created similar schools during the twentieth century to offer high-quality programs for talented students.

In the 1960s and 1970s, the magnet idea gained additional momentum as a method to racially desegregate schools voluntarily. For example, an arts magnet school established in a predominantly African American neighborhood would draw interested white students from other neighborhoods or towns, and the result would be an integrated school. Once again, real life didn't always match the theory. While the *schools* integrated, many of the *classrooms* did not. Often, African American magnet school students were enrolled in the standard high school classes, while white students were enrolled in the magnet classes. As U.S. communities themselves grow more segregated by race and socioeconomic class, magnet schools are less able to integrate students.

Magnet schools offer specialized programs that build student talent.

©Hill Street Studios/Getty Images

Pearl-Cohn Entertainment Magnet (part of Metro Nashville Public Schools) is the first U.S. high school with its own student-run record label. Relentless Music Group partners with Warner Music Nashville to produce original student songs, music videos, and more. Donors gave the school a recording studio, control room, and two editing suites. Demonstrating a magnet school's innovative possibilities, Pearl-Cohn students use audio engineering problems to learn Algrebra-2.[52]

About 2.6 million students attend roughly 4,000 magnet schools today. Unfortunately, many suffer from underfunding, especially for essential services like student transportation (less glamourous than recording studios). Nevertheless, magnet schools tend to be more effective and racially integrated than public neighborhood or charter schools.[53]

Full Service Schools for the Whole Child

Who do you think is the most important person living in New York City? According to former Mayor Michael Bloomberg, it wasn't Jay Z, Sarah Jessica Parker, or even Donald Trump. Bloomberg named educator and community advocate Geoffrey Canada, who created the Harlem Children's Zone (HCZ), a nearly 100-block area of upper Manhattan known for its rich African-American and Latino culture–and its legacy of poverty. HCZ's community-based charter schools serve more than 12,000 children, but don't rely solely on teachers and principals. They also have dentists, nutritionists, drivers to help with transportation, and counselors helping parents and children create productive lives.

Nearly every U.S. community has a school, so school buildings are strategically located to provide non-academic community services. Creating such **full-service schools** can be tough in low-income neighborhoods, where school buildings are often underfunded and left in disrepair. Programs like HCZ tackle the challenge anyway. These schools are open most of the day and 11 months a year, recognizing that children cannot learn if their families are in distress or if they come to school tired, hungry, or abused.

How would you feel about teaching in a virtual school? What are the advantages and disadvantages?

©Tetra Images/Getty Images RF

"In communities where kids are failing in record numbers, you can't just do one thing," Canada says. "We start with children at birth and stay with them until they graduate from college. . . . In the end, you have to create a series of supports that really meet all of their needs."[54] Unfortunately, full-service schools are rare. The concept challenges educators *and* communities to radically shift their notions of what a school can do. Whether public or charter, full-service schools are expensive, impressive, and necessary.

Virtual Schools

"Distance learning" has been around since the invention of snail mail. As Internet use expanded, virtual learning exploded. Major universities now offer free Massive Open Online Courses (MOOCs) and degree programs, while virtual public and private schools offer courses and programs that students can complete on their home computers. In theory, **virtual schools** provide access to a wealth of online learning from pre-school through to university, without brick-and-mortar costs like maintenance of buildings, playgrounds, parking lots, and the like. Virtual schools are now an important–and controversial–part of school reform.

Virtual schools usually begin with specific goals in mind. Occasionally, they start by chance. In 2004, hedge fund analyst and MIT graduate Salman Khan received an urgent SOS from his young cousin Nadia. She was struggling with math in her Louisiana school, and didn't want to be put in a lower math track. Khan understood and began tutoring Nadia by phone (successfully) from a thousand miles away. Soon word got around the family: free tutoring from Salman. Before long, 15 cousins were on the phone. To lighten the load, Kahn created a Web site with instructional *YouTube* videos. Eventually, he and some colleagues created Khan Academy (www.khanacademy.org/), teaching 5,000 STEM courses and tutoring millions of students of all ages, at home, at school, and around the world—for free.[55]

FOCUS QUESTION 5

What are the advantages and disadvantages of teaching in a virtual school?

REFLECTION: Visit www.thevirtualhighschool.org/ and other virtual learning sites. What do you think of the pros and cons of K-12 online learning?

However, Khan Academy is an exception, rather than the rule. For instance, for-profit companies provide management, teacher training, curriculum, and assessment to about two-thirds of online charter schools. Like other charters, taxpayer, corporate, and philanthropic funding can make virtual schools profitable. At the same time, corporate support for online learning *in traditional schools* is growing rapidly. Millions of students and teachers use Google Apps, Skype, and other online tools in school. Facebook introduced a free student-directed learning system in partnership with the nonprofit Summit charter school network, while Amazon Inspire offers free instructional materials to teachers. (Chapter 10 explores problems with corporate-supported curricular materials.)[56]

Many virtual learning programs are organized as full-time charter high schools, offering an entire curriculum online. Some students find these schools to be quite personal, interactive, innovative, and well-suited to their learning styles. Advocates argue that virtual schools fill an important need and may hold the answer to a growing teacher shortage. They say that virtual learning is the future of education—especially if inexpensive models like MOOC begin to replace traditional college campuses.

Critics argue that distance education isolates students and deprives them of important, in-person social interactions. In addition, the data on virtual school effectiveness is discouraging. Comprehensive studies of about 200 online charter schools (serving 200,000 students in 26 states) found that more than two-thirds of the schools had weaker academic progress than similar brick-and-mortar schools. For instance, researchers said that math gains were statistically "as though the student did not go to school for the entire year." On average, annual online student achievement was equivalent to 180 fewer days of math learning and 72 fewer days in reading. While online charters have relatively high student-to-teacher ratios, they simultaneously have low student engagement, high student mobility, and limited live student–teacher contact. Most operate with no or very few tutors, teacher aides, instructional assistants, guidance counselors, and other support for students and their families. Synchronous teaching (with technologies like web conferencing, Skype, and phone calls) can replicate some in-person teaching interactions, but its potential remains largely untapped: "[S]tudents in a typical online charter school have less synchronous instructional time in a week than students in brick-and-mortar schools have in a day."[57]

A California investigation of one large, for-profit virtual school company found that less than 50 percent of the students who enroll in its online high schools "earn diplomas, and almost none of them are qualified to attend the state's public universities." The same report showed that "teachers were asked to inflate attendance and enrollment records," which then could artificially increase per-pupil taxpayer funding.[58] The virtual school model—individual students and teachers working in physical isolation—presents unique challenges for states, school districts, and families to monitor transparency and accountability.

These results should put a lot of pressure on state governments, local districts, and the for-profits and non-profits operating virtual schools to show rapid improvement. So far, it doesn't look like learning will outgrow school buildings anytime soon.

Home Schools

Thirteen-year-old Taylor works at the kitchen table, sorting out mathematical exponents. Travis, 10, is absorbed in *The Story of Jackie Robinson*, while Henry practices Beethoven's *Minuet in G* on his acoustic guitar. Last week, the three brothers saw a local performance of a musical comedy, attended a seminar on marine life, and (after hearing a news report) participated in a lively debate about corporal punishment in Singapore. They actively work with their parents and other adults in a homeschooling model that fosters self-directed, spontaneous learning. Henry, Travis, and Taylor spend more time with mom than dad, because he makes his living teaching other children at a local public high school.[59]

Homeschooling is a paradoxical form of school choice: the decision to educate a child at home, rather than send her or him to a neighborhood or any other school. About three percent of the school-age population was homeschooled in the 2011–12 school year. The highest percentage was white (83 percent), followed by Hispanic (7 percent), black (5 percent), and then Asian/ Pacific Islander (2 percent). Parents' most frequently stated reason for homeschooling their child (91 percent) is a concern about the environment of other schools.[60] Government regulation of homeschool families varies widely by state (see http://www.hslda.org/hs/ for specific state information). In 25 states, homeschool students don't undergo outside evaluation (like standardized testing); 14 states don't require specific subjects in a homeschool curriculum, and 11 don't even make homeschool families register with state or local education agencies.[61]

Many misconceptions persist about homeschooling, such as most homeschooling families are religious fundamentalists. While there are religious reasons for homeschooling families, there are other reasons as well. Some families opt for homeschooling to resist gender inequity, age segregation, lack of individualized attention, drugs, bullying, and peer pressure in schools. While hundreds of thousands of families homeschool, educational approaches differ. Some families may use a fixed curriculum seven hours a day, a fixed curriculum two or three hours a day, no curriculum at all (see A Closer Look: A World without Schools), online learning, classes or activities in a homeschooling group, classes or activities at a local high school or college, formal or informal service learning, or a combination of approaches.[62]

Critics point out that children learning in a physically isolated homeschool environment are also isolated from people with diverse beliefs and backgrounds. Such isolation could undermine the national cohesion goal for public schools to meld a single nation from people with differing backgrounds.[63] Homeschool advocates answer by citing how homeschooling's flexibility allows for volunteering, part-time employment, travel, and other non-traditional learning–with a wide range of social interaction with people of many backgrounds and ages.[64]

Several things put homeschooling out of reach for many families. Homeschooling usually requires that the entire family has flexibility–along with the motivation and means–to interact with children during the day. That is why the median annual income is between $75,000 and $80,000; over 80 percent of homeschool mothers do not work outside the home, and most homeschooling parents have a college degree.[65]

Some critics also express concern about homeschoolers using religious-influenced curricula that disparage evolution.[66] However, homeschooled children do quite well

A CLOSER LOOK

A World without Schools

In *Deschooling Society*, Ivan Illich compared schools to a medieval church, performing a more political role than an educational one. The diplomas and degrees issued by schools provide society's "stamp of approval," announcing who shall succeed, who shall be awarded status, and who shall remain in poverty. By compelling students to attend, by judging and labeling them, by confining them, and by discriminating among them, Illich believed that schools harm children. He would replace schools with lifelong and compulsory learning "networks." For Illich, waking up to a world without schools would be a dream fulfilled.

Education reformer John Holt agreed, and coined the term "un-schooling" to describe an education where kids, not parents or teachers, decide what they will learn. Holt believed that children do not need to be coerced into learning; they will do so naturally if given the freedom to follow their own interests and a rich assortment of resources. For unschooled kids, there are no mandatory books, no curriculum, no tests, and no grades. Children are given complete freedom to learn and explore whatever they choose—from Chinese to aesthetic mathematics to tuba lessons to the Burmese struggle for civil rights.

SOURCE: Ivan Illich, *Deschooling Society* (New York: Harper & Row, 1973); John Holt, *Instead of Education* (New York: Dutton, 1976).

REFLECTION: How are schools more a political than an educational institution? What would your community be like if it were de-schooled?

on school achievement tests and earn higher GPAs in college than conventionally schooled students. Professors describe them as more self-directed and willing to take risks than the traditional student. Even U.S. military academies, beginning with the Air Force Academy in the 1990s, accept homeschooled students.[67]

RAP 2.8

Visit a "Choice" School

While homeschooling may remain controversial—and impractical for many families—educators should avoid unsubstantiated myths, and consider using homeschool methods that can improve classroom learning.

Public Schools as Profit Centers

As we discussed above, numerous businesses are seizing opportunities for profit-making enterprises in school reform—especially charter and virtual schools. This trend is called **privatization:** transferring a public service, like education or prisons, to a private, for-profit business. Even within traditional neighborhood schools, businesses have a big stake in textbooks, transportation services, equipment like smart boards, security apparatus and personnel, tutoring services, standardized tests (and scoring those tests), and even performing clerical tasks like writing report cards.[68]

Business interests and wealthy individuals also influence the expansion of school reform that might become profitable. For example, Washington State voters soundly defeated a statewide initiative to establish public charter schools in 1996. They did so again in 2000. And again in 2004. But in 2012, a fourth public charter school initiative squeaked by with 50.69 percent of the vote. A small group of tech and retail billionaires spent more than six dollars per signature to get the 2012 initiative on the ballot, and millions on pro-charter advertising.[69]

Why are businesses so interested in schools? More than $500 billion is spent every year on K–12 education in the United States. Overall, education accounts for nine percent of the gross domestic product. The growing number of charter schools under private management has contributed to substantial profits.[70] However, charter

YOU BE THE JUDGE

For-Profit Schools

ARE A GOOD IDEA BECAUSE...

COMPETITION LEADS TO BETTER SCHOOLS

For-profit schools will break down the public-school monopoly by creating competition and choice. As schools compete, parents (particularly poor parents) will finally have alternatives to the neighborhood school. Just as in business, weak schools will lose students and declare "bankruptcy." The stronger schools will survive and prosper.

SCHOOLS CAN REWARD GOOD TEACHERS, AND REMOVE WEAK ONES

Today's public school bureaucracy protects too many incompetent teachers through tenure, and does not recognize teaching excellence. Using sound business practices, for-profit schools will reward superior teachers through profit-sharing incentives, retain competent teachers, and terminate ineffective teachers.

BUSINESS EFFICIENCY WILL IMPROVE SCHOOL PERFORMANCE

Education needs the skills and experience of successful businesses. For-profit schools will use a business culture to implement the most effective educational strategies. Top-heavy school management will be replaced by a handful of administrators, and empowered teachers will be driven to greater productivity through profit incentives.

FOCUSED PROGRAMS AND INVESTOR OVERSIGHT LEAD TO ACADEMIC SUCCESS

For-profit schools will improve education because they provide a focused and proven instructional plan. These schools avoid the public school pitfall of trying to offer "something for everyone." And if they falter and profits disappear, investor pressure will get them back on track.

ARE A BAD IDEA BECAUSE...

COMPETITION LEADS TO WEAKER SCHOOLS

Transplanting businesslike competition into the education arena would be a disaster. In addition to competition, business brings false advertising, "special" promotions, and "feel-good" experiences. Marketplace hucksterism will mislead and shortchange students and their parents. Worse yet, local public schools, which hold a community together, will be lost.

TEACHERS WILL LOSE THEIR INFLUENCE AND ACADEMIC FREEDOM

Teachers will have a brief career if they speak out against the company, or teach a controversial or politically sensitive topic. The business community talks a lot about teachers sharing in the profits but says little about what happens to teachers, facilities, and programs during economic hard times.

PROFITS AND EDUCATION DO NOT MIX

When the interests of for-profit school investors clash with the interests of children, investors will prevail. Market forces leave students, families, and educators with little leverage when stockholders fire business executives or cut educational resources to get better return on investment, or to get through economic and market fluctuations.

FOCUSED PROGRAMS MEANS KEEPING SOME STUDENTS OUT

For-profit schools' one-size-fits-all approach might be good for efficiency, but it's bad for individual students. More challenging students—like those with special needs, non-native speakers of English, or those who need special counseling—will be left behind for underfunded public schools to educate.

connect YOU DECIDE...

Do you believe that business and schools are a good or a bad match? Explain. Do you believe that profits should or could be made in schooling the nation's children? As a teacher, would you want to work for a for-profit school? Now here is your chance to be the author! What additional advantages and disadvantages of for-profit schools can you add to these lists?

school privatization hasn't led to better student achievement.[71] Many unsuccessful for-profit schools close and investors lose their money. For now, outsourcing discrete school services to businesses is a lot less risky and more profitable than creating, operating, and being accountable for a privatized charter school.[72] (What do you think about the notion of for-profit schools? See "You Be the Judge: For-Profit Schools.")

Environmentally friendly schools like this one in Denmark can enhance teaching and learning.

©Adam Mork/ArcaidImages/Getty Images

Green Schools

About half of U.S. schools have unsatisfactory indoor environmental conditions, one in five has unhealthy air quality, and about a third have school buildings that need extensive repairs. Many of the 60 million students, teachers, administrators, and staff spend their days in unhealthy school buildings—threatening their health and inhibiting effective learning.

Green schools, on the other hand, offer healthier environments with clean air and water, nourishing and natural foods, nontoxic cleaners, and regular outdoor activities. Green schools are a focal point of the environmental movement, reducing teacher and student illness and sick days. They promote energy efficiency and sustainability through recycling, solar and wind energy, and alternative means of transportation.

The U.S. Department of Education promotes this education reform by awarding a Green Ribbon to schools that do exemplary work in promoting environmental and sustainable education, use energy effectively, and create a healthy school climate. (For more, visit http://www.greenribbonschools.org/.) "Green" education doesn't necessarily mean retrofitting buildings or building new ones. For instance, Maryland joined the green school movement by requiring that all high school graduates be environmentally literate. Maryland schools have a great deal of independence in designing interdisciplinary programs to promote environmental understanding and action. Sustainability, smart growth, and the health of our natural world are now part of core subjects like science and social studies.[73]

GLOBAL VIEW

What country is doing the most to green its schools? Where is the lack of green schools particularly problematic?

A green school also uses its "greenness" to provide relevant learning opportunities. As part of Whitmore Lake (MI) High School's "Green Tech" program, students design shoebox-size cars that work on solar power, and investigate wind power.[74] The Chesapeake Bay Foundation created the No Child Left Inside program to overcome "nature deficit disorder." No Child Left Inside works with schools to develop a green curriculum and more active learning.[75] Most students (and teachers) embrace the green movement, and the Earth Day Network has the goal of greening all America's schools within a generation. Teacher retention and student test scores are higher in the healthier green school environments.

What Makes Schools Effective?

FOCUS QUESTION 6

What are the characteristics of effective schools?

As we've seen, both traditional schools and alternative schools can work really well—or very poorly. We believe that no single "form" of school holds the answer for every student. We also believe that every form of school must contain a core substance, or set of characteristics, if it hopes to serve its students effectively.

Imagine two different schools, Washington and Madison, located in the same neighborhood. They are about the same size, serve the same community, and have identical student populations. However, in Madison school, state test scores are low and half the students drop out. In Washington school, student test scores exceed the state average and nearly every student graduates. Why are the outcomes so different, when the schools have so many similarities?

Puzzled by this question, researchers attempted to determine what factors create successful schools. Several studies uncovered **five characteristics of effective schools**.[76]

RAP 2.3
Effective Schools

Factor 1: Strong Leadership

In her book *The Good High School*, **Sara Lawrence Lightfoot** drew portraits of six effective schools.[77] Atlanta's George Washington Carver High School and John F. Kennedy High School in the Bronx were inner-city schools. Highland Park High School outside Chicago and Brookline High School near Boston were upper- middle-class and suburban. Milton Academy (also near Boston) and St. Paul's High School in Concord, New Hampshire were elite preparatory schools. Despite the tremendous difference in their styles, textures, and environments–from a pastoral, rural campus to crowded inner-city blocks–these six schools all had strong, inspired leaders.

When Robert Mastruzzi started working at Kennedy High in the Bronx, there was no school. Workers built walls around him as he sat in an unfinished office and contemplated the challenge of opening a new school–while being a principal for the first time ever. During his years as principal of John F. Kennedy, Mastruzzi's leadership style has been collaborative, actively seeking faculty participation. He wants and expects his staff to participate in decision making. He encourages them to try new things, and use their right to fail. For example, one teacher organized a school rock concert but failed to have precautionary plans in place (800 adolescents showed up, many high or inebriated). Mastruzzi realized that the teacher learned from the experience, and let her try again. The second concert was a great success. "He sees failure as an opportunity for change," the teacher said. Other teachers describe him with superlatives, such as "he is the lifeblood of this organism" and "the greatest human being I have ever known."[78]

Researchers say that students make significant achievement gains in schools in which leaders:

- Articulate a clear school mission
- Are a visible presence in classrooms, hallways, and elsewhere
- Hold high expectations for teachers and students
- Spend a major portion of the day working with teachers to improve instruction
- Are actively involved in diagnosing instructional problems
- Create a positive school climate[79]

Factor 2: A Clear School Mission

In effective schools, even extremely busy principals somehow find time to develop and communicate a vision of what that school should be. Successful leaders clearly articulate the school's mission, and stress change, innovation, and improvement. In contrast, less effective principals are vague about their goals and focus on maintaining the status quo. They make such comments as, "We have a good school and a good faculty, and I want to keep it that way."[80]

Factor 3: A Safe and Orderly Climate

Good schools have safe environments.

©Thomas Barwick/Getty Images

Before students can learn or teachers can teach, schools must be safe. Despite horrific headlines about school shootings, today's classrooms and hallways are safer than they have been in years. Between 1992 and 2014, total school victimization rates for students ages 12–18 declined 82 percent. That follows the overall, decades-long reduction of violent crime across the United States; between 1992 and 2014, victimization of students ages 12–18 *away* from school dropped 86 percent.[81] Most teachers and students report feeling safe in school.[82] There are notable exceptions; for example, LGBTQA students are three times more likely than their peers to feel unsafe in school.[83]

Despite popular beliefs, metal detectors and school guards don't create a safe learning environment. Safe schools focus on academic achievement, the school mission, family and community involvement, and creating an environment of respect for teachers, students, and staff. Student problems are identified early, before they deteriorate into violence. School psychologists, special education programs, family social workers, and school-wide programs increase communication and reduce school tension.

In some of America's most distressed neighborhoods, safe schools provide a vital refuge for students. One John F. Kennedy High School student had no money for a winter coat or glasses to see the chalkboard, but she rode the subway 1 hour and 40 minutes each way to attend school. She never missed a day, because Kennedy was her harbor of hope, where she could learn in safety.[84]

GLOBAL VIEW

"Safe" schools are relative. Compared with children in 25 other industrialized countries, U.S. children are at greater risk. Every day in the United States, eight children or teens are killed by firearms, 186 children are arrested for violent offenses, and 368 children are arrested for drug offenses. Schools are safer, but not yet safe. Source: Children's Defense Fund, July 2011, www.childrens defense.org/factsfigures_ america.htm.

Factor 4: Monitoring Student Progress

As the researcher walked through the halls of Clearview Elementary School,[85] she noted attractive displays of student work mounted on the walls, alongside profiles clearly documenting class and school progress toward academic goals. Students had a clear sense of how they were doing in their studies by keeping progress charts in their notebooks. While interviewing faculty members, the researcher heard teachers talk about individual strengths and weaknesses of their students. Teachers referred to student folders that contained thorough records of student scores on standardized tests, as well as samples of classwork, homework, and performance on weekly tests.

The same researcher's visit to Foggy Bottom Elementary[86] disclosed striking differences. Bulletin boards and walls were attractive, but few student papers were posted, and there was no charting of progress toward academic goals. Interviews with students showed that they had only vague ideas of how they were doing or how to improve their academic performance. Teachers also seemed unclear about individual student progress. When pressed for more information, one teacher sent the researcher to the guidance office, saying, "I think they keep some records like the California Achievement Tests. Maybe they can give you what you're looking for."

The researcher's summary report stated: "A very likely reason that Clearview students achieve more than Foggy Bottom students is that one school carefully monitors student progress and communicates this information to students and parents. The other school does not."

Effective schools carefully monitor student progress with:

- Norm-referenced tests comparing individual students with others in a nationwide norm group (e.g., the Stanford, the Iowa Test of Basic Skills, or the SAT).
- Objective-referenced tests measuring whether a student has mastered a designated body of knowledge (e.g., state assessment tests).
- Teachers asking students to track their own progress in reaching course objectives—so they assume more responsibility for their own learning. These important measures of student learning are often overlooked.[87]
- Homework, which increases student achievement scores from the 50th to the 60th percentile. When teachers grade and comment on homework, achievement jumps to nearly the 80th percentile.[88] (How much homework to assign and what constitutes the most effective homework tasks continue to be points of contention.)

Factor 5: High Expectations

The teachers were excited. After eight months of work, a group of their gifted students received extraordinary scores on a test predicting intellectual achievement during the coming year—just as the teachers hoped and expected. But there was a catch—the teachers had been duped as part of a research project. The students identified as "gifted" had been selected completely at random. Nevertheless, these students showed significantly greater total IQ gains than a control group of children *not* identified as gifted. Without realizing it, the teachers created a self-fulfilling prophecy.

This famous experiment by researchers Robert Rosenthal and Lenore Jacobson seemed to show that students learn as much—or as little—as teachers expect.[89] While Rosenthal and Jacobson's 1968 methodology is often criticized, there is now extensive evidence showing that high **teacher expectations** do, in fact, produce high student achievement—and low expectations produce low achievement.[90]

When we recognize the incredible power of expectations, it's essential to examine how teacher, staff, and administrators' judgments (conscious or unconscious) shape expectations. For example, good-looking, well-dressed students fit a certain stereotype, so educators (and others) tend to think those students are smarter than their less attractive peers. Often, male students are thought (thus, expected) to be brighter in math, science, and technology, and girls are viewed (and expected) to do better in language skills. Students of color are sometimes perceived as less capable or intelligent—and hampered by lower expectations. One or two student "errors" can also influence expectations. Poor performance on a single standardized test (perhaps due to illness, stress at home, or an "off" day) can lead teachers to inaccurately belittle a student's ability for months or years to come. Even casual comments in the teachers' lounge can shape the expectations of other teachers throughout the school. When teachers hold low expectations for students, they often treat these students differently, in unconscious and subtle ways. Typically, they offer such students:

- Fewer opportunities to respond in class
- Less praise
- Less challenging work
- Fewer nonverbal signs of acknowledgment (eye contact, smiles, positive regard)

When our judgments, stereotypes, and assumptions remain unexamined, any resulting low expectations profoundly affect individual children—and undermine schools' social mobility and national cohesion goals.

In effective schools, educators hold high expectations that students can learn, and teachers translate those expectations into their behavior inside and outside the classroom. They set objectives, work toward mastery of those objectives, spend more time on instruction, and actively monitor student progress. They are convinced that students can succeed.

Equally key is whether *students* believe that high expectations are real—rather than lip service. If students don't know the expectations, or trust their integrity, the expectations are unlikely to work. Unfortunately, there is substantial disconnect between expectation beliefs in schools. Only 25 percent of students believe their secondary school holds high expectations for them, compared to 39 percent of teachers—but more than half of principals.[91] We need to do a better job of communicating these expectations to students and making certain that these expectations truly challenge students.

There is also evidence that when teachers hold high expectations for their own performance, the entire school benefits. At Brookline High School, "star" teachers were viewed as models to be emulated. Always striving for excellence, these teachers felt that no matter how well a class was taught, next time it could be taught better.[92]

Beyond the Five Characteristics

New research offers us additional factors and insights into what influences effective schooling:[93]

- *Early start.* The earlier schools start working with children, the better children do. High-quality programs during the first three years of life include parent training, special screening services, and developmentally appropriate learning opportunities for children. Such programs are rare, but those that are in operation have significantly raised IQ points and have enhanced language skills. However, school-based activities shouldn't overshadow the developmental and learning benefits of unstructured play away from school and natural family interaction at home. Estimates suggest that every dollar spent in early intervention programs saves school districts $7 in special programs and services later on.
- *Focus on reading and math.* When children can't read at grade level by the end of the first grade, they face a one-in-eight chance of ever catching up. Students who do not master basic math concepts also play catch-up throughout their school years. Effective schools identify and correct such deficiencies early, before student performance deteriorates.
- *School size.* Some studies find that, when compared to those attending large schools, students in small schools learn more, are more likely to pass their courses, are less prone to resort to violence, and are more likely to attend college. Studies also show that disadvantaged students in small schools outperform their peers in larger schools. Many large schools respond to these findings by reorganizing themselves into smaller units, or schools within schools. But this may be a bit simplistic, because students in some very large schools also do very well. More research is needed to clarify the importance of school size.
- *Smaller classes.* Although the research on class size is less powerful than the research on school size, some studies indicate that smaller classes are associated with increased student learning, especially in the earlier grades. Children in classes of 15 outperform students in classes of 25, even when the larger classes have a teacher's aide.
- *Increased learning time.* Though not an amazing insight, research tells us what we already suspect: More study results in more learning. Longer school days, longer

school years, more efficient use of school time, and more graded homework are all proven methods of enhancing academic learning time and student performance.

- *Professional Development.* Researcher Linda Darling-Hammond reports that the best way to improve school effectiveness is by investing in teacher training. Stronger teacher skills and qualifications lead to greater student learning. Conversely, students pay an academic price when they are taught by unqualified and uncertified teachers.
- *Parental involvement.* Learning is a cooperative venture, and a strong school–home partnership can build a more positive attitude toward academic achievement and social well-being. Such partnerships also build the trust needed for greater success. Not surprisingly, teachers' expectations for student success rise when parents become more engaged in school life. Technology can support school–home connection, although low-income and rural communities may have less digital access. Some schools use texting services, Twitter and/or other messaging platforms to engage families in school life.
- *Parent education and support.* Wealthy parents invest more time and money in their children, while poor families, often single-working-parent families, are stretched for time and resources. Schools and society need to close these gaps by taking a more active role in enriching the educational and social experiences poor children receive outside of school. If we don't, we risk creating or extending a two-tiered educational system, one for the wealthy, and a second-rate system for the poor.

From working with parents to monitoring student progress, research and experience will continue to offer insights into that pressing question, "What makes a school effective?" But the effort to reform U.S. education will not wait for all these relevant questions to be answered.

FOCUS QUESTION 7

What are the roles of teachers and students in reforming our schools?

Teachers and Reform

Are ineffective schools due to ineffective teachers—especially those unfortunately protected by tenure and unions, as critics argue?[94] Teacher salaries and job security are determined by unions, tenure, seniority, and advanced degrees. But graduate degrees and many years in a classroom do not equal teaching effectiveness. Both Democratic and Republican presidents have challenged tenure and teacher unions. "To say that we're under attack is an understatement," explained a Los Angeles union leader.[95]

Older teachers or teachers with graduate credits are not necessarily the most skilled. Let's take **tenure** as an example. Historically, if you teach well for your first three years or so, you will earn tenure, a job protection that guarantees or enhances your continued employment. Tenure has proven essential to **academic freedom** by protecting teachers from arbitrary dismissal if they teach an inconvenient fact, discuss an unpopular idea, or have a personality conflict with an administrator. But tenure also has been used to protect incompetent teachers. If you have had such a teacher, you know how bad the experience can be.

Recently, the focus of teacher evaluation has started to shift toward classroom performance. Teacher evaluations and salaries were linked to student test scores.[96] This approach is called **value added**—that is, how much value each teacher added to the student's education. In theory, value-added metrics would objectively determine which teachers are rewarded (with extra pay, for example) and which teachers are replaced. But as we've already learned, theory often sounds better in the description than in the reality.

Despite its popularity, dependence on student test scores to measure teacher effectiveness is fraught with problems. Many students don't test well, regardless of what they learned. Even if tests were perfect measures, test scores represent only one dimension of a person's education (more on this in Chapter 10). Then again, teachers are not the only factor influencing student scores. Fortunately, some teacher unions, administrators, researchers, and politicians are working together to develop more comprehensive and equitable evaluation methods, e.g., combining videotaped samples of teaching with student test scores to assess teacher effectiveness.[97] Other useful teacher evaluation data might include how class time is used, a nurturing and respectful classroom climate, and the quality of questions asked by both teacher *and* students. As one researcher put it: "Value-added scores don't seem to be measuring the quality and content of the work that students are doing in the classroom."[98]

Blaming teachers is a simplistic and discomforting part of the reform movement—particularly while few teachers are asked for their ideas for improving schools.[99] To begin addressing that problem, the nonprofit Education Sector surveyed more than 1,000 teachers on how they view the reform movement.[100] They found that most teachers support reform and change. Teachers (especially younger ones) reported that they do not feel comfortable in a system that rewards longevity rather than competence. Many teachers report knowing at least one colleague who should be fired, but they fear that firing incompetent teachers might put all teachers (and academic freedom) at risk. Meanwhile, in their effort to improve and/or gain more control over schools, many states have raised the bar for earning tenure, and in some cases, eliminated tenure entirely.[101] The erosion of tenure protection sets fear in motion for teachers, who have doubts that the changes will be fair to them and their students.

Another plan to bring accountability to teaching is **merit pay,** which bases a teacher's salary on performance. Merit pay certainly sounds fairer than seniority, but many merit pay systems base merit salary raises to a great extent on student test scores—a one-dimensional evaluation metric, as we discussed above.[102]

The Education Sector survey reported that almost 80 percent of teachers want a stronger teacher evaluation system, along with financial incentives for superior teachers—if they are fair. Many teachers, particularly young ones, are excited about the possibility of a higher salary and feel that too many weak teachers are paid the same as stronger ones. However, merit pay can strain relationships among teachers, raise serious questions about measuring classroom success, fan the fear of "playing politics," and create a sense of being manipulated by outside forces. Influential teacher organizations cautiously support merit pay, but don't want it based solely on student test scores.[103] They want local teachers involved in planning merit pay systems, and oppose plans that penalize teachers who work in under-resourced schools.[104]

History suggests that linking teacher pay to student performance may not work in the long term. Merit pay was first tried back in 1710 in England, with teacher salaries tied to student test results. You can probably predict the outcome: schools became all about test preparation.[105] Historians David Tyack and Larry Cuban write: "The history of merit performance-based salary plans has been a merry-go-round" as districts initially embrace merit pay, only to drop it after a brief trial. Despite these failures, school officials keep "proposing merit pay again and again."[106] Will it work this time? Will tenure disappear? Will skeptical teachers join the reform movement? It boils down to trust.

The Importance of Trust

After almost a decade of studying Chicago public schools, researchers found something both startling and obvious: Meaningful school governance, improvement, and reform depend on **trust**.[107] Teachers in schools without trust naturally cling to job security (like tenure) for protection and are unlikely to try new strategies. If we expect teachers to help reform their schools, they need to feel safe and trusted. They must also be genuinely part of the process. Teachers in trusting schools thrive, and so do their students. The researchers found that student academic performance improves when trust is present in a school.

You probably already know what a trusting school looks like. People respect one another, even when they disagree. Rude behavior is not tolerated. Teachers and parents listen carefully to each other, and they keep their word. Tenure is not used to protect weak teachers, and competent teachers are recognized for their talents. Educators willingly reach out to students, parents, and one another. Nothing is more important than the welfare and education of the students. We hear a great deal about school reform but too little about creating trust in schools. Clearly, if reform is going to work, teachers need to be trusted partners at the center of the effort. That isn't happening often enough, at least not yet.

Students and School Reform

If teachers feel left out of school reform, just imagine how students feel. Their opinions are rarely sought; their voices rarely heard. Elementary students who are asked to draw pictures of typical learning situations sketch teachers, chalkboards, and books, but not themselves. Their drawings show how disengaged elementary students feel from traditional classroom instruction. But when asked to draw learning activities they like, the children draw themselves as central in those activities.[108] Do children enjoy learning most when they are away from teachers and classrooms?

Nor do things improve at the high school level, where one in four students frequently arrives at school without paper, pencil, or homework.[109] Some call this "pretend attend," a situation where student bodies are in school but their minds and their interests are elsewhere. Many college students also are disengaged.

Many college students feel disengaged from classroom instruction. Visit "A Vision of Students Today" on YouTube to get a sense of their alienation.

Source: Michael Wesch, Kansas State University

Students in a Kansas State University anthropology class created a video titled "A Vision of Students Today," based on a survey of 200 college students. Students sitting in a large lecture hall depict the survey results by holding up signs like: "My average class size is 115." "18% of my teachers know my name." "My neighbor paid for this class, but never comes." "I spend two hours a day on my cell phone." "I Facebook through most of my classes." And then a close-up of a question written on the back of a chair: "If students learn what they do, what are they learning sitting here?" While the video, created in 2007, features some "old" technology (no tablets or smartphones), it remains a stunning example of college student alienation. Ironically, the students who produced it were probably very engaged in the activity. (See www.youtube.com/watch?v=dGCJ46vyR9o.)

Statistics suggest that students drop out of school more from boredom than from academic failure.[110] If students were engaged in education reform, what changes would they envision? Here's a sample of how middle and high school students throughout the United States and Canada answered that question:

- Take me seriously.
- Point me toward my goal.
- Challenge me to think.
- Make me feel important.
- Nurture my self-respect.
- Build on my interests.
- Show me I can make a difference.
- Tap my creativity.
- Let me do it my way.
- Bring out my best self.[111]

Some schools where trust is strong *do* listen to students.[112] In these rare schools, students participate in textbook selection, writing school behavior policies, and designing new school buildings. In some high schools, students participate in hiring the principal, teaching others how to use technology, mentoring younger children, researching their dream careers, and organizing school forums.

Too often, schools ignore students' social, emotional, psychological, and developmental needs. The Carnegie Council on Adolescent Development warns that a quarter of adolescents do not have caring relationships with adults, guidance in facing often overwhelming biological and psychological changes, the security of belonging to constructive peer groups, and the perception of future opportunity. Students report that when they feel sad or depressed, they turn for help to friends (77 percent) or family (63 percent) first. Only 33 percent of the time do they seek out educators.[113]

Connection between students' life experiences and their school relationships is crucial. Sadly, so is disconnection, as shown in the following incident at an elite school in a wealthy Midwest suburb:

> A student with a history of depression . . . had been seeing a local psychiatrist for several years. For the last few months, however, she had discontinued her psychotherapy and seemed to be showing steady improvement. Since September, her life had been invigorated by her work on *Godspell*—a student production that consumed her energies and provided her with an instant group of friends.
>
> After Godspell, her spirits and enthusiasm declined noticeably. After a visit to her psychiatrist, she killed herself.
>
> The day after, the school buzzed with rumors as students passed on the gruesome news—their faces showing fear and intrigue. . . . But I heard only one teacher speak of it openly and explicitly in class—the drama teacher who had produced *Godspell.* Her words brought tears and looks of terror in the eyes of her students. "We've lost a student today who was with us yesterday. We've got to decide where our priorities are. How important are your gold chains, your pretty clothes, your cars? . . . Where were we when she needed us? Foolish old woman that I am, I ask you this because I respect you. . . . While you still feel, damn it, feel . . . reach out to each other."[114]

FOCUS QUESTION 8

What are the unintended consequences of school reform?

Rethinking Reform

We conclude this chapter with some of our own thoughts on school reform. After decades of reform efforts and new education technology, today's schools still operate remarkably like the schools of a century ago. History teaches us that many past education reform efforts have fizzled, and we believe that the current reform movement is not doing well. We think the first step is to scrutinize many fundamental assumptions about public education (and how it can be improved)[115]:

Charter schools will improve education.

Some charter schools are impressive and successful. But, charters are no panacea. For example, most families and students making the extra effort to attend charter school are already highly motivated–which may explain a big part of charter success. National research strips away much of charter schools' glamour, documenting that about 80 percent perform at a level comparable to or "significantly" weaker than local public schools. We do not believe that charter schools alone are likely to improve the nation's schools.

Private schools are better than public schools.

This largely unchallenged assumption has prompted some state governments to increase private school enrollment through vouchers. Yet there is little evidence that students are better prepared academically or do better later in life because of a private school education. Parents' education, race, wealth, and other demographic factors are more predictive of academic and future success than the kind of school a child attends.

Merit pay will improve teaching and learning.

Many states have adopted teacher evaluations and merit pay as the path to better schools, but research does not support the concept that merit pay leads to better student achievement. In fact, most teachers are drawn to teaching for reasons other than salary–which, of course, doesn't justify paying them poorly. Most teachers also prefer cooperating rather than competing with their colleagues. Later in the text, we will explore what truly motivates teachers and students (hint: it is not merit pay).

Unions protect weak teachers.

Teacher unions fail when they protect incompetent teachers. But most unionized teachers are competent and work hard to promote student achievement. Teachers are not the only factor critical to student success. Some schools are in terrible shape, without basic facilities, instructional materials, or even adequate heat, plumbing, and insulation. In addition, students bring a myriad of dilemmas to school, including neglect; hunger; economic, medical, mental, and emotional problems; homelessness; and linguistic difficulties. It takes more than teachers to resolve these fundamental social problems. Most teachers are doing an admirable job, sometimes under difficult circumstances. While critics complain that teacher unions exist in some of the nation's weakest school districts, they also exist in the nation's strongest school districts. Many other nations that score high on international tests also have strong teacher unions. Finland, for example, trusts its unionized teachers to be at the center of education decision making, doesn't use standardized tests to evaluate teachers, and still comes out near the top of international testing scores.[116] It is illogical to cast unions as the culprit.

Schools are in deep decline.

As we discussed in Chapter 1, U.S. schools have not entered a new age of dramatic deterioration, despite the media headlines. For decades, the percentage of

Americans earning a high school diploma has risen. While U.S. students—especially those who are poor and English language learners—lag behind many students in Asia in some subject areas, many U.S. schools are performing well on the world stage. Since 1995, the typical U.S. elementary and middle school student scores have improved.

Test scores tell us which students, teachers, and schools are doing well.

Are the scores on high-stakes standardized tests the measure of an education? We believe that this measure of a person's education is short-sighted. An education should also honor a student's unique gifts, talents, creativity, and insights (more about this in the next chapter).

We must train workers to successfully compete in the world economy.

This goal brings us back to the central question we asked you at the beginning of this chapter: What is the purpose of schools? The current reform movement assumes a single, overarching purpose: to prepare workers to compete in a global economy. This is certainly a goal, but should it push aside all other goals? The many challenges facing our nation deserve schools' attention: the growing gap between the rich and the poor, a divided electorate, assimilating immigrants, overcoming racism and sexism . . . the list can go on and on. And every item on the list forces us to find multifaceted answers to the question: What's a school for?

CONNECT FOR *TEACHERS, SCHOOLS, AND SOCIETY*

connect

Check out Connect, McGraw-Hill Education's interactive learning environment, to:

Read Current and Historical Articles

Tackling the Toughest Turnaround—Low-Performing High Schools, by Daniel L. Duke and Martha Jacobson, *Phi Delta Kappan,* February 2011.

The Power of Personal Relationships, by Thomas S. Mawhinney and Laura L. Sagan, *Phi Delta Kappan,* February 2007.

Questionable Assumptions about Schooling, by Elliot Eisner, *Phi Delta Kappan,* May 2003.

Teaching against Idiocy, by Walter Parker, *Phi Delta Kappan,* January 2005.

Analyze Case Studies

Amy Rothman: A high school resource room teacher is confronted by a parent during a staffing meeting about a gifted, autistic student in her resource room for whom the parent wants a service not provided by the school district.

Chris Kettering: A teacher finds to his dismay that his white, middle-class students are not interested in social activism and that he is unable to promote awareness and openmindedness in them.

Watch Teachers, Students, and Classrooms in Action

Our **Online Video Album** for contemporary videos related to this chapter.

KEY TERMS AND PEOPLE

academic freedom, 268
acculturation, 245
charter school, 250
cultural transmitter, 249
five characteristics of effective schools, 264
Freire, Paulo, 246
full-service school, 258
Goodlad, John, 247
green schools, 263
homeschooling, 260
Lemon v. Kurtzman, 256
Lightfoot, Sarah Lawrence, 264
magnet school, 257
merit pay, 269
open enrollment, 256
privatization, 261
reconstructing society, 249
school goals, 244
service learning, 246
social cohesion, 245
teacher expectations, 266
tenure, 268
trust, 270
value added, 268
virtual schools, 258
voucher, 255
Waronker, Shimon, 254
Zelman v. Simmons-Harris, 256

DISCUSSION QUESTIONS AND ACTIVITIES

1. Discuss your list of school goals that you recorded with your classmates. Which goals seem to be most important to your peers? To your instructor? Which do you consider most important? Give reasons for your priorities.
2. Congratulations! You have been put in charge of designing the next charter school in your district. Describe the charter school that you would design. Be sure to include the research on effective schools in your description. Going beyond the current research, what unique factor(s) would you make part of your school because you believe they would contribute to an effective school?
3. Reform movements are not new, but the current one has been under way for a quarter of a century, and still has a great deal of momentum. How would you describe the strengths and weaknesses of this movement? Explain whether you believe it will succeed and strengthen U.S. schools—or come up short.
4. What do you think of private businesses contracting to run schools? What factors would cause you to seek or avoid teaching for a corporation? Would you feel secure in your job, even without tenure?
5. Does your local public school district have an official (or unofficial) policy concerning homeschooling? Do homeschooled students participate in any school activities or receive any school resources? How do you feel about these (un)official policies?

> *The difference between school and life? In school, you're taught a lesson and then given a test. In life, you're given a test that teaches you a lesson.*
>
> TOM BODETT

chapter 10

Curriculum, Standards, and Testing

Focus Questions

1. What is the formal curriculum taught in schools?
2. How does the invisible curriculum influence learning?
3. What is the place of the extracurriculum in school life?
4. What forces shape the school curriculum?
5. How does the Every Student Succeeds Act (ESSA) influence U.S. schools?
6. Why has the Common Core become so controversial?
7. What problems are created by high-stakes testing, and what are the alternatives?
8. How are cultural and political conflicts reflected in the school curriculum?
9. How has technology affected the curriculum?
10. What are some potential directions for tomorrow's curriculum?

Chapter Preview

"We shape our buildings and afterwards our buildings shape us," said Winston Churchill. Had the noted statesman been a noted educator, he might have rephrased his epigram: "We shape our curriculum and afterwards our curriculum shapes us." What children learn in school today shapes the kind of adults they will become and the kind of society they will help create. In fact, the long-term influence of curriculum makes it a powerful political topic—often detaching curriculum development from the realms of philosophy, research, and education practice.

Children learn through the formal curriculum, made up of objectives and textbook assignments. Reflect on your own schooling, and you'll recognize that students also learn important and often subtle lessons from the hidden, null, and extracurriculum. This chapter explores the process of deciding what should be taught in the nation's schools.

Several trends are pushing schools toward a more standardized curriculum: the indomitable textbook, technology in schools, and national emphasis on education goals, testing, and school accountability. Anti-test protests (no pun intended) have been growing against the increasing influence of standardized tests in general, and the notion of national (versus local) standards for public schools. The assumptions and problems of the Every Student Succeeds Act (ESSA), Common Core Standards, and high-stakes tests are explored in this chapter, as are more positive and creative ways of looking at curriculum, evaluation, and teacher accountability.

What We Teach

What do we want children to learn? Should the skills and information we teach change over time? If so, how much should it change? And who decides?

To help us understand these questions, take a few moments and write out your answers to this examination:

NOTE: Your Penmanship will be graded.

Grammar

1. Give nine rules for the use of capital letters.
2. Define verse, stanza, and paragraph.
3. What are the principal parts of a verb? Give principal parts of the verbs *do*, *lie*, *lay*, and *run*.

Arithmetic

1. District No. 33 has a valuation of $35,000. What is the necessary levy to carry on a school for seven months at $50 per month, and have $104 for incidentals?
2. What is the cost of a square farm at $15 per acre, the distance around which is 640 rods?
3. Write a bank check, a promissory note, and a receipt.

U.S. History

1. Give the epochs into which U.S. History is divided.
2. Tell what you can of the history of Kansas.
3. Describe three of the most prominent battles of the Rebellion.

Orthography

1. What are the following, and give examples of each: trigraph, subvocals, diphthong, cognate letters, lingual

2. Give four substitutes for caret "u."
3. Mark diacritically and divide into syllables the following, and name the sign that indicates the sound: card, ball, mercy, sir, odd, cell, rise, blood, fare, last.

Geography

1. Name and describe the following: Monrovia, Odessa, Denver, Manitoba, Heela, Yukon, St. Helena, Juan Fernandez, Aspinwall, and Orinoco.
2. Name all the republics of Europe and their capitals.
3. Describe the movements of the Earth. Give the inclination of the Earth.

Physiology

1. How does nutrition reach the circulation?
2. What is the function of the liver? Of the kidneys?
3. Give some general directions that you think would be beneficial to preserve the human body in a state of health.

How did you do? Well, if you bombed it, don't feel too badly; few of today's PhDs would pass. However, in 1895, Saline County, Kansas students had to pass this exam to qualify for graduation from *eighth grade*.[1] (The original exam is even longer!) Don't fret about your not-so-terrific answers, we know you are eighth-grade worthy! The deeper question: What does this test teach us?

It underscores how society's notion of what is important to learn can—and will—change. Yet, we also want to retain some level of basic and shared cultural knowledge. So, there will always be tension in schools and society around questions like how much emphasis teachers give to:

1. Shakespeare
2. Diphthongs
3. Computer science
4. Family life skills
5. Geometry
6. Post-Einsteinian physics
7. The North American conflict of 1861–1865 (also known as the Civil War, the War between the States, the Southern Rebellion, or the War of Northern Aggression)

The list could be much longer, and (see no. 7) we may not even agree what to call a subject area!

Much of what is taught in schools is tradition and conventional wisdom, representing curricular inertia rather than careful thought. It's not easy to find balance among the often-competing goals and values of conveying our cultural heritage, preparing children for an unknown future, and keeping curricula from obsolescence. If we did poorly on Saline County's exam, does that mean that today's schools are weaker than ones in 1890s (or 1980s)? If we failed, are we not truly educated? Or is "important knowledge" from one era not so important after all? How much of today's "critical" information will be merely a curious footnote in the years ahead? These crucial questions underlie every curriculum discussion.

FOCUS QUESTION 1

What is the formal curriculum taught in schools?

The Visible Curriculum

A **curriculum** refers to the set of courses, and their content, offered at a school or university. (It derives from the Latin verb "currere," meaning "to run or proceed," an understandable origin for the path of courses we expect students to proceed through.)

If you ask a teacher for a copy of the curriculum, you will likely be handed a curriculum guide, a description of courses offered, or perhaps syllabi describing what students are supposed to be learning in each subject at each grade level. If you ask the teacher for a more detailed curriculum, you might receive specific lesson plans for classroom activities that will enable students to meet those objectives. Educator Hilda Taba emphasized the importance of a school curriculum: "Learning in school differs from learning in life in that it is formally organized. It is the special function of the school to arrange the experiences of children and youth so that desirable learning takes place."[2]

GLOBAL VIEW

"Educational isolationism" is the term used to describe a lack of knowledge or interest in how others approach education. How can you avoid being an educational isolationist and learn about the curriculum in other schools, states, and nations?

A more accurate way to name textbooks, lesson plans, and arranged classroom experiences for learning is the **formal** or **explicit curriculum**. If you could go back in time (and in this text, you just did!), you soon realize that the formal curriculum changes with the values and needs of the time. If you were a student in colonial America in the 1660s, your formal curriculum would focus on religion and reading, the "two Rs." If you were a student in the 1960s, you would explore courses like Multicultural Education, Peace Studies, Ecology, and Women's Studies. But by the 1980s, schools were eliminating many of these electives and increasing the number of required courses. By the 2000s, emphasis shifted to more frequent testing. At each moment in history (including today), some concerned people inside and outside of schools protest the dominant educational approach.

FOCUS QUESTION 2

How does the invisible curriculum influence learning?

The Invisible Curriculum

Let's face it, some of the most powerful curricular lessons taught in school are not to be found in the formal curriculum at all. This "invisible curriculum" has two parts, and by describing each we hope to make it more visible for you. Let's start with what educators sometimes call the **implicit** or **hidden curriculum**–learning that is not *always* intended but emerges as students are shaped by the school culture, including the attitudes and behaviors of teachers. As an example, here is an analysis of a fourth-grade spelling bee offered by anthropologist Jules Henry, as he viewed the hidden curriculum of the elementary school: Team members were chosen by two team captains. When a student spelled a word correctly on the board, a "hit" was scored. When three spelling errors were made, the team was "out." Students cheered or groaned, depending on the outcome for their team. Do you see the hidden curriculum?

Henry says these students were learning powerful lessons: the importance of winning, the pain of losing, how competition can turn a friend into an adversary, the joy of being chosen early for a team, and the embarrassment and rejection of being chosen last. Some of the more thoughtful students may have seen the absurdity of a spelling lesson being taught as a baseball game.[3] Schools teach many powerful but hidden lessons, from the importance of punctuality to following the rules, from social conformity to respecting authority. Although some hidden lessons are useful, others can be destructive. The first step in evaluating the appropriateness of the hidden curriculum is to actually see it, then figure out what it is teaching. (See A Closer Look: Seven Forms of Bias).

Let's remove the veil from another part of the invisible curriculum, the many things that you do not learn in school. When a person or group decides that some

A CLOSER LOOK

Seven Forms of Bias

Although yesterday's starkly racist and sexist texts are thankfully gone, subtle bias persists. Here are descriptions of seven forms of bias that emerge in today's texts. These categories can identify bias toward racial and ethnic groups, the elderly, English language learners, females, gays and lesbians, and others. We will select examples from different groups to illustrate how bias emerges. By teaching your students about forms of bias, you can help them to become critical readers, detect bias when it occurs, and develop an important skill for lifelong learning and citizenship.

Invisibility: Before the 1960s, African Americans, Latinos, Asian Americans, women, and Native Americans were not even included in texts. Today, those with disabilities or gays and lesbians are often invisible in texts.

Stereotyping: When rigid roles or traits are assigned to all or most members of a group, a stereotype is born. Examples include portraying all African Americans as athletes, Mexican Americans as laborers, and women only in relation to their families.

Imbalance and Selectivity: Texts can perpetuate bias by presenting only one side of an issue; for example, describing how women were "given" the vote. In fact, women endured physical abuse and other sacrifices in their struggle to *gain* this and other civil rights. They were not "given" anything.

Unreality: Curricular materials often paint a shiny and unblemished portrait of the nation. (That's true for textbooks in other nations, too!) History and civics texts often ignore past unjust national actions, class differences, the lack of basic health care for tens of millions, as well as ongoing racism, classism, and sexism.

Fragmentation and Isolation: Have you ever seen a chapter or a section along the lines of "Ten Famous Asian Americans"? When texts isolate groups in this way—segregate them into a separate box or chapter—they subtly suggest that those groups are not part of society's mainstream.

Linguistic Bias: Consider texts using words like "roaming" and "wandering" to describe Native American culture. That language (inaccurately) suggests non-directed behavior and relationships, which helps implicitly justify the seizure of native lands for white Americans to "settle" or "civilize." Other examples are word choices like "men and their wives."

Cosmetic Bias: Cosmetic bias offers the "illusion of equity" to lure educators into purchasing books that appear current, diverse, and balanced. A science textbook brandishes many photos of women and people of color on its pages, and a female scientist on the cover. Further investigation reveals that there is little or no content on female or minority scientists inside. (That's right, you can't tell a book by its cover—or its photos.)

SOURCE: Myra Sadker and David Sadker developed this framework for Title IX equity workshops.

REFLECTION: These forms of bias emerge throughout our culture, and not just in textbooks. Choose a television program, a Web site, a movie, or a news show, and see how many of these biases you can identify.

topic is unimportant, inappropriate, too controversial, or not worth the time, that topic is never taught and becomes part of the **null curriculum**. Most of us experience the null curriculum when our history class does not get us to the present. If, for example, your American History class runs out of time at the end of the year and does not get to the Vietnam War, the students would not have learned about two Gulf Wars and the longest war in American history in Afghanistan; the fall of communism; a presidential impeachment; humanitarian disasters in Somalia, Syria, Haiti and elsewhere; widespread corporate corruption; the technology revolution; the September 11, 2001 attacks; several economic recessions; the election of the first African American President; and a rising populism (of both the left and the right) in the political sphere. But running out of time in school is not the only part of the null curriculum. The null curriculum takes a darker turn when there is a *conscious attempt to ensure that students do not learn a compelling topic that adults do not want them to learn*. When a school board decides not to teach about **climate change** (significant change in climate measurements lasting for an extended period[4]), **evolution** (the process of living organisms developing from earlier forms during the history of the earth[5]), or sex education (no parenthetical explanation needed here), the board's censorship makes these topics part of the rich, but invisible null curriculum. Imagine what students would learn if some enterprising educators created a charter school to focus on the null curriculum!

RAP 2.2
Curriculum Bias Detectors

CONTEMPORARY ISSUES

A View from the Field: Hear the Music

While schools across the country eliminate many extracurricular activities, Eric Schopmeyer, 36, an elementary school music teacher in Portland, Oregon, is fighting back. Despite the lack of any financial support from his school, Eric developed an extracurricular program that touches the lives of children.

Eric created a Zimbabwean-style marimba program for fourth to seventh graders at Marysville School. Though marimbas may not seem to be the intuitive choice for students just learning to play an instrument and read music, Eric explains that they have been a part of music education for years, albeit not in the United States. "This style of contemporary Zimbabwean marimba actually began as an educational tool in that country's schools about 50 years ago. Now, as more schools in the region incorporate marimba into their music curriculum, it is once again serving its original purpose."

Eric began the program in his second year of teaching, after earning a BA in music and a master's in education from Portland State University. Like many music teachers, Eric uses the Orff approach to music education. Not a strict methodology, the Orff approach attempts to engage a child's intrinsic creativity and playfulness. Observing a colleague playing his own marimba for a group of kids, Eric says that he "immediately recognized a strong resonance between the Orff ideas and marimba. The accessibility of the music to children may be the strongest advantage that a marimba band has."

The program has been wildly successful with the students. A recent look at test scores showed that almost all the children making the most significant academic improvements over the course of a year participated in the marimba band. The program only has room for half of the students who sign up, and being in the band has social significance among the students. "It's a dose of self-esteem," Eric says, "even for kids struggling academically. It's one place in school where they are excited and engaged. Seeing the way marimba ignites kids' creativity is one of the most amazing parts of teaching. There is great beauty in giving children the power to get their communities dancing."

Courtesy of Eric Schopmeyer.

The Extracurriculum

FOCUS QUESTION 3

What is the place of the extracurriculum in school life?

Now let's look at a vibrant ingredient of school life and learning not often perceived as curriculum at all. The **extracurriculum** teaches students lessons in school activities such as recess, sports, clubs, governance, and the student newspaper—all places where a great deal of learning occurs without tests or grades. A majority of students participate in at least one extracurricular activity, with students from smaller schools and with stronger academic records the most likely to be involved.[6] In high school, varsity sports attract more than half of the boys and about 40 percent of the girls.[7] Involvement in extracurricular activities reduces behavior problems and increases students' sense of belonging and academic engagement while also teaching lessons in leadership, teamwork, persistence, diligence, and fair play.[8] Though it may surprise some, the fastest-growing high school sport for both girls and boys is bowling, defying the perception that it is a sport of a bygone era.[9] About one student in four participates in music and drama, and about the same percentage joins academic clubs in science, languages, computers, debate, and the like—clubs that enhance both academic learning and social skills.

High school seniors involved in school activities are less likely to cut class, three times as likely to have a GPA of 3.0 or higher, and more likely to attend college when compared to students not involved in school activities.[10] Nationwide programs such as Odyssey of the Mind, National Forensics Study, and Scholars Bowl promote cross-curricular interests and creative problem-solving skills. (Such programs are far more likely to be found in suburban and urban schools serving white and wealthier children than elsewhere.) Advocates see these activities as so important that they refer to them not as the extracurriculum but as the cocurriculum, and believe that their value goes far beyond the high school years.

Participation in extracurricular activities is correlated with:

- Enriched student life and learning
- Higher student self-esteem, school completion, and civic participation

- Improved race relations
- Higher grades and SAT scores
- Better health and less conformity to gender stereotypes
- Higher career aspirations, especially for boys from poor backgrounds[11]

Extracurricular activities enrich student life and learning.

©2A Images/Getty Images RF

But the extracurriculum is not without problems. The underrepresentation of low socioeconomic students is evident in many programs, as are gender differences in participation in performing arts, athletics, school government, and literary activities.[12] Skeptics suggest that "the effects of extracurricular participation on secondary school students' personal development and academic achievement are probably positive, but very modest, and are definitely different among students with different social or intellectual backgrounds."[13] Given the current emphasis on test scores and academic standards, some people view extracurricular activities as little more than a distraction.[14] In Texas and other states, "no pass, no play" rules deny students in poor academic standing the right to participate in varsity sports. In other communities, budget tightening means "pay to play," in which a fee is required for sports participation, posing a serious problem for low-income families and students. Such policies raise complex questions and issues. Should academic performance and financial constraints be factors in deciding who participates in extracurricular activities? The top academic students, more likely to be wealthy and white, already dominate the extracurriculum, so will "pay to play" and "pass to play" regulations make extracurriculum even more exclusive, driving deeper divisions between the haves and the have-nots and further segregating racial and ethnic groups?

Textbooks: Curriculum Bedrock

Although all three curriculums are powerful, the public and the press typically focus on the most visible—the formal, or explicit (also called the official) curriculum—when evaluating schools. Given the current emphasis on standards and testing, and recurrent controversies (e.g., whether to include climate change, evolution, or religion in the curriculum), the official curriculum is constantly in the news.

The textbook is the most visible element of the formal curriculum. In many ways, the textbook functions as our current de facto national curriculum. Students around the nation study from the same books, do the same exercises, and are expected to master the same material. Studies reveal that students spend as much as 95 percent of classroom time using textbooks. Teachers base more than 70 percent of their instructional decisions and as much as 90 percent of homework assignments on the text.[15]

Textbook publishing is also big business, with potential customers in the United States of 13,000-plus public school districts, 132,000 schools, 3.2 million teachers, and 50 million students annually.[16] No wonder some believe that textbooks rule.

However, many people are frustrated with the quality of textbooks. The story starts with textbook adoption states. About half the states, located mainly in the South and the West, require local districts to select their texts from an official, state-approved list (see Figure 10.1). To a large degree, these "textbook adoption" states (including big states like California, Florida, and New York) determine textbook content nationwide; it's more profitable to publishers to sell "Florida-approved" books to Oklahoma then it is to customize texts for smaller states (see Digging Deeper: The Power of the Textbook).

FIGURE 10.1

Textbook adoption states. Although some school districts are free to choose any text, others are limited to state-approved textbooks.

SOURCE: State Instructional Materials Review Association, 2014.

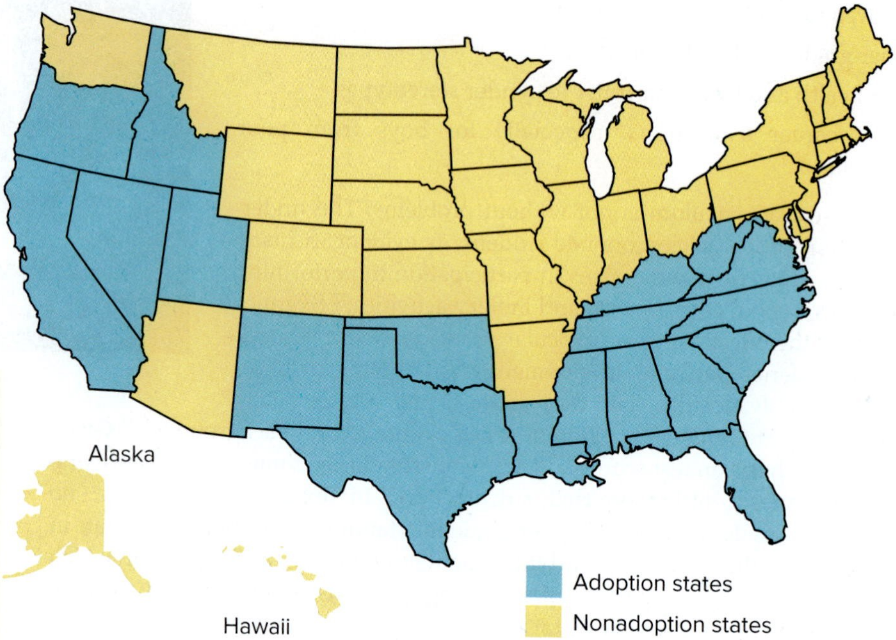

REFLECTION: What patterns do you notice in the states that require texts be selected from an approved list? Would such state adoption procedures be a factor in deciding where you might teach? Visit the site for updates at www.publishers.org.

Who and What Shape the Curriculum?

FOCUS QUESTION 4

What forces shape the school curriculum?

As a future teacher, it makes a lot of sense for you to begin thinking about who decides *what* you should teach. In fact, what you teach is decided by competing interest groups, and the final product sometimes seems bland and/or a hard-to-swallow stew. (See Figure 10.2.) Anyone from the President of the United States to an individual parent can have an impact on what is taught in your classroom. Let's take a brief tour of some of the chefs working to add or subtract from the curricular recipe.

Teachers

Teachers develop curriculum formally and informally. They may serve on textbook selection committees that determine the materials a school purchases, or they may help develop a district's curriculum. In less formal but still powerful ways, classroom teachers interpret and adapt the official text or curriculum guide, stressing certain points, giving scant attention to other points, and/or supplementing texts(s) with teacher-made materials or directing students to the Internet.

Students

During the 1960s and 1970s, student protests demanded curricular relevance. While overt protests have waned, most students still have some curricular choice in selecting topics for independent projects, research papers, book reviews, and authentic learning.

State Government

States are now assuming a larger role in education under the federal Every Student Succeeds Act (more on ESSA below), and their interest in curriculum matters has sharpened through state standards and tests, curriculum guides, and frameworks

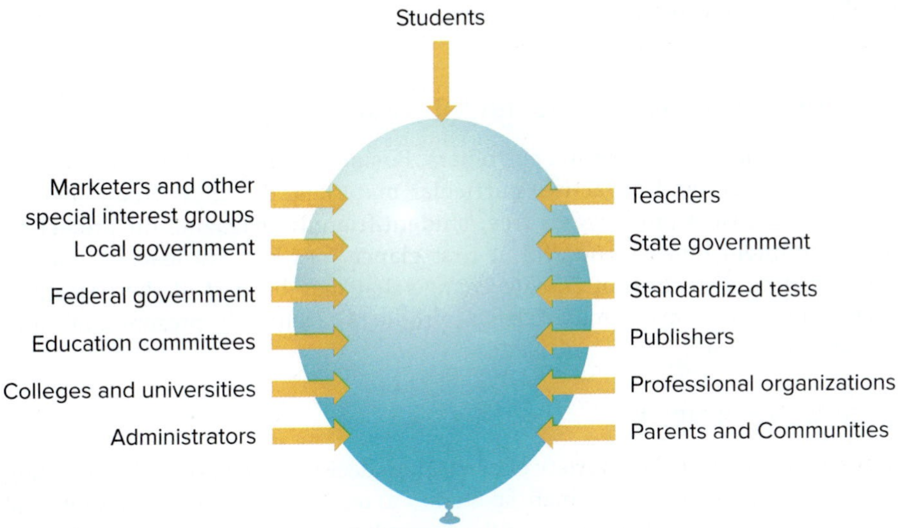

FIGURE 10.2
Numerous, sometimes opposing, groups shape the curriculum.

REFLECTION: What groups today exert the most influence on the curriculum? Do you see all these groups as a mark of democratic participation, or an inappropriate intrusion in curricular decision making?

for all schools to follow. In some states, textbook adoption committees have a large role. Tensions flow from debates on including or excluding religion, science, cultural diversity, and other hot-button issues.

Standardized Tests

The results of state and national tests (including legally mandated annual tests, state graduation tests, AP exams, SATs, and ACTs) influence what is taught in school. If students perform poorly in one or more areas of these standardized tests, government and/or public pressure pushes school officials to raise those test scores.

Publishers

The major goal of textbook publishers is—not surprisingly—to sell books. That is why textbooks are attractively packaged and chock full of terms and names deemed important at the time (including this text!). Many elementary and secondary schools must choose from a list of state-approved textbooks, limiting choices and options. To get onto those lists, publishers may forego in-depth coverage of topics and avoid unpopular points of view. Teachers need to remember that textbooks are published to meet market demands, and not necessarily to offer objective or complex viewpoints.

Professional Organizations

Professional organizations (e.g., Association for Supervision and Curriculum Development, Association for Educational Communications and Technology, International Society for Technology in Education, and International Reading Association) publish journals and hold conferences on curriculum development. Their programs and materials help teachers and administrators in several areas, from technology to authentic learning.

Parental and Community Groups

Parents can advocate for more rigorous academic courses, higher scores on standardized tests, greater access to technology, or other practices. Conservative parents and communities may object to the absence of Christian values in the curriculum, while liberal families and communities may demand elimination of gender and racial stereotypes in the curriculum.

Marketers and Other Special Interest Groups

GLOBAL VIEW

How does the peopling of America affect schools? Visit the *Americans All* Web site at www.americansall.com/ to see its large and inclusive electronic database on our immigration history.

Today's students are tomorrow's customers. Businesses seeking future customers may provide free (and attractive) curricular materials. But these free materials come with a cost. Company X's free, student-friendly magazine on protecting the environment looks wonderful at first glance, but how do teachers handle self-promoting distortion of climate change that may be part of the narrative? Teachers need to examine materials and products carefully to present a fair and accurate view.[17]

Local Government

Local school boards make a variety of curriculum decisions, requiring or prohibiting courses from sex education to financial literacy to technology. Supporters want local school boards to have a strong voice in the curriculum, because they are closest to the needs of the local community and the interests of the students. Others feel that local elected school board members often lack the professional training to make informed curricular decisions.

Federal Government

The federal government influences the curriculum through judicial decisions, financial incentives, and legislation. ESSA and federal support of a common core of standards for all states is one recent example of the power it can exert.

Education Commissions and Committees

GLOBAL VIEW

Perestroika, a Brazilian school, has placed student personal experiences, societal needs, and an emphasis on doing at the heart of its education programs, allowing students to shape their own learning. Visit www.perestroika.com.br/.

Nonprofits and local, state, and/or national governments have created various committees to study education at many points in U.S. history. In 2010, for example, the Council of Chief State School Officers and the National Governors Association developed **Common Core State Standards**, identifying the math and English skills and knowledge students should master at each grade level from kindergarten to grade 12 (more on this later). Most states adopted these standards.

Colleges and Universities

Post-secondary institutions influence curricula through their entrance requirements, which spell out courses high school students must take to gain admittance. As A. Bartlett Giamatti noted when he was president of Yale University:

> The high schools in this country are always at the mercy of the colleges. The colleges change their requirements and their admissions criteria and the high schools . . . are constantly trying to catch up with what the colleges are thinking. When the colleges don't seem to know what they think over a period of time, it's no wonder that this oscillation takes place all the way through the system.[18]

Administrators

Principals and other administrators can set the school's priorities, from raising test scores (all too common) to investing (or eliminating) arts education.

FOCUS QUESTION 5

How does the Every Student Succeeds Act (ESSA) influence U.S. schools?

Every Student Succeeds Act (ESSA) and the Testing Culture

When the federal **Every Student Succeeds Act** (ESSA) became law in late 2015, some supporters hoped for an end to the controversial effects of **No Child Left Behind** (NCLB), the 2001 law designed to raise school standards and accountability nationwide. Historically, the individual states were responsible for their own schools' quality, so NCLB (supported by both Republicans and Democrats) represented the increased federal government emphasis on student achievement. The Department of Education would provide more money to encourage states to test students and punish schools where students did not test well. Widely heralded at first, NCLB's approach proved neither popular nor effective.

Under NCLB, a school that continually posted weak test scores would be labeled "underperforming" (some said "failing"). When that happened, NCLB called on states to close or reorganize the failing school, and/or fire its teachers and principal. Students at the "failed" school would then have to attend other schools—which would themselves face greater risk for "failure" and shutdown, as they tried to absorb blocks of new students with low test scores. The ripple effect led to even more schools labeled as failing. The lives of students, teachers, administrators and parents were continually affected by test scores—and not in a good way!

Even some early NCLB advocates turned against the law. Former Undersecretary of Education Diane Ravitch (part of the team that initially implemented NCLB) later became a harsh critic, saying it funneled money away from public schools and to private companies that sell tests or run charter schools—without any evidence that either approach improves education. She railed against creating test-takers, rather than improving real learning, and lamented the elimination of arts, physical education, foreign language, and history in the curriculum. She no longer believed that **high-stakes tests** led to improved schools.[19]

One problem was dramatic inconsistency in test scores from state to state (more about this below in "Common Core"). Meanwhile, after years of NCLB, American students continued to score well below their European and Asian peers in reading, science, and math. According to the 2015 Program for International Student Assessment (PISA), United States 15-year-olds performed well below other developed nations in math, ranking 36 out of 69 countries. Almost a third of U.S. 15-year-olds fell in the "low-performing" category in math, and our percentage of *high-performing* math students (5.9 percent) was far below the international average (10.7 percent).[20] Sounds terrible, but it is also important to point out that national averages hide significant differences among schools and communities. Some of our school districts, often the wealthier ones, score near the top on these international tests, while our poorest schools score near the bottom. The public does not always understand such statistical subtleties, and therefore often believe that "bad" U.S. test scores on international exams mean that our schools are not doing well.

Deeper evaluation of PISA results shows a more complex and useful picture than simplistic year-to-year comparisons of how the U.S. is doing. Years of analysis by the Organization for Economic Cooperation and Development indicates that a country's students tend to score higher if the country:

- Make the teaching profession more selective and prestigious
- Enroll children in high-quality preschools
- Provide more resources to the neediest children

- Establish school cultures of constant improvement
- Apply consistent and rigorous standards in every classroom

Political leaders and educators were faced with a major challenge: How would they improve student learning and the nation's test scores? Federal lawmakers opted for a modified approach with ESSA, with its reduced emphasis on test scores and the drastic consequences that low test scores had triggered.

While ESSA is less draconian and detailed than NCLB, it is still intended to identify schools in need of improvement. For example, ESSA makes "failing" schools subject to state takeover, without specifying what a takeover means.[21] Under ESSA, a failing school is defined as one that:

- Is in the bottom 5 percent of assessment test scores
- Has student subgroups which consistently underperform on standardized tests
- Graduates fewer than 67 percent of students

Once these schools are identified, states are expected to develop their own strategies to improve them. This might include penalties or additional investments in the school, a stick or a carrot approach.

When signing ESSA into law, former President Obama criticized NCLB because it "often forced schools and school districts into cookie cutter reforms that didn't always produce the kinds of results that we wanted to see."[22] While ESSA returns more decision making to the states, some worry that the testing culture will continue unabated. Others are concerned that the Trump administration will go in the opposite direction and decrease school accountability. This new federal administration, less enamored with federal regulations, might simply look the other way if schools are failing, allowing states to look the other way as well. If states avoid all testing, schools in minority and poor neighborhoods might be left to falter, with students put in even greater jeopardy. We need testing to know what is going on, but we need to avoid over-testing that is self-defeating.

Here are some other important aspects of ESSA:

Less federal accountability of state performance: States have almost all the responsibility for school, student, and teacher accountability. For instance, ESSA prohibits the federal government from mandating how to perform teacher evaluations, or what grades students need to obtain on a test. While the U.S. Department of Education retains some oversight, ESSA reduces the power of the Secretary of Education to dictate specific mandates.

Annual testing flexibility. ESSA initially required standardized reading and math tests in grades 3–8 and once in high school. However, it promises more flexibility than under NCLB. For example, parents can choose to have their children skip standardized tests. Schools can break up one critical test into smaller tests, or develop alternative methods to measure student learning differently. States might weaken or eliminate tests entirely, influencing graduation rates. [23]

Eliminates Adequate Yearly Progress (AYP). NCLB's rigid and nationally mandated Academic Yearly Progress system strove to reach 100 percent proficiency in math and reading. ESSA allows states to determine more their own scoring targets.

As ESSA replacing NCLB demonstrates, political and policy winds change direction, sometimes quickly and sometimes slowly. By the time you read this, ESSA might be well established and implemented—or weakened, ignored, and for all practical purposes eliminated by a new administration. Will ESSA and/or other

A CLOSER LOOK

Common Core Standards

What do the Common Core's mathematics and English standards look like? They can be quite broad, allowing room for teachers, publishers, and school districts to develop a curriculum to meet the goals. Here's a sample:

MATHEMATICS

- Make sense of problems and persevere in solving them.
- Reason abstractly and quantitatively.
- Construct viable arguments and critique the reasoning of others.
- Attend to precision.
- Use appropriate tools strategically.
- Look for and make use of reasoning.

ENGLISH AND LANGUAGE ARTS

- Read and comprehend why complex individuals, events, and ideas develop and interact over the course of a text.
- Read and comprehend complex literary and informational texts independently and proficiently.
- Integrate and evaluate content presented in diverse formats and media, including visually and quantitatively, as well as in words.
- Develop and strengthen writing as needed by planning, revising, editing, rewriting, or trying a new approach.
- Use technology, including the Internet, to produce and publish writing and to interact and collaborate with others.

REFLECTION: How do you feel about the idea of teaching to national standards? What is lost, and what is gained? For more information, visit www.corestandards.org.

reforms radically change the face of U.S. education, solve NCLB's problems, or create new ones? Will states loosen standards so much that they become meaningless, or implement meaningful reform? Your guess is as good as ours. In terms of your own career, you might want to explore the specific state where you plan to teach. How is it evaluating schools and students under ESSA? After all, you have a lot at stake in the laws and controversies likely to continue roiling education.[24]

FOCUS QUESTION 6

Why has the Common Core become so controversial?

The Common Core

As we have seen, our school curriculum is a hodge-podge, developed by different groups and varying from state to state. Test results reflect that confusion. For instance, almost every student in Mississippi was passing the *state* mathematics exam on the first attempt, while 35 percent of the students in Arizona were failing. Were Mississippi's students brighter, or harder working than Arizona's? Or was something else going on? Here's a clue: on *national* tests, Mississippi students performed poorly. Why are some state test results so different from national outcomes? Clearly, some state tests were less demanding, the passing score was lower, and students were learning less. There was little consistency on student performance from state to state, a situation that was both unprofessional and embarrassing.

RAP 2.4 State and National Curricular Standards

To address these problems, governors and other leaders from 48 states, two territories, and the District of Columbia met in 2009 to develop a single set of **Common Core State Standards** for curriculum in all states. (See A Closer Look: Common Core Standards. You can also visit www.corestandards.org for more information.) Many educators and policymakers cheered: "About time!" Usually referred to as the **Common Core**, the standards aim to ensure that all students, regardless of where they live, will graduate from high school with "a consistent, clear understanding" of

YOU BE THE JUDGE

A Common Core of Standards

IS DESIRABLE BECAUSE . . .

EDUCATORS WILL BE HELD ACCOUNTABLE

Testing all students in all schools on the same standards will enable us to compare school effectiveness in different regions of the country. We will discover who is learning adequately and who is not.

IT MAKES US MORE COMPETITIVE

Many of today's high school graduates lack basic literacy skills, a result of weak standards and poor accountability. To compete in world markets, we must have strong national standards and tests to ensure a first-class labor force.

TEACHERS WORK COLLABORATIVELY RATHER THAN IN ISOLATION

A common set of standards promotes cooperation. Teachers and principals work together to identify problems, develop instructional solutions, and collaborate as a professional team working to ensure that all the standards are met.

IT BINDS OUR CITIZENS

Common Core Standards unify students in our common heritage. One set of standards will coalesce the nation's diverse ethnic and cultural communities.

IS A MISTAKE BECAUSE . . .

STANDARDIZED TESTS DETRACT FROM LEARNING

Schools take time away from interesting learning activities to prepare for a high-stakes test. This flies in the face of authentic education and ignores all that we have learned about multiple intelligences and individual differences.

FOR SOME, THE NATIONAL STANDARDS ARE A STEP BACKWARD

Standards in the nation's best school districts exceed this common core, so focusing on weaker core standards can lower the quality and excellence of their students' education.

TEACHERS WORK COMPETITIVELY RATHER THAN COOPERATIVELY

Student test scores are used to evaluate teachers, so many teachers feel that test preparation is necessary to ensure that their students score high enough for the teacher to avoid career problems. Survival of the fittest becomes the norm.

IT WILL DIVIDE THE NATION

In the end, all states are unlikely to agree on a single set of standards in subjects like history and science. The futile effort to create core standards will make it apparent to all that we are a divided people.

PROFILE IN EDUCATION

Alfie Kohn

Alfie Kohn is an active

proponent for engaged learning. He challenges high-stakes testing, arguing that every hour spent on such exam preparation is an hour not spent helping students to think creatively, to tackle controversial issues, and to love learning.

Both teachers and students often find that a testing culture diminishes education to a test score.

Read a full profile of Alfie Kohn on Connect.

Source: Courtesy of Alfie Kohn

connect

the key concepts and skills they need. But sometimes good ideas go awry, and the Common Core has become a disappointing national controversy.[25]

The Common Core is intended to bring more rigor to the curriculum, and reflect a national consensus on what all American students should learn. Fewer topics would be covered, but greater depth and mastery required. Each state still retains the freedom to define the curriculum and identify the materials appropriate for its own students. They agree on the skills and knowledge students should possess, but how to reach those outcomes is left to the states to decide. (See You Be the Judge: A Common Core of Standards.) Supporters point out that Common Core Standards lead to high school graduates better prepared for college and careers, allow more accurate state-to-state comparisons of schools performance, and ease the transition for students moving from one state to another.[26]

Finally, a more coherent, nationwide approach to improving our schools. Or is it? There are real doubts that core standards pave a path to a better education. Critics say the mandated standards and associated testing are onerous and handcuff teachers. During a Clifton, New Jersey school board election debate, every candidate criticized Common Core for turning teachers into "trainers," hurting education, and diverting education funding to private curriculum and testing companies. "If we care about our students, we'll protest it and fight back for real education," one candidate said.[27]

As you can detect from such comments, time has not been an ally of the Common Core. Both conservative and liberal politicians have voiced objections, as well as some respected educators.[28] Here are some of those concerns (with new ones emerging on a regular basis!):

There is not a consensus on the core standards. Different states want stronger standards for fiction reading, feel the math standards are too weak, or oppose topics like climate change and evolution (more on this later in the chapter). Some states even hold different views of what the history standards should be! The idea of a consensus on core curriculum standards has evaporated.[29]

Not all states sign on. While most states are onboard, not all are, and some are abandoning ship. Some states invest little time or resources in preparing their schools and teachers to put the standards into practice, and so there are implementation problems.[30]

Some question whether preparation for college admission or employment should be the only focus of K–12 schooling.[31] A well-rounded education features the arts, social sciences, active citizenship, physical education, caring human relations, creativity, and health concerns—but these and other goals are being submerged in Common Core's narrowed focus.

Is a single set of Common Core Standards desirable? Critics like Alfie Kohn (see Profiles in Education on Connect) wonder if it's wise to require students from different states, backgrounds, skills, and talents to meet one set of standards. He fears that common standards will simply lead to standardization, not quality education. He is not alone.[32]

Are Common Core Standards the right direction for U.S. schools? A common set of standards is no educational panacea. Stanford University professor Linda Darling-Hammond points out that students from Finland learn without such detailed standards, yet do strikingly well on international tests. In fact, Finland improved its students' test scores by doing quite the opposite, shifting "to a more localized system in which highly trained teachers design curriculum around very lean national standards."[33] Students from countries with national standards scored at both *the bottom and the top* on international tests in math and science. So, while the standards movement is popular with some, it doesn't guarantee better schools. (See A Closer Look: The Common Core: Myths and Buts).

GLOBAL VIEW

The Council of Foreign Relations issued a report in 2012 that warned the failure of the nation's schools to produce quality graduates "undermine[s] American security" and economic well being in the future. Do you agree?

The Problem with High-Stakes Standardized Tests

FOCUS QUESTION 7

What problems are created by high-stakes testing, and what are the alternatives?

Although it may sound as if we are anti-testing, we are not. Standardized tests can help educators analyze the curriculum and teaching methods to see what's working or what needs to be changed. A **standardized test** requires all test takers to answer the same questions, so that student and teacher performance can be compared. Students who do not do well or teaching methods that are not working can be identified and corrected. But high-stakes standardized tests are another story. **High-stakes tests** are used to make important decisions about students, educators, schools, or districts. Such tests are used to determine punishments (like reduced school funding), accolades (the "best" schools, teachers, or students), advancement (graduation), or salary increases. These tests are more likely to create havoc and hurt than to solve problems.[34]

Take the case of a New York City middle school preparing for a state-mandated, multiple-choice math test. The principal asked all teachers (regardless of subject area) to spend 15 minutes a day with students practicing how to answer test questions. When a language teacher protested, the principal insisted, because he, the school, the teachers, and the students would all be measured by this high-stakes test. As you might suspect, the plan failed, and fewer than one in four of these students passed the exam.

A CLOSER LOOK

The Common Core: Myths and Buts

MYTH 1: THE COMMON CORE IS A FEDERAL TAKEOVER OF PUBLIC EDUCATION.

Several nonprofits and the states, including the National Governors Association and the Council of Chief State School Officers, came together to create and promote the Common Core. The Common Core was not spearheaded by the federal government.

BUT the federal government is a major supporter and proponent of the Core.

MYTH 2: THE COMMON CORE IS A NATIONAL CURRICULUM.

The core is a set of *standards,* not a curriculum. Common Core identifies, in a general way, what students should know and be able to do from grade school through high school.

BUT it can become a curriculum. Curriculum guidelines tied to Common Core have emerged from several sources, and textbook publishers and school districts in different states have developed and often use the same prepackaged lessons.

MYTH 3: THE BUSINESS COMMUNITY IS NOT INVOLVED IN THE COMMON CORE.

The business community may or may not have been a major player originally.

BUT the Common Core is creating a national marketplace for vendors of textbooks, software and hardware, and testing companies. Businesses are exploring the goods and services they can provide on a massive scale to schools throughout the nation.

MYTH 4: COMMON CORE WILL USE A BETTER TESTING PROGRAM.

The hope and intention of the Core and ESSA is to create fairer, more challenging, and sophisticated testing programs than the ones used in NCLB.

BUT such tests have a history of problems. If test results are used to evaluate teachers or schools, additional problems will almost certainly arise.

MYTH 5: THE COMMON CORE DOWNGRADES FICTION LITERATURE.

The standards call for nonfiction texts to make up 50 percent of reading assignments in elementary schools, and 70 percent by grade 12.

BUT prescribing how much time should be spent on fiction versus nonfiction is an example of how the Common Core intrudes on teachers' curricular decision making.

MYTH 6: THE COMMON CORE IS A NATIONAL SET OF STANDARDS.

The Common Core Standards are not a national requirement; each state decides whether or not to participate.

BUT some states did not join and others have withdrawn. The Common Core is neither required nor followed by all the states, so it falls short of setting national standards.

REFLECTION: Do you believe that the Common Core is here to stay, or like No Child Left Behind, it is a program doomed to fail? How might you approach education reform differently?

SOURCES: William Bushaw, and Shane Lopez, "Highlights of the 2013 PDF/Gallup Poll," *Phi Delta Kappan*, September 2013; Lesli A. Maxwell "Common-Core Needs Dominate Districts' Curriculum Priorities, Survey Finds" *Ed Week*, December 2, 2013; Valerie Strauss, "Five Myths about the Common Core," *Washington Post*, December 13, 2013; Joseph P. Williams "Who Is Fighting Against Common Core?" and "Who Is Fighting for Common Core?" *US News and World Report*, February 27, 2014; Ravitch, Diane, "Why I Cannot Support the Common Core Standards," www.dianeravitch.net, February 26, 2013.

All this test preparation taught students a powerful lesson about the school's hidden curriculum: test scores mattered more than English or Italian, teachers did not make the key instructional decisions, principals and teachers feared tests, and the most important thing going on in school was improving test scores. (Another powerful lesson emerged when one-third of the students in the protesting teacher's class stopped attending school once the test was over, skipping the last five weeks of the school year.[35])

Twenty-five miles north in the upscale suburb of Scarsdale, two-thirds of public school students did not show up for the exam.[36] Baltimore public school juniors and seniors walked out of the classroom to protest standardized testing, gathering at Baltimore City school headquarters. They said the test provided a narrow, misleading measure of what students can do, and called it a mechanism of institutional racism.[37] In Massachusetts, some local school boards defied the state and issued diplomas to students they believed were being unfairly denied graduation because of the state-mandated test.[38]

Why are teachers, students, and parents protesting? What's wrong with measuring academic progress through such tests? Here are some reasons high-stake tests are problematic:

1. *Poorer students are at greater risk.* Because students do not receive equal educations, holding identical expectations for all students places the poorer ones at a disadvantage. States use the same tests for students in well-funded posh schools *and* students trying to learn in underfunded, ill-equipped schools. This approach is grossly unfair, with predictable outcomes. For example, one year, two out of three low-income Georgia students failed the state's math, English, and reading competency tests. Every student in well-to-do counties passed the tests, and more than half exceeded standards. Unfortunately, many states don't ensure a level playing field by providing all students with appropriate educational resources, competent teachers, and modern technology. Meanwhile, real barriers to achievement–racism, poverty, sexism, low teacher salaries, language differences, and inadequate facilities–get lost in the sea of testing and inadequate funding.

   Why do even moderate income differences affect test scores? Wealthy students are more likely to grow up with intellectual advantages at home (books, travel, technology), and arrive at school with many of the academic skills commonly measured on standardized tests. For them, teachers can focus on valuable higher-level thinking skills. Many poor and minority children, on the other hand, lack these home resources and must learn basic academic skills at school. Meanwhile, common assets that minority and poor students *do bring* to school are not honored or developed, much less tested–including being multi-lingual, knowing other cultures, oral storytelling, and unique music and artistic experiences.[39] The rhetoric of the standards movement asserts that a rising tide raises all ships. In reality, some ships do not rise without adequate resources or valuing "alternative" knowledge and skills.[40]

2. *Lower graduation rates.* A Harvard University study found that students in the bottom 10 percent of achievement were 33 percent more likely to drop out of school in states that required graduation tests. That data may seem paradoxical, but when standards-based testing is linked to promotion and graduation, higher dropout rates logically follow. Adding to the problem, a school's average test score rises when a weak student drops out–generating a false-positive rate success when the real picture is failure.[41]

3. *Rationing Time and Resources.* With limited resources, schools resort to triage or rationing. Strong students get less special attention, since mandated tests are geared to measure minimal skills, not excellence. The weakest students can be left behind, because they need more time and resources than many schools have. So-called

GLOBAL VIEW

A World-Class Education: Learning from International Models of Excellence and Innovation by Vivien Stewart offers some insights and good ideas for discussion about school practices around the world and how the United States might do schooling differently.

"bubble kids" get disproportionate attention because they are closest to clearing the high-stakes test "passing" hurdle. A Texas teacher poignantly captures this dilemma:

> Ana's got a 25 percent. What's the point in trying to get her to grade level? It would take two years to get her to pass the test, so there's really no hope for her. I feel like we might as well focus on the ones there's hope for.[42]

4. *Higher test scores do not mean more learning.* For many educators, teaching has become test preparation, with learning measured by test scores. But this pits teachers against their values, knowledge, and skills. Only 28 percent of teachers see standardized tests as an essential or very important gauge of student achievement, and only one in four teachers believes that these tests accurately reflect student learning. About half of the teachers believe that students do not take these tests seriously, and therefore do not try to do their best.[43] The students themselves may be on to something:
   - A study of 18 states found that when state standardized tests were given, student performance dropped on ACT, SAT, and NAEP math tests. The study concluded that higher state test scores were most likely due to direct test preparation rather than increased student learning.[44]
   - During a RAND study in Washington State, three-quarters of fourth-grade teachers and most principals said they believe that better test preparation (rather than increased learning) was responsible for most of the score gains.[45]
   - A group of neuroscientists from the Massachusetts Institute of Technology, Harvard, and Brown University, funded by the Gates Foundation and the National Institutes of Health, found that strategies schools used to boost high-stakes standardized test scores did nothing to help students improve development of logical thinking, cognitive gains, and "fluid intelligence" skills (the ability to analyze novel problems).[46]
5. *Standardized testing shrinks the curriculum.* Many teachers believe that their schools give less attention to subjects absent from the state test. The timing of state tests also drives teaching: "At our school, third- and fourth-grade teachers are told not to teach social studies and science until March."[47] Indeed, a study by the Center on Education Policy found that about 62 percent of school districts increased the time spent in elementary schools on English/language arts or math, while 44 percent of districts cut time on science, social studies, art and music, physical education, lunch, or recess.[48] Such a narrow view of the curriculum is self-defeating.

   Educator Alfie Kohn advises parents to ask an unusual question when a school's test scores increase: "What did you have to sacrifice about my child's education to raise those scores?"[49] While the global economy demands innovation and fluid intelligence, too often the narrow perspective of test scores is driving schools. Ironically (or sadly), schools with the arts as part of the core curriculum tend to produce self-motivated students, improved social and emotional development, greater parental involvement, intensified student and teacher engagement, stronger collegiate aspirations, greater civic engagement, and respect for cultural differences.[50]
6. *Teacher stress.* Although teachers support high standards, they object to measuring learning by a single test.[51] Not surprisingly, a national study reported nearly seven in ten teachers felt test stress, and two out of three believed that preparing for the test took time from teaching important topics not on the tests.[52] Another study found that 70 percent of educators think state-mandated

FIGURE 10.3

A teacher's impression of the testing movement.

SOURCE: Tripalavanam Ganesh, http://ganesh.ed.asu.edu/aims. See also Tirupalavanam Ganesh, "Held Hostage by High-Stakes Testing: Drawing as Symbolic Resistance," *Teacher Education Quarterly* (2002).

REFLECTION: Try your own hand at drawing an image of how you feel when you are about to take a high-stakes test.

assessments are not developmentally appropriate.[53] Fourth-grade veteran teachers were requesting transfers, saying that they could not stand the pressure of administering the high-stakes elementary exams, and teachers recognized for excellence were leaving public schools, feeling their talents were better utilized in private schools where test preparation did not rule the curriculum.[54] When 80 Arizona teachers and teacher educators were asked to visually depict the impact of standardized tests, their drawings indicated test-driven classrooms where boredom, fear, and isolation dominate. (See Figure 10.3 for one of those drawings.) Teachers feel that tests are driving them to shortchange schoolchildren out of a love for learning.

7. *Tests can fail.* Tests themselves are often flawed, and high-stakes errors become high stakes disasters. Stories continue to mount as the crush of millions of new tests overwhelms the handful of testing companies. In 2014 alone, one testing company printed New York state math assessment tests with missing questions and blank pages, admitted it wrongly scored tests taken three years earlier, and faced penalties from Florida's education commissions after schools in 26 counties had to suspend computerized testing when logins failed, screens froze, and servers failed.[55] A flawed answer key incorrectly lowered multiple-choice scores for 12,000 Arizona students, erred in adding up scores of essay tests for students in Michigan, and forced the re-scoring of 204,000 test essays in Washington State. Another error resulted in nearly 9,000 New York City students being mistakenly assigned to summer school, and $2 million in achievement awards being denied to deserving students in Kentucky. And a Massachusetts

Both teachers and students often find that a testing culture diminishes education to a test score.

©David Jennings/The Image Works

high school senior spotted an alternative answer to a math question, propelling 449 fellow students over the passing mark. [56] Given the flawed history of the testing industry, is it wise or fair to reward or punish students, teachers, and schools primarily (or solely) on such high-stakes test scores?[57]

Evaluating Teachers by Student Test Scores

GLOBAL VIEW

Singapore's minister of education explains that his country would never evaluate teachers by student test scores because doing so would create bad incentives and undermine collaboration. In Portugal, when merit pay was based on test results, that is exactly what happened: teacher collaboration decreased. Why do you think that American policymakers so rarely consider the impact of their decisions on teacher collaboration?

In addition to tracking students' progress through test scores, policymakers use those same scores to evaluate teachers' performance. Find the teachers generating the most (and the least) year-to-year improvement to a student's test results, and (so the theory goes) bingo, states and school districts can readily determine which teachers and schools to reward, and which to penalize. We talked about *value added* earlier in the book—how much value a teacher adds to a student's education. But can anyone assess that ephemeral added value based only on tests administered to millions of students from many thousands of schools?

Take the case of five talented fifth-grade teachers at Public School 146 in Brooklyn, one of New York City's highest-achieving elementary schools. These teachers won grants to study in Ghana, Mexico, and Peru and a Guggenheim Museum arts award. They also worked for Columbia University to help educate other teachers. They often stayed until 7 or 8 at night to work with students, and their principal believed them to be among the most gifted and hard-working fifth-grade teachers she ever had on staff. There was no surprise when 96 percent of their fifth-graders tested proficient in English, and 89 percent in math in 2009, among the highest scores in the city. The surprise was that a year later, those scores were slightly lower than the *2008* scores, so the teachers were penalized. Emphasis on year-to-year numbers distorts the concept of "value added," and gives negative evaluations to teachers adding excellent value to their students' lives.[58]

One year's test scores are a flawed and inadequate measure of teacher effectiveness. Yet test scores can become 40 or 50 percent of a teacher's evaluation in some states.[59] In most cases, standardized test scores reveal more about a student's world than the teacher's. As we discussed above, student achievement is influenced by health issues, home life, class size, curriculum materials, school attendance, other teachers, peers, parenting, neighborhood environment, and of course, the wealth or poverty of the student and school. With so many factors in play, it is not surprising that teacher "ratings" vary from the top one year to merely average (or worse) in following years. As one Houston teacher put it: "I teach the same way every year. [My] first year got me pats on the back. [My] second year got me kicked in the backside. And for year three, my scores were off the charts. I got a huge bonus. What did I do differently? I have no clue."[60]

In some countries, rigid test policies can spark extreme and deadly responses. In Mexico, for example, a new mandatory testing program led to a deadly clash between police and protesting teachers in Oaxaca. Four people died and dozens were injured.[61] Thankfully, test-related violence hasn't erupted in the United States, but other disconcerting problems, like cheating, have. For instance, eleven Atlanta Public School (APS) officials, including the superintendent and three school reform team executive directors, were convicted on criminal charges stemming from widespread alteration of answers on mandated state tests. To drive up test scores, teachers and administrators gave children answers, erased incorrect answers, hid and altered documents, offered monetary incentives to encourage staff cheating, and punished employees who refused to cheat. A grand jury charged 35 school employees, including Dr. Beverly

Hall, once an American Association of School Administrators Superintendent of the Year, with falsely inflating APS's performance. (Hall died before going on trial.)

Meanwhile, the *Atlanta Journal-Constitution* found that 196 of the nation's 3,125 largest school districts (or 7 percent) had suspicious test results suggesting adult tampering. For 33 of these districts, the odds of their test scores occurring naturally were greater than one in a million. Cheating scandals have emerged in nearly 40 states and the District of Columbia.[62]

Why is cheating happening? Statisticians have an answer: **Campbell's law,** named for social scientist Donald T. Campbell, who wrote: "The more any quantitative social indicator is used for social decision-making, the more subject it will be to corruption pressures and the more apt it will be to distort and corrupt the social processes it was intended to monitor."[63] In other words, the more important test scores become, the more likely it is that people will cheat.

Even the criminal indictment in Atlanta acknowledged the incentive to avoid state and federal penalties by reaching test score goals:

> Over time, the unreasonable pressure to meet annual APS targets led some employees to cheat on the CRCT [Criterion Referenced Competency Tests]. The refusal of Beverly Hall and her top administrators to accept anything other than satisfying targets created an environment where achieving the desired end result was more important than the students' education.

When such tests are used to determine firing, tenure, and merit decisions in any field, some people will rebel and break the rules.[64]

Changing test answers is pretty egregious, but other kinds of "cheating" aren't so clearly recognized. Does a teacher cheat her students if she focuses her class time on learning only what the test calls for—instead of learning all kinds of things? Such practice is now commonplace. Students learn less content in this scenario, but the standardized test results suggest (incorrectly) that students are learning more. As one teacher explains, "Teaching to the test is still third-degree [cheating] in my mind."[65]

So what's the alternative? As in professions like medicine and law enforcement, evaluation of teachers should be ongoing and conducted by experts. Most teachers agree that student progress over the year should be a factor, but not the only one. To effectively evaluate teachers—and help them improve—schools should use classroom observations, assessment of student classroom work, and ongoing exams in all subject areas. Assessment of students and teachers should move beyond high-pressure, high-stakes, standardized, fill-in-the-bubble tests; we should consider a variety of ways to measure learning.

Alternatives to High-Stakes Testing

Why are standardized tests so popular? They are less expensive than other assessments, offer apparently clear results, and can be rapidly implemented. But as we often learn in life, you get what you pay for. High-stakes standardized tests are plagued with problems. Will these problems result in an end to high-stakes standardized testing? There are some signs that we may be reaching what author Malcolm Gladwell calls a *tipping point*, "the moment of critical mass, the threshold, the boiling point" when change occurs.[66] For instance, the American Psychological Association's testing guidelines now specifically prohibit basing any consequential decisions about an individual on a single test score.[67] Most educational organizations, measurement experts, and teachers agree; they believe that they get a far more accurate assessment of student performance with multiple tools: tests, class participation, portfolios, formal

RAP 2.6

Memoirs of a Time-Tested Student

exhibitions, independent student projects, and teacher evaluations. One such measure of deeper learning is authentic assessment. **Authentic assessment** (also called alternative or performance-based assessment) captures actual student performance, not a structured test setting.

Authentic assessment encourages students to produce and reflect on their own work. The student might demonstrate what has been learned by using a portfolio (like the RAPs found on Connect) or journal, undergoing an interview, conducting an experiment, or giving a presentation. Authentic assessment offers a focused and intense insight into student learning, quite different from the answers to standardized test questions.[68] Authentic assessment is similar to learning a sport. A tennis player practices her backhand, and absorbs nuanced feedback from her coach and teammates. Then, it is time for the authentic assessment: not a multiple-choice quiz about tennis; but her actually playing tennis! Many states are exploring authentic methods of assessment in different subject areas.[69]

The Coalition of Essential Schools, founded by prominent educator Theodore Sizer, uses authentic assessment. The coalition encourages schools to define their own model for successful reform, guided by nine basic principles that emphasize the personalization of learning. These principles include the requirement that students exhibit their knowledge concretely. The high school curriculum is structured around demanding, creative tasks, which may include:

- Completing an Internal Revenue Service (IRS) tax return for a family whose records you receive, working with other students in a group to ensure that everyone's IRS forms are correct, and auditing a return filed by a student in a different group
- Designing a nutritious, attractive lunch menu for the cafeteria within a specified budget, and defending your definitions of "nutritious" and "attractive"
- Designing and building a wind instrument from metal pipes, then composing and performing a piece of music for that instrument
- Exploring one human emotion in an at least four different ways, including (but not limited to): essays, examples from literature and history; creating drawings, paintings, sculptures, films, photographs, video, or music; or performing a pantomime, dance, story, or play that you create[70]

Increased authentic assessment may contribute to a greater classroom focus on critical thinking and personal development. Authentic assessments may help us go beyond our current dependence on efficient and "cheap" high-stakes standardized tests to more accurately determine the competence of students and the success of schools.

Tension Points

FOCUS QUESTION 8

How are cultural and political conflicts reflected in the school curriculum?

You can read a curriculum the way you read today's newspaper or watch tonight's news, because in it you can see the fractures and tensions in our society. Often, the curriculum becomes a battleground for competing political and cultural ideas. Here are some examples.

Evolution, Climate Change, Religion, and Science

The Bible was the major text in colonial New England schools and religious instruction was the center of the curriculum. But the new nation's Constitution changed all that.

Or did it? From prayer in school to sex education, courts continually debate the role of religion in school. For example, students in a Virginia public school had to list six proofs that the Bible is God's word.[71] A California public school system textbook once taught that God helped Columbus discover America, that Native American accomplishments were "worthless" because they had no knowledge of the "true" God, described non-Christian religions as "cults," and asked students to punctuate this sentence: "The Hebrew people often grumbled and complained."[72] Because the First Amendment prohibits government from promoting or denigrating any religion, the examples are illegal in public schools.[73] (See Chapter 8 for a detailed discussion on the role of religion in schools.)

In 1987, the U.S. Supreme Court overturned a Louisiana statute that outlawed teaching evolution in public schools without also teaching creation science or intelligent design—the position that God created the universe in six 24-hour periods as described in the Bible. Yet, decades later, public schools were still teaching biblical creationism. Youngstown, Ohio, public schools announced that "beginning this 2016–2017 school year, any reference to intelligent design, creationism, or any like concepts are eliminated from the science curriculum."[74] At the same time, the Texas State Board of Education was working to reaffirm biblical beliefs in the schools and arguing against its own science committee's recommendation to challenge the theory of evolution.[75] The debate over teaching the theory of evolution remains heated and polarizing.

The subtlety of language is partially responsible for this tension point, because "theory" has two distinct meanings. In everyday usage, "theory" means an idea or a hunch. But in science, theory is a thoroughly tested belief unlikely to change, such as the theory of gravitation or cell theory.[76] Scientific theories are the result of decades or centuries of insights drawn on many interconnected observations, ideas, and replicated tests. The theory of evolution—that animals and plants have their origin in other preexisting types and that there are modifications in successive generations—is a well-founded scientific explanation, not a hunch.

A significant number of people believe that evolutionary theory does not explain the origin of life on its own—or at all. Some argue for **intelligent design**, the idea that nature's complexity (perhaps including evolution, or perhaps not) springs from an unnamed intelligence or designer (perhaps supernatural), rather than resulting from an undirected process. Many Christian fundamentalists believe in **creationism**, the notion that God created all life and the world in seven days, as described in the book of Genesis.[77] Supporters of intelligent design and creationism say public schools should teach one or both explanations instead of—or at least alongside—evolution.

So, should the theory of evolution be taught as the only explanation of life's origins? Many scientists and civil liberties advocates argue that intelligent design and creationism are religious and unscientific. Meanwhile, polls indicate that a large segment of the public is comfortable with the notion that students deserve to hear competing theories.[78] While science refutes a literal biblical interpretation of the earth's age, not all scientists refute a spiritual or higher intelligence at work. Perhaps intelligent design works through evolution. The bottom line is that we still have much to learn. It is unfortunate that such debates create pro- and anti-science camps.

More than a dozen states (a number likely to grow) are either considering passing or have already passed legislation requiring that when evolution and other scientific subjects (e.g., climate change) are taught, criticism and/or alternative explanations, including the supernatural, be included as well. Tennessee, for example, provides teacher guidelines for answering student questions that challenge established scientific theories and the state guarantees that teachers won't be disciplined for ignoring the tenets of science.[79]

FIGURE 10.4

Climate change and human activity.

SOURCE: "Global Trends 2014," Ipso Mori Research, UK, www.ipsosglobaltrends.com/environment.html.

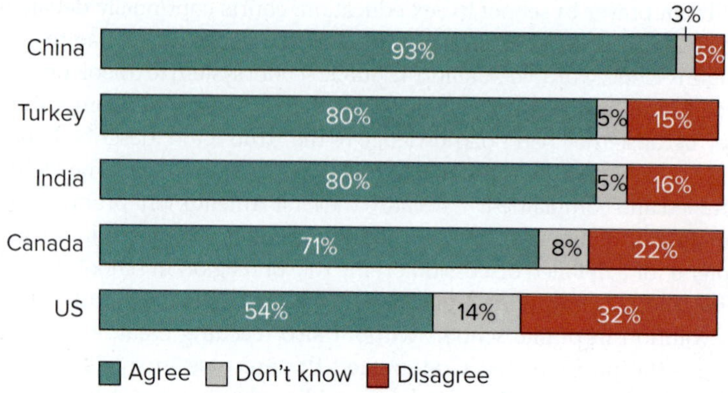

REFLECTION: Why do you think the percentage of Americans who believe that climate change is the result of human activity is so much lower than in many other countries? How would you go about changing these attitudes?

The Portland, Oregon school board voted to "abandon the use of any adopted text material that is found to express doubt about the severity of the climate crisis or its root in human activities." The decision acknowledges the wide scientific consensus that climate change is real, influenced by humans, and accelerating dangerously. Nevertheless, the National Coalition Against Censorship (NCAC) quickly responded with a warning that Portland's decision "undermine[s] public education." NCAC says curricular decisions that appear to result from political pressure are suspect, "no matter from which political side the pressure comes."[80] Another critic wrote: "I have never seen a case for homeschooling more clearly put forward. This is further proof that public schools are not interested in education, only political indoctrination."[81](See Figure 10.4: Climate Change and Human Activity.)

Unfortunately, these controversies frighten some teachers. Teaching should be about opening minds, not indoctrination. Teaching the theory of evolution is important; so is teaching about different religious traditions. Promoting or disparaging religious or political beliefs is inappropriate in public schools. Regrettably, many teachers, fearful of the consequences, avoid teaching about religion or politically contentious scientific issues.[82]

Censorship and the Curriculum

Teachers, parents, administrators, the public, elected officials, and special interest groups want a say about what is and is not in the school curriculum. No matter what content a textbook or course of study contains, someone is likely to consider it too conservative or too liberal, too traditional or too avant-garde, racist, sexist, anti-Semitic, violent, un-Christian, or pornographic.[83] When this happens, pressure to censor the offending materials soon follows. According to the American Library Association (ALA), more than 500 books are challenged at schools and libraries in a typical year.[84] There is no such thing as a totally safe, acceptable, uncontroversial book or curriculum. Each of the following has been subjected to censorship at one time or another:

- E. B. White's *Charlotte's Web*: "Morbid picture of death"
- Dr. Seuss's *Hop on Pop*: "Promotes violence"

- *The Holy Bible*: "Religious viewpoint"
- Jules Verne's *Around the World in 80 Days*: "Very unfavorable to Mormons"
- J. R. R. Tolkien's *The Hobbit*: "Subversive elements"
- Mark Twain's *The Adventures of Huckleberry Finn*: "Racism, insensitivity, and offensive language"
- *Webster's Dictionary*: "Contains sexually explicit definitions"[85]

The *School Library Journal*'s Controversial Books Survey finds that nearly all librarians rely heavily on reviews when purchasing books, while 67 percent of teachers consider the diversity of the student population and community as the most important factor in selecting instructional material.[86]

A wider problem is incidence of **self-censorship**, or **stealth censorship,** in schools, which happens more often than public suppression. Stealth censorship occurs when educators or parents quietly remove a book from a library or a course of study in response to informal complaints—or to avoid controversy. Teachers practice the same sort of self-censorship when they choose not to teach a controversial topic or discuss a difficult issue. While data on the frequency of self-censorship are impossible to obtain, we can tally up the number of books officially removed or placed on restricted-access shelves in schools and libraries. The ALA (www.ala.org) tracks challenged and censored books, issuing a new report annually. Once again, the tension centers on the First Amendment, which guarantees freedom of speech, of the press, and—by implication—of reading. For instance, challenges to books that include homosexuality are commonplace today. Critics say such books promote homosexuality and/or other sexual orientations, unacceptable topics for school. Others assert that neither books nor education can change a person's sexual orientation, so fear of "promotion" is unfounded. They believe that such books teach tolerance for individual differences.[87]

Supporters of censorship or prudent selection argue that adults have the right and obligation to protect children from harmful influences. Censorship opponents say that our purpose as educators is to expose students to a variety of views and perspectives, not to indoctrinate them. But "harmful influences" are in the eye of the beholder. Deciding what students should be able to read, and at what age, continues to be a difficult challenge for teachers, parents, and students. It has been made even more difficult by the Internet and social media, which opens wide the schoolhouse door. Teachers at all levels wonder how best to introduce potentially provocative material emerging as "trigger warnings, microaggressions and tweeting."[88] While some school Internet access is filtered or blocked, technology makes all types of information available in homes, libraries, and hot spots.[89] That means censorship challenges at school will continue in the years ahead. For helpful advice in dealing with these challenges in your classroom, visit www.ala.org.

What's Worth Knowing? The Case for Cultural Literacy

Aldous Huxley's *Brave New World* (1932) and George Orwell's *1984* (1949) were both pessimistic about what's worth knowing. "What Orwell feared was those who would ban books," writes *Teaching as a Subversive Activity* author Neil Postman. "What Huxley feared was that there would be no one who wanted to read one."[90] Neither classic novel imagined that today's great debate would revolve around which books are most worth reading.

Proponents of **core knowledge**, also called **cultural literacy**, argue for a common set of such books, a course of study for all students, one that ensures that all

GLOBAL VIEW

How could the enormous diversity of this nation be evident in any school curriculum? Provide positive (or negative) examples of how different racial, ethnic, or religious groups are portrayed in curricular materials, including your own college classes.

educated people know the same basic cultural information. This core of information is far more specific in content than the core curricular standards discussed earlier in the chapter. In fact, it is sometimes called a *curricular canon*. (The word "canon" is rooted in religion, referring to a list of books officially accepted by a church or a religious hierarchy.) The curricular canon refers to the notion that there is a central core of information that schools should teach. This includes famous figures, great works of art and music and, particularly, great works of literature. Common understanding of our civilization is an important way to bind our diverse people together.

Some argue that we have the opposite right now. In *The Closing of the American Mind* (1987), University of Chicago professor of social thought Allan Bloom famously took aim at the university curriculum as a series of often-unrelated courses lacking a vision of what an educated individual should know. He called this a canon-less curriculum. Bloom claimed that his university students were ignorant of music and literature, and charged that too many students graduate with a degree but not an education.[91]

In his book *Cultural Literacy*, Professor E. D. Hirsch, Jr. basically agreed, but included more contributions from women and various ethnic and racial groups than Bloom's canon did. In fact, Hirsch believes children from poverty and children of color would benefit most from a cultural literacy curriculum. In 1991, Hirsch published the first volume of the core knowledge series, *What Your First Grader Needs to Know*. Other grades followed in these mass-marketed books directed at both educators and parents.[92]

But the challenge is who gets to decide what should be included. Should a blue-ribbon committee of "Very Smart People" like Hirsch, Bloom, and others get to choose? Where does that leave the scores of nonacademic cultural influences (such as oral traditions and folk art)? Why are so many proposed curricular canons predominantly white, male, and Eurocentric?

Those who support multicultural education say that students of color and females like learning better, achieve more, and have higher self-worth when they are reflected in the visible curriculum. (In Chapter 3, we discuss multicultural education in depth.) And let's not forget white male students. When they read about people other than themselves in the curriculum, they are more likely to honor and appreciate their diverse peers, and less likely to see themselves as the center of the world. Educator and author James Banks calls for increased cultural pluralism:

> Many educators, people of color, women, and other marginalized groups are demanding that their voices, visions, and perspectives be included in the curriculum. For example, they ask that Western civilization acknowledge the debt it owes to Africa, Asia, and indigenous America. This does not mean eliminating Aristotle, Shakespeare, or Western civilization from the school curriculum. That would reject important aspects of their own cultural heritages, experiences, and identities.[93]

FOCUS QUESTION 9

How has technology affected the curriculum?

The Technology Revolution

Imagine a new **technology** that made human teachers obsolete, ending their centuries at the core of education. The invention is first used at home and then in more affluent schools. Eventually, all schools had the technology. Slowly but surely, the classroom teacher was replaced. New information tools took students where they had never been before, did things no human could do, and shared an unlimited reservoir of information. Clearly, this technological breakthrough had potential to teach more effectively (and at a far lower cost) than human teachers. Some even predicted the replacement of schools themselves!

Thinking computers? Think again. These predictions were made in the 1950s, amid popular perceptions that educational television would reshape the classroom, revolutionize schools, and perhaps put a few million teachers out of work. Although television reshaped much of the cultural landscape (not all for the good), predictions about its impact on schools were greatly exaggerated. Consider the following soothsayers from earlier eras:

> "The motion picture is destined to revolutionize our educational system, and . . . in a few years it will supplant largely, if not entirely, the use of textbooks."
>
> **—Thomas Edison (1922)**

> "The time may come when a portable radio receiver will be as common in the classroom as is a blackboard."
>
> **—William Levenson, director of Cleveland Public School's radio station (1945)[94]**

What about the predictions—and promises—associated with bringing revolutionary twenty-first century digital innovations to schoolrooms?

Technology brings students instant information, but educators wonder about its ultimate impact on learning.

Technology in the Classroom

So far, the large investments in school-based digital technologies have not been matched by significant gains in student achievement. In fact, researchers are divided on the academic benefits of technology. Perhaps more effective learning will occur with more sophisticated future technology—or perhaps not.[95] Technology offers a tremendous assist for some students, including homeschooled ones. But there are downsides as well. Students who become too dependent on calculators before understanding mathematical concepts can see their mathematics test scores tumble.[96] Word processing has produced longer, higher-quality writing by students, but teachers complain about how texting shortcuts impact student spelling and grammatical skills.[97] Technology creates some serious ethical dilemmas as well. Nearly 40 percent of college students cut and paste text from the Internet into their own work. Text messaging has been used to share information during exams. But high-tech cheating is rarely reported by students.[98]

Perhaps the biggest technological classroom problem is smartphone distraction. According to a 2015 Pew Research Center study, 88 percent of U.S. teens ages 13 to 17 have, or have access to, a mobile phone, and 73 percent have smartphones. Not only that, 24 percent of teens say they are online "almost constantly" during the day (including school hours).[99] In theory, easy access to mobile tools could help students and teachers actively participate in and enhance classroom learning. In practice, students too often use apps and Web access to tune out teachers and peers. And what about young people starting their teaching career after years of extensive screen use? How will they resist or break habits of digital distraction?

Meanwhile, school policies on smart devices vary dramatically. In Massachusetts, Boston schools ban smartphones during school hours, but Melrose lets each teacher decide whether to let them into the classroom, while Burlington purchased iPads for every elementary, middle, and high school student.[100] In China, teachers and parents

GLOBAL VIEW

Eighty-five percent of European youth agreed that they "would rather spend a great day outside than a great day online." Would US students agree? Would you? Is cyberspace a way of life, a useful tool, or an interesting diversion?

believe that phones disrupt learning, while students see them as a support for their schoolwork; but adults and children both agree that mobile devices should be banned during classes and exams.[101] Technology will continue to bring students instant information, and educators will continue to wonder about its ultimate impact on learning.

The Digital Divide

As with other school (and community) resources, the technology gap between haves and have-nots is substantial. For years, African American, Hispanic, and female students had fewer computers and less access to or interest in the Internet, a **digital divide** with serious educational implications.[102] While the price of laptops, tablets, and smartphones has fallen, that may not matter to a family struggling to pay rent or buy food. The number of computers in schools is growing, but that doesn't bridge after-school digital divides. In addition, classrooms in wealthier communities are more likely to have up-to-date technology with high-speed broadband than classrooms in poorer communities.[103] The impact radiates beyond public schools; the majority of computer science majors and professionals continue to be whites, Asians, and males.[104]

Geography also matters, even in the digital age. For example, running fiber-optic cables to rural communities is an expense that telecommunications companies often avoid. Some school Internet connections still use slow acoustic modems, making it almost impossible for students participating in online classes. Even when school buildings have high-speed Internet access, inadequate *internal* wiring and networks may choke off full classroom access. This digital divide is known as the **last mile problem**.[105]

Finally, let's focus on a digital divide that goes beyond issues of access: how technology is used.[106] Some schools use technology to promote drill and practice, while other schools use it to challenge students. Professor Henry Jay Becker warns, "Efforts to ensure equal access to computer-related learning opportunities at school must move beyond a concern with the numbers of computers in different schools [and] toward an emphasis on how well those computers are being used to help children develop intellectual competencies and technical skills."[107] Although technology can awe us, in the end it is how well we use the technology that matters.

It is unlikely that education will be redefined completely before you graduate college, yet technology's influence is growing demonstrably. Consider technology mastery as part of your professional development. Attend relevant courses and workshops, and observe colleagues applying technology—but do not lose your skepticism. Be wary of simple "magic bullet" solutions to complex educational problems.

FOCUS QUESTION 10

What are some potential directions for tomorrow's curriculum?

Suggestions for Tomorrow's Curriculum

Now let's take a moment to do some critical thinking of our own. Imagine that you are in charge of taking the nation's schools down an educational path. What path would you trail blaze? What content or skills do you see as most critical? Tough question, and it's not fair to ask you such a question if we are not ready to answer it ourselves. So here are some of our ideas:

Using and evaluating digital information. Technology brings us both true and phony information. It's essential to teach students how to separate the important from the insignificant and the real from the fake. We favor a curriculum that helps students effectively evaluate and use information, a curricular challenge for life and citizenship.

Critical thinking skills. Students spend a lot of time memorizing information that can be easily retrieved. More time is needed for comparing, interpreting, observing, summarizing, classifying, decision making, creating, and criticizing. Using more of these critical-thinking skills in subjects from mathematics to history increases our higher-order thinking—our ability to think clearly.[108]

Media "literacy." Inside and outside of schools, screen time is exploding. Life in a marketing culture requires understanding of how media can be helpful and promote wellbeing, and also how it could be harmful.

Financial literacy. Virtually all high schools teach geometry and calculus; but only 17 states require high school students to take a personal finance course covering math life skills like checkbook balancing, understanding compound interest, and managing credit card debt.[109] High school students who are required to take personal finance courses average better credit scores and debt delinquency rates as young adults.[110] We'd like to see wider adoption of financial literacy.

Physical fitness. Lifelong fitness activities—yoga, walking, Pilates, climbing, kickboxing, basketball, dance, biking, and so on—can be enjoyed today and promote wellness for life. We must reverse cutbacks in physical and kinetic learning. As one student explained: "I love it [lifelong fitness activities] because it's fun. I'm not an athlete, so I used to dread P.E. Now I am learning new activities that I enjoy and keep me healthy and I am not embarrassed about my body."[111]

Civics education. Responsible citizenship is difficult in an environment of hyperbolic and misleading news outlets, ubiquitous marketing, political gridlock, money's influence in politics, and denigration of our republic's political process itself. More than 80 percent of eighth-graders are not proficient in civics knowledge and skills. "Ultimately, schools are the guardians of democracy," and we advocate a more robust civics education throughout the curriculum to protect and nourish our nation's noble experiment in self-governance.[112]

Creativity. People in our society have created (and continue to create) groundbreaking art, media, technology, ideas, and countless inventions. Yet with so much focus on testing, too few educators explore how to promote and honor creativity in schools.

Collaboration and human relations. Too often our world is marked by misunderstanding and anger; cultural, class, and religious conflict; widespread poverty; physical deprivation; and interpersonal and international clashes. This calls for proactive curriculum commitment to Human Relations. Here are our suggestions:

- *Human Relations 1: Understand Yourself*. Knowing only our own family history, cultural and religious beliefs, gender challenges, and view of our national heritage leaves us less prepared for the modern world. We lack a healthy appreciation of how our backgrounds have shaped our lives and our worldview. Only through greater self-insight can we begin to understand our perceptions and motivations, our strengths and weaknesses, our limits and potential, why we behave and think as we do, and our purposeful place in the world.
- *Human Relations 2: Celebrate Others*. Self-understanding excites curiosity about and insights from other peoples and cultures. This is far richer than mere tolerance. We believe that diversity should be celebrated. Cultural, racial, ethnic, gender, spiritual, ability, and religious differences offer us wondrous insights into the human experience. We can learn so much from one another. We must learn to learn from our differences, not fear them.

TEACHING TIP

Students on My Mind

One of the things that has been most important to me in my daily work is to remember that I am not teaching a subject, but that I am teaching students. In these days of standards, clearly defined and often prescribed teaching objectives, it is hard to remember sometimes that the most important thing isn't the "standard"—it is the student. When I remember this, it calls me to use skills that aren't always written in my lesson plan. I have to be open-minded in my approach to students, remembering that their knowledge, experiences, and concerns are not what I might expect or predict. Remembering to teach to the student, I also call on the gifts of humor, patience, and creativity. While these are not written into any of my daily lesson plans, they are critical to reaching the students that I teach in authentic and transforming ways.

DIANE Petteway is the International Baccalaureate Middle Years Program coordinator at East Millbrook Magnet Middle School in Raleigh, North Carolina.

Courtesy of Diane Petteway.

REFLECTION: Can you construct a different kind of standard for your own teaching? Build your standard not around content, but on your connection with your students.

- *Human Relations 3: Encourage Individual Talents.* Schools should prepare students to live purposeful and satisfying lives. (See Teaching Tip: Students on My Mind.) To do this, students need to learn and develop their own unique interests, abilities, skills, and talents. By measuring all students against standardized yardsticks of literacy and numeracy, we lose and/or denigrate individual creativity and talents. We would like to see more individualization in the curriculum.
- *Human Relations 4: Promote Purposeful Lives.* Pioneering education reformer Horace Mann told Antioch College's 1859 graduating class: "Be ashamed to die until you have won some victory for humanity."[113] The real measure of an education is what people do after graduation—not their grades, assignments, or extracurricular activities. Are students living and working ethically? Are adults caring for one another? Do we treat children, families, colleagues, and especially strangers with love, compassion, and forgiveness? This will be the true measure of our teaching, our schooling, and our society.

Those are some of the keystones to our curriculum. What are the keystones to yours?

connect CONNECT FOR *TEACHERS, SCHOOLS, AND SOCIETY*

Check out Connect, McGraw-Hill Education's interactive learning environment, to:

Read Current and Historical Articles

Worthy Texts: Who Decides? by Barry Gilmore, *Educational Leadership,* March 2011.

Curriculum Theory and Practice: What's Your Style? by Donna L. Miller, *Phi Delta Kappan,* April 2011.

Why Has High-Stakes Testing So Easily Slipped into Contemporary American Life? by Sharon Nichols and David Berliner, *Phi Delta Kappan,* May 2008.

International Education: What's in a Name? by Walter Parker, *Phi Delta Kappan,* November 2008.

All Our Students Thinking, by Nel Noddings, *Educational Leadership,* February 2008.

Analyze Case Studies

Elaine Adams: A student teacher near the end of her assignment observes her cooperating teacher give the students help while administering the district-mandated standardized tests. She finds herself unsure how to deal with the situation.

Melinda Grant: A teacher who has developed an innovative curriculum is concerned because another teacher continually warns her that she will be held responsible for her students' end-of-year standardized test scores.

Watch Teachers, Students, and Classrooms In Action

Our **Online Video Album** for contemporary videos related to this chapter.

KEY TERMS AND PEOPLE

authentic assessment, 296
Campbell's law, 295
climate change, 279
Common Core State Standards, 284, 287
core knowledge, 299
creationism, 297
cultural literacy, 299
curriculum, 278
digital divide, 302
evaluating teachers, 294
Every Student Succeeds Act (ESSA), 285
evolution, 279
extracurriculum, 280
formal or explicit curriculum, 278
high-stakes tests, 285, 289
implicit or hidden curriculum, 278
intelligent design, 297
last mile problem, 302
No Child Left Behind Act (NCLB), 285
null curriculum, 279
standardized tests, 289
stealth or self-censorship, 299
technology, 300

DISCUSSION QUESTIONS AND ACTIVITIES

1. For some students, the hidden curriculum and the extracurriculum are most central to their school experience. Define the roles of these unofficial curricular experiences in your own education. If you were placed in charge of a school today, how would you change these hidden and extracurricular experiences? How might your changes be evident in elementary, middle, and high schools? Why?

2. What subject areas spark the greatest debate and controversy over creating a single, national curriculum? What strategies could help reach a consensus on these issues? How might a national history curriculum written today differ from one written a century from now? A century ago? Why?
3. Collect textbooks from your local elementary and secondary schools, and analyze them according to the following criteria:
   - Do they include instructional objectives? Do these require students to use recall of factual information as well as analytical and creative thinking skills?
   - Were readability formulas used in the preparation of the textbooks? If so, did this appear to have a negative or a positive impact on the quality of the writing?
   - Are under-represented group members included in the textbooks' narrative and illustrations? Are differently-abled people included?
   - When various individuals are included, are they portrayed in a realistic and balanced way, or in a stereotyped manner?
4. If you were developing a standards-based curriculum with assessment tools, where would you go to identify standards? What kinds of tests would you use? What kinds of tests would you avoid? What subjects and skills do you consider crucial? Why?
5. Do you believe that children's educational materials should be censored? Are there any benefits to censorship? Any dangers? What kinds of materials would you refuse to let elementary school students read? Middle or high school students? Postsecondary students?

Design Elements: Blue pencil: ©C.O.T/a.collectionRF/Getty Images RF; Pencils: ©Darren Greenwood/Design Pics RF; Gavel: ©Siede Preis/Getty Images RF; Students Huddled Together: ©Digital Vision/Getty Images RF; Pens with blue background: ©chiarito/Getty Images RF

One child, one teacher, one book, one pen can change the world.

MALALA YOUSAFZAI

chapter 11

Becoming an Effective Teacher

Focus Questions

1. Are teachers born or made?
2. How is learning time organized in the classroom?
3. What classroom management skills foster academic achievement?
4. What are the roles of teachers and students in the pedagogical cycle?
5. How can teachers set a stage for learning?
6. What questioning strategies increase student achievement?
7. How can teachers use technology to support effective instruction?
8. What are several salient models of instruction?

Chapter Preview

Albert Einstein believed that they awakened the "joy in creative expression and knowledge." Ralph Waldo Emerson believed that they could "make hard things easy." About whom are these talented geniuses talking? You guessed it: teachers. Some individuals seem to take to teaching quite naturally. With little or no preparation, they come to school with a talent to teach and touch the lives of students. Others bring fewer natural talents to the classroom yet, with preparation and practice, become master teachers, models others try to emulate. Most of us fall in the middle, bringing some skills to teaching but also ready to benefit and grow from teacher preparation and practice teaching.

In this chapter, we present recent research findings on effective instruction and classroom management, focusing on a core set of skills that constitute good teaching. We also detail the prevailing models of instruction, such as cooperative learning, problem-based learning, and differentiated instruction—classroom approaches that have become particularly popular in recent years. You may draw on these skills and models in your own classroom, selecting those that best fit your subject, students, and purpose.

Are Teachers Born, or Made?

FOCUS QUESTION 1

Are teachers born, or made?

Think about the best teacher you ever had: Try to evoke a clear mental image of what this teacher was like. How do your memories compare with what some of today's teachers say about their favorite teachers from the past?

- The teacher I remember was charismatic. Going to his class was like attending a Broadway show. But it wasn't just entertainment. He made me understand things. We went step-by-step in such a clear way that I never seemed to get confused—even when we discussed the most difficult subject matter.
- I never watched the clock in my English teacher's class. I never counted how many times she said uh-huh or okay or paused—as I did in some other classes. She made literature come alive—I was always surprised—and sorry—when the bell rang.
- When I had a problem, I felt like I could talk about it with Mrs. Garcia. She was my fifth-grade teacher, and she never made me feel dumb or stupid—even when I had so much trouble with math. After I finished talking to her, I felt as if I could do anything.
- For most of my life, I hated history—endlessly memorizing those facts, figures, dates. I forgot them as soon as the test was over. One year I even threw my history book in the river. But Mr. Cohen taught history in such a way that I could understand the big picture. He asked such interesting, provocative questions—about our past and the lessons it gave for our future.

The debate has been raging for decades: Are teachers born, or made? Is teaching an art or science? What do you think?

If you think it is a combination of both, you are in agreement with most people who have seriously considered this question. The science of teaching gives attention to specific teaching techniques, a core curriculum, testing and accountability. Science also helps us to understand how the brain develops and processes information. On the other hand, creativity, communication, and the ability to build relationships that honor individuality and facilitate learning are thought to be artistic inspirations of good teaching.

Some individuals are naturally gifted teachers. Their classrooms are dazzlingly alive. Students are motivated and excited, and their enthusiasm translates into academic achievement. For these truly talented educators, teaching seems to be pure art or magic. But behind even the most brilliant teaching performance, there is usually well-practiced skill at work. Look again at those brief descriptions of favorite teachers: Each of them used proven skills—structure, motivation, clarity, high expectations, and effective questioning.

- "We went step-by-step in such a clear way that I never seemed to get confused—even when we discussed the most difficult subject matter." *(structure and clarity)*
- "She made literature come alive." *(motivation)*
- "After I finished talking to her, I felt as if I could do anything." *(high expectations)*
- "He asked such interesting, provocative questions—about our past and the lessons it gave for our future." *(questioning)*

Although there is ample room for natural talent, most teaching is based on "tried and true" practices. And we know that good teachers matter: A study that followed 2.5 million students over 20 years found that teachers who helped improve their students' achievement also had positive effects on those students' lives beyond academics, including lower teenage pregnancy rates, less obesity, greater college matriculation, and higher adult earnings.[1]

In this chapter, we describe what research tells us about teaching skills and models of instruction that raise student achievement. If you decide to teach, it will be your responsibility to keep up with the expanding and sometimes shifting teacher effectiveness research through conferences, coursework, and education journals. For now, let's explore the current findings supporting teacher effectiveness.

Learning Time

FOCUS QUESTION 2

How is learning time organized in the classroom?

One constant in schools is time. What is startling is how differently teachers use their classroom time. For example, a large study showed that one teacher in a California school system spent 68 minutes a day on reading, while another spent 137 minutes; one elementary school teacher in Florida spent only 16 minutes per day on mathematics, while another spent more than three times that amount.[2] Similarly, John Goodlad's comprehensive research study, *A Place Called School,* found that some schools devote approximately 65 percent of their time to instruction, whereas others devote almost 90 percent.[3] The variation is enormous.

Research shows that students who spend more time pursuing academic content achieve more. That's the commonsense part, and it's hardly surprising. Although allocating adequate time to academic content is obviously important, making time on the schedule is not enough. How this allocated time is used in the classroom is the real key to student achievement. To analyze the use of classroom time, researchers have developed the following terms: allocated time, engaged time, and academic learning time.

Allocated time is the time a teacher schedules for a subject—for example, 30 minutes a day for math. The more time allocated for a subject, the higher student achievement in that subject is likely to be.

Engaged time is that part of allocated time in which students are actively involved with academic subject matter (intently listening to a lecture, participating in a class discussion, writing an essay, solving math problems). When students daydream, doodle, write notes to each other, talk with their peers about nonacademic topics, or simply wait for instructions, they are not involved in engaged

Academic learning time is engaged learning time in which students have a high success rate. When working independently, as here, the success rate should be particularly high.

©Fuse/Getty Images RF

time. When there is more engaged time within allocated time, student achievement increases. As with allocated time, the amount of time students are engaged with the subject matter varies enormously from teacher to teacher and school to school. In some classes, engaged time is 50 percent; in others, it is more than 90 percent.[4]

Academic learning time is engaged time with a high success rate. Many researchers suggest that students should get 70 to 80 percent of the answers right when working with a teacher. When students are working independently, and without a teacher available to make corrections, the success rate should be even higher if students are to learn effectively. Some teachers are skeptical when they hear these percentages; they think that experiencing difficulty challenges students and helps them achieve. However, studies indicate that a high success rate is positively related to student achievement.[5]

In the following sections, you will learn about research-based teaching skills that you can use to increase academic learning time and student achievement. Because much time can be frittered away on organizational details and minor student disruptions, we will look first at effective strategies for classroom management. Then we will consider the instructional skills that seem consistently to produce higher academic achievement in students.

Classroom Management

FOCUS QUESTION 3

What classroom management skills foster academic achievement?

When done well, classroom management goes unnoticed. When done poorly, it is about the only thing that is noticed. If you teach, you will develop your own style and techniques to manage a classroom. The style you select will reflect much about your own teaching philosophy. Why do you believe students misbehave? Should the focus of management be teacher control or the development of student self-control? Can misbehavior be avoided by exciting lessons and a class that feels a sense of community, or is there an overriding need for a firm set of rules and consequences? What kind of classroom climate can make both teacher and students comfortable? How can teachers create a positive learning space? What role will your students take in building a safe, creative classroom environment?

While there is no single best strategy for classroom management, the good news is you can begin thinking about what approach appeals to you. To assist you on this journey, visit Connect where we describe several of the best-known management models in the feature Digging Deeper: Models of Classroom Management. Let's also study the following classroom scene.

The observer walked to the back of the room and sat down. It seemed to him that the classroom was a beehive of activity. A reading group was in progress in the front of the room while the other children were working with partners on math examples. The classroom was filled with a hum of children working together, and in several languages—but the activity and the noise were organized and not chaotic.

The observer had been in enough schools over the past 20 years to know that this well-managed classroom did not result from magic but that carefully established and maintained procedures were at work. The observer scrutinized the classroom, searching for the procedures that allowed twenty-six students and one teacher to work together so industriously, harmoniously, and effectively.

First he examined the reading group, where the teacher was leading a discussion about the meaning of a story. "Why was Tony worried about the trip he was going to take?" the teacher asked (a few seconds' pause, all the children with eyes on the teacher, several hands raised). "Sean?"

As Sean began his response, the observer's eyes wandered around the rest of the room, where most of the children were busy at work. Olivia and U-Mei, however, were passing notes surreptitiously in the corner of the room.

During a quick sweep of the room, the teacher spotted the misbehavior. The two girls watched the teacher frown and put her finger over her lips. They quickly returned to their work. The exchange had been so rapid and so quiet that the reading group was not interrupted for even a second.

Another student in the math group had his hand raised. The teacher motioned Omar to come to her side.

"Look for the paragraph in your story that tells how Tony felt after his visit to his grandmother," the teacher instructed the reading group. "When you have found it, raise your hands."

While the reading group looked for the appropriate passage, the teacher quietly assisted Omar. In less than a minute, Omar was back at his seat, and the teacher was once again discussing the story with her reading group.

At 10:15, the teacher sent the reading group back to their seats and quietly counted down from ten to one. As she approached one, the room became quiet and the students' attention was focused on her. "It is now time for social studies. Before you do anything, listen carefully to *all* my instructions. When I tap the bell on my desk, those working on math should put their papers in their cubbies for now. You may have a chance to finish them later. Then all students should take out their social studies books and turn to page 67. When you hear the sound of the bell, I want you to follow those instructions." After a second's pause, the teacher tapped the bell, and the class was once again a sea of motion, but it was motion that the teacher had organized while the students were now taking responsibility for their own learning.

The observer made some notes. There was nothing particularly flashy or dramatic about what he had seen. But he was satisfied, because he knew he had been witnessing a well-managed classroom.

Good classroom management requires constant monitoring of student behavior.

©Bananastock/age fotostock RF

Can you remember from your childhood those activity books in which you had to find the five things wrong in a picture? Let us reverse the game: Try re-reading this classroom vignette and look for all the things that are *right* with the picture. Underline four or five examples of what the teacher did well.

The teacher in this vignette used several strategies to avoid interruptions and to keep instruction proceeding smoothly and keep students on task. Did you notice that[6]:

1. The teacher used a questioning technique known as *group alerting* to keep the reading group involved. By asking questions first and then naming the student to respond, she kept

A CLOSER LOOK

Times of Transition

Teachers must manage more than many major transitions every day. During these transitions, discipline problems occur twice as often as in regular classroom instruction. Classroom management expert Jacob Kounin identified five common patterns that can derail classroom management during *times of transition:*

- *Flip-flops.* In this negative pattern, the teacher terminates one activity, begins a new one, and then flops back to the original activity. For example, in making a transition from math to spelling, the teacher says, "Please open your spelling books to page 29. By the way, how many of you got all the math problems right?"
- *Overdwelling.* This bad habit includes preaching, nagging, and spending more time than necessary to correct an infraction of classroom rules. "Anna, I told you to stop talking. If I've told you once, I've told you 100 times. I told you yesterday and the day before that. The way things are going, I'll be telling it to you all year, and, believe me, I'm getting pretty tired of it. And another thing, young lady . . . "
- *Fragmentation.* In this bumpy transition, the teacher breaks directions into several choppy steps instead of accomplishing the instructions in one fluid unit—for example, "Put away your reading books. You shouldn't have any spelling books on your desk, either. All notes should be off your desk," instead of the simpler and more effective "Clear your desk of all books and papers."
- *Thrusts.* Classroom momentum is interrupted by *non sequiturs* and random thoughts that just seem to pop into the teacher's head. For example, the class is busily engaged in independent reading, when their quiet concentration is broken by the teacher, who says, "Where's Roberto? Wasn't he here earlier this morning?"
- *Dangles.* Similar to the thrust, this move involves starting something, only to leave it hanging or dangling—for example, "Richard, would you please read the first paragraph on page 94. Oh, class, did I tell you about the guest speaker we're having today? How could I have forgotten about that?"

SOURCE: Dominique Smith and Douglas Fisher, *Better than Carrots and Sticks: Restorative Practices for Positive Classroom Management* (Alexandria, VA: ASCD, 2015).

REFLECTION: Because each of these patterns represents a problem, can you reword the dialogue to produce a more effective transition?

all the students awake and on their toes. If she had said, "Sean, why did Tony feel concerned about his trip?" the other students in the group would have been less concerned about paying attention and answering the question. Instead, she asked her question first and then called on a student to respond.

2. The teacher seemed to have "eyes in the back of her head." Termed *withitness* by researcher Jacob Kounin, this quality characterizes teachers who are aware of student behavior in all parts of the room at all times. While the teacher was conducting the reading group, she was aware of the students passing notes and the one who needed assistance.
3. The teacher was able to attend to interruptions or behavior problems while continuing the lesson. Kounin calls the ability to do several things at once *overlapping.* The teacher reprimanded the students passing notes and helped another child with a math problem without interrupting the flow of her reading lesson.
4. The teacher managed routine misbehavior using the principle of *least intervention.* Because research shows the time spent disciplining students is negatively related to achievement, teachers should use the simplest intervention that will work. In this case, the teacher did not make a mountain out of a molehill. She intervened quietly and quickly to stop students from passing notes. Her nonverbal cue was all that was necessary and did not disrupt the students working on math and reading. The teacher might also have used some other effective strategies. She could have praised the students who were attending to their math ("I'm glad to see so

many partners working well on their math assignments"). If it had been necessary to say more to the girls passing notes, she should have alerted them to what they *should* be doing, rather than emphasize their misbehavior ("Olivia and U-Mei, please attend to your own work," *not* "Olivia and U-Mei, stop passing notes").

5. The teacher managed the transition from one lesson to the next smoothly and effectively, avoiding a bumpy transition, which Kounin termed *fragmentation.* When students must move from one activity to another, a gap is created in the fabric of instruction. Chaos can result when transitions are not handled competently by the instructor. Did you notice that the teacher gave a clear transition signal, either the countdown or the bell; gave thorough instructions so her students would know exactly what to do next; and made the transition all at once for the entire class? These may seem simple, commonsense behaviors, but countless classes have come apart at the seams because transitions were not handled effectively.

Preventing Problems

Effective classroom management requires planning, and research underscores that good behavioral managers are good instructional planners.[7] Effective classroom managers are waiting at the door when the children arrive, rather than entering a room late after noise and disruption have had a chance to build. Starting from the very first day of school, they teach standards or norms of appropriate student behavior, actively and directly. Often they model procedures for getting assistance, leaving the room, going to the pencil sharpener, and the like. The more important rules of classroom behavior are posted, as are the consequences of not following them.[8]

RAP 4.3
Rules, Rituals, and Routines

In traditional teacher-centered schools, rules usually mean obeying the teacher, being quiet, and not misbehaving. When schools move away from autocratic teaching styles, student responsibility and ownership of rules (or as one teacher calls them "Habits of Goodness") are embraced. Some teachers like to develop the list of rules together with their students; other teachers prefer to present a list of established practices and ask students to give specific examples or to provide reasons for having such rules. The bottom line: When rules are easily understood and convey a sense of moral fairness, most students will comply. We can create a productive learning community when rules are (1) few in number, (2) fair and reasonable, and (3) appropriate for student maturation.

Even the best rules need to be tied to consequences or the class can quickly deteriorate into chaos. Each consequence needs to be thoughtfully considered. A weak consequence might encourage rather than discourage a behavior, and a too-tough consequence might reflect an angry teacher's overreaction. Unfair consequences alienate a class and earn a teacher the reputation of being unfair. Never doubt the ability of students to detect injustices. Teachers rarely notice that they tend to penalize boys more harshly than girls for the same misbehavior. Students pick that up quickly. Subtle gender and race favoritism is alive and well in today's classrooms. Many teachers find it helpful to post a description of class rules and consequences and to send that list home to parents to forge a consistent home–school partnership on appropriate behavior.

Now is a good time to consider a question too few ask: Is the purpose of consequences to punish inappropriate behavior? More and more educators believe that we should move beyond punishment and use consequences to solve behavior issues.[9] For example, let's say a student, we'll call him David, is not paying attention in class. (We know, this is a highly improbable situation in your class, but let's just pretend for the moment.) Rather than the teacher imposing a punitive consequence (reprimand, time-out, no recess, detention, call to parents, etc.), the teacher can invite the class to brainstorm useful suggestions to help David stay on task. For example, David's desk could be moved closer to the teacher's desk, discouraging off-task behaviors. David could be paired with a student who can model on-task behavior, perhaps even work with David sharing ways to stay on task. Students might suggest something as obvious as a vision or hearing exam to make certain David is getting the instructions. If we had a real class of students brainstorming constructive interventions right now, they could offer us many other potential solutions to help David. The point to remember is that consequences can be constructive rather than negative.

Good managers also carefully arrange their classrooms to minimize disturbances, provide students with a sense of confidence and security, and make sure that instruction can proceed efficiently. They set up their rooms according to the following principles[10]:

- *Teaching eye-to-eye.* Teachers should be able to see all students at all times. Research shows that students who are seated far away from the teacher or the instructional activity are less likely to be involved in class discussions. As teachers intentionally move about the room, they can short-circuit off-task student behavior. Placing instructional materials (SMART board, demonstration activity, flip chart, lab station, and the like) in various parts of the room also gives each student "the best seat in the house" for at least part of the teaching day.
- *Teaching materials and supplies should be readily available.* Arranging a "self-help" area so that students have direct access to supplies encourages individual responsibility while freeing up the teacher to focus on instructional activities.
- *High-traffic areas should be free of congestion.* Place student desks away from supply cabinets, pencil sharpeners, and so on. Minor disturbances ripple out, distracting other students from their tasks.
- *Procedures and routines should be actively taught in the same way that academic content is taught.* Initial planning for classroom management is often rewarded with fewer discipline problems and smooth transitions to classroom routines and procedures. For students who come from chaotic home environments, these routines offer a sense of stability. Once established, they allow teachers and all students more time for academic learning.

A child's misbehavior—from minor classroom disruptions to emotional outbursts to violence—is often rooted in trauma, feelings of powerlessness, or even "normal" daily events beyond a teacher's control. Yet, teachers must understand and manage student anger and aggression. Several classroom strategies can help[11]:

- *Choice.* Constantly taking away privileges and threatening punishment can cause students to feel intimidated and victimized. Teachers can provide appropriate options to give a student a sense of some control and freedom. Encouraging a student to select a lunch mate or to choose a project topic offers a reasonable decision-making opportunity and can help avoid minor disruptions as well as aggressive acts.

RAP 4.1
Developmental and Psycho-Social Stages of Students

- *Responsibility.* Rechanneling student energy and interest into constructive activities and responsibilities can reduce misbehavior. When instruction is meaningful and worthwhile, boredom and fooling around are less likely to occur. When students are empowered, they are less likely to act out.
- *Laughter.* Learning doesn't have to always be so serious, nor do we or our students. Sometimes, when tensions are high, like during testing or when difficult things are happening out in the world, we need to laugh with our students.
- *Kindness.* Take every opportunity to model kindness. Students will follow.

- *Community.* Routinely include strategies and activities in your lessons that allow students to express their thoughts and ideas, build relationships, and practice collaboration. This will help grow and maintain a feeling of emotional safety in your classroom.
- *Voice.* Listening to young people is one of the most respectful skills a teacher can model. Students who feel they are not heard feel disrespected. Hearing and honoring students' words (and feelings) reduce the likelihood of misbehavior.

Listening to students was exactly what Kathleen Cushman did when she wrote *Fires in the Bathroom.* Adolescents from around the nation were asked to tell teachers what they would like to see in their classrooms. Students advised teachers to: share your plans with me and tell me how I will be evaluated, be excited about what you teach, be firm when rules are broken, treat me fairly but remember I am an individual, give me feedback and encouragement, don't say "please" too much, and don't push yourself into my personal life.[12]

Although we can't always detect the signs of danger, we can be on the lookout and can create management plans to handle small distractions as well as major incidents. As educator David Berliner says, "In short, from the opening bell to the end of the day, the better classroom managers are thinking ahead. While maintaining a pleasant classroom atmosphere, these teachers keep planning how to organize, manage, and control activities to facilitate instruction."[13] Berliner makes an important connection between management and instruction. Effective teachers, in addition to being good classroom managers, must be good organizers of academic content and instruction.

The Pedagogical Cycle

FOCUS QUESTION 4

What are the roles of teachers and students in the pedagogical cycle?

How does one organize classroom life? Researcher Arno Bellack analyzed verbal exchanges between teachers and students and offers a fascinating insight into classroom organization, likening these interactions to a pedagogical game.[14] The game is so cyclical and occurs so frequently that many teachers and students do not even know that they are playing. There are four moves:

1. *Structure.* The teacher provides information, provides direction, and introduces the topics.
2. *Question.* The teacher asks a question.
3. *Respond.* The student answers the question, or tries to.
4. *React.* The teacher reacts to the student's answer and provides feedback.

These four steps make up a **pedagogical cycle,** diagrammed in Figure 11.1. Teachers initiate about 85 percent of the cycles, which are used over and over again in classroom interaction. When teachers learn to consciously enhance and refine each of the cycle's moves, student achievement is increased.[15]

Clarity and Academic Structure

Have you ever been to a class where the teacher is bombarded with questions? "What are we supposed to do?" "Can you explain it again?" "What do you mean?" When such questions are constant, it is a sure sign that the teacher is not setting the stage for instruction. Students need a clear understanding of what they are expected to learn, and they need motivation to learn it. Effective *academic structure*

FIGURE 11.1

Pedagogical cycle and sample classroom dialogue.

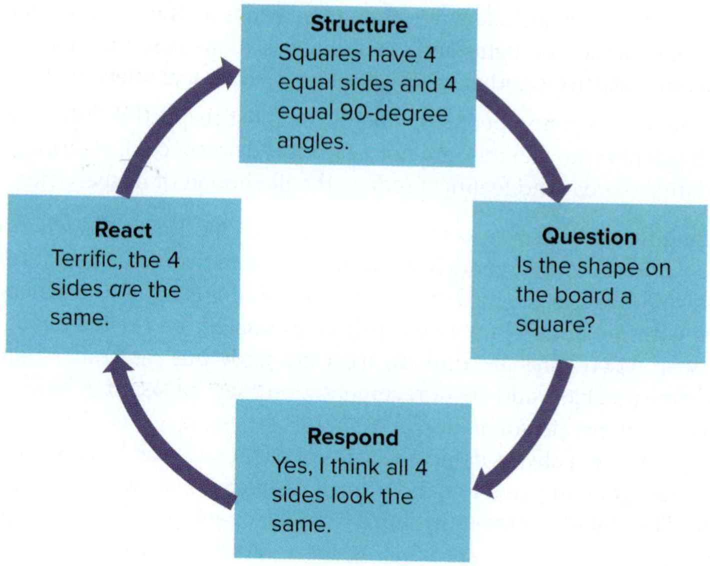

REFLECTION: Continue the classroom dialogue around the cycle again. What might the teacher and the student(s) say?

sets the stage for learning and occurs mainly at the beginning of the lesson. Although the specific structure will vary depending on the students' backgrounds and the difficulty of the subject matter, an effective academic structure usually consists of[16]:

FOCUS QUESTION 5

How can teachers set a stage for learning?

- *Objectives.* Let the students know the objectives (or purpose) of each lesson. Students, like the teacher, need a road map of where they are going and why.
- *Review.* Help students review prior learning before presenting new information. If there is confusion, reteach.
- *Motivation.* Create an "anticipatory set" that motivates students to attend to the lesson. Consider throwing out an intriguing question, an anecdote, a joke, or a challenging riddle.
- *Transition.* Provide connections to help students integrate old and new information.
- *Clarification.* Break down a large body of information. (This is sometimes called "chunking.") Do not inundate students with too much too fast. This is particularly true for young children, English language learners, and slower learners.
- *Scaffolding.* Step-by-step practice and well-crafted questions support and encourage student understanding.
- *Examples.* Give several examples and illustrations to explain main points and ideas.
- *Directions.* Give directions distinctly and slowly. If students are confused about what they are supposed to do, repeat or break information into small segments.
- *Enthusiasm.* Demonstrate personal enthusiasm for the academic content. Make it clear why the information is interesting and important.
- *Closure.* Close the lesson with a brief review or summary. If students are able to provide the summary, so much the better, for it shows that they have really understood the lesson.

Through effective and clear structure, the stage is set for the remaining steps of the pedagogical cycle.

Questioning

Good questioning is at the very core of good teaching. Using an interactive whiteboard, having students work independently or in cooperative groups, lecturing, or using technology in the classroom can all be engaging and meaningful. But designing good questions is key to success in any lesson format. As John Dewey said,

> To question well is to teach well. In the skillful use of the question more than anything else lies the fine art of teaching; for in it we have the guide to clear and vivid ideas, and the quick spur to imagination, the stimulus to thought, the incentive to action.[17]

FOCUS QUESTION 6

What questioning strategies increase student achievement?

Questioning is key in guiding learning, and all students should have equal access to classroom questions and academic interaction. Yet sitting in the same classroom taught by the same teacher, students experience significant differences in the number of questions they are asked. Research shows that male students are asked more questions than female students, and white students are asked more questions than nonwhite students. One of the reasons boys get to answer questions as well as to talk more is that they are assertive in grabbing teacher attention. Boys are more likely than girls to call out the answers to the questions. In addition, when boys call out the answers to questions, teachers are likely to accept their responses. When girls call out the answers, teachers often remind them to raise their hands. Teacher expectations also play a role and are frequently cited as one of the reasons white students (perceived as higher achievers) receive more questions and more active teacher attention than students who are members of other racial and ethnic groups.[18]

If you want all students, not just the quickest and most assertive, to answer questions, establish a protocol for participation. For example, make a rule that students must raise their hands and be called on before they may talk. Too many classes offer variations of the following scene:

> TEACHER: How much is 60 + 4 + 12? *(Many students raise their hands–both girls and boys.)*
>
> TONY: *(Shouts out)* 76!
>
> TEACHER: Okay. How much is 50 + 9 + 8?

What strategies will you use to ensure that all students are heard in your classroom?

©Purestock/SuperStock RF

This scene, repeated again and again in classes across the country, is a typical example of the squeaky wheel–not necessarily the most needy or most deserving student–getting the educational oil. Once you make the rule that students should raise their hands before participating, *hold to that rule.*

Many teachers are well intentioned about having students raise their hands, but, in the rapid pace of classroom interaction, they sometimes forget their own rule. If you hold to that "wait to be recognized" rule, you can make professional decisions about who should answer which questions and why. If you give away this key to classroom participation, you are abandoning an important part of your professional decision making in the classroom.

Although the distribution and ownership of questions are important, the type of question asked is also meaningful. This section provides more information about the different levels of classroom questions, as well as strategies for using them fairly and effectively.

FIGURE 11.2
Bloom's taxonomy.

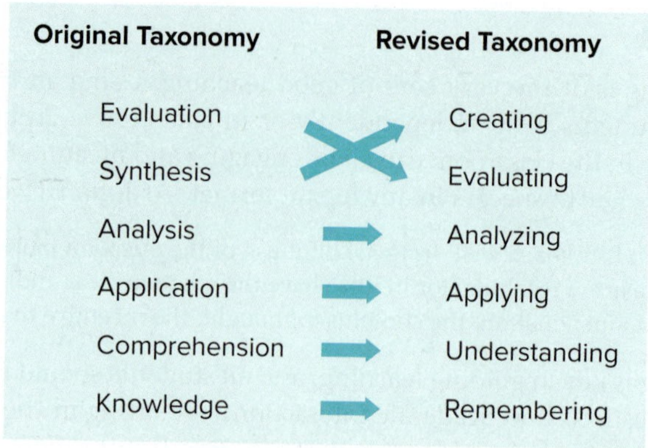

REFLECTION: Why do think the authors of the revised version decided to use verbs instead of nouns to describe each level? The revised version puts "Creating" as the highest level, indicating it is a more demanding intellectual activity than "Evaluating." What do you think?

Many educators differentiate between factual, lower-order questions and thought-provoking, higher-order questions. The oldest and most widely used system for determining the intellectual level of questions is Benjamin **Bloom's taxonomy,** which proceeds from the lowest level of questions, remembering, to the highest level, creating.[19] (By the way, *taxonomy* is another word for *classification.*)

Several years ago, some educators revised Bloom's taxonomy, transposing and renaming some of the categories.[20] Take a look at the original and revised versions and see what similarities and differences you find. (See Figure 11.2.)

The six levels of Bloom's original and revised taxonomy represent questions that require a different kind of thought process. In a sense, Bloom is offering us a blueprint of how we think, from simple (lower-order questions) to complex (higher-order questions). Teachers should be able to formulate questions on each level so that their students can engage in a range of cognitive processes, from lower-to higher-order questions. (See A Closer Look: Bloom's Revised Taxonomy Applied to Questioning Levels on p. 319.)

A **lower-order question** can be answered through memory and recall (levels I and II of the taxonomy). For example, "What is four plus one?" or "What is the name of the largest Native American nation?" are lower-order questions. Without consulting outside references, one could respond with the correct answer only by remembering previously learned information. (The answer to the second question is Cherokee, for those who do not recall.) Either students know the answer or they don't. Research indicates that 70 percent to 95 percent of a teacher's questions are lower order.

A **higher-order question** demands more thought and usually more time before students reach a response (generally, levels III through VI of the taxonomy). These questions may ask for evaluations, comparisons, causal relationships, problem solving, or creative, open-ended thinking. Following are examples of higher-order questions:

1. What similarities in theme emerge in the three Coen brother movies: *True Grit, No Country for Old Men,* and *Fargo?*
2. What could happen if our shadows came to life?

Although higher-order questions have been shown to produce increased student achievement, most teachers ask very few of them.[21]

A CLOSER LOOK

Bloom's Revised Taxonomy Applied to Questioning Levels

LEVEL I: REMEMBERING

Requires student to recall or recognize information. Student is not asked to manipulate information, but to rely on memory or senses to provide the answer. To answer a question on this level, the student must simply remember facts, observations, and definitions.

SAMPLE QUESTIONS What does "quixotic" mean?

List the first ten presidents of the United States.

Sample cue words define, list, review, who, what, where, when

LEVEL II: UNDERSTANDING

Requires student to go beyond simple recall and to demonstrate sufficient comprehension to organize and arrange information mentally. Student must use previously learned information by putting it in his or her own words and rephrasing it.

SAMPLE QUESTIONS In our story, the author discusses why the family left oklahoma. Can you summarize why in your own words?

Explain the main idea of this chart.

Sample cue words describe, explain, compare, contrast, rephrase, summarize

LEVEL III: APPLYING

Requires student to apply previously learned information to answer a problem. At this level, the student uses a rule, a definition, a classification system, or directions in solving a problem with a specific correct answer.

SAMPLE QUESTIONS Identify the proper noun in the following sentences. *(applying a definition)*

Solve the quadratic equation. *(applying a rule)*

Sample cue words choose, classify, demonstrate, diagram, illustrate, solve

LEVEL IV: ANALYZING

Requires student to use three kinds of cognitive processes: (1) to identify causes, reasons, or motives (when these have not been provided to the student previously), (2) to analyze information to reach a generalization or conclusion, and (3) to find evidence to support a specific opinion, event, or situation.

SAMPLE QUESTIONS Why do you think King Lear misjudged his daughter? *(identify motives)*

What generalizations can you make about the climate of Egypt near the Nile River basin? *(analyze information to reach a conclusion)*

Many historians think that Abraham Lincoln was our finest president. What evidence can you find to support this statement? *(find evidence to support a specific opinion)*

Sample cue words investigate, justify, support, why

LEVEL V: EVALUATING

Requires student to judge the merits of an aesthetic work, an idea, or the solution to a problem.

SAMPLE QUESTIONS Which U.S. senator do you think is most effective? Support your selection.

Decide why young children should or should not be allowed to read any book they want. Explain your answer.

Sample cue words argue, conclusion, decide, do you agree, explain

LEVEL VI: CREATING

Requires student to use original and creative thinking: (1) to develop original communications, (2) to make predictions, and (3) to solve problems for which there is no single right answer.

SAMPLE QUESTIONS Write a short story about life on another planet. *(developing an original communication)*

What do you think life would be like if Germany had won World War II? *(making predictions)*

How would you measure the height of a building without being able to go into or onto it? *(solving problems for which there is no single right solution)*

Sample cue words imagine, improve, predict, synthesize, what would happen if . . .

REFLECTION: Create a question for each level of Bloom's taxonomy. Were some levels easier than others? Why or why not?

Different questioning levels stimulate different levels of thought. If you ask a fifth-grade student to define an adjective, you are working on lower-level basic skills. If you ask a fifth-grade student to write a short story, making effective use of adjectives, you are working on a higher level of student achievement. Both lower-order and higher-order questions are important and should be matched to appropriate instructional goals:

Ask Lower-Order Questions When Students Are

- Being introduced to new information
- Working on drill and practice
- Reviewing previously learned information

Ask Higher-Order Questions When Students Are

- Working on problem-solving skills
- Involved in a creative or affective discussion
- Asked to make judgments about quality, aesthetics, or ethics
- Challenged to manipulate already established information in more sophisticated ways

Student Response

If you were to spend a few minutes in a high school English class, you might hear a classroom discussion go something like this[22]:

> TEACHER: Who wrote the poem "Stopping by Woods on a Snowy Evening"? Tomás?
>
> TOMÁS: Robert Frost.
>
> TEACHER: Good. What action takes place in the poem? Kenisha?
>
> KENISHA: A man stops his sleigh to watch the woods get filled with snow.
>
> TEACHER: Yes. Michael, what thoughts go through the man's mind?
>
> MICHAEL: He thinks how beautiful the woods are and how he would like to stay and watch. *(Pauses for a second)*
>
> TEACHER: Yes—and what else? Emma? *(Waits half a second)* Well, why does he feel he can't stay there indefinitely and watch the woods and the snow?
>
> EMMA: He knows he's too busy. He's got too many things to do to stay there for so long.
>
> TEACHER: Good. In the poem's last line, the man says that he has miles to go before he sleeps. What might sleep be a symbol for? Krista?
>
> KRISTA: Well, I think it might be . . . *(Pauses for a second)*
>
> TEACHER: Think, Krista. *(Waits for half a second)* All right then—Ethan? *(Waits again for half a second)* Alex? *(Waits half a second)* What's the matter with everyone today? Didn't you do the reading?

The teacher is using several instructional skills effectively. His is a well-managed classroom. The students are on task and engaged in a discussion appropriate to the academic content. By asking a series of lower-order questions ("Who wrote the poem?" "What action takes place in the poem?"), the teacher works with the students to establish an information base. Then the teacher builds to higher-order questions about the poem's theme and meaning.

If you were to give this teacher suggestions on how to improve his questioning techniques, you might point out the difficulty students have in answering the more complex questions. You might also note the lightning pace at which this lesson proceeds. The teacher fires questions so rapidly that the students barely have time to think. This is not so troublesome when they are answering factual questions that require a brief memorized response. However, students begin to flounder when they are required to answer more complex questions with equal speed.

Describe the classroom interaction patterns in this classroom. What are the strengths? weaknesses? As a teacher, what would you change?

©LWA/Dann Tardif/Getty Images RF

Although it is important to keep classroom discussion moving at a brisk pace, sometimes teachers push forward too rapidly. Slowing down at two key places during classroom discussion can usually improve the effectiveness and equity of classroom responses. In the research on classroom interaction, this slowing down is called **wait time**.[23]

Mary Budd Rowe's research on wait time shows that after asking a question, teachers typically wait only one second or less for a student response (wait time 1). If the response is not forthcoming in that time, teachers rephrase the question, ask another student to answer it, or answer it themselves. If teachers can learn to increase their wait time from one second to three seconds to five seconds, significant improvements in the quantity and quality of student response usually will take place.

There is another point in classroom discussion when wait time can be increased. After students complete an answer, teachers often begin their reaction or their next question before a second has passed (wait time 2). Once again, it is important for teachers to increase their wait time from one second to three to five seconds. On the basis of her research, Mary Budd Rowe has determined that increasing the pause after a student gives an answer is equally important as increasing wait time 1, the pause after the teacher asks a question. When wait time 1 and wait time 2 are increased, classroom interaction is changed in several positive ways.

Changes in Student Behavior

- More students participate in discussion.
- Fewer discipline problems disrupt the class.
- The length of student response increases dramatically.
- Students are more likely to support their statements with evidence.
- Speculative thinking increases.
- There are more student questions and fewer failures to respond.
- Student achievement increases on written tests that measure more complex levels of thinking.

Changes in Teacher Behavior

- Teacher comments are less disjointed and more fluent. Classroom discussion becomes more logical, thoughtful, and coherent.
- Teachers ask more sophisticated, higher-order questions.
- Teachers begin to hold higher expectations for all students.

TEACHING TIP

Ways Not to Use Questions

This is really an "un-tip" on how to avoid some common pitfalls as you begin crafting your effective questioning style. Here are some examples of how not to use questions:

- *To control misbehavior.* Some teachers use questions to prevent or stop misbehavior. Rather than reducing student disruptions, this "question as punishment" approach actually serves to reward misbehaving students with extra instructional attention. And guess who gets ignored: students who are behaving well and trying to stay engaged in the lesson. Questions need to involve everyone in a class—not used to manage a few. Here's a bonus: effective questioning that keeps all students on-task *reduces* the likelihood that management problems will emerge.
- *To "put down" a student.* The converse of controlling misbehavior occurs when teachers use question as a tool of humiliation, a way to put down a difficult student with a really tough question, a zinger few could answer. Good questions are not weapons.
- *To manipulate answers.* Some teachers take great liberties in restating student answers in order to move the lesson along a predetermined path. As a result, the teacher's idea rather than the student's is heard. Such manipulation of paraphrasing devalues students and can create an unsafe learning environment.

REFLECTION: Have you been in a classroom where questions were used poorly? How did it feel?

Research indicates that teachers give more wait time to students for whom they hold higher expectations. A high-achieving student is more likely to get time to think than is a low-achieving student. If we do not expect much from our students, we will not get much. High expectations and longer wait times are positively related to achievement. Researchers suggest that white male students, particularly high achievers, are more likely to be given adequate wait time than are females, English language learners, students with a disability, quiet students, and students of color. Students who are quiet and reserved or who think more slowly may especially benefit from increased wait time. In fact, a key benefit of extended wait time is an increase in the quality of student participation, even from students who were previously silent.[24]

Usually when teachers learn that they are giving students less than a second to think, they are surprised and have every intention of waiting longer. But that is easier said than done! In the hectic arena of the classroom, it is all too easy to slip into split-second question-and-answer patterns.

Teachers can adopt self-monitoring cues to slow themselves down at the two key wait-time points. For example, one teacher says that he puts his hand behind his back and counts on his fingers for three seconds to slow himself down. Another teacher says that she covers her mouth with her hand (in a thoughtful pose) to keep herself from talking and thereby destroying "the pause that lets them think."

As mentioned previously, wait time is more important in some cases than in others. If you are asking students to repeat previously memorized math facts and you are interested in developing speed, a three- to five-second wait time may be counterproductive. However, if you have asked a higher-order question that calls for a complicated answer, be sure that wait times 1 and 2 are ample. Simply put, students, like the rest of us, need time to think, and some students may need more wait time than others. For example, when a student speaks English as a newly acquired language, additional wait time could help that student accurately translate and respond to the question. And many of us could profit by less impulsive, more thoughtful responses, the kind that can be engendered by longer wait times.

When teachers allow more wait time, the results can be surprising. As one teacher said, "I never thought Andrea had anything to say. She just used to sit there like a bump on a log. Then I tried calling on her and giving her time to answer. What a difference! Not only does she answer, she asks questions that no one else has thought of."

GLOBAL VIEW

Some linguists suggest that fast-paced communication with very little wait time is typical of American classrooms. Ask your international classmates about interaction patterns in classrooms of their homeland: Do students sit silently until called upon? Would interruptions or calling out be acceptable? Is it okay to ask the teacher a question?

Reaction or Productive Feedback

"Today," the student teacher said, "we are going to hear the story of *The Three Billy Goats Gruff.*" A murmur of anticipation rippled through the kindergarten children comfortably seated on the carpet around the flannel board. This student teacher was a favorite, and the children were particularly happy when she told them flannel-board stories.

RAP 4.4

Teaching Is Learning

"Before we begin the story, I want to make sure we know what all the words mean. Who can tell me what a troll is?"

A 5-year-old nicknamed B.J. raised his hand. "A troll is someone who walks you home from school."

"Okay," the teacher responded, a slightly puzzled look flickering over her face. "Who else can tell me what a troll is?"

Another student chimed in, "A troll is someone with white hair sticking out of his head."

"Okay," the teacher said.

Another student volunteered, "It hides under bridges and waits for you and scares you."

"Uh-huh," said the teacher.

Warming to the topic, another student gleefully recounted, "I saw a green troll named Shrek who lives in the woods."

"Okay," the teacher said.

Wide-eyed, B.J. raised his hand again, "I'm sure glad we had this talk about trolls," he said. "I'm not going home with them from school anymore."

"Okay," the teacher said.

This is a classroom in which several good teaching strategies are in operation. The teacher uses effective academic structure, and the students are on task, interested, and involved in the learning activity. The teacher is asking lower-order questions appropriately, to make sure the students know key vocabulary words before the flannel-board story is told. The problem with this classroom lies in the fourth stage of the pedagogical cycle: This teacher does not provide specific reactions and adequate feedback. Did you notice that the teacher reacted with "uh-huh" or "okay," no matter what kind of answer the students gave? Because of this vague feedback and "okay" teaching style, B.J. was left confused about the difference between a troll and a patrol. This real-life incident may seem amusing, but there was nothing funny to B.J., who was genuinely afraid to leave school with the patrol.

Recently, attention has been directed not only at how teachers ask questions but also at how they respond to student answers. When Myra and David Sadker analyzed classroom interaction in more than one hundred classrooms in five states, they found that teachers generally use four types of reactions[25]:

1. *Praise.* Positive comments about student work, such as "Excellent, good job."
2. *Acceptance.* Comments such as "Uh-huh" and "okay," which acknowledge that student answers are acceptable. These are not as strong as praise.

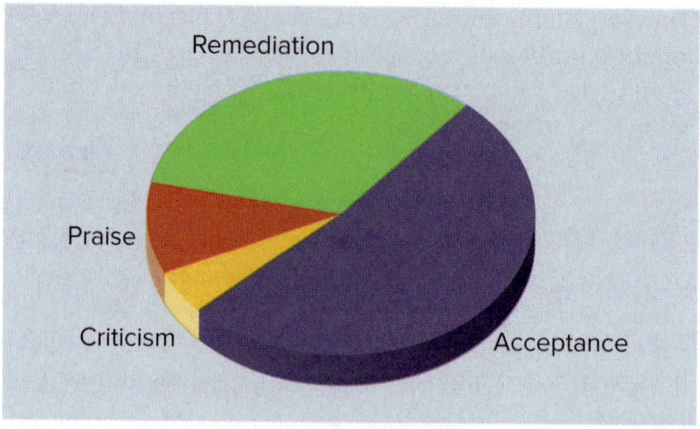

FIGURE 11.3
Teacher reactions.

REFLECTION: Most teacher reactions fall in the acceptance category. Suggest three reasons this might occur and how learning is influenced.

3. *Remediation.* Comments that encourage a more accurate student response or encourage students to think more clearly, creatively, or logically. Sample remediation comments include "Try again," "Sharpen your answer," and "Check your addition."
4. *Criticism.* A clear statement that an answer is inaccurate or a behavior is inappropriate. This category includes harsh criticism ("This is a terrible paper"), as well as milder comments that simply indicate an answer is not correct ("Your answer to the third question is wrong").

Which of these reactions do you think teachers use most frequently? The Sadkers' study found that acceptance was the most frequent response, accounting for more than half of all teacher reactions from grade school to graduate school. The second most frequent teacher response was remediation, accounting for one-third of teacher reactions. Used infrequently, praise made up only 11 percent of reactions. The rarest response was criticism. In two-thirds of the classrooms observed, teachers never told a student that an answer was incorrect. In the classrooms where criticism did occur, it accounted for only 5 percent of interaction. (See Figure 11.3.)

In *A Place Called School,* John Goodlad writes that "learning is enhanced when students understand what is expected of them, get recognition for their work, learn about their errors, and receive guidance in improving their performances."[26] But many students claim that they are not informed or corrected when they make mistakes.[27] Perhaps this is caused by overreliance on the acceptance response, which is the vaguest kind of feedback that teachers can offer. Because there is more acceptance than praise, criticism, and remediation combined, some educators are beginning to wonder: "Is the 'okay' classroom okay?"

Because achievement is likely to increase when students get clear, specific productive feedback about their answers, it is important for teachers to reduce the "okay" reaction and to be more varied and specific in the feedback they provide. Researchers have studied the links between praise and student achievement and found that praise is most effective when[28]:

1. *Praise is contingent upon student performance.* Praise should closely follow student behavior the teacher wants to recognize.
2. *Praise is specific.* When teachers praise, they should clearly indicate what aspect of the student behavior is noteworthy (e.g., creative problem solving or good use of evidence to support an argument).
3. *Praise is sincere.* Praise should reflect the experiences, growth, and development of the individual student. Otherwise, it may be dismissed as being disingenuous.

4. *Praise lets students know about their competence and the importance of their accomplishments*—for instance, "The well-documented review of studies on your Web site and the connection you made between the two tobacco filters may eventually have an impact on the industry."
5. *Praise attributes success to ability or effort*—for example, "Your analysis of the paintings of the Impressionists is excellent. I'll bet you spent a long time studying their work in the museum" *(attribution to effort)*. Or "This story is fantastic. You've got a real flair for creative writing" *(attribution to ability)*. When praise is attributed to abilities or effort, students know that successful performance is under their own control.
6. *Praise uses past performance as a context for describing present performance*—for example, "Last week you were really having trouble with your breast stroke kick. Now you've got it together—you've learned to push the water behind you and increase your speed."

When praise does not embody these characteristics, it can be detrimental. A growing body of research shows that easy, unearned praise does not help students and instead interferes with learning and emotional well-being. In study after study, children rewarded for being smart become more likely to shy away from hard assignments that might tarnish their star reputations. But children praised for trying hard or taking risks tend to enjoy challenges and find greater success. Children also perform better in the long term when they believe that their intellect is not a birthright but something that grows and develops as they learn new things.[29]

Just as students need to know when they are performing well, they need to know when their efforts are inadequate or incorrect. If students do not have information about their weak areas, they will find it difficult to improve. Here are some tips for effective feedback:

1. *Constructive feedback is specific and contingent on student performance.* The teacher's comments should closely follow the student behavior the teacher wants to improve.
2. *Critical comments focus on student performance and are not of a personal nature.* All of us find it easier to accept constructive criticism when it is detached from our worth as a person, when it is not personal, hostile, or sarcastic.
3. *Feedback provides a clear blueprint for improvement.* If you merely tell a student that an answer is wrong and nothing more, the student has clear feedback on level of performance but no strategies for improvement. Effective feedback suggests an approach for attaining success, such as "Check your addition," or "Let's conjugate this verb in both French and English, to see where the error is."
4. *An environment is established that lets the student know it is acceptable to make mistakes.* "We learn from our errors. Hardly any inventions are perfected on the first try."
5. *Constructive feedback relates eventual success to effort.* "Now you have demonstrated the correct sequence in class. Give yourself a solid half-hour tonight working on this, and I bet that you will get most of it correct. I'll check with you tomorrow."
6. *Constructive feedback recognizes when students have made improvements in their performance.* "Last week you were having trouble identifying which of Newton's laws are applicable in each of these time motion studies. Now you've mastered the skill. You've done a good job."

An "okay classroom" allows student error and misunderstanding to go uncorrected; it lets B.J. think that the patrol will eat him up after school. In classrooms where there is appropriate use of remediation and constructive criticism, students know not only when they have made mistakes but also how to correct them. They also recognize that this process leads to growth and achievement.

Technology as a Tool for Effective Teaching

FOCUS QUESTION 7
How can teachers use technology to support effective instruction?

Today's technology transports students around the world via virtual field trips, provides individualized tutorials and drill-and-practice of certain skills, and instantly and inexpensively adds millions of books, articles, and videos to a teacher's curriculum. Technology holds the potential to profoundly reshape education, and currently about forty states require formal teacher training in technology. Educators today use technology to[30]:

RAP 4.9

Web site of the Month

GLOBAL VIEW

YouTube for Schools is a wonderful free resource designed for teachers of all grade levels. Lessons, lectures, and interactive conversations from across the curriculum and the world are available. Check out learning possibilities from around the globe at www.youtube.com/user/teachers.

- *Motivate students* through multimedia materials that capture their interest.
- *Increase basic skills* in math, reading, and writing, as well as content areas, through sample quizzes, drill-and-practice, and additional course-related information.
- *Promote higher-order thinking and increased content understanding* by introducing simulations, problem-based learning, Internet research, collaborative work, and student authoring programs.
- *Increase academic resources* by bringing the unlimited written and visual assets of the Internet into local schools.
- *Increase responsiveness to different learning styles,* including children with special needs or students for whom the typical classroom culture means academic and/or social distress.
- *Improve workplace preparation* as students learn keyboarding skills, software applications, video production and other technological operations common to future employment.
- *Save work for teachers* by creating a class Web site, class Facebook page, or Twitter account. Homework assignments, worksheets, notes, and exam dates can be posted online. Parent communication can be accomplished through e-mail, social media, or texting. Grading software can track attendance, average grades, and chart the results while even more cutting-edge programs use artificial intelligence, such as the Intelligent Essay Assessor (IEA), to grade essays.
- *Strengthen student learning* by adding resources, such as SMART boards or online videos to create more dramatic and effective teacher presentations.
- *Modernize the school culture* by moving beyond pencil and paper, chalk and chalkboards to the world's digital resources.

Computers can be used for basic skills or for more high-order thinking and creative activities.

©Ron Nickel/Design Pics/Getty Images RF

Teachers can discover online an enormous amount of curriculum in a variety of formats, including audio and video pieces. Helpful sites include:

- Discovery Education's Lesson Plan Library (http://school.discoveryeducation.com/lessonplans).

Technology—Educational Marvel or Menace?

TECHNOLOGY IS A *MARVEL* BECAUSE IT . . .

IMPROVES LEARNING

With technology we can individualize instruction, grant students autonomy, and empower them to learn at their own pace, while offering a global perspective on the curriculum. Each learner benefits from having an omnipresent tutor to individually tailor schoolwork to putting the focus on learning rather than teaching.

REACHES MORE STUDENTS

Computers, the Internet, smartphones, and social media expand the educational horizons of children in rural communities and those with limited resources, as well as homebound and disabled learners. Students fearful of going to school because of bullying or violence can learn safely at home using technology.

OFFERS STUDENTS A WEALTH OF RESOURCES

Students have so much more than a school or local library when they can use technology to tap into resources around the world. Students can now access limitless books, articles, pictures, sound clips, and newspapers; follow links to experts or virtual field trips; and participate in real-time communications across the globe.

PREPARES STUDENTS FOR THE FUTURE

Technology encourages interdisciplinary and collaborative efforts, facilitates problem-based learning, and encourages student creativity; the skills many believe will be in high demand in the future economy. Students at ease with technology will be assets to future employers.

TECHNOLOGY IS A *MENACE* BECAUSE . . .

EFFECTIVE TEACHING IS COMPROMISED

Good teaching requires a personal connection. A teacher gazing at a student who is gazing at a computer is not a productive connection. Technology also often competes with teachers. Too many students become distracted from academic pursuits by cell phones, tablets, and iPods. When this happens, focus is lost and even the most effective teachers are compromised.

IT MAY LEAVE MORE STUDENTS OUT OF THE LOOP

Technology does not equalize many disparities, and in some cases amplifies economic inequalities. Children from families with means and resources, children with high-tech homes attending well-resourced schools have technological advantages not available to poorer students and schools. Poor students soon discover technology's unwelcome mat tripping them up at the door of most career options.

STUDENTS ARE FLOODED WITH MISINFORMATION

Many of today's youngsters can surf the Internet but are unable to sort truth from fiction. The Internet is home to countless narrow-interest groups that promote political and other causes by disseminating misinformation. While some books and periodicals might have done this in the past, technology has made all kinds of misinformation accessible to impressionable children who can be easily misguided.

WE MAY BE BUILDING A NOT-SO-WONDERFUL FUTURE

Technology is creating a world of superficial friendships and shallow learning. Computer health risks include increased eyestrain, repetitive motion injury, and obesity that come from a more sedentary lifestyle. What other dangers lurk in a more technological world?

connect YOU DECIDE...

Do you believe that technology is an educational marvel or menace? Or somewhere in between? Explain.

In what ways has your education been enriched—and diminished—by technology?

- TeachersFirst.com (www.teachersfirst.com/index.cfm).
- Khan Academy (https://www.khanacademy.org/)
- TeachThought (http://www.teachthought.com/)

Technology also offers an array of tools for effective instruction. As examples, teachers can engage students in Twitter-like classroom discussions with Edmodo, bring experts into the classroom via Skype, guide students in creating digital portfolios with Mahara, and take virtual field trips around the world using Google Earth.

Doesn't all this sound exciting? We Americans love our technology, and cool computers are high on our gadget love list. Unfortunately, in all this tech-glitz, perspective can get lost. (See You Be the Judge: Technology—Educational Marvel or Menace?) Surely technology has enormous potential to help teachers improve instruction and enrich student learning. But we believe educators must be wary of focusing on technology rather than people. Computers cannot create a culture of excellence and push students to meet high expectations. Computers cannot visit students' homes to get to know their families and engage them in school activities. Software developer and educator George Brackett reminds us, "Thoughtful, caring, capable people change schools, sometimes with the help of technology, sometimes not, and sometimes even despite it."[31] Technology should be seen as a teacher's tool, and not the other way around. The first step is deciding how best to use that tool.

RAP 4.7

Technology in the Classroom: Bane or Boon?

In the following section, we describe some well-known models of instruction, from direct teaching to differentiated instruction, and include examples of how each model is used in a classroom. When appropriate, we also describe how technology can offer instructional support.

RAP 4.2

Observing Different Teaching Strategies

Models for Effective Instruction

FOCUS QUESTION 8

What are several salient models of instruction?

Part of the challenge for teachers is knowing which model of instruction to choose for particular educational purposes. The following models differ dramatically from one another, yet each may be helpful in your classroom.

Direct Teaching

Also called *active* or *explicit teaching,* the **direct teaching** model emphasizes the importance of a structured lesson in which presentation of new information is followed by student practice and teacher feedback. In this model, which has emerged from extensive research, the role of the teacher is that of a strong leader, one who structures the classroom and sequences subject matter to reflect a clear academic focus.

With direct instruction, teachers present a carefully structured lesson, such as this chemistry lesson on molecular structures.

©Fuse/Getty Images RF

Researchers put forward seven principles of effective direct teaching.[32]

1. *Daily review.* At the beginning of the lesson, teachers review prior learning. Frequently, teachers focus on assigned homework, clarify points of confusion, and provide extra practice for facts and skills that need more attention.
2. *Anticipatory set.* This is also known as a "grabber" and is a way to get students' attention and interest. This could be a teacher demonstration, a video, a story, a puzzle, or a handout before the actual lesson. The anticipatory set builds a bridge from previous knowledge to new information. If successful, the anticipatory set will get students mentally or physically ready for the lesson.

TEACHING TIP

Classroom Clicks

How many times has a teacher wanted to ask a great question to all the students in the class? But of course, after one student provides an answer, the power of that question for others is diminished. Here comes technology to the rescue: Clickers (also known as Classroom Response Systems or Student Response Systems).

Clickers look like a simple TV remote that allows each student to respond to a question embedded in a specially designed PowerPoint-like presentation. Each student clicks the answer he or she thinks is correct, and those responses are shown to the instructor. Often teachers post, via a SMART board or computer projector, class summaries of student responses in real time, so the entire class can view the results. Interested in exploring clickers? Here are some thoughts for you to consider:

Why and when to use clickers: Clickers allow instructors to encourage active student learning and small group interactions, even during lectures. Ask clicker questions sparingly, but strategically, to highlight the concepts you most want to emphasize.

Clicker questions: Clickers work well for presenting multiple-choice questions, such as selecting the best answer, or opinion polling.

- Keep questions short to optimize legibility in a slide.
- Offer no more than five answer options.
- Avoid requiring complex calculations that may encourage students to guess rather than think through the question.

How to use clickers: Encourage active discussion among students. Post a question and ask students to discuss their answers with each other before collecting answers. Before revealing the correct answer, discuss the answer options and allow students to explain their reasons for choosing various answers. Be sure to allow time for discussion—thinking, not clicking, is the goal.

Assessing learning: Student responses enable teachers (and often students as well) to evaluate learning progress and gaps:

- Pre-assessments: before a new topic
  - What do students already know?
  - What are students' misconceptions?
- Mid-assessments: in the middle of a topic or lecture
  - Do students understand this concept?
  - Has student thinking changed?
- Post-assessments: at the end of a topic or class
  - Can students synthesize the concepts to solve problems?
  - How has students' understanding changed?

REFLECTION: Describe some advantages and disadvantages of using clickers.

3. *New material.* Teachers begin by letting students know the objectives to be attained. New information is broken down into smaller bits and is covered at a brisk pace. Teachers illustrate main points with concrete examples. Teachers ask questions frequently to check for student understanding and to make sure that students are ready for independent work using new skills and knowledge.
4. *Guided practice.* Students use new skills and knowledge under direct teacher supervision. During guided practice, teachers ask many content questions ("What is the definition of a paragraph?") and many process questions ("How do you locate the topic sentence in a paragraph?"). Teachers check student responses for understanding, offering prompts and providing corrective feedback. Guided practice continues until students answer with approximately 70 to 80 percent accuracy.
5. *Specific feedback.* Correct answers to questions are acknowledged clearly, so that students will understand when their work is accurate. When student answers are hesitant, the teacher provides process feedback ("Yes, Eva, that's correct because . . ."). Teachers correct inaccurate responses immediately, before errors become habitual. Frequent errors are a sign that students are not ready for independent work, and guided practice should continue.

PROFILE IN EDUCATION

Larry Cuban

Having assumed various roles in education over the past 50 years—from classroom teacher to professor to superintendent—Larry Cuban has had a first-hand view of how education has changed. Interestingly, he argues that, save for some minor reforms, it has not.

Read a full profile of Larry Cuban on Connect.

©Lee L. Jacks/Professor Emeritus of Education/Stanford University

connect

6. *Independent practice.* Similar to guided practice, except that students work by themselves at their seats or at home. Independent practice continues until responses are assured, quick, and at a level of approximately 95 percent accuracy. Cooperative learning (see the next section) and student tutoring of one another are effective strategies during independent practice.
7. *Weekly and monthly reviews.* Regular reviews offer students the opportunity for more practice, a strategy related to high achievement. Barak Rosenshine, a pioneering researcher in developing the principles of direct teaching, recommends a weekly review every Monday, with a monthly review every fourth Monday.

Direct teaching works well when you are teaching skill subjects, such as grammar or mathematics, or helping students master factual material. The direct teaching model is particularly helpful during the first stages of learning new and complex information, but it is less helpful when imaginative responses and student creativity are called for.

Technology can often enhance direct instruction. Presentation software, such as PowerPoint or Prezi, are some of the more ubiquitous programs that can organize and add energy to teacher presentations. Savvy teachers also use these presentation tools with more esoteric technology, such as digital microscopes, or bring an expert speaker into the classroom through a webcam or Skype.

Direct teaching can sometimes make it difficult for teachers to engage all students in class discussions. Technology can encourage student participation. For example, students can use a handheld computer, or "clicker," to answer instructor-initiated questions. Teachers using such devices report that along with increasing participation, students are more attentive and better prepared. (See Teaching Tip: Classroom Clicks on p. 329.)

Flipped Instruction

When do students most need teacher attention? When a subject is being explained (i.e., a lecture)? Or when students are asked to apply new information? For some subjects and learning styles, lecturing via direct instruction is a great match. But other students need teacher support most when trying to understand and apply new information or skills. They need an engaged learning environment that targets their specific needs. That's the idea behind flipped instruction.

Flipped instruction (*or flipped classroom*) encourages teachers to combine their creativity with technology to "flip" student learning.[33] Students access their lessons outside of class time via online videos. Perhaps it is a teacher-made video, a YouTube broadcast, a podcast, a blog, or the online Khan Academy that presents the information. When classrooms are flipped, students can learn anywhere–at home, at work, at the beach–and at their own pace. Strong students can breeze through the instructional video; others can watch it over and over until concepts become clearer. How well do students learn? Ah, we find that out in school. Flipped instruction creates in-class time for students to solve problems and work with their new knowledge. The terms "flipped instruction" and "flipped classroom" may initially suggest a video that students watch at home as the essential ingredient. It's not. It's about how to effectively create in-class time with students.

So what does flipped instruction look like? Instead of starting off with a lecture, a class might begin with question-and-answer time. Students come to class with at least one interesting question about the video lesson. The teacher gets to interact

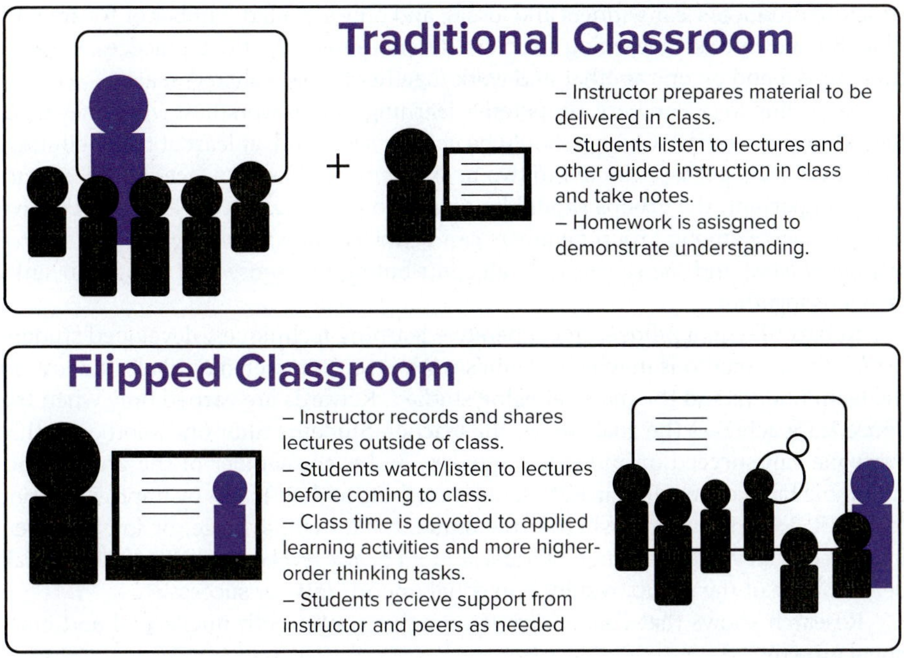

FIGURE 11.4
The flipped classroom.

REFLECTION: What words can you add to this graphic that further describe the flipped classroom? Create your own graphic to describe a flipped classroom.

with each student, and students get to point out things they don't understand or simply wonder about. Let's say that before coming to class, students viewed a video about voting rights. The teacher might open the class with a clicker poll or other check for understanding. After addressing students' questions, the teacher might select classroom activities based on student needs. For example, some students may need to review the basic requirements of the Fifteenth Amendment and subsequent Voting Rights Acts. Some students may be ready to debate contemporary voting rights issues. Still others might create a social justice project that helps all individuals in their community have access to voting. As students work independently or in small groups, the teacher has the opportunity to speak with each student about his or her understanding. The teacher is engaged in continual formative assessment, diagnosing on the spot each student's understanding and modifying instruction for each student as needed (see Figure 11.4: The Flipped Classroom).

Not all lessons lend themselves to flipping. But many do. As a teacher, how might you flip your classroom?

In cooperative learning, students work together to gain new understandings on a topic, such as this chemistry lesson on molecular structures.
©Corbis/age fotostock RF

Cooperative Learning

In a classroom using **cooperative learning,** students work on activities in small, heterogeneous groups, and they often receive rewards or recognition based on the overall group performance. Although cooperative learning can be traced back to the 1920s, it seems startling or new because the typical classroom environment is frequently competitive. For example, when grading is done on a curve, one student's success is often detrimental to others. This competitive structure produces clear winners and losers, and only a limited number of A's are possible. But a cooperative learning structure differs from competitive practices, because students depend on one another and work together to reach shared goals.

According to researchers, cooperative learning groups work best when they meet the following criteria.[34] Groups should be *heterogeneous* and, at least at the beginning, should be *small,* perhaps limited to two to six members. Because face-to-face interaction is important, the groups should be *circular* to permit easy conversation. Positive *interdependence* among group members can be fostered by a *shared group goal, shared division of labor,* and *shared materials,* all contributing to a sense that the group sinks or swims together.

Robert Slavin, a pioneer in cooperative learning techniques, developed student team learning methods in which a team's work is not completed until all students on the team understand the material being studied. Rewards are earned only when the entire team achieves the goals set by the teacher. Students tutor one another so that everyone can succeed on individual quizzes, and each member of the group is accountable for learning. Because students contribute to their teams by improving prior scores, it does not matter whether the student is a high, average, or low achiever. Increased achievement by an individual student at any level contributes to the overall performance of the group, resulting in equal opportunity for success.[35]

Research shows that cooperative learning promotes both intellectual and emotional growth:

- Students make higher achievement gains; this is especially true for math in the elementary grades.
- Students have higher levels of self-esteem and greater motivation to learn.
- Students have a stronger sense that classmates have positive regard for one another.
- Understanding and cooperation among students from different racial and ethnic backgrounds are enhanced.[36]

GLOBAL VIEW

Taking ITGlobal encourages students to collaborate with peers from around the world to share and discuss various educational, health, political, environmental, and social issues from a wide range of cultural perspectives. Visit www.tigweb.org.

However, the practical realities of cooperative learning can be challenging. Some students, accustomed to starring roles in full class instruction, continue to dominate the small groups. Accurate grading requires an analysis of both the individual and the group performance. And even the most committed practitioners acknowledge that cooperative learning may take more time than direct teaching. Still, educators are growing increasingly interested in cooperative learning as a strategy for working successfully with mixed-ability groups and diverse classroom populations.

Mastery Learning

Mastery learning programs are committed to the credo that, given the right tools, all children can learn. Stemming from an individualized reward structure, these programs are used from early childhood to graduate school. For example, after years of dismal test scores and lack of student motivation, the Chugach School District in Alaska adopted a student-centered, mastery learning approach. Unlike the standard grade-level system where students worry about passing into the next grade, with school-wide mastery learning, each student moves at an individual pace and focuses on becoming proficient in ten specific academic areas, such as reading, mathematics, and service learning, as well as nonacademic subjects such as cultural awareness and career development. Some students achieve proficiency and graduate at age 14; some do not get there until 21. Not only are test scores and attendance greatly improved, but students also report feeling motivated to learn.[37]

Mastery learning programs require specific and carefully sequenced learning objectives. The first step is to identify a **behavioral objective,** a specific skill or academic task to be mastered. Students are taught the skill or material in the objective; then they are tested to determine if the objective has been reached. Students who complete the test successfully go on for acceleration or enrichment, while the students who fail to demonstrate mastery of the objective receive corrective instruction and are retested. The success of mastery learning rests on *instructional alignment,* which is a close match between what is taught and what is assessed.

In mastery learning, students typically work at their own pace, often with individualized written or digital materials. The teacher provides assistance and facilitates student efforts, but mastery still remains a student responsibility. (Are you seeing similarities between mastery learning and flipped classrooms?) Studies have shown that many students, particularly younger ones, find it hard to take charge of their own instruction, so mastery learning programs highlight the role of the teacher as instructional leader, motivator, and guide.

Studies suggest that mastery learning can be beneficial across grade levels and subject areas. In mastery learning classrooms:[38]

- Teachers have more positive attitudes toward teaching and higher expectations for their students.
- In general, students have more positive attitudes about learning and their ability to learn.
- Students achieve more and remember what they have learned longer.

Problem-Based Learning

Focusing on authentic or real-life problems that often go beyond traditional subject areas is at the heart of **problem-based learning (PBL).** As you might imagine, real problems are not bound by a single subject field or even by the school building. This emphasis is apparent in the other terms used to describe PBL: *experience-based education, project-based instruction,* and *anchored instruction* (because it is "anchored" in the real world). In this instructional model, a crucial aspect of the teacher's role is to identify activities that fuel students' interest, such as

- Design a plan for protecting a specific endangered species.
- How can we stop bullying and harassment in this school?
- Develop a set of urban policies to halt the deterioration of a central city.
- Formulate solutions that might have kept the United States from engaging in the Civil War.

Finding scintillating questions and projects to excite and motivate students is critical, but it is only one aspect of PBL. Other characteristics include[39]:

- *Learner cooperation.* Similar to cooperative learning, PBL often depends on small groups or pairs of students collaborating as they explore and investigate various issues. This approach de-emphasizes competition. For teachers, the goal is to guide and challenge a dozen such small groups simultaneously.

Problem-based learning allows students to discover answers to real-life issues, such as how to improve children's nutrition by growing and harvesting healthy foods.

©Jim West/Alamy

- *Higher-order thinking.* Exploring real and complex issues requires students to analyze, synthesize, and evaluate material.
- *Cross-disciplinary work.* PBL encourages students to investigate how different academic subjects shed light on one another. In exploring ecological issues, for example, students touch not only on biology and chemistry but also on economics, history, sociology, and political science.
- *Artifacts and exhibits.* Students involved in PBL demonstrate what they learn in a very tangible way. Students may produce a traditional report or may create a video, a physical model, a digital portfolio of artifacts, or even a presentation, such as a play or a debate. Teachers might organize a class or school-wide exhibit to share the progress made by PBL students.
- *Authentic learning.* Students pursue an actual unresolved issue. They are expected to define the problem, develop a hypothesis, collect information, analyze that information, and suggest a conclusion, one that might work in the real world.

Differentiated Instruction

It would make a teacher's life easier if all students learned the same way, but they do not. Student needs, learning styles, life experiences, and readiness to learn differ. To connect effectively with all your students, you will need to abandon the notion that all students fit comfortably into a particular teaching or testing style. **Differentiated instruction** responds to student differences by offering multiple options for instruction and assessment. Carol Ann Tomlinson, a pioneer in the field, defines differentiated instruction broadly as "doing whatever it takes to ensure that struggling and advanced learners, students with varied cultural heritages, and children with different background experiences all grow as much as they possibly can."[40]

Differentiated instruction organizes instructional activities around student needs rather than content. At first glance, this may seem to be in conflict with the current emphasis on standards-based instruction, but Tomlinson sees it as quite complementary. As she describes it, standards-based curriculum tells us *what* curriculum to teach; differentiation tells us *how* to teach any curriculum well. Notes Tomlinson,

> Typically, what we're being asked to teach kids are facts and skills, but you can wrap them in understanding. You give kids a sense of how this makes sense in the world, how it all fits together, and what they can do with it as people. . . . No one would ask teachers not to teach what they feel responsible for. But you can teach those things in ways that are more meaningful and richer.[41]

Differentiation can show us how to teach the same standards to diverse learners by using different teaching and learning approaches, so teaching becomes a blend of whole-class, group, and individual instruction. Differentiated instruction creates a classroom climate where all students—from the gifted to special needs—can learn together. To help you see how this works, compare the following differentiated instructional approaches with traditional instructional practices[42]:

Traditional/Standardized Instruction	Differentiated Instruction
Literature is not Ethan's favorite class. Class discussions focus on analyzing the themes, characters, symbols, and writing styles of classic novels. Ethan struggles to see how these novels relate to his life, and his interest wanes.	Ethan's teacher works hard to link literacy concepts and skills with student interests. For example, students examine how the rules of writing vary in novels, journalism, music, science, and so on. They also explore how the concept of interdependence is exhibited in athletics, the arts, science, families, governments, and literature, their primary content area.
Latisha has a learning disability. She understands ideas well but has difficulty reading quickly and writing clearly. Nearly all assessments in Latisha's class are written. Most tests and papers have strict time limits. Latisha struggles to earn a passing grade.	Latisha and her teacher work together to establish timetables for her written assignments. This flexibility enables her to write with less tension and to proofread her work. The teacher also provides more than one way to express ideas. For example, Latisha and other students can use diagrams, sketches, oral presentations, or hands-on demonstrations to show their knowledge and skill.

Variety in Process and Content

Have you ever listened to a lecture for an hour and found your initial interest lapsing into daydreams? Have you ever watched a class begin a seatwork assignment with active concentration and found, after 30 minutes, that involvement turning into passing notes and doodling? Variety is the spice of life, the saying goes—the spice of instruction, too. From the teaching models described above, we hope you can easily see how variety can enhance both teaching effectiveness and student achievement. Students learn more when joy and excitement are part of classroom life (but we bet you knew that).[43]

As any savvy teacher knows, student interest can be maintained by moving from one activity to another during a single lesson. For example, a 60-minute lesson on the American Revolution might begin with a 10-minute overview providing the structure for the class, then move into a 15-minute question-and-answer session, then change to a 25-minute video, and conclude with a 10-minute discussion and closure. Another motivation to vary content and process in teaching is to accommodate different student learning styles. Some students might miss what is said in a lecture (not being auditory learners) but easily get it when the teacher shows pictures (because the visual connection is clear). Research on different ways of learning (introduced in Chapter 2) offers strong arguments for instructional variety. Following is a sample of some of our favorite tools and activities that teachers can use to maintain student interest by varying the pattern of the lesson. We encourage you to begin creating your own!

Discussions
Lectures
Films, DVDs
PowerPoint
Role plays
Simulations
Small-group activities
Guided practice
Guest speakers
Independent seatwork
Student presentations
Tests
Podcasts
Silent reading
Games
Field trips
Creative writing
Theater and drama
Community service
Learning centers
What would you add?
Music activities
Art activities
Creating digital portfolios
Spot quizzes
Panel discussions
Brainstorming sessions
Peer tutoring
Debates
Cooperative learning activities
Storytelling

Many of these activities can be described as "hands-on" or active learning and can be captivating for students, but more is needed. Variety alone will not produce achievement: Connections with content must be made, or variety will be reduced to mere activity. This is no easy task. Consider an elementary student happily pasting animal pictures on charts, but unable to explain what (if anything) he is learning about animal families. Students in a middle school may be dressing up for an evening on the *Titanic,* and from the lower to the upper decks, their clothing and accents reflect different social classes. Yet, if students have not connected their dress with social class and deck classifications, then they may miss learning about the relationship between social class and survival rate. Challenging students with engaging activities is admirable, but the effort must clearly connect the activity to both the content and the student.

A Few More Thoughts on Effective Teaching

Teaching is hard. Teaching well is fiercely so. Often confronted by too many students, a schedule without breaks, a pile of papers that regenerates daily, and incessant demands from every educational stakeholder, teachers can become predictable and mundane in their practices. Nevertheless, innovative, engaged, and reflective teaching is the path to effective teaching. Here are some ideas for you to consider.

"Less is more" is an aphorism attributed to education reformer Ted Sizer. According to Sizer, today's schools are misguided in their emphasis on "covering" material. The goal seems to be teaching a vast body of information, in order to have a sense of accomplishment or to score well on the ever-growing number of standardized tests. But international tests in science, for example, show that although U.S. students have studied more science topics than have students in other countries, they have not studied them in depth, and their lower test scores reflect this superficiality. In Sizer's vision of effective instruction, good teachers limit the amount of content they introduce but develop it sufficiently for students to gain in-depth understanding.

RAP 4.8
Memories of a Teacher

This direction for teaching and schooling marks a radical departure from the current emphasis on uniform standards, test performance, and competition. In marked contrast to the superficial nature of such test-centered curriculum, Sizer advocates deep teaching. In *deep teaching,* teachers work to organize their content around a limited set of key principles and powerful ideas and then engage students in discussing those concepts. The emphasis is on problem solving and critical thinking, rather than on memorizing.[44]

The classroom as a learning community creates an emotionally safe and intellectually engaged space for collective inquiry.

©Hill Street Studios/Blend Images LLC RF

This vision of deep teaching highlights the social nature of learning and of the classroom. As the builder of a classroom **learning community,** the teacher is called on to be a guide or facilitator, skillful in conducting discussions, group work, debates, and dialogues. In this way, the teacher empowers the students to talk with one another and to rehearse the terminology and concepts involved in each discipline. Learning becomes a community effort, not an individual competition.[45]

It is not surprising, therefore, that educators are reconceptualizing schools to create more nurturing learning communities. When learning communities work well, students and teachers get to know each other well and they can develop shared academic goals. Learning communities can be encouraged through several strategies, including looping and block scheduling. In *looping,* schools "promote" teachers along with their students, a process that allows the teacher an extra year or more to get to know students in depth, to diagnose and meet their learning needs, and to develop more meaningful communication with their parents and families. Looping offers students an increased sense of stability and community. Similarly, *block scheduling* increases teacher–student contact by increasing the length of class periods. The longer periods allow teachers to get to know these students better, and the students benefit from an uninterrupted and in-depth academic study. If you were to teach in a school with block scheduling, you might have 75 students on any given day or in a particular semester, instead of 150.

This notion of a learning community, like deep teaching, contrasts sharply with many current practices that emphasize state- and school-mandated curriculum followed by standardized testing. It points to a more thoughtful classroom, one in which the teacher is a reflective practitioner. **Reflective teachers** continually and intensely analyze their own practices to improve performance. Reflective teachers ask themselves such questions as these:

- What teaching strategies did I use today? How effective were they? What might have been even more effective?
- Were my students engaged with the material? What seemed to motivate them the most? If I were to reteach today's class, how could I get even more students involved?
- What did I do to help my students think more deeply during today's lesson? How can I further develop their critical thinking skills?
- What values and attitudes did my students cultivate from today's learning?
- How did I assess my students' learning today? Would there have been a better way to measure their learning? How well did the students grasp the main points of today's lesson? Do I need to reteach some of these concepts?
- What did I learn today? What did my students teach me?
- Can I fine-tune tomorrow's or next week's lessons to capitalize on the gains made today?

Such questions are designed to raise consciousness, encourage self-scrutiny, and move you toward more effective teaching. Becoming a reflective teacher involves growing beyond your current concerns with instructional and management techniques, the "how to" questions (where many beginning teachers naturally start) and moving toward "what" and "why" questions, the questions and answers that transform teachers into insightful and gifted instructors.[46]

Reflection has many paths. A teaching journal is one way to record each day's reactions and insights. Reviewing the journal over time will hopefully provide a record of your professional growth. Asking a colleague to observe your teaching and share his or her insights can initiate a useful professional dialogue. Returning the favor and observing your colleagues can provide ideas not only for your colleagues, but for you as well. Of course, you can be your own observer through the magic of technology.

Video record your teaching behaviors and do your own analysis. As you see, there are many valuable routes to reflection.

You don't have to wait until student teaching to start being a reflective teacher. You can start right now by asking yourself:

- What roles, official and unofficial, does a teacher have?
- What roles, official and unofficial, does a student have?
- What qualities do good teachers have?
- What teaching strategies do I prefer?
- What is the purpose of school?
- How will I motivate myself to be a reflective teacher in the years ahead?

You also don't have to wait until your student teaching placement or that exciting first job to begin planning for your first day as the teacher (take a deep breath!). Let's explore a few ideas to get you started.

Your First Day: Creating a Productive Classroom Climate

The way you organize your classroom on that very first day sends a powerful message about who you are as a teacher. If that first day is done well, you are on your way to a smoother teaching year. On the other hand, any mistakes made early in the year enter an echo chamber—they keep returning until the year (finally) ends. Here are some suggestions for creating a productive class climate.

Physical Considerations Before school starts, look around your classroom and ask yourself: "What do I want my room to say to the students?" Some of the physical features, such as doors, windows, and built-ins, are beyond your control. But there is still much you can do. Did you ever hear the phrase "If the walls could talk"? Guess what—they do. What do you want displayed on your classroom walls? Multicultural images of males and females, images of creative ideas, motivational statements, and fascinating facts can send powerful messages. (Blank walls convey their own messages, don't they?) When students walk into a thoughtfully prepared room, they appreciate the effort. But there are times when even a blank area of the wall can be positive—if it is designated as a student display area, postings that students will manage in the future. Walls do talk.

Do you want student desks all facing the front, or arranged for students to work in groups, or in a circle around the room, or changing as activities change? You will also need a space for your instructional materials, a place easy to get to so there are no long delays as you move from one class activity to another. Where will you be positioned? You should select a place where you can see the entire class, a place with no blind spots so you can spot a student who needs help—or is causing a disturbance. Some teachers plan to teach from different areas of the room, placing their desk in one place, audiovisual equipment in another, the day's agenda in yet another area, and even their water, tea, or coffee in yet another place. This ensures that they will be visiting different areas, be near different students, and not be locked in the front of the room. Have you thought about any special touches that you want to bring in? Plants, carpets, pillows, posters? It is your room, and you get to create the ambience for you and your students.

TEACHING TIP

Advice for Your First Day and Beyond

Education World asked second-year teachers to reflect on their first year in the classroom, their successes and failures, and offer advice for new teachers:

- *Take charge.* Have a clear management plan, with well-defined rewards and consequences. Explain it to the students, send it home to the parents, and ask for signatures on the plan.
- *Keep students busy and engaged.* Have a number of potential class activities available. Bored kids get into trouble; busy kids stay out of trouble.
- *Get peer support.* If you are not assigned an official mentor, find an unofficial one.
- *Get parental support.* From extra supplies to celebration plans, parents are a hidden teacher resource, but only if they are pulled into class activities.
- *Organize yourself.* Develop a system that will keep you organized. There is a lot going on in teaching, grading, and monitoring dozens of children for hours each day.
- *Organize your students.* Teach students how to organize their homework, notebooks, desks, etc.
- *Write and reflect.* Keep a journal to help you reflect on your first year, and become a stronger teacher your second year.
- *Have fun.* Teaching is not only stressful; it is joyful. Get into it and have fun!
- *Renew.* Enjoy an interest outside of teaching.

SOURCE: Education World (www.educationworld.com).

REFLECTION: Compare this advice with the more formal areas of teacher effectiveness cited in the research and by the National Board for Professional Teacher Standards described in Chapter 1. What are the similarities and differences?

Know Your Students Do you remember how it felt when the teacher called you by a wrong name, or no name at all—almost as if you did not exist? Don't forget that feeling, and dedicate yourself to learning your students' names. This is an easier assignment for teachers with one class of students than it is for a teacher with five classes a day, but the sooner teachers learn the names of all their students the smoother the class will run. Seating charts can help, as well as name signs on desks. You may hear student grunts at your suggestion for student name signs (anonymity can be a student strategy), but you can explain that the signs will disappear when everyone knows each other's name. And here is a special reminder: If a student is from another culture and has an unfamiliar-sounding name, work to learn the correct pronunciation. It will be much appreciated by the student and will help you grow as well.

Prepare for a Strong First Day This first class creates a first impression, and first impressions happen only once. Take the time to plan some exciting and meaningful activities for that first day. You may also want to share your vision and goals for the entire year with the class: what students will be learning and why that is important. An exciting and thoughtful beginning to the school year can create the tone for the weeks and months that follow.

Although you've reached the end of this text (congratulations!), your learning will continue. (See Contemporary Issues: A View from the Field on p. 340.) We wish you and your students an inspired future.

CONTEMPORARY ISSUES

A View from the Field: Your Future Classroom

We hope that these *Contemporary Issues* features inspire you to do amazing things in the classroom. For this last one, let's think about tomorrow's schools, the ones you may be working in.

Daniel Pink's *A Whole New Mind: Why Right-Brainers Will Rule the Future* describes major changes he believes will reshape America in the years ahead. Pink contends that the courses we think are so important—science, technology, math—will be less central in the future. To compete in the twenty-first century, he believes our schools should focus more on right-brain skills, the skills we often neglect. Here are some examples:

Boundary crossers. These are creative people who are comfortable working in different disciplines, cultures, and languages. A physician using both allopathic medicine and homeopathic treatments to heal patients, a businessperson helping American companies work more effectively with Indian computer experts, and a teacher working with students to improve the environment are all boundary crossers.

Design. We have lots of products that work well, so we now choose products that appeal to us. We buy a car or a laptop in part because we enjoy how it looks. We will need people with fine arts skills to design attractive and pleasing products, and perhaps they too can be boundary crossers by working with sustainable materials that honor the earth.

Joy. "People rarely succeed at anything unless they are having fun," is a Southwest Airlines motto. More and more companies are realizing that happiness, yes happiness, is an important goal. Incorporating games, humor, laughing, and play into our businesses (and schools!) may increase productivity, satisfaction, and health.

Materialism vs. Meaning. Americans have acquired much material wealth, but many are still unhappy. People have confused material wealth with happiness. Pink believes that in the future, Americans will seek more meaningful lives. He cites the increase in meditation, yoga, public service, and spirituality as examples of our search for meaningful lives.

Intuition. Perhaps our greatest scientist, Albert Einstein, had it right when he wrote: "The intuitive mind is a sacred gift; the rational mind, its servant." Why do schools honor the servant (rational thinking) and disregard the sacred gift (intuition)? How can schools help people develop and honor their intuition?

REFLECTION: How will these new priorities change our world, our schools, and your classrooms? How might schools best combine the sciences and the arts to develop integrated learning?

connect — CONNECT FOR *TEACHERS, SCHOOLS, AND SOCIETY*

Check out Connect, McGraw-Hill Education's interactive learning environment, to:

Read Current and Historical Articles

Classroom Misbehavior Is Predictable and Preventable, by Timothy J. Landrum, Amy S. Lingo, and Terrance M. Scott, *Phi Delta Kappan*, October 2011.

The Perils and Promises of Praise, by Carol S. Dweck, *Educational Leadership*, October 2007.

Mapping a Route Toward Differentiated Instruction, by Carol Ann Tomlinson, *Educational Leadership*, September 1999.

Learning to Love Assessment, by Carol Ann Tomlinson, *Educational Leadership*, December 2007.

Exemplary Teacher Voices on Their Own Development, by Rachael Gabriel, Jeni Peiria Day, and Richard Allington, *Phi Delta Kappan*, May 2011.

Lina's Letter: A 9-Year-Old's Perspective on What Matters Most in the Classroom, by David Pratt, *Phi Delta Kappan*, March 2008.

Analyze Case Studies

Ken Kelly: A teacher having trouble with questioning and with discussion teaching visits a teacher who is holding a Socratic discussion with a fourth-grade class. He questions the applicability of her methods to his situation.

Judith Kent: A teacher engages her students in whole-class discussion, and then the students work with partners on an assignment. She explains the planning process she went through to reteach the lesson after it had not worked in the previous class.

Christie Raymond: A mature woman in the first month of her first full-time position teaching music in an elementary school loves the work as long as the children are singing, but dislikes the school's emphasis on and her part in disciplining the students. The case describes Christie's classroom teaching in detail as well as her after-school bus duty.

Melissa Read: An enthusiastic young student teacher struggles to gain the respect and improve the behavior of her senior-level composition class and is devastated by one of her students' papers, which is full of vindictiveness and hatred toward her.

Watch Teachers, Students, and Classrooms in Action

Our **Online Video Album** for contemporary videos related to this chapter.

KEY TERMS AND PEOPLE

academic learning time, 310
allocated time, 309
behavioral objective, 333
Bloom's taxonomy, 318
cooperative learning, 331
differentiated instruction, 334
direct teaching, 328
engaged time, 309
flipped instruction, 330
higher-order question, 318
learning community, 336
lower-order question, 318
mastery learning, 332
pedagogical cycle, 315
problem-based learning (PBL), 333
reflective teaching, 337
Rowe, Mary Budd, 321
Slavin, Robert, 332
wait time, 321

DISCUSSION QUESTIONS AND ACTIVITIES

1. Do you think teachers are born, or made? Debate a classmate who holds the opposite point of view. Interview elementary and secondary teachers and ask them what they think about this question. Do some of them say that it is a combination of both? If so, why? Which part is art, which part skill?
2. Why do you think there is so much variation in how different teachers and schools use time for learning? Observe in your own college classrooms to determine how much time is used productively and how much is wasted. For each class observed, keep a fairly detailed record of how time is lost (students 6 minutes late, class ends 15 minutes early, PowerPoint presentation takes 4 minutes to set up, and so on).
3. Research suggests that to achieve, students should be functioning at a very high success rate. Do you agree that this is likely to lead to higher achievement? Or do you think that students need to cope with failure and be "stretched" to achieve? Defend your position.
4. Analyze teacher reactions to student answers in elementary and secondary classrooms where you are an observer and in the college classrooms where you are a student. Are most of these classrooms "okay" classrooms? Why do you think some teacher reactions are vague and diffuse? What observations can you make about the use of praise, remediation, and criticism?
5. What do you look for in a mentor? What strategies can you use to recruit such a mentor in your first teaching job?

Glossary

A

ability grouping The assignment of pupils to homogeneous groups according to intellectual ability or level for instructional purposes.

academic freedom The opportunity for teachers and students to learn, teach, study, research, and question without censorship, coercion, or external political and other restrictive influences.

academic learning time The time a student is actively engaged with the subject matter and experiencing a high success rate.

academy A classical secondary school in colonial America that emphasized elements of Latin and English grammar schools and by the nineteenth century became more of a college preparatory school. Also the name of the ancient Greek school founded by Plato.

accelerated program The more rapid promotion of gifted students through school.

accountability The obligation of schools and teachers to be held responsible for student performance.

accreditation Certification of an education program or a school that has met professional standards of an outside agency.

acculturation The acquisition of the dominant culture's norms by a member of the nondominant culture. The nondominant culture typically loses its own culture, language, and sometimes religion in this process.

achievement tests Examinations of the knowledge and skills acquired, usually as a result of specific instruction.

adequate education A legal approach that ensures educational opportunities for poorer students based on state constitution guarantees for an efficient, thorough, or uniform education. Calls for adequate education have replaced previous calls for equal educational expenditures.

Advanced Placement (AP) A curriculum that offers college-level courses to high school students. Students who score high enough on a qualifying exam can earn college credit.

aesthetics The branch of philosophy that examines the nature of beauty and judgments about it.

affirmative action A plan by which personnel policies and hiring practices reflect positive steps in the recruiting and hiring of women and people of color.

allocated time The amount of time a school or an individual teacher schedules for a subject.

American Federation of Teachers (AFT) A national organization of teachers that is primarily concerned with improving educational conditions and protecting teachers' rights.

American Spelling Book An early elementary textbook written by Noah Webster that focused on the alphabet, grammar, and moral lessons.

appropriate education A part of Public Law 94-142 that protects the right of students with disabilities to an education that reflects an accurate diagnosis.

assimilation See **enculturation**.

authentic assessment A type of evaluation that represents actual performance, encourages students to reflect on their own work, and is integrated into the student's whole learning process. Such tests usually require that students synthesize knowledge from different areas and use that knowledge actively.

B

back to basics During the 1980s, a revival of the back-to-basics movement evolved out of concern for declining test scores in math, science, reading, and other areas. Although there is not a precise definition of back to basics, many consider it to include increased emphasis on reading, writing, and arithmetic, fewer electives, and more rigorous grading.

behavior modification A strategy to alter behavior in a desired direction through the use of rewards.

behavioral objective A specific statement of what a learner must accomplish to demonstrate mastery.

behaviorism A psychological theory that interprets human behavior in terms of stimuli-response.

bilingual education Educational programs in which students of limited or no English-speaking ability attend classes taught in English, as well as in their native language. There is great variability in these programs in goals, instructional opportunity, and balance between English and a student's native language.

block grants Federal dollars provided to the states, with limited federal restrictions, for educational aid and program funding.

Bloom's taxonomy A classification system in which each lower level is subsumed in the next higher level. The Bloom's taxonomy describes simple to more complex mental processes, and usually is used to classify educational objectives or classroom questions.

board of education Constituted at the state and local levels, an agency responsible for formulating educational policy. Members are sometimes appointed, but more frequently are elected at the local level.

bond A certificate of debt issued by a government guaranteeing payment of the original investment plus interest by a specified future date. Bonds are used by local communities to raise the funds they need to build or repair schools.

Brown v. Board of Education of Topeka U.S. Supreme Court ruling that reversed an earlier "separate but equal" ruling and declared that segrated schooling was inherently unequal and therefore unlawful.

Buckley Amendment The 1974 Family Educational Rights and Privacy Act granting parents of students under 18, and students 18 or over the right to examine their school records.

busing A method for remedying segregation by transporting students to create more ethnically or racially balanced schools. Before busing and desegregation were linked, busing was not a controversial issue, and, in fact, the vast majority of students riding school buses are not involved in desegregation programs.

C

Campbell's law The more any quantitative social indicator is used for social decision making, the more subject it will be to corruption pressures and the more apt it will be to distort and corrupt the social processes it was intended to monitor.

career ladder A system designed to create different status levels for teachers by developing steps one can climb to receive increased pay through increased responsibility or experience.

career technical education A program to teach elementary and secondary students about the world of work by integrating career awareness and exploration across the school curriculum.

Cartesian dualism The belief that reality is composed of both materialism and idealism, body and mind.

categorical grant Financial aid to local school districts from state or federal agencies for specific purposes.

certification State government's or a professional association's evaluation and approval of an applicant's competencies.

character education A model composed of various strategies that promote a defined set of core values to students.

charter school A school established by a charter between a local school board or a state government and a group of teachers, parents, and even businesses. A charter school is exempt from many state and local regulations. Designed to promote creative new schools, the charter represents legal permission to try new approaches to educate students. The first charter legislation was passed in Minnesota in 1991.

chief state school officer The executive head of a state department of education. The chief state school officer is responsible or carrying out the mandates of the state board of education and enforcing educational laws and regulations. This position is also referred to as *state superintendent.*

child abuse Physical, sexual, or emotional violation of a child's health and well-being.

child-centered instruction (individual instruction) Teaching that is designed to meet the interests and needs of individual students.

classroom climate The physical, emotional, and aesthetic characteristics, as well as the learning resources, of a school classroom.

Coalition of Essential Schools (CES) A reform effort founded by Theodore Sizer that creates smaller schools, learning communities, and more in-depth study of the curriculum.

Coleman report A study commissioned by President Johnson (1964) to analyze the factors that influence the academic achievement of students. One of the major findings of James Coleman's report was that schools in general have relatively little impact on learning. Family and peers were found to have more impact on a child's education than the school itself did.

collaborative action research (CAR) A program that connects teaching and professional growth through the use of research relevant to classroom responsibilities.

collaborative decision making An effort to empower teachers in which teachers share power with the school principal and actively participate in curricular, budgetary, and other school policy decisions.

collective bargaining A negotiating procedure between employer and employees for resolving disagreements on salaries, work schedules, and other conditions of employment. In collective bargaining, all teachers in a school system bargain as one group through chosen representatives.

Comer model A program created and disseminated by James Comer of Yale that incorporates a team of educational and mental health professionals to assist children at risk by working with their parents and attending to social, educational, and psychological needs.

Common Core State Standards Identifies the skills and content a student should master at each grade level from kindergarten through grade 12.

common school A public, tax-supported school. First established in Massachusetts, the school's purpose was to create a common basis of knowledge for children. It usually refers to a public elementary school.

community schools Schools connected with a local community to provide for the educational needs of that community.

compensatory education Educational experiences and opportunities designed to overcome or compensate for difficulties associated with a student's disadvantaged background.

competency The ability to perform a particular skill or to demonstrate a specified level of knowledge.

comprehensive high school A public secondary school that offers a variety of curricula, including vocational, academic, and general education programs.

comprehensive values education An approach to moral education that integrates traditional and progressive strategies for teaching values.

compulsory attendance A state law requiring that children and adolescents attend school until reaching a specified age.

computer-assisted instruction (CAI) Individualized instruction between a student and programmed instructional material stored in a computer.

computer-managed instruction (CMI) A recordkeeping procedure for tracking student performance using a computer.

consolidation The trend toward combining small or rural school districts into larger ones.

constructivism With roots in cognitive psychology, an educational approach built on the idea that people construct their understanding of the world. Constructivist teachers gauge a student's prior knowledge, then carefully orchestrate cues, classroom activities, and penetrating questions to push students to higher levels of understanding.

content standards The knowledge, skills, and dispositions that students should master in each subject. These standards are often linked to broader themes and sometimes to testing programs.

cooperative learning An instructional model in which students work on activities in small groups and receive rewards based on the overall group performance.

copyright laws (Copyright Act) A federal law that protects intellectual property, including copyrighted material. Teachers can use such material in classrooms only with permission, or under specific guidelines.

core curriculum A central body of knowledge that schools require all students to study. This common core curriculum goes beyond common core standards because it includes specific course content.

core knowledge Awareness of the central ideas, beliefs, personalities, writings, events, etc. of a culture. Also termed *cultural literacy.*

corporal punishment The physical disciplining of a student by a school employee.

covert power This is the unofficial power wielded in schools by parents, vocal individuals, a school secretary, businesses, community and other groups not a part of official school governance.

creationism The position that God created the universe, the earth, and living things on the earth in precisely the manner described in the Old Testament, in six, 24-hour periods.

critical pedagogy An education philosophy that unites the theory of critical thinking with actual practice in real-world settings. The purpose is to eliminate the cultural and educational hegemony and encourage students to apply critical thinking skills to the real world, becoming agents for social change.

critical thinking skills Higher-order intellectual skills such as comparing, interpreting, observing, summarizing, classifying, creating, and criticizing.

cultural difference theory A theory that asserts that academic problems can be overcome if educators study and mediate the cultural gap separating school and home.

cultural literacy Knowledge of the people, places, events, idioms, and informal content of the dominant culture.

cultural pluralism Acceptance and encouragement of cultural diversity.

culturally responsive teaching An approach to multicultural education that recognizes that students learn in different ways, and that effective teachers recognize and respond to those differences. This approach also mediates the frequent mismatch between home and school cultures and honors cultural heritages.

culture A set of learned beliefs, values, and behaviors; a way of life shared by members of a society.

curriculum (formal, explicit) Planned content of instruction that enables the school to meet its aims.

curriculum (implicit, hidden) Hidden curriculum refers to the unwritten, unofficial, and often unintended values, and perspectives students learn in school. While the "formal" curriculum consists of the intentional lessons, the hidden curriculum consists of the unspoken or implicit academic, social, and cultural messages that schools teach students.

curriculum development The processes of assessing needs, formulating objectives, and developing instructional opportunities and evaluation.

D

dame schools Primary schools in colonial and other early periods in which students were taught by untrained women in the women's own homes.

de facto segregation The segregation of racial or other groups resulting from circumstances, such as housing patterns, rather than from official policy or law.

de jure segregation The segregation of racial or other groups on the basis of law, policy, or a practice designed to accomplish such separation.

decentralization The trend of dividing large school districts into smaller and, it is hoped, more responsive units.

deductive reasoning Working from a general rule to identify particular examples and applications to that rule.

deficit theory A theory that asserts that the values, language patterns, and behaviors that children from certain racial and ethnic groups bring to school put them at an educational disadvantage.

delegate representative Form of representative government in which the interests of a particular geographic region are represented through an individual or "delegate." Some school boards are organized so that members act as delegates of a neighborhood or region.

descriptive data Information that provides an objective depiction of various aspects of school or classroom life.

desegregation The process of correcting past practices of racial or other illegal segregation.

differentiated instruction An approach to teaching in which instructional activities are organized in response to individual learning differences. Teachers are asked to carefully consider each student's needs, learning style, life experience, and readiness to learn.

digital divide A term used to describe the technological gap between the "haves" and the "have-nots." Race, gender, class, and geography are some of the demographic factors influencing technological access and achievement.

direct teaching A model of instruction in which the teacher is a strong leader who structures the classroom and sequences subject matter to reflect a clear academic focus. This model emphasizes the importance of a structured lesson in which presentation of new information is followed by student practice and teacher feedback.

disability A learning or physical condition, a behavior, or an emotional problem that impedes education. Educators now prefer to speak of "students with disabilities," not "handicapped students," emphasizing the person, not the disability.

distance learning Courses, programs, and training provided to students over long distances through television, the Internet, and other technologies.

due process The procedural requirements that must be followed in such areas as student and teacher discipline and placement in special education programs. Due process exists to safeguard individuals from arbitrary, capricious, or unreasonable policies, practices, or actions. The essential elements of due process are (1) a notice of the charge or actions to be taken, (2) the opportunity to be heard, (3) and the right to a defense that reflects the particular circumstances and nature of the case.

E

early childhood education Learning undertaken by young children in the home, in nursery schools, in preschools, and in kindergartens.

eclecticism In this text, the drawing on of elements from several educational philosophies or methods.

educable child A developmentally disabled child who is capable of achieving only a limited basic learning and usually must be instructed in a special class.

educational malpractice A new experimental line of litigation similar to the concept of medical malpractice. Educational malpractice is concerned with assessing liability for students who graduate from school without fundamental skills. However, many courts have rejected the notion that schools or educators be held liable for this problem.

educational partnership A business relationship between schools and corporations through which companies offer schools services and products and often have their corporate names used in the schools.

Eight-Year Study Educator Ralph Tyler's study in the 1930s that indicated the effectiveness of progressive education.

elementary school An educational institution for children in grades 1 through 5, 6, or 8, often including kindergarten.

emergency license A substandard license that recognizes teachers who have not met all the requirements for licensure. It is issued on a temporary basis to meet the needs of communities that do not have licensed teachers available.

emotional intelligence (EQ) A new human dimension that measures personality characteristics, such as persistence. Some believe that EQ scores may be better predictors of future success than IQ scores.

empiricism The philosophy that maintains that sensory experiences, such as seeing, hearing, and touching, are the ultimate sources of all human knowledge. Empiricists believe that we experience the external world by sensory perception; then, through reflection, we conceptualize ideas that help us interpret the world.

enculturation The process of acquiring a culture; a child's acquisition of the cultural heritage through both formal and informal educational means.

endorsement The extension of a license through additional work to include a second teaching field.

engaged time The part of time that a teacher schedules for a subject in which the students are actively involved with academic subject matter. Listening to a lecture, participating in a class discussion, and working on math problems all constitute engaged time.

English as a Second Language (ESL) An immersion approach to bilingual education that removes students from the regular classroom to provide instruction in English.

English Classical School The first free public high school, established in Boston in 1821. The school initially enrolled only boys.

English grammar schools Private schools that taught commerce, navigation, engineering, and other vocational skills. The demand for a more practical education in eighteenth-century America led to the creation of these schools.

English language learners (ELL) Students whose native language is not English and are learning to speak and write English. Also referred to as *limited English proficiency* or LEP.

environmental education The study and analysis of the conditions and causes of pollution, overpopulation, and waste of natural resources, and of the ways to preserve Earth's intricate ecology.

epistemology The branch of philosophy that examines the nature of knowledge and learning.

equal educational opportunity A term that refers to giving every student the educational opportunity to develop fully whatever talents, interests, and abilities he or she may have, without regard to race, color, national origin, sex, disability, or economic status.

equity Educational policy and practice that are just, fair, and free from bias and discrimination.

essentialism An educational philosophy that emphasizes basic skills of reading, writing, mathematics, science, history, geography, and language.

establishment clause A section of the First Amendment of the U.S. Constitution that says that Congress shall make no law respecting the establishment of religion. This clause prohibits nonparochial schools from teaching religion.

ethics The branch of philosophy that examines questions of right and wrong, good and bad.

ethnic group A group of people with a distinctive culture and history.

ethnicity A term that refers to shared common cultural traits such as language, religion, and dress. A Latino or Hispanic, for example, belongs to an ethnic group, but might belong to the Black, Caucasian, or Asian race.

ethnocentrism The tendency to view one's own culture as superior to others, or to fail to consider other cultures in a fair manner.

evaluation Assessment of learning and instruction.

Every Student Succeeds Act (ESSA) Like the No Child Left Behind Act which it replaced, ESSA is a reauthorization of the 1965 Elementary and Secondary Education Act, describing the federal government's role in public education.

evolution As put forth by Charles Darwin, a keystone of modern biological theory and postulates that animals and plants have their origin in other preexisting types and that there are modifications in successive generations.

exceptional learners Students who require special education and related services to realize their full potential. Categories of exceptionality include retarded, gifted, learning disabled, emotionally disturbed, and physically disabled.

existentialism A philosophy that emphasizes the ability of an individual to determine the course and nature of his or her life and the importance of personal decision making.

expectation theory First made popular by Rosenthal and Jacobson, a theory that holds that a student's academic performance can be improved if a teacher's attitudes and beliefs about that student's academic potential are modified.

expulsion Dismissal of a student from school for a lengthy period, ranging from one semester to permanently.

extracurriculum The part of school life that comprises activities, such as sports, academic and social clubs, band, chorus, orchestra, and theater. Many educators think that the extracurriculum develops important skills and values, including leadership, teamwork, creativity, and diligence.

F

failing school The term given to a school when a large proportion of its students do not do well on standardized tests or other academic measures. Critics charge that students attending such schools are not receiving their constitutionally guaranteed adequate education.

fair use A legal principle allowing limited use of copyrighted materials. Teachers must observe three criteria: brevity, spontaneity, and cumulative effect.

First Amendment The constitutional Amendment that protects freedom of religion and speech. An important part of this Amendment is the establishment clause, which prohibits schools and the government from promoting or inhibiting religion in schools.

five-factor theory (five characteristics) of effective schools A theory, developed through school effectiveness research, that emphasizes five factors: effective leadership, monitoring student progress, safety, a clear vision, and high expectations.

fixed mindset A theory developed by Carol Dweck that views intelligence as finite, determined at birth, and unchangeable.

Flanders Interaction Analysis An instrument developed by Ned Flanders for categorizing student and teacher verbal behavior. It is used to interpret the nature of classroom verbal interaction.

flipped instruction (flipped classroom) An instructional method that essentially reverses direct instruction. Instead of lectures occurring in the classroom and assignments being done at home, the opposite occurs. Lectures are viewed at home by students, via videos or podcasts (found online or created by the teacher), and class time is devoted to assignments or projects based on this knowledge.

formal or explicit curriculum A school's official curriculum that is reflected in academic courses and requirements.

Fourteenth Amendment: The constitutional provision that ensures due process and equal protection under the law. This amendment also grants state and federal citizenship to all persons born or naturalized in the United States regardless of race.

Fourth Amendment: The constitutional provision that protects and individual's basic privacy and security from unreasonable searches and seizures of property.

Franklin Academy A colonial high school founded by Benjamin Franklin that accepted females as students and promoted a less classical, more practical curriculum.

full-service school Schools that provide a network of social services from nutrition and health care to parental education and transportation, all designed to support the comprehensive educational needs of children.

G

gatekeeping Philip Jackson's term describing how teachers control classroom interactions.

gender bias The degree to which an individual's beliefs and behavior are unduly influenced on the basis of gender. See also sex discrimination.

gender similarities hypothesis A theory suggesting that males and females are more alike than different on most psychological and intellectual variables and therefore do not demonstrate gender-specific learning styles that require unique teaching approaches.

gendered career A term applied to the gender stereotyping of career and occupational fields. Teaching, for example, was initially gendered male but today is gendered female, particularly at the elementary school level.

generalizations Broad statements about a group that offer information, clues, and insights that can help a teacher plan more effectively. Generalizations are a good starting point, but as the teacher learns more about the students, individual differences become more educationally significant.

giftedness A term describing individuals with exceptional ability. The National Association for Gifted Children defines five elements of giftedness: artistic and creative talents, intellectual and academic abilities, and leadership skills. There, however, continues to be great variance in definitions of the "gifted."

global education Because economics, politics, scientific innovation, and societal developments in different countries have an enormous impact on children in the United States, the goals of global education include increased knowledge about the peoples of the world, resolution of global problems, increased fluency in foreign languages, and the development of more tolerant attitudes toward other cultures and peoples.

Golden Mean The doctrine put forth by Aristotle asserting that virtue lies in the middle ground between two extremes.

Great Books The heart of the perennialists' curriculum that includes great works of the past in literature, philosophy, science, and other areas.

green school Schools recognized by the U.S. Department of Education as offering healthier learning environments with clean air and water, nourishing and natural foods, nontoxic cleaners, and more outdoor activities. Academic performance often improves in green schools, and absenteeism decreases.

growth mindset A theory developed by Carol Dweck that views intelligence as developing throughout an individual's life.

Gun-free Schools Act Legislation enacted by Congress in 1994 that requires states receiving federal funds to establish laws regarding firearms. Schools can lose federal funds if they do not have a zero-tolerance policy mandating one-year expulsions for students bringing firearms to schools. The vast majority of schools report zero-tolerance policies for firearms.

H

Head Start Federally funded pre-elementary school program to provide learning opportunities for disadvantaged students.

hidden government The unofficial power structure within a school. It cannot be identified by the official title, position, or functions of individuals. For example, it reflects the potential influence of a school secretary or custodian.

high-stakes tests These tests are used to make important educational decisions that impact students, educators, schools, and school districts. These tests may determine rewards or penalties for educators and students alike.

higher-order questions Questions that require students to go beyond memory in formulating a response. These questions require students to analyze, synthesize, evaluate, and so on.

homeschooling A growing trend (but a longtime practice) of parents educating their children at home, for religious or philosophical reasons.

homogeneous grouping The classification of pupils for the purpose of forming instructional groups having a relatively high degree of intellectual similarity.

hornbook A single sheet of parchment containing the Lord's Prayer and letters of the alphabet. It was protected by a thin sheath from the flattened horn of a cow and fastened to a wooden board—hence the name. It was used during the colonial era in primary schools.

humanistic education A curriculum that stresses personal student growth; self-actualizing, moral, and aesthetic issues are explored.

I

idealism A doctrine holding that knowledge is derived from ideas and emphasizing moral and spiritual reality as a preeminent source of explanation.

ideologues Homeschool advocates focused on avoiding public schools in order to impart their own set of values.

immersion A bilingual education model that teaches students with limited English by using a "sheltered" or simplified English vocabulary, but teaching in English and not in the other language.

implicit or hidden curriculum What students learn, other than academic content, from what they do or are expected to do in school; incidental learnings.

in loco parentis Latin term meaning "in place of the parents"; that is, a teacher or school administrator assumes the duties and responsibilities of the parents during the hours the child attends school.

inclusion The practice of educating and integrating children with disabilities into regular classroom settings.

independent school A nonpublic school unaffiliated with any church or other agency.

individualized education program (IEP) The mechanism through which a disabled child's special needs are identified, objectives and services are described, and evaluation is designed.

individualized instruction Curriculum content and instructional materials, media, and activities designed for individual learning. The pace, interests, and abilities of the learner determine the curriculum.

Individuals with Disabilities Education Act (IDEA) Federal law passed in 1990 that extends full education services and provisions to people identified with disabilities.

inductive reasoning Drawing generalizations based on the observation of specific examples.

informal education A practice that, in many cultures, augments or takes the place of formal schooling as children learn adult roles through observation, conversation, assisting, and imitating.

infrastructure The basic installations and facilities on which the continuance and growth of a community depend.

instruction The process of implementing a curriculum.

INTASC The Interstate New Teachers Assessment and Support Consortium, an organization that has identified competency standards for new teachers.

integrated curriculum (interdisciplinary curriculum) Subject matter from two or more areas combined into thematic units (e.g., literature and history resources to study civil rights laws).

integration The process of educating different racial and ethnic groups together, and developing positive interracial contacts.

intellectual property It refers to creations of the mind, such as inventions; literary and artistic works, such as poems and books and art, as well as names and images used in commerce.

Intelligent Design The argument that instances in nature cannot be explained by Darwinian evolution, but instead are consistent with the notion of an intelligent involvement in the design of life.

interest centers Centers that provide independent student activities related to a specific subject. Usually associated with an open classroom.

International Baccalaureate (IB) An internationally recognized curriculum for students ages 3 through 19 that includes rigorous science, math, and foreign language requirements along with diverse cultural studies. The IB program is designed to develop the intellectual, emotional, and social skills students need to learn, live, and work in our increasingly connected globalizing world.

J

junior high school A two- or three-year school between elementary and high school for students in their early adolescent years, commonly grades 7 and 8 or 7 through 9.

K

Kalamazoo, Michigan, case An 1874 U.S. Supreme Court decision that upheld the right of states to tax citizens to provide public secondary education.

kindergarten A preschool, early childhood educational environment first designed by Froebel in the mid-nineteenth century.

L

labeling Categorizing or classifying students for the purposes of educational placement. One unfortunate consequence may be that of stigmatizing students and inhibiting them from reaching their full potential.

Laboratory Schools Schools often associated with a teacher preparation institution for practice teaching, demonstration, research, or innovation.

land grant colleges State colleges or universities offering agricultural and mechanical curricula, funded originally by the Morrill Act of 1862.

Land Ordinance Act A nineteenth-century federal law that required newly settled territories to reserve a section of land for schools.

language submersion A bilingual education model that teaches students in classes where only English is spoken, the teacher does not know the language of the student, and the student either learns English as the academic work progresses or pays the consequences. This has been called a "sink or swim" approach.

last mile problem A digital divide in which geography is a factor, in part because running fiber-optic cables to rural schools is often an expense that telecommunications companies avoid. See also digital divide.

latchkey (self-care) kids A term used to describe children who go home after school to an empty house; their parents or guardians are usually working and not home.

Latin grammar school A classical secondary school with a Latin and Greek curriculum preparing students for college.

learning communities The creation of more personal collaboration between teachers and students to promote similar academic goals and values.

learning disability An educationally significant language and/or learning deficit.

learning styles The belief that students have diverse ways of learning, comprehending, and using information and have different preferences, ranging from preferred light and noise levels to independent or group learning formats.

least-restrictive environment The program best suited to meeting a disabled student's special needs without segregating the student from the regular educational program.

LGBTQA This acronym refers to Lesbian, Gay, Bisexual, Transgender, and Queer/Questioning, with the A referring to a number of possible words, including Asexual, Allies, and/or Advocates.

liability This term refers to being legally responsible for something.

limited English proficiency (LEP) A student who has a limited ability to understand, speak, or read English and who has a native language other than English.

locus of control A concept wherein learners attribute success or failure to external or internal factors. "The teacher didn't review the material well" is an example of attribution to an external factor and represents an external locus of control. In this case, the learner avoids responsibility for behavior. When students have an internal locus of control, they believe that they control their fate and take responsibility for events.

logic The branch of philosophy that deals with reasoning. Logic defines the rules of reasoning, focuses on how to move from one set of assumptions to valid conclusions, and examines the rules of inference that enable us to frame our propositions and arguments.

lower-order questions Questions that require the retrieval of memorized information and do not require more complex intellectual processes.

M

magnet school A specialized school open to all students in a district on a competitive or lottery basis. It provides a method of drawing children away from segregated neighborhood schools while affording unique educational specialties, such as science, math, and the performing arts.

mainstreaming The inclusion of special education students in the regular education program. The nature and extent of this inclusion should be based on meeting the special needs of the child.

maintenance (developmental) approach A bilingual model that emphasizes the importance of acquiring English while maintaining competence in the native language.

malfeasance Deliberately acting improperly and causing harm to someone.

mastery learning An educational practice in which an individual demonstrates mastery of one task before moving on to the next.

materialism A philosophy focused on scientific observation and the belief that existence is experienced only in the physical realm.

McGuffey Reader A reading series that, for almost 100 years, promoted moral and patriotic messages and set the practice of reading levels leading toward graded elementary schools.

McKinney Vento Homeless Assistance Act The primary piece of federal legislation dealing with the education of homeless children in public schools.

merit pay A salary system that bases a teacher's pay on performance.

metacognition Self-awareness of our thinking process as we perform various tasks and operations. For example, when students articulate how they think about academic tasks, it enhances their thinking and enables teachers to target assistance and remediation.

metaphysics The area of philosophy that examines the nature of reality.

microteaching A clinical approach to teacher training in which the teacher candidate teaches a small group of students for a brief time while concentrating on a specific teaching skill.

middle schools Two- to four-year schools of the middle grades, often grades 6 through 8, between elementary school and high school.

misfeasance Failure to act in a proper manner to prevent harm.

moral stages of development A model of moral development promoted by Lawrence Kohlberg in which individuals progress from simple moral concerns, such as avoiding punishment, to more sophisticated ethical beliefs and actions.

Morrill Act Federal legislation (1862) granting federal lands to states to establish colleges to promote more effective and efficient agriculture and industry. A second Morrill Act, passed in 1890, provided federal support for "separate but equal" colleges for African Americans.

multiple intelligences A theory developed by Howard Gardner to expand the concept of human intelligence to include such areas as logical-mathematical, linguistic, bodily-kinesthetic, musical, spatial, interpersonal, intrapersonal, and naturalist.

multiracial A term that pertains to people whose ancestry consists of more than one race. This is the fastest-growing student demographic in the United States.

N

National Assessment of Educational Progress (NAEP) Program to ascertain the effectiveness of U.S. schools and student achievement.

National Board for Professional Teacing Standards (NBPTS) An organization designed to award *board certification* to extraordinary teachers whose skills and knowledge indicate their high level of achievement.

national curricular standards Nationally prescribed or recommended standards, content skills, and testing.

National Defense Education Act (NDEA) Federally sponsored programs (1958) to improve science, math, and foreign language instruction in schools.

National Education Association (NEA) The largest organization of educators. The NEA is concerned with the overall improvement of education and of the conditions of educators. It is organized at the national, state, and local levels.

networking The term used to describe the intentional effort to develop personal connections with individuals who could be helpful in finding positions or gaining professional advancement.

neuroplasticity The ability of our brain to change itself and create new neural pathways.

New England Primer One of the first textbooks in colonial America, teaching reading and moral messages.

No Child Left Behind (NCLB) A federal law passed in 2001 that emphasized high-stakes standardized testing. By 2012, the federal government allowed many states to opt out as an emphasis on national core standards took hold.

nondiscriminatory education A principle, based on the Fifth and Fourteenth Amendments of the U.S. Constitution, that mandates that children with disabilities be fairly assessed so that they can be protected from inappropriate classification and tracking.

nonfeasance Failure to exercise appropriate responsibility that results in someone's being harmed.

nongraded school A school organization in which grade levels are eliminated for two or more years.

nonverbal communication The act of transmitting and/or receiving messages through means not having to do with oral or written language, such as eye contact, facial expressions, and body language.

norm-referenced tests Tests that compare individual students with others in a designated group.

normal school A two-year teacher education institution popular in the nineteenth century. Many normal schools were expanded to become today's state colleges and universities.

Northwest Ordinance (1785, 1787) Federal legislation that provided for the sale of federal lands in the Northwest territory to support public schools.

null curriculum The curriculum that is not taught in schools.

O

objective The purpose of a lesson expressed in a statement.

objective-referenced tests Tests that measure whether students have mastered a designated body of knowledge rather than how they compare with other students in a norm group.

Old Deluder Satan Law (1647) Massachusetts colony law requiring teachers in towns of fifty families or more and that schools be built in towns of one hundred families or more. Communities must teach children to read so that they can read the Bible and thwart Satan.

open classroom A system of education, that involves not only an informal classroom environment but also a philosophy of education. Students pursue individual interests with the guidance and support of the teacher; interest centers are created to promote this individualized instruction. Students may also have a significant influence in determining the nature and sequence of the curriculum. It is sometimes referred to as *open education.*

open enrollment The practice of permitting students to attend the school of their choice within their school system. It is sometimes associated with magnet schools and desegregation efforts.

open-space school A school building without interior walls. Although it may be designed to promote the concept of the open classroom, the open-space school is an architectural concept rather than an educational one.

oral tradition Spoken language is the primary method for instruction in several cultures around the world. Word problems are used to teach reasoning, proverbs to instill wisdom, and stories to teach lessons about nature, history, religion, and social customs.

outcome-based education (OBE) An educational approach that emphasizes setting learning outcomes and assessing student progress toward attaining those goals, rather than focusing on curricular topics.

P

paraprofessional A layperson who serves as an aide, assisting the teacher in the classroom.

parochial school An institution operated and controlled by a religious denomination.

pay-for-performance A salary method that attempts to make teaching more accountable by linking teacher and student performance to teacher salary. See also merit pay.

peace studies The study and analysis of the conditions of and need for peace, the causes of war, and the mechanisms for the nonviolent resolution of conflict. Also referred to as *peace education.*

pedagogical cycle A system of teacher–student interaction that includes four steps: structure—teacher introduces the topic; question—teacher asks questions; respond—student answers or tries to answer questions; and react—teacher reacts to student's answers and provides feedback.

pedagogy The science of teaching.

peer review The practice of having colleagues observe and assess teaching, as opposed to administrators.

perennialism The philosophy that emphasizes rationality as the major purpose of education. It asserts that the essential truths are recurring and universally true; it stresses Great Books.

performance standards Statements that describe what teachers or students should be able to do, and how well they should do it.

permanent license Although some variation exists from state to state, a permanent license is issued after a candidate has completed all the requirements for full recognition as a teacher. Requirements may include a specified number of courses beyond the bachelor's degree or a specified number of years of teaching.

philosophy The love of or search for wisdom; the quest to understand the meaning of life.

phonics An approach to reading instruction that emphasizes decoding words by sounding out letters and combinations of letters (as contrasted with the whole language approach).

Plessey* v. *Ferguson An 1896 Supreme Court decision that upheld that "separate but equal" was legal and that the races could be segregated. It was overturned in 1954 by *Brown v. The Board of Education of Topeka.*

political philosophy An approach to analyzing how past and present societies are arranged and governed and how better societies may be created in the future.

portfolio Compilations of work (such as papers, projects, videos, online activities) assembled to demonstrate growth, creativity, and competence. Often advocated as a more comprehensive assessment than test scores.

pragmatism A philosophical belief that asserts truth is what works and rejects other views of reality.

praxis The doctrine that actions should be based on sound theory and values. (It is no accident that the term *praxis* is also the name given to the teacher competency tests required by many states.)

primary school A separately organized and administered elementary school for students in the lower elementary grades, usually grades 1 through 3, and sometimes including preprimary years.

private school A school controlled by an individual or agency other than the government, usually supported by other than public funds. Most private schools are parochial.

privatization The movement toward increased private sector, for-profit involvement in the management of public agencies, including schools.

probationary teaching period A specified period of time in which a newly hired teacher must demonstrate teaching competence. This period is usually three years for public school teachers and six years for college professors. Generally, on satisfactory completion of the probationary period, a teacher is granted tenure.

problem-based learning (PBL) An approach that builds a curriculum around intriguing real-life problems and asks students to work cooperatively to develop and demonstrate their solutions.

procedural due process The right of children with disabilities and their parents to be notified of school actions and decisions; to challenge those decisions before an impartial tribunal, using counsel and expert witnesses; to examine the school records on which a decision is based; and to appeal whatever decision is reached.

professional development School district efforts to improve knowledge, skills, and performance of its professional staff.

progressive education (progressivism) Educational practices emphasizing democracy, student needs, practical activities, and school–community relationships.

progressivism An educational philosophy that organizes schools around the concerns, curiosity, and real-world experiences of students.

property tax Local real estate taxes (also cars and personal property) historically used to fund local schools.

provisional license Also referred to as a *probationary license,* a provisional license is frequently issued to beginning teachers. It may mean that a person has completed most, but not all, of the state requirements for permanent licensure. Or it may mean that the state requires several years of teaching experience before it will qualify the teacher for permanent licensure.

Public Law 94-142 Passed in 1975, this was the first law to require schools to provide free and appropriate public education to every child with special needs. This law evolved into today's Individuals with Disabilities Education Act (IDEA).

R

race Refers to a group of individuals sharing common genetic attributes, physical appearance, and ancestry.

racial discrimination Actions that limit or deny a person or group any privileges, roles, or rewards on the basis of race.

racism Attitudes, beliefs, and behavior based on the notion that one race is superior to other races.

rationalism The philosophy that emphasizes the power of reason and the principles of logic to derive statements about the world. Rationalists encourage schools to emphasize teaching mathematics, because mathematics involves reason and logic.

readability formulas Formulas that use objective, quantitative measures to determine the reading level of textbooks.

reciprocity A mutual exchange of rights or benefits. For example, a teacher's license in one state is recognized as valid in another.

reconstructionism (reconstructionist) A view of education as a way to improve the quality of life, to reduce the chances of conflict, and to create a more humane world. Also called *social reconstructionism.*

reflective teaching Thoughtfully analyzing one's own teaching practices and classroom.

regular education initiative The attempt to reduce the complications and expense of segregated special education efforts by teaching special needs students in the standard educational program through collaborative consultation, curricular modifications, and environment adaptations.

résumé A summary of a person's education and experiences, often used for application to school or employment.

revenue sharing The distribution of federal money to state and local governments to use as they decide.

Robin Hood reformers State legislators favoring the redistribution of revenue from wealthier to poorer communities to equalize educational funding.

romantic critics Critics such as Paul Goodman, Herbert Kohl, and John Holt who believed that schools were stifling the cognitive and affective development of children. Individual critics stressed different problems or solutions, but they all agreed that schools were producing alienated, uncreative, and unfulfilled students.

rubric A scoring guide that describes what must be done, and often describes performance levels ranging from novice to expert, or from a failing grade to excellence.

S

scaffolding Taking from the construction field, scaffolding provides support to help a student build understanding. The teacher might use cues or encouragement or well-formulated questions to assist a student in solving a problem or mastering a concept.

school boards Elected or appointed officials who determine educational policies for school systems.

school choice The name given to several programs in which parents choose what school their child will attend.

school financing A term that refers to the ways in which monies are raised and allocated to schools. The methods differ widely from state to state, and many challenges are being made in courts today because of the unequal distribution of funds within a state or among states.

school infrastructure The basic facilities and structures that underpin a school plant, such as plumbing, sewage, heat, electricity, roof, masonry, and carpentry.

school-to-prison pipeline describes practices implemented by educational institutions, specifically zero tolerance policies and the use of police in schools, which often moves children away from school and into the juvenile and adult criminal justice systems. The impact disproportionately affects Latino and Black students, increasing the rates of incarceration.

school superintendent The chief administrator of a school system, responsible for implementing and enforcing the school board's policies, rules, and regulations, as well as state and federal requirements. The superintendent is directly responsible to the school board and is the formal representative of the school community to outside individuals and agencies.

School to Work Opportunities Act Federal legislation that authorizes the funding of programs that link school learning to job settings, often developed in partnerships between school and industry.

school-based management The recent trend in education reform that stresses decision making on the school level. In the past, school policies were set by the state and the districts. Now the trend is for individual schools to make their own decisions and policies.

schools without walls An alternative education program that involves the total community as a learning resource.

second-generation segregation The separation of a school's multiracial populations through tracking, extracurricular activities, and informal social events.

secondary school A program of study that follows elementary school and includes junior, middle, and high school.

secular humanism The belief that people can live ethically without faith in a supernatural or supreme being. Some critics have alleged that secular humanism is a form of religion and that publishers are promoting secular humanism in their books.

separate but equal A legal doctrine that holds that equality of treatment is accorded when the races are provided substantially equal facilities, even though those facilities are separate. This doctrine was ruled unconstitutional in regard to race.

service credit or service learning By volunteering in a variety of community settings, from nursing homes to child care facilities, students are encouraged to develop a sense of community and meet what is now a high school graduation requirement in some states.

sex discrimination Any action that limits or denies a person or group of persons opportunities, privileges, roles, or rewards on the basis of sex.

sex-role stereotyping Attributing behavior, abilities, interests, values, and roles to a person or group of persons on the basis of sex. This process ignores individual differences.

sexism The collection of attitudes, beliefs, and behavior that results from the assumption that one sex is superior to the other.

sexual harassment Unwanted, repeated, and unreturned sexual words, behaviors, or gestures prohibited by federal and some state laws.

simulation A role-playing technique in which students take part in re-created, lifelike situations.

site-based (school-based) management A school governance method that shifts decision making from the central district office to individual schools.

social Darwinism A belief similar to Darwin's notion of "survival of the fittest," that contends that society is a natural sorting system which rewards the talented and places the less deserving at the bottom of the social and economic pecking order.

social reconstructionism See reconstructionism.

sociogram A diagram that is constructed to record social interactions, such as which children interact frequently and which are isolates.

Socratic method An educational strategy attributed to Socrates in which a teacher encourages a student's discovery of truth by questions.

special education Programs and instruction for children with physical, mental, emotional, or learning disabilities or gifted students who need special educational services to achieve at their ability level.

stages of teacher development A presentation of four stages that teachers pass through as they become more skilled in their craft.

standardized test A standardized test requires all test takers to answer the same questions and is scored in a "standard" or consistent manner. Test takers are often compared to one another according to their performance.

standards-based education Education that specifies precisely what students should learn, focuses the curriculum and instruction (and perhaps much more) on meeting those standards, and provides continual testing to see if the standards are achieved.

state adoption The process by which members of a textbook adoption committee review and select the books used throughout a state. Advocates of this process say that it results in a common statewide curriculum that unites educators on similar issues and makes school life easier for students who move within the state. Critics charge that it gives too much influence to large states and results in a "dumbed down" curriculum.

state board of education The state education agency that regulates policies necessary to implement legislative acts related to education.

state department of education An agency that operates under the direction of the state board of education, accrediting schools, certifying teachers, appropriating state school funds, and so on.

stealth censorship (self-censorship) The quiet removal of a book from a library shelf or a course of study to avoid possible problems and parental complaints. Teachers practice the same sort of self-censorship when they choose not to teach a topic or not to discuss a difficult issue.

stereotype threat A measure of how social context, such as self-image, trust in others, and a sense of belonging, can influence academic performance.

stereotypes Absolute statements applied to all members of a group, suggesting that members of a group have a fixed, often inherited set of characteristics.

street academies Alternative schools designed to bring dropouts and potential dropouts, often inner-city youths, back into the educational mainstream.

student-initiated questions Content-related questions originating from the student yet consisting of only a small percentage of the questions asked in a typical class.

superintendent of schools The executive officer of the local school district.

T

taxonomy A classification system of organizing information and translating aims into instructional objectives.

Teach for America A program that places unlicensed college graduates in districts with critical teacher shortages as they work toward attaining a teacher license.

teacher certification State government's or a professional association's evaluation and approval of an applicant's competencies.

teacher expectations may vary based on gender, class, racial and ethnic background of students. As a result, these students may be taught differently and their academic performance suffers.

teacher flexibility The capability to adapt a variety of skills, abilities, characteristics, and approaches, according to the demands of each situation and the needs of each student.

teacher's license A teaching credential issued by a state government that grants the legal right to teach, not unlike a driver's license, which grants the legal right to drive.

Tenth Amendment The constitutional Amendment that establishes that areas not specifically mentioned in the Constitution as federal responsibilities are left to state authority. Since education is not mentioned, each state is free to create its own school system.

tenure A system of employment in which teachers, having served a probationary period, acquire an expectancy of continued employment. The majority of states have tenure laws.

textbook adoption states States, most often those in the South and West, that have a formal process for assessing, choosing, and approving textbooks for school use.

Title I Section of the Elementary and Secondary Education Act that provides federal funds to supplement local education resources for students from low-income families.

Title IX of the Education Amendments (1972) A provision of the 1972 Educational Amendments that prohibits sex discrimination in any educational program receiving federal financial assistance.

Title VII of the Civil Rights Act (1964) Section that prohibits employment discrimination based on race, color, religion, sex, or national origin.

tracking The method of placing students according to their ability level in homogeneous classes or learning experiences. Once a student is placed, it may be very difficult to move up from one track to another. The placements may reflect racism, classism, or sexism.

transitional bilingual education A bilingual education program in which students are taught for a limited time in their own language as well as English. The goal is to move students into English-only speaking classrooms.

trustee representatives School board members viewed as representatives of the entire community, rather than of the narrower interests of a particular group or neighborhood. This conception of a school board member's role differs from the delegate approach.

tuition tax credits Tax reductions for parents or guardians of children attending public or private schools.

two-way immersion These programs enroll both native English speakers and native speakers of another language. English-speaking students learn a second language and non-English speakers learn English. Classes are taught to all students in both languages.

U

U.S. Department of Education Federal cabinet-level agency responsible for establishing national education policies, prohibiting discrimination in education, and collecting data on student achievement and other educational issues.

unobtrusive measurement A method of measuring without affecting what is measured; indirect elicitation of data.

V

value-added A statistical measure showing the contribution of teachers and schools toward growth in student achievement. Value-added measures are increasingly used to determine which teachers are rewarded and which teachers are replaced.

values clarification A model, comprising various strategies, that encourages students to express and clarify their values on different topics.

virtual school A type of distance education offered through the Internet. Virtual schools provide asynchronous learning and may offer specialized courses not typically found in traditional schools.

voucher A coupon, issued by the government, representing money targeted for schools. In a voucher system, parents use educational vouchers to "shop" for a school. Schools receive part or all of their per-pupil funding from these vouchers. In theory, good schools would thrive and poor ones would close for lack of students.

W

wait time The amount of time a teacher waits for a student's response after a question is asked and the amount of time following a student's response before the teacher reacts.

whole language approach An approach to reading instruction that emphasizes the integration of language arts skills and knowledge, with a heavy emphasis on literature (as contrasted with a phonics approach).

women's studies Originally created during the 1970s to study the history, literature, psychology, and experiences of women, topics typically missing from the traditional curriculum.

Z

zero reject The principle that no child with disabilities may be denied a free and appropriate public education.

zero-tolerance policies Rigorous rules that offer schools little or no flexibility in responding to student infractions related to alcohol, drugs, tobacco, violence, and weapons. These policies have been developed by both local school districts and a number of state legislatures, and in most cases, students who violate such policies must be expelled.

zone of proximal development The area where students can move from what they know to new learning, a zone where real learning is possible.

Notes

CHAPTER 1: THE TEACHING PROFESSION AND YOU

1. Frederick Buechner, *Wishful Thinking: A Seeker's ABC* (San Francisco: Harper, 1993), p. 119.
2. Eric McIntyre, "Should Teachers Be Paid Based on Performance?" *Education Dive*, May 2, 2016, http://www.educationdive.com/news/should-teachers-be-paid-based-on-performance/418398/; Kim Marshall, "Is Merit Pay the Answer?" *Education Week* 29, no. 15 (December 15, 2009), pp. 22, 28; Bryan Toporek, "Poll: Americans in Favor of Teacher Merit Pay," www.teachermagazine.org (retrieved September 16, 2010).
3. Richard D. Kahlenberg, "Teacher Tenure Has a Long History and, Hopefully, a Future," *Phi Delta Kappan* 97 (March 2016), pp. 16–21; Trip Gabriel and Sam Dillon, "G.O.P. Governors Take Aim at Teacher Tenure," *New York Times*, February 1, 2011, pp. A1, A3; Jeremy P. Meyer, "Colorado Renews Teacher-Tenure Debate," *Denver Post*, April 13, 2010.
4. Shane Lopez, "Wanted: Inspiring Teachers and Professors," *Gallup*, **February 17, 2015**, http://www.gallup.com/opinion/gallup/181610/wanted-inspiring-teachers-professors.aspx.
5. Frank Bruni, "Can We Interest You in Teaching?" *New York Times*, August 12, 2015, https://www.nytimes.com/2015/08/12/opinion/frank-bruni-can-we-interest-you-in-teaching.html?_r=0; Thomas Newkirk, "Stress, Control, and the Deprofessionalizing of Teaching," *Education Week*, October 21, 2009; Jillian N. Lederhouse, "Show Me the Power," *Education Week*, June 13, 2001.
6. Ron Brandt, "On Teacher Empowerment: A Conversation with Ann Lieberman," *Educational Leadership* 46, no. 8 (May 1989), pp. 23–24; *The MetLife Survey of the American Teacher: Expectations and Experience: A Survey of Teachers, Principals, and Leaders of College Education Programs* (September 26, 2006), www.metlife.com/WPSAssets/8182140270116050587 1V1F2006MetLifeTeacherSurvey.pdf (retrieved January 31, 2008).
7. Adopted from Robert Howsam et al., *Educating a Profession, Report on the Bicentennial Commission of Education for Profession of Teaching* (Washington, DC: American Association of Colleges for Teacher Education, 1976), pp. 6–7; See also *The Changing Teacher Preparation Profession: A Report from AACTE's Professional Education Data System* (Washington, DC: American Association of Colleges for Teacher Education) 2013.
8. Daniel Pink, *Drive: The Surprising Truth About What Motivates Us* (New York: Riverhead, 2009), p. 142.
9. For more information on the development and status of teacher education programs, see Autumn A. Arnett, "New Ed Dept. Teacher Prep Regulations Target Equity, Accountability" *Education Dive*, October 12, 2016, http://www.educationdive.com/news/new-ed-dept-teacher-prep-regulations-target-equity-accountability/428139/; Scott Stephens and Edith Starzyk, "Colleges Use Programs as Cash Cows, with Few Standards, Critics Say," *Cleveland Plain Dealer*, May 25, 2008, http://groups.google.com/group/oregon-arts-education/msg/a764bcd3a00d2bb7?pli51 (retrieved February 20, 2009); Jay Mathews, "Breaking Down the Ivy Tower: Study Finds Schools of Ed in Poor Shape," *Washington Post*, October 31, 2006, p. A8; Doug Selwyn, "Teacher Quality: Teacher Education Left Behind," *Rethinking Schools* 20, no. 2 (Winter 2005/2006), www.rethinkingschools.org/archive/20_02/left202.shtml (retrieved May 10, 2008).
10. Retrieved on January 1, 2017, from www.nbpts.org.
11. Roland S. Barth, David C. Berliner, Frederick M. Hess, Susan Moore Johnson, Barnett Berry, and Charlotte Danielson, "The Time Is Ripe (Again)," Leveraging Teacher Leadership, *Educational Leadership* 71, no. 2 (October 2013), pp. 10–16.
12. Anya Kamenetz, "Teacher Training As 'Part Theater, Part Sport,'" *NPR Ed*, October 18, 2016, http://www.npr.org/sections/ed/2016/10/18/497516106/teacher-training-as-part-theater-part-sport; Christie Blazer, "What the Research Says about Alternative Teacher Certification Programs," *ERIC*, February 2012, ED536506; Lisa W. Foderaro, "Alternate Path for Teachers Gains Ground," *New York Times*, April 18, 2010; National Center for Education Information, "Alternative Routes Are Attracting Talented Individuals from Other Careers Who Otherwise Would Not Become Teachers," www.ncei.com/part.html (retrieved February 12, 2009). See also Wendy Kopp, *One Day All Children Will Triumph: The Unlikely Story of Teach for America and What I Learned along the Way* (New York: Public Affairs, 2003).
13. Emma Brown, "Teach for America Retools Efforts to Recruit Graduates from Top Colleges," *Washington Post*, May 31, 2016, www.washingtonpost.com; Retrieved January 22, 2014 from www.teachforamerica.org/sites/default/files/2013_top_college_contributors.pdf; Valerie Strauss, "Why One School System Is Dropping Teach For America," Report Card, *Washington Post*, September 1, 2014; Will Dobbie, "Teacher Characteristics and Student Achievement: Evidence from Teach For America," July 2011, www.people.fas.harvard.edu/~dobbie/research; Morgaen L. Donaldson and Susan Moore Johnson, "Teach For America Teachers: How Long Do They Teach? Why Do They Leave?" *Phi Delta Kappan* 93, no. 2 (October 2011), pp. 47–51; Linda Darling-Hammond, "Teacher Preparation Is Essential to TFA's Future," *Education Week* 30, no. 24 (March 14, 2011), pp. 25–26, 36; Stephen Sawchuk, "Teach For America Elaborates Its Response to NEA Criticism," Education Week/Teacher Beat blog, July 22, 2011, http://blogs.edweek.org/edweek/teacherbeat/2011/07/teach_for_america_elaborates_o.html.
14. Jackie Mader, "What Happens When Teachers Spend More Time in a Classroom—Before Teaching?" *The Atlantic*, April 15, 2016, www.theatlantic.com; Stephen Sawchuk, "Teacher Residents Seen Outpacing Peers in Later Years," *Education Week* 31, no. 15 (published online: December 15, 2011); Stephen Sawchuk, "Teacher Residencies Make Strides, Encounter Obstacles," *Education Week* 30, no. 36 (published online: July 8, 2011).
15. "Traditional vs. Alternative Routes to Teaching: Is One More Effective?" Georgia State University, Economics, March 3, 2014, http://economics.gsu.edu/traditional-vs-alternative-routes-teaching-one-effective/(retrieved October 18, 2016); Debra Viadero, "Panel Finds No Favorite in Teacher-Prep Pathways," *Education Week* 29, no. 31 (April 29, 2010); Jill Constantine,

Daniel Player, Tim Silva, Kristin Hallgren, Mary Grider, and John Deke, *An Evaluation of Teachers Trained through Different Routes to Certification* (Washington, DC: U.S. Department of Education, February 2009).

16. Charlotte Danielson, "A Framework for Learning to Teach," *Education Leadership* 66, June 2009, www.ascd.org/publications/educational-leadership.aspx (retrieved May 2010); Bill Keller, "An Industry of Mediocrity," *New York Times,* October 20, 2013, http://www.nytimes.com/2013/10/21/opinion/keller-an-industry-of-mediocrity.html (retrieved January 1, 2014); Susan Moore Johnson and Sarah Birkeland, "Fast-Track Certification: Can We Prepare Teachers Both Quickly and Well?" *Education Week* 25, no. 23 (February 15, 2006), pp. 37, 48; "Research-Based Characteristics of High-Quality Teacher Preparation," *ASCD Smart-Brief* 1, no. 4 (February 19, 2003).
17. Valerie Strauss, *Washington Post* blog: The Answer Sheet, "What's right—and very wrong—with the teacher education debate," December 16, 2013, http://www.networkforpubliceducation.org/ (retrieved January 2, 2014); David C. Berliner, "A Personal Response to Those Who Bash Teacher Education," *Journal of Teacher Education* 51, no. 5 (November/December 2000), pp. 358–371; Suzanne M. Wilson, Robert E. Floden, and Joan Ferrini Mundy, "Teacher Preparation Research: An Insider's View from the Outside," *Journal of Teacher Education* 53, no. 3 (May/June 2002), pp. 190–204.
18. D. C. Berliner, "A Personal Response," p. 363. See also College Board, "2005 College-Bound Seniors," www.collegeboard.com/prod_downloads/about/news_info/cbsenior/yr2005/2005-college-bound-seniors.pdf (retrieved February 20, 2017).
19. Gary M. Chesley and Janice Jordan, "What's Missing from Teacher Prep: Supporting Beginning Teachers," *Educational Leadership 69,* no. 8 (May 2012), pp. 41–45.
20. C. Emily Feistritzer, *Profile of Teachers in the U.S. 2011* (Washington, DC: National Center for Education Information, 2011), p. 30.
21. Pam Grossman and Emily Davis, "Mentoring That Fits," *Ed Leadership* 69, no. 8 (May 2012), pp. 54–57; Deborah Bieler, "What New Teachers Want from Colleagues," *Ed Leadership* 69, no. 8 (May 2012), pp. 46–49.
22. Sharon Feiman-Nemser, "Beyond Solo Teaching," *Ed Leadership* 69, no. 8 (May 2012), pp. 10–16.
23. Lilian Katz, "The Development of Preschool Teachers," *The Elementary School Journal* 73, no. 1 (October 1972), pp. 50–54; John L. Watzke, "Longitudinal Study of Stages of Beginning Teacher Development in a Field-Based Teacher Education Program," *Teacher Educator* 38, no. 3 (Winter 2003), pp. 209–229.
24. Linda Darling-Hammond, "Keeping Good Teachers: Why It Matters What Leaders Can Do," *Educational Leadership* 60, no. 8 (May 2003), pp. 7–13.
25. Lapointe quoted in Gerald W. Bracey, "The Second Bracey Report on the Condition of Public Education," *Phi Delta Kappan* (October 1992), pp. 104–117, cited in David C. Berliner and Bruce J. Biddle, *The Manufactured Crisis* (Reading, MA: Addison Wesley, 1995), p. 54.
26. A chart of 2009 College-Bound Seniors Average SAT Scores, FairTest Web site, www.fairtest.org/ (retrieved February 2, 2009); Nation's Report Card, *Reading Scores* http://nces.ed.gov/nationsreportcard/reading/ (retrieved February 2, 2009); College Board, *The 5th Annual AP Report to the Nation,* www.collegeboard.com/html/aprtn/pdf/ap_report_to_the_nation.pdf (retrieved February 2, 2009); See also Berliner and Biddle, *The Manufactured Crisis,* pp. 13–64.
27. "Survey Gauges Teens' View of Tech Future," *LemelsinMIT Invention Index,* Massachusetts Institute of Technology, January 12, 2006, web.mit.edu; William Bushaw and Shane Lopez, "Highlights of the 2013 PDF/Gallup Poll," *Phi Delta Kappan* 95, no. 1 (September 2013), pp. 8–25, www.pdkpoll.org.
28. Diane Ravitch, *Reign of Error: The Hoax of the Privatization Movement and the Danger to America's Public Schools* (New York: Random House, 2013); See Fairtest.org for testing reform updates, including "Back-To-School Report Tallies 2016 Testing Reform Victories" September 6, 2016, http://www.fairtest.org/report-tallies-2016-testing-reform-victories; Diane Ravitch, *The Death and Life of the Great American School System: How Testing and Choice Are Undermining Education* (New York: Basic Books, 2010); Berliner and Biddle, *The Manufactured Crisis,* p. 146. See also Richard Rothstein, *The Way We Were? The Myths and Realities of America's Student Achievement* (Washington, DC: Century Fund, 1998); Sara Mead, *The Evidence Suggests Otherwise; The Truth about Boys and Girls* (Washington, DC: Education Sector, 2006), pp. 14–16.

YOU BE THE JUDGE NOTES

1. Amy DePaul, *What to Expect Your First Year of Teaching* (Washington, DC: U.S. Department of Education, September 1998), p. 28. There are also some worthwhile contemporary teaching experiences and insights described on the Internet. See, for example, "10 Things to Expect & Not Expect Your First Year of Teaching," at http://specialedandme.wordpress.com/2009/08/31/10-things-to-expect-not-expect-your-first-year-of-teaching-easier/.
2. Quoted in Ann Lieberman and Lynn Miller, *Teachers, Their World and Their Work* (Alexandria, VA: Association for Supervision and Curriculum Development, 1984), p. 22.
3. Valerie Strauss, "U.S. Teachers' Job Satisfaction Craters—Report." *The Washington Post,* February 21, 2013, at www.washingtonpost.com (retrieved January 2, 2014); William Bushaw and Shane Lopez "Highlights of the 2013 PDF/Gallup Poll", *Phi Delta Kappan* 95, no. 1 (September 2013), pp. 8–25.
4. Ann Lieberman and Lynne Miller, *Their World and Their Work,* p. 47.
5. William Lyon Phelps, quoted in Oliver Ikenberry, *American Education Foundations* (Columbus, OH: Merrill, 1974), p. 389.
6. Quoted in Myron Brenton, *What's Happened to Teacher?* (New York: Coward, McCann & Geoghegan, 1970), p. 164.
7. Stephen Gordon quoted in "What Keeps Teachers Going?" *Educational Leadership* 60, no. 8 (May 2003), p. 18.
8. Shane Lopez and Sangeeta Agrawal, "Teachers Score Higher than Other Professionals in Well-Being," Gallup Poll, December 23, 2009, www.gallup.com/poll/124778/ teachers-score-higher-professionals.aspx.
9. Valerie Strauss , "Pay for Veteran Teachers 'Painfully Low' in States Like Colorado, Where Truckers Earn More," *Washington Post,* July 24, 2014; Quote from Myron Brenton, *What's Happened to Teacher?* p. 97.

CHAPTER 2: DIFFERENT WAYS OF LEARNING

1. Autumn A. Arnett, "Promoting growth mindset means checking biases at the door, experts say," *Education Dive,* March 23, 2016, http://www.educationdive.com; Carol Dweck, "Growth Mindset, Revisited," *Education Week* 35, no. 5, (September 23, 2015), pp. 20, 24; Sarah Sparks, "Growth Mindset Gaining Traction as Education Strategy," *Education Week,* September 11, 2013, www.edweek.org.
2. Dweck, "Growth Mindset, Revisited."
3. Howard Gardner and Thomas Hatch "Multiple Intelligences Go to School: Educational Implications of the Theory of Multiple Intelligences," *Educational Researcher* 18, no. 8 (November 1989), p. 5; Howard Gardner, *Frames of Mind: The Theory of Multiple Intelligences,* 3rd ed. (New York: Basic Books, 2011).
4. Gardner, *Frames of Mind: The Theory of Multiple Intelligences;* Kathy Checkley, "The First Seven . . . and the Eighth: A Conversation with Howard Gardner," *Educational Leadership* 55, no. 1 (September 1997), pp. 8–13.
5. Richard Louv, *The Nature Principle: Human Restoration and the End of Nature-Deficit Disorder* (New York: Algonquin Books, 2011); Ellin Holohan, "Active Teens Are More Happy Teens: Study," *HealthDay* (June 22, 2012), http://consumer.healthday.com.
6. Naphtali Hoff, *Redefining Smart,* http://smartblogs.com/education/2015/06/01/redefining-smart/?utm_source=brief, (June 1, 2015); Gardner, *Frames of Mind: The Theory of Multiple Intelligences;* Thomas Armstrong, *Multiple Intelligences in the Classroom,* 3rd ed. (Alexandria, VA: Association for Supervision and Curriculum Development, 2009).
7. Matt Renwick, *Digital Student Portfolios: A Whole School Approach to Connected Learning and Continuous Assessment* (New York: Theory and Practice, 2015).
8. Howard Gardner, *Five Minds for the Future* (Cambridge, MA: Harvard Business School Press, 2006); Howard Gardner and Katie Davis, *The App Generation: How Today's Youth Navigate Identity, Intimacy, and Imagination in a Digital World* (New Haven: Yale Press, 2014).
9. Nancy Gibbs, "The E.Q. Factor," *Time,* October 2, 1995, pp. 60–68.
10. Daniel Goleman, *Working with Emotional Intelligence* (New York: Bantam Books, 2000); Daniel Goleman, "Emotional Intelligence: Why It Can Matter More Than IQ," *Learning* (May/June 1996), pp. 49–50; Daniel Goleman, "The Socially Intelligent Leader," *Educational Leadership* 64, no. 1 (September 2006), pp. 76–81.
11. Emma Brown, "If You Want Your Children to Succeed, Teach Them to Share in Kindergarten," *The Washington Post* online (July 16, 2015), https://www.washingtonpost.com/local/education/want-your-kids-to-go-to-college-and-get-a-job-make-sure-they-learn-how-to-share-in-kindergarten/2015/07/16/4c30726a-2b4e-11e5-a250-42bd812efc09_story.html?utm_term=.ca69865f3e91.
12. Dale Schunk, *Learning Theories: An Educational Perspective* 7th edition. (Upper Saddle River, NJ: Pearson, 2015); Alan Pritchard, *Ways of Learning: Learning Theories and Learning Styles in the Classroom* 3rd edition, (New York: Routledge, 2013); Heather Wolpert-Gawron, "The Bunk of Debunking Learning Styles," *Teacher Magazine,* February 17, 2010, www.teachermagazine.com.
13. Pritchard, *Ways of Learning*; Schunk, *Learning Theories.*
14. Angela Duckworth, *Grit: The Power of Passion and Perseverance* (New York: Scribner's, 2016).
15. Pritchard, *Ways of Learning.*
16. Norman Doidge, *The Brain's Way of Healing: Remarkable Discoveries from the Frontiers of Neuroplasticity* (New York: Penguin, 2015); Norman Doidge, *The Brain That Changes Itself* (New York: Viking Press, 2007); Sarah Sparks, "Scientists Find Learning is Not 'Hard-Wired,'" *Education Week* 31, no. 33 (June 6, 2012), pp. 1, 16–17.
17. Donna W. Tileston, Ten Best Teaching Practices: How Brain Research and Learning Styles Define Teaching Competencies; Pashler, McDaniel, Rohrer, and Bjork, "Learning Styles: Concepts and Evidence": Sparks, "Scientists Find Learning in Not 'Hard-Wired.'"
18. Janet Hyde, "New Directions in the Study of Gender Similarities and Differences," *Current Directions in Psychological Science* 16 (2007), pp. 259–263; Lise Eliot, *Pink Brain, Blue Brain: How Small Differences Grow into Troublesome Gaps—and What We Can Do About It* (Boston: Houghton Mifflin, 2010).
19. David Sadker and Melissa Koch, "Gender Insights Coming to Your Classroom," *Educational Leadership* 74, no. 3 (November 2016), pp. 62–68; Diane Halpern, "The Pseudoscience of Single-Sex Schooling," *Education Forum* (September 22, 2011), pp. 1706–1707; Caryl Rivers and Rosalind Barnett, *The Truth About Girls and Boys: Challenging Toxic Stereotypes About Our Children* (New York: Columbia Press University, 2011); Lise Eliot, *Pink Brain, Blue Brain: How Small Differences Grow Into Troublesome Gaps—And What We Can Do About It.*
20. Hyde, "New Directions in the Study of Gender Similarities and Differences"; Diane Halpern, *Thought and Knowledge: An Introduction to Critical Thinking* 5th ed. NY: Psychology Press, 2014.
21. Pamela Davis-Keen, *Dads Influence Daughters' Interest in Mathematics.* Paper presented at Education a STEM Workforce: New Strategies for U-M and the State of Michigan, Ann Arbor, MI, 2007; Erik W. Robelen, "Girls in Science: Gender Gaps Still Persist in STEM Subjects," *The Christian Science Monitor* (June 27, 2012), www.CSMonitor.com.
22. Joshua Bolkan, "Research: Child Gender Informs Parental Attitudes about Tech," *The Journal*, March 30, 2015, http://thejournal.com/.
23. Eliot, *Pink Brain, Blue Brain: How Small Differences Grow Into Troublesome Gaps—And What We Can Do About It*; Michael Kimmel, *Sexualities*. United Kingdom: Oxford University Press, 2014.
24. Doidge, *The Brain That Changes Itself.*
25. These categories build on the ones described by Sara Bicard and William Heward, "Educational Equality for Students with Disabilities," in James Banks and Cherry Banks (eds.), *Multicultural Education,* 9th ed. (San Francisco: Jossey Bass, 2016), pp. 213–234.
26. Michael Janofsky, "Some New Help for the Extremely Gifted," *New York Times* online, October 26, 2005, http://www.nytimes.com/2005/10/26/education/some-new-help-for-the-extremely-gifted.html?_r=0.
27. Erin McIntrye, "Identifying Gifted and Talented Students with Equity Proves Difficult," *Education Dive*, February 10, 2016, http://www.educationdive.com/news/identifying-gifted-and-talented-students-with-equity-proves-difficult/413434/; Walt

Gardner, "Gifted Children Are Stepchildren in School Reform," *Education Week,* May 7, 2010, www.edweek.org.

28. Valerie Strauss, "Looking for a Few Wise Children, *The Washington Post,* September 17, 2002, p. A11.
29. National Association for Gifted Children, *What Is Gifted?* www.nagc.org/ (retrieved June 3, 2016), Erin McIntrye, "Identifying Gifted and Talented Students with Equity Proves Difficult"; United States Department of Education, *2013-2014 Civil Rights Education Data Collection: A First Look* (Washington, D.C: U.S. Department of Education, 2016); Jill Barshay, "Bright black students taught by black teachers are more likely to get into gifted-and-talented classrooms," *The Hechinger Report*, January 19, 2016, http://hechingerreport.org/bright-black-students-who-are-taught-by-black-teachers-are-more-likely-to-get-into-gifted-and-talented-classrooms/.
30. Tamara Fisher, "I Don't Want to Be a Smarty Anymore," *Education Week* online (June 30, 2010); Eric Cohen, "Motivating Gifted Learners," *Educational Update* 55, no. 5 (May 2013), pp. 1–6–7; Erin McIntrye, "Identifying Gifted and Talented Students with Equity Proves Difficult."
31. Fisher, "I Don't Want to Be a Smarty Anymore."
32. Erin McIntrye, "Identifying Gifted and Talented Students with Equity Proves Difficult"; Katie McClarty, "They'll Be Fine," *Research Network* (March 17, 2014), http://researchnetwork.pearson.com/college-career-success/theyll-fine-educational-opportunities-gifted-learners.
33. Erin McIntrye, "Identifying Gifted and Talented Students with Equity Proves Difficult"; United States Department of Education, *2013-2014 Civil Rights Education Data Collection: A First Look.*
34. Joseph Renzulli, *Reflections on Gifted Education: Critical Works.* Waco, TX: Prufrock Press, 2015; Christine Fonseca, *I'm Not Just Gifted: Social-Emotional Curriculum for Guiding Gifted Children.* Waco, TX: Prufrock Press 2015.
35. Owen Phillips, "Skip A Grade? Start Kindergarten Early? It's Not So Easy," *NPR*, April 30, 2015. http://www.nagc.org/resources-publications/resources/definitions-giftedness, National Association for Gifted Children, "What is Gifted?."
36. Tamara Fisher, "On the Up-Side," *Education Week* online (July 7, 2010)
37. Ibid.
38. Sara Bicard and William Heward, "Educational Equality for Students with Disabilities," in James Banks and Cherry Banks (eds.), *Multicultural Education,* 9th ed. (San Francisco: Jossey Bass, 2016).
39. Patrick Schwarz "Special Education: A Service, Not a Sentence," *Educational Leadership* 64, no. 5 (February 2007), pp. 39–42; Bicard and Heward, "Educational Equality for Students with Disabilities."
40. Sara Bicard and William Heward, "Educational Equality for Students with Disabilities," in James Banks and Cherry Banks (eds.), *Multicultural Education,* 9th ed. (San Francisco: Jossey Bass, 2016).
41. Ibid.
42. U.S. Department of Education, National Center for Education Statistics, "Children and Youth with Disabilities," *Condition of Education 2016,* http://nces.ed.gov/programs/coe/.
43. U.S. Department of Education, National Center for Education Statistics, "Children and Youth with Disabilities"; Alan Schwartz, *ADHD Nation: Children, Doctors, Big Pharma, and the Making of an American Revolution.* New York: Scribner's, 2016.
44. U.S. Department of Education, National Center for Education Statistics, "Children and Youth with Disabilities"; Bicard and Heward, "Educational Equality for Students with Disabilities."
45. Sara Bicard and William Heward, "Educational Equality for Students with Disabilities," in James Banks and Cherry Banks (eds.), *Multicultural Education,* 9th ed. (San Francisco: Jossey Bass, 2016).
46. U.S. Department of Education, National Center for Education Statistics, "Children and Youth with Disabilities."
47. Quoted in David Milofsky, "Schooling the Kid No One Wants," *The New York Times Magazine,* January 2, 1977, pp. 24–29.

CHAPTER 3: TEACHING YOUR DIVERSE STUDENTS

1. "Disrupting Inequity," *Educational Leadership* 74, no. 3 (November 2016).
2. James A. Banks, "Multicultural Education: Characteristics and Goals," in James Banks and Cherry Banks, eds., *Multicultural Education,* 9th ed. (San Francisco: Jossey Bass, 2015), pp. 2–23.
3. Sarah E. Fiarman, "Unconscious Bias; When Good Intentions are Not Enough," *Educational Leadership* 74, no. 3 (November 2016), pp. 10–15.
4. Jason Okonofua and Jennifer Eberhardt, "Two Strikes: Race and Disciplining of Young Students" *Psychological Science* 26, no. 5 (April 8, 2015), pp. 715–741.
5. James Ford, "The Root of Discipline Disparities," *Educational Leadership* 74, no. 3 (November 2016), pp. 42–46; Constance A. Lindsay and Cassandra M. D. Hart, "Teacher Race and School Discipline," *Education Next* 17, no. 1 (Winter 2017). Retrieved at http://educationnext.org/.
6. Rich Morin, *Exploring Racial Bias among Biracial and Single Race Adults: The IAT*. Washington D.C.: Pew Research Center, 2015.
7. Andrew Hacker, *Two Nations: Black, White, Separate, Hostile, Unequal* (New York: Charles Scribner's, 1992), pp. 31–32.
8. Jason A. Okonofua, David Paunesku, and Gregory Watson, "Brief Intervention to Encourage Empathic Discipline Cuts Suspension Rates in Half among Adolescents, *Proceedings of the National Academy of Sciences* (2016). Retrieved at DOI: 10.1073/pnas.1523698113.
9. Jessica Bennett, "She? Ze? They? (Hmm?) What's In a Gender Pronoun?" *New York Times*, January 31, 2016, p. ST2.
10. Gay, Lesbian, and Straight Education Network, www.glsen.com; Ian K. Macgillivray, *Gay-Straight Alliances: A Handbook for Students, Educators, and Parents* (Binghampton, NY: Haworth Press, 2007).
11. Benoit Denizet-Lewis, "Coming Out in Junior High School," *New York Times Magazine,* September 27, 2009, pp. 36–41, 52, 54–55; Zach Ford, "As 2015 Sees a Record Number of Documented Transgender Murders, a Glimmer of Hope," *Think Progress,* November 20, 2015. Retrieved from at https://thinkprogress.org/as-2015-sees-a-record-number-of-documented-transgender-murders-a-glimmer-of-hope-bb39567fc672#.ypxw7j4ys; Ryan Lacey, "Teachers lead charge against LGBTQ bullying," *District Administrator*, Novembers 14, 2016. Retrieved at www.districtadministration.com/article/teachers-lead-charge-against-lgbtq bullying.
12. Ian Lovett, "California to Require Gay History in Schools," *New York Times,* July 14, 2011, retrieved online at http://www.nytimes.com/2011/07/15/us/15gay.html.

13. James Crawford, ed., *Language Loyalties: A Source Book on the Official English Controversy* (Chicago: University of Chicago Press, 1992); see also Jonathon Zimmerman, "A Babel of Tongues," *U.S. News & World Report,* November 24, 1997, p. 39.
14. Richard Rothstein, "Bilingual Education: The Controversy," in James W. Noll ed., *Taking Sides* (Dubuque, IA: McGraw-Hill/Dushkin, 2005), pp. 290–301.
15. James Lyon, *Legal Responsibilities of Education Agencies Serving National Origin Language Minority Students* (Chevy Chase, MD: Mid-Atlantic Equity Center, 1992), www.maec.org/lyons/contents.html (retrieved May 9, 2008).
16. Population Reference Bureau, analysis of data from the U.S. Census Bureau, Census 2000 Supplementary Survey, 2001 Supplementary Survey, 2002 through 2015 American Community Survey. Updated October 2016.
17. Tom Stritikis and Manka M. Varghese, "Language Diversity and Schooling," in Banks and Banks, eds., *Multicultural Education,* pp. 297–325.
18. Christine Bennett, *Comprehensive Multicultural Education: Theory and Practice,* 6th ed. (Boston: Allyn & Bacon, 2006).
19. Jens Manuel Krogstad, "Branstad: Bilingual Education Gives Students Leg Up in Global Economy," *The Des Moines Register,* November 15, 2011, retrieved online at http://blogs.desmoinesregister.com.
20. James Crawford, *Hold Your Tongue: Bilingualism and the Politics of "English Only"* (New York: Addison-Wesley, 1992), pp. 111–112.
21. Anya Kamenetz, "6 Potential Brain Benefits of Bilingual Education," *nprEd*, November 29, 2016. Retrieved online November 29, 2016 at http://www.npr.org/sections/ed/2016/11/29/497943749/6-potential-brain-benefits-of-bilingual-education; Claude Goldenberg, "Teaching English Language Learners, What the Research Does—and Does Not—Say," *American Educator,* Summer 2008; Virginia Collier and Wayne Thomas, *Creating Dual Language Schools for a Transformed World: Administrators Speak* (Albuquerque, NM: Dual Language Education of New Mexico, Fuente Press, 2014); "The Effects of Bilingual Education Programs on English Language Learners," *ASCD Research Brief* 2, no. 5 (March 2, 2004); Emma Brown, "New Federal Guidelines Highlight Civil Rights of English Language Learners," *Washington Post*, January 7, 2015, available at https://www.washingtonpost.com/local/education/new-federal-guidelines-highlight-civil-rights-of-english-language-learners/2015/01/07/870f952e-961f-11e4-8005-1924ede3e54a_story.html?utm_term=.02338d24cbaf.
22. Michael Winerip, "Closing the Achievement Gap Without Widening a Racial One," *New York Times,* February 13, 2011, retrieved online at http://www.nytimes.com/2011/02/14/education/14winerip.html.
23. Ana Maria Villegas, *Culturally Responsive Pedagogy for the 1990s and Beyond* (Washington, DC: ERIC Clearing-house on Teacher Education, American Association of Colleges for Teacher Education, 1991).
24. Amy Chua and Jed Rubenfeld, *The Triple Package: How Three Unlikely Traits Explain the Rise and Fall of Cultural Groups in America* (New York: Penguin, 2014); Paul Toug, *How Children Succeed: Grit, Curiosity, and the Hidden Power of Character* (New York: Mariner Books, 2013).
25. Israel Zangwill, *The Melting Pot* (play), 1909, cited in Pamela Tiedt and Iris Tiedt, *Multicultural Education* (Needham Heights, MA: Allyn & Bacon, 1999), p. 2.
26. Frederick M. Hess, "Schools of Reeducation," *Washington Post,* February 5, 2006, p. B7.
27. Education Research Center, *Cities in Crisis Education Week,* April 2008; Christopher B. Swanson, *The Real Truth about Low Graduation Rates, An Evidenced-Based Commentary* (Washington, DC: The Urban Institute, 2004); U.S. Department of Education, *The Condition of Education 2007* (Washington, DC: National Center for Education Statistics, 2007), (NCES 2007-064), Indicator 23, 2007; Gary Orfield and Chungmei Lee, *Racial Transformation and the Changing Nature of Segregation* (Cambridge, MA: The Civil Rights Project, Harvard University, 2006); Erica Frankenberg and Gary Orfield, *Lessons in Integration: Realizing the Promise of Racial Diversity in America* (Charlottesville, VA: University of Virginia Press, 2007).
28. Christine Sleeter, "Curriculum Controversies in Multicultural Education," in Margaret Early and Kenneth Rehage, eds., *Issues in the Curriculum: A Selection of Chapters from Past NSSE Yearbooks, Ninety-Eighth Yearbook of the National Society for the Study of Education* (Chicago: University of Chicago Press, 1999), p. 261; Banks, "Multi-cultural Education: Characteristics and Goals."
29. Banks, "Multicultural Education: Characteristics and Goals."
30. James Banks, "Approaches to Multicultural Curriculum Reform," in Banks and Banks, *Multicultural Education: Issues and Perspectives,* pp. 247–269.
31. Justin Britt-Gibson, "What's Wrong with this Picture?" *Washington Post,* March 18, 2007, p. B01; Peter Schmidt, "New Survey Discerns Deep Divisions Among U.S. Youths on Race Relations," *Education Week,* March 25, 1992, p. 5.
32. Cristina Fernandez-Pereda, "Media Falls Flat in Covering Race Relations, New Survey Says," *New America Media,* February 19, 2009, http://news.newamericamedia.org/news/view_article.html? article_id5fa22894b6bee1753da1e89c189126106.
33. Gary Orfield, Jongyeon Ee, Erica Frankenberg, and Genevieve Siegel-Hawley, "Brown at 62: School Segregation by Race, Poverty and State", The Civil Rights Project, UCLA, May 16, 2016. Retrieved Nov 16, 2016 at https://www.civilrightsproject.ucla.edu/research/k-12-education/integration-and-diversity/brown-at-62-school-segregation-by-race-poverty-and-stat.
34. Bennett, *Comprehensive Multicultural Education: Theory and Practice;* Gloria Ladson Billings, *Crossing Over to Canaan: The Journey of New Teachers in Diverse Classrooms* (San Francisco: Jossey Bass, 2001); Gloria Ladson-Billings, "But That's Just Good Teaching," *Theory into Practice* 34, no. 3 (Summer 1995), pp. 159–165.
35. Geneva Gay, "Achieving Educational Equality Through Curriculum Desegregation," *Phi Delta Kappan* 72, no. 1 (September 1990), pp. 56–62.
36. Carol Gilligan, *In a Different Voice: Psychological Theory and Women's Development* (Cambridge, MA: Harvard University Press, 1982); David Sadker, Myra Sadker, and Karen Zittleman, *Still Failing at Fairness: How Gender Bias Cheats Girls and Boys in School and What We Can Do about It* (New York: Charles Scribner's, 2009). See also Mary Field Belenky, Blythe McVicker Clinchy, Nancy Rule Goldberger, and Jill Mattuck Tarule, *Women's Ways of Knowing: The Development of Self, Voice, and Mind* (New York: Basic Books, 1986).
37. Julie Chlebo, "There Is No Rose Garden: A Second Generation Rural Head Start Program," unpublished doctoral dissertation, 1999, quoted in Christine I. Bennett, *Comprehensive*

Multicultural Education: Theory and Practice, 4th ed. (Needham Heights, MA: Allyn & Bacon, 1999), p. 259.

38. Joshua Aronson, "The Threat of Stereotype," *Educational Leadership* 62, no. 3 (November 2004), pp. 14–19.
39. Joshua Aronson, "The Effects of Conceiving Ability as Fixed or Improvable on Responses to Stereotype Threat," unpublished manuscript, New York University, 2004.
40. Aronson, "The Threat of Stereotype"; Carol Dweck, *Self Theories: Their Role in Motivation, Personality and Development* (Philadelphia: Taylor & Francis, 1999).
41. Bennett, *Comprehensive Multicultural Education: Theory and Practice;* Carlos Cortes, *The Children Are Watching: How the Media Teach About Diversity* (New York: Teachers College Press, 2000), pp. 149–150; Barbara J. Shade, Cynthia Kelly, and Mary Oberg, *Creating Culturally Responsive Classrooms* (Washington, DC: American Psychological Association, 1997).
42. *Common Core Data, 2005–06* (Washington, DC: U.S. Department of Education, NCES), http://nces.ed.gov/ccd/ (retrieved February 27, 2008); Children's Defense Fund, www.childrensdefense.org (retrieved February 27, 2008).
43. The information about generalizations and different group learning styles is drawn from a variety of sources, including Bobby Ann Starnes, "What We Don't Know Can Hurt Them: White Teachers, Indian Children," *Phi Delta Kappan* 87, no. 5 (January 2006), pp. 384–392; Banks and Banks, *Multicultural Education: Issues and Perspectives;* Bennett, *Comprehensive Multicultural Education: Theory and Practice;* Kenneth Cushner, *Human Diversity in Action: Developing Multicultural Competencies for the Classroom* (New York: McGraw-Hill, 2006); Gary A. Davis and Sylvia Rimm, *Cultural Diversity and Children from Low Socioeconomic Backgrounds* (Boston: Allyn & Bacon, 1997); K. M. Evenson Worthley, "Learning Style Factor of Field Dependence/Independence and Problem Solving Strategies of Hmong Refugee Students," master's thesis, University of Wisconsin–Stout, July 1987 (cited in Bennett, *Comprehensive Multicultural Education: Theory and Practice*); Norene Dresser, *Multicultural Manners: New Rules of Etiquette for a Changing Society* (New York: John Wiley & Sons, 1996); Education Alliance at Brown University, *The Diversity Kit: An Introductory Resource for Social Change in Education* (Providence, RI: Northeast and Islands Regional Educational Laboratory–LAB at Brown University, 2002); Rowena Fong and Sharlene B. Furuto, *Culturally Competent Practice: Skills, Interventions, and Evaluations* (Needham Heights, MA: Allyn & Bacon, 2001); Eleanor W. Lynch and Marci J. Hanson, eds., *Developing Cross-Cultural Competence: A Guide for Working with Children and Their Families* (Baltimore, MD: Paul H. Brookes, 2004); Ian K. Macgillivray, *Sexual Orientation and School Policy: A Practical Guide for Teachers, Administrators, and Community Activists* (Lanham, MD: Rowman & Littlefield, 2004).
44. We thank Louise Wilkinson for this poignant quote. We couldn't have said it better.
45. Kent L. Koppelman with R. Lee Goodhart, *Understanding Human Differences: Multicultural Education for Diverse America* (Boston: Pearson Education, 2005), p. 344.
46. Nancy P. Gallavan, "I, Too, Am an American: Preservice Teachers Reflect upon National Identity," *Multicultural Teaching,* Spring 2002, pp. 8–12.

CHAPTER 4: STUDENT LIFE IN SCHOOL AND AT HOME

1. Kathleen M. Cashin and Bruce S. Cooper, "Remaking Schools as Positive, Social Places," *Education Week* 33, issue 6 (October 2, 2013), pp. 27–28; Elena Silva, *On the Clock: Rethinking the Way Schools Use Time* (Washington, DC: Education Sector, January 2007), www.educationsector.org/; Tamar Lewin "John I. Goodlad, Progressive Educator, Dies at 94," *New York Times* (January 2, 2015), p.B11; Valerie Strauss, "Teacher Spends Two Days as a Student and Is Shocked at What She Learns," *The Washington Post* (October 24, 2014), https://www.washingtonpost.com/news/answer-sheet/wp/2014/10/24/teacher-spends-two-days-as-a-student-and-is-shocked-at-what-she-learned/?utm_term=.e54045a864ec.
2. Ibid.; The Gallup Blog, *The School Cliff: Student Engagement Drops with Each School Year* (January 7, 2013), http://thegallupblog.gallup.com/2013/01/the-school-cliff-student-engagement.html.
3. Carol Ann Tomlinson, "Notes from an Accidental Teacher," *Educational Leadership* (December 2010/January 2011), pp. 22–26; Leila Christenbury, "Flexible Teacher," *Educational Leadership* (December 2010/January 2011), pp. 46–50; Silva, *On the Clock: Rethinking How Schools Use Time;* Kathleen M. Cashin and Bruce S. Cooper, "Remaking Schools as Positive, Social Places;" The Gallup Blog, *The School Cliff: Student Engagement Drops with Each School Year.*
4. Quoted in Ernest L. Boyer, *High School* (New York: Harper & Row, 1983).
5. Erik Gleibermann, "Teaching Even 100 Hours a Week Leaves Children Behind," *Phi Delta Kappan* 88, no. 6 (February 2007), pp. 455–459; Strauss, "Teacher Spends Two Days as a Student and Is Shocked at What She Learns."
6. Jackson, *Life in Classrooms;* Silva, *On the Clock: Rethinking How Schools Use Time;* David Sadker, Myra Sadker, and Karen Zittleman, "Questioning Skills," in James M. Cooper, ed., *Classroom Teaching Skills,* 10th ed. (Belmont, CA: Cengage, 2013), pp. 119–197.
7. Strauss, "Teacher Spends Two Days as a Student and Is Shocked at What She Learns"; Kristiina Kumpulainen, *Investigating Classroom Research* (Rotterdam, the Netherlands: Sense Publishers, 2009); David Sadker, Myra Sadker, and Karen Zittleman, "Questioning Skills."
8. Peter DeWitt, "Only 46% of Students Feel Valued in Their School," *Education Week* (January 26, 2016), http://blogs.edweek.org/; Shane J. Lopez, "The Highs and Lows of Student Engagement," *Phi Delta Kappan* (October 2011), pp. 72–73; John Goodlad, *A Place Called School* (New York: McGraw-Hill, 1984/2004); Kathleen M. Cashin and Bruce S. Cooper, "Re-making Schools as Positive, Social Places"; The Gallup Blog, *The School Cliff: Student Engagement Drops with Each School Year.*
9. Talcott Parsons, "The School as a Social System: Some of Its Functions in Society," in Robert Havinghurst and Bernice Neugarten eds., *Society and Education* (Boston: Allyn & Bacon, 1967), pp. 191–214; Jeannie Oakes, "The Tracking Wars," in *Keeping Track: How Schools Structure Inequality,* 2nd ed. (New Haven, CT: Yale University Press, 2005), pp. 214–221; Michael J. Petrilli, "The Diversity Dilemma," *Educational Leadership* 70, no. 8 (May 2013), pp. 44–48; Jill

Barshay, "Brainy Black and Hispanic Students Might Benefit Most from 'Honors' Classrooms," *Hechinger Report* (March 28, 2016), http://hechingerreport.org/finding-benefits-tracking/; Sonali Kohi, "Modern Day Segregation in Public Schools," *The Atlantic* (November 14, 2014).

10. Jeannie Oakes, "Keeping Track: Structuring Equality and Inequality in an Era of Accountability," *Teachers College Record* 110, no. 3 (2008), pp. 12–13 (ID Number: 14610), www.tcrecord.org; Jeannie Oakes, *Keeping Track*; Jeannie Oakes, "Embrace the "Hurly Burly," *Education Week,* 35 Issue 17, (January 13, 2016), p. 26; Carol Burns, *On the Same Track: How Schools Can Join the Twenty-first Century Struggle Against Resegregation.* (Boston: Beacon Press, 2015).
11. Jeannie Oakes, "Keeping Track: Structuring Equality and Inequality in an Era of Accountability"; Michael J. Petrilli, "The Diversity Dilemma"; Kohi, "Modern day segregation in public schools."
12. Michael J. Petrilli "The Diversity Dilemma"; Jeannie Oakes, "Keeping Track: Structuring Equality and Inequality in an Era of Accountability"; Kohi, "Modern day segregation in public schools"; Burns, *On the Same Track.*
13. "Foreword," in Anne Wheelock, *Crossing the Tracks: How Untracking Can Save America's Schools* (New York: New Press, 1993), p. xiii.
14. Halley Potter, "Boosting Achievement by Pursuing Diversity," *Educational Leadership* 70, no. 8 (May 2013), pp. 38–44; Oakes, "Keeping Track: Structuring Equality and Inequality in an Era of Accountability"; Michael J. Petrilli, "The Diversity Dilemma"; Burns, *On the Same Track*.
15. Carol Ann Tomlinson, "Differentiating Instruction for Academic Diversity," in James M. Cooper, ed., *Classroom Teaching Skills,* 10th ed. (Belmont, CA: Cengage, 2013), pp. 167–207; Oakes, "Embrace the Hurly Burly."
16. Lisa Rosen and Linda Rubin, "Beyond Mean Girls: Identifying and Intervening in Episodes of Relational Aggression," *Teachers College Press,* (May 8, 2015), http://www.tcrecord.org ID Number: 17959; Kelsey Felton and Patrick Akos, "The Transition Years," *Educational Leadership* (April 2011), pp. 28–31; Raphaela Best, *We've All Got Scars* (Bloomington: Indiana University Press, 1983).
17. Rosen and Rubin, "Beyond Mean Girls: Identifying and Intervening in Episodes of Relational Aggression."
18. Cindy Sobieski and Tabitha Dell'Angelo, "Sociograms as a Tool for Teaching and Learning: Discoveries From a Teacher Research Study," *The Education Forum* 80, no. 4 (2016), http://www.academia.edu/27963304/Sociograms_as_a_Tool_for_Teaching_and_Learning_Discoveries_From_a_Teacher_Research_Study.
19. Anna Kamenetz, "Sixth Grade Is Tough: It Helps to be 'Top Dog,' *National Public Radio,* http://www.npr.org/sections/ed/2016/09/19/494232646/sixth-grade-is-tough-it-helps-to-be-top-dog (September 19, 2016); Sarah Sparks, "Study Links Academic Setbacks to Middle School Transition," *Education Week* online (November 28, 2011).
20. Ibid.
21. Shane J. Lopez, "The Highs and Lows of Student Engagement," *Phi Delta Kappan* (October 2011), pp. 72–73; DeWitt "Only 46% of Students Feel Valued in Their School."
22. Karen R. Zittleman, "Gender Perceptions of Middle Schoolers: The Good and the Bad," *Middle Grades Research Journal* 2, no. 2 (Fall 2007), pp. 65–97.
23. Girls Inc., *The SuperGirl Dilemma: Girls Feel the Pressure to Be Perfect, Accomplished, Thin, and Accommodating* (New York, 2006/2012).
24. K. M. Pierce, "Posing, Pretending, Waiting for the Bell: Life in High School Classrooms," *High School Journal* 89, no. 2 (December 2005/January 2006), pp. 1–15; Annie Murphy Paul, "Does High School Determine the Rest of Your Life?" *Time,* (November 18, 2013); Jessica Holsman, *The High School Survival Guide* (Coral Gables, Florida: Mango, 2016).
25. Quoted in Jeremy Iverson, *High School Confidential: Secrets of an Undercover Student* (New York: Atria Books, 2007), p. 202.
26. David Owen, *High School* (New York: Viking Press, 1981).
27. Iverson, *High School Confidential: Secrets of an Undercover Student.*
28. Vicki Abeles, *Beyond Measure: Rescuing an Overscheduled, Overtested, Underestimated Generation* (New York: Simon & Schuster, 2015).
29. Abeles, *Beyond Measure: Rescuing an Overscheduled, Overtested, Underestimated Generation.*
30. Abeles, *Beyond Measure: Rescuing an Overscheduled, Overtested, Underestimated Generation*; Sean Slade, "Relationships Matter," *Huffington Post* (November 23, 2011), https://www.google.com/search?q=Sean+Slade%2C+%E2%80%9CRelationships+Matter%2C%E2%80%9D+Huffington+Post+%28&ie=utf-8&oe=utf-8.
31. Federal Interagency Forum on Child and Family Statistics, *America's Children: Key National Indicators of Well-Being, 2016,* www.childstats.gov/americaschildren/; Kathleen M. Ziol-Guest, Greg J. Duncan and Ariel Kalil, "One-Parent Students Leave School Earlier," *Education Next* 15, no. 2 (Spring 2015), pp. 36–41; Julie Vogtman and Karen Schulman, *Set Up to Fail: When Low-Wage Work Jeopardizes Parents' and Children's Success,* (Washington DC: National Women's Law Center, 2016).
32. Federal Interagency Forum on Child and Family Statistics *America's Children: Key National Indicators of Well-Being, 2016*; *Statistics on Stepfamilies in the United States* (New York: The Stepfamily Foundation, 2016), www.stepfamily.org/statistics.html.
33. U.S. Census Bureau, Current Population Survey, 2015; Vogtman and Schulman, *Set Up to Fail: When Low-Wage Work Jeopardizes Parents' and Children's Success.*
34. Federal Interagency Forum on Child and Family Statistics, *America's Children: Key National Indicators of Well-Being, 2016*; Vogtman and Schulman, *Set Up to Fail: When Low-Wage Work Jeopardizes Parents' and Children's Success.*
35. American Association of University Women, *The Simple Truth about the Gender Pay Gap* (Fall 2016), http://www.aauw.org/resource/the-simple-truth-about-the-gender-pay-gap/.
36. Quoted in John O'Neil, "A Generation Adrift?" *Educational Leadership* 49, no. 2 (September 1991), pp. 4–10.
37. Steve Suitts, "Students Facing Poverty: The New Majority," *Educational Leadership* (November 2016), pp. 36–40; Claire Cain Miller, "Class Divisions Growing Worse, from Cradle On," *New York Times* (December 18, 2015), p.A1.
38. Miller, "Class Divisions Growing Worse, from Cradle On," *New York Times*; Vogtman and Schulman, *Set Up to Fail: When Low-Wage Work Jeopardizes Parents' and Children's Success.*

39. Eduardo Porter, "Education Gap Between Rich and Poor Is Growing Wider," *New York Times* (September 23, 2015) p.B1; Miller, "Class Divisions Growing Worse, from Cradle On," *New York Times*.
40. Norman Doidge, *The Brain That Changes Itself* (New York: Viking Press, 2007); Miller, "Class Divisions Growing Worse, from Cradle On," *New York Times.*
41. Oscar Lewis, *La Vida; A Puerto Rican Family in the Culture of Poverty—San Juan and New York* (New York: Random House, 1966); Porter, "Education Gap Between Rich and Poor Is Growing Wider"; Miller, "Class Divisions Growing Worse, from Cradle On".
42. Suitts, "Students Facing Poverty: The New Majority"; Porter, "Education Gap Between Rich and Poor Is Growing Wider."
43. Anya Kamenetz, "As the Number of Homeless Students Soars, How Schools Can Serve Them Better," *National Public Radio* (June 13, 2016), http://www.npr.org/sections/ed/2016/06/13/481279226/as-the-number-of-homeless-students-soars-how-schools-can-serve-them-better.
44. National Association for the Education of Homeless Children and Youth, *Facts and Resources about the Education of Children and Youth Experiencing Homelessness* (2016), http://www.naehcy.org/sites/default/files/dl/homeless-ed-101.pdf.
45. Ibid.
46. Lisa Damour, "Myths about Teenagers and Risk Taking," *New York Times* (July 13, 2016), https://well.blogs.nytimes.com/2016/07/13/myths-about-teenagers-and-risk-taking/.
47. Paul Tough, *How Children Succeed: Grit, Curiosity, and the Hidden Power of Character* (Boston, MA: Mariner Books, 2013); Emma Brown, "You Don't Have to be Mother Teresa to Help a Kid," *The Washington Post* (September 16, 2015); National Center for Education Statistics, *Trends in High School Dropout and Completion Rates,* (Washington DC: United States Department of Education, (October 2016).
48. Adria Steinberg and Lili Allen, "Putting Off-Track Youths Back on Track to College," *Phi Delta Kappan* 92, no. 5 (February 2011), p. 23.
49. National Center for Education Statistics, *Public High School Four-Year On-Time Graduation Rates and Event Dropout Rates*, Washington, DC: U.S. Department of Education, (October 2016).
50. National Center for Education Statistics, *Public High School Four-Year On-Time Graduation Rates and Event Dropout Rates*; Brown, "You Don't Have to be Mother Teresa to Help a Kid,"; Center for Promise, *Don't Quit on Me: What Young People Who Left School Say about the Power of Relationships* (September 16, 2015), http://www.americaspromise.org/program/center-promise.
51. United States Department of Health and Human Services, *Trends in Teen Pregnancy and Childbearing,* (June 2016), http://www.hhs.gov/ash/oah/adolescent-health-topics/reproductive-health/teen-pregnancy/trends.html.
52. Rashea Hamiltion, Megan Sanders, and Eric M. Anderman, "The Multiple Choices of Sex Education," *Phi Delta Kappan* 94, no. 5 (February 2013), pp. 34–39; Sexuality Information and Education Council of the United States, *Fact Sheet,* (April 2016), www.siecus.org.
53. Federal Interagency Forum on Child and Family Statistics, *America's Children: Key National Indicators of Well-Being, 2016,* https://www.childstats.gov/pdf/ac2016/ac_16.pdf.
54. Ibid.
55. Ibid.
56. Lisa Damour, "Myths about Teenage Risk Taking," *New York Times*, http://www.nytimes.com/section/well (July 13, 2016); Flavio F. Marsiglia, "Keepin' it REAL," Office of Juvenile Justice and Delinquency Prevention, https://www.ojjdp.gov (April 2012).
57. Ibid.
58. Centers for Disease Control and Prevention, *Childhood Obesity Facts* (2016), http://www.cdc.gov/healthyyouth/ obesity/facts.htm.
59. United States Department of Agriculture, *Healthy, Hunger-free Kids Act* (October 4, 2016), http://www.fns.usda.gov/school-meals/healthy-hunger-free-kids-act; United States Department of Agriculture, *National School Lunch Program* (August, 18, 2016), http://www.fns.usda.gov/nslp/national-school-lunch-program-nslp.
60. Eating Disorders Coalition, *Stats About Eating Disorders: What the Research Shows,* November 2016, www.eating.-disorderscoalition.org.
61. Eating Disorders Coalition, *Eating Disorders in Men,* November 2016, www.eating.-disorderscoalition.org.
62. Sarah Shulkind, "Reframing Bullying in Middle Schools," *Education Spotlight on Bullying,* 2010, p. 7.
63. StopBullying.gov, *Facts about Bullying* (2016), http://www.stopbullying.gov.
64. Douglas Fisher, Nancy Frey, and Dominique Smith, "After Sticks, Stones, and Hurtful Words," *Educational Leadership* 74, no. 3, (November 2016), pp. 54–58; Melissa Johnson, "Empty Plates: Kids are Being Bullied to Skip Lunch at School," *Yahoo News* (August 24, 2015), https://www.yahoo.com/news/empty-plate-kids-being-bullied-skip-lunch-school-110000836.html?ref=gs; StopBullying.gov, *Facts about Bullying*.
65. Jennifer Holladay, "Cyberbullying," *Teaching Tolerance,* Fall 2010, pp. 43–44.
66. Sameer Hinduja and Justin W. Patchin, "High-Tech Cruelty," *Educational Leadership,* February 2011, pp. 48–52; Jennifer Holladay, "Cyberbullying," *Teaching Tolerance,* Fall 2010, pp. 43–46.
67. Fisher, Frey, and Smith, "After Sticks, Stones, and Hurtful Words," Dakarai I. Aarons, "Efforts to End Bullying, A Challenge to Leaders, Gains Momentum," *Education Spotlight on Bullying,* 2010, pp. 1–3.
68. Ibid.
69. Lyn Mikel Brown, "Ten Ways to Move Beyond Bullying Prevention (and Why We Should Do It)," *Education Spotlight on Bullying,* 2010, pp. 10–11.

CHAPTER 5: THE MULTICULTURAL HISTORY OF AMERICAN EDUCATION

1. Joel Spring, *American Education,* 17th ed. (New York: McGraw-Hill, 2015).
2. Joel Spring, *Deculturalization and the Struggle for Equality: A Brief History of the Education of Dominated Cultures in the United States*, 8th ed. (New York: Routledge 2016).
3. L. Dean Webb, *The History of American Education: A Great American Experiment* (Upper Saddle River, NJ: Prentice Hall, 2005); See also Spring, *American Education.*
4. Webb, *The History of American Education: A Great American Experiment*; Spring, *American Education.*

5. John H. Best, *Benjamin Franklin on Education* (New York: Teachers College Press, 1962); Spring, *American Education.*
6. Gabriel, Compayre, *Horace Mann and the Public School in the United States* (London: Forgotten Books, 2012); Webb, *The History of American Education: A Great American Experiment.*
7. Lawrence Cremin, *The Transformation of the School: Progressivism in American Education, 1876–1957* (New York: Alfred A. Knopf, 1961).
8. Spring, *Deculturalization and the Struggle for Equality: A Brief History of the Education of Dominated Cultures in the United States*; Webb, *The History of American Education: A Great American Experiment.*
9. K. Tsianina Lomawaima and Teresa McCarthy, *To Remain an Indian* (New York: Teachers College Press, 2006); Spring, *Deculturalization and the Struggle for Equality: A Brief History of the Education of Dominated Cultures in the United States.*
10. Terry Huffman, *Theoretical Perspectives on American Indian Education: Taking a New Look at Academic Success and the Achievement Gap* (Lanham, MD: AltaMira Press, 2010); Lomawaima and McCarthy, *To Remain an Indian;* National Center for Education Statistics, *Public High School Four-Year On-Time Graduation Rates and Event Dropout Rates*, Washington, DC: U.S. Department of Education, October 2016.
11. Jackie M. Blount, "Spinsters, Bachelors and Other Gender Transgressors in School Employment, 1850–1990," *Review of Educational Research* 70, no. 1 (Spring 2000), pp. 83–101; A. Durst, *Women Educators in the Progressive Era: The Women Behind Dewey's Laboratory School* (United Kingdom: Palgrave Macmillan, 2016).
12. Mark Kelly, *Learning to Stand and Speak: Women, Educators and Public Life America's Republic* (Chapel Hill: The University of North Carolina Press, 2008); Spring, *American Education.*
13. Blount, "Spinsters, Bachelors and Other Gender Transgressors in School Employment, 1850–1990," p. 94.
14. Spring, *American Education.*
15. National Commission on Excellence in Education, *A Nation at Risk: The Imperative for Educational Reform* (Washington, DC: U.S. Government Printing Office, 1983), p. 1.
16. Susie King Taylor, *Reminiscences of My Life in Camp with the 33rd U.S. Colored Troop Late First S.C. Volunteers* (1902; reprinted, New York: Amo Press, 1968).
17. W.E.B. Du Bois, "The United States and the Negro," *Freedomways,* 1961.
18. Spring, *American Education.*
19. National Advisory Commission on Civil Disorders, *Report of the National Advisory Commission on Civil Disorders* (Washington, DC: U.S. Government Printing Office, 1968), p. 369. See also Andrew Hacker, *Two Nations Black and White, Separate, Hostile, Unequal* (New York: Charles Scribner's, 1992).
20. David Schimmel, Leslie Stellman, and Louis Fischer, *Teachers and the Law,* 9th ed. (Boston: Allyn & Bacon, 2014); Gary Orfield, and Erica Frankenberg, *Educational Delusions* (Berkeley: University of California Press, 2013); Michael Katz and Mike Rose, *Public Education under Siege* (Philadelphia: University of Pennsylvania Press, 2014).
21. Orfield and Frankenberg, *Educational Delusions;* Katz and Rose, *Public Education under Siege.*
22. Orfield and Frankenberg, *Educational Delusions;* Katz and Rose, *Public Education under Siege.*
23. Richard M. Merleman, "Disintegrating American Public Schools," *Education Week,* May 19, 2002, p. 37; Orfield and Frankenberg, *Educational Delusions.*
24. U.S. Census Bureau, *Hispanic Americans by the Numbers,* 2016, www.census.gov.
25. Meyer Weinberg, *A Chance to Learn* (Cambridge, UK: Cambridge University Press, 1977).
26. U.S. Census Bureau, *Hispanic Americans by the Numbers.*
27. U.S. Census Bureau, *Hispanic Americans by the Numbers*; Center for Puerto Rican Studies, Edwin Melendez and Carlos Vargas-Ramos, *The State of Puerto Ricans 2013* (Chicago: Centro Press, 2013).
28. U.S. Census Bureau, *Hispanic Americans by the Numbers.*
29. Much of the information on the history of Asian Americans is adapted from James Banks and Cherry Banks, eds., *Multicultural Education,* 9th ed. (San Francisco: Jossey Bass, 2016).
30. Much of the information on Arab Americans is adapted from James Banks and Cherry Banks, eds., *Multicultural Education,* 9th ed. (San Francisco: Jossey Bass, 2016); for more information about Arab Americans, visit the Web site of the American-Arab Anti-Discrimination Committee at www.adc.org.
31. Ibid.
32. David Sadker, Myra Sadker, and Karen R. Zittleman, *Still Failing at Fairness: How Gender Bias Cheats Girls and Boys in School and What We Can Do about It* (New York: Charles Scribner, 2009).
33. M. Carey Thomas, "Present Tendencies in Women's Education," *Education Review* 25 (1908), pp. 64–85; quoted in David Tyack and Elisabeth Hansot, *Learning Together: A History of Coeducation in American Schools* (New Haven, CT: Yale University Press, 1990), p. 68.
34. Adapted from "Opening the Schoolhouse Door" and "Higher Education: Peeking behind the Campus Curtain," in Sadker, Sadker, and Zittleman, *Still Failing at Fairness.*

CHAPTER 6: PHILOSOPHY OF EDUCATION

1. Nel Noddings, *Philosophy of Education,* 4th ed. (Boulder, CO: Westview Press, 2015); William Bagley, "The Case for Essentialism in Education," *National Education Association Journal* 30, no. 7 (1941), pp. 202–220.
2. Noddings, *Philosophy of Education,* 4th ed.
3. Mortimer Adler, *Reforming Education* (Boulder, CO: Westview Press, 1977), pp. 84–85.
4. Robert M. Hutchins, *The Higher Learning in America* (New Haven, CT: Yale University Press, 1962), p. 78.
5. John Dewey, *Experience and Education* (New York: Macmillan, 1963).
6. Tom Little and Katherine Ellison, *Loving Learning: How Progressive Education Can Save America's Schools* (New York: W.W. Norton & Co., 2016); Noddings, *Philosophy of Education,* 4th ed.
7. Bill Ferriter, "Using Digital Tools to Make a Difference," *SmartBlog on Education* (November 1, 2012), http://classroom-aid.com/category/youth-thinkers/; Alia Wong, "The Renaissance of Student Activism," *The Atlantic* (May 21, 2015), http://www.theatlantic.com/; Audrey Osler, *Human Rights and Schooling: An Ethical Framework for Teaching Social Justice* (New York: Teachers College Press, 2016).
8. Paulo Freire, *Pedagogy of the Oppressed* (New York: Continuum Press, 1989).

9. Maxine Greene, *Landscapes of Learning* (New York: Teachers College Press, 1978). See also Maxine Greene, "Reflections on Teacher as Stranger," in C. Kridel (ed.), *Books of the Century Catalog* (Columbia, SC: University of South Carolina, Museum of Education, 2000); and *Releasing the Imagination: Essays on Education, The Arts, and Social Change* (Hoboken, NJ: Wiley, 2000).
10. Noddings, *Philosophy of Education,* 4th ed.
11. Noddings, *Philosophy of Education,* 4th ed.; Jay Mathews, "Educators Blend Divergent Schools of Thought," *The Washington Post,* May 9, 2006, p. A12.
12. Robert Perk and Alistair Thomson, *Doing Oral History*, 3rd ed. (New York: Routledge, 2015); Timothy Reagan, *Non-Western Educational Traditions: Alternative Approaches to Educational Thought and Practice* (Mahwah, NJ: Lawrence Erlbaum Associates, 2004).
13. *Aristotle, Politics,* trans. and intro. by T.A. Sinclair (Middlesex, U.K.: Penguin, 1978).

CHAPTER 7: FINANCING AND GOVERNING AMERICA'S SCHOOLS

1. Rebecca Klein, "Teachers Spend Way Too Much of Their Own Money on School Supplies, and Here's Proof," *Huffington Post*, Sept. 3, 2015. Retrieved at http://www.huffingtonpost.com/entry/teacher-spending-school-supplies_us_55e49091e4b0c818f618a6c7.
2. Mark G. Yudof, David L. Kip, and Betsy Levin, *Educational Policy and the Law,* 3rd ed. (St. Paul, MN: West, 1992), p. 658; Betsy Levin, Thomas Muller, and Corazon Sandoval, *The High Cost of Education in Cities* (Washington, DC: The Urban Institute, 1973).
3. Barry Siegel, "Parents Get a Lesson in Equality," *Los Angeles Times* (Washington edition), April 13, 1992, pp. A-1, A-18, A-19.
4. *Robinson v. Cahill,* 69 N.J. 133 (1973); *Abbott v. Burke,* 119 N.J. 287 (1990) (known as *Abbott I); Abbott v. Burke,* 153 N.J. 480 (1998) (known as *Abbott V*).
5. Catherine Gerwitz, "Though N.J. Funding Formula Upheld, Abbott Intact," *Education Week* 8, no. 33 (June 10, 2009), p. 10; Peter Enrich, "Leaving Equality Behind: New Directions in School Finance Reform," *Vanderbilt Law Review* 48 (1995), pp. 101–194. For a description of this movement to adequacy arguments, visit http://nces.ed.gov/edfin/litigation/Contents.asp. For a discussion of the impact in Wisconsin, see Daniel W. Hildebrand, "2000 Significant Court Decisions," *Wisconsin Lawyer* 74, no. 6 (June 2001). Similar analyses are available in other such law updates.
6. "Financing Better Schools: Too Often, Traditional Methods of Paying for Schools Come Up Short," *Education Week* 24, no. 17 (January 6, 2005), p. 7.
7. John Wisely, "State of Michigan Says Literacy Is Not a Fundamental Right," *Detroit Free Press,* November 21, 2016. Retrieved at http://www.freep.com/story/news/education/2016/11/21/state-michigan-says-literacy-not-fundametal-right/94218364/; Alan Odden and Lawrence O. Picus, *School Finance: A Policy Perspective,* 4th ed. (New York: McGraw-Hill, 2007).
8. Lori Montgomery, "Maryland Seeks 'Adequacy,' Recasting School Debate," *Washington Post,* April 22, 2002, p. A1.
9. Liz Bowie, "As State Increased Aid, Grades Went Up," *Baltimore Sun,* January 8, 2009, www.goodschoolspa.org/pdf/news_articles/Baltimore%20Sun%201-8-09.pdf (retrieved May 15, 2009); The high rankings continued for years; visit www.edweek.org/ew/qc/2012/16src.h31.html for an update.
10. Kate Zernike, "An F minus for America's Schools from a Fed-Up Judge," *New York Times*, September 8, 2016. Retrieved at http://www.nytimes.com/2016/09/09/nyregion/crux-of-connecticut-judges-grim-ruling-schools-are-broken.html?_r=0; Elizabeth A. Harris, "Judge, Citing Inequality, Orders Connecticut to Overhaul Its School System," *New York Times*, September 7, 2016. Retrieved at https://www.nytimes.com/2016/09/08/nyregion/connecticut-public-schools-inequality-judge-orders.html.
11. Christina A. Samuels, "Study Tallies a District's Return on Investment," *Education Week,* December 5, 2011, http://www.edweek.org/ew/articles/2011/12/07/13econimpact.h31.html (retrieved March 5, 2012). While Maryland was first in 2011, other states, like Massachusetts, ranked first in following years. While first place alternates, states with regressive funding practices seem to continually lag behind.
12. Cory Turner, "Why America's Schools Have a Money Problem" *National Public Radio*, April 18, 2016; Robert L. Borosage, "Sending Kids the Bill for the Mess Left By Wall Street," *Huffington Post,* October 13, 2011, www.huffingtonpost.com/ (retrieved October 30, 2011); Michael A. Rebell, "The Recession—and Students' Rights," in Michael A. Rebell, Allan Odden, Anthony Rolle, and James W. Guthrie, "Four Takes on Tough Times," *The Resourceful School* 69, no. 4 (December 2011/January 2012), pp. 11–18.
13. Judy Lin, "How Much Has California School Spending Grown in the Last 5 Years?" *CALmatters*, Jan 4, 2016. Retrieved at https://calmatters.org/articles/how-much-has-californias-education-spending-grown-in-last-5-years/.
14. Paul Takahashi, "As Scrutiny of School Funding Formula Grows, a Discussion of What's Fair," *Las Vegas Sun,* March 7, 2014; David Sciarra and Wade Henderson, "What's the Matter with Kansas' Schools?" *New York Times,* January 7, 2014; Trevor Graff and John Eligon, "Court Orders Kansas Legislature to Spend More on Schools," *New York Times,* March 7, 2014; Will Weissert, "Judge's Ruling on School Funding Could Cost Texas Billions," *Fort Worth Star-Telegram,* February 5, 2013; Sean Cavanagh, "States Dogged by Lawsuits on K–12 Funding," *Ed Week* 31, no. 17 (January 18, 2012), pp. 1, 2; April Castro and Paul J. Weber, "Texas Schools Sue State, Saying Funding Is Unfair," October 11, 2011, *San Diego Union Tribune,* October 13, 2011, http://www.sandiegouniontribune.com/sdut-texas-schools-sue-state-saying-funding-is-unfair-2011oct11-story.html (retrieved October 30, 2011); James W. Guthrie, "Fine-Tuning the Cuts," in Michael A. Rebell, Allan Odden, Anthony Rolle, and James W. Guthrie, "Four Takes on Tough Times," *The Resourceful School,* 69, no. 4 (December 2011/January 2012), pp. 11–18; Morgan Smith, "Rural District Is Struggling to Make Improvements," *New York Times,* April 7, 2012, http://www.nytimes.com/2012/04/08/us/in-rural-texas-shrinking-district-battles-to-make-improvements.html (retrieved April 26, 2012); Ben Wolfgang, "No Cuts Left Behind as Schools Squeeze Most Out of Budgets," *The Washington Times,* November 14, 2011, http://www.washingtontimes.com/news/2011/nov/14/no-cuts-left-behind-as-schools-squeeze-most-out-of/; (retrieved April 21, 2012); Kimberly Hefling, "Schools Brace for More Budget Cuts," *TIME.com,* October 24, 2011, https://www.google.com/search?q=Kimberly+Hefling%2C+%E2%80%9CSchools+

Brace+for+More+Budget+Cuts%2C&ie=utf-8&oe=utf-8 (retrieved January 4, 2012).

15. Kevin Carey and Elizabeth A. Harris, "It Turns Out Spending More Probably Does Improve Education" *New York Times,* Dec. 12, 2016. Retrieved at http://www.nytimes.com/2016/12/12/nyregion/it-turns-out-spending-more-probably-does-improve-education.html?_r=0.
16. C. Kirabo Jackson, Rucker C. Johnson and Claudia Persico, "Boosting Educational Attainment and Adult Earnings," *Education Next, 15,* no. 4 (Fall 2015).
17. Natasha Ushomirsky and David Williams, *Funding Gaps 2015* (Washington, DC: Education Trust, March 2015); Bruce J. Biddle and David C. Berliner, "Unequal School Funding in the United States," *Education Leadership 59,* no. 8 (May 2002), pp. 48–59; Diana Jean Schemo, "Neediest Schools Receive Less Money, Report Finds," *New York Times,* August 9, 2002; Odden and Picus, *School Finance: A Policy Perspective.*
18. Stephen Sawchuk, "Out-of-Field Teaching Called Worse in Poor Schools," *Education Week* 28, no. 15 (November 25, 2008).
19. Bruce Baker, David Sciarra, and Danielle Farrie, *Is School Funding Fair? A National Report Card,* National Law Center, Spring, 2015, www.schoolfundingfairness.org/; Kate Taylor, "Harlem Schools Are Left to Fail as Those Not Far Away Thrive," *New York Times*, Jan 24, 2017. Retrieved at https://www.nytimes.com/2017/01/24/nyregion/harlem-schools-are-left-to-fail-as-those-not-far-away-thrive.html?_r=1; "SFFF Files Public School Lawsuit," *Topeka Capital-Journal,* November 2, 2010, http://cjonline.com/news/state/2010-11-02/sfff_fi les_public_school_lawsuit; Lesli A. Maxwell, "Funding Formula Aims at Equity," *Education Week* 29, no. 37 (July 19, 2010).
20. Amanda Paulson, "Does Money Transform Schools?" *Christian Science Monitor,* August 9, 2005, www.csmonitor.com/2005/0809/p01s03-ussc.html (retrieved March 19, 2008).
21. Rebecca Klein, "School Funding Inequality Makes Education 'Separate And Unequal,' Arne Duncan Says," March 13, 2015, *HuffPost Education*. Retrieved at http://www.huffingtonpost.com/2015/03/13/arne-duncan-school-funding-disparities_n_6864866.html; Natasha Ushomirsky and David Williams, *Funding Gaps 2015.*
22. Kevin Carey and Elizabeth A. Harris, "It Turns Out Spending More Probably Does Improve Education"; Debra Viadero, "Rags to Riches in U.S. Largely a Myth, Scholars Write," *Education Week* 26, no. 9 (October 25, 2006), p. 8.
23. "Is There A Better Way To Pay For America's Schools?" *Weekend Edition Sunday*, *NPR*, May 1, 2016. Retrieved at http://www.npr.org/2016/05/01/476224759/is-there-a-better-way-to-pay-for-americas-schools; Thomas Toch, "Separate but Not Equal," *Agenda* 1 (Spring 1991), pp. 15–17; Odden and Picus, *School Finance: A Policy Perspective;* See also Kacey Guin, Betheny Gross, Scott Deburgomaster and Marguerite Roza, "Do Districts Fund Schools Fairly?" *Education Next 7, no. 4* Fall 2007. Retrieved at http://educationnext.org/do-districts-fund-schools-fairly/; Peter Keating, "How to Keep Your State and Local Taxes Down," *Money* 24, no. 1 (January 1995), pp. 86–92; Odden and Picus, *School Finance: A Policy Perspective.*
24. Bill Norris, "Losing Ticket in Lotteries," *Times Educational Supplement,* March 19, 1993, p. 17.
25. Yoohyun Jung, "How Low-Income Tucson Schools Find High-Performing Success," *Arizona Star*, Nov. 28, 2016, pp. A1, A4.
26. "Elementary and Secondary Education Section: Finance," *The Condition of Education 2016* (Washington, DC: National Center for Educational Statistics, 2016). Retrieved at https://nces.ed.gov/programs/coe/pdf/coe_cma.pdf.
27. Stephen Sawchuk and Erik Robelen, "Stimulus Guidance Spotlights Teacher Evaluations," *Education Week* 28, no. 28 (April 1, 2009); Valerie Strauss, "Schools Chief Returns Race to the Top Money—for His Teachers," *Washington Post,* November 24, 2010, http://voices.washingtonpost.com/answer-sheet/schools-chief-returns-race-to.html; Gerald Seib, "In Education, a Chance for Change," *Wall Street Journal,* March 27, 2009; "Obama Wants Stimulus to Transform Schools," *USA Today,* February 17, 2009, www.usatoday .com/news/education/2009-02-17-stimulus-schools_N.htm (retrieved May 18, 2009); Maria Glod, "Budget Outlines Funding for Teacher Merit Pay Programs," *Washington Post,* May 7, 2009, www.washingtonpost.com/wp-dyn/content/article/2009/05/07/AR2009050703786.html (retrieved May 21, 2009); "Obama Wants 5K Closed Schools to Rebound," *USA Today,* May 11, 2009, www.usatoday.com/news/education/2009-05-11-duncan-schools_N.htm (retrieved on May 18, 2009); Libby Quaid, "Plan to Fix Schools Could Help Students," *Arizona Daily Star,* January 1, 2009, p. A3; Sam Dillon, "U.S. Stimulus Plan Would Provide Flood of Aid to Education," *New York Times,* January 28, 2009, www.nytimes.com/2009/01/28/education/28educ.html (retrieved May 23, 2009).
28. Carmen Constantinescu, "Income Segregation in Schools Found to Rise by 40 Percent Since 1990," *Education Week*, July 20, 2016. Retrieved at http://blogs.edweek.org/edweek/inside-school-research/2016/07/income_segregation_in_schools_.html ; Frederick M. Hess and Linda Darling-Hammond, "How to Rescue Education Reform," *New York Times,* December 5, 2011, http://www.nytimes.com/2011/12/06/opinion/how-to-rescue-education-reform.html (retrieved January 5, 2012).
29. Juliet Schor, *Born to Buy: The Commercialized Child and the New Consumer Culture* (New York: Charles Scribner's, 2004).
30. *FTC Report Sheds New Light on Food Marketing to Children and Adolescents* (Washington, DC: Federal Trade Commission, July 29, 2008), www.ftc.gov/opa/2008/07/ foodmkting.shtm (retrieved May 30, 2009).
31. Many of the examples in this section are adapted from "Commercializing Childhood: The Corporate Takeover of Kids' Lives: An Interview with Susan Linn," *Multinational Monitor* 30, no. 1 (July/August 2008), www.multinationalmonitor.org/mm2008/072008/interviewlinn.html (retrieved May 22, 2009).
32. Ibid. See also Linda Matchan, "A Sober Look at Ads and Children," *Boston Globe,* May 17, 2009, www.boston.com/ae/movies/articles/2009/05/17/a_sober_look_at_ ads_and_children (retrieved May 22, 2009).
33. *FTC Issues Report on Marketing Violent Entertainment to Children* (Washington, DC: Federal Trade Commission, April 12, 2007), www.ftc.gov/opa/2007/04/marketingviolence.shtm (retrieved May 22, 2009).
34. Miriam H. Zoll, "Psychologists Challenge Ethics of Marketing to Children," *American News Service,* April 5, 2000.
35. Tamar Lewin, "In Public Schools, the Name Game as a Donor Lure," *New York Times,* January 26, 2006; Pam Belluck, "And for Perfect Attendance, Johnny Gets . . . a Car," *New York*

Times, February 5, 2006; Alex Molnar and David Garia, "The Battle over Commercialized Schools," *Educational Leadership* 63, no. 7 (April 2006), pp. 78–82.

36. Neil Buckley, "Obesity Campaign Eyes School Drinks," *Financial Times,* June 23, 2003; Alex Molnar, "The Corporate Branding of Our Schools," *Educational Leadership* 60, no. 2 (October 2002), pp. 74–78.
37. "School Soda Ban Has Limited Effect," *Washington Post,* November 27, 2008, www.washingtonpost.com/wp-dyn/content/article/2008/11/27/AR2008112701843.html (retrieved July 12, 2009).
38. Alfie Kohn, "The 500-Pound Gorilla," *Phi Delta Kappan* 84, no. 2 (October 2002), p. 117; Molnar and Garia, "The Battle over Commercialized Schools."
39. Linda Lou, "Money Helps Pay for Printing Costs after Budget Cuts," *San Diego Union Tribune,* November 22, 2008, www.signonsandiego.com/news/metro/20081122-9999-1mc22rbteach.html (retrieved July 12, 2009).
40. Molnar, "The Corporate Branding of Our Schools," p. 76.
41. Bill Turque, "District Considers Longer School Day," *Washington Post,* November 8, 2010, p. B01.
42. Michael A. Rebell, Allan Odden, Anthony Rolle, and James W. Guthrie "Four Takes on Tough Times," *The Resourceful School* 69, no. 4 (December 2011/January 2012) pp. 11–18; Kris Axtman, "Schools Bend under Tight Budgets," *Christian Science Monitor,* November 20, 2002; "Schools Cut Costs with 4-Day Weeks," September 11, 2002, http://cnn.com; Richard Rothstein, "Raising School Standards and Cutting Budget: Huh?" *New York Times,* July 10, 2002; Ann E. Marimow and Rosalind S. Helderman, "Taxing Times for County Budgets," *Washington Post,* March 18, 2008, p. A01; Maria Glod, "Strapped Schools May Boost Class Sizes," *Washington Post,* December 5, 2008, p. A1.
43. Michael Alison Chandler and Emma Brown, "D.C. Area Schools Turn to Parents for More Funding as Budgets are Squeezed," *Washington Post,* April 4, 2012, https://www.washingtonpost.com/local/education/dc-area-schools-turn-to-parents-for-more-funding-as-budgets-are-squeezed/2012/04/04/gIQA1l35vS_story.html?resType=accessibility&nid=menu_nav_accessibilityforscreenreader; Sam Dillon, "Districts Pay Less in Poor Schools, Report Says," *New York Times,* November 30, 2011, http://www.nytimes.com/2011/12/01/education/us-education-department-finds-salary-gap-in-poor-schools.html (retrieved January 30, 2012); Peter Schworm, "Is It Good for Education Foundations to Fund What Taxes Don't Cover?" *Boston Globe,* February 25, 2007, www.boston.com/news/local/articles/2007/02/25/what_taxes_ dont_cover/ (retrieved March 20, 2008); Jennifer Gonzalez, "Public School Endowments on the Rise," *Cleveland Plain Dealer,* June 2007, www.publiceducation.org/newsblast/June07/June15_text.htm (retrieved March 20, 2008); Rob Reich, "Not Very Giving," *New York Times,* September 4, 2013.
44. Mary Filardo, Jared Bernstein, and Ross Eisenbrey, "Creating Jobs Through FAST!, a Proposed New Infrastructure Program to Repair America's Public Schools," *The 21st Century School Fund,* Economic Policy Institute, August 11, 2011, http://web.epi-data.org/temp727/Fix%20America%27s%20Schools_Today_FINAL.pdf (retrieved April 12, 2012).
45. Bradford Chaney and Laurie Lewis, *Public School Principals Report on Their School Facilities: Fall 2005* (NCES 2007–007) (Washington, DC: U.S. Department of Education, National Center for Education Statistics; issued January 2007), http://nces.ed.gov/pubs2007/2007007.pdf (retrieved May 5, 2009).
46. Frederick M. Hess, *School Boards at the Dawn of the 21st Century* (Arlington, VA: National School Boards Association, 2002).
47. For an insightful discussion of school boards, see Joel Spring, *American Education* (New York: McGraw-Hill, 2002), pp. 178–182.
48. "The Signing of the Every Student Succeeds Act (ESSA) Is an Historic Milestone for America's School Boards", *National School Board Association*, Dec. 2016. - See more at: https://www.nsba.org/advocacy/federal-legislative-priorities/every-student-succeeds-act-essa#sthash.kJO7H9yh.dpuf; Christina A. Samuels, "School Board Members' Focus Shifting, Survey Says," *Education Week* 30, no. 20 (February 3, 2011), www.edweek.com (retrieved January 7, 2012); Chester Finn, "Reinventing Local Control," in Patricia First and Herbert Walberg, eds., *School Boards: Changing Local Control* (Berkeley, CA: McCutchan, 1992); Emily Feistritzer, "A Profile of School Board Presidents," in *School Boards: Changing Local Control;* Neal Pierce, "School Boards Get Failing Grades, in Both the Cities and the Suburbs," *Philadelphia Inquirer,* April 27, 1992, p. 11.
49. Tara García Mathewson, **"**Superintendents with Lengthy Histories in Their Districts Bring Stability, Expertise,**"** *Education Dive***,** Dec. 13, 2016. Retrieved at http://www.educationdive.com/news/superintendents-with-lengthy-histories-in-their-districts-bring-stability/432252/; Tara García Mathewson**, "**Women Outnumber Men in Ed Everywhere But the Superintendent's Office," *Education Dive*, Nov. 22, 2016. Retrieved at https://www.google.com/search?q=Women+Outnumber+Men+in+Ed+Everywhere+But+the+Superintendent%27s+Office&ie=utf-8&oe=utf-8; Daniel A. Domenech, "AASA's Status Check on the Superintendency," American Association of School Superintendents. Retrieved at http://www.aasa.org/SchoolAdministratorArticle.aspx?id=17184; Jay Mathews, "Playing Politics in Urban City Schools," *Washington Post,* September 11, 2002; American Association of School Administrators, *The State of the American School Superintendency: A Mid-Decade Study* (September 2007). Retrieved at www.aasa.org/newsroom/pressdetail.cfm?ItemNumber59401.
50. Thomas E. Glass and Louis A. Franceschini, *The State of the American School Superintendency: A Mid-Decade Study,* American Association of School Administrators, 2007*;* Catherine Gewertz, "Race, Gender, and the Superintendency," *Education Week* 26, no. 24 (February 17, 2006), pp. 1, 22, 24.
51. Cited in Spring, *American Education.*
52. Jay Mathews, "Nontraditional Thinking in Central Office," *The School Administrator*, Web Edition, *Washington Post,* June 2001; Tamar Lewin, "Leaders from Other Professions Reshape America's Schools, from Top to Bottom," *New York Times,* June 8, 2000; Nancy Mitchell, "Nontraditional School Bosses," *Denver Rocky Mountain News,* April 16, 2001; A. Goodnough, "Retired General Takes on New Mission: Schools," *New York Times,* November 6, 2002; J. Steinhauer, "Bloomberg Picks a Lawyer to Run New York Schools," *New York Times,* July 30, 2002; Timothy Waters and Robert J. Marzano, "The Primacy of Superintendent Leadership," *The School Administrator,* March 2007, www.aasa.org/publica

tions/saarticledetailtest.cfm?ItemNumber58435 (retrieved May 28, 2009).

53. Valerie Strauss, "Rhee in D.C.: The Myth of the Heroic Leader," *Washington Post,* September 9, 2010, http://voices.washingtonpost.com/answer-sheet/guest-bloggers/rheein-dc-the-myth-of-the-her.html (retrieved November 3, 2010).
54. Joanna Richardson, "Contracts Put Superintendents to Performance Test," *Education Week,* September 14, 1994, pp. 1, 12.
55. Valerie Strauss, "U.S. Teachers' Job Satisfaction Craters — Report," *Washington Post,* February 21, 2013 Retrieved January 24, 2017 at https://www.washingtonpost.com/news/answer-sheet/wp/2013/02/21/u-s-teachers-job-satisfaction-craters-report/?utm_term=.bb0db22eeed1; Debra Viadero, "Turnover in Principalship Focus of Research," *Education Week* 29, no. 9 (October 28, 2009), pp. 1, 14; Emily Wax, "A Tough Time at the Head of the Classes," *Washington Post,* June 18, 2002, p. A9.
56. Tara García Mathewson, "Study Shows Average Principal Works 60-hour Weeks," *Education Dive*, Nov. 11, 2016. Retrieved January 25, 2017 at http://www.educationdive.com/news/study-shows-average-principal-works-60-hour-weeks/430259/; Cheri Carlson, "Competing Pressures Put Strain on School Principals, Study Finds," *Educational Policy Institute,* January 2012, http://www.educationalpolicy.org/publications/etw/us/news/etwus_120106.html (retrieved April 8, 2012); Vincent L. Ferrandino, "Challenges for 21st-Century Elementary School Principals," *Phi Delta Kappan* 82, no. 6 (February 2001), pp. 440–442; Linda Borg, "The Principal Dilemma Facing Schools in R.I.," *Providence Journal,* (August 26, 2001); Jacques Steinberg, "One Principal's World (The Unscripted Version)," *New York Times,* January 1, 2003.
57. Marge Scherer, "Perspectives/How Are You Doing?" *ED Leadership* 70, no. 7 (April 2013), p. 7–7; Valerie Strauss, "U.S. Teachers' Job Satisfaction Craters — Report."
58. Ferrandino, "Challenges for 21st-Century Elementary School Principals."
59. *Perspectives, The School Principal as Leader: Guiding Schools to Better Teaching and Learning,* The Wallace Foundation, January 2012, www.wallacefoundation.com (retrieved March 6, 2012); Denisa R. Superville, "Standards for Principal Supervisors Bring Sharper Focus to Role", *Education Week*, January 5, 2017. Retrieved January 25, 2017 at http://www.edweek.org/ew/articles/2016/01/06/standards-for-principal-supervisors-bring-sharper-focus.html; Celia Baker, "Fear Not the Principal's Office: That's Where School Success Begins," *Deseret News,* April 3, 2013.
60. Elissa Gootman and Robert Gebeloff, "Principals Younger and Freer but Raise Doubts in the Schools," *New York Times,* May 26, 2009, pp. A1, A15; Carol Ann Tomlinson, "One to Grow On/Freed from the Box," *Educational Leadership* 70, no. 7 (April 2013), pp. 88–89.
61. Jenny Upchurch, "Custodians Keep Schools Running without a Hitch," *Tennessean.com,* December 30, 2007; Edmund Janko, "The Untouchables: There Are Some People You Don't Mess With, and Many of Them Work in Schools," *Teacher Magazine* 16, no. 6 (May 1, 2005), pp. 50–51.
62. James G. Cibula, "Two Eras of Urban Schooling: The Decline of Law and Order and the Emergence of New Organizational Forms," *Education and Urban Society,* 29, no. 3 (May 1997), pp. 317–341.
63. Quoted in "Building Better Business Alliances," *Instructor* (Winter 1986, special issue), p. 21. See also Diann Woodard, "The Corporate Takeover of Public Education", *Huffington Post*, June 6, 2013. Retrieved January 26, 2017 at http://www.huffingtonpost.com/diann-woodard/the-corporate-takeover_b_3397091.html; Brian Dumaine, "Making Education Work," *Fortune* (Spring 1990, special issue), pp. 12–22.
64. For a good overview of school consolidation, see Karen Irmsher, "School Size," *ERIC Digest,* no. 113 (Eugene, OR: ERIC Clearinghouse on Educational Management, July 1997) (ED414615).
65. U.S. Department of Education, "Number of Public School Districts and Public and Private Elementary and Secondary Schools: Selected Years, 1869–70 through 2010–11," *Digest of Education Statistics, 2012* Table 98. Retrieved January 25, 2017 at http://nces.ed.gov/pubs2009/2009020_2a.pdf (retrieved May 5, 2009).
66. Catherine Gewertz, "The Breakup: Suburbs Try Smaller High Schools," *Education Week on the Web,* May 2, 2001; Craig Howley, Marty Strange, and Robert Bickel, "Research about School Size and School Performance in Impoverished Communities" (Charleston, WV: ERIC Clearinghouse on Rural Education and Small Schools, December 2000); William Ayers, Gerald Bracey, and Greg Smith, "The Ultimate Education Reform? Make Schools Smaller" (Milwaukee: Center for Education Research, Analysis, and Innovation, University of Wisconsin–Milwaukee, December 14, 2000).
67. Craig Howley, Jerry Johnson, and Jennifer Petrie, "Consolidation of Schools and Districts: What the Research Says and What it Means," University of Colorado, National Education Policy Center, February 1, 2011; Elissa Gootman, "New York City Plans to Open Small Secondary Schools," *New York Times,* March 12, 2004.
68. Adam Kirk Edgerton, "Why I Quit Teaching", *Huffington Post*, June 6, 2013. Retrieved January 26, 2017 at http://www.huffingtonpost.com/adam-kirk-edgerton/teachers-unions-issues_b_1856371.html.
69. Saul A. Rubinstein and John E. McCarthy, (2012), Public School Reform Through Union-Management Collaboration, in David Lewin, Paul J. Gollan, eds., *Advances in Industrial and Labor Relations (Advances in Industrial and Labor Relations, Volume 20)* Emerald Group Publishing Limited, pp. 1–50; Patrick McCloskey, "Vocal Arrangement," *Teacher Magazine* 17, no. 1 (September 1, 2005), pp. 30–35; Jeff Archer, "S.F. School Councils Help Chart Improvement course," *Education Week* 25, no. 31 (April 12, 2006), p. 10.
70. Information about Finland drawn from Ray Bendici, "Finnish-ing Touches on Education." *District Administration,* January 20, 2017. Retrieved January 27, 2017 at https://www.districtadministration.com/article/finnish-ing-touches-education; "Singapore Tops Latest OECD PISA Global Education Survey," *OECD*, June 12, 2016. Retrieved January 27, 2017 at http://www.oecd.org/education/singapore-tops-latest-oecd-pisa-global-education-survey.htm. Diane Ravitch, "What Can We Learn From Finland?" *Education Week's blogs,* October 11, 2011, www.edweek.org (retrieved January 7, 2012); Tara García Mathewson, "What Are the Ingredients to Finland's Elementary School Success?" *Education Dive*, January 9, 2017; David Sirota, "How Finland Became an Education Leader," *Salon.com,*

July 18, 2011; Andreas Schleicher, "Is the Sky the Limit to Education Improvement?" *Phi Delta Kappan* 93, no. 2 (October 2011), pp. 58–63; Jeevan Vasagar, "Finland's Schools Flourish in Freedom and Flexibility," *The Guardian,* December 5, 2010, guardian.co.uk (retrieved April 3, 2012).

CHAPTER 8: SCHOOL LAW AND ETHICS

1. Candace Mirabile, "A Comparison of Legal Literacy among Teacher Subgroups," *VCU Digital Archives,* August 2013, https://digarchive.library.vcu.edu/handle/10156/4496; David Schimmel and Matthew Militello, "Legal Literacy of Teachers: A Neglected Responsibility," *Harvard Educational Review* 77, no. 3 (February 2007), pp. 257–284.
2. Ibid; David Schimmel, Leslie Stellman, and Louis Fischer, *Teachers and the Law,* 8th ed. (Upper Saddle, NJ: Prentice Hall, 2010); Michael Imber, "Pervasive Myths in Teacher Beliefs about Education Law," *Action in Teacher Education* 30, no. 2 (2008), pp. 88–97.
3. Louis Fischer and David Schimmel, *The Civil Rights of Teachers* (New York: Harper & Row, 1973).
4. The legal situations and interpretations included in this text are adapted from a variety of sources, including Myra Sadker and David Sadker, *Sex Equity Handbook for Schools* (New York: Longman, 1982); Schimmel, Stellman, and Fischer, *Teachers and the Law;* Michael LaMorte, *School Law: Cases and Concepts,* 10th ed. (Boston: Allyn & Bacon, 2011); Karen R. Zittleman, "Teachers, Students and Title IX: A Promise for Fairness," in David Sadker and Ellen Silber, eds., *Gender in the Classroom: Foundations, Skills, Methods and Strategies across the Curriculum* (Mahwah, NJ: Lawrence Erlbaum, 2007), pp. 73–107; Imber, "Pervasive Myths in Teacher Beliefs about Education Law."
5. Schimmel, Stellman, and Fischer, *Teachers and the Law;* Zittleman, "Teachers, Students and Title IX."
6. *Gebser v. Lago Vista Independent School District,* 96 U.S. 1866 (1998); Greg Henderson, "Court Says Compensatory Damages Available Under Title IX," UPI, February 26, 1992; *Franklin v. Gwinnett County Schools,* 503 U.S. 60 (1992). Kathy Caprino, "What to Do if You've Been Sexually Harassed in the Workplace," *Forbes*, November 8, 2016. http://www.forbes.com/sites/kathycaprino/2016/11/08/what-to-do-if-youve-been-sexually-harassed-in-the-workplace/#46827d003382.
7. Associated Press, January 20, 2017. http://www.foxnews.com/politics/2017/01/20/texas-court-hearing-case-to-limit-gay-marriage-legalization.html; Interview conducted with Asaf Orr, Esq., National Center for Lesbian Rights Staff Attorney, January 27, 2017; Kim Westheimer, "What principals need to know about gender identity and supporting transgender students." *Principal***,** January/February, 2017. https://www.naesp.org/principal-januaryfebruary-2017-equity-access-diverse-learners/gender-inclusive-schools; NASSP, "Position Statement on Transgender Students," May 10, 2016. https://www.nassp.org/who-we-are/board-of-directors/position-statements/transgender-students; *Thompson v. Southwest School District,* 483 F. Supp. 1170 (W.D.M.W. 1980); Schimmel, Stellman, and Fischer, *Teachers and the Law.*
8. *Kingsville Independent School District v. Cooper,* 611 F. 2d 1109 (5th Cir. 1980); See also Schimmel, Stellman, and Fischer, *Teachers and the Law.*
9. Legal Dictionary, Liability." *Law.com*. http://dictionary.law.com/Default.aspx?selected=1151.
10. Schimmel, Stellman, and Fischer, *Teachers and the Law.*
11. *Pickering v. Board of Education of Township High School District 205, Will County,* 391 U.S. 563 (1968); Nathan L. Essex, *School Law and the Public Schools: A Practical Guide for School Leaders,* 5th ed. (Boston: Allyn & Bacon, 2012).
12. "California: Ruling Against Anti-Creationism Teacher," *New York Times,* May 5, 2009, p. A18.
13. Javier Hernandez, "Judge Says No to Teachers' Campaign Buttons, but Yes to Certain Politicking," *New York Times,* October 18, 2008, p. A20; Jonathan Stempel, "Pennsylvania teacher fired after blog posts cannot sue: U.S. court," *Reuters*, September 4, 2015. http://www.reuters.com/article/us-pennsylvania-teacher-freespeech-idUSKCN0R41N220150904.
14. National Constitution Center, "Interactive Constitution," http://constitutioncenter.org/interactive-constitution.
15. Chuck Klosterman, "Piracy 101," *New York Times Magazine* March 30, 2014, p. 23; *Basic Books v. Kinko's Graphics Corp.,* 758 F. Supp. 1522 (S.D.N.Y.1991); pp. 26–32; Essex, *School Law and the Public Schools.*
16. Essex, *School Law and the Public Schools.*
17. Ibid.
18. LaMorte, *School Law: Cases and Concepts.*
19. Schimmel, Stellman, and Fischer, *Teachers and the Law; Owasso Independent School District v. Falvo* 534 U.S. 426 (2002).
20. Karen Grigsby Bates, "Study: Black Girls Are Being Pushed Out of School," *National Public Radio*, February 13, 2015, http://www.npr.org/sections/codeswitch/2015/02/13/384005652/study-black-girls-are-being-pushed-out-of-school (retrieved January 5, 2017.); *Goss v. Lopez,* 419 U.S. 565 (1975); *Wood v. Strickland,* 420 U.S. 308 (1975); Essex, *School Law and the Public Schools;* "Report: Minority Students Face Harsher Punishments," *Arizona Daily Star,* March 7, 2012, p. A22; The Editorial Board, "Zero Tolerance, Reconsidered," *New York Times,* January 6, 2014, p. A18.
21. Shannon Snapp and Jennifer Munely Hoenig, "Zero Tolerance in Schools Doesn't Work, but Restorative Justice Does," *Arizona Daily Star,* December 13, 2013, p. A11; The Editorial Board, "Zero Tolerance, Reconsidered."
22. Melinda D. Anderson, "Where Teachers Are Still Allowed to Spank Students: Corporal punishment is legal in 19 states," *The Atlantic,* December 15, 2015. https://www.theatlantic.com/education/archive/2015/12/corporal-punishment/420420/ (retrieved, July 7, 2017); See also Ingraham v. Wright, 430 U.S. 651 (1977).
23. *Tinker v. Des Moines Independent Community School District,* 393 U.S. 503 (1969).
24. Tony Mauro, "Why First Amendment Still Matters to Students," *USA Today,* August 28, 2013, p. 6A.
25. Howard Fischer, "Court: Schools Can Ban Hurtful T-Shirt Slogans," *Arizona Daily Star,* April 21, 2006, www.azstarnet.com/.
26. *Bethel School District No. 403 v. Fraser,* 478 U.S. 675 (1986); *J. S. v. Bethlehem Area School District,* 757A. 2d 412 (2000).
27. *Beussink v. Woodland R-IV School District,* 30 F. Supp. 2d 1175 (1998); Jamie Raskin, *We the Students: Supreme Court Cases for and about Students* (Washington, DC: CQ Press, 2000).

28. Patrik Jonsson, "Teachers Strike Back at Students' Online Pranks," *Christian Science Monitor,* February 25, 2008, https://www.csmonitor.com/USA/2008/0225/p01s02-usgn.html.
29. Lee Lawrence, "50 Years after the Ban, God and Faith More Present than Ever," *Christian Science Monitor*, June 16, 2013, https://www.csmonitor.com/The-Culture/Family/2013/0616/School-prayer-50-years-after-the-ban-God-and-faith-more-present-than-ever; "Religion in America: Facts and Figures," *Phi Delta Kappan* 93, no. 4 (December 2011/January 2012), pp. 44–45; *Engel v. Vitale,* 370 U.S. 421 (1962); *Lee v. Weisman,* 112 U.S. 2649, (1992); *Good News Club v. Milford Central Schools,* 99 U.S. 2036 (2001); *Santa Fe Independent School District v. Doe,* 99 U.S. 62 (2000); Leo Pfeffer, *West Virginia State Board of Education vs. Barnette*, in Kermit Hall, James Ely Jr., and Joel Grossman, eds., *The Oxford Guide to the Supreme Court of the United States* (New York: Oxford University Press, 2005) pp. 1083–1084; *Holocaust Encyclopedia*, "Jehovah's Witnesses." United States Holocaust Memorial Museum. www.ushmm.org/wlc/en/article.php?ModuleId=10005394.
30. *Bellnier v. Lund,* 438 F. Supp. 47 (N.Y. 1977); *New Jersey v. T.L.O.,* 105 U.S. 733 (1985); Jesse Holland, "Court Says Strip Search of Arizona Teenager Illegal," *Arizona Daily Star,* June 25, 2009, p. A1; LaMorte, *School Law: Cases and Concepts.*
31. *Hazelwood School District v. Kuhlmeier,* 108 S. Ct. 562 (1988).
32. Liam Stack, "Trump's Executive Order on Immigration: What We Know and What We Don't," *New York Times*, January 29, 2017, https://www.nytimes.com/2017/01/29/us/trump-refugee-ban-muslim-executive-order.html; Jeff Guo, "If someone doesn't like immigrants, ask them this question," *Washington Post*, January 6, 2017, https://www.washingtonpost.com/news/wonk/wp/2017/01/06/if-someone-doesnt-like-immigrants-ask-them-this-question/; Mary C. Waters and Marisa Gerstein Pineau, eds., *The Integration of Immigrants into American Society* (Washington, DC: National Academy of Sciences, 2015), https://www.nap.edu/read/21746/chapter/1; Richard A. Gambitta, *Plyler v. Doe* in Kermit Hall, James Ely Jr., and Joel Grossman, eds., *The Oxford Guide to the Supreme Court of the United States* (New York: Oxford University Press, 2005) p. 740; *Lau v. Nichols*, 414 U.S. 56 (1974); Andrew Simmons, "What Undocumented Students Bring to the Classroom." *The Atlantic*, April 13, 2015, http://www.theatlantic.com/education/archive/2015/04/what-undocumented-students-bring-to-the-classroom/390333/; *Immigrant Students' Rights to Attend Public Schools*, Washington Office of Superintendent of Public Instruction, http://www.k12.wa.us/MigrantBilingual/ImmigrantRights.aspx; *Dear Colleague*, U.S. Department of Justice and U.S. Department of Education, May 8, 2014, http://images.politico.com/global/2014/05/08/plyler_dcl_-_05-05-14.html; Amy Mazur, "What teachers need to know about undocumented students," *PBS NewsHour*, October 15, 2014, http://www.pbs.org/newshour/updates/teachers-need-know-undocumented-students/; Alice Dominguez, "Teachers Advocate for Removal of Barriers and Fear for Undocumented Students," *HomeRoom* (blog), U.S. Department of Education, April, 2016, https://blog.ed.gov/2016/04/teachers-advocate-for-removal-of-barriers-and-fear-for-undocumented-students/; Jordan Catapano, "When Undocumented Immigrants Are Your Students," *TeachHub.com*, http://www.teachhub.com/when-illegal-immigrants-are-your-students (Retrieved January 5, 2017).
33. John Nicoletti, Sally Spencer-Thomas, Christopher M. Bollinger, *Violence Goes to College: The Authoritative Guide to Prevention and Intervention* (Springfield, Ill: Charles C Thomas Publisher, Ltd., 2001), p. 134.
34. Sarah Rhinehart, Namrata Doshi, and Dorothy Espelage, "Sexual Harassment and Sexual Violence among Middle School Youth," Paper Presented at Annual American Education Research Conference (2014), http://www.aera.net/Newsroom/RecentAERAResearch/SexualHarassmentandSexualViolenceExperiences AmongMiddleSchoolYouth/tabid/15450/Default.aspx; Charol Shakeshaft, "Know the Warning Signs of Educator Sexual Misconduct," *Phi Delta Kappan* (February 2013), pp. 8–13; Jenny Anderson, "National Study Finds Widespread Sexual Harassment of Students in Grades 7–12," *New York Times,* November 7, 2011, http://www.nytimes.com/2011/11/07/education/widespread-sexual-harassment-in-grades-7-to-12-found-in-study.html.
35. Asaf Orr and Karen Komosa-Hawkins, "Law, Policy and Ethics: What Professionals Need to Know," in Emily S. Fisher and Karen Komosa-Hawkins, eds., *Creating Safe and Supportive Learning Environments: A Guide for Working with Lesbian, Gay, Bisexual, Transgender, and Questioning Youth and Families*. (New York: Routledge, 2013). p. 105.
36. The states are Alabama, Arizona, Louisiana, Mississippi, Oklahoma, South Carolina, Texas, and Utah; GLSEN (Gay, Lesbian, & Straight Education Network), "No Promo Homo Laws," http://www.glsen.org/learn/policy/issues/nopromohomo; Alabama State Code § 16-40A-2(c) (8); Daniel Pinello, "Lawrence v. Texas" in Hall, Ely and Grossman, p. 572.
37. Zittleman, "Teachers, Students, and Title IX: A Promise for Fairness."
38. Schimmel, Stellman, and Fischer, *Teachers and the Law.*
39. Ibid.; Karen Zittleman, "Title IX and Gender: A Study of the Knowledge, Perceptions, and Experiences of Middle and Junior High School Teachers and Students," *Dissertation Abstracts International* 66, no. 11 (2005) (UMI No. 3194815).
40. Josephson Institute, Center for Youth Ethics, *Report Card on the Ethics of American Youth* (Los Angeles: The Josephson Institute, 2012), https://charactercounts.org/wp-content/uploads/2014/02/ReportCard-2012-DataTables.pdf.
41. Ibid.
42. Rebecca Moore Howard and Laura J. Davies, "Plagiarism in the Internet Age," *Educational Leadership* 66, no. 6 (March 2009), pp. 64–67; Josephson Institute, *The Ethics of American Youth.*
43. W. Chonchaiya and C. Pruksananonda, "Television viewing associates with delayed language development," *Acta Paediatrica* 97, no. 7 (2008), pp. 977–982.
44. Linda S. Pagani, Caroline Fitzpatrick, Tracie A. Barnett, and Eric Dubow, "Prospective Associations Between Early Childhood Television Exposure and Academic, Psychosocial, and Physical Well-being by Middle Childhood," *Archives of Pediatrics and Adolescent Medicine* 164, no. 5 (2010), pp. 425–431, http://jamanetwork.com/journals/jamapediatrics/fullarticle/383160.
45. A.S. Page, A.R. Cooper, P. Griew, & R. Jago, "Children's screen viewing is related to psychological difficulties irrespective of physical activity," *Pediatrics* 126, no. 5 (2010), pp. 1011–1017.
46. N.D. Barlett, D.A. Gentile, C.P. Barlett, J.C. Eisenmann, et al., "Sleep as a mediator of screen time effects on children's health effects on children's health outcomes," *Journal of Children and Media* 6, no. 1 (2012), pp. 37–50.

47. L.D. Rosen, A.F. Lim, J. Felt, L.M. Carrier, N.A. Cheever, J.M. Lara-Ruiz, J.S. Mendoza, and J. Rokkum, "Media and technology use predicts ill-being among children, preteens and teenagers independent of the negative health impacts of exercise and eating habits," *Computers in Human Behavior* 35 (2014), pp. 364–375, https://www.ncbi.nlm.nih.gov/pmc/articles/PMC4338000/.
48. Amanda Lenhart, "Teens, Social Media & Technology Overview 2015," Pew Research Center, April 9, 2015, http://www.pewinternet.org/2015/04/09/teens-social-media-technology-2015/; Common Sense Media, "The Common Sense Census: Media Use by Teens and Teens," 2015, https://www.commonsensemedia.org/sites/default/files/uploads/research/census_researchreport.pdf; danah boyd, *It's Complicated: The Social Lives of Networked Teens* (New Haven, CT: Yale University Press, 2014).
49. Jason Tomassini "Teachers Seek Specialized Peer Networks," *Education Week* 32, no. 15, (January 9, 2013), pp. 1, 19; Jennifer Preston, "Rules to Stop Pupil and Teacher from Getting Too Social Online," *New York Times*, December 17, 2011, http://www.nytimes.com/2011/12/18/business/media/rules-to-limit-how-teachers-and-students-interact-online.html (retrieved February 6, 2017); Michelle Davis, "Social Networking Goes to School," *Education Week* 3, no. 3 (June 14, 2010), pp. 16, 18, 20, 22–23
50. ChildHelp, *National Child Abuse Statistics* (2014), www.childhelp.org/; U.S. Department of Health and Human Services, *Child Maltreatment 2014*, https://www.acf.hhs.gov/sites/default/files/cb/cm2014.pdf.
51. Administration on Children, Youth, and Families, U.S. Department of Health and Human Services, *Mandatory Reporter of Child Abusers and Neglect: Summary of State Laws* (2014), https://www.childwelfare.gov/systemwide/laws_policies/statutes/manda.cfm; Child Welfare Information Gateway (2016), "Mandatory Reporters of Child Abuse and Neglect," U.S. Department of Health & Human Services, https://www.childwelfare.gov/topics/systemwide/laws-policies/statutes/manda/.
52. Caralee Adams, "Character Education Seen as Student-Achievement Tool," *Education Week* 32, no. 22 (February 27, 2013), p. 7.
53. Alfie Kohn, "Encouraging Courage," *Education Week* 33, no. 4 (September 18, 2013), pp. 28, 32; Alfie Kohn, "How Not to Teach Values," *Phi Delta Kappan* 78, no. 8 (April 1997), pp. 428–437 [cited in James Noll, *Taking Sides,* 13th ed. (New York: McGraw-Hill, 2005), pp. 102–117].
54. Nel Noddings, *Caring: A Feminine Approach to Ethics and Moral Development,* 2nd ed. (Berkeley, CA: University of California Press, 2003); R.E. Muuss, "Carol Gilligan's theory of sex differences in the development of moral reasoning during adolescence," *Adolescence* 23, no. 89 (1988), pp. 229–243.
55. Anthony Holter and Darcia Narvaez, "New Moral Education," *Educational Leadership,* April 18, 2011, http:// www.education.com/reference/article/moral-education/; Nel Noddings, "Handle with Care," *Greater Good,* Spring/Summer 2006, pp. 18–21; Charles Haynes, "Teaching Social Responsibility," *Education Leadership* 66, no. 8 (May 2009), pp. 6–13.

CHAPTER 9: PURPOSES OF AMERICA'S SCHOOLS AND THE CURRENT REFORM MOVEMENT

1. John Goodlad, *A Place Called School* (New York: McGraw-Hill, 1984), pp. 35–39.
2. Sara Neufeld, "Photos Reveal Decrepit State of City Schools," *Baltimore Sun*, February 24, 2006, http://healthyschoolscampaign.org/news/media/environ/2006-0224_photos. php (retrieved April 17, 2009).
3. James Shaver and William Strong, *Facing Value Decisions: Rationale Building for Teachers* (Belmont, CA: Wadsworth, 1976); Barbara Slater Stern and Karen Lea Riley, "Reflecting on the Common Good: Harold Rugg and the Social Reconstructionists," *Social Studies* 92 (2001); Michael E. James, *Social Reconstructionism through Education* (Stamford, CT: Ablex Publishing, 1995).
4. Benjamin Steigman, *Accent on Talent—New York's High School of Music & Art*. (Detroit: Wayne State University Press, 1984); H. Fiorello, LaGuardia High School of Music & Art and Performing Arts, "Mission and History," http://laguardiahs.org/mission-history/ (retrieved November 12, 2016).
5. CollegeNet, "2015 Student Mobility Index: Opportunity through US Higher Education," http://www.socialmobilityindex.org/ and Jim Wolfston, "How Higher Education Can Improve Economic Mobility in the United States," http://bigthink.com/experts-corner/how-higher-education-can-improve-economic-mobility-in-the-united-states-2 (retrieved November 12, 2016).
6. FindLaw, "English-Only Instruction in Public Schools," http://education.findlaw.com/curriculum-standards-school-funding/english-only-instruction-in-public-schools.html; Jake Grovum, "The English-Only Debate Heats Up Again," *Governing*, August 8, 2014, http://www.governing.com/news/headlines/the-english-only-debate-heats-up-again.html; Melinda D. Anderson, "The Costs of English-Only Education," *The Atlantic*, November 2, 2015, http://www.theatlantic.com/education/archive/2015/11/the-costs-of-english-only-education/413494/(retrieved November 12, 2016).
7. Paulo Freire, *Pedagogy of the Oppressed* (New York: Herder & Herder, 1970).
8. Bill Bigelow, "The Human Lives Behind the Labels: The Global Sweatshop, Nike, and the Race to the Bottom," Phi Delta Kappan 79, no. 2 (October 1997), pp. 112–119.
9. Linda Perlstein, "'Serving' the Community Without Leaving School," *Washington Post*, June 28, 1999, pp. A1, A6.
10. Ernest L. Boyer, *High School: A Report on Secondary Education in America* (New York: Harper & Row, 1983), pp. 209–210.
11. "The Condition of Education, 2001," U.S. Department of Education; NCES, "Indicator 16: Social and Cultural Outcomes, Community Service Participation in Grades 6–12," p. 142, http://nces.ed.gov/pubs2001/2001072_2.pdf; Helen M. Marks and Susan Robb Jones, "Community Service in Transition: Shifts and Continuities in Participation from High School to College," *Journal of Higher Education* 75 (2004), pp. 307–339
12. D'vera Cohn, Gretchen Livingston, and Wendy Wang, "After Decades of Decline, a Rise in Stay-at-Home Mothers," *Pew Research Center Social & Demographic Trends*, April 8, 2014. http://www.pewsocialtrends.org/2014/04/08/

after-decades-of-decline-a-rise-in-stay-at-home-mothers/. (retrieved November 13, 2016).
13. Nicholson Baker, *Substitute: Going to School with a Thousand Kids* (New York: Penguin Random House, 2016).
14. John Taylor Gatto, *The Underground History of American Education: A School Teacher's Intimate Investigation into the Problem of Modern Schooling*. (New York: The Oxford Village Press, 2003). p. 365.
15. Goodlad, *A Place Called School*.
16. Ernest L. Boyer, *High School: A Report on Secondary Education in America* (New York: Harper & Row, 1983), p. 5.
17. Arthur Eugene Bestor, *Educational Wastelands: The Retreat from Learning in Our Public Schools* (Urbana: University of Illinois Press, 1953), p. 75.
18. Lowell C. Rose and Alec M. Gallup, "The 39th Annua! Phi Delta Kappa/Gallup Poll of the Public's Attitude toward the Public Schools," *Phi Delta Kappan* 89, no. 1 (September 2007), Table 33, pp. 33–48.
19. "American Public Education: An Origin Story." *Education News*, April 4, 2013, http://www.educationnews.org/education-policy-and-politics/american-public-education-an-origin-story/; Applied Research Center, "Historical Timeline of Public Education in the US." April 13, 2006, https://www.raceforward.org/research/reports/historical-timeline-public-education-us (retrieved November 14, 2016).
20. William J. Bushaw and Shane J. Lopez, "Which Way Do We Go?" *Phi Delta Kappan* 95, no. 1 (September 2013), http://pdkintl.org/noindex/2013_PDKGallup.pdf (retrieved April 16, 2014).
21. National Commission on Excellence in Education, *A Nation at Risk: The Imperative for Educational Reform* (Washington, DC: U.S. Government Printing Office, 1983), p. 1; David Unze, Kirsti Marohn, and Kevin Allenspach, "Open enrollment brings gains, losses." *Saint Cloud Times*, December 13, 2015, http://www.sctimes.com/story/news/2015/12/12/open-enrollment-brings-gains-losses/76664418/ (retrieved November 14, 2016).
22. Tamar Lewin, "John I. Goodlad, Progressive Educator, Dies at 94," *New York Times*, January 2, 2015. p. B11, http://www.nytimes.com/2015/01/02/us/john-i-goodlad-educator-who-led-8-year-study-underpinning-school-reforms-dies-at-94.html (retrieved November 17, 2016).
23. National Alliance for Public Charter Schools, "A Growing Movement: America's Largest Charter School Communities, Tenth Annual Edition," November 2015, p. 2, http://www.publiccharters.org/wp-content/uploads/2015/11/enrollmentshare_web.pdf (retrieved November 15, 2016).
24. Bushaw and Lopez, "Which Way Do We Go?"
25. Phi Delta Kappa International, "2014 PDK/Gallup Poll of the Public's Attitudes Toward the Public Schools," August 2014, p. 10, http://pdkintl.org/files/2014-PDK-Gallup-Poll-Presentation.pdf (retrieved November 16, 2016).
26. Alex Molnar, "Charter Schools: The Smiling Face of Dis-investment," *Educational Leadership* 54, no. 2 (October 1996), pp. 9–15; Chuck Sudetic, "Reading, Writing, and Revenue," *Mother Jones*, May/June 2001, pp. 84–95.
27. Winnie Hu, "In a New Role, Teachers Are Given the Chance to Run Poorer Schools," *New York Times*, September 7, 2010, pp. A1, A20.
28. Marta Jewson, "ReNEW hires former Jefferson superintendent in response to testing, special-ed violations," *The Lens*, February18,2016,http://thelensnola.org/2016/02/18/renew-hires-former-jefferson-superintendent-in-response-to-violations/; Douglas N. Harris, "Betsy DeVos and the Wrong Way to Fix Schools," *New York Times*, November 25, 2016, https://www.nytimes.com/2016/11/25/opinion/betsy-devos-and-the-wrong-way-to-fix-schools.html (retrieved January 12, 2017).
29. "Charter schools do not equal education reform," *Baltimore Sun*, February 27, 2015, http://www.baltimoresun.com/news/opinion/oped/bs-ed-hornbeck-charters-20150301-story.html (retrieved November 14, 2016).
30. "Choice Without Equity: Charter School Segregation and the Need for Civil Rights Standards," The Civil Rights Project, UCLA, February 4, 2010; Dave Weber, "Florida Charters Less Diverse Than Other Public Schools," *Orlando Sentinel*, April 30, 2011, www.sun-sentinel.com/news/local/breakingnews/os-charter-schools-segregation-20110430,0,4650625,full.story; Mary Ann Zehr, "Study Finds High Dropout Rates for Black Males in KIPP Schools," *Education Week* 30, no. 27 (March 31, 2011), www.educationweek.com (retrieved February 3, 2012); John Thompson, "KIPP and Its Critics Are Both Right," *Huffington Post*, April 17, 2011, www.huffingtonpost.com (retrieved February 2, 2012); Mary Ann Zehr, "KIPP Middle Schools Found to Spur Learning Gains," *Education Week* 36, no. 29 (June 22, 2010); Mary Ann Zehr, "Regular Public Schools Start to Mimic Charters," *Education Week* 30, no. 11 (November 8, 2010), pp. 1, 12, www.edweek.org/ew/articles/2010/11/10/11charter.h30.html.
31. Valarie Strauss, "NAACP ratifies controversial resolution for a moratorium on charter schools," *Washington Post*, October 15, 2016, https://www.washingtonpost.com/news/answer-sheet/wp/2016/10/15/naacp-ratifies-controversial-resolution-for-a-moratorium-on-charter-schools/ (retrieved November 14, 2016).
32. Griselda Nevarez and Evan Wyloge, "Charter student populations don't match state demographics," Arizona Center for Investigative Reporting, *The Arizona Republic*, February 3, 2016, http://www.azcentral.com/story/news/local/arizona/education/2016/02/13/charter-student-populations-dont-match-state-demographics/80294154/ (retrieved November 15, 2016).
33. Ibid.
34. American Civil Liberties Union of Southern California, "Unequal Access: How Some California Charter Schools Illegally Restrict Enrollment," August 1, 2016, https://www.aclusocal.org/wp-content/uploads/2016/07/Report-Unequal-Access-080116.pdf (retrieved November 14, 2016), http://www.nytimes.com/2011/11/07/education/widespread-sexual-harassment-in-grades-7-to-12-found-in-study.html.
35. David Brooks, "The Relationship School," *New York Times*, March 22, 2012, p. A25; The New American Academy, http://tnaacs.org/about/.
36. Rob Pecharich, "Edge High School: Executive Summary," *AdvancEd*, May 12, 2014, http://www.advanc-ed.org/oasis2/u/par/accreditation/summary/pdf;jsessionid=4787155B88A0C13E62B0B2A02D2EA9B0?institutionId=12005 (retrieved November 21, 2016).
37. Lesli A. Maxwell, "Study Finds No Clear Edge for Charter Schools," *Education Week*, June 29, 2010, www.edweek.org/ew/articles/2010/06/29/36ies.h29.html; Lesli A. Maxwell, "Study Casts Doubt on Charter School Results," *Education Week*, June 15, 2009, www.edweek.org/ew

/articles/2009/06/15/36charters.h28.html; Trip Gabriel, "Despite Push, Success at Charter Schools Is Mixed," *New York Times*, May 2, 2010, pp. 1, 22, 23.

38. Erin Richards, "Poverty Less Damaging to Public Schools' Scores than Charters', Report Finds," *Milwaukee Journal Sentinel*, December 5, 2012, www.jsonline.com/ and https://aclu-wi.org/sites/default/files/document-library/PovertyLess DamagingtoPublicSchools.pdf (retrieved November 17, 2016).
39. Leah Fabel, "Charter School Teachers More Likely to Leave Teaching," *Washington Examiner*, July 6, 2010; Jack Buckley and Mark Schneider, *Charter Schools: Hope or Hype?* (Princeton, NJ: Princeton University Press, 2007); Robin J. Lake, ed., *Hopes, Fears, and Reality: A Balanced Look at Charter Schools in 2007* (Seattle, WA: The National Charter School Research Project, December 2007), www.ncsrp.org/cs/csr/view/csr_pubs/17 (retrieved April 9, 2008); Andrew Rotherham and Sara Mead, *A Sum Greater than the Parts: What States Can Teach Each Other about Charter Schooling* (Washington, DC: Education Sector, 2007), www.educationsector.org/usr_doc /CharterSchoolSummary.pdf (retrieved April 17, 2009); Patrik Jonsson, "As New Orleans Restarts Its Schools, Most Are Now Charter Schools," *Christian Science Monitor*, September 4, 2007, www.csmonitor.com/2007/0904 /p01s08-ussc.html (retrieved April 17, 2009).
40. Winnie Hu, "Charter School Battle Shifts to Affluent Suburbs," *New York Times*, July 17, 2011, www.nytimes.com/2011/07/17/education/17charters.html?_r51&pagewanted5print (retrieved January 26, 2012); Joshua Holland, "Charter Schools Gone Wild: Study Finds Widespread Fraud, Mismanagement and Waste," *Bill Moyers Journal*, May 5, 2014, http://billmoyers.com/2014/05/05/charter-schools-gone-wild-study-finds-widespread-fraud-mismanagement-and-waste/(retrieved May 6, 2014); "Motoko Rich, "A Walmart Fortune, Spreading Charter Schools," *New York Times*, April 25, 2014, http://www.nytimes.com/2014/04/26/us/a-walmart-fortune-spreading-charter-schools.html (retrieved November 17, 2016).
41. Javier Hernandez, "Charters, Public Schools and a Chasm Between," *New York Times*, May 11, 2014, https://www.nytimes.com/2014/05/12/nyregion/charters-public-schools-and-a-chasm-between.html (retrieved May 14, 2014).
42. Christopher A. Lubienski and Sarah Theule Lubienski, *The Public School Advantage: Why Public Schools Outperform Private Schools* (Chicago, University of Chicago Press, 2013); Erin Richards, "New Data Shows Similar Academic Results Between Voucher and MPS Students," *Milwaukee Journal Sentinel*, April 7, 2010, www.jsonline.com/news/education/90169302.html; Erin Richards and Amy Hetzner, "Choice Schools Not Outperforming MPS, Latest Tests Show Voucher Scores About Same or Worse in Math and Reading," *Milwaukee Journal Sentinel*, March 29, 2011, jsonline.com/news/education/118820339.html (retrieved February 1, 2012); Dan Hardy, "Finding That Vouchers Have Little Impact on Student Achievement Do Not Deter Advocates," *Philadelphia Inquirer*, August 08, 2011, http://articles.philly.com/2011-08-08/news/29864661_1_voucher-programs-voucher-students-voucher-proposals (retrieved February 3, 2012); Timothy McDonald, "The False Promise of Voucher," *Educationa l Leadership* 59, no. 7 (April 2002), pp. 33–37; Kaleem M. S. Caire, "The Truth about Vouchers," *Educational Leadership* 59, no. 7 (April 2002), pp. 38–42; National Education Association, "Vouchers," March 22, 2006, www.nea.org/vouchers/index.html; Maria Glod and Bill Turque, "Report Finds Little Gain from Vouchers," *Washington Post*, June 17, 2008, p. B6.
43. Motoko Rich, "A Walmart Fortune, Spreading Charter Schools."
44. For more on the legal dispute, see *Jackson v. Benson* (1998), which held that vouchers used for religious school tuition did not violate the Wisconsin state constitution; Sam Dillon, "For Parents Seeking a Choice, Charter Schools Prove More Popular than Vouchers," *New York Times*, July 23, 2005, www.nytimes.com/2005/07/13/education/13voucher.html (retrieved April 7, 2008); Valerie Strauss, "The Answer Sheet: For School Choice-Loving Democrats to Consider," *Washington Post*, January 31, 2014, www.washingtonpost.com (retrieved May 1, 2014).
45. Pat Kossan and Emily Gersema, "Arizona's High Court Bans School Vouchers," *Arizona Republic*, March 26, 2009, www.azcentral.com/arizonarepublic/news/articles/2009/03/26/20090326vouchers0326.html (retrieved March 29, 2009); National Education Association, "Florida High Court Rules Against Vouchers;" Scott Elliott and Tim Evans, "Indiana Supreme Court Upholds School Vouchers," *The Indianapolis Star*, March 27, 2013; Campbell Robertson, "Judge Deals a Setback to Louisiana's Voucher Program," *New York Times*, December 3, 2012, http://www.nytimes.com/2012/12/04/us/louisiana-voucher-programs-financing-is-ruled-unconstitutional.html (retrieved November 17, 2016).
46. Jeremy P. Meyer, "Douglas County School District Considers Starting Voucher Program," *Denver Post*, November 5, 2010, www.denverpost.com/news/ci_16528490; Dillon, "For Parents Seeking a Choice, Charter Schools Prove More Popular than Vouchers"; U.S. Charter Schools, "Frequently Asked Questions," March 22, 2006, www.uscharterschools.org/pub/uscs_docs/o/faq.html.
47. Paul E. Peterson, Michael B. Henderson, Martin R. West and Samuel Barrows, "Ten Year Trends in Public Opinion from the EdNext Poll," *EducationNext* 16, no. 1 (Winter 2016), http://educationnext.org/ednext-poll/; Layen Camera, "Surprise: Democrats Also Support School Vouchers" *U.S. News and World Report*, August 23, 2016; http://www.usnews.com/news/articles/2016-08-23/surprise-democrats-also-support-school-vouchers; Jonathan N. Mills, Anna J. Egalite, and Patrick J. Wolf, *How Has the Louisiana Scholarship Program Affected Students? A Comprehensive Summary of Effects after Two Years*, Education Research Alliance of New Orleans, February 22, 2016, http://educationresearchalliancenola.org/files/publications/ERA-Policy-Brief-Public-Private-School-Choice-160218.pdf (retrieved January 12, 2017).
48. National Center of Education Statistics, "State Education Reforms, Table 4.2: Number and Types of Open Enrollment Policies, by State, 2015," https://nces.ed.gov/programs/statereform/tab4_2.asp (retrieved November 17, 2016).
49. In Littlefork, Baudette, and Virginia, Minnesota respectively, https://www.google.com/maps. (Mileage calculated November 17, 2016.)
50. David Unze, Kirsti Marohn, and Kevin Allenspach, "Open enrollment brings gains, losses" *The Saint Cloud Times*, December 13, 2015, http://www.sctimes.com/story/news/2015/12/12/open-enrollment-brings-gains-losses/76664418/ (retrieved November 17, 2016).

51. Ronald J. Iarussi and Karen H. Larwin, "The Academic Impact of Inter-District Open Enrollment in Public Schools: The Results from a Decade of Choice," 2015, http://www.ohio.com/polopoly_fs/1.571501.1425437977!/menu/standard/file/OEI%20Final%20Draft.pdf (retrieved November 17, 2016); Jeff Murray, "The Academic Impact of Inter-District Open Enrollment in Public Schools: The Results from a Decade of Choice," *Ohio Gadfly Daily*, Thomas B. Fordham Institute, March 9, 2015, https://edexcellence.net/articles/the-academic-impact-of-inter-district-open-enrollment-in-public-schools-the-results-from-a (retrieved November 17, 2016).
52. Mackenzie Ryan, "Magnet schools make a comeback," *District Administration*, May, 2015, https://www.districtadministration.com/article/magnet-schools-make-comeback (retrieved November 18, 2016).
53. A. S. Byrk, Valerie Lee, and P. B. Holland, *Catholic Schools and the Common Good* (London: Harvard University Press, 1993); *Public School Review*, "What Is a Magnet School?" www.publicschoolreview.com/magnet-schools.php (retrieved March 22, 2006); Howard Blume, "Support for Magnet Schools Waning Despite Their Success," *Los Angeles Times*, November 26, 2008, http://articles.latimes.com/2008/nov/26 /local/memagnets26 (retrieved April 1, 2009).
54. Alyson Klein, "Needs of 'Whole Child' May Factor in ESEA Renewal; Wide Range of Supports, Services, and Enrichment Seen as Vital but Costly," *Education Week* 29, no. 30 (April 28, 2010), pp. 16, 21; Sharon Otterman, "Despite Money and Attention, It's Not All A's at 2 Harlem Schools," *New York Times*, October 13, 2010, pp. A18–19; Javier C. Hernandez, "Harlem Educator Is Said to Have Rejected Schools Chancellor Job," *New York Times*, December 10, 2010, p. 10.
55. Claudia Dreifus, "It All Started With a 12-Year-Old Cousin: Salman Khan Turned Family Tutoring into Khan Academy," *New York Times*, January 27, 2014, http://www.nytimes.com/2014/01/28/science/salman-khan-turned-family-tutoring-into-khan-academy.html (retrieved November 19, 2016).
56. Natasha Singer and Mike Isaac, "Facebook Helps Develop Software that Puts Students in Charge of Their Lesson Plans," *New York Times*, August 10, 2016, p. B5, http://www.nytimes.com/2016/08/10/technology/facebook-helps-develop-software-that-puts-students-in-charge-of-their-lesson-plans.html (retrieved November 19, 2016).
57. Bill Tucker, *Laboratories of Reform: Virtual High Schools and Innovation in Public Education* (Washington, DC: Education Sector, June 2007), www.educationsector.org/research/research_show.htm?doc_id5502307 (retrieved April 10, 2008); Cavanagh, "Survey Finds Interest in Blend of Tradition and Online Courses," Moser, "Online Courses Aren't Just for Home-Schoolers Anymore"; Michelle Galley, "Despite Concerns, Online Elementary Schools Grow," *Education Week* 22, no. 16 (January 8, 2003), pp. 1, 12; Celia Baker, "Blended Learning: Teachers plus Computers Equal Success," *Deseret News*, January 5 2013, http://www.deseretnews.com/article/865569876/Blended-learning-teachers-plus-computers-equal-success.html (retrieved April 2014); Benjamin Herold, "Cybercharter Students Fall Far Behind on Academic Measures, New Study Says," *Ed Week*, November 3, 2015, http://www.edweek.org/ew/articles/2015/11/04/cybercharter-students-fall-far-behind-on-academic.html (retrieved July 6, 2017).
58. Jessica Calefati, "California Virtual Academies: Is online charter school network cashing in on failure?" *San Jose Mercury News*, April 16, 2016, http://www.mercurynews.com/2016/04/16/california-virtual-academies-is-online-charter school-network-cashing-in-on-failure/ (retrieved November 20, 2016).
59. "Live and Learn," *Harper's Bazaar*, September 1994, pp. 268–270.
60. Jeremy Redford, Danielle Battle, and Stacey Bielick, (2016), "Homeschooling in the United States: 2012 (NCES 2016-096)," National Center for Education Statistics, Institute of Education Sciences, U.S. Department of Education, November, 2016, http://nces.ed.gov/pubs2016/2016096.pdf; National Center for Education Statistics, "Number and percentage of homeschooled students ages 5 through 17 with a grade equivalent of kindergarten through 12th grade, by selected child, parent, and household characteristics: 2003, 2007, and 2012," *Digest of Educational Statistics*, Table 206.10, http://nces.ed.gov/programs/digest/d15/tables/dt15_206.10.asp (retrieved November 20, 2016).
61. Motoko Rich, "Home Schooling: More Pupils, Less Regulation," *New York Times*, January 4, 2012, P. A1, http://www.nytimes.com/2015/01/05/education/home-schooling-more-pupils-less-regulation.html (retrieved November 20, 2016).
62. J. A. Van Galen, "Schooling in Private: A Study of Home Education," doctoral dissertation, University of North Carolina, Chapel Hill, 1986; National Center for Education Statistics, "Homeschooled Students," *The Condition of Education* (May 2009), Indicator 6, http://nces.ed.gov/pubs2009/2009081.pdf; Patrick Farenga, John Holt, and Susannah Sheffer, eds., *Growing Without Schooling* (newsletter), 1977–2001. See archive at https://issuu.com/patfarenga/stacks/bb179dac91264c10bb183f89bf955935.
63. Rob Reich, "The Civic Perils of Home Schooling," *Educational Leadership* 59, no. 7 (April 2002), pp. 56–59.
64. Farenga, Holt, and Sheffer.
65. Brian D. Ray, "Homeschooling Across America: Academic Achievement and Demographic Characteristics," August 10, 2009,www.nheri.org/Latest/Homeschooling-Across-America-Academic-Achievement-and-Demographic-Characteristics.html; Gregory J. Millman, "Home Is Where the School Is," *Washington Post*, March 23, 2008, p. B1; National Center for Education Statistics, "Homeschooling in the United States: 2003"; Moser, "Online Courses Aren't Just for Home-Schoolers Anymore." For examples of online homeschooling curricula, see HomeSchool.com at www.homeschool.com/onlinecourses/and Online Learning Haven at www.learning-haven.com/. See also Nancy Trejos, "Home Schooling's Net Effect," *Washington Post*, July 16, 2000, pp. C1, C9; Alesha Williams Boyd and Sergio Bichao, "Home-Schooling Demographics Change, Expand," *USA Today*, February 15, 2012, www.USAtoday.com (retrieved May 4, 2014).
66. "Top-Selling Home-School Texts Disparage Evolution," *Arizona Daily Star*, March 7, 2010, p. A14.
67. Ibid; Brian Ray, "Customization through Homeschooling," *Educational Leadership* 59, no. 7 (April 2002), p. 50.
68. Stephanie Simon, "Privatizing Public Schools: Big Firms Eyeing Profits from U.S. K-12 Market," *Reuters*, August 2, 2012, http://www.huffingtonpost.com/2012/08/02/private-firms-eyeing-prof_n_1732856.html (retrieved April 28, 2014).

69. Erik Smith, "I-1240 May Not Tie Record After All," *Washington State Wire*, June 20, 2012, http://washingtonstatewire.com/i-1240-wont-tie-the-record-after-all-1973-initiative-likely-always-to-be-the-fastest-signature-drive-in-state-history/; Kathy Gill, "Charter Schools Initiative 1240 bankrolled by tech millionaires," *Seattle Times*, July 26, 2012, http://blogs.seattletimes.com/uwelectioneye/2012/07/26/charter-schools-initiative-1240-bankrolled-by-tech-millionaires/, (retrieved November 20, 2016).
70. Valerie Strauss, "21 Wealthy Donors Had Decisive Impact on Charter Law in Washington State—Analysis," *Washington Post*, January 30, 2014, http://www.washingtonpost.com/blogs/answer-sheet/wp/2014/01/30/21-wealthy-donors-had-decisive-impact-on-charter-law-in-washington-state-analysis/ (retrieved April 28, 2014).
71. See the Charter School and Virtual School sections above.
72. Larry Cuban quotes in Valerie Strauss, "The Failure of K-12 For-Profit Schools," *Washington Post*, October 4, 2013, http://www.washingtonpost.com/blogs/answer-sheet/wp/2013/10/04/the-failures-of-for-profit-k-12-schools/ (retrieved April 28, 2014).
73. Erik W. Robelen, "Environmental Literacy Making a Splash," *Ed Week*, October 10, 2011, www.edweek.com (retrieved January 2012); Lucy Hood, "The Greening of Environmental Ed: Teachers Focus on Complexity, Evidence, and Letting Students Draw their Own Conclusions," *Harvard Graduate School of Education Newsletter* 27, no. 1 (January/February 2011); Katie Ash, "'Green Schools' Benefit Budgets and Students, Report Says Environmentally friendly Schools Seen as Good for Bottom Line," *Ed Week*, May 24, 2011, www.edweek.org/ew/articles/2011/05/25/32greenschools_ep.h30.html (retrieved February 3, 2012); Gregory Kats, "Greening America's Schools: Costs and Benefits" (October 2006), a Capital E Report, www.cape.com/ewebeditpro/items /O59F9819.pdf; "Daylighting in Schools: An Investigation into the Relationship between Daylighting and Human Performance," Heschong Mahone Group (August 1999), www.coe.uga.edu/sdpl/research/daylightingstudy.pdf; "Healthier, Wealthier, Wiser: A Report on National Green Schools, a Report by Global Green USA," www.globalgreen.org/news/155 (retrieved April 2, 2009).
74. Rhonda Bodfield, "Schoolchildren Aware of Environmental Woes," *Arizona Daily Star*, January 3, 2009, www.azstarnet.com/metro/274326 (retrieved April 3, 2009); Sean Cavanagh, "'Green' Classes Flourish in Schools," *Education Week*, 28, no. 20 (February 3, 2009), p. 1, 13; Chelsy Killebrew, "Schoolchildren Go Green: Gardens Offer Science, Art and Enviro Lessons," *Arizona Daily Star*, September 26, 2008, pp. B1, B2; "No Child Left Inside," www.cbf.org /site/PageServer?pagename5act_sub_actioncenter_federal _NCLB (retrieved April 3, 2009); James Daly, "School Retrofits Go Green" *Edutopia*, October 28, 2009, www.edutopia.org/green-schools-retrofitting-health-budget.
75. U.S. Environmental Protection Agency, Office of Radiation and Indoor Air, "The Inside Story: A Guide to Indoor Air Quality, U.S. (6609J)," Washington, DC, cosponsored with the Consumer Product Safety Commission, EPA 402-K-93-007, www.epa.gov/iaq/pubs/insidest.html.
76. Matthew Lynch, "What Factors Make a School Effective?" *The Edvocate*, December 15, 2015. Retrieved Feb 2017 at http://www.theedadvocate.org/what-factors-make-a-school-effective/; George Weber, *Inner-City Children Can Be Taught to Read: Four Successful Schools* (Washington, DC: D.C. Council for Basic Books, 1971); Ronald Edmonds, "Some Schools Work and More Can," *Social Policy* 9 (1979), pp. 28–32; Barbara Taylor and Daniel Levine, "Effective Schools Projects and School-Based Management," *Phi Delta Kappan* 72, no. 5 (January 1991), pp. 394–397. See also Herman Meyers, "Roots, Trees, and the Forest: An Effective Schools Development Sequence," paper delivered at the American Educational Research Association, San Francisco, April 1992.
77. Sara Lawrence Lightfoot, *The Good High School* (New York: Basic Books, 1983).
78. Ibid., p. 67.
79. David Clark, Linda Lotto, and Mary McCarthy, "Factors Associated with Success in Urban Elementary Schools," *Phi Delta Kappan* 61, no. 7 (March 1980), pp. 467–470; The MetLife Survey of the American Teacher: Expectations and Experiences, Figure 3.7, p. 50 (issued September 26, 2006), www.metlife.com/ (retrieved April 23, 2009). See also David Gordon, "The Symbolic Dimension of Administration for Effective Schools," paper delivered at the annual meeting of the American Educational Research Association, San Francisco, April 1992.
80. William Rutherford, "School Principals as Effective Leaders," *Phi Delta Kappan* 67, no. 1 (September 1985), pp. 31–34; Carl Glickman, "The Courage to Lead," *Educational Leadership* 59, no. 8 (2002), pp. 41–44. See also R. McClure, "Stages and Phases of School-Based Renewal Efforts," paper presented at the annual meeting of the American Educational Research Association, New Orleans, 1988.
81. Anlan Zhang, Lauren Musu-Gillette, and Barbara A. Oudekerk, "Indicators of School Crime and Safety: 2015," National Center for Education Statistics and U.S. Department of Justice Office of Justice Programs, May 2016, http://nces.ed.gov/pubs2016/2016079.pdf (retrieved November 20, 2016).
82. *The Metropolitan Life Survey of the American Teacher 1999* (New York: Harris Interactive Inc., 2001), pp. 39, 42.
83. Lowell C. Rose and Alec M. Gallup, "The 39th Annual Gallup Poll of the Public's Attitudes toward the Public Schools," *Phi Delta Kappan* 89, no. 1 (September 2007), Table 43, pp. 33–48; "The MetLife Survey of the American Teacher: Expectations and Experiences," Figure 3.7, p. 50.
84. Lightfoot, *The Good High School*; Kevin Dwyer and D. Osher, *Safeguarding Our Children: An Action Guide* (Washington, DC: U.S. Department of Education, August 2000).
85. The name is changed for anonymity.
86. The name is changed for anonymity.
87. Wilbur Brookover, Laurence Beamer, Helen Efthim, Douglas Hathaway, Lawrence Lezotte, Stephen Miller, Joseph Passalacqua, and Louis Tornatzky, *Creating Effective Schools* (Holmes Beach, FL: Learning Publications, 1982); Harris Cooper, Jorgianne Robinson, and Erika Patall, "Does Homework Improve Academic Achievement? A Synthesis of Research," *Review of Educational Research* 76 (2006), pp. 1–62.
88. Herbert Walberg, Rosanne Paschal, and Thomas Weinstein, "Homework's Powerful Effects on Learning," *Educational Leadership* 42 (1985), pp. 76–79.
89. Robert Rosenthal and Lenore Jacobson, *Pygmalion in the Classroom* (New York: Holt, Rinehart & Winston, 1968).
90. Patrick Proctor, "Teacher Expectations: A Model for School Improvement," *Elementary School Journal*, March 1984,

pp. 469–481; Karin Spader, "The Effects of Teacher Expectations on Student Achievement," paper presented at the annual meeting of the American Sociological Association, Montreal, Canada, August 11, 2006; Robert Marzano, *What Works in Schools* (Alexandria, VA: Association for Supervision and Curriculum Development, 2003).

91. *The Metropolitan Life Survey of the American Teacher 2001* (New York: Harris Interactive, Inc., 2001), p. 61.
92. Lightfoot, *The Good High School*.
93. Alan M. Blankstein and Pedro Noguera, "What Works in School Turnarounds?" *Ed Week* 31, no. 17 (January 18, 2012), pp. 26, 32; Debra Viadero, "Study Finds Success in NYC's 'Small Schools,' " *Education Week* 29, no. 36 (June 23, 2010); Sam Dillon, "4,100 Students Prove 'Small Is Better' Rule Wrong," *New York Times*, September 27, 2010, p. A1; Lorna Jimerson, "The Hobbit Effect: Why Small Works in Public Schools" (2006), www.smallschoolsproject.org/PDFS/RSCT_hobbit-effect.pdf (retrieved April 23, 2009); Christina A. Samuels, "Study: Effective Principals Embrace Collective Leadership," *Education Week* 29, no. 37 (July 23, 2010); Jay Feldman, Lisette Lopez, and Katherine Simon, *Choosing Small: The Essential Guide to Successful High School Conversion* (San Francisco: Jossey Bass, 2006); Douglas Ready, Valerie Lee, and Kevin Welner, "Educational Equity and School Structure: School Size, Overcrowding, and Schools-within-Schools," *Teachers College Record* 106 (2004), pp. 1989–2014; Barbara Taylor, Michael Pressley, and David Pearson, "Research-Supported Characteristics of Teachers and Schools That Promote Reading Achievement," in B. Taylor and D. Pearson, eds., *Teaching Reading: Effective Schools, Accomplished Teachers* (Mahwah, NJ: Erlbaum, 2002), pp. 361–374; Marzano, *What Works in Schools*; Anne T. Henderson, *A New Wave of Evidence: The Impact of School, Family, and Community Connections on Student Achievement* (Austin, Texas: Southwest Educational Development Laboratory, 2002), www.sedl.org/pubs/catalog /items/fam33.html (retrieved April 23, 2009); Kevin Mixon, "Making Parent Involvement a Two-Way Street," *Teacher Magazine*, December 7, 2011, www.Teacher- Magazine.org (retrieved February 8, 2012); James P. Comer, "The Rewards of Parent Participation," *Educational Leadership* 62, no. 6 (March 21, 2005), pp. 38–42; Sabrina Tavernise, "Education Gap Grows Between Rich and Poor, Studies Say," *New York Times*, February 9, 2012, http://www.nytimes.com/2012/02/10/education/education-gap-grows-between-rich-and-poor-studies-show.html (retrieved November 21, 2016); Lisa Nielson, "4 Ways to Connect with Parents via Texting," *The Innovative Educator,* February 27, 2013, http://theinnovativeeducator.blogspot.com/2013/03/7-ways-to-connect-with-parents-via.html (retrieved April 16, 2014).
94. Anna Phillips, "In State of the City, Mayor Calls for an End to Seniority Layoffs," *GothamSchools.org*, January 19, 2011; "Study Questions Seniority-Based Teacher Layoffs," *Daily Caller*, December 23, 2010, Center for Education Data and Research, www.cedr.us; Steven Greenhouse and Sam Dillon, "A Wholesale School Shake-Up Is Embraced by the President, and Divisions Follow," *New York Times*, March 7, 2010, p. 18; Jason Felch, Jason Song, and Sandra Poindexter "In Reforming Schools, Quality of Teaching Often Overlooked," *Los Angeles Times*, December 21, 2010.
95. Mitchell Landsberg, "Influence of Teachers Unions in Question," *Los Angeles Times*, November 7, 2010, http:// articles.latimes.com/2010/nov/07/local/la-me-teachers -unions-20101107.
96. Dakarai I. Aarons, "Tennessee Targets Teaching with Race to Top Winnings: State Officials See Unique Chance for Big Change in Expectations for Schools," *Education Week* 29, no. 28 (April 2, 2010), p. 28; Catherine Gewertz, "Race to Top Rules Aim to Spur Shifts in Testing," *Education Week* 29, no. 29 (April 8, 2010), www.edweek.org/ew/articles/2010/04/07/29assessment_ep.h29.html.
97. Sam Dillon, "Teacher Ratings Get New Look, Pushed by a Very Rich Watcher," *New York Times*, December 4, 2010, pp. A1, A14; Nick Anderson, "Education Secretary Duncan and Teachers Unions Announce Summit," *Washington Post*, October 14, 2010, www.washingtonpost.com/wp-dyn/content/article/2010/10/14/AR2010101404094.html.
98. Kathleen Porter-Magee, "Trust but verify: The real lessons of Campbell's Law," *Common Core Watch*, February 26, 2013. Thomas B. Fordham Institute. https://edexcellence.net/commentary/education-gadfly-daily/common-core-watch/2013/trust-but-verify-the-real-lessons-of-campbells-law.html (retrieved July 6, 2017); "Casting Doubt on Linking Teacher Evaluations to Test Scores," *Los Angeles Times*, May 13, 2014, www.LATimes.com (retrieved May 14, 2014).
99. "Is America Listening to Its Teachers? Annual MetLife Teacher Survey Reveals Two-Thirds of Teachers Say Voices Unheard," *MetLife*, B2E News Alert, February 17, 2010; Steven Brill, "The Teachers' Union Last Stand," *New York Times Magazine*, May 23, 2010, pp. 32–39, 44, 46–47.
100. Ann Duffett, Steve Farkas, Andrew J. Rotherham, and Elena Silva, *Waiting to Be Won Over: Teachers Speak on the Profession, Unions, and Reform* (Washington, DC: Education Sector, May 2008).
101. Sharon Otterman, "Once Nearly 100%, Teacher Tenure Rate Drops to 58% as Rules Tighten," *New York Times*, July 27, 2011, www.nytimes.com/2011/07/28/nyregion/tenure-granted-to-58-of-eligible-teachers-in-city.html; Doug Ireland, "N.H. Tenure Change Makes Some Happy, Some Not," *Eagle Tribune*, July 19, 2011, www. eagletribune.com/newhampshire/x1241067726/N-H-tenure-change-makes-some-happy-some-not (retrieved January 15, 2012); Scott Martindale, "Survey: 1 in 5 Teachers Support Ending Unions," *Orange County Register*, August 3, 2011, www.ocregister.com/articles/teachers-310712-percent-tenure.html.
102. Barbara Martinez, "School 'Bonus' Plan Comes Up Short," *Wall Street Journal*, April 4, 2011, http://online.wsj.com/article/SB10001424052748703806304576236711724799444.html; Scott Travis, "Merit Pay Law Raises Questions for Florida's Specialty Teachers," *Sun Sentinel*, August 20, 2011, http://articles.sun-sentinel.com/2011-08-20/news/fl-electives-fcat-accountability-20110820_1_new-teacher-merit-music-teacher-drama-teacher (retrieved February 4, 2012); Jocelyn Wiener, "Teachers Wary on Risk, Rewards of Merit Pay" *Sacramento Bee*, January 18, 2005.
103. Circe Stumbo and Peter McWalters, "The Effective Educator Measuring Effectiveness: What Will It Take?" *Educational Leadership* 68, no. 4 (December 2010), pp. 10–15; Juan A. Lozano, "Houston to Link Teachers' Pay, Test Scores," *The*

Guardian, January 11, 2006, www.guardian.co.uk; Holly K. Hatcher and Terrence Stutz, "Incentive Pay Enters Classroom; Other States Watching as Texas Ties Teacher Bonuses to Test Scores," *Dallas Morning News*, June 12, 2006, www .dallasnews.com.

104. Stumbo and McWalters, "The Effective Educator Measuring Effectiveness"; "Teachers Willing to Talk about Merit Pay," *Chicago Daily Herald*, June 7, 2006.
105. John Norton, "These Things We Believe," *Teacher Magazine online*, February 10, 2010; Vivian Truen and Katherine C. Boles, "How 'Merit Pay' Squelches Teaching," *Boston Globe*, September 28, 2005.
106. Kenneth J. Cooper, "Performance Pay for Teachers Catches On," *Washington Post*, February 26, 2000, p. A4; Alfie Kohn, "The Folly of Merit Pay," *Education Week* 23, no. 3 (September 17, 2003), pp. 44, 31.77. Anthony S. Byrk and Barbara Schneider, "Trust in Schools: A Core Resource for School Reform," *Educational Leadership* 60, no. 6 (March 2003), pp. 40–44.
107. Anthony S. Byrk and Barbara Schneider, "Trust in Schools: A Core Resource for School Reform," *Educational Leadership* 60, no. 6 (March 2003), pp. 40–44.
108. Penny A. Bishop and Susanna W. Pflaum, "Student Perceptions of Action, Relevance, and Pace," *Middle School Journal* 36, no. 4 (March 2005), pp. 1–12.
109. National Center for Educational Statistics, *The Condition of Education 2007* (Washington, DC: U.S. Department of Education, 2007), Indicator 22: Student Preparedness.
110. Marge Scherer, "Perspectives/Learning: Whose Job Is It?" *Educational Leadership* 66, no. 3 (November 2008), p. 7; An example of some of this research in action is reported in Alexis Huicochea, "C. E. Rose Among 7 Top Grade Schools," *Arizona Daily Star*, April 27, 2012, http:// azstarnet.com/ (retrieved April 16, 2014).
111. "What Students Want from Teachers," *Educational Leadership* 66, no. 3 (November 2008), pp. 48–51.
112. Adam Fletcher, "Giving Students Ownership of Learning: The Architecture of Ownership," *Educational Leadership* 66, no. 3 (November 2008), www.ascd.org/publications /educational_leadership/nov08/vol66/num03/The_ Architecture_of_Ownership.aspx (retrieved April 15, 2009).
113. "Turning Points: Preparing American Youth for the 21st Century." *Journal Of Education Policy* 5, no. 3 (1990), http://dx.doi.org/10.1080/0268093900050305; *The Metropolitan Life Survey of the American Teacher 2000: Are We Preparing Students for the 21st Century?* (New York: Harris Interactive, Inc., 2000); *The MetLife Survey of the American Teacher: Expectations and Experiences*, Figure 3.9, p. 52 (issued September 26, 2006), www.metlife.com/Applications/Corporate /WPS/CDA /PageGenerator/0,4132,P2315,00.html (retrieved April 13, 2008).
114. Lightfoot, *The Good High School*. See also Anthony Jackson and Gayle Davis, *Turning Points: Educating Adolescents in the 21st Century* (New York: Teachers College Press, 2000).
115. Carrie R. Leana, "The Missing Link in School Reform," *Stanford Social Innovation Review*, Fall 2011, www.ssireview.org (retrieved February 3, 2012); Jeff Gregg and Diana Underwood-Gregg, "The Paradox of Education Reform," *Teachers College Record*, July 22, 2011, www.tcrecord.org/ (retrieved February 9, 2012); Paul Farhi, "Five Myths about America's schools," *Washington Post*, May 20, 2011, https://www .washingtonpost.com/opinions/five-myths-about-americas -schools/2011/05/09/AFunW27G_story.html?utm_term= .cdcbfb7a8e48 (retrieved February 7, 2012); David C. Berliner and Gene V Glass, *50 Myths and Lies That Threaten America's Public Schools: The Real Crisis in Education*.
116. Madeline Will, "Some of America's Top Teachers Went to Finland. Here's What They Learned," *Education Week*, July 22, 2016; http://blogs.edweek.org/teachers/teaching _now/2016/07/state_teachers_of_the_year_finland.html. (retrieved November 21, 2016).

CHAPTER 10: CURRICULUM, STANDARDS, AND TESTING

1. David Clouston, "1895 Saline County Exam Continues to Raise Interest," *Saline Journal*, February 2, 2008, www .saljournal.com/news/story/1895-Eighth-grade-testSE1-0123082008-02-22T16-03-32 (retrieved January 10, 2009). The test (and answers) can be retrieved at http://www .restoring-america.com/Documents/Graduation%20Examination%20Questions%20of%20Saline%20County.pdf.
2. Hilda Taba, *Curriculum Development: Theory and Practice* (New York: Harcourt Brace Jovanovich, 1962).
3. Stephen Hamilton, "Synthesis of Research on the Social Side of Schooling," *Educational Leadership* 40, no. 5 (February 1983), pp. 65–72.
4. "Climate Change: Basic Information," US Environmental Protection Agency, https://www.epa.gov/climatechange/climate -change-basic-information (retrieved November 4, 2016).
5. "Evolution." *Oxford Living Dictionaries*, https://en.oxford dictionaries.com/definition/evolution (retrieved November 4, 2016).
6. Women's Sports Foundation, *2008 Statistics—Gender Equity in High School and College Athletics: Most Recent Participation & Budget Statistics*, www.womenssportsfoundation.org / (retrieved April 17, 2009).
7. Ibid.
8. National Federation High School Athletic Association, *The Case for High School Activities*, http://www.nfhs.org/articles/ the-case-for-high-school-activities (retrieved October 26, 2016); Caeey A. Knifsend and Sandra Graham, "Too Much of a Good Thing? How Breadth of Extracurricular Participation Relates to School-Related Affect and Academic Outcomes During Adolescence," *Youth Adolescence* 41 (2012), p. 379, doi:10.1007/s10964-011-9737-4.
9. National Federation High School Athletic Association, "Lacrosse, Bowling among Nation's Emerging High Sports," www.nfhs.org (retrieved April 17, 2009); Staci Hupp, "As Fastest Growing High School Sport, Bowling a Hit," *Dallas Morning News*, October 23, 2007.
10. June Kronholz, "Academic Value of Non-Academics: The Case for Keeping Extracurriculars," *Education Next* 12, no. 1 (Winter 2012), http://educationnext.org/.
11. *The Case for High School Activities*; Jennifer A. Fredericks and Jacquelynne S. Eccles, "Developmental Benefits of Extracurricular Involvement: Do Peer Characteristics Mediate the Link between Activities and Youth Outcomes?" *Journal of Youth and Adolescence* 34, no. 6 (December 2005), pp. 507–520; John Holloway, "Extracurricular Activities and

Student Participation," *Educational Leadership* 60, no. 1 (September 2002), pp. 80–81.

12. National Center for Education Statistics, *Trends Among High School Seniors, 1972–2004* (Washington, DC: U.S Department of Education, 2008); Women's Sports Foundation, *Go Out and Play: Youth Sports in America* (October 2008), www.womenssportsfoundation.org.
13. John Hoffman, "Extracurricular Activities, Athletic Participation, and Adolescent Alcohol Use: Gender-Differentiated and School-Contextual Effects," *Journal of Health and Social Behavior* 47 (September 2006), pp. 275–290; Fredericks and Eccles, "Developmental Benefits of Extracurricular Involvement."
14. Sean Cavanaugh, "Electives Getting the Boot? It Depends on Where and What," *Education Week* 35, no. 2 (April 19, 2006), p. 7
15. Bobbi Ann Starnes, "Textbooks, School Reform, and the Silver Lining," *Phi Delta Kappan* 86, no. 2 (2004), pp. 170–171; L. Fan and G. Kaeley, "The Influence of Textbooks on Teaching Strategies," *Mid-Western Educational Researcher* 13, no. 4 (2000), pp. 2–9; A. Woodward and D. L. Elliot, "Textbook Use and Teacher Professionalism," in D. L. Elliot and A. Woodward, eds., *Textbooks and Schooling in the United States, 89th Yearbook of the National Society for the Study of Education* (Chicago: University of Chicago Press, 1990), pp. 178–193.
16. Association of American Publishers, "How Publishers Present Contemporary Milestones," http://publishers.org/our-markets/prek-12-learning/how-publishers-present-contemporary-milestones. (retrieved October 24, 2016).
17. Tamar Lewis, "Children's Publisher Backing Off Its Corporate Ties," *New York Times*, July 31, 2011, www.nytimes.com/2011/08/01/education/01scholastic.html (retrieved April 4, 2012).
18. Paul Barry, "Interview: A Talk with A. Bartlett Giamatti," *College Review Board* (Spring 1982), p. 48.
19. Diane Ravitch, *The Death and Life of the Great American School System: How Testing and Choice Are Undermining Education* (New York: Basic Books, 2010); Alexis Hulcochea, "Education Expert Knocks Reform in Schools, Standardized Testing," *Arizona Star*, February 19, 2011, p. A5.
20. David Kastberg, Jessica Ying Chan, Gordon Murray, and Patrick Gonzales, "Performance of U.S. 15-Year-Old Students in Science, Reading, and Mathematics Literacy in an International Context: First Look at PISA 2015," National Center for Educational Statistics, U.S. Department of Education, December 2016, http://nces.ed.gov/pubs2017/2017048.pdf (retrieved December 6, 2016); David Nagel, "PISA Results: Math Down, Science and Reading Flat for U.S. Students," *The Journal*, December 6, 2016, https://thejournal.com/articles/2016/12/06/pisa-results-math-down-science-and-reading-flat-for-u.s.-students.aspx (retrieved December 6, 2016).
21. Gregory Korte, "The Every Student Succeeds Act Vs. No Child Left Behind: What's Changed?" *USA Today*, December 11, 2015, http://www.usatoday.com/story/news/politics/2015/12/10/every-student-succeeds-act-vs-no-child-left-behind-whats-changed/77088780/ (retrieved October 20, 2016).
22. Alyson Klein, "States, Districts Will Share More Power Under ESSA." *Education Week* 35, no. 1 (January 6, 2016), pp. 10-11.
23. Ibid; NEA, "Why Educators Support the Every Student Succeeds Act (S. 1117)," December 2015, p.2, http://educationvotes.nea.org/wp-content/uploads/2015/12/Why-educators-support-the-Every-Student-Succeeds-Act.pdf (retrieved October 20, 2016).
24. Helen Cooper, "Obama Urges Education Law Overhaul," *New York Times*, March 15, 2011, p. A22; Gail Russell Chaddock, "No Child Left Behind: Why Congress will Struggle to Hit Obama Deadline," *Christian Science Monitor*, March 14, 2011; Michele McNeil, "Majority of States Say They'll Seek Waivers Under NCLB," *Education Week*, October 13, 2011, www.educationweek.com (retrieved March 12, 2012); "The Wrong Fix for No Child Left Behind," *New York Times*, October 26, 2011, www.nytimes. com (retrieved March 12, 2012); Peter DeWitt, "What Would You Do If You Were U.S. Secretary of Education?" *Education Week*/Finding Common Ground (blog), February 22, 2013, http://blogs.edweek.org/edweek/finding_common_ground/ (retrieved January 3, 2014); Tara Garcia Mathewson, "Ed Dept. Releases Final ESSA Assessment Regulations," *EdDive*, December 8, 2016, http://www.educationdive.com/news/eddeptreleasesfinalessaassessmentregulations/431960/ (retrieved December 8, 2016).
25. Common Core State Standards Initiative, www.corestandards.org/ (retrieved February 17, 2011). These standards were developed by the Council of Chief State School Officers and the National Governors Association; Catherine Gewertz, "Gates Awards 15 Grants for Common-Standards Work," *Education Week* 29, no. 22 (February 18, 2010), www.edweek.org/ew/articles/2010/02/18/22gates.h29.html (retrieved January 19, 2011); David Keyes, "Classroom Caste System," *Washington Post*, April 9, 2007, p. A13.
26. Robert Rothman, "Five Myths About the Common Core State Standards," *Harvard Education Letter* 27, no. 5 (September/October 2011); Nancy Badertscher, "Teachers See Change Coming in Common Core State Standards," *Atlanta Journal-Constitution*, September 27, 2011, www.ajc.com (retrieved March 15, 2012); University of Virginia, "Students Benefit from Depth, Rather than Breadth, in High School Science Courses," *ScienceDaily*, March 10, 2009, www.sciencedaily.com/releases/2009/03/090305131814.htm (retrieved April 19, 2009); see also Kelly Gallagher, "Why I Will Not Teach to the Test: It's Time to Focus on In-Depth Learning, Not Shallow Answers," *Education Week* 30, no. 12 (November 17, 2010), pp. 29, 36; Alice Bidwell, "The History of Common Core State Standards," *US News and World Report*, February 27, 2014, www.usnews.com (retrieved May 13, 2014); Kenneth Chang, "With Common Core, Fewer Topics but Covered More Rigorously," *New York Times*, September 2, 2013, www.nytimes.com (retrieved May 13, 2014).
27. Jessica Presinzano, "Clifton School Board Candidates Discuss Common Core," *Clifton Journal*, October 21, 2016, http://www.northjersey.com/news/education/school-board-candidates-discuss-common-core-1.1680883 (retrieved October 24, 2016).
28. Diane Ravitch defends Louis C.K., takes down silly *Newsweek* piece: "Your belief . . . has no research to support it, nor is there any real-world evidence," May 9, 2014, www.salon.com (retrieved May 14, 2014).
29. Catherine Gewertz, "Districts Gear Up for Shift to Informational Texts," *Education Week*, March 13, 2012, www.edweek.org (retrieved March 15, 2012); Tennille Tracy, "School Standards Wade into Climate Debate," *Wall Street Journal*, March 11, 2012, www.wallstreetjournal.com (retrieved March 15, 2012); Sarah

D. Sparks, "Experts Say Social Sciences Are 'Left Behind'," *Education Week*, November 30, 2011, www.edweek.org/ew/articles/2011/11/30/13social.h31.html (retrieved March 21, 2012).

30. Catherine Gewertz, "Few States Cite Full Plans for Carrying Out Standards," *Education Week* 31, no. 17 (January 12, 2012), www.edweek.org (retrieved March 17, 2012); Catherine Gewertz, "Preparedness For Common Standards: A Work in Progress," *Education Week*, March 19, 2012, www.edweek.org (retrieved March 20, 2012); Stephanie Hirsh, "Common-Core Work Must Include Teacher Development; Standards Movement Must Embrace Teacher Professional Learning," *Education Week*, January 31, 2012, www.educationweek.com (retrieved March 26, 2012); Erik W. Robelen, "Literacy Wins, History Loses in Federal Budget; Foreign-Language, Civics, Economics Aid also Scrapped," *Education Week*, January 6, 2012, www.edweek.org (retrieved April 5, 2012); Valerie Strauss, "More States Delay Common Core Testing as Concerns Grow," *New York Times*, November 24, 2013, www.nytimes.com (retrieved May 12, 2014).
31. Michael Alison Chandler, "Montgomery County Is Paving the Way for New School Standards," *Washington Post*, September 3, 2011, www.washingtonpost.com (retrieved March 12, 2012); Fernando Santos, "A Trial Run for School Standards That Encourage Deeper Thought," *New York Times*, April 24, 2011, www.nytimes.com (retrieved March 13, 2012); Catherine Gewertz, "Academics Find Common Standards Fit for College, But Academics Maintain Some Skills Are Missing," *Education Week* 31, no. 2 (August 25, 2011), pp. 1, 12–13; Andrew Hacker and Claudia Dreifus, "Who's Minding the Schools?" *New York Times*, June 8, 2013, www.nytimes.com (retrieved May 13, 2014); Paul Barnwell, "Will the Common Core Derail True College and Career Readiness?" *Education Week* Teacher, June 25, 2013, www.edweek.org (retrieved May 3, 2014).
32. Alfie Kohn, "Debunking the Case for National Standards," *Education Week* 29, no. 17 (January 14, 2010), pp. 28, 30; Ze'ev Wurman and W. Stephen Wilson, "The Common Core Math Standards: Are They a Step Forward or Backward?" *Education Next* 12, no. 3 (Summer 2012); Catherine Gewertz, "Critics Post 'Manifesto' Opposing Shared Curriculum; More Than 100 Critics Sign Opposing Document," *Education Week*, May 9, 2011, updated May 17, 2011, www.educationweek.com (retrieved March 21, 2012); Lesli A. Maxwell, "Common-Core Needs Dominate Districts' Curriculum Priorities, Survey Finds," *Ed Week*, December 2, 2013, www.blogs.edweek.org (retrieved May 15, 2014).
33. Linda Darling-Hammond, *The Flat World and Education: How America's Commitment to Equity Will Determine Our Future* (New York: Teachers' College Press, 2010).
34. Sharon Nichols and David Berliner, *Collateral Damage: How High-Stakes Testing Corrupts America's Schools* (Cambridge, MA: Harvard Education Press, 2007).
35. John Merrow, "Undermining Standards," *Phi Delta Kappan* 82, no. 9 (May 2009), p. 655.
36. Kate Zernike, "Scarsdale Mothers Succeed in First Boycott of 8th-Grade Test," *New York Times*, May 4, 2001, http://tv.nytimes.com/learning/general/specials/testing/04SCAR.html (retrieved January 16, 2005); "Wary of Standardized Testing, Parents Are Increasingly Opting their Kids Out of Exams," *Washington Post*, September 8, 2013, www.washpost.com (retrieved May 13, 2014).
37. Lisa Robinson, "City Students Protest Validity of PARCC Testing." *WBAL-TV*, April 15, 2016, http://www.wbaltv.com/education/city-students-protest-validity-of-parcc-testing/39050762 (retrieved October 24, 2016).
38. Michael A. Fletcher, "High Stakes Rise, School Group Put Exam to Test," *Washington Post*, July 9, 2001, p. A1; Michele Kurtz, "Berkshire District to Flout MCAS Rule," *Boston Globe*, February 21, 2003, p. B5; David Hoff, "Teacher Probed for Role in Anti-Testing Activity," *Education Week* 21, no. 36 (May 15, 2002), p. 3.
39. David Keyes, "Classroom Caste System," *Washington Post*, April 9, 2007, p. A13; Marc Tucker, Linda Darling-Hammond, and John Jackson, "Fewer, Better Tests Can Boost Student Achievement," *Education Week*, October 7, 2013, edweek.org (retrieved January 14, 2014).
40. Monty Neill, "The Dangers of Testing," *Educational Leadership* 60, no. 5 (February 2003), pp. 43–46; Nichols and Berliner, *Collateral Damage: How High-Stakes Testing Corrupts America's Schools*.
41. Alfie Kohn, *The Case Against Standardized Testing: Raising Scores and Ruining Schools* (Portsmouth, NH: Heinemann, 2000); Dalia Zabala, *State High School Exit Exams: Patterns in Gaps in Pass Rates* (Center on Education Policy, February 2008), www.cep-dc.org/ (retrieved April 27, 2008); The Civil Rights Project at Harvard and the Urban Institute, "Only '50-50' Chance of High School Graduation for U.S. Minority Students, Weak Accountability Rules Found," February 25, 2004, http://www.prnewswire.com/news-releases/study—only-50-50-chance-of-high-school-graduation-for-us-minority-students-weak-accountability-rules-found-71822462.html (retrieved February 6, 2017).
42. Jennifer Booher-Jennings, "Rationing Education," *Washington Post*, October 5, 2006, p. A33.
43. "Primary Sources: 2012: America's Teachers on the Teaching Profession," A Project of Scholastic and the Bill & Melinda Gates Foundation, March 2012, www.scholastic.com/primarysources/download.asp (retrieved April 6, 2012); Anthony Rebora, "Teachers Place Little Value on Standardized Testing" *Education Week* 31, no. 26 (March 28, 2012) p. 14; The report is available at www.scholastic.com/primarysources/pdfs/Gates2012_ full.pdf.
44. Diane Rado, "New ISAT Lets Kids Pass with More Wrong Answers," *Chicago Tribune*, October 18, 2010, www.chicagotribune.com/news/education/ct-met-isat-answers-20101018,0,308277.story; Ben Feller, "Gaps Appear in State, Federal Test Scores," *Boston Globe*, March 3, 2006; Susan Saulny, "Meaning of 'Proficient' Varies for Schools Across Country," *New York Times*, January 19, 2005; Nichols and Berliner, *Collateral Damage: How High-Stakes Testing Corrupts America's Schools*; David Sadker and Karen Zittleman, "Test Anxiety: Are Students Failing Tests—or Are Tests Failing Students?" *Phi Delta Kappan*, 85, no. 10 (June 2004), pp. 740–751.
45. Nichols and Berliner, *Collateral Damage*; Sadker and Zittleman, "Test Anxiety."
46. Valerie Strauss, "Study: Test-Score Gains Don't Mean Cognitive Gains," *Washington Post*, December 16, 2013, www.washpost.com (retrieved May 3, 2014).
47. James Hoffman, Assaf Czop, Lori Paris, and Scott Paris, "High-Stakes Testing in Reading: Today in Texas, Tomorrow?" *The Reading Teacher* 54, no. 5 (February 2001), pp. 482–492.

48. Alex Kingsbury, "Schools Cut Other Subjects to Teach Reading and Math," *U.S. News and World Report*, July 25, 2007, www.usnews.com/usnews/edu/articles/070725/25nclb.htm (retrieved April 19, 2009).
49. Connie Langland, "Tests No Help to Learning," *Philadelphia Inquirer*, May 29, 2003.
50. Fran Smith, "Why Arts Education Is Crucial and Who Is Doing It Best," *Edutopia*, February 18, 2009, www. edutopia.org /arts-music-curriculum-child-development; Stephanie Perrin, "Why Arts Education Matters," *Education Week* 27, no. 21 (January 30, 2008), pp. 26–27; Shirley Dang, "Schools Pile on English, Math Classes," *Contra Costa Times*, May 19, 2007.
51. Michele Kurtz, "Teachers' Views Mixed on Testing," *Boston Globe*, March 5, 2003, p. B5; "Why Arts Education Matters"; Sarah M. Fine, "Consumed by Failure," *Education Week* 28, no. 25 (March 18, 2009), pp. 22–23
52. Kathleen Kennedy Manzo, "Protests over State Testing Widespread," *Education Week*, May 16, 2001; Howard Blume, "L.A. Teachers' Union Calls for Boycott of Testing," *Parajo Valley Federation of Teachers*, January 18, 2009, www.pvft.net.
53. "Survey: 70 Percent of Educators Say State Assessments Not Developmentally Appropriate," *NEAToday*, February 18, 2016, http://neatoday.org/2016/02/18/standardized-tests-not-developmentally-appropriate/.
54. Abby Goodnough, "Strain of Fourth-Grade Tests Drive Off Veteran Teachers," *New York Times*, June 14, 2001, http://www.nytimes.com/2001/06/14/nyregion/strain-of-fourth-grade-tests-drives-off-veteran-teachers.html (retrieved February 6, 2017); Liz Seymour, "SOL Tests Create New Dropouts," *Washington Post*, July 17, 2001, pp. A1, A8.
55. "Florida School Districts Suspend Online FCAT After Glitches." *Tampa Bay Times,* April 22, 2014, http://www.tampabay.com/news/education/k12/pasco-hernando-schools-battling-computer-problems-during-fcat/2176268; "A History of Pearson's Testing Problems Worldwide." *Washington Post*, May 6, 2014, https://www.washingtonpost.com/news/answer-sheet/wp/2014/05/06/a-history-of-pearsons-testing-problems-worldwide/ (retrieved October 26, 2016).
56. Nancy Kober, "Teaching to the Test: The Good, the Bad, and Who's Responsible," *TestTalk for Leaders*, June 2002; Michele Kurtz and Anand Vaishnav, "Student's MCAS Answer Means 449 Others Pass," *Boston Globe*, December 5, 2002, p. A1.
57. Diana B. Henriques and Jacques Steinberg, "Right Answer, Wrong Score: Test Flaws Take Toll," *New York Times*, May 20, 2001, http://www.nytimes.com/2001/05/20/business/right-answer-wrong-score-test-flaws-take-toll.html (retrieved February 6, 2017); Thomas M. Haladyna, "Perils of Standardized Achievement Testing," *Educational Horizons* 85, no. 1 (Fall 2006), pp. 30–43. See also the National Center for Fair and Open Testing, www.fairtest.org; Catherine Gewertz, "More Testing Seen for High School Students," *Education Week* 30, no. 15 (December 21, 2010).
58. Kathleen Kennedy Manzo, "Protests over State Testing Widespread," *Education Week*, May 16, 2001; Howard Blume, "L.A. Teachers' Union Calls for Boycott of Testing," *Parajo Valley Federation of Teachers*, January 18, 2009, www.pvft.net.
59. "Primary Sources: 2012: America's Teachers on the Teaching Profession." Scholastiic Pubications, retrieved at https://www.scholastic.com/teachers/collections/teaching-content/primary-sources-2012/.
60. Linda Darling-Hammond, "Value-Added Evaluation Hurts Teaching," *Ed Week* 31, no. 24 (March 5, 2012), www.edweek.com (retrieved March 6, 2012).
61. "Clashes Between Police, Teachers After Protest Against Mandatory Testing Leave 4 Dead in Mexico," *Associated Press*, June 19, 2016, http://www.timesfreepress.com/news/breakingnews/story/2016/jun/19/clashes-between-police-teachers-after-protest-against-mandatory-testing-leaves-4-dead-mexico/371810/.
62. "Report of the Office of the Governor," Special Investigators, June 30, 2011, www.courthousenews.com/2011/07/27/APS1.pdf; "Suspicious Test Scores Across the Nation," *Atlanta Journal-Constitution*, March 25, 2012, www.ajc.com/news/may-2012-suspicious-test-scores-across-the-nation/tqQClmddqVKAnoZepPd8ql/; "APS Cheating Scandal," *Atlanta Journal-Constitution* (undated summary), www.ajc.com/news/school-test-scores/; "Atlanta Educators Convicted in School Cheating Scandal," *New York Times*, April 1, 2015, www.nytimes.com/2015/04/02/us/verdict-reached-in-atlanta-school-testing-trial.html.
63. "Trust but verify: The real lessons of Campbell's Law," *Common Core Watch*, February 26, 2013. Thomas B. Fordham Institute. https://edexcellence.net/commentary/education-gadfly-daily/common-core-watch/2013/trust-but-verify-the-real-lessons-of-campbells-law.html (retrieved July 6, 2017; "How and Why Convicted Atlanta Teachers Cheated on Standardized Tests," *Washington Post*, April 1, 2015, www.washingtonpost.com/news/answer-sheet/wp/2015/04/01/how-and-why-convicted-atlanta-teachers-cheated-on-standardized-tests/.
64. Christina A. Samuels, "Cheating Scandals Intensify Focus on Test Pressures," *Ed Week*, August 4, 2011, www.edweek.com (retrieved April 4, 2012).
65. Ibid.
66. Malcolm Gladwell, *The Tipping Point: How Little Things Can Make a Big Difference* (New York, Back Bay Books, 2002), p. 12.
67. Richard Elmore, "Testing Trap," adapted from *Education Next* 105 (September/October 2002), p. 35; Barbara Gleason, "ASCD Adopts Positions in High-Stakes Testing and the Achievement Gap," *ASCD Conference News*, March 20–22, 2004.
68. Grant Wiggins, "Healthier Testing Made Easier," EDUTOPIQ George Lucas Educational Foundation, April 6, 2006, www.edutopia.org/magazine/.
69. "Primary Sources: 2012: America's Teachers on the Teaching Profession"; Sonja Steptoe, "How Nebraska Leaves No Child Behind," *Time*, May 30, 2007; Winnie Hu, "Schools Move toward Following Students' Yearly Progress on Tests," *New York Times*, July 6, 2007, www.nytimes.com/2007/07/06/education/06test.html (retrieved May 21, 2008).
70. Theodore Sizer, *Horace's School: Redesigning the American High School* (New York: Houghton Mifflin, 1992).
71. Craig Timberg, "Bible's Second Coming," *Washington Post*, June 4, 2000, p. A1.
72. "Public School Drops Christian Textbooks," *Washington Post*, September 17, 1999, p. 2.
73. Lee C. Bollinger and William G. Ross, "First Amendment," in Kermit L. Hall, et al (eds.), *The Oxford Guide to the Supreme Court of the United States* (New York: Oxford University Press, 2005), p. 346.

74. "CEO Cuts 'Creationism' from Youngstown School Classrooms," *WFMJ*, September 10, 2016, http://www.wfmj.com/story/33007921/ceo-cuts-creationism-from-youngstown-school-classrooms.
75. "How Evolution is Taught in Texas Schools May Stir New Fight," *Austin (TX) American-Statesman*, September 25, 2016, http://www.mystatesman.com/news/news/state-regional-govt-politics/will-creationism-be-stripped-from-texas-curriculum/nsfKZ/.
76. Steve Olson, "An Argument's Mutating Terms," *Washington Post*, March 20, 2005, p. B01.
77. Stephen Meyer, "Intelligent Design vs. Evolution," PBS, *Think Tank with Ben Wattenberg* (aired 10/12/2006), http://www.pbs.org/thinktank/transcript1244.html (retrieved November 4, 2016).
78. Mark Sappenfield and Mary Beth McCauley, "God or Science?" *Christian Science Monitor*, November 23, 2004; Lisa Anderson, "Darwin's Theory Evolves into Culture War Kansas Curriculum Is Focal Point of Wider Struggle Across Nation," *Chicago Tribune*, May 22, 2005, www.religionnewsblog.com/11267/darwins-theory-evolves-into-culture-war (retrieved March 5, 2008); Scott Stephens, "Panel OKs Disputed 10th-grade Biology Plan," *Cleveland Plain Dealer*, March 10, 2004, www.cleveland.com/debate/index.ssf?/debate/more/1078914742102330.html (retrieved July 18, 2007).
79. "Tennessee Monkey Bill Becomes (Unsigned) Law," *Wall Street Journal*, April 11, 2012, www.wsj.com (retrieved April 12, 2012).
80. Alison Flood, "Free-Speech Group Slams Portland Schools' Ban on Books That Question Climate Change," *The Guardian*, June 6, 2016, https://www.theguardian.com/books/2016/jun/06/portland-schools-ban-on-books-questioning-climate-change-national-coalition-against-censorship-ncac (retrieved October 25, 2016).
81. Shasta Kearns Moore, "Portland school board bans climate change-denying materials," *Portland Tribune*, May 19, 2016, http://portlandtribune.com/sl/307848-185832-portland-school-board-bans-climate-change-denying-materials (retrieved October 25, 2016).
82. David Van Biema, "The Case for Teaching the Bible," *Time*, March 22, 2007, www.time.com/time/magazine/article/0,9171,1601845,00.html; G. Jeffrey MacDonald, "Now Evolving in Biology Classes: A Testier Climate," *Christian Science Monitor*, May 3, 2005, www.csmonitor. com/2005/0503/p01s04-legn.html.
83. Michael Alison Chandler, "Two Guys and a Chick Set Off Tiff over School Library Policy," *Washington Post*, February 17, 2008, p. C06. For an extensive discussion on censorship and intellectual freedom, see the American Library Association, http://www.ala.org/advocacy/intfreedom/censorshipfirstamendmentissues/ifcensorshipqanda and http://www.ala.org/advocacy/intfreedom/censorshipfirstamendmentissues (retrieved January 9, 2017).
84. American Library Association, "Frequently Challenged Books," http://www.ala.org/bbooks/frequentlychallengedbooks (retrieved January 9, 2017).
85. Ibid and "Librarians Pressed to Ban Dr. Seuss 'Hop on Pop' for Violent Undertones," *Washington Times*, April 30, 2014, http://www.washingtontimes.com/news/2014/apr/30/librarians-pressed-ban-dr-seuss-hop-pop-violent-un/.
86. Joan Bertin and Millie Davis, "Comparing Librarians' and Teachers' Self-Censoring Patterns," *School Library Journal*, September 26, 2016, http://www.slj.com/2016/09/censorship/comparing-librarians-and-teachers-self-censoring-patterns/.
87. Chandler, "Two Guys and a Chick Set Off Tiff over School Library Policy."
88. Michael Bugeja, "The Fuss," *Inside Higher Ed*, October 25, 2016, https://www.insidehighered.com/advice/2016/10/25/teaching-controversial-topics-age-microaggressions-trigger-warnings-and-tweeting.
89. Winnie Hu, "A Call for Opening Up Web Access at Schools," *New York Times*, September 28, 2011, www. nytimes.com (retrieved April 4, 2012).
90. Quoted in Lynne Cheney, *Humanities in America: A Report to the President, Congress and the American People* (Washington, DC: National Endowment for the Humanities, 1988), p. 17.
91. Allan Bloom, *The Closing of the American Mind* (New York: Simon & Schuster, 1987), p. 63.
92. E. D. Hirsch Jr., *Cultural Literacy: What Every American Needs to Know* (New York: Vintage Books, 1988); *What Your First Grader Needs to Know and What Your Second Grader Needs to Know* (New York: Doubleday, 1991).
93. James Banks, "Multicultural Education: For Freedom's Sake," *Educational Leadership* 49, no. 4 (December 1991/ January 1992), pp. 32–36.
94. Todd Oppenheimer, "The Computer Delusion," *Atlantic Monthly*, July 1997, pp. 45–48, 50–56, 61–62.
95. Andrew Trotter, "Major Study on Software Stirs Debate," *Education Week*, April 4, 2007; Greg Toppo, "Computers May Not Boost Student Achievement," *USA Today*, April 11, 2006; North Central Regional Educational Laboratory (2005), "Critical Issue: Using Technology to Improve Student Achievement," www.ncrel.org/sdrs/areas/issues/ methods/technlgy/te800.htm (retrieved April 17, 2008).
96. Trotter, "Major Study on Software Stirs Debate."
97. "The Effects of Computers on Student Writing: What the Research Tells Us," *ASCD SmartBrief* 1, no. 7 (April 1, 2003), www.ascd.org; Jennifer Lee, "I Think, Therefore IM" *New York Times*, September 19, 2002, http://www.nytimes.com/2002/09/19/technology/i-think-therefore-im.html (retrieved February 6, 2017); Victoria Irwin, "Hop, Skip . . . and Software?" *Christian Science Monitor*, March 11, 2003.
98. Regan McMahon, "Everybody Does It," *San Francisco Chronicle*, September 9, 2007, http://www.sfgate.com/education/article/Everybody-Does-It-2523376.php (retrieved January 9, 2017); Don McCabe, "Levels of Cheating and Plagiarism Remain High," *Center for Academic Integrity* (June 2005), www.academicintegrity.org.
99. "Teens, Social Media & Technology Overview 2015," *Pew Research Center*, April 9, 2015, http://www.pewinternet.org/2015/04/09/teens-social-media-technology-2015/.
100. "Schools Seek Balance for Cellphones In Class," *Boston Globe*, June 16, 2015, https://www.bostonglobe.com/lifestyle/style/2015/06/15/cellphones-school-teaching-tool-distraction/OzHjXyL7VVIXV1AEkeYTiJ/story.html.
101. Qiufeng Gao, Zheng Yan, Chuqian Wei, Yuying Liang, and Lei Mo, "Three different roles, five different aspects: Differences and similarities in viewing school mobile phone policies among teachers, parents, and students," *Computers & Education* 106, March 2017, pp. 13–25, http://www.sciencedirect.com/science/article/pii/S0360131516302305.

102. Andrew Trotter, "Closing the Digital Divide," *Education Week* 20, no. 35 (2001), pp. 37–38, 40; Maisie McAdoo, "The Real Digital Divide: Quality Not Quantity," in David T. Gordon, ed., *The Digital Classroom* (Cambridge, MA: Harvard College, 2000), pp. 143–151; U.S. Department of Education, National Center for Education Statistics, "Computers and Technology," *Digest of Educational Statistics*, 2008, Tables 427–432 (issued March 2009), http://nces.ed.gov.
103. U.S. Department of Education, National Center for Education Statistics, "Computers and Technology"; Chris Rother, "Teachers Talk Tech," *Technological Horizons in Education* 33, no. 3, (2005), pp. 34–36; Trotter, "Minorities Still Face Digital Divide," p. 14.
104. Ellen McCarthy, "Where Girls and Tech Make a Match," *Washington Post*, March 20, 2003, p. E1; Trotter, "Closing the Digital Divide," pp. 37–38, 40; Andrew Trotter, "Minorities Still Face Digital Divide," *Education Week* 26, no. 3, (2006), p. 14.
105. Glen Bull and Joe Garofalo, "Internet Access: The Last Mile," *Learning and Leading with Technology* 32, no. 1 (September 2004), pp. 16–18, 21.
106. Larry Cuban, "Growing Instructional Technology in U.S. Classrooms" (J. George Jones and Velma Rife Jones Lecture: University of Utah, Salt Lake City, 2005).
107. Tamar Lewin, "Children's Computer Use Grows, but Gaps Persist, Study Says," *New York Times*, January 22, 2001, p. A11, http://www.nytimes.com/2001/01/22/us/children-s-computer-use-grows-but-gaps-persist-study-says.html (retrieved February 6, 2017).
108. Selma Wasserman, "Teaching for Thinking: Louis E. Raths Revisited," *Phi Delta Kappan* 68, no. 6 (February 1987), pp. 460–666; Valerie Strauss, "Relentless Questioning Paves a Deeper Path," *Washington Post*, February 18, 2008, p. B2.
109. Council for Economic Education, "2016 National State of Financial and Economic Education," http://www.surveyofthestates.com/.
110. Alexandra Brown, J. Michael Collins, Maximilian Schmeiser, and Carly Urban, "State Mandated Financial Education and the Credit Behavior of the Young," Financial Industry Regulatory Authority Investor Education Foundation, January, 2016, http://www.finrafoundation.org/web/groups/foundation/@foundation/documents/foundation/p602381.pdf.
111. Scott Melville, "Implications of the Physical Educators' Wellness Role," *Journal of Physical Education, Recreation, and Dance* 80, no. 2 (February 2009), p. 58.
112. Erik Robelen, "U.S. Must Bolster Civic Learning in Schools, Report Says," *Education Week*, September 19, 2011, www.educationweek.com (retrieved April 5, 2012); Erik W. Robelen, "Most Students Lack Civics Proficiency on NAEP," *Education Week*, May 4, 2011, www.edweek.org (retrieved April 5, 2012).
113. Joseph L. DeVitis, John Martin Rich, *The Success Ethic, Education, and the American Dream*, (Albany: State University of New York Press, 1996) p. 68.

CHAPTER 11: BECOMING AN EFFECTIVE TEACHER

1. Jeff Marshal, *The Highly Effective Teacher: 7 Classroom-Tested Practices That Foster Student Success* (Alexandria, VA: ASCD, 2016), Annie Lowrey, "Big Study Links Good Teachers to Lasting Gain," *New York Times* (January 6, 2012), http://www.nytimes.com/2012/01/06/education/big-study-links-good-teachers-to-lasting-gain.html.
2. Robert Shostak, "Involving Students in Learning," in James M. Cooper, ed., *Classroom Teaching Skills,* 10th ed. (Belmont, CA: Cengage, 2014), pp. 89–118; Marshal, *The Highly Effective Teacher.*
3. John Goodlad, *A Place Called School,* 2nd ed. (New York: McGraw-Hill, 2004).
4. Deborah Loewenberg Ball and Francesca M. Forzani, "Teaching Skillful Teaching," *Educational Leadership,* December 2010/January 2011, pp. 40–45; Shostak, "Involving Students in Learning"; Carol Weinstein and Wilford Weber, "Classroom Management," in James M. Cooper, ed., *Classroom Teaching Skills,* 10th ed. (Belmont, CA: Cengage, 2014), pp. 238–282.
5. Marshal, *The Highly Effective Teacher*; Shostak, "Involving Students in Learning."
6. Dominque Smith and Douglas Fisher, *Better than Carrots or Sticks: Restoration Practices for Positive Classroom Management*, (Alexandra, VA: ASCD, 2015); Weinstein and Weber, "Classroom Management."
7. Weinstein and Weber, "Classroom Management"; C. M. Charles, *Building Classroom Discipline,* 11th ed. (Upper Saddle River: Prentice Hall, 2013).
8. Smith and Fischer, *Better than Carrots or Sticks;* Weinstein and Weber, "Classroom Management."
9. Smith and Fischer, *Better than Carrots or Sticks*"; Jane Nelson, Lynn Lott, and H. Stephen Glenn, *Positive Discipline in the Classroom: Developing Mutual Respect, Cooperation, and Responsibility in Your Classroom*, 4th ed. (New York: Three Rivers Press, 2013).
10. Smith and Fischer, *Better than Carrots or Sticks*; Weinstein and Weber, "Classroom Management."
11. Ibid.
12. Kathleen Cushman, *Fires in the Bathroom: Advice for Teachers from High School Students* (New York: The New Press, 2005).
13. David Berliner, "What Do We Know About Well- Managed Classrooms? Putting Research to Work," *Instructor* 94, no. 6 (February 1985), p. 15.
14. Arno Bellack, *The Language of the Classroom* (New York: Teachers College Press, 1966); David Sadker, Myra Sadker, and Karen R. Zittleman, "Questioning Skills," in James Cooper, ed., *Classroom Teaching Skills*, 10th ed. (Belmont, CA: Cengage, 2013), pp. 119–167.
15. Several of the sections on the pedagogical cycle are adopted from Sadker, Sadker, and Zittleman, "Questioning Skills."
16. Sadker, Sadker, and Zittleman, "Questioning Skills."
17. John Dewey, *How We Think,* rev. ed. (Boston: D. C. Heath, 1933), p. 266.
18. Tara García Mathewson, "Teacher Expectations Top List of Effects on Student Achievement," *The Dive* (July 5, 2016), http://www.educationdive.com/news/teacher-expectations-top-list-of-effects-on-student-achievement/422029/;Sadker, Sadker, and Zittleman, "Questioning Skills"; Marshal, *The Highly Effective Teacher.*
19. Benjamin Bloom (ed.), *Taxonomy of Educational Objectives, Handbook I: Cognitive Domain* (New York: David McKay, 1956); Lorin Anderson and David Krathwohl, *A Taxonomy for Learning, Teaching, and Assessing: A Revision of Bloom's*

Taxonomy of Educational Objectives (Upper River Saddle, NJ: Pearson, 2013).

20. Anderson and Krathwohl, *A Taxonomy for Learning, Teaching, and Assessing: A Revision of Bloom's Taxonomy of Educational Objectives;* Sadker, Sadker, and Zittleman, "Questioning Skills".
21. Marshal, *The Highly Effective Teacher;* Sadker, Sadker, and Zittleman, "Questioning Skills".
22. David Sadker, Myra Sadker, and Karen R. Zittleman, "Questioning Skills," in James Cooper, ed., Classroom Teaching Skills, 10th ed. (Belmont, CA: Cengage, 2013), pp. 119–167.
23. Mary Budd Rowe, "Wait Time: Slowing Down May Be a Way of Speeding Up!" *Journal of Teacher Education* 37 (January/February 1986), pp. 43–50; Sadker, Sadker, and Zittleman, "Questioning Skills."
24. Ibid.
25. Sadker, Sadker, and Zittleman, "Questioning Skills."
26. John Goodlad, *A Place Called School,* 2nd ed. (New York: McGraw-Hill, 2004).
27. Grant Wiggins, "Seven Keys to Effective Feedback," *Educational Leadership* 70, no. 1 (September 2012), pp. 10–16; Marshal, *The Highly Effective Teacher.*
28. Barbara Blackburn, "The Six Characteristics of Effective Praise," *MiddleWeb* (December 6, 2015), https://www.middleweb.com/26483/the-6-characteristics-of-effective-praise/; Marshal; *The Highly Effective Teacher*; Wiggins, "Seven Keys to Effective Feedback."
29. Stephen Brookfield, *The Skillful Teacher* (San Francisco: Jossey Bass, 2015). Carol Dweck, *Mindset: The New Psychology of Success* (New York: Ballantine, 2007).
30. Benjamin Herold, "Technology in Education: An Overview," *Education Week* (February 5, 2016), http://www.edweek.org/ew/issues/technology-in-education/; Victor Luckerson, "Too Cool for School: Disruptive Tech Is Changing How Kids Learn," *Time* (September 22, 2014, p. 16).
31. George Brackett, "Technologies Don't Change Schools—Caring, Capable People Do," in David T. Gordon, ed., *The Digital Classroom* (Cambridge, MA: Harvard College, 2000), pp. 29–30.
32. Marshal, *The Highly Effective Teacher*; Stephen Brookfield, *The Skillful Teacher* (San Francisco: Jossey Bass, 2015; Barak Rosenshine, "Principles of Instruction: Research-Based Strategies That All Teachers Should Know," *American Educator* (Spring 2012), pp. 12–19, 39.
33. D. Frank Smith, "10 Reasons Why Flipped Classrooms Could Change Education," *EdTech*, https://edtechmagazine.com/k12/article/2015/03/cosn-2015-10-reasons-flipped-classrooms-could-change-education, March 17, 2015; Aaron Sams and Jonathan Bergmann, "Flip Your Students' Learning," *Educational Leadership* 70, no. 6 (March 2013), pp. 16–20.
34. Mary Leighton, "Cooperative Learning," in James M. Cooper, ed., *Classroom Teaching Skills,* 10th ed. (Belmont, CA: Cengage, 2014), pp. 283–329.
35. Leighton, "Cooperative Learning"; Robert E. Slavin, "Cooperative Learning in Middle and Secondary Schools," *Clearinghouse* 69, no. 4 (March/April 1996), pp. 200–204.
36. Leighton, "Cooperative Learning."
37. Jay Matthews, "Students Move at Own Pace toward Proficiency," *The Washington Post,* June 13, 2006, p. A8.
38. Tina Rosenberg, "In 'Flipped' Classrooms, a Method for Mastery," *New York Times* (October 23, 2013), http:// opinionator.blogs.nytimes.com/2013/10/23/in-flipped-classrooms-a-method-for-mastery; Laura Greenstein, *Assessing 21st Century Skills: A Guide to Evaluating Mastery and Authentic Learning* (Thousand Oaks, CA: Corwin, 2014).
39. John Lamar, *Setting the Standard for Project-Based Learning: A Proven Approach to Rigorous Classroom Instruction* (Alexandria, VA: ASCD, 2015); Andrew Miller, "Six Affirmations for PBL Teachers," *Edutopia* (May 3, 2012), http://www.edutopia.org /blog/affirmations-for-pbl-teachers-andrew-miller.
40. Anthony Rebora, "Making a Difference: Carol Ann Tomlinson Explains How Differentiated Instruction Works and Why We Need It Now," *Teacher Magazine* 2, no. 1 (September 10, 2008), pp. 26, 28–31.
41. Ibid., p. 28.
42. Carol Ann Tomlinson, "Differentiated Instruction for Academic Diversity," in James M. Cooper, ed., *Classroom Teaching Skills,* 10th ed. (Belmont, CA: Cengage, 2014), pp. 168–207; Carol Ann Tomlinson and Tonya Moon, *Assessment and Student Success in a Differentiated Classroom* (Alexandria, VA: ASCD, 2014).
43. Kristine Mraz and Christine Hertz, *A Mindset for Learning: Teaching the Traits of Joyful, Independent Growth* (Portsmouth, NH: Heinemann, 2015); Judy Willis, "The Neuroscience of Joyful Education," *Educational Leadership* 4, no. 9 (Summer 2007); Brookfield, *The Skillful Teacher.*
44. Julie Stern, *Tools for Teaching Conceptual Understanding: Designing Lessons and Assessments for Deep Learning* (Thousand Oaks, CA: Corwin Press, 2017); Kenneth Leithwood, *Teaching for Deep Understanding: What Every Educator Should Know* (Thousand Oaks, CA: Corwin Press, 2006).
45. Arina Bokas, *Building Powerful Learning Environments: From Schools to Communities* (Lanham, MD: Rowman and Littlefield, 2016).
46. James Cooper, "The Effective Teacher," in James M. Cooper, ed., *Classroom Teaching Skills,* 10th ed. (Belmont, CA: Cengage, 2014), pp. 1–22.

Index

D

I

J

K

L

M

Q

R

T

Z